Psychology and Law

A Critical Introduction

Psychology and Law provides a comprehensive, up-to-date discussion of contemporary debates at the interface between psychology and criminal law. The topics surveyed include critiques of eyewitness testimony; the jury; sentencing as a human process; the psychologist as expert witness; persuasion in the courtroom; detecting deception; and psychology and the police. Kapardis draws on sources from Europe, North America and Australia to provide an expert investigation of the subjectivity and human fallibility inherent in our system of justice. He also provides suggestions for minimising undesirable influences on crucial judicial decision-making. International in its scope and broad-ranging in its research, this book is the authoritative work on psycho-legal enquiry for students and professionals in psychology, law, criminology, social work and law enforcement.

Andreas Kapardis is Professor of Legal Psychology, University of Cyprus.

Dedication

This book is dedicated in gratitude to my wife Maria and children Konstantinos, Elena and Dina, and the memory of my parents Kostas and Sofia.

Psychology and Law

A Critical Introduction

Second edition

ANDREAS KAPARDIS

University of Cyprus

CAMBRIDGE UNIVERSITY PRESS

CAMBRIDGE UNIVERSITY PRESS
Cambridge, New York, Melbourne, Madrid, Cape Town, Singapore, São Paulo

Cambridge University Press
477 Williamstown Road, Port Melbourne, VIC 3207, Australia

Published in the United States of America by Cambridge University Press, New York

www.cambridge.org
Information on this title: www.cambridge.org/9780521531610

First published 2003
Reprinted 2003, 2005

Printed in Australia by Ligare Pty Ltd

Typeface Times (*Adobe*) 10/12 pt. *System* QuarkXPress® [PH]

A catalogue record for this publication is available from the British Library

National Library of Australia Cataloguing in Publication data
    Kapardis, Andreas.
    Psychology and law: a critical introduction
    2nd ed.
    Bibliography.
    Includes index.
    ISBN-13 978-0-521-53161-0 paperback
    ISBN-10 0-521-53161-6 paperback
    1. Law – Psychological aspects. 2. Psychology, Forensic.
    3. Judicial process. I. Title.
340.19

ISBN-13 978-0-521-53161-0 paperback
ISBN-10 0-521-53161-6 paperback

Contents

Case studies

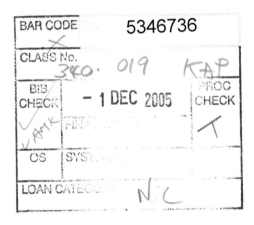

Acknowledgements

I wrote the first edition of this book in 1995–1996 encouraged by my students at La Trobe University in Melbourne, Australia. Having moved back to Europe, I decided to accept CUP's suggestion for a second edition encouraged both by the success of the first edition as well as by the knowledge that a great deal had meanwhile happened in legal psychology. I have, again, tried to draw on European and Australian work as well as on more traditional North American sources, and give sufficient of the legal framework to provide a proper context for the psycholegal research that is discussed. Inevitably, the book reflects on my own background and interests in psychology, legal studies, criminology and law enforcement. I hope it will be used as a textbook and will be of interest to undergraduate and graduate students as well as to professionals in psychology, law, law enforcement and social work.

As the manuscript goes to print, a sense of gratitude goes to my parents who taught me early on in life that where there is a will there is a way. While working on different parts of the manuscript I benefited from discussions with David Farrington, Ray Bull, Graham Davies, Aldert Vrij and Ian Freckelton. I consider myself fortunate to have enjoyed the excellent facilities and helpful assistance of the staff at the Radzinowicz Library, Institute of Criminology, Cambridge University, especially Helen Krarup for tracking down at very short notice numerous invaluable references. I wrote parts of the manuscript while staying at Clare Hall, my own college. I could not have wished for a more conducive environment. A special thanks goes to Ray Bull and Graham Davies for supplying me with material about their experiences as expert witnesses. I am grateful to Lee White and Paul Watt for their editorial comments. Of course, none of the individuals or institutions is responsible for any weaknesses, mistakes or opinions expressed in this work.

Finally, this book would not have been possible without the tremendous support and patience of my wife Maria. In appreciation, this book is dedicated to her and to our three children.

Foreword

It is a great pleasure to welcome this second edition of Andreas Kapardis' textbook, *Psychology and Law*. The first edition rapidly became recognised as a classic and has been widely used in undergraduate and postgraduate courses in legal and forensic psychology. My own students have found it incredibly useful and informative.

This second edition is even better. Although it follows the successful organisation of the first edition, this book has been completely revised and updated, especially the chapters on children as witnesses and on the psychologist as an expert witness. Novel features include margin notes, case studies and revision questions. Like the first edition, this book is scholarly, detailed, wide-ranging and up-to-date, but nevertheless very readable. There is no comparable modern textbook with such an international coverage of research on psychology and law.

The international coverage reflects the fact that Andreas Kapardis is a very international person. He completed Masters and PhD theses under my supervision at Cambridge University about 20 years ago and then taught and carried out research for a long time in Australia. Now he is pioneering research and teaching in legal and forensic psychology in Cyprus. Dr Kapardis is exceptionally knowledgeable about psychology and law throughout the world, as readers of this book will soon discover.

Forensic psychology is expanding very quickly in many different countries and there is an increasing need for trained scholars and practitioners. The value of applying the theories and methods of psychology to key issues arising in law and legal processes is now widely accepted. This book will be extremely valuable in training, as a source of the latest information about such important topics as eyewitness testimony, children as witnesses, jury decision-making, detecting deception and psychology as applied to law enforcement (to mention only a few of the issues covered). I am delighted to welcome Andreas Kapardis' book as an important contribution to knowledge. It should be essential reading for all legal and forensic psychologists.

David P. Farrington
Professor of Psychological Criminology
University of Cambridge

1 Psycholegal Research: An Introduction

'Although the roots of law and psychology were planted at the turn of the century, the "tree" has been slow to grow and only has begun to bear fruit recently.' (Ogloff and Finkelman, 1999:17)

'In the recent past psychologists' claims to knowledge and fact finding ability were altogether too forceful, and lawyers' reluctance to use psychological evidence, insights and sophisticated techniques altogether too irrational.' (Clifford and Bull, 1978:19)

'However relevant they may be to each other, the offspring of the relationship between psychology and law is still an infant and doubts are still cast upon its legitimacy.' (Carson and Bull, 1995a:3)

'The issues are not the relevance of psychology and law to each other but the extent to which the law and legal system should and are prepared, to embrace psychology and the extent to which psychologists should, and are prepared, to adapt their work to the needs and requirements of the legal system.' (Carson and Bull, 1995a:4)

Introduction: Development of the Psycholegal Field

The plethora of applications of psychology to law can be differentiated in terms of what has been defined as:[1] (a) *'psychology in law'*; (b) *'psychology and law'*; and (c) *'psychology of law'*. According to Blackburn (1996:6), psychology in law refers to specific applications of psychology within law: such as the reliability of eyewitness testimony, mental state of the defendant,[2] and a parent's suitability for child custody in a divorce case. *Psychology and law* is used by Blackburn (1996) to denote, for example, psycholegal research into offenders (see Howells and Blackburn, 1995), lawyers, magistrates, judges and jurors. Finally, *psychology of law* is used to refer to psychological research into such issues as to why people obey/disobey certain laws, moral development, and public perceptions and attitudes towards various penal sanctions. As far as the term *forensic psychology* is concerned, Blackburn (1996:6) argues convincingly it should only be used to denote the 'direct provision of psychological information to the courts, that is, to psychology in the courts' (see also Gudjonsson, 1996).[3] While there is no generally acceptable definition of *'legal psychology'*, the following one put forward by Ogloff (2000:467) is sufficiently broad and parsimonious, as he maintains, to reduce some of the confusion that surrounds this field: 'Legal psychology is the scientific study of the effects of law on people; and the effect people have on the law. Legal psychology also includes the application of the study and practice of psychology to legal institutions and people who come into contact with the law.'

Psycholegal research involves applying psychology's methodologies and knowledge to studying jurisprudence, substantive law, legal processes and law breaking (Farrington et al., 1979b:ix). Research into, and the practice of, legal psychology has a long tradition exemplified since the beginning of the twentieth century by the work of such pioneers[4] as Binet (1905), Gross (1898), Jung (1905), Münsterberg (1908) and Wertheimer (1906). In fact, Münsterberg has been called 'the father of applied psychology' (Magner, 1991:121).[5] The reader should note in this context that, as Ogloff (2000:461) reminds us, a number of well-known psychologists expressed an interest in applying psychology's findings to law as early as the 1890s. More specifically, Ogloff mentions Cattell's (1895) article in *Science* which was concerned with how accurately one could recall information; Freud's (1906) lectures to judges in Vienna on the merits of psychology for law in establishing facts; Watson's (1913) view that judges could utilise psychological findings and Paynter's (1920) and Burt's (1925) research into trademark and trade name infringements which was presented in court; Hutchins and Slesinger's (1928, 1929b) published work on psychology and evidence law and, finally, the Russian psychologist Luria's (1932) work on the affect in newly arrested criminals, before being interrogated by police, in order to differentiate the guilty from the innocent (Ogloff, 2000:461).

Regarding publications in law and psychology, the following appeared in the early part of the twentieth century: Brown's (1926) *Legal Psychology:*

> Even though well-known psychologists expressed an interest in applying psychology's findings to law as early as the 1890s, the truth is the psycholegal field really began to expand in the 1960s.

Psychology Applied to the Trial of Cases, to Crime and its Treatment, and to Mental States and Processes; Hutchins and Slesinger's (1929a) article on 'legal psychology' in the *Psychological Review*; McCarty's (1929) *Psychology for the Lawyer* and Cairns' (1935) *Law and Social Sciences*.

The psycholegal field has been expanding at an impressive rate since the mid 1960s, especially in North America, since the late 1970s in the UK and in Australia since the early 1980s. In fact, on both sides of the Atlantic, research and teaching in legal psychology has grown enormously since the mid 1970s (Lloyd-Bostock, 1994). More recently, the field of psychology and law has also been expanding in Europe, especially in the Netherlands, Germany and Spain (see Lösel et al., 1992a:509–53; Davies et al., 1996:579–601). As the chapters in this volume show, since the 1960s psychology and law has evolved into a single applied discipline and an often-cited example of success in applied psychology. Ogloff (2001:4) maintains that, 'Despite its long history, though, the legal psychology movement has had limited impact on the law, and until recently, it was focused primarily in North America'. However, the contents of this book attest to the fact that the legal psychology movement has had more than 'limited impact on law' on both sides of the Atlantic and, in contrast to Ogloff's assertion, it has not been mainly focused in North America. There appears to be an unfortunate, strong tendency among psycholegal researchers in the United States to be uninformed or, if informed, to avoid acknowledging, relevant work in Britain and on continental Europe – an example of what Ogloff (2001:7-8) identifies as 'jingoism' and one of the 'evils' of the legal psychology movement in the twentieth century. In this context, Haney (1993) points to psycholegal researchers having tackled some very crucial questions in society and, *inter alia*, been instrumental in improving the ways eyewitnesses are interviewed by law-enforcement personnel; the adoption of a more critical approach to the issue of forensic hypnosis evidence in the courts; psychologists contributing to improving the legal status and rights of children; and, finally, generally making jury selection fairer (p. 372ff). Furthermore, the impact of legal psychology has not just been one way (Davies, 1995:187).

Despite the early publications in legal psychology mentioned above, and while most lawyers would be familiar with forensic psychology, traditionally dominated by psychiatrists, it was not until the 1960s that lawyers in the United States came to acknowledge and appreciate psychology's contribution to their work (see Toch, 1961, *Legal and Criminal Psychology*; Marshall, 1969, *Law and Psychology in Conflict*).[6] Since the 1970s a significant number of psycholegal textbooks have appeared in the United States,[7] in England,[8] and some have been written by legal psychologists on continental Europe (Lösel et al., 1992a; Wegener et al., 1989). In addition, following Tapp's (1976) first review of psychology and law in the *Annual Review of Psychology*, relevant journals have been published, such as *Law and Human Behavior* which was first published in 1977 as the official publication of the American Psychology-Law Society (APLS) (founded in 1968) and is nowadays the journal of the American Psychological Association's Division of Psychology and Law.

Other journals are: *Behavioural Sciences and the Law*; *Expert Evidence*; *Law and Psychology Review*; *Criminal Behaviour and Mental Health*. New psycholegal journals continue to be published. The first issue of *Psychology, Crime and Law* was published in 1994 and those of *Legal and Criminological Psychology and Psychology, Public Policy, and Law* in 1996 in the UK and the United States respectively.

Despite the fact that in the UK lawyers and psychologists have been rather less ready than their American colleagues to 'jump into each other's arms', the push by prison psychologists and increasing interest in the field (for example, at the Social Science Research Centre for Socio-Legal Studies at Oxford, the Psychology Departments of the University of East London [previously North-East London Polytechnic], the London School of Economics and Political Science and Nottingham University, as well as at the Institute of Criminology at Cambridge) had gathered enough momentum by 1977 for the British Psychological Society to establish a Division of Criminological and Legal Psychology. By the early 1980s empirical contributions by legal psychologists at Aberdeen University added to the momentum. Annual conferences at the Oxford Centre formed the basis for Farrington et al.'s (1979a) *Psychology, Law and Legal Processes* and Lloyd-Bostock's (1981a) *Psychology In Legal Contexts: Applications and Limitations*, and these 'established a European focus for collaboration between the two disciplines, attracting scholars from many different countries' (Stephenson, 1995:133) and paved the way for the more recent annual European Association of Psychology and Law (EAPL) Conferences. These two publications, together with Clifford and Bull's (1978) The *Psychology of Person Identification* and other British works published in the 1980s and early 1990s, have established psychology and law as a field in its own right in Britain, despite the fact that in 1983 the Social Science Research Council, under a Conservative government, ceased funding conferences for lawyers and psychologists (King, 1986:1). Following a suggestion made at the EAPL conference in Siena, Italy, in 1996 by Professor David Carson of Southampton University, a very successful conference indeed was held at Trinity College, Dublin, jointly organised by APLS and EAPL. The conference was attended by over 600 delegates from twenty-seven countries, and produced two excellent books, namely *Psychology in the Courts: International Advances in Knowledge* by Roesch et al. (2001) and *Violent Sexual Offenders* by Farrington et al. (2001).

> With its emphasis on law in a social context, sociological jurisprudence has created a climate within law which has been conducive for the development of legal psychology.

Psychological associations outside the UK also set up relevant divisions, for example, in the United States in 1981 and in Germany in 1984 (see Lösel, 1992). In 1981 the American Psychological Association founded Psychology and Law as its forty-first Division (Monahan and Loftus, 1982). A significant development in the United States was the inclusion in 1994 of law and psychology in the *Annual Survey of American Law*. Besides a spate of international conferences on legal psychology that have been held in the UK and on continental Europe, there now exist both undergraduate and post-graduate programs in legal psychology (Lloyd-Bostock, 1994:133). Finally, a number of universities on both sides of the Atlantic have recognised the importance of legal psychology by dedicating chairs to the subject in psychology departments and law schools (Melton et al., 1987; Ogloff, 2000). It must not be forgotten, however, that while, by the beginning of the 1980s, one-quarter of graduate programs in the United States offered at least one course and a number had begun to offer forensic minors and/or PhD/JD programs (Freeman and Roesch, 1992), few psychology departments offered courses in psychology and law prior to 1973 (Diamond, 1992; Ogloff, 2000).

1 Bridging the Gap Between Psychology and Law: Why It has Taken so Long

The development of sociological jurisprudence (Holmes, 1897), with its emphasis on studying the social contexts that give rise to and are influenced by law, posed a challenge to the 'black-letter' approach to studying law which was based on the English common law and had been the linchpin of the legal system in North America. Sociological jurisprudence provided conditions within law that were favourable to the development of legal psychology, as did subsequent movements in law such as 'legal realism' (Schlegel, 1970).

In his book, *On The Witness Stand*, Münsterberg (1908:44–5) was critical of the legal profession in the United States for not appreciating the relevance of psychology to its work. However, Münsterberg was overselling psychology and his claims were not taken seriously by the legal profession (Wigmore, 1909; Magner, 1991). In addition, according to Cairns (1935 – cited by Ogloff, 2000: 461), there was opposition from within the discipline of psychology by such scholars as Professor Edward Titchener of Cornell University, who maintained that psychologists should not seek to apply their findings but should confine themselves to conducting pure and scientific research. Not surprisingly, therefore, 'the initial foray into law and psychology ... did not generate enough momentum to sustain itself' (Ogloff, 2000: 462).

The rather unfortunate legacy left by Ebbinghaus (1885) and his black-box approach to experimental memory research – best exemplified by his use of nonsense syllables – contributed to the state of knowledge in psychology at the time and was one significant factor that negated the success of Münsterberg's attempt. Fortunately, the dominance of the black-box paradigm in experimental psychology came to an end with the publication in 1967 of Neisser's futuristic *Cognitive Psychology* book. In the ensuing six decades, whilst behaviourism (on the one hand) and the experimental psychologists' practice (on the other) of treating as 'separate and separable' perception, memory, thinking, problem solving and language (Clifford and Bull, 1978:5) permeated and limited psychological research greatly, the early interest in psycholegal research fizzled out. As Ogloff (2000) points out, the continuing development of legal psychology after the 1930s was not only prevented by forces within psychology but, also, by a 'conservative backlash in law which limited the progressive scholars in the field ... The demise of legal realism had a chilling effect on legal psychology ...' (463).

Ogloff lists the following possible lessons to be learned, and to avoid, from the demise of legal psychology after 1930: a small number of people working and publishing in law; lack of training programmes for students; no identifiable outlet for psycholegal research; that those supporting the psychological status quo did not look favourably upon psycholegal research and, finally, the fact that legal psychologists were not formally organised (p. 462). By the late 1960s, as psychology matured as a discipline and, amongst other developments, social psychology blossomed in the United States, the experimental method came to be applied to problems not traditionally the concern of psychologists. Psychologists began turning their attention to understanding deception and its detection, jury decision-making, the accuracy of eyewitness testimony and sentencing decision-making as human processes. Most of the early psycholegal researchers with a strong interest in social psychology focused on juries in criminal cases, those with an affinity to clinical psychology concerned themselves with the insanity defence, while cognitive psychologists examined eyewitness testimony. These same areas continue to be of interest to psycholegal researchers today, but the questions being asked are more intricate and the methods used to answer them are more sophisticated (Diamond, 1992:vi). More recently, Ogloff (2001:14), like Carson and Bull (1995a: 9), has urged legal psychologists to broaden their research interests to include more areas of law, including: administrative law, antitrust, civil procedure, corporate law, environmental law, patent law, and family law. The somewhat narrow focus of psycholegal research caused enough concern to Saks (1986) for him to remind such researchers that 'the law does not live by eyewitness testimony alone' and for Diamond to urge them 'to explore underrepresented areas of the legal landscape' (Diamond, 1992:vi). It is comforting for psychologists to know that, with the general growth and maturity of their discipline, major industrialised society has come to realise the wide-ranging benefits of psychology (McConkey, 1992:3).

Why, then, has it taken so long for the field of psychology and law to develop when, as some authors would argue,[9] psychologists and lawyers do have a lot of common ground? Both disciplines focus on the individual (Carson, 1995a:43). Yarmey (1979:7) wrote that 'both psychology and the courts are concerned with predicting, explaining and controlling behaviour', while according to Saks and Hastie (1978:1): 'Every law and every institution is based on assumptions about human nature and the manner in which human behaviour is determined'. Achieving 'justice' is the concern of law and lawyers, while the search for scientific truth is the concern of psychologists (Carson and Bull, 1995a:7). Diamond (1992:vi–vii) went as far as to state that 'on grandiose days, I think that law should be characterised as a component of psychology, for if psychology is the study of human behaviour, it necessarily includes law as a primary instrument used by society to control human behaviour. Perhaps this explains why laws are such a fertile source of research ideas for psychologists'. Similarly, Crombag (1994) argues that law may be considered a branch of applied psychology because the law mainly comprises a system of rules for the control of human social behaviour. Listing law as a component of psychology, however convincing the arguments put forward for it might be, is not a suggestion that will endear psycholegal researchers to lawyers. A more realistic position to adopt than that of Crombag's is that 'to the extent that every law has as its purpose the control or regulation of human behavior, every law is ripe for psychological study' (Ogloff, 2001:13–14).[10]

While the law relies on assumptions about human behaviour and psychologists concern themselves with understanding and predicting behaviour, both psychology and law accept that human behaviour is not random. More specifically, research in psychology relates to various aspects of law in practice (Lloyd-Bostock, 1988:1). As in other countries, the legal profession in Australia, justifiably, perhaps, has been rather slow to recognise the relevance of psychology to its work. Compared to law, psychology is, chronologically speaking, entering its adulthood and, given a number of important differences between the two disciplines, it comes as no surprise to be told that there is tension, and conflict between the two disciplines (see Marshall, 1966) that persists (Carson and Bull, 1995b; Diamond, 1992:viii). Bridging the gap between the two disciplines on both sides of the Atlantic, in Australia, New Zealand and Canada, as well as, for example, in Spain and Italy (see Garrido and Redodo, 1992; Traverso and Manna, 1992; Traverso and Verde, 2001) has not been easy. In fact, there is a long way to go before the remaining ambivalence about psychology's contribution to academic and practising lawyers and ethical issues of such a function will be resolved (Lloyd-Bostock, 1988). Admittedly, 'Different psychologists have different ideas about what psychology should be about' (Legge, 1975:5) and 'Law, like happiness, poverty and good music, is different things to different people' (Chisholm and Nettheim, 1992:1). The simple fact is that there are significant differences in approach between psychology and law. This point is well-illustrated by eight issues which, according to Haney (1980)[11] are a source of conflict between the two disciplines, namely:

- The law stresses conservatism; psychology stresses creativity.
- The law is authoritative; psychology is empirical.
- The law relies on adversarial process; psychology relies on experimentation.
- The law is prescriptive; psychology is descriptive.
- The law is idiographic; psychology is nomothetic.
- The law emphasizes certainty; psychology is probabilistic.
- The law is reactive; psychology is proactive.
- The law is operational; psychology is academic.

It can be seen that the two disciplines operate with different models of man. The law, whether civil or criminal, generally emphasises individual responsibility in contrast to the tendency by a number of psychological theories to highlight 'unconscious and uncontrollable forces operating to determine aspects of individuals' behaviour' (King, 1986:76). In addition, 'The psychologists' information is inherently statistical, the legal system's task is clinical and diagnostic' (Doyle, 1989:125–6). As Clifford (1995) has

> Psychology and law have a great deal in common but they also differ in a number of significant ways. Furthermore, conflict is endemic in the relationship between the two disciplines.

put it: 'the two disciplines appear to diverge at the level of value, basic premises, their models, their approaches, their criteria of explanation and their methods' (p. 13).

In a submission to the Australian Science and Technology Council in the context of its investigation into the role of the social sciences and the humanities in the contribution of science and technology to economic development (see McConkey, 1992:3) it is stated that: 'Psychology discovers, describes and explains human experience and behaviour through the logic and method of science. Psychological research and application is based in a logical, empirical and analytical approach, and that approach is brought to bear on an exceptionally wide range of issues.'

On the other hand, 'Tradition is important to lawyers' (Carson and Bull, 1995a:29) and, as Farrington et al. (1979b:xiv) put it, law 'is a practical art, a system of rules, a means of social control, concerned with the solving of practical problems'. Furthermore: 'The law is based on common-sense psychology which has its own model of man, its own criteria ... its own values. Common-sense explanation in the law is supported by the fact that workable legal processes have evolved under constant close scrutiny over many centuries. It is in this sense "proven". But this is quite different from explanation in terms of psychological theory backed by empirical evidence of statistically significant relationships' (p. xiii).

Finally, whereas the image of human beings projected by American social psychologists is that of the 'nice person', the law, and especially the criminal law, is characterised by a more cynical view of human nature and this view tends to be adopted by those who work within and for the legal system (King, 1986:76).

Psycholegal researchers (for example, in eyewitness testimony) have utilised a variety of research methods including incident studies, field studies, archival studies and single case studies (see Clifford, 1995:19–24; Davies, 1992). Many psychologists rely a great deal on the experimental method, including field experiments, to test predictions and formulate theories that predict behaviour and are sceptical of lawyers' reliance on common-sense generalisations about human behaviour based on armchair speculation, however ratified by conceptual analysis (Farrington et al., 1979b:xiii). A feature that unifies a lot of psychological research is its preference for subjecting assertions to systematic empirical research and, where possible, testing them experimentally. This will often involve randomly allocating persons to different conditions who, at the time, are normally not told the aim of the experiment. Clifford (1995) provides an excellent account of contemporary psychology's premises and methods. Many psychologists who favour experimental simulation tend not to also consider the issue of values in psychological and psycholegal research in general, and in particular whether psychologists can indeed avoid value judgements by demonstrating the 'facts'.

Theoretical models of man espoused by experimental psychologists have involved man as a black box, a telephone switchboard and, more recently, man as a computer. These models, which are different from the lawyer's notion of 'free will', have been rejected by cognitive psychologists because they do not take into account man as a thinking, feeling, believing totality (Clifford and Bull, 1978:5), as someone who interacts with the environment in a dynamic way.

For many a psychologist, a great deal of information processing is done without people being aware of it; the lawyer, on the other hand, operates a model of man as a free, conscious being who controls his/her actions and is responsible for them. What the law, based on a lot of judicial pronouncements, regards as 'beyond reasonable doubt' is rather different from the psychologist's conclusion that an outcome is significant at a 5 per cent level of statistical significance. One interesting aspect of this, for example, is the lawyer's reluctance to quantify how likely guilt must appear to be before one can say that such doubt as exists is not reasonable. The lawyer in court is often only interested in a 'yes' or 'no' answer to a question asked of a psychologist who is appearing as an expert witness, while, at best, the psychologist may only feel comfortable with a 'maybe' response. It should be noted, however, that the answers of interest to a practising lawyer might vary according to whether it is examination in chief or cross-examination. In the former, the lawyer is interested in a story, whereas in the latter, the lawyer is interested in questions that require a 'yes' or 'no' answer (see chapter 8). Also, lawyers look at the individual case they have to deal with and highlight how it differs from the stereotype; they try hard to show in court that one cannot generalise, whereas psychologists talk about the probability of someone being different from the aggregate.

> Lawyers, on the one hand, focus on their individual client and emphasise how he/she differs from the stereotype and that one cannot generalise. On the other hand, however, psychologists talk about the probability of someone being different from the aggregate.

In addition to significant differences between psychology and law (see Carson, 1995b), there is the fact that the approaches of various branches of psychology differ in the degree to which they are based on what might be called scientific experiments. Furthermore, some psychologists have cast doubt on the practical utility of findings from controlled laboratory experiments that reduce jury decision-making, for example, to a few psychology undergraduates reading a paragraph-long, sketchy description of a criminal case and making individual decisions on a rating scale about the appropriate sanction to be imposed on the defendant (see Bray and Kerr, 1982; King, 1986; Konečni and Ebbesen, 1992; Bornstein, 1999). Rabbitt (1981) pointed out that 90 per cent of the studies quoted in standard textbooks on the psychology of memory then available only tested recognition or recall of nonsense three-letter syllables. More recently, Konečni and Ebbesen (1992: 415–16) have argued that: 'It is dangerous and bordering on the irresponsible to draw conclusions and make recommendations to the legal system on the basis of simulations which examine effects independently of their real-world contexts' (that is, on the basis of invalidated simulations or those that are not designed to examine the higher-order interactions). More recent research on the jury (see chapter 5) includes protocol analyses, in-depth interviews with jurors after they have rendered verdicts in real cases, elaborate simulations involving videotaped trials and juror respondents, and even randomised field experiments (see Heuer and Penrod, 1989). Similarly, eyewitness testimony researchers have been making increasingly greater use of staged events and non-psychology students as subjects, as well as utilising archival data (see chapters 2 and 3).

King (1986) has also criticised legal psychologists' strong reliance on the experimental method, arguing that there is a tendency to exaggerate its importance; that treating legal factors as 'things' and applying to them experimental techniques and statistical methods gives rise to at least four problems, namely, inaccessibility, external validity, generalisability and completeness (p. 31). King has also argued that exclusive reliance on experimental simulation also encourages legal psychologists to focus on inter-individual behaviours without taking into account the social context to which they belong (p. 7); that Karl Popper's (1939) refutability has been shown by philosophers of science to be a questionable criterion for defining whether a theory is scientific. Furthermore, King contends that the real reasons for legal psychologists' continued use of the experimental method as the prime or sole method for studying legal issues is: (a) a belief by psychologists that using the experimental method enables them to claim they are being 'scientific' in carrying out their research; (b) a need felt by psychologists for recognition and acceptability; and (c) a belief by psychologists that they are more likely to be accepted and recognised as 'experts' if they are seen to be 'scientific'. Finally, neo-Marxist critics of the use of the experimental method (see Wexler, 1983) 'see the failure to pay attention to the context of social behaviour as a political act perpetrated by psychologists in order to obscure the true form and content of social interaction' (King, 1986:103). King has advocated a shift 'away from the restrictive and self-aggrandising notions of what constitutes "scientific" research which have tended to serve as a starting point for much of what passes for legal psychology' (p. 82). No doubt many psychologists would disagree both with Wexler's (1983) picture of them as involved in a political conspiracy informed by a particular ideology and with King's (1986) push to get them to use the experimental method less in favour of ethnomethodology as their preferred method of enquiry.

Highlighting the dangers inherent in studying eyewitness testimony under rather artificial conditions in the laboratory, Clifford and Bull (1978) reminded their readers that such research could lead psychologists to advance knowledge that is, in fact, the reverse of the truth, as in the case of the influence of physiological arousal on recall accuracy. A theory of recall, or any other psychological theory for that matter, arrived at on the basis of grossly inadequate research could hardly be expected to be taken seriously by lawyers.[12]

According to Hermann and Gruneberg (1993:55), in the 1990s memory researchers no longer presumed that a laboratory procedure would or would not extrapolate to the real world because the ecological validity issue in memory research had largely been solved. Hermann and Gruneberg proposed that: 'It is time now to move beyond the ecological validity issue … to the next logically appropriate issue – applied research'. In so doing legal psychologists in the new millennium should heed Davies' (1992) words that: 'no one research method can of itself provide a reliable data base for legislation or advocacy. Rather, problems need to be addressed from a number of perspectives, each of which makes a different compromise between ecological validity and methodological rigour.' (p. 265)

Another reason why problems arise when psychology and law meet is that, as Lösel (1992:15) points out, for the psychologist the plethora of theories and perspectives in the discipline is a matter of course. In law, however, the main goal is uniformity and the avoidance of disparity. Consequently, lawyers regard the numerous viewpoints in psychology as contradictory. Taking the psychological literature on bystander intervention and using good samaritanism (that is, intervening to assist or summon assistance for people in urgent need of such assistance – see Kidd, 1985) as an example, we find two conflicting decision-making models. On the one hand, experimental simulation studies of the phenomenon (see Latane and Darley, 1970) have given rise to a cognitive decision-making model. This model assumes that people are rational decision-makers who resolve to intervene directly or indirectly in an emergency after a series of decisions: whether an incident is an emergency, whether one has personal responsibility to get involved and, finally, whether the benefits outweigh the costs of intervention. On the other hand, there exists another model of bystander intervention, partly based on experimental studies (see Piliavin et al., 1981), partly on interviews with individuals who had heroically intervened in real-life crime situations and partly on comparisons with 'non-interveners' (see Houston, 1980), which depicts intervention as 'impulsive' and not as comprising a series of rational decisions. A basic assumption in law (see Luntz and Hambly, 1992) is that helping behaviour is the result of rational decision-making. The relevant psychological literature, however, provides conflicting views regarding the validity of this assumption for bystander intervention, a situation that does not help those who advocate introducing failure-to-assist provisions into the criminal law of jurisdictions like those of England and Australia which do not have such laws (see Geis, 1991).

Greer (1971) drew attention to the fact that many psychologists attempting to investigate questions of legal relevance on their own have had a rather limited view of legal objectives and, as a result, in the case of eyewitness testimony, for example, 'they failed to appreciate the intricacies and complexities of legal procedures for eliciting testimony ... [and] tended to oversee the legal implications of their work and seemed to expect their findings to be regarded as virtual saviours of the integrity of the legal profession' (p. 142). Greer's comment applies some thirty years later to a significant amount of psycholegal research, as later chapters in this volume demonstrate. The need for legal psychologists to have an in-depth understanding of the relevant law has also been emphasised by Ogloff (2000:11).

Lloyd-Bostock (1981b) has drawn attention to another problem besides that of extrapolating from the laboratory to real life, namely, in applying general psychological principles in the individual case. She has argued that: 'It is important to distinguish between application to particular cases on the one hand, and more general applications in policy formation on the other.

Applications in individual cases (and hence expert evidence) are far more hazardous' (p. 17). Lloyd-Bostock has also maintained that while developments in the psycholegal field have paralleled more general developments within psychology, the relatively fast pace at which psychological knowledge changes and well-accepted theories are superseded detracts from the practical utility of psychological findings. As already mentioned, the prevailing legal model of man entails a conscious mind. As Lloyd-Bostock (1981b) rightly pointed out, this model is unlikely to be shifted in the face of psychological knowledge. Furthermore, even some psychologists themselves (for example, King, 1981) have opposed such a shift because the very question of 'whether the legal model should be shifted at all is a value judgement not a question of whether psychology or law is on an empirically sounder basis' (Lloyd-Bostock, 1981b:19).

Another explanation as to why it has taken a long time for psycholegal research to be embraced by both psychologists and lawyers lies in the fact that, as psychologists present themselves as experts in the courtroom, they find they have to deal with ethical dilemmas regarding, for example, the confidentiality of their clients (see Haward, 1981a). Toch (1961:19)[13] in his book *Legal and Criminal Psychology*, warned of the danger of overselling psychology, similar to that which has happened with psychiatry (see Szazz, 1957). Of course, there is the additional danger of psychologists peddling their expertise and producing a favourable opinion for a client in a legal case to whoever would pay their fee. The United States experience has shown that the field of the expert psychologist in court (see chapter 7) can be a real money-spinner.

2　Remaining Difficulties

Interestingly enough, however, as Lösel (1992:11–12) reminds us: 'Despite the generally encouraging development of recent legal psychology, a number of problems still remain'. Inter alia, Lösel highlights the importance of the following factors:

- *The Internal Situation of Legal Psychology:* Lösel identifies a great imbalance in the interest shown in various topics within legal psychology. For example, psycholegal researchers have focused on eyewitness testimony and ignored issues in civil law or custody law, cross-cultural comparisons or more multinational research.
- *The Position of Legal Psychology within Psychology:* It would appear that only a small percentage of practising psychologists in western countries work in the field of legal psychology. This is, perhaps, not surprising in view of the fact that, as Lösel (1992:13–14) points out, legal psychology does not yet belong to the big areas of applied psychology and topics that concern legal psychologists are rather heterogeneous.
- *Legal Psychology's Relation to Legal Science and Practice:* Lösel (1992:15) also rightly argues that how legal psychology will develop in the

long run will depend on its relationship with the discipline of law and, above all, the legal profession. As this chapter makes clear, this relationship is inevitably not without conflict (see King, 1986; Melton et al., 1987). Of course, the situation differs from country to country. To illustrate, unlike Australia, the United States seems readier to include legal psychology in law faculties and has even established chairs in legal psychology. In the UK, for a number of years there has existed an independent Division of Criminological and Legal Psychology within the British Psychological Society. In Australia, however, the College of Forensic Psychologists of the Australian Psychological Society, with its orthodox adherence to clinical psychology training as the prerequisite for anybody who might want to call themselves a forensic psychologist, has not, until recently, provided strong encouragement for the development of criminological and legal psychology as a field in its own right. It could be argued that such a myopic attitude towards psychology and law excludes, for example, cognitive and social psychologists as well as lawyers who have a lot to contribute to legal psychology, it discourages the teaching of legal psychology at both the under-graduate and postgraduate level and, finally, can be said to have almost stifled the development of the field in Australia. Fortunately, the pace of the discipline's development has accelerated in the last few years and looks likely to continue to do so.

- *New Psychological Findings vs Long-Term Establishments in Law:* The wheels of law turn very slowly when it comes to change and, not surprisingly, it often takes a long time for new and established findings by psychologists to be enshrined in statute or to be taken account of by judges in their case law (Lösel, 1992:16).

- *Empirical Experimentation vs Principles of Equal Treatment and Fixed Jurisdiction:* Finally, Lösel draws attention to a major constraint imposed on psychologists by the law: because of the emphasis on equal treatment of like cases and fixed jurisdiction in the justice system, some field experiments which psychologists might wish to carry out are not possible (p. 16). Examples of such field experiments are in the sentencing of criminal defendants or in the reaction to child abuse (p. 16).

> In order for legal psychology to continue to develop and mature as a discipline in its own right, certain 'evils' pointed out by Ogloff (2001) that have plagued its growth over the last one hundred years need to be addressed.

Ogloff (2001) discusses a number of '*evils*' that have plagued the development of legal psychology in the twentieth century and which need to be addressed in the light of the experience in order to ensure that legal psychology continues to develop and mature:

1 *Jingoism*, that is, focusing in a narrow way on one's own country. It would not be an exaggeration to say that psycholegal research in North America too often shows a great deal of ignorance about British and continental European legal systems and studies. As Ogloff points out, learning from the experience of other countries can only be for the benefit of both the individual researcher as well as the discipline of legal psychology (pp. 7–8).

2 *Dogmatism*, even in the face of conflicting findings, stifles creativity and progress in the field (p. 9).

3   *Chauvinism*, especially in terms of sexism and ethnocentricism. The remedy here is to broaden the populations that are studied and to be sensitive to cultural diffrences and the needs of ethnic minorities and women (p. 10).

4   *Naïveté*, that is, undue ignorance of procedural and substantive law that pertains to one's area of work. Remedying this is essential in order to achieve high external validity of one's findings and is conducive for identifying more and interesting legal questions to be investigated (p. 12) and, finally,

5   *Myopia*, that is, being interested in a few, narrow, areas of psychology such as jury decision-making or eyewitness testimony (pp. 13–14). As already mentioned above, legal psychologists need to broaden their areas of interest in law if they wish to have a significant impact on the law.

Another problem that still remains is the strong tendency by legal psychologists to be method- rather than phenomenon-orientated and to lack first-hand knowledge of the legal issue they investigate. Such first-hand knowledge could be obtained by means of participant observation, fieldwork, and/or interviews with the main protagonists over a sufficiently long period of time. Instead, most legal psychologists rely on experimental simulation as a short-cut to knowledge (King, 1986:91). Finally, the results of psycholegal research would be more likely to be accepted by members of the legal profession, academic lawyers and policy-makers alike if psychologists show greater familiarity with both common law and statutory provisions relevant to their research, as well as with different theoretical stances in contemporary legal theory (see Davies, 1994) instead of a myopic perception of a legal issue. As shown in chapter 5, there is more to the jury debate for academic and practising lawyers than simply the nature of the decision-making processes that underpin jury verdicts. Furthermore, utilising their research findings, psychologists should encourage 'constructive debate of basic jurisprudential issues of lively interest in the community' and not, rather conveniently, leave it to politicians to judge the significance of psycholegal research (Stephenson, 1995:136).

3 Grounds for Optimism

Despite differences between psychology and law, differences that have been exacerbated by the lack of communication between the two professions and the concomitant absence of collaborative research (Farrington et al., 1979b), it is comforting, perhaps, to know that the scope of psycholegal research has widened significantly beyond its early concern primarily with criminal law topics in general and with eyewitness testimony and other procedures in the courtroom in particular (Lloyd-Bostock, 1981a:ix). As Lösel (1992:10) informs us, in recent years there has been an important increase in psycholegal research into, for example, the honesty of tax-payers (see Hessing et al., 1988) and social cognition of tort law (Wiener and Small, 1992). In addition, it is nowadays well accepted that legal psychology does not have to be, as it often is, an applied field (Lloyd-Bostock, 1981b, 1988); in other words, the value of psycholegal research can be both theoretical and practical, of interest to both the practitioner and the academic psychologist and lawyer. Diamond (1992) argues, in fact, that the truly challenging, intellectual questions psychologists should be asking about law require them not to yield to the temptation to equate success with recognition by lawyers, a temptation that is the more understandable given the power of law and lawyers in society.

Raising questions about what psychology can contribute to law and the difficulties and ethical questions that occur does not mean that difficulties should be exaggerated (Lloyd-Bostock, 1981b:21). Similarly, while 'identifying and dwelling on difficulties may seem unduly pessimistic, exposing problems in a joint enterprise is not incompatible with a belief in its value' (Farrington et al., 1979b:xiii). Writing in 1981 Lloyd-Bostock pointed out that: 'Current topics of research in psychology and law are so diverse and sprawling that it is not possible even to offer an exhaustive list, let alone any idea of the type of work being done on each' (p. 2). Psycholegal research has continued to expand in both quantity and range, and to a significant degree, in quality, too.

The interested reader would be forgiven for coming to the view that the available textbooks on psychology and law contain material on such a range of topics as to render psycholegal research an applied field and to depict psychologists as only interested in questions of direct practical interest to the legal fraternity. However, a number of textbooks (for example, Brewer and Wilson, 1995; Bull and Carson, 1995; Lösel et al., 1992a; Kagehiro and Laufer, 1992; Ross et al., 1994; Davies et al., 1996; Roesch et al., 1999; Roesch et al., 2001; and Traverso and Bagnoli, 2001), including this volume, contain chapters addressing questions of interest to practising and academic lawyers, as well as law-enforcement personnel, that do have immediate policy implications. As Diamond (1992) puts it, the psycholegal field 'encompasses questions about how people exercise social control and how responsibility, resources, and risk are allocated. The capacity for basic research in psychology and law has not been fully explored.'

As we advance into the twenty-first century, some feel that the full potential of the psycholegal field will only be realised with the development of a distinctly psycholegal jurisprudence (Small, 1993). To some extent a feeling of frustration still characterises both legal psychologists and lawyers (Pennington and Hastie, 1990:103). Psychologists are appalled when lawyers continue to ignore what the psychologists consider good empirical research results and, consequently, fail to resolve issues in law. For their part, the lawyers wish the psychologists would try harder to make their work more useful by ensuring that it is more relevant to actual legal contexts and 'less convoluted' (p. 104). Legal psychologists can, nevertheless, look back on a century of existence and take pride in their achievements. The research that is considered in the following chapters provides enough evidence for the belief that, by going a considerable way in bridging the gap between psychology and law, psycholegal researchers have provided us with knowledge the total of which is more than the sum of its parts. This realisation provides, perhaps, the best basis for optimism about legal psychology's future.

The wide range of topics dealt with in this and other textbooks does not mean that psychology and law is a field comprising a loose collection of topics – psychology and law is a recognisable field. Psychology has a unique perspective – its concern with the individual in a social context – and a unique contribution to make to law. In this regard, psycholegal research differs from such related fields as sociology of law in the way it addresses issues as well as in the methodology it uses. We can now take it for granted that psychology has a contribution to make to law; indeed, as the contents of this volume and others like it attest, psychology has been and is making a significant contribution in a number of ways. While not forgetting the narrower focus of a lot of psycholegal research alluded to above, the evidence is overwhelming that psychologists offer a unique perspective on law and have shown themselves capable of transcending the narrow boundaries of early psycholegal research to also address issues of the macro-sociological level, since the vast majority of psychologists today consider behaviour to be a function of both the individual and the environment. 'Boundaries [in psychology and law] are thus seen as providing contours and emphases rather than erecting walls' (Diamond, 1992:viii). Lösel (1992:16–17) concludes his overview of legal psychology that there is justification for optimism as far as the future of legal psychology is concerned: 'In both law and psychology … there is a growing understanding for the possibilities, peculiarities and idiosyncrasies of the other side … recent legal psychology seems to be one of those fields in which psychology's relationships to neighbouring disciplines has developed relatively successfully'.

In pondering the future of psychology and law and deciding how best to move forward in the 21st century, psycholegal researchers should consider their position on the range of problems of the legal psychology movement in the twentieth century raised by Ogloff (2001 – see above), as well as an additional number of concerns raised by Haney (1993:376ff). They include: that, generally speaking, psycholegal research has not been well received by appellate courts; the discipline of psychology and law appears to have abandoned its sense of shared purpose – its mission of legal change; psycholegal researchers have a strong tendency to accept the legal status quo, thus precluding attempts to change it; researchers continue to give the impression that psycholegal research is value free and, consequently, are in no position to debate values and lack a 'coherent framework' around which to organise their research; and that the focus is on fine-tuning procedures in the legal system to make them fairer and not on the outcomes of the procedures, and thus psychologists contribute to perpetuating social inequalities and injustices.

There can be no doubt that the experimental method has a number of merits. It must not be forgotten, however, that it also has its limitations and often, in order to understand, explain adequately and predict a particular psycholegal phenomenon, the experimental method needs to be supplemented by other methods. As the chapters that follow show, there has been a general tendency for researchers in the psycholegal field to be reluctant to combine different research methods, instead relying excessively on experiments of often questionable external validity and, furthermore, failing to locate their work in a contemporary critical socio-legal context. Without ignoring the constraints under which university-based psycholegal research often has to be conducted, a first step in making good these deficits and advancing psychology and law further as a discipline in its own right inter-nationally would be a conscious effort by psychologists to increasingly use representative samples of the wider community as subjects where this is appropriate and under forensically relevant conditions, to invest more time in the field relevant to their specific research interest, familiarising themselves with actual situations, as observers, utilising archival material, and talking with practitioners. Finally, legal psychologists have also neglected public education, thus rendering themselves almost impotent in the political arena when it comes to translating their knowledge into social and legal change. The main thrust of Haney's (1993) position is that psycholegal researchers should adopt a more critical perspective on the legal issues they study (p. 386) in order to 'confront several conceptual stress points that remain in our discipline' and to resolve the conflict and confusion that still exists about professional values (p. 392).

Carson (1995b) suggests that the way forward for psychology and law is primarily through 'collaboration focused upon change' (p. 38). Carson and Bull (1995b) are more specific about what the way forward for psychology and law should be when they advocate 'finding ways in which psychology's product can – appropriately and always questioningly and critically – aid, and question, legal processes and goals' (p. 645).

4 Psychology and Law in Australia

Psycholegal research in Australia has not flourished to the extent it has done so on both sides of the Atlantic; it still involves a limited number of psychol-ogists who tend to be relatively isolated from each other. Not surprisingly, in addition to Australian psycholegal research published internationally, there has been a small number of publications in Australian psychology journals or Australian books on such topics as: eyewitness testimony (for example, Thomson, 1981, 1984, 1991; McConkey and Roche, 1989; McConkey and Sheehan, 1988; Naylor, 1989; Tucker et al., 1990; Vernon, 1991), forensic hypnosis (Evans and Stanley, 1994), the psychologist as expert witness (Cattermole, 1984; Freckelton, 1987, 1996; Freckelton and Selby, 2002; Moloney, 1986; Wardlaw, 1984), confidentiality in the psychologist–client relationship (McMahon and Knowles, 1995), recovered memories (Freckelton, 1996; Magner, 1995; Thomson, 1995b) and psychology and policing (Brewer and Wilson, 1995).

Since 1980 the main focus for Australian and New Zealand psycholegal researchers has been the annual congress of the Australian and New Zealand Association of Psychiatry, Psychology and Law (see Greig and Freckelton, 1988, 1989, 1990; Freckelton, Greig and McMahon, 1991; Freckelton, Knowles and Mulvaney, 1992). In addressing the second such congress in 1981 Justice Michael Kirby stated that 'one of the constant themes of the Law Reform Commission has been the need to bring together various specialised disciplines, particularly in the design of new laws', and, 'in an age of science and technology, this interdisciplinary communication useful at any time, becomes imperative'. The publication in 1994 of the *Psychiatry, Psychology and Law* journal in Australia and the March 1996 special issue on forensic psychology of *Australian Psychologist*, 31(1), have been significant steps in formally establishing psycholegal research in Australia as a field in its own right. The fact remains, however, that, in addition to the vastness of the Australian continent, the relatively small number of prison psychologists and small number of practising and academic forensic psychologists, the situation in Australia has really been no different from that in the UK where there is 'a deep-rooted suspicion and scepticism among both lawyers and psychologists about the value of such interdisciplinary work' (King, 1986:1). This is not surprising, perhaps, in view of the very little contact and exchange of ideas between the thousands of psychologists and lawyers in Australia.

Australia has a population of approximately 17.5 million and thirty-nine universities, two of them private. According to the Australian Psychological Society (APS), in June 1996 there were twenty-three universities offering four-year degree courses accredited for the purpose of associate membership of the Society, forty-seven university campuses were offering psychology courses consisting of an approved sequence of three years, all the universities were offering approved fourth-year courses and, finally, master's courses accredited for membership were being offered by thirty universities. At the same time, twenty-seven university campuses were offering accredited LL.B degree courses. Postgraduate degrees in forensic psychology (Masters and/or PhD) were offered at five universities, namely Edith Cowan, Melbourne, Charles Sturt, Monash and Deakin. The large number of psychology and law courses, as well as the development of the discipline of Legal Studies with its focus on law in context and an increasing number of publications by Australian law reform bodies,[14] have no doubt helped to increase awareness of the relevance of social sciences in general and legal psychology, in particular to law scholars and practitioners. Tremper's (1987a) assessment that on both sides of the Atlantic and on continental Europe 'The current state of legally oriented social science research is a mixture of success and unfulfilled promise' (p. 267) still applies, albeit to a lesser degree. It is hoped that, as psycholegal research in Australia gathers momentum, interested psychologists and lawyers will become better organised and will be able to contribute to Royal Commissions and Law Reform bodies and to the work of the courts, as their counterparts have done in the United States[15] and in Britain.[16]

5 Conclusions

In the words of Ogloff and Finkelman (1999:1), 'although progress has been made during this the field's "developmental phase", there is still much room for the field to grow and develop'. As legal psychology's maturity as a discipline continues, the arguments presented lead to the cautious conclusion that the dawn of the new millennium marks the onset of a new era in legal psychology, characterised by a certain amount of healthy tension within psychology itself as well as between psychology and law. This multifaceted tension can be said to provide both the impetus and the focus necessary for the further maturity of this rather interesting field. Ogloff and Finkelman (1999:18) predict that, '… As the law becomes more open to the empirical realities introduced by the social sciences, it is probable that psychology will become even more welcome in the legal system' (Ogloff and Finkelman, 1999:18). At the same time, however, they urge that care be taken to educate courts and legislatures to prevent them from distorting or otherwise misrepresenting social science findings (p. 18).

Those working in psychology and law can look back with a sense of pride to their discipline's development, albeit occasionally a chequered one, and its various achievements, especially regarding court procedures. They can also look forward to the discipline's promising future. At the same time, it is nice to know that the impact of psychology and law has been a two-way process (Davies, 1995). Recognising psychology's limitations regarding, for example, the external validity of a lot of experimental psycholegal research, and utilising more than one research method to study a particular phenomenon, as well as mistakes made in the effort to bridge the gap between the two disciplines (for example, overselling psychological research findings to the legal profession), and learning from them would seem to be imperative if, in Carson and Bull's (1995b) words, psycholegal researchers are to increase the legitimacy of the infant offspring of the relationship between the two disciplines. Psychology and law is by now an established discipline on both sides of the Atlantic, on continental Europe, and in Australia. One of its main pillars has been eyewitness testimony, the subject of the next chapter.

6 The Book's Structure, Focus and Aim

This book is intended to provide students at undergraduate and postgraduate level with a general overview of a number of important specific topics from the perspectives of different countries (United States, UK, Australia, New Zealand, and Canada). The topics surveyed are inevitably only part of the interface between psychology and law. The author's intention is not to provide a complete overview of psychology and law. Consequently, other areas such as psychological research into people's perceptions of decisions about justice (see Mellers and Baron, 1993), confidentiality in psychological practice (see McMahon and Knowles, 1995), clinical approaches to working with offenders (see Davies et al., 1996; Hollin, 1995, 1996; Howells and Blackburn, 1995; McGuire et al., 2000), psychological evaluations for the courts (see Heilbrun, 1992) including competency, criminal responsibility and violence prediction, and 'psychology of the law' literature, all of which deserve and have received book-length treatment of their own, are not included, and the book is not concerned with civil law.

In the remainder of the book the first six chapters, which some authors might classify under 'psychology and courts', fall within Haney's (1980) 'psychology in law' category: eyewitnesses – key issues and event characteristics; eyewitnesses – the perpetrator and interviewing; children as witnesses; the jury; sentencing as a human process; and the psychologist as an expert witness. The remaining four chapters (persuasion in the courtroom; detecting deception; witness recognition procedures; and psychology and the police) are examples of Haney's 'psychology and law' category, also known in the literature as 'psycholegal studies', where the concern is with 'behaviour within the legal system as an arena of legal interaction' (Blackburn, 1996:6).

In each specific area the book aims to provide a comprehensive up-to-date survey of the published literature, drawing upon European and Australian work as well as more traditional North American sources, also giving sufficient of the legal background to provide a proper context for the psychological research. Appropriately, for a textbook, the present author is content to let the major protagonists in the literature speak for themselves. For a number of years now, there has been no comprehensive treatment of such a broad range of areas at the interface between psychology and criminal law. The present book is intended to remedy this.

2 Eyewitnesses: Key Issues and Event Characteristics

'A witness to a crime is expected, as a civic duty, to report the crime to the police ... At a later date the witness may be asked to give oral evidence in court about what he may have seen, and answer questions during cross-examination by the defence.' (Home Office, 1998:19)

'Testimony to personal identity is proverbially fallacious.' (William James, 1890:97)

'Although such testimony is frequently challenged, it is still widely assumed to be more reliable than other kinds of evidence. Numerous experiments show, however, that it is remarkably subject to error.' (Buckhout, 1974:23)

'Human memory is a fragile and elusive creature. It can be supplemented, partially restructured, or even completely altered by post-event inputs. It is susceptible to the power of a simple word. This is not to imply that all memories are changed and no original memories remain intact.' (Loftus and Ketcham, 1983:168–9)

'Nowhere are the problems of generalizability and reliability of research findings more acute than in the study of eyewitnessing.' (Davies, 1992:265)

'It is important not to exaggerate the fallibility of human memory. Memory is often wonderfully detailed and accurate.' (Lindsay and Read, 1994:293)

Introduction

The above quotes reflect the concern over the years with the limitations of eyewitness testimony, the more recent acceptance of the fact that the whole process of observing and recalling faces and events is a complex, interactive and dynamic one and, finally, that we should not overlook the fact that such testimony can be accurate.

Eyewitness testimony is of crucial importance for both crime investigators and lawyers. Not surprisingly, therefore, within the psycholegal field, testimony, especially eyewitness testimony, has attracted a lot of attention over the years. Since the 1980s the treatment of court witnesses by the criminal justice system has begun to improve. Memory issues permeate the law and psycholegal studies of eyewitness testimony constitute one of the pillars of legal psychology. As the content of this and the next chapter indicates, more empirical studies have been reported in this area of forensic psychology than in any other area. Furthermore, assumptions about human memory are inherent in both substantial and procedural rules without which the legal system could not function.

1 Legal Aspects of Eyewitness Testimony

The great importance of eyewitness testimony in criminal law can be seen in a number of different ways (Narby and Cutler, 1994:724): the various safeguards in law to protect defendants from wrongful conviction on the basis of mistaken identification; in the evidence that eyewitness testimony influences the outcome of trials (Cutler et al., 1990; Visher, 1987); as with all evidence, the prevailing practice by courtroom lawyers to discredit the other side's witnesses in order to win (Berman et al., 1995) and, finally, the very strong interest shown in testimony by psycholegal researchers and law reform bodies alike (see Cooney, 1994, for a sociologist's analysis of the social origins of evidence).

The courtroom procedure followed in the United States, Australian, British, Canadian and New Zealand courts and in other countries with a common law system (for example, India, Malta, Cyprus) is known as the 'adversary system'. This basically means that different sides to a dispute fight it out in court in order to obtain a favourable judgement (McEwan, 1995a; Waight and Williams, 1995:2–17). This is based on the belief that the 'truth' is most likely to be discovered when the disputing parties each present their version of the facts in question to a magistrate (lay or stipendiary) or to a judge or to a judge and jury. So strong is this belief that until the US Supreme Court ruled in the case of *Maryland v. Craig* (1990) 497 US 836, a defendant's absolute right to confront his/her accuser/s face-to-face was, in fact, guaranteed by the Sixth Amendment of the Constitution. Generally speaking, unlike Royal Commissions in the UK, Canada, New Zealand and Australia, or Senate Committees, House of Representatives Committees, Presidential

Commissions or Grand Juries in the United States, for example, which follow an 'inquisitorial' procedure, a court of law in common law jurisdictions may not call its own witnesses or carry out its own investigation into the case before it; it simply arrives at a decision on the basis of the evidence and arguments put before it by the two parties according to the rules of evidence and procedure which are intended to ensure a fair trial (see Jackson, 1995; McGinley and Waye, 1994; Smith, 1995; Waight and Williams, 1995).[1]

A widely known rule, the hearsay rule, enables a court in common law countries to exclude statements by persons who are not witnesses and who, therefore, cannot be cross-examined (Gillies, 1987). In common law jurisdictions, a criminal or civil case often involves, then, a contest between two parties in which the party initiating the proceedings wants to convince the court that the defendant incurred criminal or civil liability. Typically, in non-guilty plea cases the different parties will disagree about material facts of the case, and the prosecutor in a criminal case or the plaintiff in a civil case will lead evidence to convince the court as to the existence and nature of those facts. The defendant has the choice of also 'adducing' evidence. Parties to a dispute can attempt to prove material facts by direct or circumstantial evidence. 'Direct evidence is that which goes directly to prove a material fact. Circumstantial evidence requires the fact finder to draw inferences other than that the witness is correctly reporting what their senses registered' (McGinley and Waye, 1994:9). There is a presumption that evidence should be given to a common law court in oral form (Magner, 1995:25). Therefore, oral evidence is an important feature of most trials and legal disputes in general. As Leippe (1994) rightly pointed out, the existence of an eyewitness is of importance in the investigation of a crime, in making the decision to prosecute a suspect and at trial where a confident witness could sway the jury (p. 385).

According to Doyle (1989:128–9): 'It is an article of faith among lawyers that cross-examination represents "The greatest legal engine ever invented for the discovery of the truth" (Wigmore, 1974, Sec.1367)'. A wealth of judicial opinions assert that whatever problems may exist with the eyewitness testimony, cross-examination is their solution. Each party has a right to cross-examine the other side's witnesses, to question them in order to discover other facts or in order to cast doubt on the importance the court should place on the evidence already provided by the other side's witnesses (see chapter 8). If the cross-examination discovers some new fact, then the first party may re-examine. It is up to the magistrate or the judge, as the case may be, to decide whether the evidence being led by a particular party is admissible on the basis of existing law of evidence. Of course, cross-examination of witnesses does not guarantee that there will be no wrongful convictions due to false identification. As the extensive literature cited in this chapter shows, there is indeed an 'eyewitness identification' problem. Unfortunately, some authors take a rather narrow view and write about this problem as if it were synonymous with witness error in identifying a suspect in an identification parade/line-up, a task that does not confront the great majority of witnesses in criminal investigations and prosecutions.

Psycholegal researchers run the risk of exaggerating the practical importance of their studies if they are unaware, for example, that the great majority of criminal defendants plead guilty (Willis, 1995) and, consequently, all material facts are not in dispute. Also, most criminal cases in western common law English-speaking countries are not decided by a jury and, finally, eyewitness testimony plays but a very minor role in crime detection. The last point is brought home by a study of burglary and violence offenders in Nottingham, England, by Farrington and Lambert (1993). They found that: (a) victim descriptions of suspects accounted for 2 per cent of burglary and 14.7 per cent of violence offenders arrested; and (b) witnesses' descriptions contributed 6.7 per cent and 13.3 per cent to burglary and violence arrests respectively. Also, many experimental psychologists seem to have overlooked the fact that a trial under the adversary system is not a search for ultimate truth but a means of settling disputes. Lawyers are, first and foremost, interested in winning their case in court, not in being impartial – as psychologists researching witness testimony might wish them to be. Furthermore, experimental psychologists reporting studies of the reliability of eyewitness testimony have generally failed to locate their work in a truly psycholegal context by relating their findings to the relevant law of evidence and procedure in the jurisdiction where the research has been conducted (see Konečni and Ebbesen, 1992).

Research into the reliability of witness testimony has the longest history in psychological research, its formal beginnings stretching back to the beginning of the twentieth century.[2] Interestingly enough, however, when McConkey and Roche (1989) administered a questionnaire to introductory psychology, advanced psychology, and advanced law students in Sydney, Australia, to assess their knowledge of eyewitness memory, it was found that they all had a relatively limited knowledge of the topic in question. Similar findings have been reported by American (Deffenbacher and Loftus, 1982; Sanders, 1986), Canadian (Yarmey and Tressillian Jones, 1982) and UK researchers (Bennett and Gibling, 1989; Noon and Hollin, 1987). Bennett and Gibling reported that police officers and members of the general public alike had rather poor knowledge of many important factors in eyewitness testimony (for example, the impact of violence, post-event contamination, witness confidence), indicating the need for improvement in police training. The voluminous growth of witness research is not surprising in view of the vast literature on human attention, perception, memory and narration processes involved in all testimony.

On both sides of the Atlantic and in the Antipodes experimental psychologists have been appearing in court more and more frequently as expert witnesses to tell the court and juries about the psychology of testimony in general and eyewitness testimony in particular (see chapter 7). This is an interesting development in view of the myriad of cases, both criminal and civil, in which witness testimony plays an important part. While not suggesting that witness testimony is never reliable, the fact is that such testimony is often challenged in court and, as the empirical evidence in this and the next chapter shows rather convincingly, it is subject to error. This does not stop many lawyers, police personnel and the public at large from assuming that it is more reliable than other kinds of evidence. The available psycholegal research has not as yet eradicated the belief that human perception and memory operate like a tape-recorder or a video camera, that witnesses see and hear correctly and so testify.

Of course, a witness may testify dishonestly or honestly but incorrectly, or may disappear, recant or die before the case comes on for trial (Greer, 1971). It is the honest, co-operative witness which is the concern of this chapter. As Lord Devlin (1976) put it: 'the highly respectable, absolutely sincere, perfectly coherent and apparently convincing witness may, as experience has quite often shown, be mistaken'. In most jurisdictions there is no shortage of cases of mistaken identity, including some unfortunate ones where the defendant was executed. More common are cases where people (see Hain, 1976) are arrested and prosecuted by the state on the basis of identification evidence that is subsequently discredited (Buckhout, 1974:23). According to Connors et al. (1996), DNA testing on people in the United States who had been convicted of rape and other crimes which leave biological evidence has revealed a number of cases in which innocent defendants were convicted on the basis of inaccurate eyewitness testimony, often by the victim (see Wells et al., 1998).

2 Characteristics of Human Attention, Perception and Memory

Everyday witnesses in criminal and civil cases all over the world are asked by police, lawyers and others in and out of court to recall details of events, to describe a face and so forth on the assumption that the human memory operates like a video-recorder. This misleading passive model of human attention, perception and memory has, since the late 1970s, given way to the view that these are active processes, that perception and memory are also constructive processes, that a person's knowledge of the world around them is of paramount importance in understanding what and how he/she perceives events or other stimuli and what they remember about them (Clifford and Bull, 1978).

Human attention, perception and memory are dynamic processes.

The available experimental evidence in cognitive psychology is evidence that goes back to Bartlett (1932) and his finding that perceptions are assimilated into organisations or schemata: that when we remember a story, for example, we try to 'make sense' of what we remember. Such evidence leaves no doubt that perception and memory are 'social systems' (Buckhout, 1974) with structural and functional limitations. Many aspects of eyewitness behaviour cannot be explained unless we consider what someone is, what they are trying to do and the ways their values, attitudes, expectations and motivations act not only at the time of attention and perception but also during the period of storage, and especially when they are being asked to remember. In other words, perception involves a contribution from the perceiver, human memory is both selective and constructive and 'we make sense of things and come to perceive them in terms of the sense we have made of them' (Lloyd-Bostock, 1988:5).

The mental processes by which we come to understand things is known as 'cognition' and is made possible by the combined work of attention, perception and memory. According to Davenport (1992), human attention can be thought of as a 'low capacity, single channel' operation which enables us to selectively attend to stimuli in our environment and within us (pp. 127–33). 'Perception' refers to those processes which take in, and make some sense of, all our sensations, that is, the input from our senses. Perception is an active process whereby we interpret what information we receive so that it is meaningful to us. How we interpret sensations is influenced by our age, cultural background, expectations, emotions, particular specialist knowledge and so forth (p. 135).

> There are different kinds of memory and researchers have identified different processes that comprise a 'central executive'.

In a matter of a few years memory researchers have shifted from proposing a somewhat monolithic view of long-term memory to a view which differentiates different kinds of memory. Drawing on Gray (1999), the *modal model theory of the mind* (Atkinson and Shiffrin, 1968) has proved a useful framework for thinking and talking about the mind. This model posits: (a) that the mind combines three memory stores, namely a sensory memory, a working or short-term memory) and and a long-term memory; and (b) that the processing of information within stores and the movement of information between stores is governed by the following three central processes that comprise the *central executive* by controlling the flow of information:

- *Attention* – from the sensory store into the working memory.
- *Encoding* – from the short-term memory into the long-term memory.
- *Retrieval* – from the long-term memory into the working memory (Gray, 1999:322).

The available research evidence points to an impressive degree of specialisation in how information is stored (Gray, 1999:484). Finally, when psychologists distinguish between different kinds of memory, this is best understood 'as reflecting the different processes that can be used to access a common memory trace' (p. 482). While memory appears to be organised into separate stages or processes, the fact remains that its short-term storage lasts for less than 20 seconds, by which time new input will displace existing information, the memory can hold no more than seven items at one time unless information is passed into the long-term store for permanent storage, from where it can be retrieved (Davenport, 1992:153–4). Failure to retrieve information from our memory may reflect: failure to store information correctly; that information may have been displaced; the memory trace has simply faded away or decayed with the passage of time; or there may have been interference from later input which sounded similar and impacted negatively on the short-term memory or is semantically similar and interfered with information in the long-term memory (Davenport, 1992; Gray, 1999). In addition, many clinicians would argue that forgetting can be due to repression, that is, a process by which the mind pushes into the unconscious a memory of a traumatic experience. However, despite attempts to integrate the cognitive and the psychodynamic unconscious (see Epstein, 1994), as the discussion of the justifiably generalise findings about witness testimony from studies using such methodology. The desirability of research that allows a lot of control of the laboratory, while at the same time being forensically relevant, cannot be overemphasised (see Yuille et al., 1994, for an example of such research).

3.1.3 Field Studies

There are, of course, limits on the types of factors which can be examined by innocuously deceiving subjects involved in field studies and as they go about their daily routines. However, as already mentioned, there exists a strong argument for researchers attempting to replicate findings (first obtained in the laboratory with student subjects) in field studies. A finding obtained by using both methods is undoubtedly more convincing evidence (Konečni and Ebbesen, 1992:421). Admittedly, it is not possible to research the impact on witness accuracy of all variables that might be of interest to a researcher in a field because of both logistical and ethical constraints on such research. As Davies (1992:268) reminds us, in order to examine enough variables field studies need to be supplemented by archival research and case studies which paint a better picture of the reality of witnessing.

3.1.4 Archival Studies

Here the researcher examines, for example, police files to identify crucial variables. Illustrating with an example, Macleod (1987) examined 379 witness statements associated with 135 cases of assault. In support of earlier experimental findings (Clifford and Scott, 1978), it was found that, where injury occurred women gave fewer details of their assailant than did men. In addition, MacLeod (1987) also found that bystanders gave less information about both events and appearance than did victims – findings of some interest as laboratory studies have tended not to address the victim vs. bystander accuracy comparison. Davies (1992:269) also cites archival research which has confirmed the overwhelming saliency of a suspect's hair and upper facial features relative to lower ones, for example. The major limitation of archival studies of witness accuracy are: the absence of information on the accuracy of the descriptions provided by witnesses to the police in cases where the perpetrator has not been apprehended or has been acquitted and lack of control of potentially key variables which lead to confounding of data (Van Koppen and Lochun, 1997) For example, a researcher analysing data from official police records will not find details of the style used to interview the witness a factor which, as shown in the next chapter, has been shown to impact on eyewitness testimony accuracy.

3.1.5 Single Case Studies

In view of the limitation of archival studies mentioned, Yuille and Cutshall (1986) and Yuille and Kim (1987) in Canada and Davies (1992) in England have examined the statements of a number of witnesses in a serious crime for which someone has been convicted. Yuille and Kim (1987) found that, contrary to what laboratory testimony researchers would have us believe, the testimony of witnesses to serious crime is reliable. Yuille and Kim, however, were only able to interview a self-selected minority of the witnesses to a gun-shop shooting in Burnaby, Vancouver, four to five months later, a limitation that casts doubt on the veracity of their findings. Davies' case study of an armed robbery in Birmingham in which shots were fired and which involved fourteen witnesses being summoned to the identification parades, concluded that his findings 'accord much more closely with the view of witnessing which emerges from laboratory research than that arising from [Yuille and Cutshall's, 1986] the Burnaby study' (p. 271). Davies (1992) concludes: 'Case studies, however crucial and illuminating, do not open the doors to some alternative reality which will overturn the findings of more traditional research' (p. 272). It becomes clear that no method for studying witnessing is 'the best' since different methods have different merits and defects. While the slide presentation is easy to carry out in the laboratory and lends itself to a good control of variables, staging an event in the laboratory is an easy way to attempt to simulate the dynamics of a crime but comes with poor control of variables involved. Staging events out in the field allows the researcher good control of variables while, finally, both case studies and archival studies are high on realism but poor on control of relevant variables. The dictum for psychological researchers is to ensure that their findings about the reliability of witness testimony are replicated across a range of paradigms, or to risk broad acceptance of their research results (Davies, 1992).

Ultimately, the findings of experimental research into eyewitness testimony must be generalisable to real-life situations. However, such psychological research has had a 'deserved credibility problem' because, according to Malpass and Devine (1981), notwithstanding a great deal of findings relevant to the operation of the criminal justice system, 'the empirical base of our contribution is derived from studies that appear to only remotely reflect the conditions experienced by witnesses to actual criminal events' (p. 348). The empirical eyewitness literature consists, in the main, of studies in which subjects are uninvolved, bystander, undergraduate student volunteers; memory for an event in such studies is commonly tested, at most, a few days later and, above all, there are no consequences for the 'witnesses' (Yuille (1992:207–9). As Yuille emphasises, these conditions are in real contrast to what real-life witnesses experience – they are often victims of the crime they are asked to recall, crimes are often complex, fast-moving and 'absorbing' events and memory is tested months later (p. 208). Furthermore, often there exist long delays, ranging from months to years, between the event giving rise to a dispute and the trial. An extreme example is Longman's case (*Longman v. R* (1989) 64 ALJR 73) where the delay was twenty-six years (Magner, 1995:25).

Unfortunately for the discipline of psychology and law, the great majority of eyewitness researchers do not seem to share the serious concern about the external validity of experimental simulation studies (Davies, 1992; Konečni and Ebbesen, 1992; King, 1986; Malpass and Devine, 1981; Yuille, 1992). In a climate of 'publish or perish', the majority of researchers will, understandably perhaps, continue to rely on experimental studies of often questionable ecological validity, journals will continue to depend largely on such studies for their continued existence, and eyewitness testimony 'experts' will continue basing their status (and fees) on having carried out and published such research and a minority will continue voicing their concerns about all this. This chapter emphasises the proposition that the discipline of psychology and law is better served by a combination of both sound laboratory research and fieldwork as well as archival research. It does appear that the few psycholegal researchers who have expressed grave concern about the generalisability of a lot of experimental eyewitness research are researchers who have had first-hand experience of actual cases. The majority of those who apparently adhere blindly to experimental simulation as their only research method do not seem to consider familiarity with real cases important, or if they do, they choose not to invest time and resources to achieve it by spending time in the field, whether with operational police and/or practising lawyers and/or ex-jurors and/or crime witnesses. One partial solution might be for psychology students to be granted credit points towards their degree courses for exactly such involvement in the field. Rather than adopt entrenched positions, psychologists in both camps will go a longer way in bridging the remaining gap with lawyers if they take the middle ground rather than the high moral ground.

The 'credibility problem' referred to became less serious by the late 1990s than it had been in the early 1980s, primarily because in recent years many eyewitness researchers have made use of the simulated crime methodology or used real-life events instead of presenting subjects with pictures depicting a crime scene or face photographs of suspects. Such simulations have involved, for example, subjects viewing a video of a staged 'crime' or subjects 'coming across' a 'crime' being committed, being asked questions about what they have seen/witnessed and, where applicable, also being debriefed. As a result, better-designed applied testimony research, despite the limitations mentioned above, is not as scarce as it used to be, especially as more researchers have come to focus on 'system' variables rather than continue to report findings pertaining solely to 'estimator' (witness) variables as showing that a human witness is a limited-capacity processor of information (see below).

4 Variables in the Study of Eyewitness Memory

Wells (1978) made an important distinction between 'system' variables (that is, those factors the criminal justice system can do something about, procedures used to enhance the accuracy of eyewitness testimony) and 'estimator' variables (that is, characteristics of the witness which influence witness accuracy that the criminal justice system cannot do anything about). Wells et al. (1999) stress the crucial importance of *system variables* because for them, 'much of the problem with the accuracy of witness testimony owes to the system and the methods used to obtain the information from these witnesses'. While the distinction suggested by Wells is an important one when considering policy implications of research findings, it needs to be remembered that in the real world of crime victim and crime witnesses interviewed by police, the distinction between 'estimator' and 'system' variables is not always as clearcut as it appears. For example, the time when a witness is to be interviewed by particular police personnel is often the result of a little negotiation between the volunteer witness and police over the telephone to accommodate each other's preferences. Similarly, 'refreshing a witness' memory' is something which inevitably occurs as eyewitnesses discuss their experience with lawyers, friends, family members and others. However, it is also a common practice for the police officer who has the conduct of the case to 'refresh the memory' of a prosecution witness by ensuring the witness has reviewed the statement he/she made to the police at the first possible opportunity before going into the witness box (Magner, 1995:26). In the English case of *R v. Da Sylva* ([1990] 1 WLR 3; 1989 90 Cr App R 233), after entering the witness box a witness was allowed to refresh his memory by reading the statement he had made to the police a year earlier. As Magner (1995:29) points out, psychologists have not addressed the question of the effect of refreshing memory from a document and the question whether such legal procedures 'exaggerate or mitigate the misleading information effect which might otherwise occur' (p. 33).

Drawing on a taxomony of variables first used by Clifford (1981:21), Hollin (1989) categorised eyewitness memory variables under the heading of 'social' (attitudes, conformity, stereotypes, prejudice, status of interrogator), 'situational' (complexity of event, duration of event, illumination, time delay, type of crime), 'individual' (age, cognitive style, personality, race, sex, training) and 'interrogational' (artists' sketches, computer systems, identification parades, mugshots, photofits). As Hollin pointed out, eyewitness researchers have been concerned with the effects of these variables at the stages of acquisition, retention and retrieval. Other attempts to classify eyewitness testimony variables have included Ellis' (1975) distinction between 'stimulus' factors (for example, length of viewing time) and 'subject' factors (for example, sex of the witness) and Loftus' (1981) distinction between 'event' and 'witness' factors. Clifford (1979) suggested the additional category of 'interrogational'. In this context, it is worth noting that Wells' (1978) 'system' variables overlap with Ellis' (1975) 'stimulus' factors and Loftus' (1981) 'event' factors, while Wells' 'estimator' category overlaps with Ellis' 'subject' and Loftus' 'witness' category.

In reviewing studies of eyewitness testimony authors in the 1980s such as Goodman and Hahn (1987), Hollin (1989), Loftus (1981), and Penrod et al. (1982) drew upon the three memory stages of acquisition, retention and retrieval. These three stages have traditionally been identified in memory research and correspond to the stages involved in: (a) witnessing an event; (b) time taken before giving evidence; and (c) giving evidence. In reality, of course, these three stages are not distinct. For example, while waiting to give evidence, a witness may see a police artist's sketch of the suspect on television and/or may talk about the incident with other witnesses. As will be seen below, in the course of such exposure to information about the crime, a witness acquires information that becomes part of the memory to be retained for later recall. Furthermore, the terms 'event' and 'witness' variables are not always mutually exclusive. For example, 'type of event' and a witness' level of physiological arousal are closely related, while 'number of witnesses' can be both an 'event' and a 'witness' variable. Table 2.1 shows the variables considered in the literature reviews that follow below and in the next chapter under the categories of 'event', 'witness' and 'interrogational'.

In considering classifications of such factors it should also be remembered that memory errors are of two types: errors of omission and errors of commission. Errors of omission stem from inherent limitations of the way the human memory is structured and processes information.

Before reviewing available empirical evidence that a number of factors impact on the accuracy of eyewitness testimony, it should be noted that the empirical literature on witness testimony deals almost exclusively with the accuracy of identification rather than non-identification or misidentification (see Twining, 1983, on the issue of identification and misidentification in legal processes). A small number of researchers have examined the impact on mock juror verdicts of non-identification, that is, when the witness says: 'No, that's not the person I saw'. According to Wells and Lindsay (1980:776): 'Non-identifications generally are considered uninformative because of the belief that there are multiple plausible causes for non-identification (for example, memory failure)' and Williams et al. (1992:152) suggest that a non-identification may be construed as a 'non-event' rather than as an important piece of evidence. Leippe (1985) reported that the probability of a defendant being found guilty by mock jurors in an experiment was reduced from 53 per cent to

> Eyewitness testimony variables can be classified into 'event', 'witness', 'perpetrator' and 'interrogational'.

Table 2.1 Variables in the study of eyewitness testimony by category

Event	**Frequency, time, duration, illumination, type of event, weapon.**
Witness	Fatigue, physiological arousal, chronic anxiety, neuroticism, extroversion, reflection-impulsivity, need for approval/affiliation, morning–evening type, self-monitoring, field-dependence, breadth of categorising, levelling-sharpening, mood, alcohol, age, race, gender, schemas/stereotypes, physical attractiveness, whether also victim of the crime, confidence, whether witness is a police officer, collaborative testimony.
Perpetrator	Gender, body size, height, ethnicity, gait.
Interrogational	Retention interval, type of recall, efforts made to recall, leading questions, memory retrieval therapy, cognitive interview.

14 per cent by a non-identifying witness even if it was in contrast to two witnesses who positively identified the defendant. It was also found that the impact of a non-identifying witness was completely negated if such a witness elected not to testify and the information was conveyed to the mock jurors by the lawyer. Finally, Bekerian (1993) has rightly argued against the notion of a typical eyewitness situation or typical eyewitness because psychologists 'might be asked to identify one in court' (p. 575).

5 Variables that Impact on Eyewitness' Testimony Accuracy

There already exist a number of works that provide excellent reviews of the eyewitness literature (Cutler and Penrod, 1995; Davies, 1993a; Memon and Wright, 2000; Thomson, 1995a; Wells et al., 1999; Williams et al., 1992). The aim of the discussion of the literature that follows is to reach conclusions about the importance of a number of 'event' factors in eyewitness' accuracy, considering the findings in a broader sociolegal context as much as possible, drawing on contemporary criminology and relevant law. A literature review of the categories of 'witness', 'perpetrator' and 'interrogational' variables is the subject of the next chapter.

In *Neil v. Biggers*, 1972, the US Supreme Court outlined five criteria on which evaluations of eyewitness identifications should be based: certainty, view, attention, description and time. Interestingly, an experimental study by Bradfield and Wells (2000) found that each of the five *Biggers* factors contributes some amount to the overall impression of witness accuracy and, also, that the amount contributed by one factor is independent of the other factors.

5.1 Event Characteristics

Passage of time: the interval between witnessing an event and being questioned about it can vary from a few minutes to months and even years. It is very well established in eyewitness testimony research that both children and adults forget things over time (Flin et al., 1992). In a Dutch study, Van Koppen and Lochun (1997) used archival data from official police records to examine both the completeness and accuracy of witnesses' descriptions of commercial robbery offenders. As would have been expected, it was found that more complete descriptions were associated with a shorter delay between the crime and the reporting of the description. The reader should note, however, that a person's meory of an event, of someone's appearance, can be wonderfully accurate weeks later or even longer. It is well established, of course, that recognition is more accurate than recall. The following case illustrates accurate eyewitness recall of an event at a busy airport on Christmas Day that helped police investigators convict a homicide offender.

Case Study

A Christmas Day murderer who did not get away

On Christmas Day 1997 Jacqueline arrived at Larnaca International Airport in Cyprus on Alitalia flight AZ816 for a week's holiday in the sun. The island is a popular holiday destination for millions of European tourists every year and there were many flights that day. Jacqueline was due to return to France on New Year's Day. On 8 January 1998 the French embassy in Nicosia notified the Cyprus Police that she had failed to return home and had been reported missing as she had made no contact and could not be contacted since she left for her holiday. The case shocked Cypriots who take pride in the fact that their country has one of the lowest crimes rates in the world. Intensive police investigations revealed that Jacqueline had caught a taxi from the airport. On 21 January 1998 a taxi driver saw Jacqueline's photograph in a newspaper and told the police he could remember which taxi driver had picked her up outside the airport while waiting in the taxi-rank. Armed with the witness' description of the suspect and additional information he was able to recall with accuracy, such as the colour of the suspect's car, the police soon arrested the suspect who confessed to robbing Jacqueline of her valuables before killing her and disposing of her body. Later in the same year, he was convicted of homicide and sentenced to twenty years' imprisonment.[6]

Frequency: in some cases a bank-teller has spoken to the suspect of an armed robbery when he/she came into the bank to carry out surveillance and/or to do a 'dry run', or a suspect may have been seen at least once before in the vicinity of premises that have been broken into. Powel and Thomson (1994)[7] found that the greater the frequency of an event, the better people will remember it as having occurred and details about it. However, if people are asked to remember a specific occasion when a recurring event took place, the accuracy of recall decreases the more times it has occurred.

Time: remembering accurately when an event actually took place would add to the credibility of an eyewitness' recall of event information, including identification of a suspect alleged to have been involved in the event. A witness' recall of an event, or a description of an offender's face, exists in a time framework. Despite the fact that 'Time is a richly elaborated concept, one that is resistant to analysis' (Friedman, 1993:44), there is a body of literature on memory for time. Both life memory studies and laboratory studies have reported the 'forward telescoping' phenomenon. Forward telescoping refers to a 'tendency to give estimates that are too recent for events that are among the oldest in the range tested ... Respondents seem to import events that really took place before the cutoff in the question' (Friedman, 1993:51). It has also been found that judgements of time are more accurate when there is a more temporary structure to an unusual interval than when people's activities are more uniform (Tzeng and Cotton, 1980); when two items belong to the same semantic category, such as 'sofa' and 'chair', and when two items are strongly associated, as in 'smoke' and 'tobacco' (Winograd and Soloway, 1985). A number of theories have been put forward to account for such findings (see Friedman, 1993, for a discussion). Friedman groups theories according to the type of information that each theory emphasises as the basis for memory of dates.

Duration: the time it takes to commit a particular crime can range from a few seconds to a few minutes or even longer. An assault may be over in a fraction of a second, an armed robbery of a bank or of a person in the street may well be over in less than a minute (Kapardis, 1989), while a brawl between two street gangs or an abduction or a rape could last for much longer. According to Williams et al. (1992), in *Neil v. Biggers*, 1972, the US Supreme Court accepted the proposition that there is a strong correlation between a witness' memory accuracy and an opportunity for the witness to observe. In fact, the same court 'accepted this notion as a criterion for judging every witness' reliability' (p. 143). In the English case of *R v. Turnbull* (1977) 65 Cr App R 242, Lord Widgery stated that a defining feature of 'good' quality witness identifications (as opposed to 'poor' ones) is that the witness had ample time to get a good look at the suspect. This common-sense belief is supported by the literature. The Dutch study by Van Koppen and Lochun (1997) reported that more complete descriptions of offenders were associated with a shorter distance between the witness and the robber. A survey of 836 members of the public and 477 undergraduates in Kingston, Ontario, found that duration of crime was rated by potential jurors as the fourth most important determinant of eyewitness identification accuracy out of twenty-five variables (Lindsay, 1994a:372). In an experiment by Clifford and Richards (1977) policemen were asked to recall details of a person who had approached and conversed with them for either 15 or 30 seconds. They found better recall in the 30 seconds than in the 15 seconds exposure to the target person. In view of the existence of selective attention, however, greater exposure duration to an offence will not necessarily mean greater accuracy. It has been found that people tend to overestimate significantly short temporal duration, a tendency that is more likely to manifest itself when the event in question is complex or the person is stressed (Sarason and Stroops, 1978; Schiffman and Bobko, 1974). A bank-teller may say the robber pointed his sawn-off shotgun at him/herself for 2 minutes when, in fact, the time involved was no more than 30 seconds.

Illumination: crimes take place round the clock and illumination, the amount of light available at the scene of the crime, is undoubtedly a relevant factor. Illumination was considered by the potential jurors in Lindsay's (1994a) survey as the fifth most important determinant of eyewitness identification accuracy out of the twenty-five variables examined. Kuehn (1974) reported that witnesses could remember less about an incident that took place at twilight rather than during the day or at night and, similarly, Yarmey (1986b) found that accuracy of incident details and recognition of the people involved was better during daytime than at the end of twilight or during the hours of darkness. Van Koppen and Lochun (1997) found that the only factor which, to a significant degree, influenced the accuracy of commercial robbery eye-

Need for Approval/Affiliation: human beings vary in the extent to which their everyday lives are characterised by grouping. This process of grouping is also known as 'affiliation'. Affiliation refers to 'forming associations involving cooperation, friendship and love' (Davenport, 1992:123). Schill (1966) reported that persons high in need for affiliation (n-Aff) showed greater perceptual sensitivity to face-related stimuli than those low on n-Aff (Atkinson and Walker, 1955) and, similarly, persons high in need for approval (n-App) performed better in a memory task for faces than those low in n-App.

Morning–Evening Type: different people prefer different schedules in their daily lives. More specifically, morning-type individuals (known as 'larks') are said to reach their arousal peak 3 hours before the evening-type ones – known as 'owls' (Kerkoff, 1985). In fact, in free recall, 'larks' perform better in the morning and the 'owls' perform better in the evening (Lecont, 1988).[2] Where a person is located in the 'morningness–eveningness' dimension can be measured by Horne and Ostberg's (1976) questionnaire.

In an interesting experiment Diges et al. (1992) showed morning- and evening-type subjects a very brief film of a traffic accident at 10 a.m. or 8 p.m. Utilising two measures of arousal from McNair et al.'s (1971) *Profile of Mood States*, they found that the main factor affecting witness testimony is time; in other words, accuracy of recall is significantly better when people are more aroused. Diges et al. also found, however, that there was a systematic superiority of the 10 a.m. (testing time) as compared with the evening test at 8 p.m. Finally, evening-type subjects in the morning test failed to discriminate as much accurate from irrelevant information. The authors explained the last finding in terms of evening-type individuals' tendency to be extroverts (Kerkhoff, 1985). The owls' low basal level of arousal in the morning, Diges et al. argue, is related to 'scarce cognitive resources' that permit them to 'catch' a lot of accurate details of the event but they do not guarantee that the details will be properly integrated in a factual way. Being extroverts, more assertive and self-confident, the same authors suggest, explains why 'owls' differ in the way they face their task as witnesses: 'owls' seem to have a lower decision criterion when they recall details of an event. Consequently, they were found to write longer reports, to perform hurriedly and make mistakes when trying to integrate the information (p. 320). It is obvious that researchers are a long way from closing the chapter on individual differences in arousal and witness accuracy.

Intelligence: no relationship has been found between intelligence (when it falls within normal ranges) and the accuracy of eyewitness testimony (Brown et al., 1977; Feineman and Entwhistle, 1976).

Self-Monitoring: Snyder (1979, 1987) has distinguished between persons who are high self-monitors (HSMs) and low self-monitors (LSMs). This attribute refers to 'the extent to which people observe, regulate and control their public presentation of self in social situations and in their interpersonal relationships'

(Hosch, 1994:329–30). Thus, HSMs care about social situations within which they interact, and put considerable effort into monitoring and controlling the way in which they present themselves and the images they project (p. 330). Since HSMs are more attentive to the social environment, one might expect them to be more accurate eyewitnesses than low LSMs. In a number of studies Hosch and his co-workers have examined differences in eyewitness identification as a function of differences in one's degree of self-monitoring ability (see Hosch and Cooper, 1982; Hosch and Platz, 1984; Hosch et al., 1984). Hosch (1994) concludes that while HSMs appear to be more accurate as eyewitnesses on identification tasks, the relationship between witness accuracy and degree of self-monitoring ability 'is not necessarily a simple one' (p. 332). HSMs have been found to be more accurate (but no more confident) witnesses when they are the 'victims' of a staged crime instead of bystanders (p. 332). Snyder (1987) has argued that individual differences in self-monitoring are biologically based. In support of this view, Pannell et al. (1992)[3] found significant differences in evoked potentials between HSMs and LSMs in a facial recognition task, suggesting important differences in the way the two types of individuals search their memory and decide such a task.

Cognitive Style: Kogan (1971) defined 'cognitive style' as a characteristic way of perceiving, storing, transforming and utilising information. A widely cited example of cognitive style in psychology is field dependence/field independence. This construct describes one's ability to discriminate parts from the whole in which they are embedded. The same construct is referred to as articulated vs. global psychological differentiation (Hosch, 1994:341). Field independence has been theoretically linked with facial identification accuracy. Witkin et al. (1962, cited by Hosch, 1994:342) maintained that field-dependent persons should be better at recognising faces than field-independent ones because they are generally more attentive to faces. Studies that have tested this hypothesis have reported conflicting findings (see Hosch, 1994:341–3, for reviews). Durso et al. (1985) reported that field-dependent persons are more likely than field-independent ones to confuse memories of actual and illusory events. This finding lends support to the view that field-dependent individuals differentiate self less sharply from non-self compared to field-independent ones.

Breadth of categorising is another cognitive characteristic which has been considered in eyewitness identification accuracy (Kogan and Wallach, 1967)[4] and 'refers to a preference for being inclusive, when establishing an acceptable range for specified categories' (Hosch, 1994:338). Thus, if a witness is over-inclusive, then he/she would be more likely to pick a foil in a line-up. Hosch (p. 339) cites empirical evidence that breadth of categorising is positively related to facial recognition accuracy (Messick and Damarin, 1964) and is predictive of eyewitness accuracy (Hosch et al., 1990; Hosch et al., 1991).

Levelling-Sharpening: Hosch (1994:343–4) has also suggested that a witness' position on this dimension could be related to suggestibility to unconscious interference (see Ross et al., 1994) and the misinformation effect (see Lindsay, 1994b; Weingardt et al., 1994, and below in this chapter). 'Levelling-sharpening' refers to reliable individual variations in assimilation in memory (Gardner et al., 1959).[5] Levellers have been described as tending to blur similar memories and to merge perceived objects or events with similar but not identical events recalled from previous experience (Hosch, 1994:343).

Mood: It has long been known in cognitive psychology that people find it easier to recognise something than to recall and describe it. In accounting for the difference between recall and recognition, context is of paramount importance (Geiselman et al., 1986; Gudjonsson, 1992a; Lloyd-Bostock, 1988). Cues to recognition may be present within the witness when reliving the original incident and feeling the same way they did at the time (see Haaga, 1989; Schare et al., 1984) and/or in the external environment (Davies, 1986; McGeoch, 1932). McGeoch (1932)[6] termed the first context 'intra-organic condition' of the learner and the second 'stimulus properties of the external environment'.

The 1980s saw a burgeoning of research on the relation between emotional states and cognitive processes (Ellis and Ashbrook, 1991:1). Researchers have examined the hypothesis that a person's mood at encoding will subsequently serve as a retrieval cue for the learned information during recall. This is known as state-dependent effect (Mayer and Bower, 1986). On the basis of their discussion of relevant empirical studies, Ellis and Ashbrook (1991:14) concluded that state-dependent effects seem to occur seldom and the results are often impossible to replicate. The same authors reported stronger support for the 'mood-congruency effect', that is, the view that individuals retrieve more easily material which is congruent with the mood state prevailing at the time of encoding. According to Ellis and Ashbrook, this phenomenon is quite robust across a broad range of experimental conditions. Support for both state-dependent and mood-congruency effects has been reported by clinical studies (see Weingartner et al., 1977; Ingram and Reed, 1986; Blaney, 1986).[7] However, studies of the effects of emotional states on the retrieval of personal experiences in one's childhood or more recently have reported contradictory findings (see Ellis and Ashbrook, 1991:16). Network theory (Bower, 1981, see below) and the resource allocation or capacity model (see Ellis and Ashbrook, 1988) have been applied to the literature on mood and memory. Ellis and Ashbrook (1991) do not consider these two theoretical approaches as competing but rather as complementary.

According to Gudjonsson (1992a), the basic idea is that people find it easier to remember an event if they are in a similar mood (Haaga, 1989) or under the influence of a particular drug (Overton, 1964) or alcohol (Lisman, 1974) as when they witnessed the event. As far as the facilitating effect of cues in the external environment is concerned, the important finding is that reinstating the witness in the original context (for example, returning the witness to the scene of the crime, showing the witness photographs of the scene of the crime or asking him/her to form an image of the crime scene) enhances recall by maximising retrieval cues (Gudjonsson, 1992a:90; see also 'cognitive interview' below). Cutler and Penrod (1988) found, for example, that identification accuracy can be increased if police reinstate strong physical context cues associated with the offender, such as his/her voice, posture and gait.

The effect of context on memory can be explained by Bower's (1981) 'associative network theory' which holds that one's emotions serve memory units and are linked to what has been seen and experienced. In other words, one maximises retrieval cues by reliving the original context (Gudjonsson, 1992a:90). Reinstating the context is a crucial component of one particular technique for enhancing witness memory, namely, the 'cognitive interview technique' (see below).

Alcohol: alcohol abuse afflicts many societies (see De Luca, 1981; Saunders, 1984) and very few would doubt that, in addition to its astronomical social cost, alcohol also impairs many sensory motor and cognitive functions. Generally, the more alcohol consumed the greater the impairment, but this relationship is 'subject to a host of task, instructional, cognitive process and individual variables' (Read et al., 1992:427). Alcohol, of course, features frequently in the commission of a large volume of such criminal offences as homicide, rape, serious assault, robbery and culpable driving (Feldman, 1993:276–7; Kapardis, 1989; Kapardis and Cole, 1988; National Committee on Violence, 1990). It is often a requirement for judges in jury trials in common law countries to direct the jury that intoxication could render a witness' recollections inaccurate.[8]

> Researchers have reported conflicting findings regarding the impact of alcohol on memory performance.

Empirical studies of the impact of alcohol on memory performance have reported conflicting findings. On the one hand, Steele and Josephs (1990) and Yuille and Tollestrup (1990) found that alcohol interferes with the acquisition and encoding of information and Read et al. (1992) reported that it significantly impairs subjects' recall of peripheral information. On the other hand, Parker et al. (1980) found that consuming alcohol during the retention interval correlated with better recognition and recall performance than when subjects did not. More research is needed before the alcohol-memory performance relationship is elucidated. Lindsay's (1994a:372) survey found that the level of witness intoxication during the crime was ranked tenth by potential jurors in importance as a determinant of eyewitness identification accuracy out of twenty-five variables.

Alcohol is one kind of drug. A commonly taken drug that is illegal in many countries is cannabis. It has been found that being high on cannabis interferes seriously with one's recall accuracy of recent events (Thomson, 1995a:127). On the basis of what is known in psychological pharmacology, such illicit drugs as heroin, cocaine, and amphetamines can only be expected to influence adversely both a witness' initial perception of an event and his/her memory of it (Spiegel, 1989). Also, given the large number of people in society who are on such prescribed drugs as antidepressants and barbiturates and so forth, there is a need for research into how such individuals' performance as eyewitnesses is affected by their medication.

Age: in view of the increasing concern in recent years about abuse of children in general and their sexual abuse in particular, a lot of empirical literature on the relationship between the age of a witness and accuracy of recall has focused on child evidence (see chapter 4). At the same time, largely due to improvements in medical care, an increasing proportion of the general population, especially of western countries, comprises elderly people. The last few years have also witnessed an increasing concern about the abuse of elderly people in the home, in institutions, and as vulnerable victims of crime (Groth, 1979), who often live in fear of crime even though they are the least likely to be victimised by strangers (Kapardis, 1993; Kennedy and Silverman, 1990; Parker and Ray, 1990). In criminal law, the fact that a victim of an offence is of advanced age is regarded as an aggravating factor at the sentencing stage (Kapardis, 1985:103–5; Thomas, 1979).

According to Light (1991): 'Older adults complain more about memory than younger adults' (p. 333). Laboratory studies of memory[9] have found that persons over the age of 60 perform less well than persons in their twenties on free recall, recognition of lists of words or sentences. Light also reported that older adults on forensically relevant tasks remember less of buildings along the main roads in towns they have lived in for a long time, about what coins and telephones look like, activities they have participated in, names and faces of people and, finally, they have poorer memory for prose (p. 334). There is also ample evidence pointing to 'cognitive slowing' with aging, that is, that as one gets older one gets slower as far as the rate of rehearsal during a memory task, scanning in memory search tasks, or responding in primary and secondary memory tasks is concerned (Light, 1991:361). Apparently, also, older people are disadvantaged if their recall accuracy is tested by means of multiple-choice questions instead of 'yes' 'no' answers (List, 1986; Yarmey and Kent, 1980).

There is disagreement among researchers as to whether there is a peak age beyond which memory does not improve and may decrease. Diamond and Carey (1977) claimed to have found that memory peaks at the age of ten years while Carey (1981) and Chance et al. (1982) reported that adult-like levels of face recognition on performance may not, in fact, be achieved until about 16 years of age.[10] There is agreement, however, that elderly people of 70 years or older have poorer perceptual and memorial faculties (Wallace, 1956). A common loss suffered is in short-term memory retention (Craik, 1977) and in visual acuity for both near and distant objects, as well as the ability to discriminate colours adequately. Elderly people have also been shown to have a strong tendency to emphasise the accuracy of what they say at the expense of the speed in saying it (Botwinick and Shock, 1972); are less able than younger subjects to pay attention to stimuli on the periphery when driving (Manstead and Lee, 1979); have less confidence in their testimony and may well approach memory tasks differently (Yarmey and Kent, 1980).

The available literature also indicates that the elderly are also more prone to recognition errors for faces seen only once before (Bartlett and Leslie, 1986; Bartlett and Fulton, 1991; Smith and Winograd, 1978). However, this age-related deficit disappears if a face has been seen from a number of viewpoints (Bartlett and Leslie, 1986; Yarmey and Kent, 1980). Bartlett and Leslie (1986) reported that there may be an age-related deficit where the suspect is young and/or is seen only at a glance. Another defect which the elderly suffer is in free recall of events they have witnessed (List, 1986). Finally, it should be noted that studies reporting no significant differences between elderly and young subjects (Tickner and Poulton, 1975) defined 'elderly' to mean an average age of 50 years while others reporting differences (Yarmey and Kent, 1980) used 'elderly' to refer to subjects aged 65 to 90 years. For American potential jurors, however, the age of the witness is not considered an important determinant of eyewitness identification accuracy. Lindsay (1994a:372) reported that it was ranked eighteenth in importance out of the twenty-five factors considered. Ross et al. (1990) carried out three experiments on mock-jurors' perception of the average 74-year old's credibility as a witness compared to an average 24-year old and reported inconsistent results. There was general agreement, however, that elderly witnesses are honest.

In her review of the literature on memory and aging Light (1991) discussed four classes of explanation for age-related decrements in memory, namely: (a) metamemory (in terms of deficient knowledge about memory; deficient strategy use; memory monitoring); (b) semantic deficit (for example, in terms of richness, extensiveness and depth of encoding; encoding inferences); (c) impairment of deliberate recollection; and (d) reduced processing resources. Light concluded that, whether separately or combined, these hypotheses do not account adequately for what is known about the memory performance of elderly people (p. 366). In other words: 'Memory impairment in older adults does not seem to be accounted for by deficiencies in strategies used, or by problems in language comprehension' (p. 366). Future research into memory and aging needs, for example, to clarify the concepts of 'attention' and 'effort' in evaluating the attention capacity hypothesis (p. 363). Such research would also need to investigate further whether the same mechanisms underlie problems in recalling recent events and in remembering old information. At the same time, the need for such research in forensic contexts cannot be overemphasised. On the basis of his literature review, Bornstein (1995) suggests the following means of improving elderly eyewitnesses' memory: use recognition; ask precise questions; avoid leading questions; emphasise that a high degree of certainty is needed before deciding to select someone out of a lineup; present a line-up sequentially and, finally, make use of the cognitive interview technique (see below).

> People are generally better at identifying members of their own race but seasoned basketball fans are equally good at identifying faces from other races.

Race: as criminologists are not tired of reminding us, 'blacks [in the United States] are vastly over-represented in prison populations, in the official statistics of arrest and in victim reports of robbery and assault' (Feldman, 1993:69). Aborigines in Australia are also over-represented in official criminal statistics (National Committee on Violence, 1990:36–8; Walker and McDonald, 1995) as are West Indians in Britain (Ouston, 1984). A substantial body of research spanning more than two decades has been reported that focuses on racial and cross-racial identification. The general conclusion is that cross-racial identifications are more difficult, less accurate and thus less reliable than within-race identifications by adult witnesses.[11] A meta-analysis by Bothwell et al. (1989) on cross-racial identifications found that the own-race bias is consistent for both white and black subjects. In other words, testimony will be of doubtful validity when the race of the witness and the suspect is not the same. Differences in frequency and quality of contact between members of different races go a long way towards explaining the cross-race identification difficulty. Support for this was provided by Dunning, Li and Malpass (1998) who found that seasoned basketball fans were as accurate in identifying African–American faces as European ones but that novice basketball fans were not. Cross-racial identification is also characterised by a higher rate of false identifications (Thomson, 1995a:136). Interestingly, race of the witness and the criminal was rated as one of the least important factors (twentieth out of twenty-five) in eyewitness identification accuracy in the Lindsay (1994a:372) study. The issue of the cross-race effect is discussed further in the context of line-ups (see chapter 10).

Gender: according to Wootton (1959): 'If men behaved like women, the courts would be idle and the prisons empty' (cited by Feldman 1993:66). The gender gap in criminal offending has been known in criminology for a long time and victimisation surveys confirm it (Feldman, 1993:66; Blackburn, 1993:50–2). A number of studies have focused on gender as an influencing variable in eyewitness identification/facial recognition. Levine and Tapp (1971)[12] interviewed informally members of a large police force in the United States and found they seemed to prefer female to male witnesses. But how important is gender in witness testimony? (See Loftus et al., 1987c, for a review.) It is established that, generally, people tend to overestimate the duration of an event but it appears that females exhibit the tendency more than males (Loftus et al., 1987c). Males, on the other hand, are significantly more likely to suffer colour deficiency (Hurvich, 1981) and hearing loss (Corso, 1981), deficiencies which inevitably have a detrimental effect on their accuracy as witnesses. In addition, a witness' gender has been found to influence the types of details that are remembered from an incident. Powers et al. (1979) reported that females are more accurate in their memory recall than males for 'female-oriented' details and vice versa, suggesting that a witness' interest (see below) may well be another important factor in testimony. Lindsay (1994a:372), however, found (without taking type of crime into account) that the potential jurors in his study considered the gender of the witness to be rated the least important variable in eyewitness identification accuracy of all the twenty-five examined.

A series of other studies of the importance of gender have yielded inconsistent findings. While some (Cunningham and Brigham, 1986; Lindsay, 1986) found no gender differences in identification/facial recognition accuracy, others reported that females have higher accuracy of recall and are better than males in identifying a bystander (Howels, 1983; Lipton, 1977;

Shapiro and Penrod, 1986; Yarmey and Kent, 1980). There is also some evidence (contradicted by Cross et al., 1971) that accuracy is greater for same-gender than cross-gender targets (Jalbert and Getting, 1992; Shapiro and Penrod, 1986).

As far as violent incidents and the effects of arousal are concerned, Clifford and Scott (1978) found that female subjects were less accurate than male subjects about event details but were equally accurate as male subjects after viewing a non-violent incident. MacLeod and Shepherd (1986) compared 379 witness reports for assaults that involved either physical injury or no physical injury to the victim. They found no differences in the kinds and amount of details reported by male and female witnesses when the victim was not physically injured. However, when the victim sustained physical injury, female witnesses reported significantly fewer details about the perpetrator's appearance than did male witnesses. Finally, Jalbert and Getting (1992) reported a tendency by male subjects to make more false identifications than females, irrespective of the race of the suspect. In considering contradictory findings on gender and person identification we should note that different studies have used different events: rape (Yarmey, 1986b; Yarmey and Jones, 1983), a robbery (Loftus et al., 1987a) or a non-criminal event or a snatch-theft of a satchel (Sanders and Warnick, 1981). Also, as Foster et al. (1994:110) point out, none of the studies just mentioned examined consequentiality or type of line-up instructions. We can see that while gender does appear to be an important factor in the reliability of eyewitness testimony, for the most part the often contradictory findings reported do not allow any definitive conclusions to be drawn other than the weight of the evidence points to a same-gender bias.

Schemas/Stereotypes: social psychologists are particularly interested in social perception/cognition. For a number of years now, it has been known that in some circumstances (for example, of ambiguity, as when one has got a glimpse of a robbery being committed in a matter of seconds) people tend to report seeing what they expect to see, or desire or need to see (Whipple, 1918; Hollin, 1980). In Hollin's (1980) study the target person had blond hair, green eyes and a fair complexion. Of the 93 per cent who correctly recalled the hair colour (blond), almost half reported blue eyes! In other words, the subjects remembered the information originally encoded but combined it with stereotypical information, with information from their own scripts (Bower et al., 1979). As Buckhout (1974:26) put it: 'Expectancy is seen in its least attractive form in the case of biases or prejudices'. Very relevant to the impact of people's expectations on their testimony is their social schemas, that is, mental representations of social categories. Schemas can refer to persons, social events, and social roles (see Lilli, 1989; Wippich, 1989). They include some knowledge about a particular object or person, some information about the relationships among the various thoughts concerning that object or person, as well as some specific examples (Taylor and Crocker, 1980). Our social schemas often influence the impressions we have of others. Once we have decided that a person fits a particular category then our mental representations evidence has also been advocated by Thomson (1984:111) in Australia on the grounds that evidence can only be useful if it is accurate and by admitting the original account as the primary evidence will also prevent a dishonest witness from making up a story.

Type of Recall: a witness may be asked to tell everything they saw happening during an incident in their own words and at their own pace. This is known as 'free recall' and it would be normal police practice to follow it with cued, 'interrogative' recall. According to Hollin (1989) the distinction between 'free' and 'interrogative' recall was made by Binet (1900). Experiencing difficulty in remembering, a witness may well hesitate. Rather unwisely, police investigators may encourage a hesitant witness to 'have a guess' in furnishing a physical description of the suspect, for example, or in picking him/her out from a photospread, an identification parade or in a 'show-up' (see chapter 10). Such encouragement has been shown to have an adverse effect on accuracy later on.

Psychologists have known for a long time that, generally speaking, an interrogative recall produces a greater range of information (that is, it is more complete) than free recall, but it is less accurate. In contrast to what early researchers (for example, Binet, 1900; Gardner, 1933; Stern, 1939; Whipple, 1909) reported, the picture for the effect of mode of recall on testimony is more complex; interrogative, structured questions can lead to more complete recall but also produce more inaccuracy when asking a witness about difficult items of information (see Clifford and Scott, 1978). In other words, from the point of view of law-enforcement personnel, testimony accuracy and completeness are directly related to how specific a question is as well as how difficult is the information being asked of the witness. Police investigators, therefore, need to be aware of the trade-off here.

Number of Efforts Made to Recall: first-hand knowledge of how crime victims/witnesses are processed by police personnel leaves no doubt that it would be most unusual for a witness to be asked only once to recall details of the offender's face or of an incident. Repeatedly recalling stories was an issue that attracted the attention of Bartlett (1932), and its significance was noted by Penrod et al. (1982), for example, but the number of studies devoted to it are few in number (for example, Dunning and Stern, 1992; Jobe et al., 1993; Scrivner and Safer, 1988). Both laboratory and survey studies have found that the amount of cognitive effort influences the quality of recall (Jobe et al., 1993:573). Hypermnesia, first observed by Ballard (1913),[19] is a phenomenon of improved memory performance with repeated testing. In fact, one of the recommendations of the architects of the cognitive interview technique (see Fisher and Geiselman, 1992) that enhances eyewitness accuracy is to solicit multiple recalls from witnesses in order to increase the amount of information provided (see below). Payne (1987) suggested that 'hypermnesia' be used to refer to increases in net recall in successive trials and 'reminiscence' as referring to gains in gross recall.

As would have been expected on the basis of the literature on the useful-ness of the cognitive interview, in a series of experiments Turtle and Yuille (1994) obtained evidence supporting the reminiscence notion, that 'multiple eyewitness recalls can be beneficial in terms of overall recall without a severe increase in errors' (p. 268). As for how hypermnesia and reminiscence occur, Turtle and Yuille (1994:261) accept a process, put forward by Estes (1955), as stimulus sampling, that is, as witnesses repeatedly attempt to access their memory they obtain different samples from a population of potential infor-mation about the trace in question. Like Turtle and Yuille (1994), Otani and Hodge (1991) found no support for hypermnesia in two forced-choice recognition experiments. Otani and Hodge, however, found support for hypermnesia in two cued recall experiments and explain their findings in terms of relational processing that increases the availability of retrieval cues and thus aids recall of target words (see Hunt and Einstein, 1981). Turtle and Yuille (1994) remind us that while repeated recall may well produce more accurate information for the police investigation, any inconsistencies between successive accounts by the witness will be useful ammunition for the lawyers in court to discredit such a witness. This concern, they point out, will be counterbalanced by the fact that repeated recall will yield more facts about the case and, also, that 'a unified position on how it is affected by multiple-retrieval attempts should make people aware that gaining and losing details on successive recall is typical of how memory works' (p. 269).

Post-Event Interference: it is common police practice to ask witnesses to a crime for a verbal description of the suspect/s, to assist in making a photofit or an artist's impression with or without the aid of a computer, and to also ask witnesses to take a look at photographs of known offenders and try and identify the suspect they have seen. In addition, police may later ask a witness to identify the suspect in an identification parade/line-up (see chapter 10). It is interesting to note in this context that the Devlin Committee (1976) examined all line-ups in England and Wales in 1973 and they found that 347 cases were prosecuted when the only evidence was identification by one or more eye-witnesses. Three-quarters of the accused were convicted. The significant impact of eyewitness testimony on findings of guilt is also documented by experimental studies (see Loftus, 1974; Wells et al., 1979). According to Milne and Shaw (1999), 'The proper use of questions is itself a complex skill. The complexity arises because different types of question produce different types of answer and it is essential that particular classes of question are used in their correct way' (p. 129). In asking witnesses questions the police may inadvertently contaminate the witness' memory.

A very popular paradigm for eyewitness testimony researchers since the mid 1970s has been the use of the 'misinformation' paradigm to study how and when information encountered after an event contaminates a wit-ness' memory and makes it unreliable. The considerable interest in the misin-formation effect is evident by studies[20] in the United States (for example, Belli, 1989; Metcalfe, 1990), in Australia (Sheehan, 1989), in Germany

(Köhnken and Brockman, 1987) and in Holland (Wegener and Boer, 1987). In such studies, planting misinformation on subjects has been found to lead to misrecall, a witness remembering a car as being of a different colour, a 'give-way' sign as a 'stop' sign, seeing broken glass and even a barn never seen (Williams et al., 1992:149). Similarly, as a result of misinformation, a man with a moustache, straight hair, a can of Coca-Cola and breakfast cereal were recalled as clean shaven, curly hair, a can of peanuts and eggs respectively (Hoffman et al., 1992:293). There is disagreement among cognitive psychologists whether the later information causes an irrevocable alteration of the original memory, or whether the original memory is retrievable under appropriate circumstances (see below). There is, however, consensus among researchers that memory can be contaminated by means of leading questions.

Leading Questions: during a trial a lawyer is generally not allowed to ask leading questions either in examination-in-chief or in cross-examination, that is, questions suggesting how a lawyer wishes a witness to answer them (Waight and Williams, 1995:251). However, according to Archbold (2000:1058), the answers to leading questions are per se inadmissible (*Moor v. Moor* [1954] 1 WLR 927) although the weight which can properly be attached to them may be substantially reduced (*R v. Wilson*, 9 Cr.Ap.R.124, CCA). It is stated in Archbold that there are exceptions to this general rule: (a) if a witness swears to a certain fact and another witness is called in order to contradict him, the latter witness may be asked directly whether the fact did occur; and (b) counsel for the party which has called a witness may ask him leading questions if he has leave from the court to treat him as hostile (p. 1058). Practising lawyers might be interested to know that, from a psychologist's point of view, asking a witness a question is analogous to an experimental treatment situation and the type of question and manner of asking it impacts on the answer given (Lilli, 1989:223–4).

An easy way of contaminating someone's memory of an event (that is, introducing errors) is to ask them a leading question containing a false piece of information supposedly present in the original incident.

   A very common method of contaminating someone's memory of an event (that is, introducing errors) is to ask them a leading question containing an item of information that never existed in the original incident.

> In a study by Loftus and Palmer (1974) subjects viewed a film of a car accident and were asked to estimate the speed of the car at the moment of impact. It was found that estimates of speed varied as a function of the verb used to describe the accident. Asking subjects how fast the cars were travelling when they 'contacted' one another as opposed to when they 'smashed' into each other yielded speed estimates of 31.8 mph and 40.8 mph respectively. Furthermore, when subjects were later asked to describe the accident it was found that those exposed to the 'smash' condition were more likely to report having seen broken glass at the scene of the accident when, in fact, none existed.

The literature on post-event misinformation has given rise to an ongoing controversy regarding whether the new information changes the original memory – the 'integration' view – or whether the effects found by Loftus et al. (1978) are attributable to the processes used rather than to permanent changes in memory.

It is now well established that subjects exposed to misleading post-event information are likely to report such information on subsequent memory tasks and to do so confidently (see Holst and Pozdek, 1991; Lindsay, 1994b; Loftus et al., 1978; Loftus et al., 1989; Weingardt et al., 1994). Loftus et al. (1978) found that the greatest post-event contamination/misinformation effect occurs when the misleading information is introduced following a long delay after acquisition and before recall. Dristas and Hamilton (1977)[21] reported that post-event information interferes more easily with peripheral, rather than central, features of one's memory of an incident. The available literature leaves no doubt that asking a witness questions can influence their memory of an event. Loftus and Zanni (1975) reported that the presence of the indefinite article ('a') instead of the definite article ('the') gives rise to different expectations about the existence of an object. Using 'the' significantly increases the percentage of subjects who say they saw something that was not present in a film.

The literature on post-event misinformation has given rise to an ongoing controversy regarding whether the new information changes the original memory – the 'integration' view (see Loftus and Ketcham, 1983) – or whether the effects found by Loftus are attributable to the processes used rather than to permanent changes in memory (see McCloskey and Zaragoza, 1985; Zaragoza and Koshmider, 1989: Zaragoza et al., 1987). Zaragoza and Koshmider (1989) have argued that misinformation-based responses do not necessarily mean that the witnesses actually believe the details concerned happened in the original event; that subjects' responses are indicative of 'demand characteristics'. McCloskey and Zaragoza (1985), in fact, believe that memory for an original incident is not impaired by post-event contamination and advocate the 'coexistence' theory, that is, that the original memory could become accessible under appropriate circumstances at retrieval.

Bonto and Payne (1991) examined the effect of varying the context of presentation of the original event and the post-event information and found it did not have an effect on subjects' performance. The robustness of the misinformation effect has been further reinforced by Weingardt et al.'s (1994) study which found that even when subjects were instructed to exclude suggested items from their recall lists they continued to include them. This finding led them to conclude that 'Witnesses can exhibit strong beliefs in their memories, even when those memories are verifiably false' (p. 25). Lindsay and Johnson's (1987) own work in this area has produced results that are consistent with Loftus and her associates. Lindsay and Johnson (1987) and Lindsay, D. S. (1994), however, proposed that a satisfactory explanation for the misinformation effect lies in what they term 'source misattribution' by witnesses in terms of their source monitoring processes, that is, that although the original event and the post-event information may exist in the memory, misled subjects may experience confusion as far as sources of the two types of information is concerned.

Watkins (1990) has suggested that cognitive psychology may not be able to resolve the question of whether misleading post-event information does, in fact, alter memory traces or simply makes them less likely to be retrieved. It is unlikely this fierce debate between the 'integration' and 'coexistence' view of post-event influences on memory will be resolved in the very near future. It is, therefore, worth remembering that both sides to the dispute are in agreement that post-event misleading information can have a significant effect on what a witness remembers and the accuracy of his/her testimony. Finally, available research indicates that post-event contamination by interviewing police officers is more likely when a witness believes the police know exactly what happened (Smith and Ellsworth, 1987). This finding is of particular importance when it is remembered that both developmentally handicapped and mentally disordered witnesses are particularly vulnerable to the misinformation effect (Gudjonsson, 1995; Perlman et al., 1994).

4 Misinformation due to source monitoring error

Cognitive psychologists (Johnson et al., 1993) use the term 'source monitoring error ' to refer to cases where a witness confuses what he/she has experienced with what he/she has seen on television or heard about from other people, he/she confuses what is real and what is imaginary. The result is that the witness remembers misinformation. A real-life example of this type of error was provided by Crombag et al.'s (1996) study of witnesses in the wake of the Israeli airline El Al Boeing 747 crashing into apartment buildings in Amsterdam. Even though no one had filmed the crash, the researchers found that 60 per cent said they saw the plane crash on television and many of those gave detailed answers to questions. It would appear that people in the study pieced together what they had heard about the crash from different sources to construct an image of the crash and accepted the suggestion that they had watched it on television.

5 Repressed or False-Memory Syndrome?

Until the early 1980s reports of abuse, especially sexual abuse, said to have taken place many years earlier in childhood and not reported for years, were rare indeed. Since then, however, such reports have become increasingly more common. Therapists use a diversity of alternatives to 'assist' their clients to 'recover' their allegedly repressed memories including: Eye Movement Desensitisation and Reprocessing (EMDR), age regression, psychodrama, visualisation, guided imagery, body work, art therapy, group therapy, dream interpretation, having the client read popular books on the subject, and various drugs. Jurors have also been found to rely on a witness' repressed memory of a crime in order to convict a defendant of murder (see Brahams, 2000, for an American case). The focus here, however, is on recovered alleged cases of childhood sexual abuse.

The following case from Western Australia, cited by Freckelton (1996), illustrates the use of a series of psychotherapeutic interventions in repressed memory syndrome. In the *Bunbury* case (*R v. Jumeaux* (unreported, Supreme Court, WA, 23 September 1994)), claiming their memories had been repressed, two daughters made sixty-five allegations of sexual abuse against their father. Daughter A underwent psychotherapy after her depression had not responded to antidepressants. Earlier on she had described uncomfortable feelings after recovering from an anaesthetic. During psychotherapy she experienced 'abreaction', that is, a free expression or release of an emotion that has been repressed. She also later had flashbacks of abuse, both in and outside therapy. While daughter A was undergoing psychotherapy, her sister sought the help of a medical doctor out of concern that her own memories of sexual abuse might have been repressed. She came to 'recover' memories of such abuse after being hypnotised a number of times and seeing two medical practitioners. At the trial a number of experts testified on the topic of repressed memory syndrome. Justice Seaman stated that, 'evidence based upon memories by various forms of counselling and psychotherapy have similar inherent dangers; namely, the production of false evidence by means of suggestion' (cited in this context by Abadee J. in *Tillott v. The Queen* (unreported, Crt Crim App, NSW, 1 September 1995, cited by Freckelton, 1996)). In *R v. Bartlett* [1996] 2VR 687, the Court of Appeal of the State of Victoria established the legitimacy, in certain circumstances, for the defence in criminal trials to adduce suitably qualified expert evidence about the unreliability of recovered memories of abuse (see also chapter 7 in this volume).

Broughton (1995:93) points out:

- The mental health of most survivors of sexual assault deteriorates significantly as a result of their participation in the criminal justice system.
- Such survivors are degraded and humiliated immensely during the cross-examination.
- In most cases, if the offender pleads not guilty, he is acquitted.

Victims of childhood sexual abuse who pursue legal redress because they want justice, are, therefore, advised by experienced criminal lawyers specialising in sexual assault (for example, Broughton, 1995, in Melbourne, Australia) to apply, instead, to the Criminal Injuries Compensation Tribunal, after reporting the crime/s to the police.

Mock-jurors in the United States have been found to be more likely to believe a plaintiff in a repressed memory of sexual assult case if the number of assaults was thirty rather than one; if the victim reported the assault/s to the police immediately rather than if there was a twenty-year delay (Golding et al., 1999). Coleman, Stevens and Reeder (2001), too, investigated what makes recovered-memory testimony compelling to mock-jurors and found that they considered the victims' testimony as more accurate and credible and decided in favour of the victim if the therapist had used hypnosis. The opposite was found if the therapist was being sued for having used hypnosis to influence a client's recall of false memories of abuse.

Given cognitive psychologists' belief in the malleability and suggestibility of memory, it comes as no surprise to be told they have been at loggerheads with psychotherapists over the issue of recovered memories of childhood sexual abuse (see Thomson, 1995b, and Freckelton, 1996, for a discussion of the false memory syndrome). Whilst not disputing that child sexual abuse exists and is serious, Read and Lindsay (1994:430) have argued that 'memory recovery therapy, like ECT in the 1940s, is being used too often, too indiscriminately, with overly large "doses", and with insufficient safeguards for the well-being of clients, and that it has consequently harmed some of the people it was intended to help'. The concern expressed by some cognitive psychologists is that memory recovery therapies may lead clients of psychotherapy to, in fact, create illusory memories and that there exists a high rate of false diagnosis of child sexual abuse (Ceci and Loftus, 1994; Loftus, 1993; Lindsay and Read, 1994; Read and Lindsay, 1994; Slovenko, 1993). As already mentioned, concern about recovered memories of abuse has been expressed by the judiciary in Australia (see, also, *R v. Thorne* (unreported, Crt Crim App, Victoria, 19 June 1995). According to Freckelton (1996), the same concern has also been voiced in judicial judgements in the United States (see *New Hampshire v. Hungerford and Morahan* (unreported, Superior Court, New Hampshire, Hillsborough County, 23 May 1995)) and in Canada (see *R v. Norman* (1993) 87 CCC (3d) at 168–9). However, 'The admissibility of expert evidence about repressed memory syndrome and false memory syndrome remains to be authoritatively determined throughout common law jurisdictions' (Freckelton, 1996:122), and 'Repressed memory syndrome could not at this stage qualify as reliable under the [US] *Daubert* test of falsifiability, the test that governs the admissibility of scientific evidence generally under the United States Federal Rules of Evidence' (p. 29).

Concerned that false memories of childhood sexual abuse may be falsely implanted or encouraged by mental health professionals without regard for their accuracy, Slovenko (1993) has argued the need for corroborating evidence of abuse in order to justify the application of the discovery rule in such cases in the United States. For its part, the Australian Psychological Society (1995) in its *Guidelines Relating to the Reporting of Recovered Memories* exhorts psychologists to exercise 'special care' in dealing with allegations of past abuse (see also American Psychiatric Association, 1993, *Statement on Memories of Sexual Abuse*). The American Psychiatric Association warned in its 1993 position paper that repressed memories could be false, especially if recovered in the context of therapy. In the UK the Royal College of Psychiatrists' Working Group on Recovered Memories published its Guidelines for Practice in 1996, rejecting the concept of massive repression. According to Brandon (1999), the Working Group 'did not find convincing evidence that repeated sexual abuse is ever completely forgotten'. As shown in the next chapter, it is well established in the empirical psychological literature that memory for early childhood events is poor. Furthermore, as Thomson (1995b:200) reminds us, 'There is an inherent difficulty in any study that attempts to examine childhood memories'.

Lindsay and Read (1994:294–8) and Loftus (1993:525–6) attribute the alleged high rate of false diagnosis to both popular publications on child sexual abuse (for example, *The Courage to Heal* by Bass and Davis, 1988) and poorly trained therapists who unintentionally, perhaps, suggest to their clients that they must have been sexually abused as children on the basis of insufficient evidence, leading: (a) to numerous legal cases on both sides of the Atlantic involving allegations of child sexual abuse (in the main, incest) by men and women in the wake of memory recovery therapy (see Bulkley and Horowitz, 1994; Wakefield and Underwager, 1992); and (b) to legal reforms permitting plaintiffs to sue for recovery of damages for injury suffered as a result of child sexual abuse within a period (up to three years in Washington, for example) of the time they remembered the abuse (see Sales et al., 1994, regarding the admissibility of child sexual abuse memories in the United States) and to even bring criminal charges against their alleged abusers many years later (see Loftus, 1993:520–1). Such critics of memory recovery therapies point to the evidence for suggestibility of memory, and suggest that not only is repression a rare phenomenon (Read and Lindsay, 1994:418) but it also lacks scientific support (Loftus, 1993:519) and is therefore problematical as an explanation for recovered memories (Thomson, 1995b:101). It has also been argued that there is no conspicuous syndrome of child sexual abuse (Ceci and Loftus, 1994:354) and that memory recovery therapists make very questionable assumptions about the human memory (for example, that people can remember events in their childhood that took place before the age of 5, despite the evidence for 'infantile amnesia' – see Fivush and Hamond, 1990) that are not consistent with the weight of the empirical evidence provided by cognitive psychologists (Lindsay and Read, 1994:284, 286). In the light of the various arguments against repression as an explanation for recovered memories of abuse, Thomson (1995b) has argued that an explanation of such memories in terms of 'suppression' (that is, when someone chooses not to report a particular event they are aware of and remember it for one reason or another) is more convincing than repression (p. 202).

Undoubtedly, a major criticism that has been levelled against memory recovery therapists is that they are subject to 'confirmatory bias' (that is, that they tend to search for evidence that confirms rather than disconfirms their own hunches) and, thus, lead their client's memory with suggestions about childhood sexual abuse (Loftus, 1993:530). Research in Australia by Thomson (1995b) has also found that such therapists' own expectations of what may have happened affects the types of questions they ask which, in turn, influence what the interviewee reports of the original event. In other words, 'people's memory of a particular event can be shaped in more subtle ways via direct suggestions' (p. 104). Finally, Thomson (1995b) found there is no scientific evidence that memory recovery therapy is effective. Accepting these arguments casts serious doubt on a range of legal changes introduced, perhaps prematurely, to facilitate criminal and civil action against the alleged abusers (Wakefield and Underwager, 1992).

The Recovered or False Memory Debate: Two Contrasting Views

At the basis of the controversy surrounding recovered memories of child sexual abuse are two contrasting schools of thought. On the one hand, there are those who are prepared to rely on assumptions, to infer internal psychological states and mental processes even though they lack scientific support. The psychotherapists who identify with this school of thought tend to accept without question what clients tell them and/or to encourage such 'revelations' by means of suggestive questioning (Wakefield and Underwager, 1992:503). On the other hand, there are those cognitive psychologists who are concerned about the claims being made by therapists regarding recovered memories of child sexual abuse because they espouse a constructive model of human memory, in the Bartlett (1932) tradition.

A number of authors, however, have defended memory recovery therapists against the onslaught by the cognitive psychologists. Berliner and Williams (1994) point out that the polarised debate is really a dispute between academic researchers and clinicians, with each group pursuing their different goals (pp. 384–5), and argue that Lindsay and Read (1994) exaggerate the significance of a few studies, claiming that these studies have produced false reports (p. 380), charge them with selective use and evaluation of studies (p. 381) and maintain that: 'While there is evidence based on laboratory studies for the fallibility of memory, suggestibility and inaccuracy, it has not been proven that full-blown memories for traumatic childhood experiences can be created from nothing' (p. 385). Berliner and Williams suggest that if cognitive psychologists spent more time investigating the effects of trauma on memory as well as alerting us to the dangers of some clinical practices, the debate would be less polarised (pp. 385–6). Redzek (1994), in her comment on the Lindsay and Read (1994) article, in the same special issue of *Applied Cognitive Psychology*, also disputes some of their claims and, in an attempt 'to generate more light than heat', proposes recasting the real vs. illusory memory debate by replacing the 'all true vs. all false' approach with a Signal Detection Model that distinguishes the signal (true memory) from the noise (illusory memory). In their rejoinder to the commentaries by Berliner and Williams (1994) and Redzek (1994), Read and Lindsay (1994) defend the claims they make about memory recovery therapists, make the point that a minority of such therapists (who use highly suggestive techniques and are in need of some retraining and education by cognitive psychologists) contribute a disproportionate number of 'tragic false alarms' but concede that 'some cases of inaccurate delayed accusations might be better characterised as involving false beliefs rather than illusory memories. The reason this is important is that it is probably much easier to induce false beliefs than it is to induce full blown illusory memories' (p. 429). On the basis of there being 250 000 therapists in the United States, 10 per cent of whom, with caseloads of twenty clients per year, use highly suggestive techniques that are applied to non-abused patients 10 per cent of the time and create illusory beliefs and memories of child abuse in only 10 per cent of such cases, Read and Lindsay (1994:416) estimate 5000 cases of false alarms a year, that is, a rate of one per 100 recovery therapy clients 'treated' by such memory recovery therapists.

While the basis of the controversy surrounding recovered memories of child sexual abuse are two contrasting schools of thought, the fact is, of course, that, as seen earlier in this chapter, there are competing models of memory and the constructionist cognitive psychologists' case is not as convincing as is presented (see Davies, 1993a). The constructionist camp, however, can point to some hard evidence supporting their model of memory and thus justify their concern to some extent and the ringing of alarm bells about the innocent individuals whose lives are destroyed as a result of accepting what therapists claim. The legal system has been shown to be an ineffective answer to a broad range of societal problems, ranging from alcohol abuse, violence (both domestic and public) and criminal behaviour in general. Finally, there is a crucial sociolegal question about the whole issue: how valid is the assumption that adults claiming to have recovered memories of childhood abuse stand to benefit more by taking legal action, civil and/or criminal instead of resolving their psychological harms in therapy? Bulkley and Horowitz (1994) pose this very question and, after a lot of serious discussion of the arguments for and against, conclude the answer is a cautious negative one.

Following the excessive claims made for memory recovery therapy in the 1980s, Read and Lindsay (1994) provided a well-argued, well-intended and timely reminder to psychotherapists to at least be careful with their use of techniques to help their clients recover suspected memories of childhood sexual abuse (pp. 430–1). As a step in the right direction, Ceci and Loftus (1994) suggest that in attending to the needs of true abuse survivors, therapists need to be very conscious of the dangers of suggestive questioning and that failure to be so results in false alarms that cast doubt on the therapists themselves and undermine sympathy for the unfortunate victims of childhood abuse (p. 362). Meanwhile, 'Because there is no clear way of discriminating between authentic and fabricated memories' (Thomson, 1995b:104), there is an urgent need to subject the various techniques used by proponents of recovered memory therapy to procedural safeguards or guidelines as have been adopted, for example, for the use of hypnosis in the *Evidence Code of California* (Freckelton, 1996). In addition, the need for research into how best to discriminate between accurate and illusory memories cannot be over-emphasised (Raskin and Esplin, 1991). For therapists, it may be a consolation to know that they can pay and attend workshops advertised as providing adequate knowledge and skills in how best to handle memories-of-abuse cases and so minimise their risk of legal liability, against the backdrop of guidelines issued by their psychological society. Finally, in some jurisdictions like Victoria, Australia, those victims, whose allegations were believed by juries not warned of the difficulty faced by the accused in proving innocence on uncorroborated and dated sexual abuse charges based on 'recovered' memories of sexual abuse, can keep the money awarded them as compensation for their injuries despite the fact that the accused is subsequently acquitted (Arndt, 1995).

Of course, there remains the crucial question of interest to therapists and ethics committees alike, namely whether the process of reviving memories of past traumas is more harmful than helpful for the client. Australian researchers Brabin and Berah (1995) interviewed 257 mothers and 160 fathers who had a stillborn baby years earlier and found that, of the small proportion (18 per cent) who found the interview distressing, almost all reported that it had also been helpful to them. While Brabin and Berah's finding is interesting, what they studied is rather different from a victim of child sexual abuse in the family context whose repressed memory is recovered years later and has to learn to cope with the new knowledge and emotions that come with it.

Meanwhile, the optimistic student of legal psychology can take comfort in the fact that in psychology, as in other disciplines, often knowledge is advanced through three stages (Watkins, 1993:309): (a) thesis (that is, when a finding such as recovered memories of childhood sexual abuse is made in the context of therapy – and there is a spate of studies reported, books published, etc. supporting the basic finding); (b) antithesis (that is, when the earlier reports are challenged by methodologically more robust studies of suggestive questioning); and (c) synthesis, when researchers proceed to resolve the issue by somehow integrating valuable knowledge generated during the thesis and antithesis stages. The synthesis stage in dealing with recovered memories of childhood sexual abuse will involve researchers finding 'ways of distinguishing verifiable from fantasized or contaminated memories' (Watkins, 1993:310), undoubtedly a tall order.

Perry and Gold (1995) reported that 15 000 cases of false accusations of sexual abuse had been recorded in the United States in the previous few years, over 300 in Canada and as many in the UK. The tidal wave of 'repressed/recovered-memory' cases peaked in the United States in the early 1990s and fanned the debate on the 'false memory syndrome'. In 1992 the False Memory Syndrome Foundation was founded in Philadelphia and soon had a membership of 18 000 families (Brahams, 2000:79). The British False Memory Society was established in 1993 and soon had a membership of 900 families. The ferocity of the debate has been subsiding since then, largely because many US insurance companies have refused to fund repressed memory therapy and many US medical institutions prohibit such techniques on their premises. Consequently, Brahams (2000) has pointed out, 'the therapy loses its status and the claims are killed at cause' (p. 80). Wells et al. (1999) conclude their discussion of the credibility of recovered memories by expressing the view that, 'it might be wise to inform clients about the possibility that they were not abused, and about the possibility that they could develop illusory memories. Perhaps this caution helps people maintain separation between imagined events and events that they actually experienced' (p. 80).

6 Interviewing Eyewitnesses Effectively

Interviewing crime victims/witnesses is a crucial part of evidence gathering in law enforcement investigations. It is essential, therefore, that when various professionals interview witnesses they obtain the maximum accurate recall but without contaminating the recollection of the witness. The cognitive interview technique and forensic hypnosis are two aids to recall that have attracted a lot of researchers' attention.

6.1 Using Neuro-linguistic Programming to Build Rapport

Neuro-linguistic programming (O'Connor and Seymour, 1990) is being used by the FBI to train its special agents in developing skills for building rapport with eyewitnesses with traumatic experiences (Sandoval and Adams, 2001). The basic idea is that the interviewer develops a personal bond with the interviewee that is conducive to trust. This, in turn, encourages the witness to provide information. The personal bond is achieved by the interviewer leaning forward, being attentive and subtly and continuously matching the following characteristics of the witness: (a) language (that is, use of similar visual, auditory or kinesthetic phrases); (b) kinesics (non-verbal behaviour/body language, that is, gestures, posture, movement of the hands, arms, feet and legs); and, finally, (c) paralanguage (choice of words, how something is said, the speech rate, volume, and pitch of speech). The aim is for the witness to feel the interviewer is genuinely interested in him/her as an individual, thus increasing rapport and enhancing communication, resulting in the witness providing crucial information about the crime in question (Sandoval and Adams, 2001:5).

6.2 Cognitive Interview (CI)

Until recently a police officer was expected to learn interviewing skills 'on the job'. It is also known that police spend a large part of their time talking to people and that frequently witnesses do not provide police with all the information they require for an investigation (Köhnken et al., 1999). The availability, therefore, of an effective technique for interviewing witnesses can only assist police and other investigators. Such a procedure now exists, is known as the cognitive interview (CI) technique, and has been adopted by police forces on both sides of the Atlantic, on continental Europe and in Australia, as well as by other professionals (for example, social workers) whose work involves interviewing people, including children.

By now there is anecdotal evidence regarding the success of the CI in assisting police investigators to catch criminals. Milne and Shaw (1999) reported that the CI helped detectives in the United States to elicit detailed information pertaining to sightings of a missing girl aged 7 years old and it was used successfully in the police investigation of the bombing incident in Bournemouth, England, in 1993.

The CI has been largely the work of American psychology professors Fisher and Geiselman (see Fisher and Geiselman, 1992; Geiselman et al., 1984). They have utilised four principles derived from the empirical literature on information retrieval (Bower, 1967; Tulving, 1974) which increase recall accuracy without increasing the amount of inaccurate information remembered. According to Geiselman et al. (1984), the four principles (mnemonic aids) are: (a) reinstate the context (see Clifford and Gwyer, 1999), that is, the conditions under which the event in question was encoded; (b) report everything, however trivial it may seem; (c) recount the event in different orders; and (d) recount the event from different perspectives.

Geiselman et al. (1984) compared the CI with the hypnotic interview along the lines suggested by Orne et al. (1984) and a 'standard police interview' in a study in which student subjects saw a video showing an armed robbery. The hypnotic interview and the CI were found to yield 35 per cent more accurate information than did the standard police interview, without an increase in inaccurate and fabricated information. The CI has also been shown to significantly reduce the impact of misleading questions on witness accuracy (Geiselman et al., 1986). In the light of studies with serving police officers, the original CI was revised by Fisher et al. (1987). The enhanced CI was developed to overcome such difficulties as anxious and inarticulate witnesses and poor interviewing strategies used by interviewing police officers (George, 1991). The enhanced CI incorporates techniques like rapport building, transferring control of the interview to the interviewee, appropriate use of pauses and non-verbal behaviour. The revised version places less importance on asking the witness to recall, using different perspectives and in different order and stresses the importance of repeated recall and listening skills. Fisher et al. (1987) found the revised version produced significantly more (45 per cent) accurate information in police detectives' interviews of crime witnesses without increasing inaccurate recall. Subsequent laboratory and field studies with both children and adult eyewitnesses and a meta-analysis by Köhnken (1992) have reported findings in support of the CI as a superior interview technique with crime witnesses (Fisher and Geiselman, 1992; Memon and Bull, 1991). British researchers Clifford and George (1995) reported a field study with twenty-eight experienced policemen and policewomen interviewing real crime victims/witnesses which compared three methods of investigative interviewing: CI, conversation management (CM) and a combination of both. Their findings provide strong support regarding the ecological validity of the CI as a superior investigative interviewing technique. Findings supporting police use of the CI were also reported by Kebbell et al. (1999) who established that a serious problem was that many police officers in the UK do not have the time to conduct a full cognitive interview.

Köhnken et al. (1999) reported a meta-analysis of the CI literature since 1984, a total of fifty-five experimental comparisons of the CI and the standard interview from forty-two empirical reports, both published and unpublished, representing 2447 interviewees. They concluded that the CI 'generates substantially more correct details compared to a structured (or unstructured) interview … Moreover, no experiment has been reported yet where a cognitive interview has resulted in fewer correct details compared to a standard interview' (p. 20). Köhnken et al. found that the memory enhancing effect of the CI on the recall of correct details is even greater in the more ecologically valid studies. The CI has been shown to compare favourably with other interview procedures (see also Memon and Highman, 1999, for a literature review) such as the standard police interview, the guided memory interview (Malpass and Devine, 1981), the structured interview (Memon et al., 1997) and hypnosis (Geiselman et al., 1995). Milne et al. (1999) reported a study which compared forty-seven adults with mild learning intellectual disabilities attending day-centres and thirty-eight adults from the general population. The subjects were shown a video-recording of an accident and were interviewed a day later using the CI or the structured interview. It was found that for both groups of subjects the CI was more effective than the structured interview in enhancing witnesses' recall. However, with the learning disabilities group the CI also produced a disproportionate increase in the reporting of person confabulation. Granhag and Spjut (2001) compared the structured interview, the standard interview and the enhanced cognitive interview with thirty-two children as subjects aged 9 to 10 years who watched a 15-minute perfomance by a professional fakir. They found children recalled more correct information (and no more incorrect information) with the enhanced cognitive interview than with any of the other other techniques.

> The cognitive interview is a very good example of the application of psychological theory from the laboratory to the field.

However, a number of ecologically-valid studies have failed to find support for the CI as a superior interviewing technique and point to difficulties in training experienced police investigators to use the technique (Memon et al., 1995). Some researchers have also failed to find evidence that all four techniques used in the CI increase witness accuracy significantly. Boon and Noon (1994) reported that the changing perspectives mnemonic did not facilitate recall of accurate information by student subjects. Finally, Milne et al. (1995) examined the degree to which the CI helps children to resist the impact of misleading questions. It was found that whilst the CI enhanced children's recall of person and action details, it increased their person errors and confabulations; children were significantly more likely to resist script-inconsistent than script-consistent misleading questions and, finally, the CI enhanced children's resistance to misleading questions only when the questions were presented after the CI. The CI is a very good example of the transfer of psychological theory from the laboratory to the field. However, despite the fact the CI is routinely taught to police officers in Britain, for example, many of the officers are reluctant to apply the CI, especially to interview traumatised victims (Croft, 1995). Shepherd et al. (1999) advocate the use of spaced cognitive interview (SCI) which, they argue on the basis of case studies, has therapeutic effects on traumatised victim-witnesses. The SCI 'combines standard prolonged exposure procedures with explicit memory retrieval techniques of context-reinstatement, focused and extensive retrieval, especially reverse order recall. Since it aimed at maximising the individual's experience, he or she is not asked to report the events from another standpoint or perspective' (Shepherd et al., 1999:130).

The available empirical evidence shows that while it enjoys a number of merits, it also has to overcome a number of apparent defects, especially when used with child witnesses, before being unreservedly recommended for adoption by law-enforcement investigators and other categories of investigators whose work includes interviewing witnesses. The need for additional ecologically-valid studies to maximise the effectiveness of the CI becomes more important when we remember the lack of usefulness of such aids to recall (such as the Identi-Kit, E-Fit, and FACE), all of which have been found to be of limited use in apprehending offenders (Clifford and Davies, 1989; Davies, 1983; Kapardis 1994). Finally, as far as mock-jurors' perceptions of the CI are concerned, Fisher et al. (1999) had ninety-one college subjects listen to cognitive interviews and standard police interviews of 7-year-old children who were attempting to describe an earlier session of playing the game of 'Simon Says'. While no relationship was found between the type of interview used and perceived credibility of the witness, the CI interviewer was judged to be less manipulative than the standard police interviewer.

6.3 Forensic Hypnosis

Haward (1990) defined forensic hypnosis as 'Hypnotic techniques applied to information-gathering for evidential purposes' (p. 60). Reiser (1989) is a strong advocate of the view that hypnosis could be used to enhance witness memory accuracy. Orne (1979), however, sees hypnotic techniques to be most appropriately utilised in the investigative context. Hypnosis itself, of course, has a long and impressive history as a therapeutic tool in psychiatry and clinical psychology. In the early days of hypnosis in the first half of the nineteenth century the law's interest was in controlling its use, but since the second half of the nineteenth century the law's interest has been in the field of forensic hypnosis (Evans, 1994). At the start of the new millennium, an unsatisfactory state of affairs still characterised the relationship between hypnosis and the law.

Hypnosis interviews by police to assist witnesses to remember were first used in the United States in the early 1950s and by 1975 experienced detectives were being trained in hypnosis. Within one year trained Los Angeles detectives handled seventy major crime cases and the practice spread to other police departments (Reiser, 1989). In the UK (see Gudjonsson, 1992a) and in Australia (see McConkey and Sheehan, 1988; Judd et al., 1994) hypnosis is usually conducted by psychiatrists and qualified psychologists and, in stark contrast to the United States, never by police officers. In compliance with the Home Office Regulation 66/1988, it is in the most exceptional of crimes that British authorities would resort to the use of hypnosis and hypnosis cannot be used on a murder suspect to obtain a confession (Berry et al., 1999).

Reiser (1989:151) describes a few cases to illustrate the usefulness of investigative hypnosis. In one such case in California, a 15-year-old female hitch-hiker accepted a lift from a man driving a van. The driver tied her up, raped her, cut off her forearms with an axe and forced her into a highway drainage tunnel. When he left, the victim managed to crawl out, stopped a passing car and was taken to the hospital. Because of her extremely traumatic experience her memory of the suspect and of the events was rather limited. When interviewed under hypnosis, however, she was able to recall the suspect's name, his occupation, described the van and helped a police artist construct a composite drawing of the suspect. The offender was arrested and convicted.

Haward (1981b:110) points out a number of constraints on the use of hypnosis: admissibility of hypnotic evidence and the reimposition of amnesia; not all victims are willing to be hypnotised; some people are poor hypnotic subjects; age-regression requires considerable time; parents may not consent to their children (especially if female), who have been victims of crime, being hypnotised and, finally, hypnosis is powerless to obtain recall if the memory of a particular fact simply no longer exists. In addition, individuals can and do lie under hypnosis (Virgo, 1991) and some individuals are able to simulate an hypnotic trance (Wagstaff, 1993). Sheehan (1994:66–7) has also drawn attention to another major issue in forensic hypnosis, namely, the civil rights of the person who is hypnotised, especially when the individual is under suspicion of a crime. One concern is, for example, that such a person may report incriminating evidence under hypnosis which comes to the attention of the police (p. 67). On the question of whether hypnosis could interfere with a witness' memory of an event, Gudjonsson (1992a:170) points out three risks: witness' vulnerability to confabulation, to suggestibility and to overconfidence. Gudjonsson adds, however, that the experimental evidence on confabulation, susceptibility to leading questions and overconfidence as a result of hypnosis is not unequivocal (p. 171).

Regarding the extent to which the hypnosis interview increases the accuracy of witness recall, McConkey (1995) concludes his assessment of the laboratory evidence on hypnotic hypermnesia and hypnotic pseudomemory stating that: 'there is no guarantee that any benefits (such as increased accurate recall) will occur, and there is a likelihood that some costs (such as inaccurate recall, and inappropriate confidence) may be incurred when hypnosis is used to enhance memory ... [and] ... A similar conclusion comes from using hypnosis in the forensic setting' (p. 2).

Taking hypnotised subjects back to the scene of the crime and methodically questioning them about various aspects of the event may indeed help some witnesses to remember more details. This is not surprising because the technique involved is similar to the CI technique. However, when there is no external corroborative evidence there is the difficulty of not knowing in such a situation what is accurate and what is not (Haward, 1981b). It is, therefore, not possible to decide whether forensic hypnosis solves more problems than it creates. It is, of course, necessary that the hypnosis be carried out by a properly qualified professional such as a psychiatrist, a psychologist or medical practitioner who is trained in witness interviewing techniques and who is not involved in the case, preferably with the whole session being videotaped continuously.

Despite its popularity among police investigators, especially in the United States, the use of forensic hypnosis has had a mixed treatment in psychology (see McConkey, 1995). Some authors (for example, Haward, 1981b) have attacked the practice of training police investigators on a brief course to use hypnosis. Two of the concerns expressed in this context include protection of the mental health of the witness, as well as the possibility of inadvertently planting items of information, pseudo-memories, which become part of what a hypnotised witness will remember later (Haward, 1981b). Lloyd-Bostock (1988) concluded that: 'Hypnosis is not ... the wonder tool it has been held to be. There is no video-recording faithfully stored in the brain awaiting to be uncovered and played back at the convenience of the forensic hypnotist: the appearance of full and clear recall under hypnosis can be spurious despite the best intentions of witnesses and hypnotist' (p. 19).

Kebbell and Wagstaff (1998) pointed out that while for some authors hypnotic techniques may have the potential to enhance eyewitness testimony in police investigations into criminal offences, experimental research shows that hypnosis is associated with decreases in accuracy, false confidence in incorrect information, increased suggestibility to leading questions and, finally misleading post-event information – factors that limit the usefulness of hypnosis as a witness interviewing technique.

> Evidence obtained by forensic hypnosis should be viewed with caution and it should only be allowed to be used under strict guidelines.

In view of strong arguments against the admissibility of hypnotically enhanced testimony, one could argue that it should not be allowed to be used as a method for 'creating' an eyewitness whose memory has been reconstructed by hypnosis and, furthermore, that such a witness should not be allowed to testify to this new memory in the court. It is possible, of course, for one to agree to hypnosis being used selectively and under safeguards to assist during the investigation process but not to its being admitted as evidence by the courts.

Since the mid 1980s, many law-enforcement officers have embraced hypnosis as a panacea for the frailties of human memory, a tool that would greatly assist them to clear up more serious crime. However, the enthusiasm by law-enforcement agencies, some forensic psychologists and the public at large about forensic hypnosis seems to be unwarranted in the light of both the experience with crime detection and hard facts from psycholegal research.

On the basis of the existing literature it can be safely stated in conclusion that: 'Properly controlled hypnosis may be very useful in appropriate cases [with witness victims in cases where memory recall is inhibited by emotional trauma], but indiscriminate use and a false impression of its power can do a great deal of harm' (Lloyd-Bostock, 1988:21). Evidence obtained by forensic hypnosis should, therefore, be viewed with a great deal of caution. Finally, forensic hypnosis should only be allowed to be used under strict guidelines (including the video-taping of such hypnotic interviews), like those provided in the Californian legislation regulating the admissibility of post-hypnotic evidence and approved in New Zealand in *R v. Felin* [1985] 2NZLR 750 at 753 (Freckelton, 1996).

7 Conclusions

At best, what can be confidently stated is that psychologists have identified a number of important correlates of eyewitness identification inaccuracy to do with the witness, the perpetrator, and how witnesses are interviewed by law-enforcement personnel. Admittedly, the empirical evidence is more convincing for some variables than for others. Unfortunately, psychologists have not yet tackled the question of how different crimes or different aspects of a crime are remembered by different eyewitnesses, or how, for example, disguises worn by armed robbers affect witness accuracy, as has been suggested by Clifford (1981). Research, especially of a non-laboratory nature, is badly needed to examine whether and how different variables that have been identified as important indicators of witness identification accuracy interact to impact on eyewitnesses.

McCloskey and Egeth's (1983) article in the *American Psychologist* entitled 'Eyewitness identification: What can a psychologist tell a jury?' concluded 'not much'. Ten years later, in the same journal, in answering the question 'What do we know about eyewitness identification?', Wells (1993) focused on system variables and concluded that in line-up and photospread identification: 'Scientific research methods used by psychologists in conjunction with bodies of knowledge in memory, cognition, social perception, and social influence provide powerful methods and theories that make research psychologists uniquely well suited to contribute to the eyewitness identification problem' (p. 568). Egeth's (1993) article, in the same journal, on 'What do we not know about eyewitness identification?' was concerned with both estimator and system variables and concluded that both the quantity and quality of psychological research into eyewitness testimony has increased in the intervening years, to the extent where psychologists appearing as expert witnesses may not be able to enlighten jurors about much to do with the crime but may have something valuable to communicate to the police (p. 579).

The psychological literature discussed permits the following conclusions:

1 A range of witness characteristics, namely, personality, cognitive style, age, gender, race, stereotypes, whether the witness is also a victim of the crime and the number of witnesses have been shown to be important indicators for psychologists who testify as experts in the courtroom.

2 Factors relating to the perpetrator have been neglected by psycholegal researchers. What limited evidence there is indicates that physical attractiveness, gender, body size and height are related to how an eyewitness will perceive and remember a crime suspect.

3 The police would do well to remember that the length of the delay between the commission of an offence and when they interview eyewitnesses impacts on witnesses' accuracy as does the number of efforts made to recall. Also, being a police officer does not confer superior perceptual or memory capabilities but comes with a 'mental' set to selectively perceive and interpret an event as to even impute and remember 'criminal' details that, in fact, never existed. The practice of permitting one police officer to represent a group of police eyewitnesses is a dubious one. When they ask witnesses leading, suggestive questions, police may well construct the answers they will get. The police also need to take note of evidence from studies of actual police interviews of witnesses where they use directive

questioning, a significant part of which is often characterised by inappropriate, counter-productive questioning, such interviews treating witnesses worse than criminal suspects (McLean, 1995).

4 As far as the whole debate about recovered memories of childhood sexual abuse is concerned, therapists, like the police, need to be sensitive to, and guard against, the potential problem that is endemic in suggestive questioning.

5 The effectiveness of the CI technique in enhancing the accuracy of eyewitness recall provides further support for the view that experimental psychologists have a great deal to contribute to law enforcement in general and crime suspect identification in particular.

6 While not denying that forensic hypnosis can be crucial in obtaining crucial evidence from eyewitnesses in appropriate cases, in view of the fact that hypnosis has been shown to have a number of limitations its use needs to be strictly regulated by statute.

7 Finally, a major challenge for psycholegal researchers is to determine whether and how particular combinations of event, witness, perpetrator and interrogational factors impact on the accuracy of identification accuracy.

The psychological knowledge presented should also serve to dispel myths adhered to by the legal profession, law-enforcement personnel and the public alike that human perception and memory behave like a video-recorder. Notwithstanding the fact that the work of psychologists contributes to reducing the risk of false identifications which, as Wells (1993:568) pointed out, cause double injustice because they penalise the innocent, their friends and relatives but also mean the real culprit remains free, the same knowledge should also help to remind psychological researchers that not all eyewitness evidence is unreliable.

Psychologists in the United States (for example, Loftus, Buckhout), in the UK (for example, Bull, Clifford, Davies, Gudjonsson) and in Australia (for example, Byrne) have advised as expert witnesses in cases involving witness testimony. As shown in chapter 7, the courts in the United States, UK, Canada, Australia and New Zealand have broadened the scope for the evidence of psychologists as experts on eyewitness testimony. In the early 1990s, the British Academy of Forensic Sciences organised a seminar in London on eyewitness testimony for judges, lawyers and other professionals involved in the criminal justice field. The seminar was chaired by the chairman of the Criminal Committee of the Judicial Studies Board (see Heaton-Armstrong, 1995a). The question of whether psychologists are justified in testifying as experts in courts of law is discussed in chapter 7. It is sufficient here to emphasise that the very best psychologists can do is draw the attention of magistrates, judges and jurors to the kinds of factors that contribute to the unreliability of eyewitness identification accuracy. Understandably, some expert witnesses may find this conclusion rather difficult to accept but the empirical evidence presented in this chapter does not justify their doing more than sound general warnings. Also, psychologists would do well to remember that, while different category variables are important in eyewitness evidence

(Cutler et al., 1987), defence lawyers are more likely to accept findings pertaining to system variables.

On the basis of the empirical evidence on mistaken identification and a small number of known miscarriages of justice due to such misidentification, Davies (1996:232–41) believes it is now time to reconsider Lord Devlin's (1976) recommendation that a positive identification should stop being the primary or principal premise on which someone can be prosecuted. Also, Davies argues for the adoption in England and Wales of the Scottish legal position whereby all identifications must be independently corroborated. Davies' suggestion warrants serious consideration by the legal fraternity, researchers and the public alike.

Revision Questions

1 Which personality attributes are important in eyewitness accuracy?
2 What do we know about elderly people as eyewitnesses?
3 What is the relationship between eyewitness confidence and accuracy? What factors influence it?
4 What do we know about police officers as eyewitnesses?
5 How accurate are eyewitnesses as far as a perpetrator's non-facial characteristics are concerned?
6 What explanations have been put forward for post-event misinformation?
7 What are two contrasting schools of thought concerning the controversy about recovered memories of child sexual abuse?
8 How useful is the cognitive interview in enhancing the accuracy of eyewitness testimony?
9 What are some of the dangers in using forensic hypnosis? How can one guard against them?

4 Children as Witnesses

'… Scientific truth … must come about by controversy … Without fighting you get science nowhere … ' (Boring, 1963:68).

'Children have a right to justice and their evidence is essential if society is to protect their interests and deal effectively with those who would harm them.' (Jack and Yeo, 1992)

'To permit adult witnesses to relate children's unrecorded hearsay from investigative interviews is to tolerate listener distortion, foster professional ineptitude, and again to frustrate justice.' (McGough, 1995:385)

'The demonstrable fact that investigative interviews with young children can be rendered worthless by inept practice should not blind us to the substantial literature demonstrating that reliable information can be elicited from young children who are competently interviewed, however.' (Lamb et al., 1995:446)

'… Despite the rhetoric, consistency in findings is not always present, … in the fields of stress and arousal, suggestibility, and misleading information, … there is scope for methodological developments which could serve to further empower the child within the criminal justice system.' (Clifford, 2002:334)

Introduction

Psycholegal research into children as witnesses has a history going back to the beginning of the twentieth century (Binet, 1900). Since the 1970s there has been an increasing interest in western countries in victims of crime, especially sexual abuse. Since the 1990s there has been an alarming increase in the number of sex crimes against children that are reported to the police (Sedlak and Broadhurst, 1996; US Bureau of Census, 1994). Such crimes are very difficult to investigate and prosecute successfully because often the only evidence available is that of the victim and the alleged offender. Therefore, the child's testimony is of crucial importance. There is now a voluminous literature on children's testimony (see Westcott et al., 2002). A great deal of research has now been done into the accuracy of young children's memories and how reports of sexual abuse can be interfered with by the interviewer. Allegations of sexual abuse are also made in the context of divorce and custody disputes (Byrne and Maloney, 1991; Wakefield and Underwager, 1991). Contrary to popular belief, however, McIntosh and Prinz (1993) in the United States found that a survey of 603 family court files pertaining to divorces involving children revealed that in only 2 per cent of cases in which custody or access was contested were sexual abuse allegations made. The focus on and the concern with child victims and child witnesses since the 1980s by the media and researchers alike has been instrumental in the legislatures in various countries responding to demands that the law of evidence and procedure become more sensitive to the needs of victims in general and female and child victims in particular.[1] However, despite all the attention paid by a broad range of professionals to the topic of the child witness and the enactment in many countries of mandatory reporting laws for child abuse, there is a noticeable lack of adequate training for child protection services workers (Doris et al., 1995).

> We know a great deal about child witnesses and significant progress has been made in the law's treatment of them in western common law countries but a lot remains to be done.

The empirical evidence discussed in this chapter leads to the inescapable conclusion that children as young as 3 to 4 years old can provide us with reports about an alleged incident that are of significant potential forensic usefulness but, like adults, the child's performance is also influenced by situational demands. We know a great deal about child witnesses and significant progress has been made in the law's treatment of child witnesses in western common law countries, but a lot remains to be done.

1 Legal Aspects of Children as Witnesses

Police Standing Orders and statutory provisions in various jurisdictions[2] require that where a child is questioned, a parent, guardian, relative or, in special circumstances, a responsible adult be present except where it is impracticable or for other sufficient reasons. Not surprisingly, too, the courts have routinely scrutinized confessional evidence of young persons with particular care.[3] Traditionally, the law in the UK (see Flin, 1995; Smith, 1995;

Spencer and Flin, 1990, 1993), the United States (Myers, 1993), and Australia (see Byrne, 1991; Waight and Williams, 1995) 'has taken a very restrictive use of child witnesses, regarding them as inherently unreliable. When children have been permitted to testify they have done so on adults' terms' (Naylor, 1989:82). These suspicions about the reliability of child witnesses are seen in the competency requirement and the requirement for corroboration still in existence in various jurisdictions. In fact, it would not be an exaggeration to say that until very recently 'children were treated as second-class citizens in the eyes of the law' and, not surprisingly, only a small proportion of offenders who have sexually abused children have been successfully prosecuted (Davies, 1991:178–9). However, as Clifford (2002:334) points out, as a result of the research into witness testimony and the socio-political drive to get children's voices heard in court, a paradox has evolved between adult witnesses being challenged (whereas the law has traditionally considered them reliable) and child witnesses' status in the court being strengthened (whereas historically the law considered them unreliable). Many countries, including the United States and Canada, still make use of competency examinations for children under the age of 14. In such examinations, a child's competency will be decided following a *voir dire*.

Whether a person is competent to testify in court is a question of fact and it is for the judge to decide where a doubt is raised about competency. The judge will normally decide the issue by questioning the witness and, in exceptional circumstances, he/she may hear evidence regarding the witness' capacity. Everybody is presumed competent unless there is something to suggest otherwise. According to the well-known authority on evidence law in Britain, Sir John Smith (1995), 'A person is incompetent if, because of youth, mental illness, or any other cause, he is incapable of recollecting relevant matters, of understanding questions and giving rational answers, or knowing that he ought to tell the truth ... In the case of a prosecution witness he [the judge] must be satisfied beyond reasonable doubt that the witness is competent' (p.147). In England and Wales as in other common law countries, 'There is no prescribed age under which a child is incompetent' (p. 147) and the competence of children (under 14 years of age) is determined, as for other persons. More specifically, Schedule 9 (para. 33) of the *Criminal Justice and Public Order Act* (1994) provides that, 'A child's evidence shall be received unless it appears to the court that the child is incapable of giving intelligible testimony'.[4]

> Legal rules concerning children's competency as eywitnesses in western common law countries have been relaxed in recent years.

The field of children's evidence has been in turmoil since about the early 1980s. This is seen, for example, in the plethora of publications in the United Kingdom,[5] in the United States,[6] in Australia,[7] New Zealand[8] and Germany.[9] The turmoil has also been reflected in a number of legal reforms largely intended to relax the rules pertaining to children's competency. Examples of such reforms are amendments to the *Criminal Code of Canada Evidence Act* to allow children under 14 years to provide either sworn or unsworn testimony (Ruck, 1996). In the United States, various grounds of witness incompetence, including age, have been eliminated by Rule 601 of the *Federal Rules of*

Evidence, the consequence of which is that child witnesses are treated by the courts like witnesses generally as far as competency is concerned. In other words, the basic test is: does the witness understand the difference between lying and telling the truth in court and does the witness, whether on oath or in affirmation, also understand the duty of telling the truth? Similar reforms to children's testimony requirements have included the abolition of the corroboration requirement in New South Wales, Australia, in 1985; the abolition in the *Criminal Justice Act* 1988 in England and Wales of the rule that there could be no conviction on the unsworn evidence of children, and the *Criminal Justice Act* of 1991 which allows for a video-recorded interview with a child witness to be shown in court as the child's evidence-in-chief. A court in England and Wales, however, has the power not to show part or all of a video-recording if the interview has not been carried out in compliance with relevant legislation. More recently, the *Youth Justice and Criminal Evidence Act*, 1999, in an attempt to assist young witnesses, included for certain categories of witnesses, the pre-trial videotaping of cross-examination and the use of intermediaries. However, as Esam (2002) argues, a number of problems and gaps which remain within the system in England and Wales mean that, in a real sense, there is no justice for young witnesses.

Despite the importance of children's own understanding of providing testimony in legal contexts, there has been very little research 'pertaining to those situations where the child may be motivated or influenced to withhold the truth' (Ruck, 1996:104). In order to examine the development of children's understanding of telling the truth in court Ruck presented short story vignettes to children aged 7, 9, 11, and 13. The main character in the vignettes was a child who had either witnessed, been involved with, or committed a crime, and who was required to testify in court and faced the dilemma of whether to tell the truth or to lie. It was found that younger children (aged 7 to 9) were more likely to perceive telling the truth when giving testimony in court as a way of avoiding punitive consequences while older children (aged 11 to 13) were more concerned with upholding the laws and rules of society. More knowledge about why children decide to tell the truth in court could suggest ways of assessing children's reasoning and competence in both civil and criminal proceedings, especially since 'the *voir dire* (interview) is an imperfect metric of a child's understanding of telling the truth in court' (Ruck, 1996:115).

The 1988 English *Criminal Justice Act* also abolished the mandatory caution from judges in dealing with children's evidence in their summing up and introduced the principle of the live video-link as a means by which children could simultaneously communicate with the courtroom without having to confront the accused (see Davies and Noon, 1991, 1993; Flin, 1992). According to Davies and Noon (1993:22), the 'Live Link', as it became known, is available to children under the age of 14 in cases involving violence and to those under 17 in cases involving sexual assault. In England and Wales the link has enabled a child to give evidence from a smaller room adjacent to the courtroom, in the company of a court-approved supporter. A child witness can see the particular person speaking to them and those in the court can see the child giving evidence. The same piece of legislation raised the age limit for the video-link from 14 to 17.[10] Closed circuit television is also available in most jurisdictions in Australia (Cashmore, 1991; Waight and Williams, 1995:46).[11] More specifically, as in England and Wales, in New South Wales, Western Australia, Tasmania and the Australian Capital Territory there is a rebuttable presumption that a child giving evidence in a sexual or serious assault case can use closed-circuit television (Australian Law Reform Commission and Human Rights and Equal Opportunity Commission, 1997, para. 14.103).

The introduction of closed-circuit television for child witnesses in a number of different jurisdictions has been done with the intention of avoiding a situation where the victim has to confront the defendant in court, as well as to save the child the traumatic experience of testifying in the formal and anxiety-provoking atmosphere of the courtroom (Goodman et al., 1992). As application must be made to the court for some means of separation, such as closed-circuit television, to ensure that a child does not meet a criminal defendant face-to-face in the courtroom, there is scope for psychologists to conduct psychological evaluations regarding the potential trauma a child may experience in confronting the accused in a criminal trial (see Howells et al., 1996; Small and Melton, 1994).

However, it was the United States that pioneered the use of closed-circuit television for child witnesses in criminal cases in 1983. The Supreme Court in *Maryland v. Craig* 497 US 836 (1990) upheld the use of one-way closed-circuit television procedure to question child witnesses. In a majority decision in that case it was held that the Sixth Amendment does not guarantee a defendant's absolute right to meet with the witnesses against him/her face-to-face except 'Where an important public policy is furthered and where the reliability of testimony is otherwise assured' (Small and Melton, 1994:229). The Supreme Court outlined three criteria that must be satisfied for the state to show 'necessity', a finding that is required to allow a child to testify via a video-link. According to Small and Melton (1994:228), by 1990 thirty-seven states allowed the use of videotaped testimony of alleged sexually abused children, twenty-seven states authorised the use of one-way television testimony in such cases, and eight states permitted the use of a two-way video-link. It should be noted in this context, however, that despite a number of important legal reforms on both sides of the Atlantic in Australia, New Zealand and Canada (see O'Neil, 1992), 'Videotechnology offers one approach to alleviate some of the difficulties that child witnesses face as part of the court process, … [However] … It is … not the panacea that some had hoped for and is not without problems, not the least of which are the attitudinal barriers of the professionals involved in the court process' (Cashmore, 2002:214). Consequently, Spencer and Flin's (1990:38) assessment that, 'The most important class of legally incompetent witnesses that remains is little children' is, alas, still valid.

While a minority of children prefer facing the accused in court (Cashmore, 1992; Davies et al., 1995) and some have argued that children should have the choice of testifying on closed-circuit television or in open court, available evidence shows that what child witnesses testifying in court fear most is being watched by the accused (American Psychological Association, 1990; Flin et al., 1988). Edelstein et al. (2002) has reviewed the research on children's reactions to the legal system and concluded that, 'forensic interviewing, court involvement generally, and/or its anticipation specifically may be stressful experiences for children' which may continue as a source of upset for up to three years and possibly twelve to fourteen years later (p. 269). Despite such evidence, Montaya (1995) has argued that shielding child witnesses: does not invariably produce "better evidence"', it 'may impair a defendant's right to represent a defense' and, finally, recommends that 'the judge should personally interview child witnesses before determining the need for shielding' (pp. 366–7). Suggestions for reducing the impact of legal stressors on children involved in prosecutions have included: videotaping forensic interviews the first time they are conducted; alternatives to testifying in court (for example, closed-circuit television); and programmes that provided children with knowledge of the legal system before they enter the courtroom (see Edelstein et al., 2002; Goodman et al., 1999). But how effective are such video-links in protecting child witnesses?

2 Evaluations of the 'Live Link'/Closed-Circuit Television

Child witnesses of sexual abuse who are protected from the presence of the accused during the trial are less stressed and provide more complete and accurate information. However, closed-circuit television provides a partial solution to the child witness' problem of having to testify in court in the presence of the defendant. The emotional repercussions of the trial for a child witness of sexual abuse are not resolved with the conclusion of the trial.

One such evaluation study was carried out for the British Home Office by Davies and Noon (1991; Davies and Noon, 1993). The researchers monitored the scheme during its first twenty-three months during which time they surveyed courtroom personnel (judges, prosecutors and barristers) as well as a smaller number of police officers and social workers. Observational data were collected from 100 trials involving 154 children (100 girls and 54 boys) testifying via the 'Live Link'. The performance of children in court was assessed using rating scales provided by Gail Goodman. The average age of the witnesses was 10 years and 1 month and the great majority (89 per cent) were alleged victims (96 per cent of sexual abuse) rather than bystanders. It was found that the majority of the courtroom personnel thought favourably of the link, 74 per cent of the children were rated as happy when testifying and most were rated as giving their evidence effectively. Davies and Noon (1993:24) concluded that their data 'present a consistent picture of the advantages accruing to children testifying via closed-circuit television and clearly justify the extension of the scheme currently under way'. The question of the scheme's effectiveness, however, needs to be answered against the knowledge that only 8 out of the 154 children studied had met their counsel prior to being examined on the link; children waited an average of ten months for their case to come to trial; despite arriving at the start of court business, they had to wait an average of 2 hours 28 minutes before giving evidence and, finally, no measures were taken to ensure that a child could not come into contact with and be intimidated by the accused or their supporters[12] during recess in the corridors of the court or in the canteen (Davies and Noon,

1993:24–5). It can be seen that schemes such as the 'Live Link' on their own can only provide a partial solution to the child witnesses' problem of having to confront the accused when they are testifying in court.

Wade (2002) reported a study of forty children at one Crown Court Centre in England and Wales. All but one concerned sexual offences against children. The children comprised twenty-six children complainants and fourteen bystander witnesses. Nineteen of the children were aged 7 to 12 years and twenty-one between 13 and 18 years. The researchers observed each trial and a detailed transcript was taken of the proceedings. Also, in-depth interview data were obtained for at least one child in all but one of the cases examined. It was found that some children felt they could not have testified if the link had not been available but 'the response of others was more equivocal' (p. 225). The bystander witnesses, who were all aged 13 years or above, were anxious while waiting to go into court but their anxiety diminished when they started answering questions. In contrast to bystander witnesses, children who were the complainants were distressed by the cross-examination. Wade found that, 'the emotional repercussions of the trial were not resolved with the conclusion of the court case' (p. 228). Therefore, it is interesting to note that, despite the stress involved for many of the children in Wade's study in testifying against the accused, overall the children viewed the criminal justice process with respect (p. 229).

Evaluations of the effect of 'Live Link' (cited by Cashmore, 2002) on: (a) children witnesses in court proceedings have also been reported in the Australian Capital Territory (Cashmore and Dhaas, 1992) and in Western Australia (O'Grady, 1996), in Scotland (Murray, 1995): and (b) there have also been experimental and court simulation studies (for example, Goodman et al., 1998) and court observation studies (Murray, 1995). In support of earlier research, Cashmore's literature review concludes that the findings reported 'indicate that child witnesses who are less stressed are able to provide more complete and accurate information, particularly when they are protected from the presence of the accused' (p. 208).

Videotaping a child's statement about the alleged offence means the child will be interviewed less, his/her trauma in testifying will be reduced and the accused may well decide to plead guilty when faced with such a videotape (Cashmore, 2002:210). Furthermore, a videotaped statement allows the fact-finder, perhaps months later, to see the child's age, and facial expression when making the statement to police officer or social worker and so forth. Finally, such a videotape reduces the scope for the defence lawyer to undermine the child's credibility as a witness by blaming him/her for inconsistencies in his/her testimony before and during the trial (Milne and Shaw, 1999:133).

Videotaped interviews in England and Wales (which save a child aged under 14 years in the cases of physical violence or under 17 years in cases of sexual assault from giving their evidence-in-chief at trial) must be conducted by a police officer or a social worker. Such interviews are governed by the *Memorandum of Good Practice* jointly issued by the Home Office and the Department of Health in 1992 (see below). An evaluation in the early 1990s of videotaped interviews with child witnesses for the British Home Office by

Davies et al. (1995) from Leicester University reported the following: of the 1199 trials (predominantly indecent assault cases), that took place in England and Wales during the 21-month period (October 1992 to June 1994 inclusive) involving children witnesses, 640 (53 per cent) included an application to show a videotaped interview, 73 per cent of those applications were granted and in 43 per cent of those cases the tape was in fact played in court – in other words, a tape-recorded interview was played in court in 17 per cent of the total number of trials during the period in question. It was also reported that judges were significantly more positive in their evaluation of videotaped interviews than were barristers, while 98 per cent of police officers and all social workers surveyed believed the main advantage was a significant reduction in stress for the child. Examination of forty videotaped interviews, most of which had been conducted by female police officers, revealed that generally the interviews were conducted in accordance with the guidelines provided in the *Memorandum of Good Practice* (1992)[13] but in more than enough cases children were not allowed sufficient opportunity to describe the incident in their own words; the evidential quality of the majority of the tapes (75 per cent) was judged to be satisfactory (that is, gave a clear account of the incident). Finally, those interviewing a child on tape (mainly female police officers) were generally more supportive and more likely to adjust their questioning to the child's linguistic style and, in such cases, the child was rated as less anxious than in interviews conducted during the trial by lawyers.

Mock-juror research by Ross et al. (1994) in the United States has reported that subjects (psychology students) who observed a two-hour video based on a real trial and showing a 10-year-old girl give evidence in open court (as opposed to doing so behind a screen or video-link) against her father accused of sexual and physical abuse and who never got to give evidence himself, were more likely to convict the defendant. Ross et al. concluded that the use of protective shields and video-link, devices aimed at protecting children from trauma in the courtroom, do not impact adversely on the interests of defendants. Davies et al. (1995) found no significant differences between videotaped evidence and live examination-in-chief as far as actual jury verdicts in England and Wales are concerned. Davies et al. also reported that children waited an average of five months for their case to go to trial; waited 2 hours and 20 minutes inside the courtroom to testify; most of them were given a tour of the courtroom before testifying and a minority were introduced to the 'Live Link', but 30 per cent received no such preparation. Finally, most children would not have preferred to have given their evidence at trial. On the basis of their findings, Davies et al., inter alia, recommend improving interviewer training so that a greater percentage of such interviews will comply with the guidelines provided in the *Memorandum of Good Practice*; fast-tracking cases involving children as witnesses to avoid delays; and, finally, encouraging judges to be more effective in protecting children from inappropriate or intimidating tactics by counsel (see also Davies, 1994; Walker, 1993; Westcott, 1995). Delays and confronting the accused are not the only stressors for child witnesses. Kelly (2002) also mentions: public exposure; understanding the significantly worse in a photo line-up identification task of a familiar person than eight- and eleventh-grade children.

The literature review by Fivush (1993) of the amount and accuracy of children's autobiographical recall concluded that the empirical evidence shows even young preschoolers to be rather accurate and to retain over considerable time information about events they experienced themselves (p. 8). The same studies,[15] however, show that preschoolers' recall is not as detailed or as exhaustive as older children's recall; preschool children recall better with the assistance of cues, prompts and so forth and they do not recall as much information spontaneously, irrespective of the length of the retention interval (Fivush, 1993:9); and, finally, unlike older children or adults, preschoolers focus on and remember different aspects of an event (p. 17). Almost a decade later, Fivush (2002) concludes her discussion of autobiographical memory stating that, 'By age 3, children's memories are remarkably accurate and enduring. Moreover, children seem able to recall stressful experiences at least as well as more mundane occurrences. However, we must be cautious in drawing implications for forensic settings. Not all events are recalled in the same way' (p. 65). Fivush goes on to add that how an event is remembered and narrated by a child is influenced both by the level of stress experienced and at what age the child had that experience as well as by whether the child has discussed the experience/s with others and, finally, 'Events which are distinctive, public, and openly discussed will most likely be well recalled, but the fate of memories of private, undisclosed events is still in question' (p. 65).

Of course, as Fivush (1993) reminded her readers, if a child requires numerous specific questions to remember an event in the courtroom, the less credible such testimony will be seen, a factor that no doubt will be exploited in cross-examination. Furthermore, if a child is asked cued questions, they may well be objected to as being 'leading questions' or even misleading, while if the child's recall is in response to open-ended questions only then is his/her testimony likely to be incomplete and to be perceived as inaccurate. It is in such a context, having to strike a balance between the two types of questioning with their respective dangers, that a technique like the 'cognitive interview' is useful (see chapter 3 and below).

Another factor that may very well impact on a magistrate's, judge's or juror's perception of a child's testimony accuracy is the degree of consistency (that is, stability over time) that characterises a child's recall of the same event on different occasions.[16] Such inconsistencies seem attributable to the fact that young preschoolers have limited general knowledge, limited retrieval structures and focus on routine and general information (Hudson, 1986; Nelson, 1986, cited by Fivush, 1993:12). Consequently, even though they encode a great deal of information, they have difficulty retrieving it when interviewed and are thus vulnerable to the effects of multiple interviews. The fact is that young children (for example, aged 3 to 6) can be accurate if asked specific questions. However, if such children are asked different questions about the same event in different interviews, they are likely to yield inconsistent responses (Fivush et al., 1991), even though they are not likely to

> Even 3-year-old children will lie when they have a motive.

incorporate much of the information supplied them by an adult during questioning into their subsequent recall of the event (Fivush, 1993:15). Let us next consider another popular belief about children, namely that they lie, as well as the detection of children's deception by adults.

5 Deception in Children

Ceci and Leichtman (1992) showed that 3-year-olds are able to misinform others by, for example, telling the interviewer that they did not know who broke a toy or claiming it had been broken by someone else. According to Vrij (2002), it is generally accepted that children are capable of telling deliberate lies at 4 years of age (Newton et al., 2000). Lewis et al. (1989) reported that about half of the 3-year-olds in America can tell lies with enough control of their facial muscles to avoid detection. Drawing on Vrij (2002), it can be said that even 3-year-old children will lie when they have a motive, such as to avoid punishment, to protect a loved one or because someone has asked them to do so, while older children may also lie for a reward. Children at a very young age misinform by concealing information. There is also some evidence that, compared to older children, younger ones will show more clearly non-verbal indicators of deceit, such as signs of nervousness or signs of hard thinking; with increasing age, children become better liars; parents are better at detecting lies in children than non-parents; it is easier to detect lies in children by listening to their voices than by looking at their faces; and, finally, observers are less likely to believe introverted and socially anxious children. Vrij concludes that 'a clear picture about children's ability to lie (in court) and people's ability to detect such lies does not exist' (p. 190). Finally, sociologists tell us that in many cultures a lot of effort is put into teaching children to be honest, for instance, some communities resort to deterrents against children telling lies by threatening them they will be struck by lightning, a tree will grow on their tongue or, like Pinocchio, that their nose will grow (Barnes, 1994). Other cultures, however (for example, the Quechna community in Peru), do not try to discourage children from lying by threatening them.

6 Factors that Impact on Children's Testimony

Researchers have established that a child's mind interacts with his/her physical and inter-personal environment (Fischer and Bullock, 1984). Therefore, it makes sense to conceptualise a child's accuracy or suggestibility as a witness, not as something the child is not capable of because of his/her level of cognitive development, but as reflecting a particular context (Batterman-Faune and Goodman, 1993:303). In other words, the extent to which a child is familiar with a particular environment and what his/her expectations are about a particular context will impact on how a child will perceive and later remember a situation. It follows that a child's age is but one important factor in evaluating children as witnesses.[17]

Past Abuse: Goodman et al. (2001) investigated the effect of child maltreatment on children's eyewitness testimony by comparing a matched sample of abused children with a non-abused group. The seventy children studied were aged 3 to 10 years old and took part in a play session with an unfamiliar adult and were tested about the experience two weeks later. As would have been expected on the basis of previous research, the reports of older children were more complete and accurate. It was also found that non-abused children were more accurate in answering specific questions and made fewer errors in identifying the unfamiliar adult in a photo identification task and (especially for younger non-abused boys), freely recalled more information. Comparing abused children themselves, Goodman et al. found that those children who had suffered more severe sexual abuse made more omission errors to specific abuse-relevant questions. Finally, past abuse experience did not make children more suggestible in response to questions that were relevant to abusive actions.

Presence of the Perpetrator: researchers have paid very little attention to the importance of sociocognitive factors such as a witness motivation, expectation in children's eyewitnessing, concentrating instead on whether children are reliable witnesses (Bussey, Lee and Grimbeck, 1993:148). Social cognitive theory emphasises the significance of a witness' anticipated outcome of disclosing an event (Bandura, 1986). Such outcome could be whether one would be believed, supported, embarrassed, shamed or punished as a result of reporting an event, especially if a witness has promised not to do so or has been warned against doing so and threatened with adverse consequences. Such concerns by children could well underpin false allegations and false denials by children. It has been found, for example, that the presence of the perpetrator makes it less likely that children aged 3, 5 and 9 years will report the perpetrator's misdeed (Bussey et al., 1991, cited by Bussey et al., 1993). Furthermore, as we have seen already, the intimidating presence of the perpetrator can influence a child's testimony itself. In a study by Peters (1991) children witnessed a staged robbery and were then interviewed alone or with the robber present. In the robber-present condition the amount and accuracy of what the children reported was significantly affected, resulting in five times less children reporting what they had seen. Findings like this provide experimental simulation support for the US Supreme Court's decision in *Maryland v. Craig*, allowing children not to have to confront the defendant. Not paying attention to motivational factors is indeed a major omission by researchers when we remember that, contrary to popular belief, children as young as 5 (Peterson et al., 1983) and even 4 years (Haugaard and Crosby, 1989, cited by Bussey et al., 1993) can correctly identify lies and can themselves intentionally lie or tell the truth.

Children can and are routinely interviewed about an alleged event in a great variety of contexts. Tulving's (1983) principle of encoding specificity emphasises the importance of reinstating the environmental context at the coding stage when asking subjects to recall an event. Providing cues specific to the context of the event in question is especially likely to facilitate children's recall (Dietze and Thomson, 1993). This finding has implications for interviews of children in legal contexts and points to the importance of social workers, police, lawyers, judicial officers and other professionals who interview children about allegations of sexual abuse, for example, being familiar with such psychological literature.

Stressful Events: like adults, children get exposed to a lot of violence in society in one way or another. As already mentioned, testifying in a courtroom is in itself a source of significant stress for most children and often impacts negatively on their testimony in terms of both the quantity and accuracy of their reports (Hill and Hill, 1987). In fact, a child may too frightened to attend court to give evidence in a trial (*Neil v. North Antrim Magistrates' Court and another* [1992] 4 All ER 846). This fact should be of great concern to all who are interested in the welfare and rights of children. While it is important to balance the rights of child witnesses with the rights of defendants, it should be remembered that children are called to testify as victims and/or witnesses to such traumatic events as sexual abuse, domestic violence, shootings, stabbings, robberies, murder,[18] even the killing of one parent by another (see Burman and Allen-Meaves, 1994), and serial murder and are psychologically affected[19] (Herkov et al., 1994). It is therefore of crucial importance to know how well children remember and testify about such experiences.

It has been reported that children's memories for such very traumatic incidents as kidnappings, killings of loved ones and a sniper firing on a school contain both accuracies and inaccuracies (see Pynoos and Eth, 1984; Terr, 1991). Warren and Startwood (1992) found that children who were more upset by the space shuttle Challenger tragedy remembered more details of the event than did children who were less upset. Similarly, a study by Steward (1992)[20] reported that children who were more upset by a painful medical procedure remembered more details and were more accurate than children who were less upset. These findings are consistent with results reported by Goodman et al. (1991). However, the relationship between anxiety and memory in the context of testifying about a stressful event is more complex than some authors (for example, Peters, 1987) have suggested. In contrast to Goodman, Hirschman, Hess and Rudy (1991) and Peters (1987), Vandermaas et al. (1993) reported a negative impact of anxiety on 3 to 8-year-olds' identification accuracy of target persons associated with a dental visit. Vandermaas et al. (1993) had children aged 4 to 5 and 7 to 8 years visit for a teeth-cleaning checkup or an operative procedure. They found that: high anxiety had a detrimental effect on the reports of the older but not the younger children; while experience with the dental event was found to mediate the influence of age and anxiety on memory, older children did not offer incorrect information spontaneously, and young children infrequently made errors of this type; asking younger children specific questions was what caused them to give incorrect information and, all children gave incorrect information in response to specific questions regarding peripheral details about a routine event (Vandermaas et al., 1993:123); and, finally, there was no difference in recall of central vs. peripheral information due to anxiety level as would have been predicted on the basis of Easterbrook's (1959) hypothesis (see chapter 2). Differences between studies in this area would seem to reflect differences in the types of events involved and children's degree of familiarity with them as well as differences in how soon subjects are asked to recall (for example, immediately or weeks later), the level of anxiety involved and how it is measured. On the basis of the existing literature no definitive conclusions can be drawn about the effects of stress on children's testimony.

Leading Questions: children can be asked to free recall an event, can be asked specific questions about it or leading and even misleading questions. One primary concern about children's testimony has been that they are susceptible to the effect of suggestive questioning, that is, they are suggestible (Bruck and Ceci, 1995; Ceci and Bruck, 1993; Spencer and Flin, 1990). Widely publicised child abuse cases like the *McMartin* case in California (cited as *People v. Buckey*, No. 750900 (Cal.Cr.Dt.Ct 1984)), portrayed in the film 'The Indictment', and *Michaels* in New Jersey (*State of New Jersey v. Margaret Kelly Michaels*, 625 A.2d 489 (N.J.Super.Ct.App.Div.1991) (see Rosenthal, 1995, for an account) and the report into child abuse in Cleveland in the UK illustrate rather convincingly the dangers that are inherent in suggestive questioning and how zealous and unethical therapists and investigators can use such interview procedures to solicit from child witnesses the answers they need, rather than the facts of the case, in order to safeguard their own vested interest and in the process also construct the case for the prosecution. Grave concern about children's suggestibility and vulnerability to suggestive questioning underpinned the *amicus* brief filed in the *Michaels* case (see Bruck and Ceci, 1995) co-signed by social scientists, psychological researchers and scholars. In *McMartin*, members of a family, including an elderly grandmother, running a child care centre, were charged, on the basis of a great deal of rather questionable evidence obtained by means of suggestive questioning, with numerous counts of child sexual abuse against many of the children at the centre. After 2489 days of the court's time and $15 million costs the case ended up with a hung jury at the retrial. Dubious procedures by one particular therapist and district attorney investigators combined with the effects of wide sensational coverage by the media ensured that the principle of the innocence of those accused until proven guilty was overridden, forever marring the lives of the children themselves and their families as well as the innocent individuals falsely accused and kept in custody for years. Since the early 1990s experimental psychologists have amassed a lot of knowledge about various potential sources of children's suggestibility. The psychological insights gained can be used to identify poor interview procedures with child witnesses that corrupt the reliability of the prosecution's evidence, and provide guidance on how to guard against suggestive interviewing which is useful in the training of various professionals.

6.1 Implanting False Information in Children

As Pedzek and Hinz (2002) remind us, the establishment of the False Memory Syndrome Foundation by Pamela Freyd in March 1992 'served as a call to action for cognitive psychologists studying memory' (p. 99). Pedzek and Hinz reviewed six research programmes in which attempts had been made to plant false events in memory: Ceci et al. (1996), Ceci et al. (1994), Huffman et al. (1997); Garry et al. (1996); Hyman et al. (1995); Loftus and Pickrel (1995); Mazzoni et al. (1999); and Pedzek and Hodge (1999). They concluded (p. 113) that:

- Under some conditions, some false events can be planted in memory.
- Plausible false events are more likely to be planted than implausible ones.
- A suggested event is more likely to be incorporated into memory if one has prior knowledge of it.
- Children are more suggestible than adults and younger children (aged 5 to 7 years) are more suggestible than older ones (aged 9 to 12 years).

> A child's self-confidence is important when considering the relationship between age and suggestibility.

Pedzek and Hinz (2002) go on to remind the reader that 'Beyond this, we have more questions than answers because the research is riddled with methodological problems' and, meanwhile, 'The call to action to cognitive psychologists provided by the False Memory Syndrome Foundation continues' (p. 114). Lee and Bussey (1999) have shown that 7-year-old children are not immune to misinformation effects even when tested on material (relationships between rooms, clothing and fruit) for which they had previously learned criteria and for which they had been tested and had a good memory.

When considering the effects of misleading questions on children's memory, it should be noted that there is an important interviewing variable, namely a child's self-esteem. Australian researchers Howie and Dowd (1996) found that children with low self-esteem (on the basis of teachers' ratings) are more disadvantaged. Empirical support for Howie and Dowd's finding has been reported by Vrij and Bush (2000) who used the Behavioural Academic Self-Esteem Scale.[21] They found that younger children (aged 5 and 6 years) are more suggestible than older ones (aged 10 and 11 years) and this difference disappeared when they controlled for children's self-confidence.

Bruck and Ceci's (1995) *amicus* brief in *Michaels* provides an excellent summary of research findings regarding children's suggestibility. The conclusions they reached then have not been altered significantly by subsequent research. They identify the following nine potential sources of suggestibility for children which they document with references to empirical studies.

6.1.1 Interviewer Bias

If an interviewer believes that a child has been sexually abused and that is the only hypothesis he/she is interested in confirming, he/she may very well bias the interview outcome by utilising one or more of the ways mentioned next in order to obtain from the child a report that is consistent with his/her blinkered view of the allegations made (pp. 273–9).

6.1.2 Repeating Questions

Repeating questions in the course of the same interview or in different interviews may lead preschoolers to change their original answers (p. 279). Leichtman and Ceci's (1995) study of eyewitness reports by pre-schoolers (3 to 6 year olds) who had been exposed to suggestive questioning showed that asking a witness the same question increased false reporting. It should also be noted in this context that studies examining the effects on children of repeated interviews in the short term have yielded mixed results and researchers have not addressed such effects in the long term (Edelstein et al., 2002:267).

6.1.3 Repeating Misinformation In Interviews

As a result of repeating misinformation in different interviews, children may well come to incorporate the misleading information in their subsequent reports and/or distort the misinformation itself (p. 280).

6.1.4 The Interviewer's Emotional Tone

Children may be led to fabricate information if they are asked in an accusatory tone 'Are you afraid to tell?', or are likewise told that 'You'll feel better if you tell' (p. 281).

6.1.5 Peer Pressure

Telling children in an interview that their peers have already answered a particular question and/or that another child victim has already named them as having been abused makes them want to change their answers so as to be consistent with their peers (pp. 283, 285). A child can also be pressured into providing the answers an interviewer wants to hear if threatened with exposure to his/her peers for being uncooperative (p. 283).

6.1.6 Being Interviewed by Adults in Authority/of High Status

Children's comprehension of legal processes is dependent on their understanding of the role and powers of legal personnel. In the case of police officers, young children's (aged 5 to 9 years) perceptions of a police officer's status are dominated by the uniform (Durkin and Jeffery, 2000). A child being interviewed by a police officer or a Youth and Family Services investigator or a sexual abuse consultant is likely to want to please such an adult figure by providing answers the child believes the authority figure would like to hear, and is also likely to accept such an adult's account of an alleged event (p. 285).

6.1.7 The Induction of Stereotypes

Suggestive interviewing may take the form of the interviewer telling a child that a particular person 'does bad things'. Such information may then be incorporated by the child into a subsequent report about his/her interaction with that individual (p. 287).

6.1.8 Ethnicity of Child Witness

In multicultural societies like the United States, UK, Canada, Australia, Germany and France the increase in the reporting of abuse cases involving children is likely to include children from ethnic communities. Ethnicity has been neglected in child witness research. British researchers Sattar and Bull (1999) compared the testimony of two groups of children (Asian and Caucasian) who were interviewed by Asian or Caucasian interviewers. The eighty-one children involved were aged 8 to 11 years and were interviewed about a magic show, during which a confederate interrupted, asking the magician for a book. No differences were found between the two groups of children as far as free recall accuracy is concerned or as a function of the ethnicity of the interviewer. However, when asked a misleading question Asian children were less likely to say they did not know the answer, probably because they considered it disrespectful to the interviewer (p. 14).

6.1.9 The Use of Anatomically Detailed Dolls

Three-year-old children interviewed with the aid of an anatomically detailed doll are likely to inaccurately report being touched and/or to insert their fingers into the anal or genital cavities in the doll even though nobody has done so to them (pp. 289–1) (see, also below).

6.1.10 Source Attribution Errors

The phenomenon of source attribution error was dealt with in the previous chapter. Young children (6-year-olds) are vulnerable to confuse what they have seen with what has been suggested to them and, consequently, to make false reports (pp. 294–6).

Bruck and Ceci (1995) go on to add that children who have been subjected to suggestive interviewing often appear highly credible and can fool even well-trained professionals (p. 301) and, furthermore, the effect of such interviewing 'may be long lasting' (p. 303). Finally, they also conclude that the interrelationships of the factors affecting children's suggestibility are complex and 'Even though suggestibility effects may be robust, the effects are not universal. Results vary between studies and children's behavior varies within studies' (p. 310). Bruck and Ceci also emphasise that 'poor interviewing procedures make it difficult to detect real abuse' (p. 310).[22]

Adults, too, have been shown to be suggestible (Gudjonsson, 1992a:143). In contrast to the popular belief that suggestibility is age-related and a personality trait, in Gudjonsson and Clark's (1986) social psychological model suggestibility is conceived of as the outcome of a complex and dynamic interaction between an individual, the environment and other important persons in that environment. Gudjonsson and Clark believe there are three factors that predispose someone to be susceptible to leading questions: uncertainty, interpersonal trust, and expectations. However, even if these factors are present in an interview, a witness is likely to resist the effect of suggestive questioning if he/she is suspicious of the interviewer (Gudjonsson and Clark, 1986; Siegal and Peterson, 1995; Warren et al., 1991). Four potential sources of suggestibility for children are: (1) demand characteristics; (2) the credibility of the misleading information; (3) repeated interviews; and (4) the linguistic form of the question (Gudjonsson, 1992a:94–5; Moston, 1990).

While some authors point to the increased suggestibility of especially preschool children (Ceci and Leichtman, 1992),[23] others emphasise children's ability to resist the influence of leading questions (Siegal and Peterson, 1995)[24] while others have found 6-year-olds more suggestible than 8-year-olds to negative (that is, suggesting incorrect 'facts') but not to positive-leading questions (Cassell and Bjorklund, 1995). Goodman et al. (1990) reported that children as young as 3 to 4 years can resist suggestive questioning of the type used in sexual abuse investigations for up to a year after the incident. A child's ability to resist the effect of suggestive questioning appears to be a function of a witness being suspicious of the interviewer (Gudjonsson and Clark, 1986; Siegal and Peterson, 1995; Warren et al., 1991). The Australian study by Siegal and Peterson examined resistance to suggestibility among 4- and 5-year-olds utilising a story about a little girl who has a stomach-ache from eating toast too fast before her first day at pre-school. It was found that presenting children with a rationale to cancel the implication conveyed in biased information (that the original details were irrelevant to producing an accurate report of the story), reduced the pre-schoolers' suggestibility. Siegal and Peterson concluded that, 'children are not inevitably vulnerable to suggestion in simple salient situations where they have a strong knowledge base' (p. 40). Support for this view was provided by Saywitz et al.'s (1991)[25] study which found that exposing children to an alternative set of expectations and beliefs about answering questions resulted in a 26 per cent decline in percentage of error when responding to misleading questions in comparison to a control group.

> Even though the testimony of young children (4 to 8 years) is not likely to be as accurate and complete as that of older children, children can provide identity information of significant potential forensic usefulness but such information must be elicited by skilled interviews and appropriate questioning (Davies, 1993b:243).

Davies (1993b) provides an excellent discussion of the empirical literature on children's identification. On the basis of his review he concludes that, even though the testimony of young children (4 to 8 years) is not likely to be as accurate and complete as that of older children, children can provide identity information of significant potential forensic usefulness but such information must be elicited by skilled interviews and appropriate questioning (p. 243). More specifically, children are least likely to show age differences in identification tasks but are most likely to do so if asked to estimate a suspect's height or weight or to furnish a description of a suspect's face for police to construct a face composite image (pp. 252–3). Finally, like adults, children's perform-ance as eyewitnesses is influenced by situational demands. In other words, both their cognitive development and how they are approached as witnesses play a significant role in their accuracy as eyewitnesses. It should be remembered, however, that the findings reported by empirical studies of child witnesses are based on group accuracy data. This should not be allowed to detract from the potential usefulness of the individual child of rather young age who has every right to be heard and evaluated as a witness in open court like everybody else (Davies, 1993b:253).

6.2 Children vs. Adults

> The completeness and accuracy of children's testimony parallels their general cognitive development with increased age.

The methodology of research into children's testimony has shifted in recent years from the laboratory to the field as slide and video presentations have been, to an extent, superseded by real-life staged events or the utilisation of naturally occurring events (Clifford, 2002:333). Children as young as 4 have been found to be as good at colour memory as adults (Ling and Blades, 1995). Generally, however, research into children's memory vs. adults' has yielded inconsistent results (Leippe et al., 1993:170). To illustrate, in a highly cued memory task Sheingold and Tenney (1982) found that school-age children could recall accurately as much as adults about the birth of a sibling when the subjects were 4 years old. However, in another study involving cued recall of being touched, Leippe et al. (1991) compared 5/6, 9/10-year-olds and adults. They reported that 5/6-year-olds performed more poorly than did the adults in free recall and when asked objective questions, but both groups of children performed significantly more poorly than did adult subjects in a line-up identification task (both in correctly identifying the person who had touched them as well as correctly rejecting a target-absent line-up (see also chapter 10).

Clifford (1993) has drawn attention to the fact that if one reads five pre-1984 textbooks in eyewitness testimony one finds they state that children are poorer witnesses than adults, presumably on the basis that they have poorer memory capabilities. This is in contrast to post-1984 literature which portrays children as being much better witnesses than was thought earlier on and in some ways as being not significantly different, if not better, than adults (p. 15).

> Whether one considers studies using children as actively involved witnesses or as mere bystanders, there is no strong evidence that young children's recall or identification performance is significantly different from that of adults.

Clifford's (1993) study reported an impressive series of six experiments concerned with comparing adults and children as eyewitnesses. The experi-ments involved the following:

- *Experiment 1:* 7/8, 11/12 and 20-32-year-olds, a 15-minute videotaped television programme ('The Wonder Years'), immediate recall in response to twenty multiple-choice questions;
- *Experiment 2:* two videos (one a dummy filler), 4-5-, 9-10- and 18-35-year-olds, fourteen objective and six misleading questions, recall immediately or after one week;

- *Experiment 3:* 7/8-, 11/12- and 15-18-year-olds, an 8-minute video clip from 'Dempsey and Makepiece', recall of actions, descriptions and verbalisations by a twenty-item questionnaire, and recognition and identification from blank and filled video parades, testing after one or five days;
- *Experiment 4:* 7/8- and 18-39-year-olds, two videos depicting people engaging in different activities for about $1\frac{1}{2}$ minutes each, testing after two days with questionnaire which did or did not include misleading questions, testing after four days for recall with yes/no questions, as well as matching actors to activities and sequencing the activities seen previously;
- *Experiment 5:* 12-year-olds and adults, a 2-minute interaction with an Asian confederate of the researcher in a McDonald's restaurant, recall tested by objective and misleading questions, identification of confederate from filled or blank photographic line-ups; and
- *Experiment 6:* 5-year-olds and adults (mean age 27.8 years), interact with a confederate for $3\frac{1}{2}$ minutes (including physical contact), free recall of event details tested a week later as well as identification of blank or filled photospread.

On the basis of his findings Clifford concluded that: whether one considers studies using children as actively involved witnesses or as mere bystanders, there is no strong evidence that young children's recall or identification performance is significantly different from that of adults. In fact, if one focuses on the more forensically relevant studies, children emerge as inferior eyewitnesses to adults; the term 'young' as used in the literature is ambiguous and needs scrutiny; 11-to 12-year-olds are comparable to adults as witnesses; and, finally, one needs to turn to the sociology of knowledge for an answer to the question of whether children are comparable to adults as eyewitnesses and why this was answered by numerous researchers in the negative until the mid 1980s but in the positive since then (p. 20).

In support of Clifford (1993), Loftus et al. (1989) reported that the amount of information free-recalled by children aged 12 or older is as good as that provided by adults and, furthermore, they are no more susceptible to the effect of leading questions. We now know (see Goodman et al., 1987) that when children's recall is influenced by leading questions, it is not with reference to central detail but rather peripheral. There are, of course, situations when children can be vulnerable. Children seem more prone than adults to false identification in a line-up of strangers they have seen briefly (Parker and Carranza, 1989). Davies et al. (1988) asked children aged 7 to 8, 8 to 9 and 10 to 11, who had helped a stranger at their school set up a film show, to try and identify him from twelve photographs. It was found that all age groups selected him 65 per cent of the time when his photograph was present in the array. However, when his photograph was absent, 87 per cent of the 7- to 8-year-olds selected a photograph compared to 50 per cent of the two older age groups; in other words, the 7- to 8-year-olds had an apparent 'urge to please' (Davies, 1991:182).

When considering the importance of a child's or a young person's testimony, it is also important to remember that a witness' age appears to be related to how credible he/she is perceived and, consequently, to the likelihood of the defendant being convicted. Nightingale (1993) reported that the number of guilty verdicts and the witness' credibility in a sexual abuse case decreased as the age of the child in the experiment increased from six to fourteen years. Nightingale also found that mock-jurors blamed the older victim more.

As far as line-up performance is concerned, children can be as good as adults in identification of a perpetrator from a target-present array (Pozzulo and Lindsay, 1998) but produce more false positive errors than adults in a target-absent line-up (Lindsay et al., 1997), a proclivity which is reduced significantly if an elimination line-up is used (Pozzulo and Lindsay, 1999). In this procedure, the child eliminates (one by one or all at once) all but one line-up member before being asked if the remaining one is the actual person.

Davies (1991:182) concluded that the completeness and accuracy of children's testimony parallels their general cognitive development with increased age. However, it is not possible to identify a particular age before which children are 'bad' witnesses. Quality of recall is largely context-dependent, that is, 'the same child may be a good witness in one situation and poor in another ... Children can be convinced that one set of photographs must be of a man they have seen before but not the same stranger who sexually assaulted them' (p. 182). While children with mild learning disabilities are vulnerable to suggestion, even when interviewed utilising the cognitive interview (Milne and Bull, 1995), Davies' conclusion that suggestibility is not some kind of universal trait with which all children are invested, is supported by Gudjonsson (1992a:94–5), Ceci and Bruck's (1993) and Clifford's (2002) reviews of the concept.

We can conclude that the available psycholegal research shows that, as Naylor (1989) put it, 'children can be good witnesses when their special needs are understood' – a conclusion that has clear legal implications (p. 82). The importance of social support for children in order to reduce stress during interviewing, an area neglected by researchers (see Moston and Engelberg, 1991), cannot be overemphasised. Meanwhile, legal psychologists should be cognisant of the importance of the 'sociology of knowledge' for the type of research they carry out and what they decide to report. By 'sociology of knowledge' in operation Clifford (1993:15) means that knowledge (that is, research and the reporting of research) does not take place in a social vacuum; on the contrary, researchers produce what society demands and/or what it accepts as valid (see Wattam, 2002, for a stimulating discussion of the sociological approach to child witness research). Clifford has argued that the cause of children is better served by an acceptance of the evidence that children and adults differ as far as their memory capacities are concerned. Such an acceptance would lead the legal system to be more sensitive to children's needs when 'placed in situations that are inherently difficult for them' (p. 20). Approximately a decade later, Clifford (2002), argues convincingly that ' "the child-as-good-as adult" card should not be overplayed' because 'We must not let our rhetoric run ahead of our results' (p. 334).

7 Enhancing Children's Testimony

We have already seen that providing contextual cues improves children's recall by aiding the retrieval process, as would be predicted on the basis of Tulving's (1983) 'encoding specificity' hypothesis. Given that children's recall of events is likely to be accurate but incomplete, findings from memory training studies can be useful to assist their recall (Saywitz and Snyder, 1993:125). In a study by Saywitz, Snyder and Lamphear (1990) children aged 7 to 11 years were trained to use external visual cues, drawn on cards, to remind them to report a specified level of detail from categories of information (setting, participants, conversations, effective states, actions and consequences)[26] that would be useful in a criminal investigation two weeks after participating in a videotaped classroom event. It was found that the training resulted in better and more accurate free and cued recall without increases in inaccuracies (Saywitz and Snyder, 1993:128). Interestingly, it was also found that merely instructing the same children to be more complete was not effective. This study shows that, without infringing on the rights of the accused, children can be assisted with providing more complete recall before they are interviewed by police or testify in a courtroom.

Saywitz and Snyder (1991) trained children to be better at monitoring how far they understood what was being communicated to them and found that, unlike a control group, when confronted with difficult-to-comprehend questions about easily recalled information they were more likely to communicate that they did not understand a question and to request that it be rephrased (p. 137). As Saywitz and Snyder point out, a great deal of additional research is required before these methods can be used in actual forensic contexts (p. 138). On the basis of existing psychological knowledge, however, the potential exists for social workers, police personnel, lawyers and judicial officers to reduce significantly the negative influence on children's testimony of their limited communication skills.

7.1 Open-ended Prompts

Hershkowitz (2001) reported an Israeli study which used the National Institute of Child Health and Human Development protocol for interviewing children that offers specific guidance on open-ended prompts. Six experienced youth investigators conducted interviews with forty girls and ten boys, alleged victims of sexual abuse in various parts of Israel. Nine of the children were 4 to 6 years of age, sixteen were 7 to 9 years of age and twenty-five were 10 to 13 years of age. It was found that open-ended prompts yielded significantly longer and more detailed responses than did focused prompts.

7.2 The Cognitive Interview Technique

The cognitive interview (CI) technique (discussed in chapter 3) which has proved to be useful with adult witnesses (Geiselman et al., 1985) has also been

The cognitive interview can indeed improve the completeness of children's recall but its use is not without some problems.

used to enhance the amount and accuracy of children's recall.[27] Geiselman and Padilla (1988) interviewed children aged 7 and 12 years three days after showing them a video of a simulated liquor store robbery. The interviews were carried out by research assistants trained in how to use the CI. It was found that, without increasing errors and confabulations, the CI produced 21 per cent more correct 'items' of information than did the standard interview where the interviewer only asked about the facts.

The study by Geiselman et al. (1990) used a 'Simon Says' touching game that involved an unfamiliar adult, one child 'victim' and one child witness. Again, it was found that significantly more facts were elicited using the CI than the standard interviewing technique with 7 to 8 and 10 to 11-year-olds. Geiselman et al. also reported, however, that (a) there were differences between the interviewers regarding the extent to which they use the CI techniques; and (b) the interviewees differed in the ease with which they used different CI techniques; more specifically, the 7-year-olds especially had difficulty understanding what was meant when the interviewer instructed him/her to 'change perspective'. Geiselman et al. (1993) used a slide presenta-tion and also staged two live events in front of groups of three or four third-graders aged 8 and 9 years and 11 and 12 years. Children were randomly assigned to a 2 by 3 matrix, that is, two grade levels and three types of inter-view (CI with practice, CI without practice and standard interview). Psychol-ogy majors interviewed the children about the live event and police detectives carried out the interviews about the slide presentation. It was found that CIs elicited more correct facts and that giving children 'practice' with the CI techniques increased their recall performance even more. Like Memon et al. (1993) (see below) Geiselman et al. (1993) also found that there were differ-ences between the interviewers regarding the frequency with which they used various CI techniques. Geiselman et al. (1993) concluded that CI techniques can improve the completeness of children's recall, that children benefit from having prior practice with CI techniques before receiving a CI and, finally, that giving children practice with the CI about an unrelated event is good invest-ment because it produces a more complete report from child witnesses and reduces the likelihood of children having to retell and relive details of traumatic experiences (pp. 88–9).

Problems in using the CI technique with children have been reported by Köhnken et al. (1991)[28] who found that the CI increased confabulation. A British study by Memon et al. (1993) used a 2 (interview type: CI, standard) by 2 (test phase: two days, six weeks) with 6 to 7-year-olds who were video-taped while having their vision tested. The cameraman was a stranger who was introduced to them by name as the children arrived for their eye test. Children were asked to recall details of the event and the appearance of the cameraman. Memon et al. found that there was no difference in the relative effectiveness of the CI when used with children as compared with the standard interview, irrespective of the measure used to assess effectiveness. The one exception to this finding was that the CI elicited significantly more information about locations of objects and people (p. 7). One weakness of the Memon et al.

study, which the authors themselves acknowledge, is that their subjects may have reinstated context when they were instructed not to do so by virtue of the fact that subjects' recall was tested in a familiar setting (p. 8).

Differences between Memon et al. (1993) and other CI studies (for example, Fisher et al., 1994; Geiselman et al., 1993) concerning the effectiveness of the CI vs. the standard interview reflect differences in how 'effectiveness' is measured. As Memon et al. (1993:7) point out, Geiselman and Fisher have always used total correct information as their measure of effectiveness when reporting the CI as more effective; however, when the 'proportion correct' measure is used, no significant differences between the effectiveness of the CI and the standard interview have been reported. In the absence of a standard scoring system for studies of this kind, inconsistent findings are inevitable and evaluations of the CI technique remain inconclusive.

Milne et al. (1994) examined the effectiveness of their revised version of the CI for children aged 8 to 10 years. They found that as far as person details are concerned, CI children showed more incorrect recall and confabulations; in questioning subsequent to an initial free recall, the CI children yielded 20 per cent more accurate information than did structured interview children. It was also reported that interviewing children with the CI reduced the impact of subsequent suggestive questioning. Another study by Wark et al. (1994) used the revised version of the CI as was used in the Milne et al. (1994) study with 8- and 9-year-old children and reported rather similar findings. Wark et al. also found, however, that there were no significant differences between CI and structured interview children when recall was tested eleven days after the event – the CI only produced more information than the structured interview did when recall was tested two days after the event. Similarly, Memon et al. (1997) found the CI led to more correct information (and errors) in open-ended recall when children were interviewed with two days' delay but not when there was a twenty-day delay. On the basis of the studies cited, it can be concluded that the empirical evidence supporting the usefulness of the CI with children is not unequivocal. This is not to deny that the CI has been shown to increase correct recall with different types of interviewees, of different ages and in different countries, namely the UK, United States, Canada, Germany, France and Spain (Milne and Shaw, 1999:131).

8 Interviewing Children in Sexual Abuse Cases

In view of the need to minimise both false allegations and false denials of child sexual abuse, the importance of conducting adequate interviews of children cannot be overemphasised (see Bull, 1995a and b; Lamb et al., 1995). It is imperative that the interviewer in such cases has adequate knowledge of sexual development, the numerous ways in which children can be sexually abused, 'as well as specialist knowledge to interact appropriately and sensitively with them' (Yuille et al., 1993:98). Yuille et al. recommend that, if

> The importance of conducting adequate interviews of children cannot be overemphasised.

an interviewer has concerns about the suggestibility of a child, he/she should ask a few questions about irrelevant issues before concluding the interview in order to decide whether the interviewee's answers can be relied upon.

In their *amicus* brief in the *Michaels* case, Bruck and Ceci (1995:309) concluded that the following reduce the risks of suggestibility effects:

- A child's report after a single interview rather than after multiple interviews.
- Asking a child non-leading questions.
- The interviewer not having a confirmatory bias, that is, not blindly following only one hypothesis.
- Not repeating closed-ended yes/no questions during the same or different interviews with a child.
- If the interviewer is patient, non-judgemental and does not try to create demand characteristics, in other words, does not in any way, subtle or otherwise, bias a child to answer a question in a particular way.

Yuille et al. (1993:99–100) advocate using their method known as the 'Step-Wise Interview'. It is a non-suggestive method of interviewing which comprises a series of nine steps during the interview, and is meant to maximise recall while minimising contamination. The nine steps are:

1 Rapport building.
2 Requesting recall of two specific events.
3 Telling the truth.
4 Introducing the topic of concern.
5 Free narrative.
6 General questions.
7 Specific questions (if necessary).
8 Interview aids (if necessary).
9 Concluding the interview (from table 5.1, p. 99).

Yuille et al. also list four major goals of an investigative interview, namely:

1 Trauma-minimisation of the investigation for the child.
2 Obtaining maximum information from the child about the alleged event/s.
3 Minimising the interview contamination effects on the child's memory for the event/s in question.
4 Maintaining the integrity of the investigative process (p. 100).

They suggest combining the step-wise method with 'Statement Validity Analysis' (see Steller and Köhnken, 1989 in chapter 9). According to Marxsen et al. (1995), 'The step-wise protocol has been officially adopted by both police and child protection workers in many parts of Canada, the United Kingdom, and the United States' (p. 454). The Pigot (1989) Report in the UK into issues concerning children's evidence, had in fact recommended the adoption of the step-wise interview method as a national standard.

Another systematic approach to gathering evidence in cases involving children in general and alleged sexual abuse in particular has been developed at Liverpool University in England. This particular model is known as the 'Systematic Approach to Gathering Evidence' (SAGE) and has been developed in response to such events in the UK as the Cleveland Inquiry and reforms regarding children's evidence introduced by the *Criminal Justice Act* (1991). SAGE has been tested within family courts (Roberts and Glasgow, 1993:10). SAGE has the following six aims:

1 To make decision-making explicit and to encourage investigators to 'opt in' to particular actions and behaviours.
2 To provide the investigation with a structure and to make clear to investigators the relevant information they need to collect.
3 To encourage communication about the child's world – experiences, significant others and abilities – not only about allegations of abuse.
4 To provide testing of the child's competence and to encourage accuracy within the process of the investigation.
5 To facilitate professional 'working together', providing practical ways of expediting this process and to provide a context of training.
6 To investigate alleged experience of child sexual abuse within a single-case methodology framework (p. 10).

SAGE aims to compare and contrast the child's response to stimuli presented in a series of planned and controlled brief sessions. As Roberts and Glasgow (1993) acknowledge, however, 'the most common criticism of SAGE is that it takes longer [several brief sessions, often no longer than 30 minutes each] than the "one or at most two" interviews recommended in the Cleveland Report'. There is undoubtedly a need for evaluation studies of the comparative strengths and weaknesses of interview methods such as step-wise and SAGE in forensically relevant contexts.

A procedure for assisting children to understand what is being asked of them in investigative interviews, known as 'felt board', was devised by Poole (1992). It entails drawing on the 'felt board' the outline of an adult's head and a child's head, the child's head containing a fair number of felt triangles of a different colour from the 'felt board'. The interviewer explains to the child that the triangles in his/her head stand for all that the child knows about the matter at hand. As the interview proceeds and the child passes on information about the incident, triangles are moved from the outline of the child's head to the interviewer's sketched head. Poole (1992) and Sattar and Bull (1994) found this procedure resulted in children giving longer (but no more accurate) responses. In addition, Poole (1992) also found that a child's recall is facilitated if an audio tape of a child's first attempt at remembering is played back to him/her.

9 Anatomical Dolls and Interviewing Children

Since the late 1980s the practice of using anatomically detailed dolls (AD dolls) when interviewing children in cases of alleged sexual abuse has become very widespread (see Koocher et al., 1995, for a literature review). Morgan (1995) points out that anatomical dolls are being used in interviews in all fifty of the states in the United States and in many other countries. Utilising data in trial court transcripts, Mason (1991) examined 122 appellate court decisions in the United States in which expert testimony on the characteristics of sexually abused children was challenged. It was found that in seven out of nine cases that involved testimony based on interviews using AD dolls, expert testimony was not admitted on the basis that the use of AD dolls was not scientifically accepted (pp. 195–7). Given the controversy surrounding this practice, what can be said about it on the basis of the existing literature? The general consensus of opinion is that first of all professionals must be trained in the use of AD dolls as an aid in child interviews about child sexual abuse. The interviewer should also establish initial rapport with the child before presenting a clothed doll. There is evidence that this is the practice followed by most professionals who use AD dolls and that most children aged 3 to 6 undress dolls spontaneously or with little encouragement from an adult (Glaser and Collins, 1989). Not forgetting that at about the age of 5 children are more likely to be able to communicate about (that is, name) body parts (Schor and Sivan, 1989), interviewers would be well advised not to give children the names of body parts or to suggest functions for them (American Professional Society on the Abuse of Children [APSAC] Guidelines, 1990).[29]

> Professionals who interview children about child sexual abuse must be trained in the proper use of AD dolls as as an aid to recall.

One crucial question is whether the use of AD dolls as demonstration/ memory aid/diagnostic tools leads young children to make false allegations of sexual abuse (see DeLoache, 1995). Some authors (for example, Bruck and Ceci, 1995; Kooch et al., 1995; Raskin and Yuille, 1989) have argued that using AD dolls, especially with pre-schoolers, increases children's suggestibility. Boat and Everson (1993:56–9), however, cite a number of studies (for example, Goodman and Aman, 1990; Saywitz et al., 1991a) that appear to allay this concern. Saywitz et al. (1991a) used free recall, AD dolls and direct, and misleading questions to investigate the memories of non-refereed 5 to 7-year-old girls a week after experiencing a medical checkup by a paediatrician that involved medical touch. It was found that not only does the use of dolls not stimulate false reports of genital contact but it also helps children to remember more information about the event. However, since children younger than 5 years of age are known to be more suggestible, the results of Saywitz et al. (1991a) cannot be generalised to younger children. Boat and Everson (1993) conclude their discussion of relevant studies stating that, as far as the question of the use of ADs as a diagnostic tool is concerned, 'The preponderance of research supports the use of anatomical dolls as an interview tool but not as a litmus test for sexual abuse. It is important to remember that the effectiveness of any tool is contingent upon the skill of its user' (p. 65). Similarly, on the basis of their literature review, Kooch et al. (1995) conclude that 'research to date mainly supports use of AD dolls as a communication or memory aid for children 5 years or older, albeit with a certain risk of contributing to some children's errors if misleading questions are used' (p. 217). Their assessment of the available empirical evidence leads Kooch et al. to recommend that 'APA reconsider whether valid "doll-centered assessment" techniques exist and whether they still "may be the best available practical solution"' (American Psychological Association, 1991, p. 722) for the pressing and frequent problem of investigation of child sexual abuse' (p. 218).

Bruck and Ceci (1995) speak for most authors in this area when they state that because AD dolls are suggestive and because one cannot draw definitive conclusions about whether or not children have been sexually abused or not on the basis of how they play with such dolls, 'The use of anatomically detailed dolls has raised skepticism, ... among researchers and professionals' (p. 290). Those professionals who prefer to err on the side of caution should heed Yuille et al.'s (1993:109) advice that AD dolls 'are to be used only after the child has disclosed details of the abuse. The dolls should never be used to obtain the disclosure, only to clarify it.' Extreme caution in the use of AD dolls in legal contexts is also urged by Skinner and Berry (1993) on the basis of their literature review. In the last week of September 1993 a group of experts from North America, Europe and the Middle East gathered in Satra Bruk in Sweden to assess what was known about how to effectively investigate child sexual abuse (Lamb, 1994). Twenty of the participants (interestingly none of them from the Middle East) signed a consensus statement which, inter alia, recommended that interviews utilising dolls should, as much as possible, be videotaped and reminded potential consumers of investigative interviews that 'there is no anatomically detailed doll "test" yielding conclusive scores quantifying the probability that a child has been sexually abused' (Lamb, 1994:154). DeLoache (1995) argues convincingly against the use of dolls with children 3 years of age or younger. On the basis of their review of the literature, Pipe et al. (2002) state that dolls should not be used with children aged 5 years or less because they 'fail to substantially increase the correct information that childern report' (pp. 165–6). Pipe et al. conclude the same about the use of any toys. Finally, whether or not AD dolls are used in child sexual abuse investigative interviews, one cannot but agree with McGough (1995) that, while the law in the United States (and in other common law countries) does not require it, it is imperative that such interviews be videotaped. Such a practice will help to improve 'the quality of the child abuse investigations, the reliability of child witness testimony, and ultimately the justice of the American [and other countries'] civil trial' (p. 386).

Finally, as far as the use of photographs is concerned, Pipe et al. (2002) cites empirical evidence (Ascherman et al., 1998; Hudson and Fivush, 1991; Paterson and Bull, 1999) that photographs can be effective retrieval cues in interviewing children, following both short and long delays.

> It is not advisable that AD dolls be used as an interview tool with children aged 5 or less and, generally, such interviews should be videotaped.

10 Conclusions

The empirical evidence considered in this chapter shows there is no justification for considering children incompetent as witnesses by virtue of their age. Edelstein et al. (2002) conclude their discussion of the effects of legal involvement on children stating that, 'In general, research on childern's reactions to the legal system suggests that forensic interviewing, court involvement generally, and testifying and/or its anticipation specifically, may be stressful experiences for children' (p. 269). In order to improve children's testimony it is important that attention is focused on elucidating jurors', judicial officers' and police officers' perceptions of children's and adolescents' credibility as eyewitnesses as well as identifying children's strengths and weaknesses and how they are treated by the legal system, the legal agents and other professionals who interact with child witnesses. There is a need for police personnel, lawyers and judicial officers to communicate with children in age-appropriate language. In view of the increasing number of children testifying in courts, relevant psychological knowledge should inform police, legal and judicial training as well as other professionals (for example, child protective services workers) whose work involves them in interviewing children in the context of abuse allegations having been made. As Doris et al. (1995) point out, however, implementing a training programme for such professionals does not of itself mean they become competent interviewers. Similarly, reforming legislation is simply not enough. Flin (1993:296) reminds us that, closed-circuit television can save a child the trauma of having to confront an offender in court face-to-face but it does nothing about long pretrial delays, the use of inappropriate language by lawyers in communicating with children (see Walker, 1993; Wilson, 1995), the cross-examination of a child by a lawyer who aims to intimidate and discredit a child as a witness (Westcott, 1995), or, finally, preventing the defendant or his/her associates intimidating a child in the environs of the courthouse. It is interesting to note in this context that one of the recommendations by Judge Piggot's committee was for a specialist child examiner to interview the child on behalf of both parties and for the benefit of the court. It was the representative of the bar who dissented from that suggestion (Flin, 1993:296).

As far as the use of AD dolls in child sexual abuse assessments is concerned, they can be a useful communication aid when used by an adequately trained professional interviewer with children of 5 years of age or older, who also remembers that 'many pressing questions about the impact of AD dolls on children's memory and suggestibility remain to be explored or have received insufficient research attention' (Koocher et al., 1995:218).

The legal system in western English-speaking common law countries can create a better socio-legal context for children's testimony by adopting some features of inquisitorial legal systems on mainland Europe, such as court-appointed child examiners (see Köhnken, 2002). The need for innovation when it comes to hearing and testing children's evidence on both sides of the Atlantic and in the Antipodes is long overdue. Such reforms should utilise both top-down and bottom-up solutions. Meanwhile some researchers have examined the importance in children's identification accuracy of children's secrets (see Pipe and Goodman, 1991), multiple interviewing (Davies, 1994:179), and ways judges regulate the questioning of children in court by lawyers (Carson, 1995). For many other researchers the behaviour of jurors/juries, the concern of the next chapter, continues to be the focus of their attention. Research into juridic decision-making is another pillar on which the edifice of legal psychology has been built.

Revision Questions

1 How has the legal status of children as eyewitnesses improved in western common law countries?
2 How effective is closed-circuit television in protecting a child victim of sexual abuse when testifying in a trial?
3 How valid are popular beliefs about children as eyewitnesses?
4 What do you know about the memory performance of pre-schoolers?
5 What factors impact adversely on the accuracy of children's memory of an event?
6 What does the empirical evidence indicate about implanting false information in children?
7 Under what circumstances are children as good eyewitnesses as adults?
8 How effective is the cognitive interview in enhancing the accuracy and completeness of children's testimony?
9 In a forensic context, how should a child be interviewed to reduce the risk of suggestibility?
10 What are some of the dangers in interviewing children in cases of alleged child sexual abuse? How can they be avoided?

5 The Jury

'No freeman shall be seized, or imprisoned, or disposed or outlawed, or in any way destroyed; nor will we condemn him, nor will we commit him to prison, excepting by the lawful judgement of his peers, or by the law of the land.' (Clause 39 Magna Carta 1215)

'A better instrument could scarcely be imagined for achieving uncertainty, capriciousness, lack of uniformity, disregard of former decisions – utter unpredictability.' (Judge Jerome Frank, 1949:172)

'The verdicts juries give may sometimes seem willfully perverse ... Stories provide answers to the pressing questions of identity, mental state, actions and circumstances that are required to establish blame. There is a story behind every verdict.' (Stephenson, 1992:196)

'Because of the problem-driven nature of most jury research, however, no overarching theoretical model has emerged around which to structure a comprehensive review of the broad empirical literature.' (Devine et al., 2001:625).

Introduction

In *The Book of Magna Carta*[1] Hindley (1990:ix–x) comments that the words in the above quotation from clause 39, which has been the basis for the institution of trial by jury, 'coined by a distant society in a half-forgotten language, have been treasured by generations of men and women in the English-speaking world as a safeguard of individual liberty'. Darbyshire (1991:742), however, reminds us that, contrary to popular belief, legal historians (for example, Holdsworth, 1903:59) have pointed out (but have gone largely unnoticed by students of the jury) that clause 39 has nothing to do with trial by jury. The notion of being tried by one's peers existed long before the Magna Carta. The conclusion reached in the pages that follow is that the weight of the evidence from both experimental simulation and studies of actual juries/jurors is that the jury system is not a reliable, sound method of determining whether a defendant is guilty or innocent. In view of the fact, however, that the jury is most highly unlikely to be abolished in western common law countries in the foreseeable future, a number of reforms are suggested to improve jury decision-making. While the focus in this chapter is primarily on the psycho-legal implications of jury research, some background information is necessary in order to place the issues considered in a broader context.[2]

> The notion of being tried by one's peers existed long before the Magna Carta in 1215. It was invented in ancient Athens.

1 A Jury of Twelve: Historical Background

An early documented example of a system of jury existed in ancient Egypt 4000 years ago (Moore, 1973).[3] However, the idea and 'The right to trial by a jury of ordinary citizens (not persons having any special position or expertise) … It was in Athens that it was invented' (McDowell, 1978:34). Allotting jurors by lottery and the number of jurors used meant that 'An Athenian jury was the Athenian people' (p. 40). From ancient Greece the concept of a jury was adopted across Europe in one form or another and was introduced to Britain in the middle of the eleventh century by the Normans (Kerr, 1987:64).[4] Trial by ordeal was abolished by the Pope in 1215 and the idea of twelve jurors developed over many centuries (Cockburn and Green, 1988; New South Wales Law Reform Commission (NSWLRC), 1985:14). While the requirement that a jury's verdict be unanimous was established in 1367, and the Star Chamber (which heard cases of immense importance to the Crown, including high treason cases where the jury had acquitted) was abolished in 1621, 'the common law bench retained the power to hold juries in summary contempt, which resulted in imprisonment or fines for the jurors' (Clarke, 2000:40). In fact, until 1670 juries were often fined or even imprisoned if their verdict was not what the judge thought it should be. Furthermore, a property qualification for jury service in Northern Ireland, for example, that excluded a substantial proportion of its citizens, especially women, from jury duty was not abolished until 1976 (Quinn, 1999).[5] Similarly, in Australia, too, it was not until relatively recently that women and indigenous peoples, for example, became

eligible for jury service (NSWLRC, 1985:16). In western common law jurisdictions with a jury system the qualification for jury service is (a) being on the
electoral role;[6] and/or (b) being a licensed driver; and/or (c) not coming under
any of the categories of disqualified or ineligible persons detailed in statutory
provisions.

2 The Notion of an Impartial and Fair Jury: A Critical Appraisal

Many civil law countries (for example, Israel, Spain, the Netherlands) have no
community participation in the guilt-determining process in serious criminal
matters. Those common law and civil law countries that have a jury system
differ regarding various aspects of their jury system (Osner et al., 1993). Such
differences pertain to whether, for example, the number of possible verdicts is
two ('guilty', 'not guilty') or, three, as in Scotland[7] ('guilty', 'not guilty' and
'not proven'); the jury comprises twelve members (as is the case in England
and Wales, the United States, NZ, Australia and Canada) or more (fifteen in
Scotland); a jury comprises just lay persons (as in England and Wales, the
United States, New Zealand, Australia and Canada) or a combination of lay
persons and judges (as in Denmark, Belgium, France, Italy, Germany and
Sweden) and the types of legal cases they decide; how lists of potential jurors
are compiled;[8] who is disqualified from or is ineligible for jury service;[9]
whether peremptory challenges are allowed and how many; and the categories
of individuals who can be excused from service as of right and how many
peremptory challenges[10] and how many challenges for cause are allowed each
side at a trial. Other important features of different jury systems[11] are what
information about potential jurors is divulged in court for either side to
challenge (in England a lawyer knows only a potential juror's name and,
therefore, unlike in the United States, the scope for 'choosing' jurors is very
limited – but see below for a judge's ruling that changes this), and whether a
judge has discretion to exclude a juror even without a challenge having been
made (as is the position in England and Wales – Buxton, 1990a and b). In
addition, the size of the jury varies between different countries and often
depends on whether it is a civil or a criminal trial. While the public in western
common law countries is well accustomed to twelve-member juries for
criminal trials, the number of lay persons sitting with judges to decide serious
criminal matters varies between civil law countries: in France, nine jurors
deliberate with three judges; in Italy six lay assessors sit with two judges; in
Germany, three career judges adjudicate with lay judges; and, finally, in
Sweden one professional judge sits with three lay judges (Osner et al, 1993).
Furthermore, while some jurisdictions require a unanimous verdict others are
content with a majority one. Some other differences are whether there is a
requirement that a jury be segregated once it has commenced its deliberations[12] and whether the judge sums up to the jury on the facts (as happens in
England and Wales, though not in the United States (Evans, 1995:95). A

crucial characteristic of some jury systems is that a jury's verdict is final while in others it is merely a recommendation to the judge, as in some parts of the United States. Finally, in some jurisdictions it is prohibited to interview jurors after a trial has been completed, as is the position in England[13] and in Australia but this is not so in the United States. Such differences between jurisdictions mean that one should not generalise findings about juror decision-making across jurisdictions without question. Despite its great significance for so many people, it has been said that the jury is 'probably the least understood branch of our system of government' (Krauss, Stanton, 1995:921). Drawing in part on Darbyshire (1991) concerning the very concept of the jury, let us next take a close and critical look at the jury, this 'quaint institution that reflects the apotheosis of amateurism' (Blom-Cooper, 1974).

> The very concept of the jury itself is problematic because trial by one's 'peers', 'representativeness' and 'impartiality' do not go together and, even if they did, they would not guarantee that a jury's verdict would be a fair one.

A thorough dissection of the jury idea reveals that, sentimental attachments aside, the very concept of the jury itself is problematic and a strong case can be made for at least drastically reforming the jury system in western common law countries. To begin with, as already mentioned above, trial by one's peers is not provided in clause 39 of the Magna Carta itself. The fact is the Latin words 'judicium parium do not refer to a trial by jury', *judicium* 'implies the decision of a judge, not a jury verdict' (Darbyshire, 1991:743)[14] and *liber homo* (translated as 'freeman' or 'freeholder') 'did not mean what it does today' and 'we should remember from school history, freemen were a limited class in the feudal system' (p. 743). Thus, the long-held belief by legal scholars (for example, Blackstone, 1776; Devlin, 1956) that *judicium parium* referred to trial by one's peers is based on a misconception (Forsyth, 1852:108). It has also been pointed out that one cannot assert, in jurisprudential terms, that there is a right to jury trial (Darbyshire, 1991:743). The Sixth Amendment of the Constitution of the United States guarantees defendants the right to a jury trial if they are charged with serious offences, which are usually defined as those carrying a possible sentence of more than six months' imprisonment.[15] The simple truth is that many criminal defendants charged with indictable offences/felonies simply do not have the choice of being tried by a magistrate/judge alone – they have to be tried by judge and jury. The view that it is desirable to be tried by one's 'peers' is based on the argument that: (a) it is good to be tried by a group of individuals who are representative of one's community; and (b) that 'representativeness' makes for impartial, objective, just and fair jury verdicts. Marshall (1975) has argued that 'the right to trial by an impartial jury' is not an ideal that can be achieved because trial by one's 'peers', 'representativeness' and 'impartiality' do not go together and, even if they did, they would not guarantee that a jury's verdict would be a fair one. For example, fairness and impartiality may not be a feature of the general public which the jury represents (see Rosen, 1992).[16]

Such arguments, however, are unlikely to be taken seriously by staunch supporters of the jury. According to Cammack (1995:407), in the United States, historically, the jury has symbolised and embodied American democracy and the Supreme Court in *Powers v. Ohio*, 499 US 400, 407 (1991) stated that, 'jury service is second only to voting in the implementation of participatory government' (p. 483) and the right to an 'impartial jury' in criminal cases is explicitly guaranteed in the Sixth Amendment (p. 428). In *Wainwright v. Witt* 469 US at 423 (1985) the Supreme Court provided a definition of a constitutionally impartial juror as someone 'who will conscientiously apply the law and find the facts' (Cammack, 1995:458). Finally, the Supreme Court stated clearly in *Holland v. Illinois* 493 US at 482 (1990) that the constitutional requirement of juror impartiality is to be achieved by means of peremptory challenges (p. 447) but these are not to be exercised on the basis of the juror's sex (*J.E.B. v. Alabama* ex rel.T.B. 114 S.Ct 1419 (1994) or race (Batson v. Kentucky 476 US 79 (1986) because to do so violates the Equal Protection Clause of the Fourteenth Amendment (p. 406). Cammack maintains that definitions of juror impartiality, as provided by the Supreme Court, have their origin in and reflect the mind-body dualism of the Enlightenment, the belief that fundamentally we can distinguish the subjective mind from the objective world and that, because there exists neutral objective reality, truth is something objective – beliefs that have been seriously questioned in linguistics, cognitive psychology and sociology (pp. 410, 463–6). As for the crucial term 'trial by one's peers', its meaning is by no means clear for the indigenous peoples of the United States, Canada, Australia and New Zealand (Antonio and Hans, 2001; Dunstan et al., 1995; Fukurai et al., 1993; Israel, 1998). According to Fukurai et al., the fact that minorities are disproportionately represented on juries poses a serious challenge to the jury system. Antonio and Hans (2001:71) list a number of arguments that can be advanced in favour of a diverse jury, namely:

- It would facilitate discussion and generate unique ideas.
- It would reduce the manifestation of prejudice.
- It would reduce the likelihood of stereotypical judgements by jurors.

> The arguments in favour for and against the jury listed below make it clear that there are two conflicting views of what the function of the jury ought to be.

In the final analysis, of course, a verdict by a racially representative jury is more likely to be accepted by the public at large. In order to provide a sufficient backdrop for the discussion of empirical studies that follows pertaining to a broad range of jury controversies, let us also consider what defenders and critics of the jury have said about it.

2.1 Arguments Against and For the Jury

The following is a list of arguments against jury trials:

- The right to trial by jury is not enshrined in a constitution.[17]
- Trial by jury is not the cornerstone of the criminal justice system.[18]
- Juries are not representative of the wider community.[19]
- Most of those eligible for jury service will never have the experience.[20]
- In some jurisdictions jury trial is very nearly extinct.[21]
- A jury does not give reasons nor is it accountable for its verdict.[22]
- A jury deliberates in secret.
- A jury establishes no precedent.[23]

- Juries are unpredictable.
- For all intends and purposes, a jury verdict is final.
- A significant number of jury trials end up in mistrials.[24]
- In a significant number of trials there is a hung jury.[25]
- Compared to a judge-alone trial, a jury trial is costly and time-consuming.[26]
- Some jury verdicts reflect jurors' emotional involvement rather than rational decision-making.[27]
- A jury can be interfered with.[28]
- Non-legal factors such as inadmissible evidence and pre-trial publicity impact on jury verdicts.[29]
- Juries are influenced by both non-legal[30] and legally-relevant[31] issues and neither judicial instructions nor deliberation reduces its impact.[32]
- Often jury verdicts are the result of persuasion tempering reason.[33]
- Many potential jurors try to avoid jury service and many of those who serve on juries report being disenchanted with the whole experience and lose confidence in the administration of justice.[34]
- In England and Wales the jury does not have to wait until the defence has finished presenting its case but can acquit the accused at any time after the prosecution has finished presenting its case.[35]
- Jury service can be a very traumatic experience.[36]
- Jurors often lack the ability to understand and judge a legal case adequately.[37]
- Jurors frequently cannot remember all the relevant facts of a case.[38]
- Juries acquit too readily.[39]
- Juries have been shown not to defy public opinion and, by failing to identify serious weaknesses in the prosecution case, convict innocent defendants.[40]
- Perverse jury verdicts are not uncommon.[41]
- Any form of *voir dire* is incompatible with both randomness and repre-sentativeness.[42]
- Allowing juries to rewrite the law has the potential for wrongful convictions.[43]
- Changing the law is the province of Parliament.[44]
- Juries do not necessarily safeguard defendants' civil liberties.[45]
- There is no longer a need for perverse jury verdicts to counter the extreme severity of penal sanctions – thieves are no longer being sent to the gallows.[46]
- There is no big difference in verdicts agreed between a jury of twelve and a judge deciding alone.[47]
- The jury's task is one for professionals, not amateurs.[48]

Interestingly, despite such a long list of serious criticisms against the jury, Sanborn (1993) argued that the juvenile peer jury that exists in youth courts in the United States (see Williamson et al., 1993) should be extended to all juvenile courts. In contrast to this, in England and Wales it has been suggested that the minimum age for jurors be raised to twenty-one years (Stone, 1990).

In response to one of the criticisms of the jury system mentioned above, in England and Wales it has recently been proposed by the Auld Report (2001) that juries should move more towards reasoned verdicts, using case summaries and a list of questions they must answer. The judge could require the jury to give a verdict on each question.

Case Study

Examples of Alarming Jury Verdicts

According to Kassin and Wrightsman (1988:99), eleven members of a jury in the United States believed that a person could be possessed by the devil. Not surprisingly, therefore, they accepted the defence of demonic possession! In a case in Britain (Stephen Young ([1988] 1WLR 430), a jury found the defendant guilty of murder. However, the conviction 'was set aside when it was discovered that four jury members had been influenced by a séance they had conducted in order to receive a post-humous message from the victim' (McEwan, 2000:113).

The following are arguments in favour of jury trials:

- Jury service is an important civic experience.
- Jurors discharge their duty with a strong sense of responsibility.[49]
- A decision by a jury of one's peers is more acceptable to most defendants than the decision of a single judge.
- It adds to the legitimacy of government authority.[50]
- It counterbalances the special interests of judges.[51]
- The jury is an antidote to tyranny.[52]
- Twelve heads are better than one.
- Unlike an experienced judge, a jury brings a fresh perception to each trial.
- Jurors make up in common sense and experience what they do not possess in professional knowledge and training.
- Jurors are interpreters of trial information and not passive recipients of evidence.[53]
- Experts do not dominate jurors' opinions.[54]
- Jurors generally stick to the evidence and are not swayed by irrelevant considerations.[55]
- It is not true that juries take too long to reach a verdict.[56]
- Jury deliberations significantly reduce any undesirable idiosyncrasies of individual jurors.
- Jurors are suitable to decide complex legal cases.[57]
- Jury damages awards are not biased against businesses and high-status defendants.[58]
- Unlike a judge, a jury can counter strict and unfair legal rules by deviating from them, motivated by its own social and ethical standards.[59]
- A jury individualises the administration of justice.[60]
- Juries act as catalysts for legal reform.
- A jury can ignore a judge's direction to acquit the defendant.[61]

- Whether a jury's verdict is 'perverse' depends on whose opinion is sought.[62]
- Most jury trial protagonists believe the jury system is a 'good system'.[63]
- A significant proportion of people who have attended for jury service have confidence in the jury system.[64]

The arguments in favour of and against the jury listed above make it clear that there are two conflicting views of what the function of the jury ought to be: (a) to return a 'correct verdict' applying the law and on the basis of the facts before the jury; and (b) to go beyond the law and the facts of the case and to mediate 'between the law and community values' (Jackson, 1996:327).

Defenders of the jury in the UK (Harman and Griffith, 1979) have pointed with great concern to the onslaught on the jury in the form, for example, of the abolition of unanimous verdicts (1978), restrictions of the right to question jurors (1973), restriction on the cases to be tried by the jury (1977), restricting the right of defence counsel to challenge jurors (1977) as well as the legitimisation of jury vetting (1978).

In the light of so many, and often conflicting and entrenched, views held by both advocates and critics of the jury system, it would seem that no amount of research evidence as to how juries behave in real life or how they compare with judges or some other tribunal will resolve the jury controversy. Findings by psycholegal researchers may abound but in the end important value judgements remain to be made. One thing is certain: the jury trial on both sides of the Atlantic and in Australia may well undergo further reforms (see below) but it will be with us for a long time to come. Its abolition 'will come only after long reflection and in the context of a complete overhaul of the administration of criminal justice' (Blom-Cooper, 1974).

Jury verdicts impact not only on individual criminal and civil defendants but can also have a significant effect on a whole community as when, for example, at the end of the Rodney King trial in Los Angeles the jury's verdict triggered riots. As Levine (1992) reminds us, the jury is a political institution, a jury verdict can also have dire economic consequences for companies made to pay large amounts in damages, can ruin a political party's popularity by finding a leading politician guilty and, finally, a jury's decision can send a strong message to a community regarding what behaviour is tolerated.

Since the Chicago Jury Project of the 1950s (Kalven and Zeisel, 1966, see below) stimulated renewed interest in the study of trial procedures and jury performances (Davis, 1989), the jury has been a very popular research topic for psychologists. Kadane (1993:234), however, draws attention to the fact that psychologists have devoted a disproportionate amount of time to studying juries and have neglected a host of other decisions in the criminal justice system, such as the decision to report a crime; the police deciding to record what has been reported; the police deciding to use their firearms; to stop and search someone; to arrest them; deciding what to charge them with and plea-bargaining decision-making processes and so forth, which impact on a far greater number of individuals within most western societies than do jury decisions. Furthermore, Lloyd-Bostock (1996) has pointed out that 'the field has been dominated by research on the jury in the United States. Its relevance to the jury in Britain and elsewhere cannot be taken for granted' (p. 349).

The fact is that the great majority of legal cases are not decided by juries but by tribunals, Magistrates' Courts,[65] judges sitting alone, and most criminal defendants plead guilty while most civil cases are settled outside courts (Baldwin and McConville, 1979; Hans, 1992:56; Willis, 1983). It should also be noted in this context, that as judicial discretion at the sentencing stage is reduced (see chapter 6) and sentences become more predictable, the scope for prosecutorial discretion increases as does the practice of plea-bargaining, thus reducing the importance of jury trials even further. In this chapter an attempt will be made to show that the jury's symbolic importance far outweighs its practical significance, that systematic jury selection is conceptually problematic and does not appear to be as 'scientific' as its advocates would have us believe and, finally, that there exists a strong case for drastically reforming the jury as it exists on both sides of the Atlantic and in Australia in both a legal and psycholegal sense. On the basis of the available behavioural research into jurors and juries some authors have argued that there is already a substantial body of knowledge relevant to attempts to improve the jury system (Pennington and Hastie, 1990).

Of course, as Hastie (1993b:6–10) and Hans (1992:56–58) point out, there are very good reasons for the popularity of jury studies, namely the very nature of jury cases, the fact that the jury's task is clear, it appeals not only to cognitive psychologists interested in higher processes but also to psychologists with other interests because of the symbolic importance and actual impact of jury decisions on people and, last but not least, because 'research on jury decisions can be profitable' (Hastie, 1993b:10). The practice of jury consulting firms, retained by wealthy defendants and their defence attorneys to construct ideal profiles of jurors who would be favourable or opposed to a defendant to be used to reject jurors during *voir dire* (a largely American phenomenon) can be criticised as being unethical.

3 Methods For Studying Juries/Jurors

Research into both jury verdicts and individual jurors has been bedevilled by the apparently insurmountable difficulty that there is no consensus about what constitutes a 'good juror' or a 'good verdict' (Cammack, 1995; Mungham and Bankowski, 1976). This fact has not prevented jury/juror research becoming one of the most popular topics for psycholegal researchers since the mid 1970s. Devine et al. (2001) used computer-assisted search of several databases (for example, Lexis, Nexis, PsycInfo), manual searches through eight well-known journals (albeit only American) for the previous ten years or more and, finally, they consulted the reference lists of recent literature reviews and selected empirical studies. They identified a total of 206 studies of jury decision-making from 1955–99.

3.1 Archival Research

Archival research enables one to collect data on real jury verdicts and is the method used, for example, by a group of Rand Corporation researchers in the United States who analysed jury verdict reporters over a twenty-year period.[66] Two limitations of archival research are that important information of interest to a researcher may well be missing, and it is not possible to draw convincing causal inferences on the basis of such data. Of course, hypotheses developed from archival research can be tested under simulated conditions. Approximately one-fifth (19 per cent) of the empirical studies identified by Devine et al. (2001) involved analysis of archival data.

3.2 Questionnaire Surveys

The best-known study using the method of questionnaire surveys is Chicago Law School's Kalven and Zeisel's (1966) pioneering study *The American Jury* which 'was a remarkable contribution and stimulated generations of scholars to undertake empirical work on the jury' (Hans, 1995:1233). Because of the great impact this study has had on psychological studies of juries/jurors, let us consider it in some detail.[67] Kalven and Zeisel sent a questionnaire to a total of 3500 judges in the United States. Of those, 555 (15.8 per cent) cooperated, providing data on 3576 trials. This oft-cited study, which provided the basis for a great deal of the jury/juror research, however, suffers a number of very serious limitations (Law Reform Commission of Victoria, 1985; Pennington and Hastie, 1990; Stephenson, 1992). To illustrate, according to the LRCV, the sample of cases surveyed comprised 3 per cent out of the total number of jury trials (60 000) during the two-year period in question in the 1950s; 50 per cent of 3576 cases were provided by only 15 per cent of the judges; the reliability and validity of the study was grossly undermined by the fact that 'at first a broadly worded questionnaire was used (2385 cases), which was changed midway to a more specific questionnaire, whilst lumping them together for the findings' (LRCV, 1985:82).

Another major limitation of the same study is that judges, and not jurors themselves, were asked to assess the jurors' competence in understanding the content of a trial. The finding, therefore, that 'by and large the jury understand the facts and get the case straight' (Kalven and Zeisel, 1966:149) can only be viewed with a lot of scepticism since we would not expect a judge to admit that he/she did a very poor job of summing up for the jury before they retired to deliberate their verdict (LRCV, 1985:83). At best, Kalven and Zeisel's conclusions 'about the motivations and psychological conditions underlying individual jurors' decisions … must be hypothetical rather than conclusive' (Pennington and Hastie, 1990:93). It is interesting to note that even though Kalven and Zeisel also carried out post-trial juror interviews in 225 cases and, in addition, went as far as to tape actual jury deliberations in five civil cases (it was legally still possible to do so then),[68] they provide no figures on jurors' responses about what they thought of the judges' summing up or how far the jurors were influenced by the weight of the evidence as they perceived it, instead of how they were said to have been influenced by it on the basis of what the judges who took part in the postal survey led the researchers to conclude.

Two very significant findings reported by Kalven and Zeisel were: firstly, and contrary to what films like 'Twelve Angry Men' might lead us to believe, most jurors decide on their verdict before they retire to deliberate and the majority view prevails. If accepted, this finding has serious policy implications, not the least in emphasising the importance of screening potential jurors during *voir dire* so as to have as many jurors as possible who will favour one's client (see below). The same finding has also led many juror researchers (see Hastie, 1993a) to concern themselves with how jurors behave before they retire to deliberate. The wisdom of so doing, however, has been challenged (see Ellsworth, 1993). Secondly, the judge agreed with the jury in 75 per cent of the cases.

Stephenson (1992:180–2) has analysed the figures on judge–jury agreement provided by the Chicago researchers and shows convincingly that the conclusion that jurors' verdicts are not significantly different from what trial judges themselves would decide is not justified. Stephenson concludes that: 'In effect, Kalven and Zeisel's work suggests that if the judges' views are taken to be the criterion against which the validity of jury decision-making is evaluated, then juries are very poor performers, and vice-versa. Judges and juries agree that a majority of defendants is guilty. Unfortunately they do not agree on whom to find not guilty' (p. 181). Stephenson shows that the judges in Kalven and Zeisel's study would have convicted 57 per cent of the 1083 defendants the juries would have acquitted (p. 180) and concludes that the police are apparently right in assuming that many criminal defendants should consider themselves lucky for having been tried by a jury and not by a more legally informed panel (p. 181).

Unlike the United States, in the UK, Australia, New Zealand and Canada the function of the jury in criminal trials is confined to deciding whether a defendant is guilty or not. It is the judge who decides on what sentence to impose. British researchers have also reported questionnaire surveys. The Oxford study by McCabe and Purves (1972b) surveyed judges, counsel and solicitors involved in 266 contested trials and reported a rate of 12.5 per cent 'perverse acquittals', that is, cases where the jury verdict is against the weight of the evidence. Zander's (1974) study of jury trials at the Old Bailey and the Inner London Crown Court reported that perverse acquittals comprised 6 per cent of the total. Finally, the well-known Birmingham jury study of 500 trials by Baldwin and McConville (1979) surveyed defence solicitors and judges (with a response rate of 84 per cent and 94 per cent respectively) as well as police and found that about one in four of the prosecuting solicitors and one-third of the judges were dissatisfied with the jury's verdict, with 12 per cent of such verdicts being considered as 'perverse'. The more recent questionnaire survey of jurors and other trial protagonists in Britain by Zander and Henderson (1994), however, found that the percentage of verdict acquittals considered 'surprising' varied depending on the category of respondents (see above). The same survey reported relatively high response rates except by defendants. Contrary to what the majority of American mock-jury researchers have reported (see below), Baldwin and McConville (1979:104) found no relationship between the social composition of juries in terms of age, social class, gender and race and their verdicts, indicating that real jury verdicts are perhaps largely unpredictable. Dunstan et al.'s (1995) assessment of the relevant literature similarly concluded that jurors' sex, age and occupation do not seem to play any important role in jury deliberations (p. 55). Negative results from studies of actual juries (see also below) challenge the external validity of a lot of mock-juror/jury studies. Of the 206 empirical studies surveyed by Devine et al. (2001) very few indeed used retrospective surveys.[69]

3.3 Mock-Juries

Mock-juror/jury studies have been the most commonly used method by students of juridic behaviour, especially in the United States, and have attracted a great deal of criticism. This method has two important advantages: (a) one can investigate a number of significant variables while controlling for extraneous influences; and (b) it allows direct access to the deliberation process. However, the use of the experimental method has attracted a great deal of criticism, especially the relevance to actual juries of findings obtained under experimental conditions. According to Nietzel et al. (1999), during 1977–74 89 per cent of the 265 jury studies examined criminal rather than civil trials and only 11 per cent used real juries or jurors. Furthermore, 'Generally, however, real-jury studies are not of the analytic type preferred by research psychologists (for a notable exception see Heuer and Penrod, 1994a), and they often are plagued by sampling problems, independent variable confounds, definitional and criterion variability and missing data that limit their variability (Vidmar, 1994)' (p. 28). In the literature review by Devine et al. (2001) two-thirds of the 206 studies involved mock juries. As has repeatedly been pointed out in the literature,[70] it is very difficult in a simulation study to reproduce both the court atmosphere and the legal issues as well as the responsibility involved in a jury trial, especially if expediency prevails and psychology undergraduates are used as subjects. As McEwan (2000) points out, since we cannot interview real jurors, 'laboratory experiments and mock trials appear to be the best alternative psychologists can adopt' but 'It would be dangerous to make too much of their findings' (p. 111). Nietzel et al. (1999) acknowledge the utility of simulation research but also urge such researchers to study real juries and jurors 'once in a while' (p. 28). It is encouraging to note in this context that Nietzel et al.'s survey of jury studies found a significant tendency for more recent research to involve real jurors, and to be based on samples that do not use student subjects (p. 29).

Mock-juror/jury studies have reported a significant amount of experimental evidence suggesting that characteristics of both the defendant and the jurors impact on jury decisions about verdict and (in the United States)

> Mock juror/jury studies have reported a significant amount of experimental evidence suggesting that characteristics of both the defendant and the jurors impact on jury decisions about verdict and (in the United States) severity of sentence.

severity of sentence. Since the early 1980s, the quality of mock-jury studies has improved in recent years in terms of its sensitivity to the social and legal context of jury decision-making, methodological subtlety and legal sophistication (Hans, 1992:60). The maturity of the field of jury research is evidenced in the use, for example, of filmed trials based on transcripts of real cases (instead of brief descriptions of fictional cases), sampling jurors from actual court jury pools (instead of using psychology undergraduates), and having them deliberate as a group under conditions that are comparable to what goes on in real trials (see Hastie et al., 1983; Hastie, 1993b).

Such improvement has come about in the wake of criticism of jury simulation research by both psychologists (for example, Konečni and Ebbesen, 1979, 1992) and judges such as Chief Justice Rehnquist in the United States in the case of *Lockhart v. McCree*, 106 S.Ct. 1758 (1986). Commenting on simulation research on the death penalty and jury verdicts (see below) Konečni and Ebbesen (1992:418) stated that, 'One is tempted to conclude that some psychologists and justices have behaved as they claim jurors do: Their private attitudes against capital punishment have caused them to ignore the strength of the evidence and to assert external validity for a conclusion the truth of which as a scientific fact has been far from being established'. It would be true to say that while, generally, mock-jury research is characterised by high internal validity, a lot of it appears to be short on external validity. In addition to the problem of artificiality in many jury simulation studies, Hans (1995b:1234) has criticised the almost exclusive reliance on one research method – experimental simulation. There is also the problem that jury researchers have failed to consider to what type of case or juror they want to extrapolate their experimental simulation findings (Kadane, 1993:233). This is not to suggest that the types of variables examined in mock-jury studies are irrelevant but, rather, that actual jury decision-making processes are more complex than laboratory studies would seem to suggest. Most mock-jury research is largely American (see Strodtbeck et al., 1957, and Chicago Law School's Jury Project – Simon, 1967 – for early examples) but jury experiments were also carried out at the London School of Economics in the late 1960s and early 1970s utilising members of the public as jurors (see Cornish, 1968; Sealy and Cornish, 1973).

3.4 Shadow juries

Given that juries deliberate in secrecy and it would be illegal to interview jurors at the end of a trial in England, McCabe and Purves (1974) of Oxford University's Penal Research Unit, as it was then known, studied thirty 'shadow juries' sitting in on actual trials. Whilst shadow jurors' verdicts were not binding on the defendants involved, the fact that they were recruited utilising the electoral roll, that they listened to the same information being presented in the course of a trial as the real jury, left the court at the same time as the real jury during *voir dires*, means that it is the closest one could get in simulating juries. Their deliberations were, of course, recorded and transcribed, and shadow jurors were interviewed subsequently. McCabe and Purves found that the verdicts of the real and shadow jury were very similar indeed. Both shadow and real jury decided on a conviction (30 per cent) and on an acquittal (30 per cent) but shadow juries opted to convict and real juries to acquit 13 per cent and, finally, shadow juries decided to acquit but real juries to convict 7 per cent, while the remaining juries were 'hung'. While the significant similarity in verdicts between the two juries supports the validity of conclusions to be drawn from this Oxford study, according to Stephenson (1992), this shadow jury study by itself does not constitute convincing evidence that juries decide whether defendants are guilty or not consistently and reliably (p. 185). Finally, the reader should note that while field studies of jury behaviour are more realistic than experimental ones, they are limited by the fact that possible confounding variables make difficult the interpretation of their findings.

3.5 *Post-trial Juror Interviews*

Post-trial interviews have been used, for example, to ascertain jurors' understanding of judges' instructions (see Costanzo and Costanzo, 1994; Reifman et al., 1992).

In jurisdictions such as Australia (but see Cadzow, 1995), Canada and England it is against the law to interview ex-jurors and even where it is allowed (as in the United States) jurors themselves may agree not to talk about their deliberations to anybody and/or the judge may discourage jurors from speaking to journalists or researchers. In England and Wales both the Royal Commission on Criminal Justice (1993) and the recent *Review of the Criminal Courts of England and Wales* under the chairmanship of Lord Justice Auld (Auld Report, 2001) recommended the amendment of section 8 of the *Contempt of Court, Act 1981* which prevents questions being asked about the deliberation process. Limitations of the interview method include the fact that verbal reports of mental events are often incomplete (Nisbett and Wilson, 1977) and, furthermore, people generally find it difficult to determine the effect different factors have had on their thinking processes. As Hans (1992:59) points out, such interviews are increasingly common but they still tend to be used with jurors in celebrated cases; jurors' memories of what was said in the retiring room is bound to be limited; different jurors may well disagree about the content of the deliberation and, finally, publicising jury deliberations will impact adversely on actual jurors' participation and freedom of expression during deliberation. Like eyewitnesses generally, jurors' recall will normally get worse over time and be susceptible to 'contamination'; their answers may well be influenced by the 'hindsight bias' (Casper et al., 1989) and the social desirability factor. To illustrate, Doob (1977) reported that even though the great majority (97 per cent) of jurors surveyed said they had found judicial instructions easy to understand, about 25 per cent could not define 'burden of proof' and in cases where this applied half of them were unable to remember that the judge had instructed them about the defendant's criminal record. Therefore, cognitive biases and limitations of ex-jurors make it difficult to obtain an accurate record of what actually happened during deliberation (Devine et al., 2001:627).

Despite its limitations, by giving jurors a voice the interview method can be fruitful in yielding very significant findings, including revelations about phenomena not initially known, especially in terms of how jurors cope with the knowledge that they are responsible for someone's execution (Hans, 1995b:1235). Lengthy in-person interviews with capital jurors carried out by university students is the chief source of data in the national Capital Jury Project (CJP) in the United States.[71] According to Bowers' (1995:1057), the objectives of the CJP have been to: (a) examine and systematically describe jurors' exercise of capital sentencing discretion; (b) identify the sources and assess the extent of arbitrariness in jurors' exercise of capital discretion; and (c) assess the efficacy of the principal forms of capital statutes in controlling arbitrariness in capital sentencing

3.6 Books by Ex-jurors

Jurors in celebrated cases are not only constantly the object of widespread media coverage (as in the O.J. Simpson trial) but individual jurors on both sides of the Atlantic have published their experiences (see Barber and Gordon, 1976; Zerman, 1977). The major limitation of such books is that they are about the experience of one or a few individuals in isolated cases. Nevertheless, books by ex-jurors can still provide an insight into the experience of serving on the jury.

4 What Do We Know About Juries?

The reader who decides to answer the question posed by locating literature reviews of empirically-based studies of juror behaviour and jury performance will find that, generally speaking, such reviews by American authors (for example, Nietzel et al., 1999) fail to include British and other European literature and are thus incomplete. This comment, however, does not apply to Devine et al. (2001). The latter authors have pointed out that, 'Because of the problem-driven nature of most research, however, no overarching theoretical model has emerged around which to structure a comprehensive review of the broad empirical literature' (p. 625).

4.1 Selecting Jurors

As already mentioned, the scope for selecting jurors is very limited in Great Britain, Australia and New Zealand. Before a trial starts, during the *voir dire* hearing both the defendant and the prosecution can reject a number of prospective jurors without giving any reason other than they do not like the look of them. The number of peremptory challenges, as this is known, varies

The use of the term 'scientific jury selection' conveys an impression of accuracy and precision. However, it is not justified by existing knowledge and methods in juror/jury research. Therefore, scepticism is warranted about· some of the extravagant claims made for it.

from jurisdiction to jurisdiction. At the time of writing in Australia, each side is allowed six peremptory challenges in Victoria but three only in New South Wales. In the two States, the two sides can also challenge a number of jurors for cause. By comparison, in England and Wales, s.118(1) of the *Criminal Justice Act* (1988) abolished peremptory challenge but the *Juries Act* (1974) preserves both a statutory and common law grounds for challenging individual prospective jurors mainly on the basis of presumed or actual partiality (see Buxton, 1990a and b). Baldwin and McConville (1980a) reported that challenging jurors was a rather uncommon practice in their Birmingham study since in only one trial in seven was the right to challenge potential jurors exercised; furthermore, where there was a challenge, it generally meant challenging one single potential juror. It thus came as no surprise to find that 'the final composition of the juries had in effect been largely unaffected by the use of challenges' (p. 39). However, in the *R v. Maxwell* trial[72] in England, which received a lot of pre-trial publicity, Phillips, J. directed that a questionnaire be administered to potential jurors by court officials to ascertain both their availability and any possibility they were unduly prejudiced against the defendant because of pre-trial publicity. His Lordship ruled that the information thus collected would be of help to him in deciding if jurors ought not to sit on that case and would also be helpful to counsel when considering challenging potential jurors for cause (Victoria Law Reform Committee, 1995:8).

By using the juror challenge procedure and such instruments as the 'Juror Bias Scale' (see Kassin and Wrightsman, 1983) an accused in the United States, especially one with a lot of money, can influence significantly the composition of the jury who will try the case and pass sentence. Both the length of the *voir dire* selection hearing and the extent to which attorneys will go in questioning potential jurors varies and often reflects the socioeconomic status of the defendant. As far as it has been possible to ascertain, in the much-publicised O.J. Simpson trial, for example, prospective jurors had to respond to a 75-page questionnaire comprising 294 questions. The whole *voir dire* process is predicated on the assumption that jurors give honest answers. However, the validity of this assumption is questionable in light of evidence reported that between 25 and 30 per cent of real ex-jurors surveyed in one study admitted to having concealed relevant information about themselves when questioned in court (Seltzer et al., 1991).

The cases that are decided by juries in English-speaking western common law countries cannot be said to be representative of criminal cases as a number of processes negate this and, similarly, the individuals who serve as jurors cannot be said to be representative of their community (Kadane, 1993). Furthermore, every jury case is unique in terms of the defendant, the victim, the attorneys and the quality of their advocacy skills, the type and strength of the evidence against the defendant, the composition of the jury, and the way in which the attorney will frame his/her arguments. The question, therefore, arises of whether 'scientific', systematic jury selection is as possible and successful in influencing trial outcome as some psychologists and jury selection experts claim. After all, such experts have a vested interest since they make a lot of money offering their services and advising attorneys about the *voir dire* selection hearing. As Lloyd-Bostock (1988:52) points out, 'Systematic jury selection has coincided with winning in a growing number of cases. However, there are good reasons to remain sceptical about some of the more extravagant claims made for it'. The use of the term 'scientific jury selection' has been criticised by Hans and Vidmar (1986) on the basis that it conveys an impression of accuracy and precision not justified by existing knowledge and methods.

The very notion of systematic jury selection is also controversial for other reasons. Its supporters maintain that jury selection per se is a justifiable practice and should be empirically based. Its critics, on the other hand, maintain that selecting jurors is incompatible with the ideal of a representative jury chosen by a random process. The controversy is one that is unlikely to be resolved in the foreseeable future. Meanwhile, students of legal psychology should note that a lot of juror research has concerned itself with how individual jurors in serious criminal cases behave before they retire to deliberate (see Hastie, 1993b and 4.6 below). This focus stems from a belief that: (a) most jurors have decided on a verdict before they retire to deliberate; and (b) that the pre-deliberation distribution of individual juror's verdict preferences is the best predictor of the final jury verdict (Kalven and Zeisel, 1966; McCabe and Purves, 1974). In considering the alleged importance of pre-deliberation distribution of individual juror verdict preferences, the reader should also remember that it is the strength of the evidence against the defendant that plays the most important role in determining trial outcome; that such characteristics of jurors as their personality and attitudes impact significantly on trial outcome if the evidence against the defendant is weak; jury deliberation tends to iron out individual juror preconceptions and, consequently, we are 'looking at quite a minor aspect of courtroom processes in looking at individual juror bias' (Lloyd-Bostock, 1988:48).

Ellsworth (1993:42), is similarly of the opinion that individual differences among jurors are not very good predictors of jury decision-making. However, Ellsworth goes on to point to a paradox in this context, namely that 'In most cases the weight of the evidence is insufficient to produce first-ballot unanimity in the jury ... Different jurors draw different conclusions about the right verdict on the basis of exactly the same evidence', and, 'first-ballot splits are the best-known predictor of final jury verdict ... The inescapable conclusion is that individual differences among jurors make a difference'. Examination of jury literature shows that: (a) some enduring characteristics of jurors are important in understanding the jury verdict; and (b) that it is the interaction of juror and case characteristics that should be the focus of the jury researcher since neither set of variables can be said to be operating alone. In the absence of sufficient such research, a certain amount of scepticism is therefore warranted when considering research findings concerning the relationship between juror characteristics and verdict. In fact, such scepticism is further supported by the knowledge that studies of real juries, such as Baldwin and McConville's (1979) study, found that in 500 non-guilty pleas dealt with by the Birmingham Crown Court in England during the period from February 1975 to September 1976, 'no single social factor [class, age, sex and race] nor as far as we could detect, any groups of factors operating in combination) produced any significant variation in the verdicts returned across the board' (p. 104).

A few studies have examined the impact on jury decisions of both the strength of the evidence against the defendant and extralegal factors. On the basis of such research it would appear that, as already mentioned, it is when the evidence against the defendant is weak that jurors will focus on legally irrelevant factors, such as a rape victim's physical appearance, in order to agree about the verdict (Reskin and Visher, 1986).

Juror empanelling in celebrated cases often provides ample material for the sensationalist print and electronic media, but the simple truth is that if there is good, hard evidence against the defendant, the likelihood is that it will be legal argument during the trial and not the composition of the jury that will win the day (see Visher, 1987). Despite their limitations, a significant contribution of mock-jury studies has been to highlight the importance of non-legal characteristics of the defendant in jury decision-making about the verdict (Stephenson, 1992:200). Before considering the reported significance of individual juror characteristics, it needs to be emphasised that their importance lies more in the fact that different jurors choose to focus on and utilise different information from what is presented to them during the trial in order to construct different narratives justifying one verdict or another. What, then, is the evidence that a number of characteristics of jurors alone, or in combination (identified during *voir dire* impact) can impact significantly on jury verdicts?

4.2 *The Reported Importance of Juror Characteristics*

One book on trial advocacy contains reference to 'time-honoured selection criteria which counsel have used in years past' (Mauet and McCrimmon, 1993:25). The same authors, however, doubt the utility of generalising theories of jury selection from the United States to Australia because of the 'cultural mosaic which characterises contemporary Australian society' (p. 26). Without any reference to any supporting empirical research, Mauet and McCrimmon emphasise the importance of having jurors with similar characteristics and backgrounds as one's client's; point out that prosecutors in a criminal case and defence counsel in a civil case prefer 'middle-aged or retired jurors who have average incomes, stable marriages, work in blue-collar or white-collar jobs, are in business or generally can hold jobs which demonstrate an adherence to the traditional work ethic' (p. 26); refer to the alleged importance of potential jurors' body language and physical appearance as a source of useful indicators in selecting jurors (p. 27) and, finally, they note the dichotomy between 'strong' and 'weak' jurors, with the latter said to be favoured by the party that has the onus of proof in a criminal or civil case (p. 27).

Regarding the *composition* of the jury, it needs to be remembered that a homogeneous jury in terms of its demographic composition would not be representative of the general population; in other words, it cannot be 'a microcosm of society'. Researchers have found that heterogeneous juries solve problems better than homogeneous ones (Zeisel, 1971; Lempert, 1975).

Studies have reported conflicting findings regarding the relationship between jurors' *gender* and verdict (Arce, 1995:566). However, the weight of the evidence shows that *female* jurors are more likely to convict a defendant charged with rape (Arce et al., 1996; Bagby et al., 1994; Brekke and Borgida, 1988; Fischer, 1997; Hans and Vidmar, 1982; McEwan, 2000:112) or child sexual abuse (Crowley et al., 1994; Gabora et al., 1993) and especially if there had been no eye-contact between the rape victim and the offender during the attack (Weir and Wrightsman, 1990). Interestingly, Brekke and Borgida reported that juror deliberation narrows such gender verdict differences. Memon and Shuman (1998) surveyed members of the public awaiting jury service in Dallas regarding possible differences in their perception of experts in civil disputes as a function of a juror's gender and found no differences. As one might have expected, *younger* jurors have been found to be more likely to acquit, but those of a higher *educational standard* have been reported as more likely to convict (Hans and Vidmar, 1982).

As far as *race* is concerned, the Auld Report (2001) recommended that in trials in England and Wales where race is an issue, at least three jurors should be from an ethnic minority group – a proposal that was quickly ruled out by the government (Gibb, 2001). The Antonio and Hans (2001) questionnaire survey of jurors found that whites, in general, were more satisfied with their jury experience than Hispanics and other racial minority groups (p. 78). Memon and Shuman (1998) reported that their predominantly white jury sample was more likely to be persuaded by a black than a white female expert (p. 189).

The US Supreme Court has stated that peremptory challenges on the basis of a juror's race are unconstitutional (see above). In the first Rodney King trial, an all-white jury in Ventura County, Los Angeles, a predominantly white suburb, acquitted the four white policemen of the charge (under State legislation) of assaulting King, an African-American. In the aftermath of the Los Angeles riots, a racially-mixed jury in Los Angeles County found two of the officers guilty of civil rights crimes the following year, casting doubt on the Supreme Court's sense of realism in pushing for sexless and colourblind jury decision-making (Hans, 1995a).

The well-known study of actual jury trials in Birmingham by Baldwin and McConville (1979) found that the racial composition of a jury was not important in explaining the verdict. It was the race of the defendant that emerged as significant – even when a jury was predominantly black, a black defendant was more likely to feature among perverse convictions than acquittals. Evidence for juror prejudice and racial discrimination has also been reported in Canada (Avio, 1988; Bagby et al., 1994). According to Stephenson (1992:198), 'Little consistent effects of race have been demonstrated'. Of course, if a criminal defendant in England, Australia or in the United States is black the chances are he/she is also of low socioeconomic status which, in turn, correlates with having a court-appointed counsel rather than a private one. Very few scholars of the criminal justice system in western countries doubt that, to a significant degree, a defendant's wealth can buy 'justice' in the courts. Devine et al.'s literature review (2001) of the racial composition of the jury concluded that, 'Jury-defendant bias has thus been observed across a number of studies and contexts and appears to be a robust phenomenon. When the evidence against the defendant is weak or ambiguous, jurors that are demographically similar to the defendant tend to be lenient; however, when the defendant's culpability is clear, juries tend to be harsher' (p. 674).

Persons high on authoritarianism are characterised by deference to authority, power-orientation, rigidity, conventional beliefs and conservativeness (Adorno et al., 1982). A juror's *authoritarianism* correlates with imposing a severer sentence but not with conviction proneness (Stephenson, 1992:198). Narby et al.'s (1993) meta-analysis of twenty studies distinguished between 'legal' and 'traditional' authoritarianism and found the latter was a better predictor of verdict preference. Finally, there is some evidence that high-authoritarian jurors are more likely to change their verdict preferences during deliberation (Krieger and Shay, 1982).

A personality trait that is similar to authoritarianism is *dogmatism*, which denotes a closed-minded person, with rigid thinking but not necessarily right-wing attitudes. A juror's dogmatism appears to correlate with the imposition of harsher sentences and convicting more often, unless the judge reminds them of their nullification capability (Shaffer and Case, 1982; Shaffer et al., 1986; Kerwin and Shaffer, 1991). However, the evidence linking jurors' authoritarianism and dogmatism and sentencing in the United States should be treated with caution because none of the studies have involved real juries. Regarding jurors' *conservatism*, studies have reported conflicting findings (Arce et al., 1992:435). The presence on a jury of jurors with *previous experience* correlates with a greater likelihood of a guilty verdict (Dillehay and Nietzel, 1985) and severer sentences in both criminal and civil trials (Himelein et al., 1991).

The relationship between one's *attitudes* and behaviour is one of the most researched areas but remains a controversial topic in social psychology (see Jonas et al., 1995, for an excellent discussion). Attitudes, Ellsworth (1993:49) reminds us, 'rarely exist in isolation. Rather they come as bundles or constellations of related beliefs, and a scientifically ineffable but intuitively sensible consistency seems to apply locally to constellations of closely related attitudes'. Baldwin and McConville (1980a) concluded that it is not so much personal or social characteristics of the foreperson or jurors that explain the verdict but 'individual attitudes, beliefs and prejudices, as they are brought out in discussions of the particular point at issue' (p. 41). A meta-analysis of the relevant empirical literature by Stephen Krauss (1995) concluded that attitudes do predict behaviour. It appears that the weight of the empirical evidence (using simulation studies) supports relationship between jurors' attitudes and their decision-making. However, there is a great need for studies of real juries/jurors like that of Baldwin and McConville (1980a) that would also explore the hypothesis that it is jurors' attitudes to the specific case at

Conflicting findings
have been reported
about death-
qualified juries and
the likelihood of
guilty verdicts.

hand that are more important from an attorney's point of view and not who the jurors are or their general attitudes (Arce, 1995: 566).

Capital juries are unique in American jurisprudence and in human experience generally because nowhere else does a group of ordinary members of the public, acting under legal authority, rationally discuss taking the life of another human being (Haney et al., 1994:149). For Weisberg (1983)[73] death penalty jurors are reminiscent of subjects in Stanley Milgram's (1974) famous obedience experiments because they are placed in a situation which is both novel and disorienting for them, experience stress, confront a moral dilemma and may well resort to 'a professional, symbolic interpretation of the situation' to get oriented.

There exists a sizeable body of literature on attitudes towards the death penalty and jury verdicts and interesting findings have already been reported by researchers participating in the Capital Jury Project (see Bowers, 1995; Bowers et al., 1998). According to Ellsworth (1993) and ForsterLee et al. (1999), attitudes towards the death penalty are generally strongly held and closely related to other attitudes about the criminal justice system (p. 48). More importantly, however, any potential jurors in the United States who are found during *voir dire* to be opposed to the death penalty in principle and thus unable to return a fair verdict would be eliminated from jury service, as stated by the US Supreme Court in *Witherspoon v. Illinois*, 1968. It has been reported that death-qualified jury candidates are influenced more by defendant characteristics than are death-penalty-excludable candidates (Williams and McShane, 1990).

However, conflicting views have been expressed about whether death-qualified juries are conviction prone. The American Psychological Association's (APA's) *amicus* brief, submitted on behalf of the defendant McCree in *Lockhart v. McCree* 106 S.Ct. 1758 (1986) concluded, on the basis of existing experimental evidence, that such juries are conviction prone. Subsequent researchers reached the same conclusion.[74] Further experimental evidence from jury simulation has been reported by Ellsworth (1993) and Mauro (1991). Interestingly, Chief Justice Rehnquist was very critical of the methodology of mock-jury research and did not accept the view expressed in the APA's *amicus* brief. Criticising the US Supreme Court for mistrusting 'social scientific evidence', Mauro (1991:252) has claimed that in *Lockhart v. McCree* 'The Supreme Court clearly did not appreciate the social scientific evidence of the biasing effects of death qualification'. Elliott's (1991) literature review of studies using brief written cases, studies based on the recall of real jurors and studies using audiotaped or videotaped trial presentation, concluded that the main assertion in the APA's *amicus* brief about the conviction proneness of death-qualified juries is not supported by the available research data; rather, 'There is support for the proposition that a weak relationship exists between death penalty attitude and predeliberation verdict preferences' (p. 263). Similarly, Nietzel et al.'s more recent literature review (1999) concluded that, 'The overwhelming amount of variance in verdicts for defendants charged with capital crimes does not appear to be associated with that they frequently change the opinions of individual jurors regarding what constitutes equitable damages in negligence cases. It may very well be the case that individual juror variables identified as important in a well-controlled experiment are not as important in the context of an actual jury where a host of factors are operating at the same time.

The foreperson can, of course, influence the outcome of the deliberation by directing discussion, timing poll votes and influencing whether poll votes will be public or secret (see below). The Spanish study by Arce (1995) found that forepersons talked the most. In another mock jury study in Spain Arce et al. (1999) used 160 persons from the electoral register (and thus eligible for jury service) in twenty (ten hung, ten unanimous) eight-member juries, balancing them for gender and with a mean age of 32.6 years to investigate the issue of hung vs unanimous juries. They found that in hung juries the foreperson (a) failed to control the deliberation in order to guide it to evaluate the evidence; (b) did not avoid destructive interventions, (c) failed to be persuasive; and (d) did not inspire either authority or respect (p. 269). In the light of their findings Arce et al. recommended that the foreperson should be trained in how to deal with the deliberation in order to be able to control destructive messages among the jurors, to guide the discussion towards evidence evaluation and to focus on verdict-evidence relationship (pp. 267–8). More research is needed on the foreperson to examine, for example, jury verdict and/or sentence severity as a function of the group-leadership style of the foreperson, the weight of the evidence against the defendant and the degree of homogeneity of the jurors in terms of relevant attitudes.

4.5 Litigation Strategies: A Joinder Effect?

Rule 8 of the US Federal *Rules* of Criminal Procedure permits a defendant to have his/her multiple charges dealt with in the same trial when the crimes he/she is charged with are of the same or similar nature or reflect the same event or revolve around the same plan or scheme. While joinder of criminal charges can be said to contribute to court efficiency and means a defendant does not have to prepare for a number of separate trials, it can also be said to carry the risk of a likely biased verdict against the defendant (Nietzel et al., 1999:41). The bias may come about as a result of jurors being confused by evidence against the defendant relating to different charges, thus leading to the conclusion that the defendant has a propensity for criminal behaviour as he/she is facing multiple charges (p. 41). Nietzel et al.'s meta-analysis of the empirical literature published in ten journals in the United States during 1977–94 led them to conclude that joinder of charges could disadvantage criminal defendants (p. 42).

4.6 Jury Deliberation

At the end of a criminal trial the judge will normally instruct the jury on both procedures and verdicts and the jury will then retire to the jury room to discuss the case and reach a verdict. The underlying belief is that 'jury deliberation is a reliable way of establishing the truth in a contentious matter' (Stephenson, 1992:179). What we know today about jury deliberation is from mock and shadow jury studies as well as from accounts by ex-jurors. None of the researchers in this area has observed real juries at their task. Whilst accounts by ex-jurors are idiosyncratic and biased (Baldwin and McConville, 1980a), most of the mock research into jury decision-making (see Hastie, 1993a; Levine, 1992; Nietzel et al., 1999, for reviews) focuses on juror behaviour at the pre-deliberation stage in the belief that most jurors have already decided on a verdict before they retire to deliberate and that first-ballot majority verdict preferences predict the final verdict reliably. This belief can be traced back to Kalven and Zeisel's (1966) reported finding that in nine out of ten juries the deliberation task is concerned with convincing a minority of jurors to change their mind and embrace the verdict of the majority. This is referred to as Kalven and Zeisel's 'liberation hypothesis'. It is established that jurors generally enter the deliberation room without a unanimous verdict and there is support for Kalven and Zeisel's liberation hypothesis. Using six-member juries, Tanford and Penrod (1986) found that in approximately 95 per cent of the time the side that had most of the votes at first ballot had the final verdict. However, the relationship between predeliberation distribution of juror preferences and jury verdict is not as simple as Kalven and Zeisel suggested (see also 4.1 above). As stated above, in addition to jury size (see below), another pertinent factor is the foreperson. As far as it has been possible to ascertain, no published simulation jury study has examined jury deliberation as a function of jury size, the weight of the evidence against the defendant and whether a majority verdict is possible or not.

Ellsworth (1993:58) disagrees with Kalven and Zeisel's generalisation about jury deliberation – that it is in only 95 per cent of the cases that the distribution of individual jurors' pre-deliberation verdict preferences does not predict the final jury verdict – and points to the finding by Hastie et al. (1983) from their mock-jury research that the verdict of one-quarter of the juries who were in a minority before deliberation managed to prevail. It is worth noting in this context that, as Ellsworth (1993:58) points out, Kalven and Zeisel provide no details of how they came to their 'liberation hypothesis' conclusion. On the basis of their own work, the well-known American researchers Pennington and Hastie (1990:102) concluded that the relationship between individual jurors' initial verdicts and the final jury verdict is more complex than the simple one proposed by Kalven and Zeisel (1966). It would appear that many a jury researcher has been unaware or has downplayed, if not ignored outright, the importance of jury research contradicting Kalven and Zeisel's much-quoted nine out of ten pre-deliberation distribution of individual juror verdict preferences. Seriously considering such contradictory evidence would call into question the usefulness of a great deal of research into the relationship between juror characteristics and verdict.

Available empirical evidence (Hastie et al., 1983) indicates that we need to distinguish between: (a) deliberations where jurors announce their verdict preferences before discussion begins in the jury room (known as 'verdict-

driven' deliberations); and (b) deliberations in which jurors' verdict preferences are expressed later in the deliberation process (known as 'evidence-
driven' deliberations). In other words, with the latter there will be discussion
before jurors have their first ballot and, consequently, first-ballot preferences
may not reflect the jurors' predeliberation preferences. In addition, there is the
possibility, for example, that jury discussion may reduce an initial majority
verdict that the defendant is guilty of first-degree murder to a final verdict of
guilty of second-degree murder (Hastie et al., 1983:59).

Additional evidence that predeliberation juror preferences are not
equivalent to first-ballot votes was reported by Davis et al. (1988) who found
that the timing of a straw poll on individual first-ballot votes (that is, whether
before any discussion or after five minutes' of discussion) makes a significant
difference in how individual jurors will change their initial verdict preferences
to their first-ballot votes. The findings by Hastie et al. (1983) and Davis et al.
(1988), as well as findings reported regarding the importance of jury size (see
below), whether jurors are instructed to reach a unanimous as opposed to a
majority verdict (Hastie et al., 1983; Kerr and MacCoun, 1985) indicate that:
(a) jurors' pre-deliberation verdict preferences do not necessarily predict their
first-ballot votes; and (b) the process by which jurors' pre-deliberation verdict
preferences are somehow synthesised to yield a jury verdict is a complex one,
probably more complex than Kalven and Zeisel or some jury researchers
would like us to think. Sandys and Dillehay (1995) tested Kalven and Zeisel's
'liberation hypothesis' utilising 142 telephone interviews of a representative
sample of ex-jurors who had decided felony cases in Lexington, Kentucky. Ex-
jurors were asked what they did first and, second, upon retiring to deliberate,
how much time they spent discussing the case before having their first ballot
and, finally, the outcome of the first ballot. Sandys and Dillehay reported that:
(a), in support of Kalven and Zeisel, a significant relationship was found
between first-ballot votes and final jury verdict (p. 184); (b) that in most of the
trials concerned the juries spent an average of 45 minutes discussing the case
before having their first ballot, and (c) in only 11 per cent of the trials the
jurors had a ballot without any discussion taking place (p. 191). Sandys and
Dillehay concluded that their results suggest that deliberation plays a more
significant role in shaping the verdicts of real juries than was conjectured by
Kalven and Zeisel (1966) in the liberation hypothesis. The same view was
expressed by Baldwin and McConville (1980a) on the basis of their study.

A number of factors have been found to influence the deliberation process
and to impact on the jury's verdict. Recognising the crucial importance of
jurors' feeling responsible for their verdict, the Eighth Amendment in the
United States prohibits providing capital jurors with misleading information
that undermines their sense of personal moral responsibility for imposing the
death penalty (Hoffmann, 1995:1138). Given that for most people deciding to
sentence someone to death is a negative consequence, the less responsible
capital jurors feel for the decision, the more likely they are to impose the death
penalty (Sherman, 1995). In order to lessen their responsibility capital jurors
may well attribute responsibility to the relevant guided discretion, the judge,

the defendant, the appeal process, they may perceive themselves as mere conduits of community values and/or finally, may feel a diffusion of responsibility to other members of the jury (Sherman, 1995:1244–5). Findings from the Capital Jury Project indicate that capital jurors try hard to distance themselves from the decision (Hans, 1995b:1235).

Socially 'successful' jurors have been found to talk more than less successful ones, men talk more than women and the foreperson talks a disproportionate amount of the time (Ellsworth, 1993:59). It has also been reported by Hastie et al. (1983) that if a jury is required to return a majority instead of a unanimous verdict, then minority jurors will participate less and will be paid less attention by the rest of the jury and that taking a vote very early on speeds up the deliberation process. Jury deliberation will take longer if the jury is evidence- rather than verdict-driven (Hastie et al., 1983) but this will not necessarily result in a different verdict. However, studies of real juries have found that the longer the retirement, the more likely it will lead to an acquittal (Baldwin and McConville, 1980a:42). More specifically, Baldwin and McConville reported that the chances of acquittal virtually doubled with juries that were out for more than three hours (p. 42). Multiple charges against the defendant correlate with a greater likelihood of a guilty verdict (Tanford et al., 1985) as does knowledge that the defendant has a prior conviction (Greene and Dodge, 1995). It has also been found that if a reasonable doubt standard of proof is emphasised, then jurors are more likely to acquit (McCabe and Purves, 1974). As a jury proceeds with their discussion, the tendency is for minority jurors to move closer to the majority view and for leniency to prevail (Kerr and Bray, 1982). Osborne et al. (1986), however, found that, following deliberation, jurors shift to a severer decision if the jury is heterogeneous rather than homogeneous. In this sense, the composition of a jury can be said to be related to its verdict.

> Small juries are more likely to hold secret ballots, to convict and they are most unlikely to be a microcosm of society. The real reason for introducing them has been economic concerns.

In the 1970s the US Supreme Court upheld the use of *six-person juries* in criminal (*Williams v. Florida*, 399 US 78, 86, (1970) and civil (*Colgrove v. Battin*, 413 US 149, 156 (1973)) cases (Cammack, 1995:435). Thomas and Pollack (1992) applied probability theory to assess how far jury size and majority verdicts could be reduced without impacting adversely on the jury as a microcosm of the general community from which it is drawn. Their findings provided support for the Supreme Court's decisions in *Williams* and *Colgrove*. However, as Stephen Krauss (1995) points out, Thomas and Pollack's results are based on the assumption that juries comprise a random sample of the relevant community of potential jurors. Real jurors cannot be said to constitute such representative bodies of their parent communities, a factor that renders Thomas and Pollack's findings 'meaningless' (Stanton Krauss, 1995:924). The sad reality is that the US Supreme Court, like the judiciary and legislatures in other western common law, has as yet to come to grips with the contradictions that are inherent in the jury concept itself.

Smaller juries such as six-member ones can only be less representative of the broader community than the conventional twelve-member jury, and their verdicts are likely to be different (Hans and Vidmar, 1986; Zeisel and

Diamond, 1987). In fact, small juries involve less communication per unit time, are less likely to recall evidence accurately or to examine the evidence thoroughly or to result in a hung jury (Saks, 1977). There are conflicting views on whether jurors in a smaller jury participate less (Saks, 1977) or more (Arce, 1995:567). Small juries are more likely to hold secret ballots and to convict (Hans and Vidmar, 1986).[80] It becomes clear that the real reason for introducing small-size juries has been economic concerns (Zeisel and Diamond, 1987:204). The fact is, of course, that the courts' wish to increase the jury's efficiency and to reduce its monetary cost inevitably has meant tampering with the psychological processes that take place during deliberation. As Wrightsman (1987:260) pointed out, what is also of particular concern is the fact that the US Supreme Court's decision in *Williams v. Florida* – that six-member juries were constitutionally acceptable (that is, could discharge their responsibility as successfully as twelve-member juries) – was handed down on the basis of a misreading of the psychological research results available. In a country with the death penalty such practices by some of its most senior judges are definitely a worry. Equally worrying is the practice of politicians who legislate to change aspects of the criminal justice system that are vital to the defendant's rights in the name of expediency alone, as was the case with the change to the ten out of twelve majority in jury verdicts in Great Britain in the 1970s.

A perception that a small jury is 'okay' because many jurors are not active has been offered as a justification for having smaller juries. However, as Arce (1995:568) points out, there is empirical evidence that '"non-active" jurors play a more decisive role in the dynamics of the jury … than is commonly conceived' (p. 568). For example, non-active jurors have been found to accept arguments contrary to their initial position (pro guilty or pro not guilty) which in turn produces disequilibrium in the jury by finally swaying the more active members of the group towards a consensus (p. 568).

Regarding how jurors reach agreement, there has been a report of at least one US jury (in the *Oliver North* case) who resorted to prayer to break an impasse in their deliberation (Rosenbaum, 1989).[81] Levine (1992) sums it up well when he states that, 'Social and psychological pressure usually suffices to bring dissenters into line … [but] … this generalization is too broad; minorities within the jury are not so powerless as they have been made to seem' (p. 155) and it is not unheard of for 'holdouts' to cause a hung jury. According to Levine, jurors have also been found to reach a compromise verdict, to indulge in 'logrolling' (that is, jurors in disagreement with each other trade off convictions involving multiple defendants and, in one case he quotes, a juror took it upon herself to mediate between two opposing groups of fellow jurors (p. 169). Of course, a juror with leadership qualities (and he/she does not have to be the foreperson) can sway even a majority to his/her point of view.

As to the question of why jurors change their minds about the appropriate verdict, according to Pennington and Hastie (1990:100), jurors do so primarily because they are influenced by information about legal issues or how legal definitions or instructions should be applied to the evidence, rather than information about the evidence and its implications for what had happened during the crime events. The trial judge can influence the verdict of the jury by, for example, sending them back to the jury room repeatedly until they reach a unanimous verdict or even by giving them a sermon (known in some parts of the United States as an 'Allen Charge') on the importance of reaching a verdict if they seem unable to do so (Levine, 1992:165).

5 Defendant Characteristics

Defence lawyers often advise their clients to look presentable in court and to watch their demeanour. But does research support such common-sense beliefs? A number of studies have reported that a defendant's *attractiveness* is a good predictor of defendant guilt in mock-jury studies (Bagby et al., 1994)[82] and whether mock-jurors will apply the reasonable doubt standard (MacCoun, 1990). Interestingly, jurors have been shown to be harsher on an attractive defendant whose good looks enabled them to commit a deception offence (Sigall and Ostrove, 1975). Of course, as Sealy (1989:164) has pointed out, a defendant's attractiveness is not a variable that can be controlled in a trial. Furthermore, in an actual trial a perception by jurors that a defendant is 'attractive' is the result of a process, sometimes over weeks or even months, of watching and listening to him/her and not on the basis of subjects being allowed a brief look at a photograph as part of an experiment. The Spanish researcher Ramon Arce found in his doctoral thesis at the University of Santiago in Spain in the late 1980s that a juror's *ideology* (progressive vs. conservative) and *attribution of responsibility* (internal vs. external) only explained 10 per cent of the variance in juror decision-making.[83] Regarding a defendant's display of remorse in the courtroom, Devine et al. (2001) concluded that, on the basis of the review of the relevant studies, no conclusions are possible due to conflicting findings reported.

6 Victim/Plaintiff Characteristics

According to Devine (2001), there is no evidence from studies of criminal trials that the *victim's suffering or attractiveness or age* are significantly related to jury verdicts. Barnet (1985) did find that juries in Georgia were more likely to impose the death penalty when the victim was a *stranger* to the defendant and, finally, Daudistel et al. (1999) reported that longer sentences were imposed when the victim and the defendant were of the same race (for example, white vs Hispanic). Regarding the importance of plaintiff characteristics in civil trials, an interaction effect between a victim's age and race has been reported by Foley and Pigott (1997) who found that when the plaintiff was young jurors considered black plaintiffs as less responsible and awarded them more damages than white plaintiffs in a sexual assault case. However, the reverse was found when the plaintiff was older.

7 Interaction of Defendant and Victim Characteristics

As documented in the next chapter, there is overwhelming evidence that blacks in the United States are disproportionately sentenced to death by juries (Baldus et al., 1998). Furthermore, black defendants who kill white victims are significantly more likely to be sentenced to death than white defendants and black defendants guilty of killing black victims.

8 Hung Juries

We saw earlier in this chapter that one of the arguments against the jury is that in a number of trials there is a hung jury, causing long delays in the administration of justice and adding to the financial cost of trials, thus undermining the role of the jury system. In order to remedy this weakness in the judicial system legislators on both sides of the Atlantic have allowed smaller juries (see *Williams v. Florida*, 399, US, 78–145 (1970)) and majority verdicts (10 out of 12) in England and Wales. In Spain, a non-guilty verdict requires a majority verdict of 5 out of 9 and a guilty verdict 7 out of 9 votes in order to eliminate hung juries (Arce et al., 1999:244). Also, since the case of *Allen v. U.S.*, 164, US, 492 (1896), a judge can ask jurors to reconsider their verdict in order to avoid a hung jury. The weight of the empirical evidence[84] indicates that the number of hung juries increases with jury size when a unanimous verdict is required and when case complexity is high. In Arce et al.'s (1999) Spanish study mock-jurors saw a video re-enactment of a real-life rape trial. The juries were balanced for gender and their mean age ranged from 18 to 65, with a medium age of 32.6 years (p. 245). It was found that, compared to unanimous juries, hung ones deliberated for significantly longer, their deliberation style was characterised by superpositions, disapprovals, orders or replies and interrupted the flow of the debate (p. 256). According to Arce et al., hung juries 'are inefficient with reference to the content and style of deliberation. In contrast, unanimous juries … aim to integrate the evidence' (pp. 256–7). It was also reported that occasionally majorities are intransigent and that it was more likely that intransigence was related to a non-guilty verdict, rather than being attributable to minorities (p. 257). The same authors urge judges to instruct the jury to discuss issues, to focus on verdict-evidence relationships, to avoid destructive messages, and to avoid trying to force minorities to conform.

9 Models of Jury Decision-Making[85]

According to Hastie (1993b), there are basically four descriptive models of jury decision-making: (a) the Bayesian probability theory model (see Hastie, 1993b:11–17); (b) the algebraic weighted average model (Hastie, 1993b); (c) the stochastic Poisson process model (Kerr, 1993); and (d) the cognitive story model (see Pennington and Hastie, 1993). The algebraic model (Ostrom et al., 1978) draws on information integration theory and posits that jurors assess and weigh each item of evidence presented during the trial and decide on guilt in a criminal, or liability in a civil, trial by averaging their evaluations of the different pieces of evidence. According to Kerr (1993), 'The word stochastic derives from a Greek root that means random, chance, or haphazard' and 'Stochastic models ... characterize processes as probabilistic or chance events ...' and 'predict a set of possible responses weighted by their probability of occurrence' (p. 116). One limitation of mathematical models of jury decision-making is that they do not cater for jurors' own 'explanation' that mediates between evidence and verdict (Pennington and Hastie, 1990:95).

In contrast to mathematical models, the story model (see Hastie et al., 1983; Pennington and Hastie, 1986) assumes that jurors actively construct explanations for the evidence presented to them and decide on a verdict accordingly. It is thus possible for two members of the same jury, exposed to the same evidence, to arrive at a different verdict because of differences in how they have understood and interpreted the same evidence. In other words, the process by which jurors selectively pay attention to, interpret and remember evidence and justify their verdict is an active and a dynamic one. Consequently, if a juror believes that the defendant is guilty, he/she will construct a story that will be consistent with the preferred verdict, or as Stephenson (1992) puts it, a juror's perception of the evidence, their preferred verdict and story construction 'reciprocally influence one another', and, 'There is a story behind every verdict' (p. 196). As might be expected, the more stories put forward early on in a jury's discussion, the longer the deliberation taken to reach a verdict, and the greater the likelihood that there may be a hung jury (p. 197). Finally, in so far as the media construct narratives of celebrated trials before, during and after trials, they have the potential to influence jurors' own stories of the trials and, ultimately, the verdict (Stephenson, 1992:200).

10 Reforming the Jury to Remedy Some of its Problems

Having to recall evidence by witnesses, lawyers and expert witnesses, provided days, weeks or even months earlier, means the chances are jurors will remember some of the facts about the case better than others and/or they will be confused about what exactly had been presented and/or explained to them in court (McEwan, 2000: 112). Poor comprehension and poor memory for the salient facts of the case, such as the legal definition of the offences and details of witness testimony, has been shown to be associated with deviant verdicts (Hastie, Penrod and Pennington, 1983). Not surprisingly, therefore, there have been a number of procedural innovations in a number of jurisdictions aimed at enhancing the jurors' competence in complex trials. These innovations include: allowing jurors to ask questions during the trial and to take notes, to discuss evidence among themselves, to have access to trial transcripts, to pre-instruct jurors, and rewriting and standardising judge's instructions to the jury.

6 Sentencing as a Human Process

'Sentencing cannot be an exact science; indeed, Lady Wootton likened the sentencer to a small boy adding up his sums but with no one to correct his answer.' (His Honour Judge P.K. Cooke, OBE, 1987:57)

'Sentencing is part of a very complex system. Many events and agencies influence the decision, and sentencing can cause anything from a ripple to a tidal wave throughout the system. And so sentencing, in common with other stages in the criminal justice process, cannot be viewed in isolation.' (Morgan et al., 1987:169)

'Most judges do not read psychology journals or scholarly books; some do not even read law reviews.' (Wrightsman, 1999:viii)

Introduction

Judges have been termed 'the gatekeepers of the legal system' (Wrightsman, 1999:vii). Since the 1970s the judiciary in western countries has undergone unprecedented expansion in both its size and power. The expanding judicial role is evident in the appointment, training and scrutiny of members of the judiciary (Malleson, 1999). At the same time there has been increasing tension between the requirement of judicial independence and accountability created by the changes that have taken place.

In imposing sentences such as terms of imprisonment, judges and magistrates inevitably make policy and can become prison reformers, for example.[1] At the same time, 'Trial judges like to think of themselves as autonomous decision-makers whom nobody bosses around', when, in fact, judges, prosecutors and defence lawyers are interdependent (Jacob, 1997:3); furthermore, 'the constraints flowing from the organisational context in which judges work affect not only their personal careers but also the distribution of cases by trial courts' (p. 4).

The judiciary worldwide enjoy a great deal of discretion[2] when it comes to imposing sentences on convicted criminal defendants. Historically, sentencing discretion and the availability of a broad range of sentencing options, both non-custodial and custodial ones, have been largely justified in the name of attempts to rehabilitate offenders (Kapardis, 1985; Victorian Sentencing Committee, 1988). By definition, rehabilitation as a penal aim requires sentences tailored to an offender's needs. This is in contrast to a more structured approach in sentencing known as 'just deserts' where the emphasis is on fixing a custodial sentence that almost exclusively reflects the seriousness of the crime committed, that is, the offender's deed/s (von Hirsch, 1995). The existence of wide judicial discretion, however, should not be taken to mean that judicial discretion is not subject to a number of important constraints and influences (Shapland, 1987). To illustrate, statutes normally provide a maximum sentence for a given offence;[3] courts in common law countries are obliged to follow precedent and to adhere to certain principles of sentencing (Thomas, 1979). In addition, in many jurisdictions judges and magistrates are provided with sentencing guidelines,[4] that, in Australia and England and Wales, for example, make it clear which are normally the mitigating (for example, a guilty plea – see Douglas, 1988; Willis, 1995) and aggravating factors to be taken into consideration (Walker and Padfield, 1996), while in the United States there exist specific sentencing guidelines (Doob, 1995; Frase, 1995). Furthermore, in Magistrates' Courts in England and Wales, the court clerk plays an important role in the form of advice he/she gives the bench (Kapardis, 1985; Corbett, 1987) and there is the possibility of appeal against the sentence. Finally, members of the judiciary in various jurisdictions participate in sentencing conferences aimed at reducing unjustifiable inconsistencies; and, in most jurisdictions sentencers are expected to provide reasons for their choice of sentence. In addition to constraints on judicial discretion, in a number of countries there has been a conscious effort to structure it by the introduction of mandatory sentences, for example.[5]

> Sentencing has been termed the 'cornerstone of the criminal justice system'.

Sentencing has been termed the 'cornerstone of the criminal justice system' (Sallmann and Willis, 1984) and the 'visible pinnacle of criminal justice decision-making' (Morgan and Clarkson, 1995:7). The fact is, however, that a lot of negotiation precedes a guilty plea, sometimes even during the trial.[6] The reader should also note in this context that: (a) plea-bargaining is a practice that is more prevalent in the United States than in the UK,[7] Australia, or New Zealand (Curran, 1991; Willis, 1995); and (b) there has been enormous growth in non-court penalties such as the infringement notice system with its powerful technological overlay (for example, speed cameras) which has transformed the very concept of sentencing itself (Fox, 1995).

1 Disparities in Sentencing

While acknowledging that a large number of criminal cases are routinely processed and disposed of in the lower courts, the task of the sentencer is often not an easy one. There are numerous reasons for this: there exist conflicting penal philosophies[8] (for example, retribution, rehabilitation, deterrence, just deserts, social protection, denunciation) and unsatisfactory guidance on how they are to be applied; the judiciary are expected to process cases at a fast rate; the volume of the cases coming before the courts has increased over the years (Thomas, 1987); particular pieces of sentencing legislation turn out to be problematic as far as implementing them is concerned (Thomas, 1987); there is public demand for harsher penalties (St Amand and Zamble, 2001) and, finally, the field of sentencing is plagued by a lack of consensus on what is meant by a 'right' sentence.[9] This state of affairs is no consolation for judges and magistrates who are often criticised for either being 'too soft on criminals' or for imposing unjustifiably harsh penalties on defendants who have already been victimised enough by an unjust society and its criminal justice system. Taking an empirical approach to the question, Farrington (1978) suggested that the 'right sentence' is the one that achieves a given penal aim for a given type of offender most effectively and efficiently, providing a challenge for researchers to enlighten judicial officers and the public alike on the issue of 'right' sentences. Researchers into sentencing, however, have a long way to go before they are in a position to provide judicial officers with such specific advice. From a traditional, narrow (and cynical) legal point of view, the 'right' sentence is the one given by the judicial authority that spoke last and highest on the matter.

While this chapter is concerned with disparities (unjustifiable inconsistencies) in sentencing, it needs to be emphasised that there is a great deal of consistency in sentencing in criminal courts. For example, the Scottish study of consistency and disparity in the custodial sentencing by ten sheriffs in three courts by Tata and Hutton (1998a) found evidence of broad consistency.

Case Study

Disparities in Sentencing: A Cause for International Concern

A random sample of fifty-two judges in Spain with a minimum of one year's experience in Appeal and High Court and average age 34.6 years were given a detailed written transcript of a real trial where the defendant was to be sentenced for raping a woman. Half the judges were against incarceration, 40 per cent were in favour of incarceration and 10 per cent did not respond. Finally, the length of the sentence varied from 5 to 25 years (Arce et al., 2001:202).

Disparities in sentencing criminal defendants are endemic in the system.[10] This is because it is a human system that involves both large numbers of cases and magistrates (more than 30 000 of them in England and Wales – Lawrence, 1993:279), judges, and (in the United States) jurors (see chapter 6). In addition, there are regional variations between urban and rural courts (Douglas, 1992; Hogarth, 1971:370); there are differences in the input to sentencers, in other words, the type of information about a case that sentencers are provided with (for example, whether there is a pre-sentence report and whether a recommendation about sentencing is made by a probation officer/social worker/psychiatrist), whether evidence is provided concerning the 'good character' of the defendant.[11] In addition sentencers differ in how they assess offence seriousness and how much importance they attribute to particular kinds of case information, how they translate offence seriousness into a penalty (Fitzmaurice and Pease, 1986), as well as in how they justify their decision about disposition of the defendant (Hood and Sparks, 1970:154). In addition, as Tata and Hutton (1998b) found in their Scottish study of consistency and disparity in the custodial sentencing by ten sheriffs in three courts, disparities may be the result of the idiosyncratic approach of one particular sentencer who systematically passes significantly longer sentences than his/her colleagues. Not surprisingly, therefore, inconsistencies in sentencing have been a cause for concern and attracted researchers' interest since the nineteenth century (Galton, 1895).

> Disparities in sentencing criminal defendants are endemic in the system.

One of the criticisms levelled against judicial discretion is that it often results in disparities in sentencing (Skyrme, 1979). Unjustifiable inconsistencies in sentencing, a ground for appeal against a sentence (Thomas, 1979), are referred to in the literature as 'disparities'. The concern about disparities in sentencing has been one factor in the shift away from rehabilitation in favour of just deserts, as the dominant penal philosophy in some western countries has resulted in attempts to structure judicial discretion.[12] According to Fox (1987) such attempts fall into two main categories: judicial self-regulation (appellate review, guideline judgements, sentencing councils or panels, judicial training, information services) and statutory regulation (restructuring penalties, presumptive sentencing, guideline sentencing). Despite such attempts (see New South Wales Law Reform Commission, 1996, for a discussion), sentencing disparities continue to be a cause for concern. Evidence for variations in sentencing policy that simply cannot go unnoticed are to be found in British Home Office figures for the 411 Magistrates' Courts in England and Wales. They reveal that, 'despite sentencing guidelines laid down by the Magistrates' Association [1993], serious discrepancies still arise' (19 November 1995, *Sunday Times*, p. 7).

Writing about the role of the sentencing scholar, Ashworth (1995) outlines the following six roles: (a) reminding politicians and the judiciary that their decisions have an impact on real people and their liberty; (b) ensuring that the sentencing system does not lose sight of the fact that it must remain committed to the principles of natural justice and to the rule of law (for example, by contributing to attempts to structure judicial discretion and to minimise disparities in sentencing); (c) informing the sentencing-effectiveness debate; (d) contributing to the development of sentencing theory; (e) researching sentencing in both theory and practice; and, finally, (f) providing a framework within which to discuss the role of sentencing in society. The empirical studies discussed in this chapter have been concerned with throwing some light on the factors that underpin disparities in sentencing and can thus be said to fulfil Ashworth's roles (b) and (d). The discussion of empirical evidence that follows concentrates on studies of actual sentencers.

There is a large amount of empirical literature on inconsistencies in sentencing and the importance of both legal and extra-legal factors in accounting for such inconsistencies. The legal factors identified by Kapardis' (1985:154) literature review of 140 studies as important (that is, that attracted an evaluation score of 2 ('of some importance') or 3 ('important') or 4 ('very important')) in explaining sentencing variation are: type of charge; defendant's: criminal record, recency of last conviction, past interaction with the criminal justice system, type of plea, age, gender, community ties; provocation by the victim; whether a court is in an urban or rural area; and probation officer's recommendation about sentence. Such a literature review today would also need to include some courts' use of Victim Impact Statements when considering sentence (see New South Wales Law Reform Commission, 1996:418–45). The extra-legal factors identified are: a defendant's pre-trial status, socio-economic status (see also Douglas, 1994), race, and attractiveness; the victim's race; a sentencer's age, religion, education, social background, cognitive complexity, constructs, politics and, finally, penological orientation (that is, whether offence- or offender-focused). There is no doubt that it is the interaction of both specific legal and extra-legal factors that best explains disparities in sentencing. Given regional differences in sentencing legislation and the large number of factors that have been found to have the potential to impact on sentence choice and severity, no generalisations are possible, especially not across different jurisdictions or over time.[13] Some of the studies of sentencing go back almost eighty years and studies utilising court records preceded experimental simulation studies on both sides of the Atlantic. The sentencing stage in the criminal justice process provides a goldmine of opportunities for psychologists interested in decision-making. Furthermore, it is an area where organised psychology (for example, the American Psychological Association) has on a number of occasions attempted to influence judicial policy-making by filing *amices curiae* ('friends of the courts') briefs (Tremper, 1987).

2 Studying Variations in Sentencing[14]

Studies of sentencing can be grouped under the following categories on the basis of the research method used to study variations in sentencing (see Kapardis, 1984, 1985, for a discussion of the merits and limitations of the different methods):

2.1 'Crude comparison' Studies

'Crude comparison' studies have compared sentences passed by different courts in the same region (Warner and Cabot, 1936), by judges in different regions (Grunhut, 1956) or by different judges in the same court (Morse and Beattie, 1932) or, finally, between sentences imposed for the same offence (Ploscowe, 1951).

2.2 'Random Sample' Studies

'Random sample' studies have simply assumed a random distribution of offence and offender characteristics between different courts and or different judges, without any justification given for the assumption being made (for example, Chiricos and Waldo, 1975).[15]

2.3 'Matching by item' Studies

For 'matching by item' studies, see Hood, 1962; Mannheim et al., 1957; Nagel, 1961; Wolfgang and Riedel, 1973. The number of variables used to match criminal cases in order to compare sentences imposed has varied, for example, from one (Nagel, 1961) to twenty-seven (Wolfgang and Riedel, 1973).

2.4 'Prediction' Studies

For 'prediction' studies, for example, Fitzmaurice et al., 1996, Hogarth, 1971).[16] In order to identify the best predictors of sentence severity, some researchers have controlled for a number of offence, offender, victim, court and community variables. To illustrate, Fitzmaurice et al. (1996) used the Parole Index prediction method (see Farrington and Tarling, 1985) to predict a total of eight different types of sentences in 4000 cases, using data on a total of thirty-two variables. Of the 3975 defendants who were sentenced, 685 (17 per cent) were sent to prison. They constructed seven prediction models and reported that: some models worked better for some disposals than for others. They concluded that: 'predicting court sentences was a perilous exercise' (p. 309) and 'the choice between models will be a trade-off and that some disposals will always be difficult to predict especially when the number is small or when the sentencing pattern which underpins them lacks in consistency' (p. 310).

> The sentencing stage in the criminal justice process provides a goldmine for psychologists, lawyers and others who are interested in decision-making. In this context six research methods have been used.

2.5 Observational studies

Aware of the inadequacy of court records and of the importance in sentencing of information about courtroom interactions which is never recorded by court stenographers, a number of researchers have utilised the observational method (for example, Stewart, 1980).[17] A major attack against the observational method was launched by Konečni and Ebbesen (1979) who claimed to have shown that, 'it is a completely inappropriate research tool to study sentencing'. The adequacy of their own findings, however, is impossible to evaluate as Konečni and Ebbesen failed to provide sufficient information about the number of judges involved in their observational study or the between-judge agreement in sentencing in cases that were not significantly different (Kapardis, 1985:42–3).

2.6 Experimental Simulation Studies

It would appear the first experimental simulation study of sentencing, using real sentencers as subjects, was by Rose (1965). Close examination of thirty-four such studies on both sides of the Atlantic by Kapardis (1985:44–57) revealed the following: in over half of them psychology students were used as subjects; British studies overall used actual sentencers as subjects but most of the studies suffer from low internal validity; and, finally, only two (Devlin, 1971; Hood, 1972) compared sentence decision-making under simulated and real-life conditions. Hood (1972) reported no differences between the two conditions while Devlin's (1971) limited comparison cannot be said to provide a test of the external validity of experimental simulation.

A comparison of real vs. simulated sentencing using 168 magistrates from five different regions in England and deciding in groups of three with the most senior chairing the discussion, as they would normally do in real situations, and nine criminal cases sentenced in the Cambridge Magistrates' Court, provided strong support for the external validity of experimental simulation (Kapardis and Farrington, 1981). It should also be noted that experimental simulation studies of inconsistencies in sentencing as a function of a large number of factors have generally failed to pay adequate attention to the legal context of actual sentencing; such researchers have demonstrated a reluctance, if not an inability, to locate such psycholegal research in the broad context of the contemporary sentencing reform debate.

In real life, sentences imposed on criminal defendants can vary from a fine, to a community-based order, to a suspended term of imprisonment or a term of imprisonment or a life-sentence. There is, therefore, a need for a scale to measure sentence severity (see Durham III, 1989; Fox and Freiberg, 1990). Such a scale was reported in the English study by Kapardis and Farrington (1981) who found significant consistency both within and between 168 magistrates in their ranking of twelve different disposals across nine cases, in other words, the type of case did not seem to have much effect on their ranking of the severity of penalties (p. 113).

3 Some Extra-Legal Factors that Influence Sentences

In considering the empirical evidence for extra-legal factors, such as a defendant's gender and race, at the sentencing stage in criminal justice one must not lose sight of the fact that the very same factors influence decision-making earlier in the process through, for example, differential access to private legal representation and the existence of stereotypes among law-enforcement personnel, factors that can be expected to influence the charges laid against a defendant and/or a defendant's ability to bargain his/her plea for fewer and/or less serious charges. According to McCarthy and Smith (1986), therefore, there is a need to view and account for sentencing in a structural context. Let us next take a close and critical look at the empirical evidence for the importance of a few interesting factors in sentencing disparities.

3.1 Defendant's Gender

Gender bias and the law and the administration of criminal justice has been an issue of concern for a number of years now. Feminist authors have argued that the theoretical underpinnings of the law is in many instances biased in favour of men and that the judiciary are guilty of sexism. In the context of sentencing, it has been argued that sexism operates to reinforce traditional gender roles and manifests itself in a paternalistic approach that aims to protect the social institution of the family (Daly, 1987).[18] It has also been suggested that while the judiciary take into consideration the family circumstances of both male and female defendants, the way they do so differs – men are portrayed as breadwinners in contrast to females who are seen as dependants and domestics, a perception that encourages gender inequality before the law; that female defendants are perceived as psychologically disturbed deviants (Gelsthorpe and Loucks, 1997), even though the evidence for such assessment is often weak or questionable (Henning, 1995). Of course, sex discrimination has been outlawed in a number of countries.[19] But what is the evidence for discrimination for or against women at the sentencing stage?

Examination of criminal statistics indicates that the judiciary discriminate in favour of women and against men. According to Ashworth (2000:203), of those defendants who were sentenced in 1998 in England and Wales, 27 per cent of adult women received a discharge. However, caution is warranted in drawing conclusions on the basis of such statistics because women in Britain: are more likely than men to commit theft, to be sentenced by a lower court (Magistrates' Court) and to be first offenders (p. 204), if recidivists, to have fewer previous convictions, and to be less likely to have independent means to pay a fine (Gelsthorpe and Loucks, 1997: ch. 4). Finally, as Gelsthorpe and Loucks found, courts may be reluctant to fine female defendants because it would make their child-care responsibilities more difficult.

In an interesting study of judges' verbal statements in real courtroom settings by Fontaine and Emily (1978) it was found that judges gave reasons for their choice of sentence more often in the case of male than female defendants. In addition, judges sought information about the defendant's circumstances when having to sentence females but about the crime when dealing with males, an indication, perhaps, that the judges considered offending by females as out-of-role and, consequently, focused more on the type of woman she was and her motives. In the case of male offenders, judges considered their behaviour 'normal' and, consequently, focused more on the seriousness of the crime than on the type of individual involved and his/her circumstances. Judicial officers' own 'theories' of criminal behaviour and their penal philosophies would seem to bias how they perceive a case before them, what information about the case they emphasise, what additional information they seek and how they justify their decision about sentence (Hogarth, 1971; Kapardis, 1984; Oswald, 1992).

A defendant's gender is stated as a relevant consideration in deciding the sentence to be imposed in both statutes and in common law in the United States, UK and Australia (Gillies, 1993; Odubekum, 1992; Thomas, 1979). The classic example of gender as a legally relevant factor in criminal law is infanticide, an offence that can only be committed by women (Laster, 1989) and which poses a serious difficulty for feminist criminological theory. It is, of course, questionable whether a criminal defendant's gender per se should be the basis for disparities in sentencing.

With one exception, British studies of gender differences in sentencing have reported that female defendants receive more lenient sentences (Allen 1987; Hedderman, 1994; Hood, 1992; Kapardis and Farrington, 1981; Mackay, 1993; Wilczynski and Morris, 1993). Kapardis' (1985:105–8) examination of three earlier British studies (Casburn, 1979; Mawby, 1977; Phillpotts and Lancucki, 1979) came to a similar conclusion. Farrington and Morris' (1983) study of sentencing in the Cambridge Magistrates' Court used the penalty-severity scale developed by Kapardis and Farrington (1981) and is the only one to have found no gender differences when taking into account offence seriousness and previous convictions. In the absence of a study of other Magistrates' Courts using the same methodology as Farrington and Morris (1983), it is impossible to say whether their negative finding reflects idiosyncratic sentencing practices of the one particular bench of magistrates in Cambridge. The British empirical evidence for gender disparities is all the more convincing when remembering that it has involved studies of both Magistrates' Courts and Crown Courts, a broad range of offences and offenders and, finally, different research methods. Wilczynski and Morris (1993) analysed data on 474 cases in which a child had been killed by a parent and found that female defendants were significantly more likely to be convicted of manslaughter rather than murder, to be dealt with on the basis of the defence of diminished responsibility, and to receive significantly more lenient sentences, especially non-custodial ones. The leniency of treatment was especially evident for the women convicted of infanticide – none of them were incarcerated. Wilczynski and Morris concluded that labelling such women's killings as 'abnormal' behaviour that contradicts sentencers' perception of women as 'inherently passive, gentle and tolerant ... nurturing, caring and altruistic' and that a woman 'must have been "mad" to kill her own child' (pp. 35–6), results in lenient treatment by the courts.

> Studies of the importance of gender at the sentencing stage in the United States have reported contradictory findings.

The relationship between gender and sentence severity has also proven problematic for American researchers. Regarding the disposition of civil cases, Goodman et al.'s (1991) jury simulation study of wrongful death awards found that male descendants were awarded substantially higher monetary damages than were their female counterparts. Goodman et al. explain their finding in terms of males enjoying a higher estimated lost income than females. Studies of the importance of gender at the sentencing stage in the United States have reported rather contradictory findings. Fourteen of them have found female defendants to be treated more leniently by the courts.[20] Eight other researchers, however, have reported no significant gender differences in sentencing.[21] Finally, Feely's (1979) study in Connecticut, like Hampton's (1979) in New Zealand, reported that female offenders were sentenced more severely. Taking into account the quality of the methodology used by researchers, Kapardis (1985) concluded that a defendant's gender is an important factor in sentencing on both sides of the Atlantic (p. 154). The more recent research mentioned above has not altered that conclusion.

3.2 Defendant's Race

'The clearest application of the principle of equality before the law is that no person should be sentenced more severely on account of race or colour' (Ashworth, 1998: 199). It has been known for some time in criminology that blacks in the United States and in the UK and the natives of Australia, New Zealand and Canada, who are disproportionately represented in criminal statistics, are differentially treated by the criminal justice system; more specifically, African-Americans are more likely to be questioned on the street (Piliavin and Briar, 1964); if questioned, they are more likely to be arrested and, if arrested, they are more likely to be prosecuted (Goldman, 1963), charged with more serious offences (Forslund, 1970) and to be remanded in custody awaiting trial. Finally, as this section shows, when sentenced, they are more likely to be given harsher sentences and to be less likely to be granted parole (Elion and Megargee, 1979). Blacks in Britain have also been shown to be more prone to be arrested than Asians or whites (Stevens and Willis, 1979). Jefferson and Walker's (1992) study of 5000 people arrested during a six-month period found that blacks have a higher arrest rate in predominantly white areas and whites have a higher arrest rate in predominantly black areas. Also, white juveniles in the UK have been significantly more likely than black juveniles to be cautioned rather than prosecuted (Landau and Nathan, 1983).

The main aim of a lot of sentencing legislation in the United States since the late 1970s (for example, *Washington Sentencing Reform Act*, 1984) has been to reduce sentencing disparities by means of determinate sentencing whereby the likely penalty severity is determined by the seriousness of the crime and the number of previous and concurrent convictions of the defendant.

Research into race and sentencing has been reported in Canada (Hagan, 1975, 1977; Rector and Bagby, 1995), Australia (Eggleston, 1976; Walker and McDonald, 1995) and New Zealand (Mugford and Gronfors, 1978). Regarding the treatment of Aborigines in Australia by the criminal justice system, Aboriginals have an imprisonment rate that is thirteen times higher than that of non-Aboriginals. Walker and McDonald (1995) have claimed, on the basis of national prison data, that courts in Australia 'may have a lenient view of indigenous offenders, biasing sentence lengths in their favour to avoid accusations of racial biases in sentencing' (p. 4). However, taking into account prisoners' 'most serious offence', when comparing 'average aggregate sentences' of indigenous (that is, Aboriginal and Torres Strait Islanders) and non-indigenous offenders is not convincing evidence that indigenous defendants are treated more leniently by the courts, as Walker and McDonald claim. While accepting that no single study can control for all relevant legal factors, the fact is that in order to provide a satisfactory account of sentencing practices and whether racial discrimination (negative or positive) exists, a number of additional relevant and important legal variables (for example, criminal record, type of plea, etc.) should be taken into account as well as a broad range of personal and social characteristics that have been shown to impact on sentence severity (Kapardis, 1985:63–155).

British researchers did not start looking into the possibility of racial discrimination at the sentencing stage until the late 1970s. Most of the published empirical studies have failed to find a positive relationship between a defendant's race and penalty severity (Brown and Hullin, 1992; Crow and Cove, 1984; Hudson, 1989; Kapardis and Farrington, 1981; Jefferson and Walker, 1992). Mair (1986) did find, however, that blacks were less likely to be given probation than whites. Given that a recommendation is more likely to be made in the case of a defendant with community ties, such as being in employment (Kapardis, 1985:154), Mair's tentative finding (due to his rather small sample) may well reflect black defendants' greater likelihood of being unemployed at the time of the trial (see Halevy, 1995:269).

Researchers in England and in the United States have found that sentencing decisions are influenced by a defendant's race.

Hood's (1992) study (in collaboration with Graca Cordovil) was undertaken for the Commission of Racial Equality and analysed data on all cases (2884 males and 433 females) tried in 1989 at five Crown Court Centres in the West Midlands. Taking into account sixteen factors related to both the offences and the offenders' criminal records, it was found that black men were 5 to 8 per cent more likely to be sentenced to a term of imprisonment than white men with similar antecedents convicted of the same crimes; Asian men were slightly less likely to be incarcerated than similarly placed whites. Blacks and Asian were more likely than whites to have pleaded not guilty, and both groups were given significantly greater terms of imprisonment than whites in similar circumstances who had also pleaded not guilty. Hood claimed that 7 per cent of the over-representation of blacks amongst those imprisoned could be attributed to direct discrimination at the sentencing stage but did not contend that racial discrimination in sentencing occurs systematically and universally. Hood also compared the five Crown Court Centres and found that discrimination against blacks, in terms of the rate of custodial sentences, was much higher at three of them – Dudley, Warwick and Stafford. Despite the fact that some criticisms have been levelled against Hood's study (for example, for failing to control for personal and social characteristics of the defendants being compared – see Halevy, 1995), which Hood (1995) has vehemently refuted, the study can be said to have made a significant contribution to the debate about racial discrimination in criminal justice in Britain (see also Gelsthorpe and McWilliam, 1993; Smith, 1994). In her review of studies of discrimination against ethnic minorities in the criminal justice system in England and Wales for the Royal Commission on Criminal Justice, Fitzgerald (1994) points out that: (a) researchers have tended to include in one category people from the Indian subcontinent (Indians, Pakistanis and Bangladeshis) as a single 'Asian' group; and (b) that small direct and indirect racial discrimination effects at various stages in the criminal justice system can have a significant cumulative impact. Finally, racial discrimination by British Magistrates has been reported by Gelsthorpe and Loucks (1997) to be attributable to magistrates' being influenced by the defendant's demeanour in court because they misinterpret the body language of black defendants as 'arrogance'. The misinterpretation then leads them to respond in an unsympathetic way to the defendant (pp.33–4).

Research into racial discrimination at the sentencing stage in criminal justice has a much longer history in the United States, where many jurisdictions provide for the death penalty for certain crimes. Blacks have consistently made up 11 per cent of the American population since 1930. US Bureau of Justice statistics show that during the period 1930–84 the execution rate of blacks for murder and rape was five and nine times respectively that of whites (Aguirre and Baker, 1990:135). Such figures, of course, do not show that differences in the execution rate are due to racial discrimination. In an attempt to deal with inconsistent findings, Kapardis (1985) reviewed a total of thirty-seven studies and found that twenty-one of them reported evidence for racial discrimination but sixteen did not. Taking the quality of the research method used into account, it was concluded that 'the weight of the evidence supports the view that non-whites (in the main the research has been concerned with blacks) are discriminated against at the sentencing stage. However, this evidence is not as overwhelming as might be expected' (1985:122). That conclusion, however, should not be used to dismiss the argument that courts in the United States discriminate against blacks in sentencing – even weak evidence should be a cause for concern, especially regarding the imposition of the death penalty. Spohn et al. (1981–82) had earlier concluded that black defendants received severer sentences than white defendants due to their more serious history of offending. Finally, a somewhat provocative view was expressed by Kleck (1985) who claimed that in the United States there is no evidence that race influences sentencing, and that the problem lies not with members of the judiciary discriminating against blacks but with the researchers who distort and grossly exaggerate the importance of race in sentencing by selecting evidence that purports to show discrimination when, in fact, it does not. Since Kleck (1985), additional and well-controlled studies have reported evidence pointing to racial discriminatory practices against blacks by the judiciary. Nelson's (1992) New York State study found such evidence for both black and Hispanic defendants. Spohn (1992) found that in Detroit black non-jury defendants were treated more harshly than non-jury white defendants. The same study also found that racial discriminatory practices were also evident in judges' decisions to incarcerate defendants who had pleaded guilty and that such decisions in less serious cases reflected the impact of both legal and extra-legal factors (Spohn and Cederblom, 1991).

Walsh's (1991) Ohio study of 712 male felony offenders sentenced during the period 1978–85 inclusive for crimes ranging from receiving stolen goods to murder, was controlled for offence seriousness and prior record and reported that whites were treated more harshly by the courts than blacks. His failure, however, to take into account such very important legal variables as a defendant's type of plea and age casts serious doubt on his findings. Sweeney and Haney (1992) reported a meta-analytic review of nineteen simulation (experimental) studies that examined the effect of a defendant's race on mock-jurors' sentencing decisions. They found strong support for anti-black cross-racial punitive bias.

As in the UK, the issue of racial discrimination does not only apply to Anglo-whites vs. blacks. Wooldredge (1998) reported a study that compared the sentences imposed on 1586 Mexican- and Anglo-American male defendants in Dona County, New Mexico, and found that the former are more likely to receive longer prison terms than the latter. Interestingly, however, unmarried Anglos received longer prison sentences than unmarried Mexican-Americans (p. 173).

Eugen, Gainy and Steen (1999) interviewed judges, deputy prosecuting attorneys and defence attorneys and also analysed data relating to 299 convicted felony drug offenders comparing the sentences imposed on white (non-Hispanic), African-American and Hispanic defendants in three counties of Washington. They found that, controlling for legal factors, Hispanic and African-American defendants were more likely to be incarcerated as opposed to being given only community supervision (p. 2). Eugen et al. also found that courts in smaller counties imposed longer sentences and were more likely to incarcerate defendants rather than give them probation.

While there still remains the issue of the external validity of mock-juror studies (see chapter 5), the studies reviewed and the conclusion by Sweeney and Haney (1992) add to the debate about (a) racial discrimination as well as (b) capital punishment, and strengthen the concern expressed by a number of authors (Aguirre and Baker, 1990; Applegate et al., 1994; Keil and Vito, 1990; Thomson, 1997; Williams and Holcomb, 2001) that, controlling for legally relevant factors, a death sentence is more likely to be imposed on black offenders by juries in the United States, especially when their victim is white. What is of particular concern in this context is the fact that racial discrimination in the use of capital punishment in the United States, and it also applies to Hispanics (Thomson, 1997), continues unabated despite attempts by the Supreme Court to thwart it by providing guidelines (*Furman v. Georgia* (1972) 408 US 238; *Gregg v. Georgia* (1976). Finally, the finding by so many researchers that a black offender is most likely to receive the death penalty if he victimises a white person adds credence to the claim that 'capital punishment serves the extralegal function of majority group protection; in other words, the death penalty acts to safeguard (through deterrence) that class of individuals (whites) who are least likely to be victimised' (Aguirre and Baker, 1990:147–8).

Regarding the controversy surrounding the use of capital punishment by the courts (see Cochran et al., 1994; Walker, 1987:84–93), it should be noted that supporters of capital punishment as the appropriate sanction in order to reduce the incidence of such crimes as murder, rape, and terrorist offences, basically assume – wrongly – that the serious violent offenders involved act rationally. To 'deter' means to discourage someone from offending through fear of consequences (Walker, 1980). In other words, deterrence theory assumes a rationally-thinking potential offender. However, as Walker (1980) points out, deterrence is inapplicable when: people do not commit certain crimes because it is against their moral scruples; when the behaviour involved is impulsive (as is often the case in homicides and armed robberies (see Kapardis, 1989; Kapardis and Cole, 1988) or compulsive; when people intentionally commit a crime to defy the law or because they are desperate, or because they are prepared to die for a cause (as is the case with suicide bombers); or, finally, when people believe they can commit a crime and remain unpunished. Penologists make a distinction between individual deterrence (that is, the penalty is directed at an individual offender convicted by the court in order to 'teach him a lesson') and general deterrence (that is, when it is hoped that by punishing severely those who are convicted and publicising the penalty imposed others will be discouraged from perpetrating the same crime). Penologists also inform us that for a deterrent to be effective, a combination of penalty severity and high subjective probability of a person being apprehended and convicted by the courts is required in most cases (Walker, 1980).

The available empirical evidence in criminology shows that capital punishment 'is no more effective as a general deterrent than long incarceration' (Walker, 1987:64). For their part, some advocates of the death penalty maintain that it is the deserved punishment for certain crimes and/or that it is the most effective way of preventing a serious violent offender from reoffending. Opponents of the death penalty, on the other hand, argue that: to allow that particular State to deliberately execute a convicted offender is no more justifiable than the crime he/she has committed; that 'it transforms assassins into martyrs, alienates ethnic communities who suspect discrimination and is bad for the morale of prisons' (Walker, 1987:64). Undoubtedly, one of the strongest arguments against capital punishment is that miscarriages of justice are known to have occurred and innocent persons have been executed. In addition, the previous chapter and this chapter show, sentencing decisions, whether by magistrates, judges or juries, are influenced by non-legal factors, including the defendant's race. Finally, a question which many consider problematical is the extent to which, if at all, the judiciary (or juries in the United States) should take public opinion into account in deciding sentence severity generally and the imposition of the death penalty in particular (see Harlow et al., 1995).

Ashworth (2000) has argued that, 'The problem of race in sentencing must be seen at two different levels, at least. First, there is the broadest level of social policy: unless there is an end to racial discrimination in society, it is likely to manifest itself in criminal justice no less than elsewhere … Second, there is the level of criminal justice policy' (p. 203). Ashworth advocates the following measures in order to reduce racial discrimination in sentencing:[22]

- Increase the proportion of people from ethnic minorities who work in the police, the courts and the probation service.
- Increase relevant training to criminal justice personnel.
- Increase racial awareness training for the judiciary.
- Greater monitoring of sentencing decisions – a reform also suggested in 2001 by the Auld Committee.

3.3 Defendant's Attractiveness

Defendants are often advised by the lawyers to look 'presentable' when appearing in court. Likewise, people are generally given the same type of advice when going for a job interview. The assumption is that magistrates', judges' and jurors' decision-making, like that by members of the public, is influenced by a person's appearance. From a legal point of view, of course, such considerations are irrelevant to decisions about guilt and sentence.

It is well established in social psychology that physical attractiveness: is the one characteristic that most determines whether a person will be liked by another (Walster et al., 1966); is equally important to both men and women (Feingold, 1990); is assumed by most people as being highly correlated with such other desirable traits as: sociability, extroversion, popularity, sexuality, happiness, and assertiveness (Eagly et al., 1991).[23] In other words, there is a stereotype that 'what is attractive is good'. However, the 'attractive is good' stereotype does not include the same traits across cultures (Wheeler and Kim, 1997). The term 'attractive' can refer to physical appearance or likeability, appeal of one's personality, or both. Social psychologists have also established that physical appearance is an important factor in impression formation. According to Bull (1974), people behave differently in the presence of a well-dressed, as opposed to poorly dressed, individual. A respectable appearance can act as a buffer against imputations of deviance (Steffensmeier and Terry, 1973). But does a defendant's appearance impact significantly on the sentence he/she receives?

As already mentioned in chapter 5, experimental mock-juror studies indicate that a defendant's attractiveness will lessen harsh punishment but will have the reverse effect if the defendant exploited his/her attractiveness to perpetrate the crime.[24] The classic jury study by Kalven and Zeisel (1966) reported that American judges attributed 14 per cent of their disagreements with the jury to jurors' impression of the defendant, the impression itself alleged by the same judges to have been influenced by whether or not a defendant was 'attractive'.

Mazzella and Feingold (1994) suggested that attractive defendants may be held to higher standards for judgement, and behaviour and, thus, may be

> The relationship between a defendant's attractiveness and sentencing severity remains unclear due to contradictory findings.

treated more harshly when they do not live up to those standards. A recent study by Abwender and Hough (2001) reported an interesting interaction effect between the gender of mock sentencers (students) and defendant attractiveness in an experiment that used a vignette describing a vehicular homicide. Female subjects sentenced the unattractive female defendant to more years in prison than was the attractive female defendant, while the male subjects showed the opposite tendency (see also *Gender of Sentencer* below).

Some studies with real sentencers also suggest that highly physically attractive/socially respectable defendants promote sympathy and attract more lenient sentences. An experimental study with twenty-five magistrates in Cambridge by Fernandez (1974 – personal communication), the observational studies of a minor traffic court in Ontario, Canada, by Finegan (1978), Stewart's (1980) in Philadelphia reported a positive relationship between defendant's attractiveness and leniency of sentence. The validity of Stewart's (1980) findings, however, is questionable because he had no relevant information about the defendants in his sample. An Australian study of sentencing variations in Magistrates' Courts by Douglas et al. (1980) found a weak positive relationship between defendants' physical appearance (described as 'well-dressed', 'average' and 'shabby') and likelihood of imprisonment, controlling for legally relevant variables. Douglas et al. (1980) and Konečni and Ebbesen (1979) indicate that attractive appearance does not necessarily correlate with being favourably treated by the courts. The inconsistent findings reported by studies of real sentencers do not allow any conclusions to be drawn about whether an attractive physical appearance is a positive asset for an offender at the sentencing stage in criminal justice as experimental psychologists and practising lawyers would claim.

3.4 The Sentencer

Both lawyers, convicted offenders and members of the judiciary share a belief that the sentence imposed on a given defendant depends to a significant degree on who the individual sentencer is (Mather, 1979). It is also commonly known that lawyers indulge in 'magistrate/judge shopping' to get one who is likely to be favourably disposed to their case (Ericson and Baranek, 1982) while judges themselves allocate those of their brethren who are known for being tough on crime to courts that hear contested cases (Hagan and Bernstein, 1979). Early 'crude' studies of sentencing variations (for example, Everson, 1919) and methodologically sophisticated ones (for example, Palys and Divorski, 1986) have claimed a relationship between sentencer and sentence severity. A few researchers, however, have reported negative findings (Konečni and Ebbesen, 1979; Rhodes, 1977). The role of the sentencer as a determinant of sentence has also received a great deal of attention by Australian researchers who have reported a positive relationship between the two (Anderson, 1987; Grabosky and Rizzo, 1983; Lawrence and Homel, 1987; Lovegrove, 1984; Polk and Tait, 1988). Douglas' (1989) study of Victorian Magistrates' Courts (ten in Melbourne and thirty-eight in the country) involving twenty-seven stipendiary magistrates, also reported a positive but weak relationship between sentencer and sentence.

The importance of sentencer characteristics in sentencing was emphasised by Everson (1919) who concluded in his study of twenty-eight Magistrates' Courts in New York that, 'justice is a very personal thing, reflecting the temperament, the personality, the education, environment and personal traits of the magistrate' (p. 98). On the basis of Kapardis' (1987) literature review and more recent studies, the following conclusions emerge:

- Inconsistent findings have been reported concerning the relationship between a magistrate's social class and their sentencing (Hogarth, 1971; Hood, 1962).
- Lay magistrates in England from small towns are more punitive than their urban counterparts (Hood, 1972).
- Legally trained, as opposed to lay, magistrates in Canada take a more flexible approach to law and focus on the offender in deciding on sentence (Hogarth, 1971).
- Older English magistrates impose severer sentences on motoring offenders (Hood, 1972) and older judges in Gibson's (1978) study discriminated against black defendants the most.

3.4.1 Gender of sentencer

With the increase in the number of women in the legal profession in western countries, 'the courtroom is no longer an almost exclusive male enclave [where women appear mainly as victims of criminal offences or in messy divorce cases]. Today, not only is the presence of professional women in the courtroom not at all unusual, but every respectable courtroom drama must now include a woman judge or at least a couple of women lawyers' (Bogoch, 1999:51). According to Heidensohn (1992), women judges appear to face the dilemma of 'defeminization or deprofessionalization' and, consequently, try to neutralise themselves and their personal style (Thornton, 1996). What, then, is the evidence for a relationship between a sentencer's gender and his/her decision making?

In an archival study Myers and Talarico (1987) analysed data on more than 27 000 cases and found that prison sentences on white and black offenders tended to be longer in courts where female judges presided. They also reported that female judges sentenced rape offenders more harshly than male judges. Another archival study by Kritzer and Uhlmann (1977) also found no differences in the way male and female judges treated male and female offenders; in other words, there was no support for the view that 'chivalrous', paternalistic male judges punish female defendants more leniently. Other archival research by Gruhl, Spohn and Welch (1981) and Myers and Talarico (1987) found a tendency (though not a statistically significant one) for female judges to impose prison sentences than did male judges. Such studies need to explore the relationship between the gender of the judge and type of sentence imposed, controlling for sentence recommendation by probation officers which has been found by Konečni and Ebbesen (1982) in archival research of over 1200 cases to be identical to the judge's choice of sentence 87 per cent of the time. Oswald and Drewniak (1996) analysed data on petty theft from the Federal Central Register in Berlin with respect to the unappealable sentences imposed by male and female criminal court judges of three Magistrates' Courts in different states of the former Federal Republic of Germany and found no differences.

Bogoch (1999) examined all cases that were decided in the District and Magistrates' Courts in Israel in 1988 and 1993, for which the maximum punishment was five years or more, in three categories of offences: bodily assault (assault and grievous bodily harm), sexual offences, and offences against life (murder, attempted murder, and manslaughter). The sample consisted of 868 defendants involved in 747 cases in five different areas. About one-fifth of the cases involved a panel of three judges, and the rest were decided by one judge. There were no trials in which three women judges presided, and women judges participated in less than one-fifth of all the cases (p. 59). In all the trials, there were twenty different female judges and fifty-eight different male judges. Bogoch found that: (a) female judges were significantly more lenient than male judges (p. 60); (b) panels that included women were more likely to impose harsher sentences than men-only panels; (c) when a man was judging, whether alone or in a panel, the sentence imposed on those convicted of sexual offences was significantly higher than that imposed on those convicted of bodily harm offences; but (d) when a woman was judging, especially in a panel, the sentence for sexual offences was lower than that handed down in bodily harm offences (p. 63). Bogoch concluded that, 'if women have a different voice, it is muted in the role of judge. While the leniency of women judging alone may be explained by a gender-related rehabilitative rather than a punitive approach, it may also derive from her still relatively marginalized position in the profession' (pp. 70–1). We see that the literature on sex biases in judges' decision-making provides an inconsistent picture about the behaviour of male and female judges.

> The judiciary themselves have been shown to be a source of disparities.

Inconsistent findings have been reported regarding not only a sentencer's gender[25] but also religion,[26] politics,[27] and penal aims,[28] and his/her sentencing decisions. As far as justices of the US Supreme Court are concerned, political scientist Glendon Schubert in *The Judicial Mind* (1965) and *The Judicial Mind Revisited* (1974) advocated that a justice's vote was a function of the relationship between his/her ideological position on the issue at hand and the type of case involved.

The available empirical evidence shows that the sentencer plays an important role as a determinant of sentence. One way of reducing the individual sentencer as a source of disparity would be to reduce his/her discretion in what sentence to impose on a given type of defendant for a given offence. While the judiciary in the United States is by now well accustomed to the 'just deserts' philosophy of sentencing curtailing their discretion, sentencers in Britain, Australia and New Zealand, however, are likely to resist such a restriction on their judicial independence; furthermore, restricting judicial discretion 'may produce reduced intra-legal disparity at the cost of reducing the ability of sentencers to make allowance for the distinctive features of particular cases' (Douglas, 1989:55). Other policy implications that would seem to follow from the findings reported about the sentencer as a source of disparities are: (a) educating sentencers about this knowledge; and (b) actively involving them in realistic sentencing exercises aimed at achieving uniformity of approach (Kapardis, 1985). Already such an approach has been used, amongst others, by the Judicial Studies Board in England and Wales and the Institute of Judicial Administration in Victoria, Australia, and, on the basis of feedback from magistrates and judges (personal communication), has proved very useful in achieving more uniformity in sentencing. A proper empirical evaluation of such attempts to reduce disparities in sentencing by targeting sentencers is long overdue.

4 Models of Judicial Decision-Making

A variety of models[29] have been proposed for judicial decision-making by both psychologists and non-psychologists. Chambliss and Seidman (1971) presented a sociological picture by identifying the effect of structural inputs (for example, court structure in appellate courts – see Coffin, 1994) and their impact on structural outcomes (that is, the court system). Two British criminologists – Hood and Sparks (1970:148–9) – suggested a more social psychological viewpoint by focusing on the court system and identifying the flow of information in the courtroom.

According to Rowland and Carp (1996, cited by Wrightsman, 1999:22), 'The attitudinal model[30] proposes that if a challenged behavior is inconsistent with a justice's ideological perspective, that justice will vote to reject the behavior' (Wrightsman, 1999:22).

The cognitive model of judicial decision-making questions the one-to-one relationship between attitudes and behaviour and makes use of schemas, in other words, 'an organised body of knowledge from past experience that is used to interpret a new experience' (Wrightsman, 1999:23). Thus, the cognitive model uses attitudes as 'filters'. As Rowland and Carp (1996) have pointed out, however, the problem with the attitudinal model is that it reflects an obsolete conception of the pivotal role of attitudes.

Michon and Pakes (1995:510–11) draw attention to a distinction between 'normative' and 'descriptive' models. The latter describe optimal decision-making behaviour while the former describe how decisions are made in real life. Descriptive models assume that a decision-maker like a magistrate or a judge is limited as to the amount of information he/she can process and, consequently, uses information selectively (p. 511). Descriptive models focus on the heuristics (that is, the processes by which they find an answer to a question) and strategies real-life decision-makers use and aim to describe the cognitive processes underpinning such decision-making. Michon and Pakes (1995) also distinguish six steps in the decision-making process: problem recognition, decision-making problem, identification of consequences, utility and likelihood assessment, long-term vs. short-term consequences and choosing between alternatives (pp. 512–13). They conclude that: (a) the complex task of judicial decision-making is performed rather well by human decision-makers, but not necessarily by using methods that would be described by normative models; and (b) judicial decision-making cannot be 'rational' in a pure sense, as the term is used in economics, for example (p. 523).

Attribution theory is concerned with how people attribute traits, abilities and motives to people on the basis of observing their behaviour (Heider, 1958; James and Davis, 1965; Kelley, 1967). A basic distinction in attribution theory (see Schneider, 1995, for an excellent account) is that between internal (that is, dispositional) and external (that is, situational) causes of behaviour. Focusing upon the sentencer as a source of variation, researchers in different countries have utilised attributional analysis (for example, Weiner 1979, 1980) in an attempt to understand how sentencers perceive a broad range of sentencing-relevant factors and how they are related to the sentence imposed (Ewart and Pennington, 1987; Oswald, 1992). According to Weiner's model, the psychological meaning of 'cause' (attribution of responsibility) results from the way an individual classifies another's behaviour in terms of locus of control, stability (that is, consistency over time) and controllability. Carroll and Payne (1977) reported that subjects imposed lenient sentences if they perceived the offender's criminal behaviour as resulting from external, unstable and uncontrollable causes. Ewart and Pennington (1987) tested Weiner's attributional model with British police officers and social workers and reported findings providing further support for the model. Bierhoff et al. (1989) also reported a significant relationship between causal attributions and punishment recommendation, with sentences becoming more lenient as situational (external) attribution increases (p. 204). Another German study by Oswald (1992) used questionnaires to survey thirty-six criminal court judges and concluded that sentencing decision-making can be usefully understood in terms of: (a) how a sentencer justifies punishments (retributive, that is, an end in itself) vs. utilitarian (a means to an end such as crime-reduction); and (b) whether sentencers act from the offender's or the victim's perspective. Oswald found that the more a judge adopted the perspective of the victim, the more likely the judge was to attribute responsibility to the offender. Future research should test experimentally Oswald's findings and attempt to synthesise Weiner's (1979) model and Oswald's offender-victim perspective dimension.

5 Conclusions

The issue of disparity in sentencing is one of public concern and has attracted considerable research. A major contributing factor to disparities is the wide discretion enjoyed by magistrates, judges and, in the United States, juries, as well as the existence of conflicting penal aims and lack of sufficient guidance on how judicial officers are to exercise their discretion. Researchers have used a range of different methods to disentangle disparities in sentencing. This chapter has focused on studies of actual sentencers and the importance of extra-legal factors, which are few in number, but controversial. The available empirical evidence shows that a criminal defendant's gender and race are significant determinants of sentence. Of particular concern is the failure of the US Supreme Court to thwart, by means of guidelines, apparently widespread racial discrimination by courts against black defendants when imposing the death penalty in cases when such defendants offend against whites. Such discriminatory practices by the courts add further support to the call for the abolition of the death penalty.

Inconsistent findings have been reported about the importance of a defendant's attractiveness. Finally, sentencers themselves have been shown to be a major source of disparity. Significant reduction of the range of sentencing options available to them, however, does not seem to be a commendable measure; educating sentencers about sources of disparity by focusing, perhaps, on how they perceive defendants and their circumstances, how they integrate different sources of information and how they attribute motives and traits to defendants who appear before them in order to select a particular sentence, and training them in how to achieve uniformity of approach by also making use of realistic sentencing exercises, appear much more promising. Both legal and extra-legal factors impact on sentencing and contribute to disparities. There is already ample empirical evidence that Justice herself is not as effectively blindfolded as some conservative lawyers and judges would have us believe. Members of the judiciary themselves, too, have come to accept this fact and already proposals are under way in the United States, UK, Australia, New Zealand and Canada to 're-educate' judges in the wake of a number of trials in which judges made rather sexist comments.

Revision Questions

1   What do you know about judicial discretion in sentencing?
2   What is meant by 'disparity' in sentencing?
3   What methods have been used to study sentencing variations?
4   Which extra-legal characteristics of defendants influence the severity of their sentences?
5   What policy implications arise from the conclusion that the judiciary themselves are a source of disparity in sentencing?
6   What models of judicial decision-making have been proposed?

7 The Psychologists as Expert Witnesses

'The law is hostage to the knowledge possessed by others; it needs data, good data. It can well do without the biases and prejudices of related disciplines – it has enough of its own to deal with.' (Allen and Miller, 1995:337)

'The use of expert witnesses in the courtroom has entered a dynamic era. Over the course of the next decade a great deal is likely to happen.' (Landsman, 1995:157)

'Expert witnesses do not just appear out of the blue. They are recommended by a city's "old boy" network over lunches, telephone calls and drinks. Or they are tried out by legal firms and insurance companies and, if successful, put on to their "panels" of suitable experts.' (Ragg, 1995)

'Psychology can play a valuable role in the criminal process, even if it must end at the door of the court.' (Sheldon and McCleod, 1991:820)

'greater numbers of expert witnesses are being permitted to testify on a broader base of subject matter than has hitherto been permitted.' (Freckelton and Selby, 2002:12).

Introduction

Experts, in the form of medical doctors, appear to have been first called upon to advise judges at the Old Bailey six hundred years ago, but it was not until around 1620 that a jury was furnished with expert testimony for the first time. By 1721 there was the first challenge to an expert witness (a surgeon) testifying for the prosecution by another expert testifying on behalf of the defendant (Landsman, 1995). However, it was not until the latter part of the eighteenth century that the role of the expert witness (as the term is generally understood by lawyers on both sides of the Atlantic) was finally shaped, as counsel came to participate more and more in questioning and cross-examining expert witnesses (Landsman, 1995:139).[1] Lawyers' and other professionals' demand for expert evidence by psychologists has increased since the 1980s, reflecting growing recognition that psychologists 'have a unique contribution to make to judicial proceedings' (Gudjonsson, 1993:120). While 'The specialty most involved in forensic psychology in practice is clinical psychology' (Blackburn, 1996:14), as shown in this chapter, forensic psychologists, including legal psychologists; have become accepted as experts on both sides of the Atlantic and in the Antipodes. An area showing increasing involvement of psychologists as experts is family law. Psychologists, of course, are called as expert witnesses in both civil and criminal cases. As seen below, the range of cases has been broader in some jurisdictions than in others.

> Demand for psychologists as expert witnesses has increased significantly since the 1980s.

The terrain traversed is dotted with very significant developments in the courts' treatment of expert testimony by psychologists in a broad range of areas. It is noted that in a major judgement (*Daubert v. Merrell Dow Pharmaceuticals* – see below) the US Supreme Court has reasoned its criteria for deciding whether expert evidence shall be admissible. Without abandoning the 27-year-old 'common knowledge and experience rule' (see below), the courts in England have opened the door to the psychologist as expert witness. Careful examination of the relevant case law in Australia, New Zealand and Canada (see Freckelton and Selby, 2002, for an in-depth analysis) shows that in a number of recent cases the courts in these countries have followed a more liberal approach to the interpretation of the common knowledge rule (Freckelton and Selby, 2002:160). This chapter does not purport to deal with the controversies about the adequacy of legal procedures for selecting or qualifying experts, whether expert testimony can be prejudicial, the objectivity of expert witnesses, the ethics of expert testimony by experimental psychologists (see McCloskey et al., 1986) or the scarcity of generally acceptable scientific methods and theories (Golding, 1992).

One of the basic assumptions in common law is that there exists a distinction between facts and the inferences that can be drawn from such facts. The distinction between 'fact' and 'opinion', however, is not without difficulties (Freckelton and Selby, 2002:10). It is the function of the magistrate, judge and jury to draw inferences. The role of witnesses is to state the facts as they have been directly observed by them. In other words, witnesses do not give their opinions. However, the law makes an exception to this basic rule in the case of an expert in cases where a tribunal of fact decides that a specific issue calls for an expert witness because the particular expertise does not fall within the knowledge and experience of the magistrate, judge or jury, and a witness qualifies as an 'expert'. In some jurisdictions (for example, the United States) an expert witness is allowed to also express an opinion on the ultimate issue, the very question which the tribunal itself has to answer. Hamlyn-Harris (1992), however, has pointed to the danger of courts coming to depend on experts' opinion on an ultimate issue before deciding the issue (p. 82). The cause for concern in this context becomes greater when one remembers that clinical psychologists and psychiatrists, for example, have been known to misrepresent their competence, falsely claiming they can predict dangerousness with a high degree of accuracy (see Faust and Ziskin, 1988, for a discussion).

The question of whether a witness is an expert is a question of fact for the judge. A particular and special knowledge of a subject that has been acquired through scientific study or experience can qualify a witness as an expert (Cattermole, 1984:126). To illustrate, in *Moore v. Medley* (*The Times*, 3 February 1995) a member of the Inner Circle of magic was allowed to testify as a highly expert magician that there were various ways 'one could have a fraudulent manipulation of coins' (Smith, 1995:113). Haward (1981) identified four roles for forensic psychologists (using the term 'forensic' in a broad sense) appearing as expert witnesses:[2]

1   *Experimental:* this could involve a psychologist informing the court (a) about the state of knowledge relevant to some cognitive process and/or (b) carrying out an experiment (for example, involving eyewitness testimony, or a defendant's claim to be suffering from a phobia) directly relevant to the individual's case before the court (Gudjonsson and Sartory, 1983).
2   *Clinical:* as already mentioned, this is the more common role for psychologists appearing in western English-speaking common law countries and involves testifying, for example, on their assessment of a client's personality, IQ, neuropsychological functioning, mental state or behaviour (Freckelton, 1990; Gudjonsson, 1985,1995b[3]:62).
3   *Actuarial:* in a civil case involving, for example, a plaintiff claiming for damages for a psychological deficit caused by someone's negligence, a psychologist may be asked to estimate the probability that such an individual could live on their own and/or be gainfully employed (Haward, 1981).
4   *Advisory:* in this role, a psychologist could be advising counsel before and/or during a trial about what questions to ask the other side's witnesses, including their expert witness/es. Knowing that there is another psychologist in court evaluating one's testimony has been reported to increase an expert's level of stress when testifying in court (Gudjonnson, 1985).

Krauss and Sales (2001) used 208 psychology undergraduates as subjects and a Texas death penalty case involving the issue of dangerousness to investigate whether mock-jurors are more influenced by clinical opinion expert testimony or actuarial expert testimony. They found that mock-jurors weigh clinical expert opinion more heavily than actuarial expert testimony. Their finding casts doubt on the validity of the assumption by some courts in the United States (for example, in Florida and California) that: (a) jurors routinely differentiate between clinical and other forms of testimony; and (b) that jurors consider clinical opinion expert testimony to be less influential than other testimony (p. 305). However, in considering the implications for the courts of this finding, the reader should note the possibility that, as Krauss and Sales themselves admit, 'Actual jurors may have reacted differently to the experimental conditions' (p. 304).

1 Five Rules for Admitting Expert Evidence

According to Freckelton and Selby (2002:2), five rules have evolved which specifically apply to the reception of expert evidence:

> Five rules have evolved in western common law countries which specifically apply to the reception of expert evidence.

1 *Expertise rule:* Does the witness have sufficient knowledge and experience to qualify as an expert who can assist the court?[4]
2 *Common knowledge rule:* Is the information sought from the expert really something upon which the tribunal needs the help of any third party or can the tribunal rely upon its general knowledge and common sense?
3 *Area of expertise rule:* Is the claimed knowledge and expertise sufficiently recognised as credible by others capable of evaluating its theoretical and experiential foundations?
4 *Ultimate issue rule:* Is the expert's contribution going to have the effect of supplanting the function of the tribunal to decide the issue before the court? If so, it is likely to be rejected.
5 *Basis rule:* To what extent can an expert's opinion be based upon matters not directly within the expert's own observations? Such reliance on material that cannot be directly evaluated by the court falls foul of a fundamental principle of evidence.

As the same authors point out, 'Not surprisingly in an era of rapid advances in knowledge, these rules are frequently being stretched as courts grapple with the problems of how to apply them to new developments in areas of expertise' (for example, survey evidence, novel psychological evidence, battered woman syndrome, victim profile evidence and parental alienation syndrome).

Allen and Miller (1995) argued that the more fact-finders defer to experts, the greater the likelihood of irrational verdicts and of expert witnesses becoming advocates. They proposed an education-centred view of the expert's proper role at trial, very much along the lines of the *amicus* brief in *Michaels* (see chapter 4).

Where parties to a dispute in a criminal or civil trial call their own expert witnesses, a 'battle' of experts can eventuate (Turnstall et al., 1982). A survey of forty-two experts (48 per cent were physicians), seventy lawyers employing them, thirteen judges hearing cases involving them and 118 jurors who decided forty civil cases over a 14-week period in 1988 in Dallas County,

Texas, by Champagne et al. (1991) reported that expert 'battles' occurred less frequently than had been suggested. The main limitations of such a postal survey, as Champagne et al. themselves acknowledge, is not knowing whether non-respondents differ from respondents – the average response rate was 37 per cent. Of course, given the high fees charged by most experts for their written or oral testimony, there is an incentive to avoid the possibility of the experts 'battling it out' in court 'by pre-trial agreements about the number of experts to be called, and pre-trial meetings of the experts. In England and Wales it is not unknown for the experts on both sides to come to court with a joint statement' (Nijboer, 1995:561–2) .

'Hired guns' are not believed by mock jurors.

Psychologists in the United States have been appearing as experts more frequently and in a larger range of cases than their counterparts in other western English-speaking common law countries.[5] Kassin et al. (1989) surveyed sixty-three leading eyewitness testimony researchers in the United States and found that over half of them (54 per cent) had testified on the subject at least once, with an average of 7.6 occasions. Kassin et al. also found that more had refused to testify at least once than said they had testified at least once. Reasons for refusing to testify included feeling that one did not have anything useful to say, having doubts about their expertise in a given case, and being concerned about not being allowed to qualify their answers. Kassin et al. also reported that experts were equally likely to testify for the prosecution as for the defence, and for both sides in a civil case. The same survey shows that although 'hired guns' exist in forensic psychology as they do in other fields, there is no justification for assuming that this is a common feature of such eyewitness experts. Regarding the 'hired gun' effect idea, a mock-juror study by Cooper and Neuhauss (2000) used 140 jury-eligible residents in New Jersey aged 18 to 72 years as subjects, and the legal case used involved the scientific issue of whether a chemical to which the plaintiff had been exposed was the immediate cause of his cancer. It was found that: (a) the experts who are highly paid for their testimony and testify frequently are perceived as 'hired guns'; and (b) they are neither liked nor believed, especially if the expert testimony adduced is complex and cannot be easily processed.

There are differences between legal proceedings in different countries and this includes the precise roles of expertise and of expert witnesses (Nijboer, 1995:556). To illustrate, in western common law countries an expert witness testifies for the side that has retained him/her and pays his/her fees. In contrast to this practice, in continental European jurisdictions expert witnesses are normally appointed by the court to assist the court. In addition, there is a difference in status between court-appointed and privately retained expert witnesses, with the former enjoying a higher status (p. 557).[6] Another important difference between continental European jurisdictions and England and Wales, for example, which Nijboer points out is the fact that the former (for example, France, Switzerland, Holland, Belgium) are characterised by 'very low thresholds for the admissibility of expert evidence. They prefer to regulate how the expert evidence, which is admitted, is regulated' (p. 559). Expert witnesses, of course, may be involved in different stages of legal proceedings:

pre-trial, trial and post-trial. This chapter is concerned with psychologists as expert witnesses in court-based legal disputes.

An interesting question concerns the way jurors perceive expert witnesses hired by each side vs. a court-appointed expert. To investigate this question, Cooper and Hall (2000) presented mock-jurors with a civil case involving a car accident and varied systematically: (a) whether the medical expert testimony about the plaintiff's injury was provided by experts hired by each side or by a court-appointed expert in addition to the two adversarial experts; (b) whether the defendant was an individual or a corporation; and (c) whether the expert witness sided with the plaintiff or the defendant. Cooper and Hall found that mock-jurors sided with the court-appointed expert in every condition except when the expert favoured a corporate defendant.

Importing non-legal knowledge into both criminal and civil trials has proven problematical in western common law countries with their adversary legal systems (Saks, 1992:185). There is no doubt that magistrates (be they stipendiary or justices of the peace), judges and jurors sometimes require assistance to establish the facts of a case before them. In this context, the expert witness can play a crucial role. In the words of Ian Freckelton, a well-known Australian practising lawyer and authority on expert testimony, 'The role of experts is vital. They supply information that can't be supplied elsewhere. They supply counter-intuitive information, myth-dispelling information, which may be essential to clear thinking' (quoted in Ragg, 1995:16). Alas, however, fact-finders have to also contend with the knowledge that expert 'evidence can be complex and hard for a jury to understand. Also, there's the danger of bias. These are hard financial times, and the forensic expert needs to be a repeat player. If they don't supply the information required, they will find they don't have as much work as they need to survive' (p. 16). Enough concern within the organised profession about the nature and the quality of expert testimony has resulted in forensic psychologists in the United States, for example, being provided with formal guidelines.[7] According to Gudjonsson (1993), 'The main theme of these guidelines is that forensic psychologists have the responsibility of providing a service which is of the highest professional standard' (p. 120). Deviating from the present author's approach in the rest of the book, expert testimony is not dealt with here by structuring the discussion thematically but on a country-by-country basis. This is done for the benefit of the reader because there are significant differences in the common law position in different countries and in the fields in which psychologists are admitted as expert witnesses.

> The gist of the United States Supreme Court in *Daubert* is that expert evidence needs to be scientific to be admissible in court.

2 United States

The practice of providing expert testimony for a fee and as a means of earning a living did not become widespread in the United States until the middle of the nineteenth century, and the test for admitting expert testimony between 1850 and 1920 was 'whether the proffered expert was appropriately "qualified" to render an opinion on the issue before the court' (Landsman, 1995:150). In the landmark decision in the case of *Frye v. United States* (293 F 1013 (1923)) the District of Columbia Court of Appeals rejected testimony by a lie-detector expert[8] that the defendant was telling the truth when he denied having committed the alleged offence on the ground that the scientific theory on which it was based was not generally accepted within the relevant professional community. Interestingly, it was not until the early 1980s that the *Frye* test came to be cited frequently in court decisions in the United States (Landsman, 1995). *Frye* was a vague ruling that was instrumental in American courts admitting expert testimony in a rather broad range of fields without much scrutiny (Landsman, 1995:155). The US Supreme Court's unanimous decision in *Daubert v. Merrell Dow Pharmaceuticals* (113 S.Ct. 2786 (1993)) held that *Frye* had not been incorporated as part of federal evidence law but had in fact been rejected when the expert testimony rules of the Federal Rules of Evidence were proclaimed in 1975 (p. 155). According to the ruling in *Daubert*, the test for expert witnesses is 'vigorous cross-examination, presentation of contrary evidence, and careful instruction' (113 S.Ct, 2786, 2798, 1993).[9] More specifically, the *Daubert* judgement stated, *inter alia*, that, 'The subject of an expert's testimony must be "scientific … knowledge" … in order to qualify as "scientific knowledge", an inference or assertion must be derived by the scientific method' (p. 2795), and, 'The criterion of the scientific status of a theory is its falsifiability, or refutability, or testability … Another pertinent consideration is whether the theory or technique has been subjected to peer review and publication.' (pp. 2796–7).

Landsman contends that the *Daubert* judgement embraced judicial managerialism, a trend evident in American courts since the mid 1980s, and 'increased trial judge authority to review challenges to scientific evidence at the expense of litigant control', and what remains to be seen is how far judges will go in exercising this authority and whether they will do so evenhandedly between all litigants (p. 156). Landsman predicts that judges will favour well-established corporate or government defendants at the expense of civil rights, discrimination and product liability plaintiffs (p. 157). For their part, Penrod et al. (1995) have argued that the *Daubert* decision 'is likely to have minimal impact on the ways in which eyewitness expert admissibility decisions are made in the federal courts. *Daubert* will have less impact on states – the decision is not binding on the states and … Several state supreme courts have explicitly rejected *Daubert* …' (p. 244). Duncan (1996) concludes her discussion of expert testimony on psychological syndrome evidence after *Daubert* stating that, 'Examination of the scientific bases for most of the psychological evidence examined in this Note exposes as unfounded the fears of those apprehensive of the legitimacy of social science evidence' (p. 770). By handing down the *Daubert* ruling the US Supreme Court has indicated its confidence in judges adequately deciding the scientific status of a theory or technique in a civil or criminal case without scientific training; in fact, both advocates and the judiciary will need to be rather sophisticated in scientific matters (Freckelton, 1993:111). To achieve this, it will be necessary for lawyers to possess 'cross-disciplinary knowledge and understanding' (p. 113). The urgent need for legal psychology courses for practising lawyers provides psychologists with a great opportunity to communicate their expertise to the legal profession and move closer to bridging any remaining gap between the two disciplines.

As would have been expected, in the wake of *Daubert*, almost a decade later, 'a large body of scholarship continues to debate the merits of the *Daubert* criteria as judicial decision-making guidelines' (Gatowski et al. (2001:434). The post-*Daubert* debate in the United States has included discussion of:[10]

- 'the relative importance of the criteria to the admissibility decision and procedures for their application …
- of the extent to which judges understand and can properly apply the criteria when assessing the validity and reliability of proffered scientific evidence …
- the potential differential application of the criteria to various domains of expert testimony and the implications of their application for the admissibility and legitimacy of different domains of knowledge' (p. 434).

In the main, such discussion has concentrated on analysing published opinions by State appellate courts and the Supreme Court.[11] Such analysis is limited, however, because it only deals with published case law and *ipso facto* justifications. This is not to deny, of course, that such analysis provides insights into the impact of *Daubert*.

The next significant Supreme Court decision was handed down in *General Electric Co. v. Joiner*, 522 US 136, 118 S.Ct. 512 (1997). The issue in that case was whether Joiner's exposure to certain chemicals caused his lung cancer. The trial judge excluded the testimony provided by Joiner's expert witnesses on the grounds that, it 'did not rise above "subjective belief or unsupported speculation"' (at 516). The appellate court reversed the trial judge's decision but the Supreme Court reversed it again, reinstating the trial judge's exclusion, stating that the legal standard for allowing expert testimony to be put to the jury is the same as that which the relevant professional community uses (Gutheil and Stein, 2000: 244).

The question of whether the *Daubert* guidelines apply to all forms of technical or otherwise specialised knowledge, or just scientific knowledge, was addressed by the US Supreme Court in *Kumho Tire Co. v. Patrick Carmichael*, 526 US, 13, 152, 119 S.Ct. 1167, 1176, (1999). *Kumho* concerned the expert testimony of an engineer and the essence of the court's decision is that: (a) the factors that a court ought to use to decide whether a scientific theory is reliable, as enunciated in *Daubert*, may apply to testimony of engineers and other experts who are not scientists; (b) the 'gatekeeping' obligation of the trial judge under *Federal Rule of Evidence* 702 (FRE 702) applies to all expert testimony because FRE 702 does not distinguish between 'scientific', 'technical' or 'other specialized knowledge'; (c) the distinction between scientific and non-scientific evidence is unclear; and, finally, (d) the judge has broad discretion as to how to discharge his/her gatekeeping role. In other words, *Kumho* clarified that the *Daubert* analysis applies not only to scientific knowledge but also to scientific, technical and otherwise specialised knowledge. Freckelton and Selby (2002) are of the view that 'This makes it likely that the Supreme Court will apply the *Daubert* analysis also to areas of specialised knowledge such as medicine and even psychology. This may have highly significant repercussions' (p. 79).

According to Foxhall (2000:38),[12] Justice Breyer who wrote the concurring opinion in *Joiner* and the majority decision in *Kumho* called on psychologists to assist the judiciary to ' "separate the sheep from the goats" in identifying valid psychological testimony for use by the courts'. As Gutheil and Stein (2000:248) have argued, now is the time for psychologists and psychiatrists to accept the 'offer of cooperative effort' (*Joiner*, at 1176) by creating a joint committee of judges and forensic clinicians to implement the recommendations in *Joiner* and *Kumho Tire* by establishing a pilot project in the courts. As far as it has been possible to ascertain, their advice has gone unheeded in the United States and elsewhere. Concluding on the significance of *Kumho*, Gatowski et al. (2001) remind their readers that, 'although on its surface *Kumho* resolved one of the central debates of *Daubert* and its application to different forms of knowledge, the decision failed to address the underlying assumption that judges are fully capable of making judgements about scientific reliability and validity of proffered scientific evidence. In fact, because bench philosophies of science – judicial definitions of what constitutes science – seem to reflect the rhetoric but not the substance of *Daubert*, Kumho may ultimately have clouded the process even further' (p. 454).

> Crucial concepts in the *Daubert* judgement (for example, 'falsifiability' and 'error rate') are not understood by the majority of American judges. This is a cause for concern.

The trilogy of *Daubert*, *Kumho* and *Joiner* assume that American judges are capable of making judgements about the scientific reliability and validity of proffered scientific evidence. However, Gatowski et al.'s (2001) empirical evidence to the contrary is undoubtedly a cause for concern and defeats the purpose of the joint effort by forensic clinicians and judges advocated by Gutheil and Stein (2000) in the light of *Joiner* and *Kumho*.

Gatowski et al. (2001) surveyed a proportionate stratified random sample of State court judges and found that:

- There was very strong support among judges in the United States for their 'gatekeeping role' as defined in *Daubert*, irrespective of the admissibility standard followed in their state.
- Many of the judges surveyed did not possess the scientific literacy apparently required by *Daubert* in order to perform the 'gatekeeping' role.
- Only 5 per cent knew the meaning of the term 'falsifiability' and only 4 per cent knew the meaning of 'error rate'.
- There was little consensus about the relative importance of the *Daubert* guidelines and judges emphasised they required more general acceptance as an admissibility criterion.
- Most did not apply judicial guidelines in differentiating between 'scientific' and 'non-scientific' expert evidence.

- Finally, the judges' own 'bench philosophy' appeared 'to reflect the rhetoric rather than the substance of *Daubert*'.

Gatowski et al.'s findings seriously: (a) challenge the assumption in *Daubert*, *Kumho* and *Joiner* that judges in the United States are capable of making judgements about the scientific reliability and validity of proffered scientific evidence; and (b) indicates to the American judiciary that they should, perhaps, make good the deficit identified by means of some kind of education programme aimed at improving their knowledge of the pertinent concepts and issues in philosophy of science.

3 England and Wales

Experts began to testify in English courts in the second half of the nineteenth century (see Hand, 1901). Interestingly, 'The general English approach to the admissibility of novel scientific or psychological evidence has been benevolent acquiescence rather than the application of any stringency in assessing the reliability or standing of techniques or theories within a particular professional community' (Freckelton and Selby, 2002:79). British courts have been rather unenthusiastic about expert evidence by psychologists (Sheldon and McCleod, 1991:818). The landmark decision in a provocation case, *R v. Turner* (1975) Q.B. 834, has meant that, unlike their American counterparts, their expert testimony has had to surmount a rather difficult impediment to admissibility, namely the 'common knowledge and experience' rule of evidence. This common law principle can be traced to the case of *Folkes v. Chadd* in 1782 in which Lord Mansfield ruled that an expert's opinion is admissible if it provides the court with information which is likely to lie outside the common knowledge and experience of the jury. Similarly, Lawton LJ stated in *Turner* that, 'If on the proven facts a judge or jury can form their own conclusions without help, then opinion of an expert is unnecessary. In such a case if it is given dressed up in scientific jargon it may make judgement more difficult. The fact that an expert witness had impressive qualifications by that fact alone [does not] make his opinion on matters of humane nature any more helpful than the jurors themselves; but there is a danger that they may think it does' (at 841).

The gist of the *Turner* decision is that a court in England and Wales does not need a psychologist's or psychiatrist's expert knowledge when it comes to psychological processes except where mental abnormality is involved. As Colman and Mackay (1993) have argued, however, 'The *Turner* rule appears to be based on an interpretation of the relation between psychology and common sense that is sufficiently wrong-headed to be called a fallacy' (p. 47). One of the underlying assumptions in *Turner* is that normal human behaviour is essentially transparent and, consequently, a jury does not need a psychologist's opinion on such behaviour since it is within their 'common knowledge and experience'. However, despite the fact that the ruling in *Turner* has largely restricted the admissibility of expert testimony, it also recognises the need for change (Thornton, 1995:147). Colman and Mackay (1993:48–9) argue convincingly that the 'human behaviour is transparent' assumption is undoubtedly false, citing psychological knowledge in the areas of the 'fundamental attribution error' (see Miller et al., 1990), obedience to authority (Milgram, 1974), group polarisation (Isenberg, 1986), cognitive dissonance (Wickland and Brehm, 1976) and bystander intervention (Latane and Naida, 1981). Colman and Mackay conclude their critique of *Turner* stating that 'expert psychological evidence should be admitted whenever it is both relevant and potentially helpful to the jury in explaining aspects of human behaviour that are not easily understood with common sense alone' (p. 49).

> Courts in England have opened the door to forensic psychologists appearing as expert witnesses.

Examination of English authorities since *Turner* shows that psychiatric or psychological evidence which is not abnormal or does not directly concern the defendant's state of mind or the issue of intent, has generally been excluded. However, there have been a number of encouraging decisions indicating greater readiness to admit psychological evidence (Thornton, 1995:144, 146). The restrictive interpretation of the rule in *Turner* was relaxed by the Court of Appeal in the case of *R v. Sally Loraine Emery* (and another) (1993). In the *Emery* case, an 11-month-old child died as a result of serious injuries inflicted over a period of weeks as a result of very severe physical abuse. *Emery*, the unmarried mother of the child, was found guilty in the Peterborough Crown Court in January 1992 of failing to protect the child from her father and was acquitted of occasioning actual bodily harm on her child. She appealed against her sentence of four years' detention in a young offender institution and had it reduced to thirty months. The prosecution appealed against the trial judge's admitting expert evidence on post-traumatic stress disorder (PTSD), 'learned helplessness' and 'the battered woman syndrome' on the grounds that the evidence concerned fell within the common knowledge rule enunciated in *Turner*. However, the Court of Appeal upheld both the trial judge's decision to admit the expert evidence on behalf of the defendant as well as the justification offered for that decision.

The effect of *Emery* is that courts in England and Wales are no longer to assume that expert psychiatric evidence is called for to assist the jury only when it deals with mental disorder, mental handicap or automatism (Colman and Mackay, 1995). In delivering the Appeal Court's decision, Lord Taylor, Lord Chief Justice, upheld the decision of the trial judge to allow expert evidence by a psychologist and a psychiatrist that the defendant had been suffering from PTSD, 'learned helplessness' and the 'battered woman syndrome', on the grounds that such evidence was complex and not known by the general public and was necessary to assist the jury to determine the facts of the case. According to Colman and Mackay (1995), 'The effect of the *Emery* judgement therefore appears to open the door to psychological evidence in a far wider range than has hitherto been the case' (p. 264). In *Frost v. Chief Constable of the South Yorkshire Police* ([1997] 1 All ER 540) police officers sued for damages for psychiatric injury, claiming negligence on the part of the Chief Constable and senior police officers in crowd control arising out of the circumstances of the Hillsborough Stadium collapse as a result of which ninety-six spectators were crushed to death and approximately 730 injured. It was claimed that the psychiatric injury sustained because they had tended to victims of the Chief Constable's negligence was responsible for their suffering from PTSD. The judgement in *Frost* showed a preparedness to extend the categories of compensability to include those in rescue efforts. However, 'the relaxed attitude of the court in equating back injury claims with PTSD claims suggests an emerging confidence in England at least that PTSD actions can be adequately evaluated in the forensic environment provided that the expert evidence placed before the tribunal of fact is of high quality and, presumably, well-tested by cross-examination' (Freckelton and Selby, 2002: 445). However, when counsel sought to adduce expert evidence about the truthfulness of children in *G v. DPP* ([1997] 2 All ER 755 at 759) the English High Court decided against its admissibility out of a concern that the role of the court would be taken over by the expert witness. It can be seen that in a number of cases in recent years courts in England have opened the door to a broader range of cases than would have been possible under the restrictive interpretation of the rule in *Turner*. The common knowledge rule itself, of course, has not been abandoned but has been interpreted more broadly than in *Turner*.

Further evidence that courts in England and Wales are readier to admit expert evidence by psychologists on matters that do not fall within abnormal behaviour is also evidenced by the fact that in a small number of cases well-known legal psychologists have now testified on eyewitness testimony issues. One such British expert is Professor Ray Bull of Portsmouth University who since the mid 1990s has provided expert testimony in three different cases (personal communication). One case concerned the possibility of 'unconscious transference' (see chapter 10) by an eyewitness in an armed robbery trial. A newsagent proprietor had his back to the door near closing time when someone grabbed him from behind and demanded money, threatening him by sticking a knife to his face. The shop-owner saw the offender from behind as he was running away from the scene of the crime. One year earlier, the same shop-owner had been robbed in the street by someone with a knife. That offender was identified, tried, convicted and sentenced to a term of imprisonment. The issue on which Professor Bull was asked to provide expert testimony was whether the eyewitness might have assumed the identity of the second robber influenced by what he had seen of the first robber; in other words, might the second robber's identification have been the result of 'unconscious transference'? There was a hung jury and a re-trial with a different jury. The expert testimony provided was held helpful.

The second of Professor Bull's cases involved a rape trial in which the major source of evidence against the defendant was the female victim and the fact that she had picked his voice out in a voice parade conducted by the police.[13] The expert was requested to express an opinion on the fairness of the parade for the benefit of the jury. The police carried out the voice parade after taking the trouble to seek the advice of a Cambridge University linguist to ensure that the suspect's voice did not differ from the rest of the voice parade in terms of accent. The voice parade constructed by the police contained segments of monologues by a number of speakers and the suspect's voice was the only one taken from an interview with the police. An experiment was carried out by Professor Bull in which subjects were asked to identify which of the voice samples came from a police interview. Subjects identified the suspect's voice at better than chance level. The testimony was admitted by the trial judge. That case ended up with a hung jury and, at the time of writing, there was to be a re-trial.

In another recent, interesting case Professor Bull was asked by the defence to write a report overviewing published research on 'unconscious transference' and 'transracial identification'. It was in relation to a case in which a girl was alleged to have been indecently assaulted while walking home from school. After the incident, she reported that she believed that the teenage boy who had assaulted her was a pupil at her school but she did not know him or his name. A day or so later at school she saw the boy whom she believed had assaulted her and pointed him out to her friend. The lawyer for the accused boy was aware that not only psychological research (see chapters 2, 3 and 4) but also prior miscarriages of justice had revealed that honest eyewitnesses can make grave errors when identifying someone as the perpetrator. When the trial commenced the prosecution did not object to any of the points made in Professor Bull's report. After hearing the prosecution's case and reading the expert report the judge said that he did not need to hear the defence case as she had decided the boy should be acquitted.

The next two cases of expert testimony have involved Professor Graham Davies, a famous forensic psychologist at Leicester University in England and a serving magistrate. They help to draw attention to a number of important points about expert testimony.

Case Study

R v. Steven Davis

This rather interesting armed robbery case from Herefordshire in England illustrates:
- How identification evidence can still form the principal plank of a prosecution for a serious offence in England and Wales.
- The importance of judges adhering to the *Turnbull* Guidelines (*R v. Turnbull and others* (1977) QB 224 at 228, 63 Cr.App.R. 132 at 137–40).
- How expert testimony on identification can be used in criminal cases and the lengths to which the courts will go to exclude it from the witness box!
  In May 1991 two men enter a specialist jewellers' shop in rural Herefordshire. Both are wearing anoraks and closely fitting caps with dark glasses. The lead man produces a sawn-off shotgun and threatens the shopkeeper and his wife and the two men make off with gems and cash, which they take from the safe. The jeweller is struck by their apparent familiarity with the location and operation of the safe. He recalls an incident in March when a stranger came into his shop during the Cheltenham Race Week and enquired about the cost of making a diamond brooch. The shopkeeper agreed to provide the stranger with an estimate. When asked his name he says 'It's Steve Davis – just like the snooker player'. The shopkeeper tells the police he thinks the lead robber and the stranger are the same person.

Police records reveal that a Steve Davis with previous convictions for armed robbery lives in East London, some 5 miles from where the robbers' car is recovered. The police decide that Davis may have inadvertently given his real name to the jeweller, and stage an identification parade later the same month for the jeweller, his wife and two workmen who saw the robbers leave the shop. All the members of the parade are dressed in the manner of the robbers. Only the jeweller picks out Mr Davis; one of the workmen declares that the men he saw were 'definitely not there'. On the basis of the one positive identification, Davis is put on trial in Hereford in November 1991. The judge in his summing up has to be prompted by defence counsel to remind the jury of the dangers of convicting on identification alone and does not apply the *Turnbull* Guidelines appropriately. After 6 hours' deliberation, the jury find Davis guilty and he is given a twelve-year sentence.

Davis goes to prison, but continues to maintain his innocence. Professor Davies is asked by Davis' solicitors to prepare a brief on the identification evidence. He points to: (a) the limited opportunity to observe the robber's appearance; (b) weaknesses in the identification evidence and in particular the importance of the witness who said the person he saw was *not* present; (c) the failure of the judge to follow *Turnbull* Guidelines in his handling of the identification evidence. The case is heard at the Court of Appeal in September 1993 and Professor Davies attends ready to give expert evidence. However, the judges after hearing legal submissions decide to quash the conviction on the basis of the procedural errors: they make it clear they do not wish to set a precedent by hearing evidence from a psychologist on identification issues. A retrial is ordered and duly takes place in Birmingham in October 1993. By this time, one workman witness has died and the other cannot be traced. The Crown decide to abandon their position that the March stranger and the May robber are one and the same person and rely on the jeweller's evidence. Professor Davies attends once again, ready to give evidence and once again, is not called, though the defence use parts of his report. At the end of the trial, the jury take just 20 minutes to find Davis not guilty.

Case Study

R v. Peter Ellis

The second case in which the services of Professor Davies were enlisted is a New Zealand case and it illustrates:

- The need for and the importance of adhering to proper guidelines in the conduct of interviews with children.
- Difficulties that can arise through multiple interviews.
- The particular problems of collecting and evaluating the evidence of very young children.
- The significant role that expert witness psychologists can take in facilitating enquiries of this kind.

Peter Ellis worked as an assistant in Christchurch Civic Crèche, New Zealand. By all accounts, he was a flamboyant character, the only male helper at the crèche. In November 1991, a 3-year-old told his father that he 'hated Peter's black penis'. This led to a wave of concern culminating in a meeting of concerned parents where a psychologist from the Social Welfare Department described the main features of child sexual abuse, asked parents to look out for these, but warned them of the dangers of questioning or interrogating their children. Subsequently, a number of children were interviewed by child protection specialists, none of whom made allegations against Mr Ellis.

However, in January 1992, a parent reported the first of a trickle of fresh allegations against Mr Ellis. The police and social services commenced a fresh round of interviews with children who had attended the crèche while Mr Ellis worked there. In all, some 118 children were interviewed, nearly all were now aged 5 to 6 years of age and were asked to describe events which had occurred some 18 months or more previously. A total of twenty children made statements about Mr Ellis that caused the investigators concern and eleven were eventually called to give evidence against Mr Ellis at his trial in the spring of 1993. The evidence of the children implicated not just Mr Ellis, but a number of other care assistants. The children alleged not only that they had been sexually abused while at the crèche, but also had been taken to various addresses in Christchurch and beyond, where they had suffered multiple abuse and been the victims of bizarre rituals. The defence pointed to the fact that most of the children had been repeatedly interviewed, one as many as six times. Moreover, many of the parents had ignored the plea not to interrogate their children and were in regular contact with other parents within the group.

The charges against the other crèche helpers were all eventually dismissed, but Ellis was found guilty of sexually abusing seven of the children and sentenced to ten years' imprisonment. He continued to maintain his innocence and mounted an appeal, based on the lack of credibility or plausibility of some of the allegations, particularly in the later interviews (one child had spoken of being abused in a busy Civic Centre in Christchurch) and that the interviewing was unnecessarily suggestive and leading. (At the time the interviews were conducted, there were no agreed guidelines for the conduct of investigative interviews comparable to the *Memorandum of Good Practice.*) The Court of Appeal rejected these claims, though it quashed the charges relating to one child who had retracted her allegations in the interim.

In 1997 and again in 1998, Mr Ellis petitioned the Court of Appeal for a free pardon, based upon allegations of defective interviewing techniques and the issue of possible contamination of the children's evidence through contact between the parents during the investigative phase. His lawyers also pointed to the developments that had taken place in the understanding of the influence of suggestive responding under questioning, particularly the work of Ceci and Bruck (1995). They emphasised the potential for miscarriages of justice as a result of a too literal reliance on the allegations as a result of multiple interviews of very young children, reflected in the Cleveland affair (Butler-Slos, 1992) and the Orkney Enquiry (Clyde, 1992). As a result, the Ministry of Justice set up an enquiry to examine again the issue of interview standards and the risks of contamination.

The Enquiry was undertaken by a former Chief Justice, Sir Thomas Eichelbaum, who in turn recruited two experts, Professor Davies and Dr Louis Sas, to examine the evidence in the light of recent research on suggestibility and contamination. In all, they were provided with thirty-five video interviews with the key witnesses, together with four packing cases full of supportive documentation. Their independent reports, though written from the different perspectives of an applied cognitive psychologist and a clinical practitioner, reached remarkably similar conclusions: the statements made by the children regarding incidents at the crèche involving Mr Ellis could not readily be attributed to undue bias or inappropriate practice by the interviewers involved. They concluded that the standard of interviewing was generally good and in accord with contemporary standards and showed an awareness of the problems of suggestibility in very young children. While some parents had undoubtedly talked to each other, others had not and there was a degree of mutual corroboration in the accounts of the different children that was difficult to explain unless they had experienced similar events. All children began by describing abusive incidents at the crèche; it was only as a result of repeated interviewing that the more bizarre allegations of

(Mason, 1991). Using data in trial court transcripts, Mason (1991) surveyed 122 appellate court decisions in both civil and criminal cases in which expert witness testimony on the characteristics of abused children provided by a total of 160 experts was challenged. Thirty-one per cent of the experts concerned were clinical psychologists. It was found that in over half of the cases (55 per cent) the expert testimony was allowed on appeal and in 9 per cent the evidence was partly admitted; in those cases where the courts rejected the expert witness testimony they did so mainly on the grounds that the testimony went to the issue of the child's credibility, something which, in evidence law, is for the jury to decide and not for an expert witness. Mason concluded that expert testimony informing the court about the weight of the evidence in the relevant literature pertaining to sexually abused children's willingness to remember, the accuracy of their recall and vulnerability to suggestive questioning, can indeed assist the judge or jury to evaluate a child's testimony.

Drawing on Krauss and Sales' (2001:274–5) discussion of the literature, researchers have reported that juror decision-making is influenced if expert testimony is presented on the following issues:

- The fallibility of eyewitness identifications.
- Clinical syndromes (for example, battered wife syndrome, rape trauma syndrome, child sexual abuse syndrome, and depressed memory syndrome).
- Insanity.
- Future dangerousness of a defendant.

However, the mechanism by which expert testimony affects juror/mock-juror decision-making 'is poorly understood' (p. 274). Available evidence suggests that an expert witness' gender may play a role in the impact of expert testimony on juror decision-making. In an Australian experimental study by Schuller, Terry and McKimmie (2001) undergraduate students were presented with a modified version of a civil trial involving anti-trust price-fixing violation by two defendant suppliers. The gender of the plaintiff's expert witness was manipulated, as was the industry within which the violation took place stating it was either: (a) the construction or (b) the women's clothing industry. It was found that expert testimony by a male expert was more influential when there is congruency between the gender of the expert and the domain of the case. One serious limitation of Schuller at al. is that the decisions of individual mock-jurors may be different from actual jury verdicts reached by jurors after deliberations (p. 77).

5.1 Adversarial vs Court-Appointed Experts' Influence on Jurors/ Mock-jurors

In a mock-juror study by Cooper and Hall (2000) subjects were presented with testimony about a plaintiff's injury in a car accident. The researchers systematically varied information about: who hired the expert (each side or court-appointed); with whom the expert sided (the plaintiff or the defendant); and, finally, the type of plaintiff involved (whether an individual or a corporation).

It was found that the mock-jurors sided with the court-appointed expert except where the expert favoured a corporate defendant.

6 Appearing as Expert Witnesses

Poor evidence by psychologists appearing as experts can be very damaging for psychologists in general, undermining the positive impact which psychologists can have on developments within the legal system, and can have a disastrous effect on individual cases, causing miscarriages of justice (Gudjonsson, 1993). For Gudjonsson, poor psychological evidence is testimony that, firstly, does not inform and, secondly, is misleading or incorrect. Furthermore, the characteristics of such poor evidence are: 'poor preparation, lack of knowledge and experience, low level of thoroughness, and inappropriate use or misinterpretation of test results' (p. 120).

Advice for forensic psychologists, like other expert witnesses,[17] who wish to avoid the embarrassing and unpleasant experience of seeing their expert testimony being distorted and their professional reputation damaged, includes:

- Being very familiar with courtroom procedure, rules of evidence, and ways of presenting psychological data to a bench or a jury, as well as being aware of the conduct expected of an expert witness (Wardlaw, 1984:135, 137).
- Having well-prepared reports and other evidence and, if inexperienced, to undertake some training in how to best handle lawyers' cross-examining (Carson, 1990; Nijboer, 1995).
- Stick to one's own area of expertise and be explicit and open (Nijboer, 1995).
- Novice expert witness psychologists can also benefit from having in mind a number of criteria by which to judge their testimony when preparing for it (see Newman, 1994) and, equally important, to be familiar with what advice is given lawyers about how to cross-examine a psychologist (see Mulroy, 1993).

Regarding cross-examination, Wardlaw (1984) lists a number of rules likely to prove helpful for the witness. Inter alia, these include:

- Answer all questions and do not allow counsel for the other side to put words in your mouth. Don't make guesses and take as much time as you need to reply to questions.
- If under attack keep calm and avoid getting angry or unreasonably defensive.
- Prepare for the cross-examination by trying to anticipate the questions by imagining that you are the one who is to cross-examine.

In providing advice on the art of advocacy, Evans (1995) reminds his readers that even experienced expert witnesses have been known to 'just come apart like wet cardboard toys when actually giving evidence' (p. 72) and urges them to remember that 'nobody – not even the ultimate leader in the field –

knows everything about his subject' (p. 165). Mauet and McCrimmon (1993) are more specific in their advice on how to best cross-examine an expert witness. They suggest first to obtain from the expert admissions favourable to one's client, then to discredit unfavourable evidence and, finally, to impeach the expert him/herself (p. 203). The same authors list a number of cross-examination techniques, including:

- Build up the expert's field of expertise and then proceed to show that it is not directly relevant to the issue facing the court.
- Use hypothetical situations to show that the expert would in fact agree with your presentation of the facts of the case or to show that the expert's credibility is doubtful because of apparent rigidity against considering other possible interpretations of the fact at issue.
- Demystify the expert's apparent self-importance by obtaining from him/her definitions of technical terms in simple, everyday language.
- Cast doubt on the thoroughness with which the expert has obtained his results.
- Get the witness to admit that in the past other experts are known to have disagreed with him/her on the issue concerned (pp. 203–6).

7 Conclusions

The courts in the United States, Canada, England, Australia and New Zealand have opened the door to psychologists to testify as expert witnesses. In a number of areas (for example, psychological research on hypnosis), however, the courts have disallowed such evidence. The psychologist as expert witness has thus far had a luckier run earlier in the United States than in the UK, Australia, New Zealand or Canada, appearing in cases involving child sexual abuse (see Mason, 1991), child custody cases (Mulroy, 1993), the battered woman syndrome (Breyer, 1992), eyewitness testimony (Elliott, 1993; Kassin et al., 1994; Loftus and Ketcham, 1991).

The significance of the US Supreme Court's important judgements in *Joiner* and *Munho*, that followed in the wake of the *Daubert* decision in 1993, is dependent on American judges' ability to understand and implement crucial concepts in *Daubert*, but empirical evidence points to the contrary for the great majority of the American judiciary. This knowledge is a cause for concern.

Gudjonsson (1995:56) reminds us that empirical research by psychologists has influenced 'legal structures, procedures and case law' in the United States in such areas as eyewitness testimony, prediction of dangerousness, forensic hypnosis and lie-detection. Similarly, legal researchers in the UK have influenced the development of police procedures in interviewing suspects and the admissibility of expert testimony on whether a witness is suggestible (pp. 56–7). In addition, a number of cases illustrate increasing readiness by English courts to admit expert evidence by a psychologist on a broader range of issues, including eyewitness and earwitness identification, the battered woman syndrome, learned helplessness and the battered woman syndrome, than would normally have been allowed by a restrictive interpretation of the rule in the 1975 case of *Turner*. Unfortunately, an opportunity to reform the law of evidence in England regarding the admissibility of expert testimony by the Royal Commission on Criminal Justice (1993) (the Runciman Report) has been missed. Despite the fact that the Commission called for a greater opportunity for experts to educate tribunals of fact, its report (a) took a myopic view of the issue of court experts, and (b) by means of 'bizarre reasoning' – that such a move would 'lead to a confusion of roles and prevent the cross-examination of expert witnesses' – rejected a proposal for a Forensic Science Service that would be independent of both the prosecution and the defence and which would be appointed by the courts (Redmayne, 1994:157–8).

As far as Australian courts are concerned, by not admitting expert testimony by mental health professionals on the working of memory, pitfalls in identification evidence, the typical behaviour of children after they have been sexually abused, or how likely it is that a record of interview presented by police was in fact made by the defendant, they deny 'the assistance of specialist information possessed by mental health professionals which may provide insights into a range of matters germane to the proof of a defendant's guilt or innocence' (Freckelton, 1990:49). The need for evidence law reform in Australia at State level (as in NSW) cannot be overstated. Explicitly abolishing the common knowledge rule in the rest of Australia's jurisdictions, in the UK and New Zealand would be a significant first step in the right direction. One cannot but agree with Freckelton that, when a theory is sufficiently acknowledged by the experts in a given field to be reliable and characterised by scientific integrity, 'surely it is only arrogance and foolhardiness for the law to close its eyes to knowledge and understanding which is germane to its decision-making practices' (p. 65).

Despite the empirical evidence that expert testimony impacts on trial outcome, for those sceptical of the need for expert testimony in court, Sheldon and McCleod (1991) list three alternatives, namely: (a) making use of a psychologist's expert report on particular legal issues pertinent to a trial to cross-examine witnesses; (b) introducing independent forensic psychologists as part of an independent forensic science service; and (c) providing lawyers with much-needed training in psychology. Writing about the judiciary in England, Thornton (1995) has also canvassed the need for judicial training in areas of forensic psychology. In the future, judgements in individual cases in England, Australia, New Zealand, but less so in Canada where there is a lesser need, may well significantly reduce current restrictions to the admissibility of expert evidence. This, however, is a process that is likely to take a long time. An alternative would be to let the tribunal of fact decide whether a particular case calls for expert evidence or not. Finally, parliament could codify the new limits of admissibility (Thornton, 1995:148). As Landsman (1995) has stated, 'a great deal is likely to happen during the next decade' in the domain of expert evidence (p. 157).

Revision Questions

1 What is the role in court of an expert witness in general, and a forensic psychologist in particular?
2 What does the term 'common knowledge rule' mean?
3 What is the gist of the US Supreme Court's unanimous decision in Daubert?
4 How do the subsequent judgements in *Joiner* and *Munho* modify the Daubert guidelines on the admissibility of expert testimony?
5 How valid is the assumption that American judges are capable of making judgements about the scientific reliability and validity of proffered scientific evidence based on adequate understanding of crucial concepts in Daubert?
6 What do you know about the admissibility of expert forensic psychological evidence in the United States, England, Australia, New Zealand and Canada?
7 Under what conditions does expert testimony by psychologists impact on trial outcome?

8 Persuasion in the Courtroom

'Appearing as an advocate in court is the most challenging thing a lawyer can do: it is the sharp end of lawyering and it calls not only for courage but a great deal of skill as well.' (Evans, 1995:vii)

'the feeling is [among practitioners] that the skills for the job of advocacy bear little or no relation to that knowledge most cherished by the law schools or by the Law Society's examining boards.' (Mungham and Thomas, 1979:174)

'Writing in a magazine in January 1889 Oscar Wilde ... complained that, with the possible exception of the speeches of barristers, lying as an art had decayed.' (Barnes, 1994:1)

'When a court hears two competing accounts about what happened it must choose between them. One account will be more persuasive than the other. But what makes it more persuasive? The facts are very important, though they need to be told in an interesting way, and the witness as storyteller needs to be believable.' (Selby, 2000:55)

Introduction

Law is a difficult course to get into at most universities. Being a practising lawyer confers social status in many countries and there is a strong tendency internationally to include judges on committees that are entrusted with important tasks in society. Such status seems to be synonymous with being a distinguished trial lawyer, a senior barrister in Great Britain and in the Commonwealth and, especially, becoming one of that elite group of Queen's Counsels who can command impressive fees. However, it should be remembered in this context that: 'The majority of cases are won or lost on their own facts despite the intervention of the finest advocacy' (Du Cann, 1964:183). Furthermore, there is also a popular perception of lawyers as liars and that enough skilled but unethical pleading by an advocate can see a patently guilty individual acquitted, causing a miscarriage of justice (p. 182).

A great deal of the perceived importance of the legal profession also comes from a perception of their main role as advocates and defenders of the innocent before the courts. Images of the lawyer as advocate, Mungham and Thomas (1979:170) pointed out, 'come down to us from reports and tales of the lives of the "great advocates" '.[1] In fact, many books on advocacy[2] give the impression that there has existed a 'golden age of advocacy' (p. 170), that the 'good old days' contain a lot of useful material for new and aspiring advocates and, finally, that 'things have changed' for the better for the novice advocate. However, Selby (2000), adopts a practical approach and explains the basic techniques of questioning in conference, in opening a case, and examination and cross-examination of witnesses, thus offering valuable advice on how to win in court. Since the 1970s a number of changes have taken place within society which have had an impact on lawyering. These changes include: the introduction of legal aid in many jurisdictions, which has expanded the practice of law and the concept of advocacy and has diversified the population of lawyers who appear in court; the increasingly heterogeneous population of law graduates; the introduction of formal teaching of advocacy; the introduction of State-initiated as well as community-based legal centres and mediation schemes; and, finally, the emphasis on conflict resolution rather than litigation. Since 'the myth that advocacy cannot be taught has been finally put to rest' (Hampel, 1993:xii), the system of pupillage for passing on advocacy skills has long been questioned and is rapidly being replaced by professional courses for barristers and solicitors in Britain (which, according to Evans (1995:vii), contribute to improving advocacy standards) as well as in Australia and New Zealand and for trial lawyers in the United States. However, as practising lawyers are not tired of telling us, the skills needed to be an advocate bear hardly any relationship to that knowledge valued by law schools and the organised profession's examining boards (Mungham and Thomas, 1979:174).

The image of the advocate in a higher court as the epitome of what most practising lawyers do most of the time has more to do with popular television shows than reality.[3] A significant proportion of law graduates end up not practising law and for the majority of those who do, the reality is they will never appear before a higher court to defend someone charged with murder, they will not have the services of an expensive team of other lawyers and trial experts, including one or more psychologists, and finally, in Great Britain, Australia and New Zealand, the average lawyer is unlikely ever to find himself/herself addressing a jury. For most 'young' lawyers, practising law means appearing in very busy lower courts in large urban centres where most defendants plead guilty to minor charges, where the main skill required of a lawyer is to know how to plea-bargain with the police and/or the prosecutor in crowded corridors, and where the blindfolded lady operates very routinely without much ritual and oratory preceding disposition by the bench, irrespective of whether the bench comprises two or more lay magistrates, more commonly known as 'Justices of the Peace' (as is the case in most Magistrates' Courts in England and Wales – see Kapardis, 1985), a stipendiary magistrate or a judge at a lower court. Lawyering means different things depending on whether one attends police stations (see Baldwin, 1994; Law Society, 1994), is dealing with private or public clients (Flemming, 1986), is a one-lawyer firm, or works within a small or a large law firm, as well as on whether one appears before a lower, higher or appeal court (see Glissan, 1991:149–57, on appellate advocacy) or a professional or non-professional court (see Evans, 1995:181–204), a juvenile court or, finally, whether one is cross-examining a social worker in the Family Court (see Moloney, 1986). A participant-observation study of a corporate law firm by Flood (1991) found that business lawyers are more involved in managing uncertainty for themselves and their clients and they do so through interaction with them rather than through appeals to the law. To place advocacy in perspective, it should be remembered that the average lawyer spends most of his/her time drafting or advising on a variety of documents before a trial can even begin, and not on advocacy (Du Cann, 1964:80).

Psychologists interested in researching advocacy need to address advocacy in context and to remember that winning a case is not objectively defined and can involve different strategies and outcomes in theory and practice. In an interesting study in Britain, Mungham and Thomas (1979) interviewed sixty solicitor advocates over a period of eighteen months and also carried out observations of Magistrates' Courts in session. They found that, if working within a large practice, solicitors would most likely have a heavy case load, would read briefs at the last minute, had to juggle appointments and negotiate adjournments, and would be rushing from one court to another. Such lawyers, whose criminal advocacy in Magistrates' Courts traditionally 'has had a low standing within the English legal profession' (p. 174), needed 'social skills and sheer physical energy' (p. 175) and would most often be called upon to argue questions of evidence rather than questions of law in contested cases. It can be seen that the concept of advocacy as the art of persuasion in the context of a trial at a higher court is too narrow and does not encompass the reality as experienced by the great majority of practising lawyers. For psychologists, a broader definition of 'advocacy' also means there is more they can offer the practising lawyer, including invaluable knowledge concerning interpersonal skills, negotiation and conflict resolution. In Britain the Law Society's (1994) training kit for legal advisers who attend police stations has been mostly written by Dr Eric Shepherd, a forensic psychologist who specialises in forensic interviewing techniques. It is not uncommon for a lawyer to know individual magistrates or judges, to be able to predict their sentencing, and adapt their advocacy accordingly.

Mauet and McCrimmon (1993:1–20)[4] point out that the need for lawyers to demonstrate their advocacy skills in the courtroom does not exist in a vacuum but is often the climax of a process that has included attempts to settle the case without going to court and the amassing of trial material. It should also be remembered that advocacy manifests itself against the backdrop of a great deal of ritual, what authors on advocacy term 'etiquette'. Such rules (see Evans, 1995:7–17; Glissan, 1991:1–19) are more evident in the higher courts and vary from country to country. In considering advice on advocacy skills the reader should also bear in mind that there are significant differences between countries. For example, unlike the United States, in Britain, Australia and New Zealand advocacy is very seldom conducted before a jury in a criminal trial and lawyers in Britain (where 'the civil jury has all but disappeared' – Evans, 1995:21) address the bench, the jury or the witness from behind the bar table and do not enjoy the freedom to move about the floor that is enjoyed by trial lawyers in the United States. Lawyers in these countries, for example, need permission from the bench to cross the floor and approach a witness in the witness box. Also, the form advocacy takes depends on whether a lawyer is arguing about evidence or on a point of law.

1 Defining Advocacy

'Advocacy' is defined in *The Oxford Companion to Law* (Walker, 1980) as 'The art and science of pleading cases on behalf of parties, particularly orally, before courts and juries. It requires a thorough appreciation of the relevant facts, a good knowledge of the law, persuasive presentation and argumentative powers'. For Mungham and Thomas (1979), however, there is 'no generally agreed upon definition of what constitutes "good advocacy"' (p. 176) largely because it is context-specific and subjective and this makes even a market test (that is, whether a lawyer retains his/her clients or not) untenable. For the same authors, in fact, in one sense all solicitors' work is advocacy (p. 189). A well-known English QC has written that the task of the advocate is to be 'argumentative, inquisitive, indignant or apologetic – as the occasion demands – and always persuasive for his client' (Pannick, 1992:1). A definition of advocacy is not considered problematic for Justice Hampel, a well-known Australian judge for whom 'Advocacy is the art of persuasion in court' (Hampel, 1993:xi). In the same vein, Glissan (1991) offers a more elaborate definition of advocacy, stating that: 'legal advocacy means the congeries of techniques which together make up the art of conducting cases in court … The art of legal advocacy is in part one of communication and in part one of persuasion … always remember they [the techniques] have to be varied (or ignored) according to time and circumstances and modified to suit one's own style' (p. 20). Such a definition makes it possible for an author to provide novice advocates with 'a small bag of tools to get you started' (Evans,

> Advocacy is the art of persuasion in court.

1995:205). The reader should also note in this context that eyewitness testimony can be described as a persuasive communication.[5] Advocacy books tend to follow the same approach: offer advice, often accompanied by examples (sometimes extracts from famous trials) on how to best approach the different parts of a trial (that is, the opening address, examination-in-chief, cross-examination, re-examination and closing arguments), as well as advice on courtroom etiquette. Du Cann (1964) reminded his readers that 'Part of the art of advocacy lies in its concealment' (p. 180). Glissan (1991) asserts that 'advocates are born not made' (p. 21). This rather brave assertion is contradicted by the example of one famous advocate, namely 'John Philpot Curran, cruelly hampered by a stammer, was unable to utter a word the first time he got to his feet in court. Yet he too rose to great heights, dominating the Irish courts' (Du Cann, 1964:46). Accepting a nature, rather than nurture, position on advocacy would also render any notions of training for advocates largely irrelevant.

The picture of the successful advocate portrayed in books on advocacy is a composite of natural talent combined with a range of skills and effective techniques. It should therefore come as no surprise to be told that the prevailing view among legal writers on advocacy is that persuasion in the courtroom is an art. Such authors, in effect, provide numerous assertions, some of them giving actual examples of good (and sometimes also bad) advocacy in practice in the higher courts. Such books do not, as a rule, contain empirical support, as such, for the assertions made, and consequently, do not advance their subject matter to the level of arguments. They do, however, provide psychologists with a large number of testable hypotheses. There is a need for psychological research into the types of individuals who, after opting to study law, go into practice, what characterises their advocacy in a broad range of sociolegal contexts, and how and why some lawyers come to be regarded by their peers as 'good advocates'. Such research could take the form of both a longitudinal study that follows a cohort of law graduates and also tests experimentally some of the assertions made by practising lawyers about persuasive communication in the courtroom and qualities said to characterise notable advocates.

2 Qualities of An Advocate: Lawyers Writing About Lawyers

Du Cann (1964:47) emphasises that eloquence is but one quality that is essential for an advocate, and provides aspiring young advocates with some food for thought when he reminds the reader that: 'The qualities essential to the successful practice of the art of advocacy cannot be acquired like pieces of furniture' (p. 46). He also considers it of crucial importance that advocates possess the right qualities (p. 183) and argues that failure to do so 'should arouse professional and public concern, for it is the lack of these which leads to incompetence and it is incompetence which leads to miscarriages of justice' (p. 183). What, then, are some of the basic qualities desired of a good advocate? In his book *The Seven Lamps of Advocacy*, His Honour Judge Parry (1923)[6] listed honesty, courage, industry, wit, eloquence, judgement and fellowship. For Lord Birkett (1962), however, 'presence' is the defining attribute of a successful advocate.

The qualities listed as essential by Du Cann are: honesty, judgement, courage, control of one's feelings, tenacity, sincerity and industry. Unlike Parry (1923), Du Cann does not consider wit a vital asset for an advocate. Those solicitor–advocates interviewed by Mungham and Thomas (1979:171–2) emphasised the following attributes: 'personality', 'projection', 'skills of persuasion', being able 'to take command of a court' and having a 'firm grasp of legal principle'. Glissan (1991:21) cites a number of qualities, mentioned in Munkman's book *The Technique of Advocacy* (1951, 1986), that should characterise an advocate: 'voice' (that is, 'A clear, distinct and interesting voice'), 'command of language', 'confidence', 'persistence' and 'mileage' (that is, experience). Finally, in addition to an advocate's acquiring preparation and technical performance skills, His Honour Justice Hampel (1993:xi–xii) considers the most important truth about advocacy is that 'a good advocate must be a good communicator'.

2.1 Qualities of an Ideal Defence Lawyer: The Client's Perspective

According to Boccaccini and Brodsky (2001:82), 'The right to the "effective"[7] assistance of counsel has long been recognised as an essential component of the right to counsel' which, in turn, is embodied in the Sixth Amendment to the US Constitution and extended by the courts. According to the same authors, research findings indicate that most prisoners are not satisfied with the services provided by their defence attorneys; prisoners represented by court-appointed attorneys are the most dissatisfied and, finally, legal training does not produce attorneys with the appropriate interpersonal skills (p. 94). Regarding the characteristics of an ideal defence attorney from the clients' perspective, Boccaccini and Brodsky investigated this issue with reference to the criminal defence lawyer in a survey of 250 prison inmates in Arkansas. They found that the respondents considered the most important attributes of an ideal attorney to be: 'loyalty' (in other words, 'a strong advocate for the client's best interests' (p. 98)), 'lawyering skills' (in other words, to be 'knowledgeable about the law and legal system, hard-working, and an effective deal maker'(p. 98)), and 'client relations skills' (p. 99).

The attorney–client relationship has become even more problematic for lawyers because it is no longer considered sacrosanct, and the attorney–client privilege (the oldest of the privileges for confidential communication known to the common law) is not a shield that protects both the client and the attorney; in fact, a number of court decisions in the United States (for example, *United States v. Cueto*, 151 F.3rd 620, 624 (7th Cir. 1998), 'mean that an attorney must act, from the beginning, as though his client is presumed to be guilty and he is presumed to know it' (Silets and Overbey, 2000:78).

3 Effective Advocacy: Some Practical Advice by Lawyers

'Contests, including court contests, are about winning and losing. Just as a game, be it a sport or cards or chess, requires skill and preparation (along with an element of luck), so the outcome of any court case reflects the quality of the preparation and the quality of performance in the court ... Hence all litigation should be seen as requiring a game plan and the skill to carry out the agreed tactics' (Selby, 2000:xii).

As Bartlett and Memon (1995) remind us, 'The importance of advocacy in court is a consequence of the trial system, particularly in adversarial proceedings which dictate that the parties are in opposition to one another: the defence seeks an acquittal; the prosecution proposes conviction. In a civil case the plaintiff seeks compensation or a special order and the defence seeks to avoid this and/or make counter-claims' (p. 544). Unlike continental European systems, the role of the judge in adversarial proceedings is deliberately kept to a minimum.[8] The way many authors have approached the question of what constitutes effective advocacy, in other words a persuasive presentation by a lawyer, is in terms of what is said, by whom and how? (see below). The successful lawyer, therefore, needs to appear competent, honest and, most importantly, correct (p. 546). Bartlett and Memon draw attention to the importance of: (a) the lawyer using impression management tactics to ensure that his/her appearance will have the desired effect on the jury and magistrates; (b) his/her presentation is persuasive and the arguments put forward are convincing (see below); (c) refuting the opponent's arguments by presenting his/her witnesses as credible and those of his/her opponent as lacking in credibility (p. 546). How these goals can be achieved is detailed below.

3.1 Opening Address

Regarding a counsel's position and delivery during a trial, Mauet and McCrimmon (1993:37) emphasise maintaining eye contact with the jury and avoiding mannerisms and fidgeting so as not to distract the jurors. As far as the opening address is concerned, despite the fact that it can, and often does, play a key role in the outcome of cases it has been rather neglected by advocates, writers and researchers alike (Glissan, 1991:32). Regarding how the opening address is best delivered, Mauet and McCrimmon remind the reader that those advocates who can make the opening speech without using notes come across as confident and have a significant advantage over the other party (p. 37).

In trials in ancient Athens speeches by advocates were subject to a time limit, the same for both sides, measured by a water-clock known as 'clepsydra' (McDowell, 1978:249). Contemporary lawyers similarly agree that an opening address should be as brief as possible. Evans (1995:66) is specific about this – no more than ten minutes – because a short address is more likely to be remembered by the jury and the counsel will appear more confident (p. 66). Writing for advocates addressing a jury, Evans advises prosecuting counsel to also attract the attention of the jury and gain their sympathy, to present him/herself as an 'honest guide', to give the jury 'a few phrases to hold on to' (p. 66) and, finally, 'Above all talk to them and not at them' (p. 64). Mauet and McCrimmon (1993:31–7) offer a rather long list of suggestions they regard as essential if one wishes to launch a case 'on the right footing'. With one omission,[9] the following is their advice:

- State the facts and be clear.
- Be forceful and positive.
- Do not be argumentative.
- 'It is essential that your opening address is delivered smoothly, without interruption.'
- Do not state personal opinions and do not overstate.
- Personalise your client and depersonalise the other side so as to reduce the likelihood of jurors identifying with them.
- Use exhibits and develop the theory of your case.
- Volunteer a weakness which is apparent and known to the other side (p. 35).
- In the case of a defence counsel, consider whether to waive the right to make an opening address at the close of the plaintiff's or the Crown's case 'If a decision has been made to move for a non-suit in a civil case, or a discharge on the basis that there is no case to answer in a criminal case' (p. 37). There is disagreement among advocates as to whether one should end an opening address reiterating the facts or arguments on which the case is based or to bring home to a jury the importance of a single issue (Du Cann, 1964:78).

> The task of the advocate can be compared to that of a music conductor and, like music interpretations, advocacy styles must reflect current tastes (Selby, 2000:91).

3.2 Examination-in-Chief

While examination-in-chief 'has become an endangered species' in civil cases in Britain (Evans, 1995:124), if successfully conducted (that is, to present the facts of the case logically and forcefully), it will significantly influence the outcome of a case (Mauet and McCrimmon, 1993:59). Glissan (1991:39) states that the aim of examination-in-chief is to prove the various elements of one's case by adducing all relevant and material evidence before judge and jury that the witness can give about the case. It is, therefore, of paramount importance that the witness be the centre of attention during this stage of the trial and be perceived and remembered as credible (see also chapter 3). Consequently, advocates would do well to remember that the credibility of a witness does not evolve around how eloquent the advocate is as a speaker and, also, that it is the strength of the case-in-chief which is more likely to determine whether one side will win the case or not rather than weaknesses in the case presented by the other side (Mauet and McCrimmon, 1993:59–60). Before commencing to elicit evidence from a witness in examination-in-chief an advocate should first consider a range of preliminary questions, such as the issues which must be proved, how many and which witnesses to call and in what order.[10] Glissan maintains that whereas one can be taught how to cross-examine witnesses effectively, conducting an examination-in-chief calls for a 'natural talent' which is in rather short supply (p. 45). Mastering this difficult art of conducting an examination-in-chief, however, is considered by Glissan a precondition if an advocate is to really establish him/herself as a trial lawyer (p. 45). Interestingly, Glissan considers the art of examining witnesses almost a lost art.

Mauet and McCrimmon (1993:59–127) provide a comprehensive account of a long list of elements deemed important to an effective examination-in-chief, also illustrating with examples. Briefly stated these elements are:

- Keep the examination simple and elicit evidence from the witness in a logical sequence.
- Get the witness to first provide detailed information about a scene and then about what took place.
- Proceed with the examination at varying speed as deemed appropriate for the issue in question.
- Do not lead the witness but ask open-ended questions to encourage the witness to give descriptive and narrative accounts.
- Only ask leading questions about matters that are not being disputed.
- If confusion arises, get the witness to clarify it at once.
- Ensure the witness is the centre of attention throughout.
- Pay attention to your own witnesses during the examination as well as to the witnesses of the other side during cross-examination (see below).
- Use a variety of exhibits effectively.

An interesting question for lawyers handling compensation cases has been addressed by Green et al. (1999). Their subjects were 122 jurors waiting to be called for *voir dire* at a local courthouse who were asked to decide in twenty-two juries the amount to be awarded in an employment discrimination case. The researchers varied whether damage awards should be presented by: (a) the plaintiff's lawyer; (b) the plaintiff's expert economist; or (c) both the plaintiff's and the defendant's expert economist. It was found that juries awarded more in damages when they heard testimony from the plaintiff's expert witness than by the plaintiff's lawyer who argued for the same amount of money. However, caution is warranted in accepting their finding because, as Green et al. themselves admit, the small number of juries in their study preclude finding significant differences between different conditions and, consequently, their findings are tentative (pp. 111, 120).

When a witness has been examined by the party who produced him/her (after first being sworn or affirmed) the other party or parties each cross-examine him/her in turn.

3.3 Cross-Examination

'Because cross examination is such an overt exhibition of control over the witness it is necessary to display that control throughout the questioning, and especially in the opening and final questions' (Selby, 2000:135–6).

Mauet and McCrimmon (1993) maintain that the term 'cross-examination' 'still commands respect ... no other area of court work generates as much uncertainty, or is shrouded in as much mystery', and that: 'Texts on the subject often point out that cross-examination is an "art" or "an intuitive skill"' (p. 163). Regarding the question of what cross-examination is, Du Cann (1964:95) cites Lord Hanworth's, Master of the Rolls, statement that: 'Cross-examination is a powerful and valuable weapon for the purpose of testing the veracity of a witness and the accuracy and completeness of his story'. Du Cann also cites Lord Macmillan's (1952) view that when 'properly used' in a court in England cross-examination 'is the finest method of eliciting and establishing the truth yet devised' (pp. 95–6). Put simply, the aim of cross-examination is to elicit evidence favourable to one's side and to cast doubt on the credibility of the witnesses of the other side. To achieve this twofold aim, Mauet and McCrimmon (1993) advise that a cross-examination should be carried out according to a predetermined structure of questioning that is logical as well as persuasive (pp. 166–7). The same authors provide a number of rather useful questions advocates should ask themselves before embarking on a cross-examination in order to think clearly and to minimise risks inherent in this part of the trial (pp. 163–4).

Evans (1995:149–50) lists four objectives of cross-examination: laying the foundation; putting your case; eliciting extra and useful facts; and discrediting the evidence. He does remind advocates, however, that they are to discredit the evidence, not the witness. One way of discrediting the evidence mentioned by Evans is by 'driving the wedge', that is, by eliciting inconsistent answers from two witnesses, a task that should not be very difficult given the limitations of eyewitness testimony discussed in chapters 2 and 3. Mauet and McCrimmon (1993) indicate that a witness' evidence can be discredited in cross-examination by casting doubt on their perception, memory or their ability to communicate.

A number of general, specific and cautionary rules to provide the advocate with some guidance in how to best carry out a cross-examination are outlined by Evans (1995:137–41). The general rules are: be kind to the other side's witnesses; every question must have a specific purpose; do not ask witnesses questions in a hostile manner but in a spirit of enquiry; do not look to a witness for assistance; and always try to give the impression that you are succeeding in your task. Evans' specific rules for the advocate (pp. 140–1) are: ask precise questions; avoid composite questions; and ask short questions that will elicit short and specific answers, thus enabling control of the witness. The cautionary rules (pp. 141–2) are: do not ask a question unless you know what the answer will be (p. 141); 'Do not suddenly draw back with a start' (p. 142); and, finally, 'ride the bumps' (p. 142). Du Cann (1964), Evans (1995), Glissan (1991) and Mauet and McCrimmon (1993) all agree that when cross-examining, an advocate would be rather unwise and seriously risk losing the case to ask the witness a leading question.

Mauet and McCrimmon (1993) also furnish advocates with guidance on how to structure and conduct a cross-examination that is similar in many respects to what Evans (1995) provides. They do, however, also emphasise the principles of primacy and recency (that is, making one's strongest points at the beginning and at the end because this is what the jury will most likely remember). The primacy effect is well documented in social psychology (Schneider, 1995:45). This basically refers to the phenomenon that the first information we get about others is more important than information we get later. Mauet and McCrimmon also advise varying the order of the subject when cross-examining and, in contrast to Du Cann (1964:128), draw attention to the importance of an advocate projecting a confident, commanding attitude but in a natural way and, finally, they stress the importance of maintaining eye

contact with the witness. Whilst some legal writers disagree about the importance of an advocate's style during cross-examination, as discussed below, the
advice on keeping control of the witness by asking short precise questions is
at variance with what has been reported by O'Barr (1982). Concerning the
allegedly misplaced importance on style, Du Cann blames authors of legal
biography who eulogise 'the subjects of their work [for] their virtues and not
their questions' and is in no doubt that what matters is effect; that, in fact, 'the
possession of a particular style can be a distinct handicap' since style is not
adaptable, and adaptability is the most essential quality for the advocate who
has to cross-examine people from very diverse backgrounds (pp. 128–9).

3.4 Re-Examination

At common law, after a witness has been cross-examined the party who has
examined may re-examine about matters raised in cross-examination or about
other matters with leave from the judge (Glissan, 1991:109). Glissan gives the
aim of re-examination as 'to explain, to complete any matter left incomplete,
and to countervail the damaging effect of the cross-examination' (p. 110). As
re-examination 'must be prepared "on the run" ' (p. 118), Glissan suggests that
an advocate should first consider whether there is a real need to re-examine at
all because of risks involved, and if re-examination is deemed necessary, to do
so aiming to 'mend fences, not holes' and to avoid letting in material that will
enable the other party to cross-examine the witness again (p. 119). Evans
(1995) advises advocates to take advantage of the opportunity and to go ahead
and re-examine a witness in cases where, during examination-in-chief or
cross-examination (at the discretion of the judge for the latter), evidence was
adduced that was inadmissible (pp. 173–6). Mauet and McCrimmon (1993)
argue strongly against the view that an advocate should always re-examine and
ask the witness at least one question so as to have the advantage of having the
last word and show this belief to be an unsubstantiated myth (p. 124).

3.5 Closing Speeches

Following re-examination, each party in a trial has a last chance to address and
communicate directly with the jury (or the presiding judge or magistrate/s if it
is a non-jury trial), in a last opportunity to provide a convincing argument for
why they should accept the case as presented by one side rather than the other
(see Mauet and McCrimmon, 1993:211–45; Glissan, 1991:130–48). Mauet
and McCrimmon point out that the importance of closing arguments lies in the
fact that they 'are the chronological and psychological culmination of a trial'
(p. 211). Du Cann (1964) highlights the importance of an advocate's style
which, unlike in the cross-examination, plays a significant part in closing
speeches; more specifically, Du Cann maintains that 'A dose of good thump-
ing sarcasm, spiced with a short, sharp rhetorical question or two, has always
been one of the most effective weapons in the advocate's armoury' (p. 171).
For psychologists, of course, such a view remains an empirical proposition.

Additional guidance offered by Du Cann is that an advocate should first sum-marise the points of argument before dealing with each one separately, showing how the arguments fit into the facts and how they paint a more persuasive picture than the other side's arguments in order to have more of an impact on any tribunal (p. 176). To achieve the same goal, Mauet and McCrimmon provide detailed guidance on how an advocate should go about the closing argument, illustrating their suggestions with examples.

Mauet and McCrimmon urge advocates to:

- Use a logical structure and argue the theory of their case.
- Argue the facts and avoid personal opinions.
- Use exhibits and weave the judge's instructions into the advocate's argument.
- Use themes and rhetorical questions.
- Use analogies and stories and make the opening and closing points without referring to notes.
- Use understatement as well as overstatement.
- Argue strengths (that is, argue one's own strengths, not the other side's weaknesses).
- Volunteer a weakness (this helps the jury to like the counsel and this is important because jurors are inclined to favour those they like. The advocate should ensure that the jury or the bench comes to like him/her and his/her client).
- Force the other side to argue its weaknesses, for example, by asking rhetorical questions.

4 Effective Advocacy in the Courtroom: Empirical Psychologists' Contribution

Trial advocacy is largely about argument-based persuasion. Advocates will be disappointed to find that while psychological research in this area has addressed Lasswell's (1948) question about 'who says what in which manner to who with what effect' (p. 37), it 'has not produced "laws of persuasion" in the form of general relationships between particular independent variables and amount of persuasion' (Jonas et al., 1995:11). Psychologists have therefore concentrated on identifying the processes underlying persuasion and have put forward a number of models (see Jonas et al., 1995, for a discussion). Drawing on Jonas et al.'s discussion, it can be said that such models emphasise the importance of systematic processing. McGuire's (1972) information-processing model suggested that persuasion requires the following processes: presentation, attention, comprehension, yielding (or acceptance), retention and behaviour (Jonas et al., 1995:12). Thus, this model highlights the import-ance of an audience having the intelligence to understand the content of a message in order to be persuaded. The message for advocates here is to tailor the complexities of their arguments according to the apparent intellectual abilities of the jurors.

The cognitive-response model stresses the importance of a message evoking favourable thoughts for the recipient in order for it to be persuasive (Petty et al., 1981). According to Jonas et al. (1995), more recent theories of argument-based persuasion maintain that people often decide to accept or reject a persuasive message, not as a result of having thought about the message, for the motivation to do so is frequently not there, but on the basis of peripheral processes, including heuristic cues (Chaiken et al., 1989). Advocates, of course, have the task of attempting to persuade the fact-finder in a trial, knowing only too well that if their arguments are not well thought out and logically consistent, the other side will capitalise on it. Unlike persuasive attempts at changing people's attitudes in order to impact on their behaviour – as happens, for example, in television advertising and which is a paradigm that has attracted a great deal of research by social psychologists – a trial is often a dynamic persuasion contest where strategies and tactics are crucial. Relevant psychological literature is, in this sense, of limited practical use to the advocate. However, what is known about how a speaker's credibility is assessed is of use to the advocate.

Drawing on Aronson et al. (2002), Lloyd-Bostock (1988:37), and Zimbardo and Leippe (1991) and focusing on 'who said what to whom' (known as 'Yale Attitude Change Approach' – Aronson et al., 2002:224), the following factors appear to influence positively the credibility and persuasiveness of the source of a communication (message), namely:

- If it is perceived as being credible by virtue of being objective and having particular expertise in the matter at hand (Hurwitz et al., 1992; Petty et al., 1981).
- Supporting a position which is against one's own interest.
- If the person providing the communication is familiar to the audience or is similar to the audience in terms of social background and attitudes.
- If the communicator is likeable and considered physically attractive by the audience (Chaiken, 1979; Petty et al., 1997).

As far as the nature of the communication itself is concerned, people are more likely to be persuaded by messages that do not appear to be structured in an attempt to influence them (Walster and Festinger, 1962), and, also, it is best to present a two-sided communication (in other words, to argue for and against one's own position) if one is confident about refuting the arguments of the other side (Crowley and Hoyer, 1994). The psychological literature also supports the view that it is a good idea to admit weaknesses in one's evidence, thus 'inoculating' the jury or the bench against the possibility of the other side 'cashing in' on the weaknesses, and having variety in the channels of communication that are used to put a message across (Lloyd-Bostock, 1988:45–7). Other factors that may influence acceptance of a message include such characteristics of the audience as knowledge about the subject-matter of the communication (Wood, 1982) and pre-existing attitudes towards it (Lord et al., 1979). The psychological literature endorses the advice given advocates to deliver a logically-structured speech in a forceful style (Petty and Cacioppo, 1984) and to maintain eye contact with their audience (Mehrabian and Williams, 1969). Finally, a fast speech rate has also been shown to correlate with persuasion (Miller et al., 1976).

Jurors themselves or the judge or magistrate/s in a non-jury trial, like ordinary members of the public, have techniques for resisting persuasive communication by witnesses or by counsel. According to Avery et al. (1984: 406–7), such techniques include: selective attention (that is, tuning out when not wanting to hear a given communication); rejecting a communication outright (that is, a 'blanket rejection' such as 'rubbish!'); distorting what is being communicated (for example, misperceiving a message as more extreme than it really is and hence it is not worth thinking about); discrediting the source (for example, during jury deliberation a juror attacks what defence counsel said about the defendant by claiming to the rest of the jury that defence counsels are notorious for lying about their clients). Avery et al. remind us that 'Attitudes and beliefs can be surprisingly resistant to change' (p. 407).

Books on advocacy and training courses for trial lawyers reiterate the importance for advocates to plan in advance and structure the arguments they will put to fact-finders, whether a jury or the bench in non-jury trial. However, in considering advice on how to present arguments and evidence strategically, an advocate would be in some serious difficulty as to how to make best use of such advice, for every jury trial is unique. As Kadane (1993) so rightly points out: 'Attorneys will frame their arguments differently depending on who is on the jury and who they think will influence whom on the jury' (p. 233). Kadane's rather mundane but crucial observation would seem to 'throw a spanner into the works' of jury researchers and legal writers on advocacy alike, most of whom will most likely choose to ignore it!

Schum (1993) has reported interesting research into how arguments are structured and also how such evidence is evaluated by fact-finders. He has identified and examined two types of structuring: temporary (that is, one whereby 'its major ingredient is the believed ordering over time of events of significance to matters at issue' (p. 176)) and relational (that is, one which is meant 'to show how one's evidence items are related to these facts-in-issue and to each other' (p. 178)). Schum has found that it is not clear how people go about these two structuring tasks and how performing one impacts on the other (p. 189). In the light of this conclusion and the limited abilities fact-finders can bring to bear on large masses of evidence, Schum and his collaborators have been working on computer-based systems that will make easier the process of structuring arguments in rather difficult inferential problems involving large amounts of evidence (pp. 189–90).

Bartlett and Memon (1995) cite interesting ethnographic research by Bennet and Feldman (1981) concerning criminal trials in Seattle, which reported that trial protagonists rearrange, update, compare and interpret information utilising 'stories' (see also chapter 5). As far as closing speeches are concerned, it appears that how much time has elapsed between the prosecution's opening speech and the judge's summing up influences whether the fact that the prosecution which is first to make a closing address (the primacy effect) is believed more than the defence which is the last to make a closing speech (the recency effect) before the judge's summing up (Lind and Ke, 1985). This finding is of importance in view of the fact that sometimes a criminal or civil trial can last for weeks, months or even more than a year. Making it possible for the jury or the bench in non-jury trials to view a video of the prosecution's/complainant's opening address would seem to be one way of not disadvantaging some defendants/plaintiffs.

We have seen that while the advocate's language style is considered important in closing arguments, there is disagreement about its importance in cross-examination. At the risk of repetition, authors on advocacy, like the ones mentioned in this chapter, provide their readers with guidance about the different stages of a trial, in effect with lists of 'do's' and 'don'ts', accompanied with examples to illustrate. How useful such advice (for example, to control the witness in cross-examination by means of short, precise questions) is in practice can only be determined empirically. O'Barr (1982) reported a very interesting interdisciplinary field simulation study of language styles ('powerful' [direct, straightforward, assertive and rational – characteristic of American white male speakers], narrative, 'hypercorrect', and simultaneous speech) which were identified by analysing tape-recordings of actual trials. O'Barr subsequently found that subjects in experiments who had been presented with the same facts of a case rated male witnesses as more truthful and convincing if they spoke in a powerful rather than in a 'powerless' style (polite and marked, for example, by the frequent use of intensifiers such as 'so' and 'surely' and hesitation forms such as 'well' and 'you know') and generally perceived witnesses more favourably if they spoke in narratives. As might have been expected, witnesses were assessed less favourably (that is, less intelligent, convincing, and less competent) if they spoke in a 'hypercorrect' style (for example, speaking in rather formal English one is not accustomed to in order to impress and thus making mistakes in the process). O'Barr also found that advocates should not try to dominate the witness, as various authors on advocacy recommend (see above), nor should they try to dominate the witness by 'hogging the floor' significantly more than the witness, because they are likely to be perceived negatively by a jury. Drawing on Bartlett and Memon (1995), let us next consider a number of specific strategies a lawyer can use to discredit a witness, thus making it more likely that a jury or a bench of magistrates would be persuaded.

4.1 How to Make One's Witnesses Seem Credible and Thus Persuade Magistrates, Judges and Juries

A lawyer could use a number of strategic devices to make his/her own witnesses seem credible and, thus, more persuasive. They include:

- Encouraging them to use rather vivid instead of bland language.
- Increasing the saliency and impact of specific pieces of information by

getting his witnesses to repeat parts of their testimony or by calling a number of witnesses who reiterate the same crucial facts.

- Causing certain inferences to be made by asking witnesses questions involving some kind of direct or indirect presupposition (for example, 'Did you see the knife?' implies there was a knife involved).
- Asking his/her witnesses to describe details of an event he/she knows they can remember.
- Articulating his/her case that the defendant is guilty or innocent in probabilistic rather than in absolute terms.[11]

4.2 How to Discredit the Opponent's Witnesses

A lawyer could make his witnesses more persuasive by making the opponent's witnesses seem unreliable by:

- Asking the opposition witnesses questions concerning particular details they are unlikely to remember.
- Challenging the credibility of a witness by showing that he/she is incompetent and, consequently, likely to be mistaken.
- Challenging the credibility of a witness especially by showing that he/she is lying and cannot be trusted.
- Transforming a witness' mistake into a lie by capitalising on the unclear distinction between a lie and a mistake.

5 Conclusions

Various developments in recent years which have changed the practice of law do not seem to have impacted on the rather narrow way many legal writers conceive of advocacy as synonymous with lawyering in the higher courts nor, it should be said, have such developments impacted on how psychologists study persuasion as it relates to legal practitioners. This is not to deny the fact that for the minority of advocates who do appear in the higher courts there is ample advice on how to handle the different parts of a trial. A lot of the practical advice given, however, is generally in the form of assertions. The empirical social psychological literature on argument-based persuasion offers some useful findings for advocates. However, there is an obvious need for persuasion research done under forensically relevant conditions, as well as for guidance on advocacy skills for all those lawyers appearing in the lower courts and in a broad range of sociolegal contexts. As a corollary, legal psychologists should take up the challenge and test, under forensically relevant conditions and with a representative sample of lawyers' clients as subjects, the wisdom of advice given by legal writers about techniques of persuasion, both at different stages of a trial and in a variety of sociolegal contexts outside the courtroom. O'Barr's (1982) work is a limited indication that advice given to advocates on how to treat and question witnesses may well be misguided.

Revision Questions

1   What factors have influenced lawyering internationally since the 1970s?
2   From the clients' point of view, what qualities should a successful defence lawyer possess?
3   What is some basic advice for lawyers regarding the opening address?
4   What is some basic advice for lawyers regarding the examination-in-chief?
5   What should a lawyer avoid during cross-examination?
6   How should a lawyer go about the closing speech?
7   What advice could psychologists give lawyers as to how to be persuasive in court?

9 Detecting Deception

'Lies are everywhere. We hear continually about lying in public and private life. Very few people would claim never to have told a lie, and even fewer would say they have never been duped by a liar.' (Barnes, 1994:1)

'Human beings hate to be deceived. It makes us feel violated, used and stupid ... The intellectual and moral traditions of Western culture have been shaped and driven by an explicit and consistent fear of deception ... but ... without such lies humanity cannot survive.' (Rue, 1994:4–5)

'Not every deception involves emotion, but those who do may cause special problems for the liar. When emotions occur, physiological changes happen automatically without choice or deliberation.' (Ekman and O'Sullivan, 1989:299)

Introduction

A moment's reflection tells us that deception implies that someone intentionally does or says something in order to induce a false belief in someone else (Ekman, 1985; Miller and Stiff, 1993:16–31; Vrij, 2000:6). Miller and Stiff have argued persuasively that a useful approach to studying deceptive communication is to conceptualise it as a general persuasive strategy, that is, as a means to an end and not an end in itself. Others, however, advocate using a discourse-centred definition rather than the intent criterion (Bavelas et al., 1990). Deception, as old as human existence, is a social phenomenon that permeates human life, irrespective of context, or one's age, gender, education or occupation. The Internet provides endless opportunity for deception. 'Deception includes practical jokes, forgery, imposture, conjuring, confidence games, consumer and health fraud, military and strategic deception, white lies, feints and ploys in games and sport, gambling scams, psychic hoaxes, and much more' (Hyman, 1989:133). Similarly, the unfair 'manipulation' of securities markets by unscrupulous individuals or entities can: wreck the life of law-abiding investors by depriving them of their personal savings; cause public companies to collapse; impact adversely on the economies of countries with dire political consequences for governments (Pickholz and Pickholz, 2001:117).

Deception makes possible sale swindles and export scandals and can cause political scandals that bring about the downfall of politicians. Deception in the form of fraudulent reporting of research data and findings has been perpetrated by well-known scientists (see Humphrey, 1992) and routine use of deception in psychological experiments has increased in popularity and given rise to ethical debate (Fisher and Fyrberg, 1994). The use of an alias is a common practice among incarcerated offenders (Harry, 1986). Deception in the form of undercover operatives is standard practice by police and security services as is disinformation (see Marx, 1988; Wright, 1991).[1] In fact, 'Lying and other deceptive practices are an integral part of the police officer's working environment' (Barker and Carter, 1994:139). Lying is obviously necessary in covert policing and has been known to be tolerated by police when used to justify police practices or to ensure the conviction of a defendant who the investigators believe to be guilty. Barker and Carter cite the example of a Boston detective who committed perjury by 'inventing' an informant. Police lying, however, 'contributes to police misconduct and corruption and undermines the organisation's discipline system' (p. 150).

> Lying is ubiquitous in some cultures and abundant in advertising and politics, for example.

A lie is a statement intended to deceive (Barnes, 1994:11, citing Bok, 1978:13; Vrij, 2000:6) and is but one mode of deception. According to Barnes, lying is ubiquitous in some cultures and is abundant in such ambiguous domains as politics, advertising, bureaucracies, courts and the police (pp. 2, 35–54). In fact, lying has been shown by DePaulo et al. (1996) to be a frequent daily occurrence for people. DePaulo et al. asked college students and members of the public in the United States to keep a diary for seven days and to record details of their social interactions of at least ten minutes' duration, including all the lies they told during those interactions. They found that lying is a frequent daily event. Of their interactions with others, they lied 25 per cent in a day, 34 per cent over a week, they felt comfortable lying, were generally successful as liars and, finally, were detected by others only 18 per cent of the time. As to why people lie, the researchers reported five reasons: to impress others/avoid embarrassment/disapproval; to obtain an advantage; to avoid punishment; to benefit others; to facilitate social relationships. As far as gender differences are concerned, DePaulo et al. found that: (a) women are more inclined to tell other-oriented lies whereas men tell more self-oriented lies; and (b) women become more uncomfortable when they tell lies than do men.

Barnes (1994) points out that the meaning generated by a written statement may vary according to the context in which it is read (p. 166), liars often dupe friends rather than enemies (p. 166); in the twentieth century lying became more institutionalised and an established practice by elite liars (p. 167) but people today are more aware of the prevalence of lying, largely because public lying is often exposed sooner than in the past (p. 1). Barnes also reminds us that a spoken or written lie can consist of 'either true or false statements or statements that are partly true and partly false' and draws attention to the fact that the truthfulness and deceit of a statement 'refers to the intention of the liar, and not the actual state of the world' (p. 12). Finally, while the focus in everyday life and in the empirical literature is on the spoken or written lie, Vrij (2000) emphasises that one does not need to use words in order to lie and gives the examples of the athlete who fakes a foot injury after a bad performance without saying anything, and the taxpayer who intentionally does not report details of additional income in his/her tax return (p. 6). Even silence can be a means of deception as seen when we speak of 'pregnant silences' (Barnes, 1994:17). Taking deception to be an act involving at least two people, this chapter will not discuss self-deception.

The law generally defines a number of both criminal and civil offences that involve deception and provide for sanctions. Criminal offences include obtaining property by deception and obtaining a financial advantage by deception. The Corporations Law also provides for such offences as fraudulent trading. Making a false complaint to the police or lying in court, if found out, are criminal offences. Most countries also have consumer-protection legislation that prohibits deceptive advertising, while the use of deceit could render a contract invalid. Deception and its detection is, without doubt, a topic of great interest to psychologists, lawyers and law-enforcement personnel alike. Whilst deception offences are not responsible for people's paralysing fear of crime in big cities, the financial cost is astronomical. This chapter is concerned with lie-detection and in parts draws on Vrij (2000).

According to Hyman (1989): 'The early years of psychology's existence as an independent science offered the strong possibility of a psychology of deception' (p. 134). However, the rise and dominance of behaviourism in the United States at the start of the twentieth century left no room for associationist, mentalistic psychology and eclipsed the promising work of pioneers like Binet (1896), Dessoir (1893), Jastrow (1900) and Triplett (1900). The focus of these early deception scholars focused exclusively on demystifying conjuring tricks.[2] Despite the significance, the enormity and heterogeneity of deception, it is disheartening to find that we cannot, as yet, speak of a psychology of deception in the same sense as we can talk about a psychology of memory. No single, coherent framework has been put forward that can adequately account for the broad range of psychological issues involved in the plethora of deception contexts 'in terms of a coherent set of interrelated psychological propositions' (Hyman, 1989:143). As this chapter shows, most of the attention by psychologists has been focused on lying (see Ekman, 1985) and lie-detection, and detection can be assisted by drawing on sub-areas within psychology such as physiological, clinical, developmental, cognitive and social psychology.[3] Interrogation techniques are discussed in chapter 11 as an example of psychology's contribution to law-enforcement.

1 Paper-and-Pencil Tests

A survey by Harding and Phillips (1986) of ten west European countries found that in nine of them people ranked honesty as the most important quality they wished to pass on to their children. Having honest employees is vital to the success of business and the public sector alike. Not surprisingly, therefore, if an employee is found to have provided false information in their employment application/interview, he/she will often be dismissed. It is well-established in criminology that theft by employees costs both the private and public sector all over the world a great deal of money, sometimes resulting in the collapse of companies. There is, therefore, a big incentive for employers to try to screen out potential thieves among job applicants. This practice is very widespread in western countries. In the United States, the *Employee Polygraph Protection Act* (1988) prohibits the use of the polygraph (see below) in screening applicants for jobs except for local, State and federal personnel, members of the armed forces and the various secret services, security personnel guarding nuclear power stations, water supply facilities and those working in financial security businesses (Camara and Schneider, 1994). Since the Act was introduced there has been a lot of interest in what are commonly referred to as integrity or honesty tests. Such paper-and-pencil tests are used at the selection stage in an attempt to identify and minimise risks pertaining to employee theft, for example. In other words, they are said to be tests of potential employee trustworthiness (Goldberg et al., 1991).

Integrity tests are also used, though to a lesser degree, in post-employment investigations of employee misbehaviour such as theft. Whether it is used in a pre- or post-employment context, some authors assume that certain characteristics of individuals are stable over time and are useful in determining whether an individual is capable of dishonest behaviour (Sackett, 1985). Other authors, however, assume that situational factors are more important in understanding why people cheat and so forth, than are characteristics of their personality (Hartshorne and May, 1928). It seems unlikely that the person vs. situation debate will be resolved in the near future, a factor that would appear to undermine the future of integrity testing.

There are two main types of integrity tests: overt and personality-based ones. The former measure attitudes towards theft. Personality-based ones, on the other hand, are supposed to measure traits such as conscientiousness

(Wooley and Hakstian, 1992). Of course, paper-and-pencil tests are but one method of testing for integrity that can be supplemented with a face-to-face interview, applicant background checks or, finally, graphology (that is, handwriting analysis, see Ben-Shakhar, 1989). The predictive utility of graphology in the pre-employment context is rather doubtful (Murphy, 1995:223–4).

According to Camara and Schneider (1994:113), a survey of publishers of integrity tests carried out as part of the Goldberg et al. (1991) study by the American Psychological Association found that the constructs measured by twenty-four such tests were: counter-productivity (15), honesty (9), job performance (9), attitudes (8), integrity (6), reliability (4) and 'other' (12). The last category, inter alia, includes: absenteeism/tardiness, admissions of dishonesty and drug abuse, credibility, dependability/conscientiousness, emotional stability, managerial/sales/clerical potential, probability of short-term turnover, stress tolerance, and substance-abuse resistance. Bernardin and Cooke (1993) inform us that different overt tests contain an honesty subscale that is based on five universal constructs, namely:

1 Thinking about stealing more often than others do.
2 Being more tolerant to those who steal than other people are.
3 Believing most people commit theft regularly.
4 Believing in loyalty amongst thieves.
5 Accepting rationalisations for theft.

Bernardin and Cooke maintain that these five constructs exist in all the overt tests but different ones measure different areas in addition to honesty. The use of integrity tests raises questions about their reliability and validity and also broader questions about civil liberty concerns, such as one's right to privacy. The validity of integrity tests is very difficult to determine irrespective of whether one validates them against background checks, self-reports of dishonest acts, contrasting those who appear to be honest with persons known to have been dishonest by virtue of their criminal records or, finally, by carrying out before-and-after testing comparisons of a company's losses (Murphy, 1995:212–15).

Given the very wide use of, and the controversy surrounding, integrity tests, the US Congress Office of Technology Assessment (OTA) (1990) undertook a close and critical look at these tests, as has the American Psychological Association (APA) (Goldberg et al., 1991). Not surprisingly, perhaps, the two bodies used different levels of validity, focused on different studies and arrived at different conclusions regarding the validity and usefulness of such tests. The OTA concentrated on five predictive validity studies. The APA report provides a review of 300 studies covering a broad range of criteria of validity. The OTA report evaluated integrity tests against 'absolute levels of validity' (Goldberg et al., 1991:7) using a detected theft or a close approximation to it as their external criterion of validity. The APA report assessed test validity in comparison, for example, with structured integrity interviews. Finally, neither of the reports examined whether such tests accurately predict total job performance (Camara and Schneider, 1994).

The OTA concluded that integrity tests over-predict dishonesty. More specifically, it found that 95.6 per cent of people who are given such tests and fail are incorrectly labelled as dishonest. In fact, the mean average percentage in the five studies examined that was detected for theft was 3 per cent. Camara and Schneider (1994:115) cite studies that used self-reported data and found theft base rates from 28 per cent to 62 per cent (see Hollinger and Clark, 1983, Slora, 1989, respectively). Consequently (and not surprisingly, the cynics might retort!), it is not possible to reach any definitive conclusions about the predictive utility of integrity tests. Camara and Schneider (1994:115) identify three major difficulties in evaluating integrity tests:

1   There is no consensus on what is meant by integrity.
2   There is an over-reliance on cut scores without the standard error of measurement and overlapping score ranges being reported.
3   Publishers are unlikely to encourage independent research into their integrity tests.

Camara and Schneider (1994)[4] conclude that: 'there is general agreement that integrity tests can predict a number of outcomes to employers and that they have levels of validity comparable to many other kinds of tests used in employment settings' (p. 117). Murphy (1995) lists the following caveats to the conclusion that integrity tests are useful: definition of integrity is problematic; the distinction between personality-based tests of integrity and other personality tests is not clear-cut; not informing examinees of integrity test scores when they are unsuccessful in their job applications poses serious ethical problems; from a psychometrician's point of view, the scoring procedure of some integrity tests is a cause for concern; and, finally, while integrity tests may help to identify high-risks among applicants they are not useful in screening the very honest individuals (pp. 215–17). Camara and Schneider (1994) remind the reader that legislation and the judiciary may one day decide what becomes of paper-and-pencil tests in general, be it personality or pre-employment tests, and that 'psychologists should wilfully participate in such public policy debates' (p. 117). One of the debates concerns the question of whether integrity tests should continue to be used in the employment setting in light of their limited predictive utility and invasion of an individual's privacy (see Stone and Stone, 1990).

2   The Social Psychological Approach

The demeanour of witnesses is relevant in judging their credibility in British courts (Stone, 1991:822): 'Hence, appeal courts are reluctant to interfere with decisions on veracity by the trial courts which saw and heard the witnesses' (p. 822). Apparently, the distinguished English judge, Lord Devlin, unlike many of his brethren on the bench, did not have much faith in his ability to determine whether a witness was lying from his demeanour (Stone, 1991:828). Of course, the judiciary is not alone in believing that lying can be detected from a person's demeanour (that is, verbal and non-verbal communication) – the general public and many leading psychologists share the same belief.

In an article in the *Police Review* Oxford (1991), a serving detective in Cambridgeshire, England, had enough confidence as a 'human polygraph' to offer advice regarding both non-verbal and verbal cues to deception, which included delayed responses and the use of phrases such as 'If I remember correctly' and 'Now let me see'. Alas, the provider of this advice betrays a rather dangerous assumption that the majority of suspects routinely lie when questioned by the police.[5] But is such confidence in one's ability to distinguish the innocent but nervous individual (who has just been brought to a police station for questioning) from the guilty suspect on the basis of verbal and non-verbal cues to deceptive communication justified in the light of the existing empirical literature? Can 'human polygraphs' achieve the high deception-detection accuracy claimed by Oxford (1991)? As this chapter shows, people generally have a grossly exaggerated belief in their abilities to detect lies in what others say and there is lack of concern about false positive errors of judgement in this context (Vrij, 2000).

> People generally have an exaggerated belief in their abilities to detect lies in what others say and there is lack of concern about false positive errors of judgement in this context (Vrij, 2000).

2.1 Beliefs About 'Lying Behaviour'

People's apparent inability to discriminate reliably between truth and deception utilising non-verbal cues seems partly attributable to their beliefs about 'lying behaviour'. Akehurst et al. (1996) used a 64-item questionnaire to survey police officers and laypeople in southern England regarding their own as well as other people's beliefs about correlates of lying. They found that: (a) people believed that such non-verbal behaviours as arm and leg movements and self-manipulations (stroking the back of the head, touching the nose, stroking or straightening the hair, pulling at threads of clothing) increase when a person is lying when, in fact, the reverse happens (see below); (b) there were no significant differences between the beliefs of laypeople and police officers; (c) there were no significant differences between the beliefs of those who had read literature on deception and those who had not; and, finally, (d) people were more accurate regarding their own than other people's lying behaviour (pp. 367–70). Similar findings have been obtained in Spain by Garrido and Masip (2001). Vrij and Semin (1996) investigated the relationships that police, detectives, patrol officers, customs officers, prisoners and prison guards believed existed between sixteen non-verbal behaviours and deception. Police officers were found to have the same, stereotyped and inaccurate beliefs about non-verbal cues to deception as non-police. Interestingly, the correctness of prisoners' beliefs was significantly higher than any of the other five groups, which did not differ significantly.

Finally, it should be remembered in this context that when a police officer interviews a witness or a suspect, he/she has some kind of preconception as to this person's credibility. Furthermore, a naïve and credulous attitude towards a witness by police have caused miscarriages of justice (see, for example, Wagenaar et al., 1993). Granhag and Stromwall (2000) investigated how observers' (125 undergraduates in Sweden) judgements of deceit or truthfulness were affected by different types of background information presented before they watched a videotaped testimony. They found that: (a) those observers who received crediting background information showed a pronounced truth-bias, whereas those who received discrediting information showed a small lie-bias; and (b) those observers who made truth-judgements used significantly more non-verbal than verbal cues than did those observers who made lie-judgements; and (c), contrary to what other researchers have reported, there was high inter-observer disagreement regarding how a large number of cues to deception are perceived and used. Granhag and Stromwall's findings indicate that studies of people's beliefs about cues to deception as well as their ability to detect deceit should also consider the important role played by one's preconceptions, the most common type of which is suspicion.

2.2 Non-Verbal Cues to Deception

A number of different feelings may accompany deception, including detection apprehension and detection guilt. Some categories of individuals may well feel no guilt about having to lie to conceal their deceptive communication. Persons diagnosed with antisocial personality disorder (previously termed psychopathy) lack remorse and shame (Hare, 1970). Many diplomats are well versed in the art of lying, as are hardened career criminals. However, for many people, lying is stressful. Strong deception guilt undermines attempts at lying because it produces non-verbal leakage or some other clues to deception (Ekman and Friesen, 1972). To choose when to feel emotions and to control whether others become aware of them is a most uncommon skill possessed only by the most accomplished of actors.

Deception, of course, may be accompanied by detection apprehension. Ekman and O'Sullivan (1989:305–6) list the following conditions that increase detection apprehension. These are: when the person to be lied to has a reputation for being difficult to deceive; is initially suspicious; when the deceiver has limited practice or no previous success; is particularly vulnerable to the fear of being caught out; is not particularly talented; possesses no special skill at lying; when the consequences of being found out are serious, or serious punishment awaits the deceiver upon being found lying; when the deceiver has not much incentive to confess because 'the punishment for the concealed act is so great'; and, finally, the person being lied to gains no benefit from the deceiver's lie.

According to Vrij (2000:24–28), liars may experience the following three different processes during deception, but this does not mean that the presence of any of these indicators necessarily indicates deception:

1   The *emotional approach:* Deceit is associated with excitement, fear, guilt.

2   The *content complexity approach* maintains that lying can be a cognitive complex task because liars find it difficult to lie. This, in turn, will manifest itself in a number of cues to deception.

Of course, liars may well be aware of their emotions and difficulty in lying and try to conceal both. Thus, the third approach is known as,

3   The *attempted behavioural control approach:* liars try to behave 'normally', to make an honest impression.

As Vrij (2000:29) reminds his readers, 'The three approaches predict different and sometimes even contradictory behaviours during deception'. In the discussion of cues to deception that follows, a distinction is made between verbal and non-verbal (vocal and non-vocal) indicators. Let us first consider the non-verbal ones.

> Non-verbal behaviours that can be used to identify liars comprise vocal and facial characteristics and movements.

Since the 1970s there has been a proliferation of empirical studies of non-verbal behaviour and there is one specialist journal dedicated to this field of study. Drawing on Vrij (2000:33), non-verbal behaviours comprise three categories:

1   Vocal characteristics: speech hesitations, speech errors, pitch of voice, speech rate, latency period, frequency of pauses and pause duration.
2   Facial characteristics: gaze, smile and blinking.
3   Movements: self-manipulations, illustrators, hand and finger movements, leg and foot movements, head movements, trunk movements and shifting position.

A broad range of paradigms has been used by deception researchers to study the non-verbal and verbal leakage that normally occurs when people lie (see Miller and Stiff, 1993:39–49). These have included: uninterrupted message presentations, asking subjects to provide truthful and deceptive reactions to stimuli (known as 'reaction assessment') and implicating subjects in a cheating incident during an experimental task. The last paradigm is known as the 'Exline procedure' (Exline et al., 1970) and has the advantage of both producing deceptive behaviour not sanctioned by the experimenter and motivating deceivers not to get detected (Miller and Stiff, 1993:43). Few researchers, however, have integrated correlates of deception with deception judgement accuracy (p. 65).

Until relatively recently psychological studies of deception have tended to use college students as subjects who lie or tell the truth about liking or not liking their friends and who are sometimes offered trivial incentives to take seriously what they are asked to do in experiments. Such mock studies are generally very low on external validity, a far cry from the real world of deception detection in a law-enforcement context (Ekman and O'Sullivan, 1989).

Vrij (2000:34–5) surveyed forty-five studies of seven vocal indicators of deception (hesitation, errors, high-pitched voice, speech rate, latency period, pauses duration, frequency of pauses) and forty-four studies of ten non-vocal indicators (gaze, smile, self-manipulations, illustrators, hand/finger movements, leg/foot movements, head movements, trunk, shifting position and eye-blinking). He concluded the following about the majority of liars, in contrast to truth-tellers:

- They tend to have a higher-pitched voice, probably caused by stress.
- They pause for longer when they speak, probably because they have to think harder.
- In most studies they show an increase in speech errors and hesitations and a slower speech rate but some studies have found the opposite pattern. These inconsistent findings appear to be attributable to variations in lie complexity.
- They do not differ significantly as far as latency period (in other words, the period of silence between question and answer) and frequency of pauses are concerned.
- They tend to make fewer movements of their arms, hands, fingers, feet and legs, probably because: of lie complexity and/or they have to think hard in order to lie and neglect their body language and/or they become rigid and inhibited in their conscious effort to make an honest impression by avoiding such body language.
- Are not characterised by: gaze aversion, smiling, self-manipulation (in other words, scratching the head, wrists, etc.), shifting position and eye blinks.

According to Vrij (2000), the fact that lying is not consistently accompanied by certain non-vocal cues to deception may well be due to liars not being nervous during the experiments concerned or that some cues may be overlooked by researchers who do not, for example, use a detailed enough scoring system (p. 39). To illustrate, the studies surveyed by Vrij indicate that smiles are not related to deception. However, if a distinction is made between felt and false smiles (Ekman et al., 1990), a false smile – characterised by the absence of the action of the orbicularis oculi muscle which 'raises the cheek and gathers skin inwards from around the eye socket, producing a bagged skin below the eyes and crow's-feet wrinkles' and the presence only of the action of the zygomatic major muscle 'which pulls the lip corners upwards towards the cheekbone' (Vrij, 2000:39) – is shown to be associated with deception.

2.3 Verbal Cues to Deception

There is no verbal behaviour that is typical of lying.

Vrij (2000:104) mentions seven objective verbal characteristics, some of which are cues to deception, namely: negative statements, plausible answers, [unsolicited] irrelevant information, overgeneralised statements (for example, 'never', 'everybody', etc.), self-references, direct answers and response length. As in the case of non-verbal behaviour, these seven verbal criteria are assumed to be influenced by emotions, content complexity and attempted control but, alas, again, there is no verbal behaviour that is typical of lying (p. 103).

2.3.1 Emotion

Since there is no typical verbal behaviour (Vrij, 2000:103), the challenge is to decide whether someone is lying by analysing both what they say or avoid saying as well as how they say it. According to Vrij, liars who feel guilty and anxious when they lie they may give indirect answers to questions, or they may overgeneralise or will not explicitly refer to themselves. In addition, guilt and anxiety are negative emotions which may well make someone irritable and uncooperative, leading them to make negative statements (for example, 'I am not a crook' instead of 'I am an honest man'.[6]

2.3.2 Content Complexity

According to Vrij (2000:105), it can sometimes be difficult to lie to someone, resulting in statements that are short, are not plausible and, consequently, not convincing. Also, if someone is lying about having been somewhere, they will avoid referring to themselves.

2.3.3 Attempted Control

A liar may well try to conceal information about that which he/she is being asked by, for example, providing irrelevant information.

2.3.4 The Reported Importance of Verbal Cues

As Vrij (2000) points out, the number of studies into verbal cues to deception is limited. Examination of twenty-eight such studies revealed that 'short statements, indirect responses and answers which sound implausible raise suspicion' (p. 109) and, also, that liars make more negative statements and make fewer self-references (p. 109). Thus, people could become better at catching liars if they pay attention to the content of someone's speech. However, some liars are very difficult to catch. To illustrate, sales people, for example, can manage to produce truthful and deceptive statements that are not significantly different, as far as their verbal differences are concerned, presumably because they are very eloquent (DePaulo and DePaulo, 1989, cited by Vrij 2000).

The cognitive perspective on deception cues posits that producing a deceptive statement requires more cognitive effort than producing a truthful one (Cody et al., 1984), and results in a number of verbal cues such as number of specific references, and vocal cues to deception like how long one waits before answering a question and the number and duration of pauses. Unfortunately, research into verbal correlates of deception has reported contradictory findings. This unsatisfactory state of affairs is largely attributable to different researchers using different paradigms. A number of studies has found evidence supporting Yerkes and Berry's (1909) hypothesis that 'pauses are associated with lying'. Alonso-Quecuty (1992) reported that the number of pauses is greater in delayed false statements. Harrison et al. (1978) and Alonso-Quecuty have also found that false statements are longer (that is, have more words) than truthful ones.

Spanish researchers have shown that the cognitive interview differentiates reliably between true and false statements intentionally made by witnesses to a crime.

According to Miller and Stiff (1993:65), however, 'The most consistent verbal correlate of deception is the number of words in a response' and, compared to truthful statements, deceptive ones tend to be shorter, more general, to contain a smaller number of specific references about people, places and the sequence in which events took place and, also, to over-generalise using words like 'all', 'every', 'none', 'nobody'. Stiff and Miller (1986) reported a significant relationship between deception and a composite measure of verbal content consisting of the following interrelated factors: clarity, consistency, concreteness and plausibility of one's verbal response.

An interesting new approach to detecting deception has been reported by two Spanish psychologists. Hernandez-Fernaud and Alonso-Quecuty (1995) carried out experimental work aimed at differentiating between true and false statements by eyewitnesses who watched a videotape of a simulated incident involving attempted car theft and threatening behaviour against the car-owner and a witness. Student subjects were instructed to give a true statement of what happened or a false one (a fabricated version to exempt one of the robbers). Subjects were interviewed using the traditional interview (TI) technique used by the Spanish police or the cognitive interview (CI) technique (Fisher and Geiselman, 1992). It was hypothesised that: (a) truthful statements would be more accurate and contain more contextual and more sensory information; (b) false accounts would contain more references to cognitive processes; and (c) the CI would enable a greater discrimination between truthful and false accounts by witnesses than the TI. It was found that witness accounts of events, persons and objects were more accurate in the CI condition (see chapter 3). It was also found that: (a) true statements contained more contextual information and more sensory details than the false ones; and (b) the CI produced greater differences between truthful and false accounts than the TI by amplifying the differences between the types of account. Finally, Hernandez-Fernaud and Alonso-Quecuty reported that false statements did not differ from true ones in terms of number of references to internal information/processes (feelings, thoughts and opinions). These findings indicate the CI is potentially very useful to those social workers and police interviewing crime victims/crime witnesses – it not only produces significantly more accurate witness accounts but it also appears to differentiate reliably between true and false statements made intentionally by witnesses to a crime.

2.4 Humans as Lie-Detectors: How Accurate?

The available empirical literature shows that humans, though generally successful in deceiving others more often than not, are generally poor lie-detectors if they rely on everyday experience alone because they have not acquired sufficient specialist knowledge about how to go about detecting lies (DePaulo et al., 1980; Kalbfleisch, 1985);[7] in fact, the average detection rate across thirty years of research is 57 per cent (Vrij, 2000). Researchers have also found that: (a) it is not easier for adults to detect deception in children than in adults; and (b) adults find it more difficult to detect deception in girls than in boys (Granhag et al., 2001; Westcott et al., 1991). Furthermore, even professionals supposedly trained to be good at detecting deception generally turn out to be no better than ordinary folk. In an interesting field study, Kraut and Poe (1980) conducted mock customs inspections in which 110 volunteer subjects who were domestic passengers waiting for their departure from Hancock Airport in New York were randomly assigned to the role of a 'smuggler' or innocent passenger and asked to try and smuggle contraband past a US customs inspector. The contraband was a miniature camera, a small pouch containing white powder, and so on and the subjects had to hide it in their person. Subjects were offered a prize of $100 if they appeared honest. The questioning of passengers by the customs inspector was videotaped. Judges watched the videotapes and decided whether to search a traveller. Kraut and Poe found that travellers were more likely to be searched if they were young and lower class, appeared nervous, hesitated before answering, gave short answers, avoided eye contact with the inspector, shifted their posture and were returning from holiday trips. In other words, the decision to search a traveller was based on their comportment. Interestingly, the researchers also found that customs inspectors were no better at detecting deceiving travellers than were members of the public.

One context in which deception by criminal offenders would be expected to occur frequently is the parole interview. The average prisoner, most of whom recidivate and are returned to prison by the courts (Walker and Padfield, 1996:160) have every reason to want to try to convince their parole officer that they have been rehabilitated by the prison experience and truly intend to lead a law-abiding life upon early release. At the same time, the accuracy of judgements of honesty and deception by parole officers can have important consequences for the prisoners (continued incarceration vs release) and the offender's potential victims in the community. Porter et al. (2000) used truthful and fabricated video clips depicting an account of a highly stressful personal experience with parole officers from the Correctional Service of Canada, who had a mean of approximately twelve years of job experience, and undergraduate students. They had three groups: (a) one that received feedback on accuracy following each judgement; (b) one that was given feedback and information on empirically based cues to deception; and, finally, (c) a control group that received neither feedback nor cue information. They found that at baseline all groups performed at or below chance levels. However, all experimental groups became significantly better at detecting deception than the control group. The parole officers' degree of accuracy increased from their baseline of 40 per cent to 76 per cent as a function of the feedback/training provided; in other words, detecting deceptive behaviour is difficult but training can improve it.

In another interesting study, Ekman and O'Sullivan (1991) investigated the deception-detection accuracy of US Secret Service, CIA, FBI, and National

Security agents, armed forces personnel, federal polygraph examiners, robbery investigators, judges, psychiatrists, college students and working adults. They reported: (a) no relationship was found between one's confidence and deceit detection accuracy; and (b) with the exception of the secret agents (whose accuracy was 64 per cent), there were no significant differences between the members of the various law-enforcement agencies and the students. When occupational group was disregarded it was found that those who were accurate were more likely to use non-verbal or non-verbal plus speech clues to decide whether someone was lying than did inaccurate observers, who seemed to have relied on speech clues alone. Regarding explanations why members of the US Secret Service were better than the rest, Ekman and O'Sullivan allude to the fact that many of them had done protection work that involved guarding important government officials from potential attackers and such work may have predisposed them to pay more attention to non-verbal behaviour. Also, such agents would have had experience questioning people who threaten to harm government officials and tend to be truthful when answering questions. By contrast, criminal justice personnel would have had experience questioning people who would have good reason for lying, leading these law-enforcement personnel to form the view that most of the people they question are liars, resulting in over-prediction of deceit and low accuracy.

Vrij and Winkel (1993) in the Netherlands showed eighty male and eleven female detectives with an average of seventeen years' experience in the Dutch police video fragments depicting subjects who had been instructed and given a monetary reward to lie about whether they were in possession of a pair of headphones. The detectives had 15 seconds to make their decision and to also indicate their degree of confidence in so doing. Given that 92 per cent of them indicated they had a lot of experience interviewing people, they were found, predictably, perhaps, to be very confident in their assessments and to agree significantly with each other about who was lying and who was telling the truth. Alas, the detectives' accuracy was less than chance (49 per cent) and, in fact, they turned out to be as inaccurate as subjects in other studies without any experience in questioning suspects. Vrij and Winkel reported that the detectives based their judgement on six criteria: less public self-conscious-ness, untidy dressing, less smiling, more social anxiety, less co-operative behaviour and more hand and arm movements during the communication the detectives deemed deceptive (p. 55). In other words, they were apparently judging on the basis of stereotypes. The crucial finding here is that erroneous preconceived notions about the nature of deceptive behaviour impairs the ability to detect deceit by non-professionals and professionals alike.

Garrido et al. (1997, cited in Garrido and Masip, 1999:16) reported a study in which police recruits and undergraduates in Spain were shown two video fragments and judged whether a videotaped female was lying or telling the truth. It was found that police: had more confidence in their lie-detection skills than the students; irrespective of their experience in the job, their accuracy in detecting deceptive statements was no better than chance; they were no better than the students in lie-detection; and, finally, the police were the least accurate in identifying truthful statements, showing a lie-bias. The ability of fifty-two British uniformed police officers to detect deception was examined in an experiment conducted by Vrij and Mann (2001). Their experiment differed from previous similar experiments because of its high-stake lie scenario. The police were exposed to videotaped press conferences of people who were asking the general public to assist in finding their relatives or the murderers of their relatives. They had all lied during these press conferences and had been found guilty of killing their own relatives. The accuracy performance of the police officers concerned was no better than chance and was not related to their degree of confidence, age, years of job experience in the police or, finally, level of experience in interviewing criminal suspects. Finally, policemen were better at detecting deception than policewomen.

> Police officers using the 'indirect method' (Vrij et al., 2001) can distinguish truth and lies.

Very encouraging results have also been reported by a team of British researchers at the University of Portsmouth. Vrij et al. (2001) had thirty-nine police officers watch a videotape of a number of truth-tellers and liars being interviewed. In one condition the subjects were asked whether a person on the videotape was lying and in another (the 'indirect method') subjects had to indicate for each person they saw on the videotape whether that person 'had to think hard', thus focusing on the cognitive load shown to be experienced liars (Vrij et al., 2000). They found that: (a) when police officers were using the indirect method they could distinguish between truths and lies; and (b) only by using the indirect method did the subjects pay attention to the cues that were actual indicators of deceit. Vrij et al. concluded that the use of the indirect method to detect deceit has the potential to become a useful tool in lie detection in legal contexts.

Being able to make an accurate judgement about whether a child is lying in what he/she is communicating would be of great help to all those professionals who work with children – parents, nursery school and primary school teachers, social workers and police. Without ignoring the importance of age differences for children (for example, 3 vs 7 years) as far as the use of deception strategies is concerned, the available empirical evidence shows that adults believe they can detect reliably when children are lying. The fact is, however, that the performance accuracy of adults in this context is only slightly better than chance (59 per cent, reported by Westcott et al., 1991). Vrij and van Wijngaarden (1994) reported two experiments in schools in which students were shown videoclips depicting children (aged 5 and 6, or 8 and 9) giving either a true or a false report. Unlike earlier studies in this area, the children were completely visible, the false statement they made was their own decision (that is, they were not instructed to do so as in other studies) and the researchers also investigated the importance of children's social skills in successfully making a false statement. In support of earlier research both experiments found that, despite subjects' confidence, the accuracy rate was little better than chance – 57 per cent in one experiment and 58 per cent in the other against a chance level of 50 per cent. Vrij and van Wijngaarden also found that observers showed higher accuracy scores for younger than for older children. One possible explanation put forward by them for the observers' apparent inability to accurately differentiate true from false statements by the children is that their student subjects had not been trained in detecting false statements by children and they speculated that nursery school teachers or child psychologists who have more experience in dealing with children might be more accurate.

Their prediction has, in fact, been borne out in a study by Chahal and Cassidy (1995) who examined how accurately social workers in the final year of their training, trainee primary school teachers and student controls could detect deception in male and female children in videotapes that focused on the child's face in a close-up but also showed the child's upper body in another shot by a different camera. It was found that no group of subjects showed overall superiority in accuracy scores, but those subjects who were parents did significantly better than non-parents. One policy implication of the latter finding is that in real-life situations calling for decisions to be made about a child's allegations, more recognition should be given to the decision-maker having had real-life experience in dealing with children (p. 243).

Stone (1991) is in no doubt about the futility of attempting to decide in the courtroom context whether someone is lying by observing their behaviour and on the basis of their apparent anxiety or calmness (pp. 827–8). He concludes that 'There is no sound basis for assessing credibility from demeanour' (p. 829). Wellborn III (1991) surveyed the social science literature on the subject and concluded that demeanour evidence does not help in detecting deception or witness errors. Ekman and O'Sullivan (1989) suggest two ways to reduce making mistakes in detecting deceit when observing a person:

1 Take account of individual differences and base one's judgement on a suspect's observed behaviour.
2 Endeavour to become aware of one's own preconceptions about the suspect (p. 319) and to consider the possibility that a person may exhibit a particular emotion not because they are lying but because they are upset by being disbelieved (p. 320). This strategy should help one to avoid committing what Ekman and O'Sullivan call the 'Othello error', that is, that a person who is telling the truth under stress may appear to be lying.

Finally, the same authors provide a very useful lying checklist, containing thirty-eight questions to be considered in evaluating or checking a lie (see pp. 324–7).

The literature from a number of countries on both sides of the Atlantic indicates that people's (including law-enforcement personnel) inability to detect deceit at a level better than would be expected by chance is attributable to their erroneous stereotyped beliefs about cues to deceptive communication. Also, there is evidence that, while detecting deceit is undoubtedly very difficult, training and feedback can enhance detection skills (Porter et al., 2000). Finally, the use of the indirect method demonstrated by Vrij et al. (2001) appears very promising and warrants further testing in the field.

3 Physiological and Neurological Correlates of Deception

3.1 Voice Characteristics: The Psychological Stress Evaluator

A person who is lying tends to have a higher-pitched voice than a truth-teller because of stress. Such differences are usually very small (only a few hertz) and can only be detected with sophisticated equipment. Mention has already been made that: (a) people believe deception is associated with an increase in speech disturbances (Akehurst et al., 1996); and (b) there is empirical evidence that liars make more speech hesitations and speech errors (compared to truth-tellers) when the lie is cognitively difficult and, also, make fewer speech hesitations (compared to truth-tellers) when the lie is easy (Vrij and Heaven, 1999). We have also seen that changes in voice pitch have been reported as a correlate of deceptive communication. The Psychological Stress Evaluator (PSE) has been a commercially available instrument which its advocates claim detects and records low frequency stress changes in the voice (Horvath, 1979). The stress changes result in micro-tremors in the vocal muscles which the PSE is said to detect. The voice sample is recorded and played back at reduced speed to the PSE which plots a graph of the speech (Brenner et al., 1979). One obvious advantage of the PSE over the polygraph (see below) is that (if we accept what its supporters claim) it can be used to detect lying without the person physically being there or being hooked up to any machine. Thus, it could be used while someone is speaking on the phone, or it can be used to examine a tape-recorded or video-recorded message and, furthermore, it can be used to analyse sentences and statements, not just 'yes' and 'no' responses. These potential uses sound very impressive but what do we know about its accuracy in identifying lying?

Brenner et al. (1979) used two conditions (stressful situations), one involving an arithmetic problem and the other the guilty knowledge task. The subjects in the guilty knowledge task were motivated to conceal the correct answer. The accuracy of the PSE was no better than chance in the guilty knowledge task, casting serious doubt on its ability to accurately detect lying. PSE detection rates not exceeding chance level were also reported by Horvath (1979) and Hollien et al. (1983). The research mentioned can be said to be limited due to low external validity but, according to Podlesny and Raskin (1977), negative findings about the PSE were reported by researchers utilising a mock-crime situation and a sample of criminal subjects. The available limited empirical evidence does not support the claims made about the PSE as a reliable means of identifying lying through voice-stress analysis (Bartol and Bartol, 1994:259). The possibility of using the PSE without a court warrant and without someone being aware of it raises serious ethical questions about its use.

3.2 The Polygraph/Lie-Detector

As most people know, anxiety is normally accompanied by physiological changes – sweating, dryness of the mouth, the heart beating faster. The belief that most people feel anxious when lying and this, in turn, is betrayed by measurable physiological changes, is as old as human existence itself, it is widely held today and forms the basis of the polygraph lie detection method. In one English police force a detective superintendent has been advising his officers attending training courses that when questioning suspects they should look out for useful cues to lying like getting uncomfortable and fidgeting and, more importantly, to observe when their blood pressure builds up to a level that the veins in their necks start protruding.[8] Noticing that when a person is anxious or afraid they do not salivate resulting in mouth dryness, the ancient Hindus would give a suspect rice to chew and spit it out. Failure to do so was taken as evidence of guilt (Harnon, 1982:341). The assumption that when people lie is evidenced in physiological changes which they do not control underpins the polygraph test for detecting deceit. The idea that changes in blood pressure and pulse accompany lying was first put forward by the pioneer Italian criminologist, Cesare Lombroso, in the nineteenth century (see Palmiotto, 1983). The polygraph itself has been available for about eighty years now. It was in use a number of years before the publication of Larson's (1932) *Lying and its Detection: A Study of Deception and Deception Tests*.

3.2.1 Expert Evidence on the Polygraph

Regarding the admissibility of expert evidence on the polygraph, according to Freckelton and Selby (2002:201), there has been no reported judgement on the use of the polygraph by a superior court in England, US, Australia, New Zealand or Canada. In the United States the preponderance of authority (for example, *People v. Lippert*, 466 NE 2d 276; 47 ALR 4th 1183 (1984 5th Dist); *State v. Kersting*, 623 P 2d 1095 (1981); *Castillo v. State*, 739 SW 2d 280; cert den and app dismd 487 US 1228 (Tex 1987), cited in Freckelton and Selby, 2002:201) is against the admission of polygraph evidence. However, the New South Wales District Court in Austalia in *R v. Murray* ((1982) 7 A.Crim.R 48), admission of expert evidence on behalf of an accused person was rejected on the basis of the common knowledge rule (see chapter 7). In Canada, in *R v. Beland* ((1987) 4 DLR (4th) 641 at 655) the majority of the court rejected admission of polygraph testimony on the grounds that it ran counter to well-established rules of evidence and its admission would serve no purpose which was not already served. Freckelton and Selby conclude that it is likely courts in Australia and New Zealand will follow the sound reasoning in the Canadian case of *R v. Beland* as to the admissibility of expert evidence based on polygraphy.

The polygraph basically measures changes in: (a) blood pressure; (b) electrodermal activity (that is, the galvanic skin reflex (GSR)); and (c) respiration. The polygraph has been traditionally used in criminal investigation, employment screening, and for security screening (Office of Technology Assessment, 1983). The GSR refers to the electrical resistance of one's skin, especially that on the palm or other hairless surfaces. The GSR varies with the activity of the sweat glands and is a convenient measure of sympathetic activity. Use of the polygraph in the US is provided in the *Employee Polygraph Protection Act* (1988). The polygraph is not used in a number of countries such as Australia, the Netherlands, the UK (except by the security service – see Russell, 1986), Germany and France but it is used in a number of countries in addition to the United States, namely Turkey, Israel, Canada, South Korea, Philippines, Taiwan, Thailand, Japan (Barland, 1988) and Poland (Wojckiewicz, 2001). In the United States, where the federal government's Department of Defence Polygraph Institute trains 100 new federal examiners each year, and where such evidence is admissible in court in thirty-two of the fifty States (see Honts and Perry, 1992), the polygraph is widely used by law-enforcement agencies as an investigative tool to verify witness statements, to clear suspects and to provide leads for interrogations (Honts and Perry, 1992). The polygraph can also be used by criminal suspects wishing to convince the police of their innocence, as did Russell Jewell who was arrested for the bomb explosion in Centennial Park in Atlanta during the 1996 Olympic Games (cited by Vrij, 2000:169). Mock-jurors are not over-whelmed by polygraph evidence against a defendant (Myers and Arbuthnot, 1997). Its wide use in some countries should not, however, blind us to the controversy surrounding its reliability as a method of detecting deception as well as a number of ethical concerns about its use.

3.2.2 Deception Detection with the Polygraph: Techniques Used

The relevant–irrelevant question test was used in the early days of the polygraph and is nowadays used in pre-employment screening. A person who is lying is expected to show stronger reactions to the relevant questions. The simple fact that an innocent person who is anxious about the outcome of the questioning would be labelled as a liar means that it is a technique that produces an unacceptable number of false positive identifications and 'is seldom used in federal law enforcement investigations in the US' (Raskin, 1989b:252).

To overcome limitations of the relevant–irrelevant test researchers developed the control question test. This technique is commonly used in criminal investigations and involves asking three types of questions: (a) relevant, 'hot', questions (for example, 'Did you drive the getaway car used in the robbery?'); (b) irrelevant, 'cold', questions (for example, 'Is your full name John Simon Smith?'); and (c) control questions (for example, 'During the first twenty years of your life, did you ever take something that did not belong to you?' (Raskin, 1989b:257)) which 'are designed to give an innocent suspect an opportunity to become more concerned about questions other than the relevant questions, thereby causing the innocent suspect to react more strongly to the control than to the relevant questions' (p. 253). The polygraph examiner compares a suspect's responses to the relevant and control questions and decides whether they indicate truthfulness or lying.[9] Strong supporters of the polygraph, such as Raskin (1989b), cite laboratory studies reporting poly-graph examination accuracy of between 93 per cent and 97 per cent and a relatively high rate (30 to 80 per cent) of confessions by criminal suspects questioned by law-enforcement personnel using this technique. The Office of Technology Assessment (1983) reported that acceptable field studies examined pointed to a 90 per cent and 80 per cent overall accuracy of the polygraph on criterion-guilty and criterion-innocent suspects respectively. In other words, at best, a polygraph examination risks labelling 20 per cent of suspects as liars who are later found to be innocent.

Raskin (1989b) reported a major field study that used data from criminal investigations conducted by the US Secret Service over a three-year period beginning in 1983. Polygraph examinations were only included in the sample if they involved: (a) a confession that inculpated or exculpated a suspect; and (b) if there was corroboration of the confession by physical evidence. The polygraphed suspects were thus 'classified as either confirmed truthful or confirmed deceptive on one or more relevant questions in the test' (p. 267). Different Secret Service polygraph examiners re-evaluated the polygraph charts blindly. It was found that the original examiners had a false negative rate of 5 per cent and a false positive rate of 4 per cent. The blind re-evaluations were found to have a 6 per cent false negative and 15 per cent false positive rate. The difference in the false positive rate was attributable to the fact that the original examiners were in a position to make judgements about deception by utilising information about the case concerned and about the demeanour of the suspect, information that was not available to the blind examiners. Raskin concluded that: 'Taken as a whole, these data provide strong support for the accuracy of control question polygraph tests when properly used in criminal investigations' (pp. 268–9).

However, caution is warranted in accepting Raskin's conclusion because: (a) a confession by a person as a result of having been given a polygraph test by an agent of the Secret Service is not a satisfactory criterion due to the likelihood that the suggestibility factor operated in a number of cases; (b) guilt had not been established beyond reasonable doubt by a properly constituted court of law; and, finally, (c) the vast majority of polygraph examiners do not possess the qualifications, do not receive the in-depth training and do not have the practical experience which apparently characterise Secret Service agents and explains their relative success at detecting deceit with and without the aid of the polygraph (Ekman and O'Sullivan, 1991). Raskin's field study is, nevertheless, a significant improvement on earlier attempts to test the effectiveness of the control question technique. Raskin (1989b) himself concedes: 'It is clear that the major weakness of the traditional control question test is its susceptibility to false positive errors'. Given that such mistakes by Secret Service agents may well be used by them to justify keeping a citizen under surveillance and so forth, false positive polygraph tests are a cause for concern.

Persons diagnosed as psychopaths (in contemporary clinical diagnosis the preferred term is 'suffering from an anti-social personality disorder') are known to have a propensity to lie, not to experience anxiety and to feel no remorse. Parrick and Iacono (1989) offered prison inmates $20 to beat the polygraph. They had forty-eight subjects, half of whom had been diagnosed as psychopaths. Half of each of those groups were instructed to steal money from a coat from a prison doctor's office and the rest in each group who were not involved in committing the theft served as controls (the innocent comparison group). Polygraph control question tests were conducted by professional polygraph examiners with over thirty years' experience between them and they scored each other's chart blindly using a semi-objective scoring method. It was found that the psychopaths had no advantage on the polygraph test. The accuracy of the control question technique with both psychopathic and non-psychopathic groups of inmates was slightly better than chance for the innocent (55 per cent) and 86 per cent for the guilty. In other words, using the control question technique polygraph examiners wrongly classified 45 per cent of the innocent subjects as guilty of the theft.

In another field study Parrick and Iacono (1991) collaborated with the polygraph division of the Royal Canadian Mounted Police (RCMP). Using information in police investigative files they identified persons who had taken a polygraph test but were subsequently shown to be innocent of a crime. The researchers had RCMP polygraph examiners score those persons' polygraph charts blindly and found that 55 per cent of them were classified as truthful. It was also reported that the RCMP conducts polygraph tests when the investigation fails to unearth evidence incriminating a suspect. The two studies by Parrick and Iacono leave no doubt that the control question technique misidentifies almost half of innocent suspects as liars.

To overcome weaknesses of the control question technique the directed lie control test has been suggested (Honts and Raskin, 1988). A typical lie question might be 'Before the age of eighteen did you ever lie to anyone about anything?' and a suspect is instructed to answer 'No' to each such question and is also told by the polygraph examiner that to deny ever having lied in the past means that he/she is lying. The assumption is that someone who is innocent and telling the truth will show stronger physiological reactions to the directed lie questions than to the relevant questions, while guilty ones will show stronger reactions to the relevant questions.

A field study by Honts and Raskin (1988) examined the validity of the directed lie test. Honts and Raskin carried out polygraph tests of criminal suspects over a four-year period and obtained twenty-five confirmed tests in which one personal directed lie was included with traditional control questions. Each of the polygraph examiners then scored blindly the charts obtained by the other examiners, including or not including the directed lie question. Honts and Raskin reported that including one directed lie question completely eliminated false positives. Raskin (1989b) concluded that the findings from experimental simulation and field studies support the view that the directed lie test has a number of advantages over the traditional control question test namely that: it is more standardised in its structure; it is easier to administer; it requires less manipulation of the subject and creates fewer problems for the subject; it is more readily explained to lawyers, judges and juries; and most important, it reduces the problem of false positives inherent in the traditional control question test (pp. 274–5). Finally, the reader should note in this context that in essence a control question test is misleading the suspect and is, thus, unethical and illegal (Vrij, 2000:186–7).

3.2.3 Scoring the Polygraph Chart

There are three approaches to scoring the polygraph chart (Raskin, 1989b):

1 *Global evaluation:* this is a subjective impression based on an examiner's overall inspection of the chart showing how an examinee answered different questions, as well as information about the case at hand and observations of the examinee's behaviour during the test. This scoring method has been shown to be inferior to the next two approaches (Raskin, 1989b:259).

2 *Numerical evaluation:* this involves assigning a score ranging from 23 to +3 to each of an examinee's three physiological responses (galvanic skin reflex, blood pressure and respiration) to indicate the difference between the response to a control question and its nearby relevant question. If the reaction to the control question is greater and the magnitude of the response is a dramatic difference then a score of +3 is assigned to that response. A score of 23 would indicate the response to the relevant question was greater. According to Raskin (1989b:260), a zero score indicates no observed difference, 1 a noticeable difference, 2 a strong difference and 3 a dramatic difference, but a score of 3 is very rarely given.

3 *Computer scoring:* using mathematics, Kircher and Raskin (1988) developed a computer method for scoring the chart that yields a probability value (ranging from 0 to +1) that an examinee was truthful on the basis of the test. According to Raskin (1989b), laboratory studies 'indicate that computer evaluations are extremely useful and are worthy of field implementation at this time' (p. 262).

The use of computer-based methods to score polygraph charts has been criticised by Furedy (1996). Given the lack of clarity in how to score polygraph charts (that is, whether the difference between a control and relevant question is 'noticeable' or 'strong' or 'dramatic'), Vrij (2000) has argued that scoring polygraph charts is indeed a subjective process (pp. 184–6).

3.2.4 The Polygraph and Ascertaining a Suspect has Direct Knowledge of Specific Information

An early method used to investigate whether a suspect has direct knowledge of particular items of information was the 'peak of tension' test. This involves comparing a suspect's physiological responses to a number of alternative answers (usually five) to a particular question, such as the type of knife used to stab a victim to death. One of the alternative answers is the correct one. What is known as the 'searching peak of tension' test can be used to establish a fact that a criminal investigator does not know but is keen to find out, such as where a body is buried or a kidnap victim is kept (Raskin, 1989b:276).

Building on the peak of tension test, Lykken (1959) proposed the 'guilty knowledge' test (GKT). This basically tests a suspect's reactions to specific items of information in the form of multiple choice questions, directly relevant to the commission of a crime of the kind that only the perpetrator would know. According to Podlesny and Raskin (1978) and Iacono et al. (1987), the galvanic skin response is the most useful measure in determining the outcome of a concealed knowledge test. One major limitation of the GKT is that the number of real-life serious crimes in which it can be used is limited (Vrij, 2000:190–1) because: (a) the only questions that can be asked are those to which only the polygraph examiner and the suspect know the answers; (b) the suspect may be found to have guilty knowledge but is innocent (for example, in a sexual assault case the suspect is found to have had sexual intercourse with the alleged victim but denies it was not without her consent); and (c) the polygraph examiner can only ask questions the answers to which would not be known to an innocent examinee. However, the frequent practice of the mass media to report intimate details of serious crimes limits the questions that can be asked of a suspect. Interestingly, however, Elaad and Ben-Shakkar's (1997) experimental 'concealed knowledge technique' (CKT) study found that merely asking the same question more than once achieves the same accuracy rate as that achieved by asking several questions. Were it to be replicated, that finding would add significantly to the effectiveness and efficiency of the CKT. It should be noted in this context that the term 'guilty knowledge technique' is being replaced by 'concealed knowledge technique' (CKT) because the latter is more defensible as someone can conceal knowledge but feel no guilt about it.

> The concealed knowledge technique can be a useful tool in criminal investigation and it protects innocent people from being falsely identified as guilty.

Laboratory studies of the guilty knowledge technique have generally reported accuracy of approximately 84 per cent with guilty and 99 per cent with innocent subjects. Elaad (1990) reported a field study of detection of guilty knowledge in a random sample of ninety-eight real-life criminal investigations conducted during 1979–85 in which the guilt and innocence of the suspects had been verified by the confession of the person who had committed the crime in question. Elaad found that 98 per cent of the innocent and 42 per cent of the guilty subjects were correctly classified. Elaad et al. (1992) used another sample of eighty actual CKT criminal polygraph records obtained from verified polygraph tests carried out during 1985–91 by the Israeli Police Scientific Investigation Unit. The verification of guilt or innocence was based on the confession of the culprit. They reported correct detection rate for guilty examinees 75.8 per cent and 94.1 per cent for the innocent. Elaad (1998) reviewed fifteen mock crime studies of the CKT and found average detection rates of 80.6 per cent for guilty examinees and 95.6 per cent for the innocent (p. 168). Also, no false positives (that is, failures to exonerate innocent subjects) were reported. Finally, further support for the CKT has been provided by Iacono and Lykken's (1997) survey of members of the American Society of Psychophysiological Research and Fellows of the American Psychological Association (division 1, general psychology) about their views on the control test and the GKT tests. Most respondents (75 per cent) favoured the GKT in terms of its scientifically sound psychological principles or theory. The empirical evidence mentioned shows that the CKT can be a useful tool in criminal investigations and that it protects innocent suspects from being falsely classified as guilty.

3.2.5 Factors Impacting on Polygraph Test Accuracy and Outcome

A number of factors can justifiably be said to influence lie-detection using the polygraph. Who the examiner is has been shown to be an important factor. Elaad and Kleiner (1990) reported an interesting field study that compared one group of examiners (N=5) with at least three years' experience in chart interpretation and a second group (N=5) of trainees in the seventh and eighth month of a ten-month training program. A random sample of fifty real-life polygraph records from the Israel Scientific Interrogation Unit were used to examine the performance of the two groups of examiners. Half the records were of innocent suspects verified by the confession of another person and the other half were of guilty suspects verified by their own confession. It was found that an examiner's length of experience correlated positively with accuracy detection rate when scoring the respiration channel but not when scoring the skin resistance or blood pressure channels.

That the polygraph can be fooled by an accomplished liar is not in doubt. The CIA agent Aldrich Ames who spied for the Soviets passed numerous polygraph tests.[10] As far as the personality of the suspect is concerned, there is some evidence that emotional stability, also known as trait anxiety, can impact on the polygraph's accuracy (Gudjonsson, 1992a:186). More specifically: 'stable subjects may react in a way that leads the examiner to make false negative errors, whereas emotionally labile subjects more commonly react in a way that results in false positive errors' (p. 186). The personality trait of psychopathy (better known today as anti-social personality disorder) has been reported by a number of studies as a correlate of criminal behaviour and is of interest to many forensic psychologists working in prisons (see Blackburn, 2000; Hare, 1996). The potential of countermeasures to influence a polygraph test outcome has attracted a certain amount of research interest.[11] In brief, the available evidence shows that it is possible, using countermeasures (for example, of the kind that augment the examinee's response to the control questions) to seriously undermine the accuracy of the polygraph (Gudjonsson, 1992a:187). For one to use such countermeasures effectively, however, special training is required (p. 187). Apparently, an easy and effective countermeasure that can be used by guilty suspects against a control question polygraph test is to serially subtract 7 from a number greater than 200 (Honts et al., 1994). Anybody wishing to attempt to beat the polygraph should remember that examiners themselves get schooled in counter-countermeasures (Gudjonsson, 1988:133–4). However, there have been no field studies on the question of how effective different countermeasures and counter-countermeasures are (Gudjonsson, 1988:134).

From the point of view of the general public, an easy countermeasure to its use would seem to be to take some drugs that will interfere with a polygraph test. Raskin (1989b) concluded his discussion of laboratory studies of the potential effects of such drugs as tranquillisers, beta blockers, stimulants and alcohol (see Iacono et al., 1987; O'Toole, 1988; Waid et al., 1981) by stating that there is no convincing evidence for such effects either with the control question or the GKT procedure (p. 285). Support for this view was later provided by Iacono et al.'s (1992) laboratory study finding that anti-anxiety drugs are not effective countermeasures to be used against the GKT. Counter-measures would seem to take on another interesting twist in the light of attempts by some researchers in recent years to infer the possession of information in persons attempting to conceal it measuring 'event-related brain potentials' (see Bashore and Rapp, 1993). According to Vrij (2000:204–5), the small number of studies does not allow conclusions to be drawn about the ability of the polygraph to detect lies told by psychopaths who are less anxious than non-psychopaths and tend not to feel remorse and, consequently, do not become aroused when telling lies.

A number of bodies have carried out assessments of the polygraph and have published reports (Irving and Hilgendorf, 1980; Office of Technology Assessment, 1983; Department of Defense, 1984; House of Commons Employment Committee, 1985; British Psychological Society [BPS] Working Group, 1986). The Royal Commission on Criminal Procedure in Britain devoted nine lines to the polygraph in its report and rejected the idea of polygraph evidence in the courts, but did not deny its value as an investigative tool for police forces. Predictably, perhaps, the US Department of Defense (1984) report claimed that: 'Without the polygraph as an investigative tool, a number of espionage cases never would have been solved' (p. 13). Two years later, the BPS Working Group Report on the use of the polygraph in criminal investigation and person-nel screening, prepared under the chairmanship of Professor Anthony Gale at the request of the Society's Scientific Affairs Board, concluded that polygraph tests are unlikely to be used in personnel selection generally in Britain; they raise serious efficacy concerns in the context of criminal investigations which need to be addressed by future research; they are irrelevant in the context of the security services; and, finally, the Working Group seriously doubted whether such evidence would ever be admissible in British courts of law (pp. 80–1).

One of the strongest criticisms levelled against the polygraph by its opponents is that 'Unlike the fictional Pinocchio, we are not equipped with a distinctive physiological response that we emit involuntarily when, and only when, we lie' (Lykken, 1989:124). Lykken, perhaps the best-known critic of the polygraph, does nevertheless accept that: 'Polygraphic detection of guilty knowledge, based on entirely different and more plausible assumptions, has proved itself in the laboratory and deserves control study in the field of criminal investigation' (p. 125).

Opponents of the polygraph also repeatedly point to its bias against the innocent, that jurors are likely to be influenced by its results (but see Cavoukian and Heslegrave, 1979; Honts and Perry, 1992), that it constitutes an invasion of people's privacy, and that although in western countries the tendency is for police storage and so forth of criminal record information to be regulated by standing orders and legislation and in some jurisdictions members of the public can apply to access such information under freedom of information provisions, the storage and potential use of polygraph charts and the information that accompanies them is wide open to abuse. Meanwhile, there is no doubt that the polygraph will continue to be used in countries like the United States and Israel in the context of criminal investigation and national security. The hope is that the courts will play a more effective role in regulating its use and enforcing strict ethical standards on its practitioners.

4 Brainwaves as Indicators of Deceitful Communication

In view of the limitations and the controversy surrounding the use of the polygraph to detect lies, researchers in the United States have identified patterns of brain activity that betray a liar. If we accept their findings it would mean police could use magnetic resonance scans to detect lies by criminal suspects. Presenting the brain with a discrete stimulus generates an electrical signal known as event-related potential which is approximately a few millionths of a volt in size (Iacono, 1995:168–70). This takes place against the brain's background electrical activity. By presenting a stimulus repeatedly about thirty times and averaging the brain's responses to the repetitions it is possible to extract the event-related potential. P3 or P300 brainwave is one particular type of event-related potential which is evoked by relatively uncommon stimuli but which have special significance for a person. A number of laboratory studies have reported using P3 waves to distinguish guilty and innocent alternatives in guilty knowledge experiments (Allen et al., 1992; Boaz et al., 1991; Farewell and Donchin, 1991; Rosenfeld et al., 1991). A research team led by Daniel Langleben at the University of Pennsylvania has carried out guilty knowledge test studies using functional magnetic imaging (fMRI) and reported that when people lie it is more likely to activate sections of the brain (anterior cingulate gyrus and parts of the prefrontal and premotor cortex) that are important in how people pay attention to, monitor and control errors than when telling the truth.[12] Field research is needed before we can conclude that measuring a person's event-related brain potential (ERP) does indeed pick up a person's signature of deceit when trying to conceal the truth and is a more reliable lie-detection method than using the polygraph. Meanwhile, what is certain is that it will be impossible for liars to learn to control the electrical impulses in their brains that generate thought because individual neurons begin to 'fire' in response to a stimulus before a person is conscious of the fact.

5 Stylometry

Drawing on Gudjonsson (1992a), stylometry is a branch of linguistics and literary studies that tries to authenticate the creator of a written or even spoken language text. It is assumed that a person's stylometric features do not change with time. Thus, the argument goes, no two individuals are significantly the same in how they express themselves through language: how often they use particular vocabulary, combinations of words, or how they structure their sentences. Stylometry can also be used to comment on the mental state of a person when he/she made a statement to the police, for example. To illustrate, it is known that people's use of the verb–adjective ratio changes according to one's emotional arousal (Gudjonsson, 1992a:194). To authenticate a document, a stylometrist might decide to count the most frequent linguistic characteristics in a document, quantitatively analyse the language structure used in terms of its vocabulary, grammar, syntax and spelling (see Morton, 1978; Morton and Michaelson, 1990).

Robertson et al. (1994) discuss case law pertaining to the admissibility of stylometric evidence in the UK and Australia and show that stylometry has had a mixed reception in the courts. It was not admitted in the well-known case of Patty Hearst[13] (*US v. Hearst*, 418, F Sup 893 (1976)) on the grounds that it failed the *Frye* test (*Frye v. United States*, 293 FR 1013 (1923) now superseded by the *Daubert* criteria – see chapter 7). Stylometric evidence was admitted in England in *The Queen v. McCrossen* (unreported, 10 July 1991 CA (Cr.D.)) and in *Mitchell* (unreported, 82/2419/E2). In Australia, stylometric evidence was rejected in Tilley ((1985) VR 505), in which Justice Beach rejected the argument that 'a person's oral utterances would be stylometrically consistent with his or her written work' (Robertson et al., 1994:646). The British forensic psychologist, Professor David Canter (1992), has argued that there is no empirical evidence showing that an individual's stylometric features are consistent over a long period of time. The future of stylometric evidence does not seem optimistic either in the UK or in Australia and we need to wait and see how courts in the United States will treat expert stylometry testimony on the basis of the *Daubert* decision, that is, whether they will regard the theory underpinning it as scientific.

6 Statement Reality/Validity Analysis (SVA)

Following a West German Supreme Court decision in 1954, German psychologists came to play an important part appearing as expert witnesses in court testifying on the truthfulness of witness statements, especially in sex cases, utilising a method known as 'statement reality analysis', developed by Undeutsch and known widely as statement analysis.[14] The theoretical basis of this technique is that people's accounts of events actually experienced are both quantitatively and qualitatively different from fictitious accounts, whether invented or coached. The SVA consists of three main elements: (a) a structured interview; (b) a criteria-based content analysis (CBCA) which assesses systematically the contents and qualities of the statement made; and (c) a set of questions (Validity Check List) that evaluates the outcome of the CBCA. Undeutsch (1982) put forward eight reality criteria (features) for deciding the objective reality, and truthfulness, of a statement. The criteria are: 'Originality; Clarity; Vividness; Internal consistency; Detailed descriptions which are specific to the type of offence alleged; A reference to specific detail that would under normal circumstances be outside the experience of the witness or victim; The reporting of subjective feelings' and, finally, 'spontaneous corrections or additional information' (Gudjonsson, 1992a:201). Steller and Köhnken (1989) have been critical of earlier work on this technique and have proposed using a total of nineteen criteria instead of Undeutsch's eight[15] which are more likely to be found in truthful than in deceptive statements.

Drawing on Vrij (2000:117),[16] the following are the nineteen CBCA criteria:

- *General characteristics:* logical structure; unstructured production; quantity of details.
- *Specific contents:* contextual embedding; descriptions of interactions; reproduction of conversation; unexpected complications during the incident; unusual details; superfluous details; accurately reported details misunderstood; related external associations; accounts of subjective mental state; attribution of perpetrator's mental state.
- *Motivation-related contents:* spontaneous corrections; admitting lack of memory; raising doubts about one's own testimony; self-deprecation; pardoning the perpetrator.
- *Offence-specific elements:* details characteristic of the offence.

Logical structure, unstructured production, quantity of details, contextual embedding, and description of interactions (see Marxsen et al., 1995, for details) are considered the minimum necessary for a statement to be coded as truthful. If any of the remaining fourteen criteria are also present, this adds to the credibility of the statement but their absence does not render a statement untruthful. At least two additional criteria are considered sufficient for a statement to be classified as credible (Marxsen et al., 1995:455).

Vrij (2000:123) lists the following eleven items that comprise the validity check-list, adapted from Steller (1989):

- *Psychological characteristics* (of the interviewee):
  1 Inappropriateness of language and knowledge.
  2 Inappropriateness of affect.
  3 Susceptibility to suggestion.
- *Interview characteristics:*
  4 Suggestive, leading or coercive questioning.
  5 Overall inadequacy of the interview.
- *Motivation:*
  6 Questionable motives to report.
  7 Questionable context of the original disclosure or report.
  8 Pressures to report falsely.
- *Investigative questions:*
  9 Inconsistency with the laws of nature.

10 Inconsistency with other statements.
11 Inconsistency with other evidence.

Using statement validity analysis, Undeutsch (1982) has claimed to have found victims to be truthful in 90 per cent of 1500 cases he examined. This finding is of interest in view of the fact that 95 per cent of the defendants involved in those cases were, in fact, convicted. Empirical support for the 'Undeutsch hypothesis' has also been reported by Yuille (1988) and Steller and Boychuk (1992) with children. Yuille found that statement analysis identified correctly 74 per cent of false and 91 per cent of true stories by children aged 6 and 8 years. Further support for statement analysis was reported by Esplin et al. (1988, cited in Raskin and Esplin, 1991) who examined forty statements, of which twenty involved child sexual abuse which had been confirmed either by a confession or medical evidence or a combination of the two, and twenty 'doubtful' (that is, there was no confession, the children withdrew the allegation, the case did not get to a court, the case was dismissed by the judge or the defendant was acquitted). Esplin et al. reported that a single person coding the statements without knowing what belonged to what category was able to differentiate perfectly between true and false cases of child sexual abuse. Marxsen et al. (1995) point out that researchers have neglected statement analysis as a useful technique with which to assess the credibility of children's statements.

Qualified support for the CBCA was reported by Horowitz et al. (1997) who used judges on two occasions and transcripts of interviews with 100 alleged victims of child sexual abuse to examine the inter-judge and test-retest reliability of CBCA for the presence of the original nineteen criteria. They found that all the criteria had adequate test-retest reliability, fourteen criteria were reliable across raters but the inter-judge reliability of individual criteria varied.

Most of the validation studies of Undeutsch's theory have been with children, but Zaparniuk et al. (1995) reported that statement reality analysis distinguished reliably (mean accuracy rate of 76 per cent) between true and false statements by adult witnesses. Akehurst et al. (2001) reported that CBCA discriminated between truthful accounts based on direct experience of an event and fabricated accounts (overall detection rate, 70 per cent). Porter and Yuille (1995) examined ten of the statement analysis criteria in a mock-crime paradigm and found three (coherence, sufficient detail and admitting lack of memory) differentiated reliably between truthful and false accounts. Parker and Brown (2000) investigated the usefulness of CBCA in determining the truthfulness or falsity of forty-three rape allegations by adults. They also compared the capability of CBCA and the ability of detectives to differentiate between true and false allegations. The validity of the allegations' veracity was assessed against forensic correctness, guilty pleas and withdrawal of complaints. CBCA was found to discriminate genuine from false statements and its predictions about the veracity of rape allegations were more accurate than those made by police detectives.

While empirical support has been reported for statement validity analysis, criticisms have also been levelled against it.

If a lie-detection technique is worth adopting, it should be possible to teach to those who are going to use it in the context of their work. According to Raskin and Esplin (1991), making CBCA valuations is a skill that can be taught in two or three days. Landry and Brigham (1992) showed the potential of training individuals to use the technique effectively with a videotape of adults who were instructed to make true or false statements about a personal traumatic experience. Joffe (1992) and Yuille et al. (1993), however, reported difficulty in training field workers to perform statement analysis. More recently, Akehurst et al. (2000) used materials provided by David Raskin and John Yuille to train police officers, social workers and students in the use of the CBCA in a 45-minute session. They found that training did not improve the detection accuracy of students and social workers while police officers performed significantly well after the training session.

Additional weaknesses of statement validity analysis have also been reported: its subjectivity, possible differences between statement analysis carried out 'post hoc from a transcript or videotape of an interview and statement analysis done during the interview by the interviewer' and the fact that brief narrations (often a characteristic of rather young children) are not amenable to analysis (Marxsen et al., 1995). In addition, expert raters, using only one aspect of the statement analysis (criterion-based content analysis) have difficulty differentiating actual events in statements by children from events in their statements persistently suggested to them during interviews over a long period of time (Huffman, 1995, cited by Ceci et al., 1995:514).

Some evidence that the CBCA should not be used in court proceedings in its present form has been reported by Santila et al. (2000). Their Finnish study examined the effects on the CBCA criteria of age, verbal ability (assessed with the Weschler Intelligence Test for Children-Revised vocabulary) and the emotional style of the interviewer. The subjects were sixty-eight children aged 7 to 8, 10 to 11 and 13 to 14 years who made a true and a false statement about a mildly traumatic event. It was found that while the correct classification rate was 66 per cent, a child's age and verbal ability increased the occurrence of some of the CBCA criteria irrespective of the truthfulness of the statements. Santila et al. also found that different criteria differentiated between true and false statements in different age-groups of children and, finally, the interviewer's emotional style affected the occurrence of the criteria.

On the basis of his survey of three field studies and twelve experimental laboratory studies of CBCA criteria, Vrij (2000:126–36) concluded that: the field studies supported the Undeutsch hypothesis; the experimental studies show CBCA is more successful in detecting truths than in detecting lies; and, finally, his literature review showed no real differences in accuracy rates between statements by children and by adults. Regarding the factors that can impact on the presence of CBCA criteria in statements made, Vrij's review identified the following: age of the style, interviewer style, number of interviews, cognitive interview and stressful events. Also based on his discussion of existing literature on the validity check-list, Vrij doubts the justification of three criteria: 'inappropriateness of affect', 'inconsistency with other statements' and 'susceptibility to suggestion' (p.139–45). Finally, Vrij lists two major limitations of SVA:

1 It is not a standardised instrument because: (a) there are no CBCA rules to determine the number of criteria that need to occur for a statement to be truthful or not; (b) there are no rules regarding the weighting of the different criteria; (c) external factors impact on the criteria; and, consequently, (d) SVA assessments are subjective; and, finally, (e) it is not clear where the method can be used.
2 It lacks theoretical underpinning.

Vrij (2000:153–6) has drawn attention to the need for future research to examine: SVA assessments; the utility of CBCA with statements made by suspects; the relevance of the technique in situations other than in a judicial context; the issue of whether people who are aware of the CBCA criteria can subsequently make false statements that mislead evaluators; cultural differences; and, finally, since the CBCA criteria are in fact cues to truthfulness, researchers should also include lie indicators to the criteria and examine their effect on detection accuracy.

The available empirical literature provides support for Undeutsch's basic proposition that the memory of someone who has had a real experience will differ in both quantity and quality from that which a person who has not had the experience could fabricate. CBCA can differentiate between truthful and fabricated statements better than chance but mistakes are made, especially as far as detecting lies are concerned (Vrij, 2000:157). The available literature shows that while the SVA can be a useful tool in police investigation of an alleged crime, especially child abuse cases for which it was specifically developed, it suffers from a number of serious weaknesses that detract from its accuracy. Therefore, it should not be admissible as evidence in the courts as has been the case in Germany; in other words, 'it must be applied in a context of pursuing multiple hypotheses and is not a sort of "no tech" lie-detector. The individual criteria must be examined further, and there is no guarantee that what will work for younger children will work with older' (Marxsen et al., 1995:458). As far as it has been possible to ascertain, there has been no legal test of the question of the admissibility of expert statement analysis testimony in British, United States or Australian courts. The results of such analysis would be particularly useful to both judges and juries in alleged sexual abuse cases.

7 Reality Monitoring

Unlike the CBCA, 'reality monitoring' includes 'lie criteria' which can be used in different settings and not only in sexual abuse cases since it focuses on memory characteristics of actual events one has experienced and imagined ones. Reality monitoring is based on the same hypothesis as CBCA, that is, that memories from experienced events differ in quality from memories of imagined events. According to Johnson and Raye (1981) and Johnson et al.

(1988), the basic premise of this particular lie-detection method is that the difference between the two types of memories is that memories of real events are clear and vivid, they derive from perceptual processes and, consequently, are more likely to contain: perceptual information (to do with the five senses); contextual information (that is, detailed information regarding when and where someone had a particular experience); and, finally, affective information (that is, details concerning how the individual felt during the experience/event in question). On the other hand, a fabricated memory/statement about an imagined event originates in an internal source and is likely to be characterised by cognitive operations like thoughts and reasonings.

Since there is no standardised reality monitoring criteria, let us, like Vrij (2000:159, table 6.1), draw on Sporer's (1997) list, as it was published in English: clarity; perceptual information; spatial information; temporal information; affect; reconstructability of the story; realism; and cognitive operations. A number of researchers have used reality monitoring criteria to detect lies (see Vrij 2000:161–5, for a review). Vrij surveyed twelve such studies and concluded that, compared to statements about fabricated events, statements about real experiences contain more perceptual information, more spatial information and more temporal information (p. 162). Regarding accuracy rates for reality monitoring, it was found by three studies that used adult subjects to be: 71 per cent (Vrij et al., 1999), 61 per cent (Hofer et al., 1996) and 75 per cent (Sporer, 1997). The accuracy of lie-detection was found by the same three studies to be 74 per cent, 71 per cent and 68 per cent respectively. It can be seen that the accuracy rates reported are much higher than chance level. It has also been found that accuracy rates using reality monitoring are affected by time-delay (Johnson et al., 1988; Sporer, 1997) and become problematic with children (Alonso-Quecuty, 1992). Thus, reality monitoring would appear to be a useful tool in the investigation stage when used with adults for recent events. Finally, Vrij (2000) recommends combining the CBCA and reality monitoring methods.

8 Scientific Content Analysis

Another method of statement analysis that has been suggested as useful in detecting deceptive communication is scientific content analysis (SCAN). This is a technique more familiar to an elite number of secret services personnel, law enforcement, armed forces and private sector investigators who have been introduced to it than to psychologists (Driscoll, 1994). The assumptions of SCAN are that: (a) there are significant differences between truthful and deceptive accounts; (b) the suspect's words must be produced without any help from the interrogator; and (c) every individual has his/her unique linguistic code, with the exception of pronouns. SCAN utilises a number of criteria to analyse the transcript or written statement of an individual. According to Driscoll (1994: 80–1),[17] these criteria include the following and show how they point to a deceptive communication: pronouns (a change or absence), spontaneous corrections (their use), emotion (if located near the peak of the story rather than throughout), connections (their use, for example, 'later on', 'the next thing I remember'), first person singular, past tense (deviations from these), time (a deceptive statement will have more lines written before the key issue or offence than after it) and, finally, changes in language use (inconsistent use of language indicates deception, as when 'a nice guy' becomes 'that man'). Driscoll reported SCAN analysis of thirty written statements given voluntarily by crime suspects prior to being given a polygraph test by the same examiner. Scoring of the statements indicated that the technique 'is capable, within limits, of differentiating between probably accurate statements and likely false statements' and compares well with the polygraph in effectiveness (p. 86). More research is needed, however, before definitive conclusions can be drawn about the forensic utility of SCAN in detecting written deceptive communication.

9 Conclusions

Despite the importance of deception as a social phenomenon, we cannot as yet speak of a psychology of deception. Early psychological research into deception was largely concerned with explaining conjuring tricks but was eclipsed by the rise of behaviourism. The wide use of integrity tests in pre-employment screening remains controversial, as different evaluations of the validity of such tests have reached rather different conclusions. There still remain serious difficulties in attempting to evaluate integrity tests, such as the absence of consensus on what is meant by 'integrity'.

A lot of research has been carried out into both non-verbal and verbal cues to deception. While studies have established a number of non-verbal correlates of deceptive communication, research into verbal cues appears to be more bedevilled by conflicting findings. Humans, including trained and experienced law-enforcement personnel (but apparently with the notable exception of US Secret Service agents), turn out to be as good as chance in detecting deception. The consolation is that most people are better than chance in deceiving others. The external validity of studies of deception-detection by law-enforcement personnel is questionable. As far as the psychological stress evaluator is concerned, research results do not support claims made for it.

Regarding the much-researched and talked-about polygraph, the main issue is its accuracy in general and the false positive rate in particular, as well as ethical concerns about its wide use. Researchers have reported false positive rates ranging from 4 per cent to 20 per cent and false negatives ones from 4 per cent to 15 per cent. The directed lie control test appears more accurate than the control question test and thus reduces even more the percentage of false positive errors. The directed lie control test, however, awaits evaluation in the field. The guilty knowledge technique has been shown by Israeli researchers to be a useful tool in criminal investigations and to protect innocent suspects from being labelled as guilty.

In considering the accuracy of the polygraph with whichever technique, it is important to remember that such factors as how experienced the examiner is, the trait anxiety of the examinee, and the use of certain countermeasures (for example, that augment one's responses to control questions) can influence the test outcome. Even strong opponents of the polygraph, like Professor Lykken, accept that, properly used, the polygraph can be a useful tool in criminal investigations. Whether a police force should be allowed to use it, let alone whether such evidence should be admissible in court, is a question left entirely to the legal systems of different countries and their parliaments to decide. The answer would seem to depend on how a society decides to balance the rights of the individual citizen on the one hand and police powers on the other. The usefulness in the field of the event-related potential method is yet to be determined by studies that will attempt to replicate the rather impressive results obtained in the laboratory. The guilty knowledge technique has been shown to have more merits than the control question technique, especially when it is used with event-related potential recordings.

As far as stylometry is concerned, despite some researchers' awarding it good marks as an effective method for authenticating the authorship of a given text, Australian courts, unlike courts in England, have shown a reluctance to allow such expert testimony, and the research that has given rise to the technique has come under attack.

Rather impressive results have been reported over the years from Germany and elsewhere regarding the usefulness of statement reality analysis in determining the truthfulness of both a child's or an adult witness' statement. It is a technique which, despite its limitations, undoubtedly deserves more attention from psychologists, lawyers and the judicial profession in common law countries. Finally, the SCAN technique appears to deserve more field testing before it is recommended for use by law enforcement investigators. Future research should also examine the comparative effectiveness of different techniques available (for example, reality monitoring or scientific content analysis) for identifying deceptive communication, both oral and written, and the merits of their theoretical underpinnings. Meanwhile, the search for new methods continues. A method which has been suggested as potentially useful in detecting deception uses electronic noses to sniff and measure differences in a person's body smells that occur when people are under stress, such as when they are lying (Coghlan et al., 1995).

Revision Questions

1   What gender differences have been reported as far as lying is concerned?
2   What are some limitations of integrity/honesty tests?
3   What vocal and non-vocal indicators of deception characterise the majority of liars?
4   Why do even experienced police investigators find it difficult to detect lies at better than chance?
5   How accurate can the polygraph be in detecting lies? Should such evidence be admissible in court? If not, why not?
6   Is the 'event-related brain potential technique' a window into a brave new world where nobody will be able to lie? If yes, what are the policy implications?
7   Should the criteria-based content analysis (CBCA) be admissible in court? If not, why not?
8   In what way is the reality monitoring method an improvement on CBCA?

10 Witness Recognition Procedures

'Few problems can pose a greater threat to free, democratic societies than that of wrongful conviction – the conviction of an innocent person.' (Huff et al., 1986)

In a democracy, the presumption of innocence is of paramount importance. Although there is sometimes a natural desire among police officers to seek to prove cases well beyond a reasonable doubt, there is very real need to ensure that such desires do not lead to behaviours that are manifestly unfair and add unjustifiable strength to the prosecution case.' (McKenzie, 1995)

'Particularly alarming is the fact that police receive little or no training on line-ups and photospreads, there are no rules or laws that prevent constructing and conducting line-ups and photospreads in ways that place an innocent suspect at risk, and courts are relatively insensitive to the ways these subtle variations in line-ups and photospreads have strong effects on the chances of mistaken identification.' (Wells et al., 1999:72)

'there are a large number of ways in which even well-intentioned witnesses can make mistakes which could result in the conviction of an innocent person.' (Ainsworth, 2000a:174)

'For the criminal justice system, the current findings suggest that police and courts should treat voice identification made by auditory-visual witnesses with caution.' (Bull and Clifford, 1999)

Introduction

Very often, the identity of the perpetrator of a crime is not an issue or it can be readily established by the prosecution. In such cases, the primary concern of police investigators is to establish the necessary points of proof regarding the charges laid against the defendant. However, in those cases where a criminal offence has been committed and the issue is whether the defendant has been identified by a witness as the person who committed it, visual witness visual identification may involve one of the following: single confrontation identification, photograph identification, photo-board identification, video-film identification and, finally, identification by means of a line-up (that is, an identification parade). Courts have discretion to exclude witness identification evidence which has been obtained illegally, unfairly or improperly, as when a suspect was forced into taking part in a line-up or a police officer somehow communicated to a witness who the suspect was before a line-up was conducted, or when a line-up should have been conducted but was not or, finally, when the suspect's photograph 'stands out' in a photo-board or video-frame.

> There is evidence from different sources that an eyewitness identification problem does exist.

We saw in chapter 2 that the issue of person identification has been of central concern to eyewitness researchers since the 1970s. At the same time, there is widespread concern about biases in police identification practices and procedures that result in the false identification of innocent citizens. Wells et al. (1998) describe forty cases in which DNA analysis established retrospectively that persons had been wrongly convicted; of those convictions, 90 per cent were based on identifications in which one or more witnesses falsely identified the accused as the perpetrator of the crime. As Wells et al. (1999) point out, 'The DNA cases are useful in showing that mistaken identification by eyewitnesses is probably the largest single cause of the conviction of innocent persons' (p. 57). Wells et al. (1994:224) list three sources of support for the basic assumption 'that there is an identification problem': empirical studies reporting high rates of false identifications; the 'sincerity' and confidence of subjects in such studies reporting false identifications; and actual cases of wrongful convictions. The following example from Britain (cited in Ainsworth, 2000a:166) shows the danger of convicting an innocent person on line-up identification:

Case Study

Line-up Misidentification

In October 1992 a man went up to a taxi-driver and threatened him with a gun. He then proceeded to place a bomb in the taxi and ordered the driver to deliver it to the street in central London where the British Prime Minister lived. Suspecting the content of the parcel in his cab, the cab-driver abandoned the taxi in Whitehall and managed to shout a warning before the bomb went off. Afterwards, the police arrested Patrick Murphy, an Irishman, who had no doubts about his innocence, did not request to see a lawyer and agreed to take part in a line-up. To Murphy's astonishment, the taxi-driver and two other witnesses identified him as the offender who placed the bomb in the taxi, he was detained in custody and the Crown Prosecution Service got on with the job of preparing the legal brief to bring him to justice. Fortunately for Murphy, he was able to prove his innocence by producing eleven witnesses who testified that at the time of the crime he had been attending a meeting of Alcoholics Anonymous. In the face of such overwhelming evidence for Murphy's alibi, the Crown Prosecution Service dropped the charges against him and he was released. As we shall see in this chapter, Patrick Murphy has not been the only innocent Irishman who has been wrongly arrested and charged; in fact, Murphy was lucky: the 'Guildford Four' and the 'Birmingham Six' spent years in prison as convicted IRA bombers before they were able to prove their innocence.

How, then, is it possible for witnesses to identify in a line-up an innocent person they have not seen before as the perpetrator of a crime and to do so with great confidence? By the end of this chapter, the reader should be able to answer this question.

Formal recognition of the dangers of misidentification is no new thing. In England and Wales, after fifteen witnesses mistakenly identified Alfred Beck, it led to a Committee of Inquiry in 1905[1] that was instrumental in establishing the Court of Criminal Appeal by the *Criminal Appeal Act 1907* (Archbold, 2000:1303). Similar concerns about miscarriages of justice as a result of mistaken eyewitness identification in the early 1970s (see Brandon and Davies, 1973)[2] led to the Devlin Committee (Devlin, 1976) making, *inter alia*, the following recommendations to avoid such misidentifications:

- If the only evidence against an accused is that of eyewitness testimony, the case should be dropped by the prosecution.
- Should such a case be brought to trial, the judge should direct the jury to acquit.

Twenty-six years later, these safeguards have not been legislated and an accused may be convicted on eyewitness evidence, albeit with a judge warning the jury about the dangers of such identification (see below). Similarly, serious concern in the United States about innocent persons getting convicted on the basis of eyewitness misidentification led Janet Reno, the US Attorney General, to set up a panel of lawyers, police officers and psychologists (see Wells et al., 1998) to provide guidelines (see below) for establishing identification by means of line-ups or photo-spreads (see below). In England and Wales such guidelines are to be found in the *Police and Criminal Evidence Act* (PACE) 1984.

> Judges are required to warn the jury about the dangers of eyewitness identification evidence.

Recognising the dangers inherent in person identification, trial judges in Britain are required to warn the jury about identification evidence of witnesses in the terms required by *Turnbull and others* ((1977) QB 224, at 228–31, 63 Cr.App.R. 132 at 137–40).[3] Such warnings are also to be taken into account by magistrates. According to Archbold (2000:1307), the *Turnbull* warning requires that a judge should:

- Warn the jury of the special need for caution before convicting on witness identification evidence.
- Instruct the jury as to the reason for such a need.
- Inform the jury that a mistaken witness can be a convincing witness, and that more than one witness may be mistaken.
- Direct the jury to examine closely the circumstances in which each identification was made.
- Remind the jury of any specific weaknesses in the identification evidence.
- If appropriate, remind the jury that mistaken recognition can occur, even mistaken identification of close relatives and friends.
- Identify to the jury the evidence capable of supporting the identification.
- Identify evidence which might appear to support the identification but which does not in fact have the quality.

As stated in *R v. Oakwell* ((1978), 66 Cr.App.R. 174), a *Turnbull* warning is generally required in all cases where identification is the sole or substantial issue. Finally, the *Turnbull* guidelines apply equally to police who are identifying witnesses (*Reid v. R* (1990) A.C. 363, PC).

Fisher (1995) drew attention to the fact that police detectives who routinely question eyewitnesses and conduct line-ups (that is, identification parades) and photo-spreads (that is, identification from an array of 'mugshots') receive little or no training on how to interview a witness. Fisher's comment would seem to apply more to the situation in the United States than in the UK because police officers there have been routinely taught the cognitive interview technique (see chapter 4) for a few years now. Admittedly, the existence of State police forces in countries like the United States, Australia and Canada makes it less likely that there will be uniformity in evidence and criminal procedure legislation and in police training, let alone in how to interview a witness or, finally, how to construct and conduct a line-up or a photo-spread.

Irrespective of federal systems, there are, of course, differences in what police officers in different countries can legally do as far as witness identification procedures are concerned. To illustrate, according to Wells and Turtle (1986) as many as a quarter of the cases in the mid-west in the United States involve a procedure whereby the police create a line-up comprising only the suspects in a crime. As Wells et al. (1994:228) put it, this procedure 'is like giving the witness a multiple choice test in which there can be no wrong answer'. Under the rules in the Code of Practice D, made under section 66 of the *Police and Criminal Evidence Act [PACE]* (1984) such a practice is prohibited in Britain.[4] The same practice is also prohibited in Australia. Also, photo-spreads (see below) are by far the most common method used in the

United States for establishing identification but are seldom, if ever, used in the UK. In addition, unlike in the United States, in the UK all police interviews with suspects are tape-recorded and line-ups are videotaped in customised identification suites located in London and elsewhere. Differences in the law of evidence and police procedures need to be borne in mind when generalising some research findings from one country to another.

Police person identification procedures, which most often involve the use of photographs, do not, of course, take place in a vacuum but in a social context. The witness has his/her memory of the event in question of which often one particular face is of special importance. At the same time, witnesses have their own expectations about the criminal investigation process they are contributing to and the evidence is overwhelming that mock-witnesses are more than ready to select a suspect from a line-up that contains only innocent foils (that is, a target-absent line-up). For their part, law-enforcement officers, often under a lot of pressure to detect (that is, clear up) crimes, are likely to have their suspicions about who the culprit is and would like the witness to confirm their suspicions. Consequently, some police officers may inadvertently and in a rather subtle, non-verbal way such as by smiling and showing approval (see Fanselow, 1975), or even quite openly (for example, in terms of the verbal instruction they give a witness to point out the criminal in the line-up), indicate to the witness who he/she should pick out from a photo-array or in a live line-up. The analogy between a methodologically sound social psychology experiment and a properly conducted line-up has guided eyewitness identification research implicitly and proven very fruitful (Wells and Luus, 1990a).

> It has been claimed that every year in the United States about 6000 people are wrongly convicted.

Estimates of the percentage of cases involving wrongful conviction vary. In an attempt to obtain a more reliable estimate of the size of the problem, Huff et al. (1986) surveyed State Attorneys General (fifty States, District of Columbia, American Samoa, Guam and Puerto Rico) and an Ohio sample which included all presiding judges of common pleas courts, all county prosecutors, all county public defenders, all county sheriffs and the chiefs of police of Ohio's seven major cities. On the basis of a 65 per cent response rate, they reported that 71.8 per cent of those surveyed believed that wrongful felony convictions in the United States was less than 1 per cent. Taking the 1981 US figure for persons arrested and charged with index offences (2 291 560) and on the basis of a 50 per cent conviction rate, Huff et al. estimated that approximately 6000 are wrongly convicted annually (p. 523). This estimate, however, is rather crude as different crimes have different conviction rates. While it is impossible to have an accurate estimate of the number of wrongful convictions,[5] the concern is twofold: an innocent person is wrongly convicted and suffers the consequences, while the real criminal is at large. Of particular interest to psychologists is the general view that eyewitness identification is considered the single most important factor leading to wrongful conviction (Brandon and Davies, 1973; Huff et al., 1986). Most members of the public would be concerned about falsely identifying an innocent person as the perpetrator of a crime. We also know that it is rather common in criminal trials for the defence and the prosecution to disagree about the fairness of police-conducted identification procedures.

Before taking a close and critical look at some well-known witness identification procedures, it is important to remember the following about the use of photographs as a means of identification which mean that both police identification procedures and empirical research using photographs sacrifice a great deal of the memory potential of witnesses asked to perform a recognition task:

- Subjects in simulation studies using photographs are asked to recognise a target person by looking at static images of different faces.
- Such studies actually require picture recognition rather than face recognition (Bruce, 1988).
- Unlike a static picture, motion (for example, rotating a picture of a face 360 degrees), gives information about a face from a variety of views as well as detailed information about the effects of illumination, and can thus 'provide information that can be used to increase identification accuracy' (Pike and Kemp, 1995:26).
- The recognition involved in such a task is based on familiarity and is not identification as such because it takes place in the absence of contextual information, such as details of the culprit's body and the crime scene (Davies, 1989). As Davies pointed out, a crime victim/witness at a live identification parade must both recognise the suspect and place him/her in the appropriate context (p. 557). Furthermore, reinstating the context of an event improves eyewitnesses' recognition accuracy (see chapter 3).
- Recognition accuracy is higher for persons seen as actors in a film showing a robbery than for static, motionless pictures depicting faces devoid of bodies (Schiff et al., 1986).
- For understandable, ethical reasons, most simulation identification studies involve student subjects who have witnessed a staged crime or who are shown a video of such an incident and subsequently are asked to pick the culprit from a set of photographs under different conditions. This is a major limitation because it has been shown that real crime victims generally produce much more information than bystanders (MacLeod, 1987).[6]

In the light of such serious limitations of a great deal of the empirical literature on face identification, one cannot but agree with Davies (1989) that relying on photo identification does not do eyewitnesses justice and empirical studies focusing exclusively on this identification procedure has very limited forensic relevance (p. 559). Davies' grave warning should not go unnoticed by psychology researchers and police alike (see also Laughery and Wogalter, 1989).

In view of the pressures under which police investigators work in busy police departments in large cities, and irrespective of the identification procedure used, they would no doubt appreciate psychologists enabling them to distinguish accurate from inaccurate eyewitness identification. Drawing on the existing literature on reality monitoring (Johnson et al., 1993), facial recognition (Sporer, 1993) and eyewitness identification, (Dunning and Stern,

1994) describe a test of eyewitness accuracy that could be applied to specific witnesses at the time they make their identifications of suspect. They hypothesised that different cognitive processes would be reported by witnesses when making accurate as opposed to inaccurate positive identification judgements. Individual mock-witnesses in four studies were shown a 3-minute videotape depicting a staged theft of money from a teacher's purse that had been left on a table. After spending 5 to 10 minutes completing a questionnaire about the scenes shown in the video (but not including the theft), the subjects were asked to pick out the perpetrator in a five-photo line-up. Subjects were also instructed to say aloud what they were thinking or doing, what sort of processes went on in their head and they were tape-recorded while making/ thinking aloud their judgements. It was found that, of those making positive identifications, accurate witnesses were significantly more likely than inaccurate ones to describe their judgements as resulting from automatic recognition (for example, 'His face just "popped out" at me'); in other words, they were relatively unable to articulate any explicit cognitive strategy that underpinned their identification judgement. A process of elimination strategy, that is, comparing the photos in a line-up to short-list suspects and so narrowing their choices, was the process significantly more frequently used by inaccurate witnesses. Dunning and Stern also reported that telling subjects about the strategy found to characterise accurate and inaccurate identifications, improved their identification performance.

1 Person Identification from Photographs

In western common law countries identification of a suspect by photograph is a lawful means of identification during a police investigation of a criminal offence or as an alternative when a suspect refuses to take part in an identification parade. The most commonly used photo identification procedure is where a witness identifies a suspect from a photo-board, comprising, in Victoria, for example, one photograph of the suspect and eleven others, such ordinary photographs (that is, not police ones) only showing facial features and which are, as much as possible, similar to the suspect's. Photo-board identification is used in criminal investigations when the identity of the suspect is not known and at the evidence-gathering stage when the suspect has been identified (*Alexander v. R* (1981) 145 CLR 395). Recently, there has been a trend towards identifying a suspect by means of video-frames or a video-film. With this form of identification, a witness views separate video-frames of twelve individuals, one of whom is the suspect. Unlike photo identification, video identification[7] provides a coloured three-dimensional photograph of a suspect instead of a two-dimensional image allowed in a photo-board. Video-frame and video-film identification, like photo and photo-board identification, is admissible evidence.

In England and Wales, the photograph of a person who has been arrested may be taken at a police station only with his/her written consent (PACE,

1984: Code D4.1) but, if certain criteria are met (see Code D4.2), it may be taken without their consent but force may not be used (Code D.4.3). Photographs of offenders known to the police are routinely kept at police stations and are used in local criminal investigations in an attempt to identify a culprit.[8] In addition, within police forces there usually exists a criminal identification unit that keeps and updates State/national collections of such photographs. A large proportion of them go back a number of years. Such photographs are carefully indexed and catalogued and kept in albums and are sometimes also available on computers for police personnel and crime witnesses to search. Unlike witnesses in simulation or staged event studies, actual witnesses to different crimes who look (browse?) through police photo albums of offenders known to the police can expect to encounter different numbers of offenders because different crimes have different clear-up rates. For some crimes, even taking age and gender into account, there will be thousands of photographs of potential suspects a witness to a crime could be asked to look at in an attempt to select the culprit whereas for other crimes there will be at most a few dozen. To illustrate, police photo albums would contain fewer photographs of paedophiles and arsonists than burglars or armed robbers. In addition, the proportion of different ethnic groups in the community varies as does their involvement in different crimes, and there are fewer offenders known to the police with red hair because there are fewer such individuals among the population at large and there is no reason whatsoever why one should expect such individuals to be over-represented among offenders.

Identification from police photographs is admissible evidence in most jurisdictions even though defence attorneys might like to argue that such evidence should be inadmissible because it implies that the defendant has a criminal record (see *Bleakley* (1993) Crim. LR 203). On the basis that photographic evidence has its dangers from the defendant's point of view, trial judges in Britain, for example, are required by *Dodson* ((1984) 1 WLR 971) to warn the jury about such evidence.[9] The following case (cited in Cutler and Penrod, 1995) shows how eyewitnesses can make mistakes where photo identification is involved, with serious consequences for the innocent.

Case Study

Witness Photo Misidentification

A blurred photograph of a robber in action was shown on television in an effort by police to apprehend the perpetrator of a number of bank robberies. Someone telephoned the police claiming the photograph shown was of Shaun Deckinga. Three bank-tellers who had been in the bank during one of the robberies identified him with confidence as the perpetrator, the jury believed the eyewitnesses and he was found guilty of two robberies. He protested his innocence but to no avail. The real robber, who had recently been released from prison, committed another almost identical robbery not later afterwards while Deckinga was in custody. This time, however, the security camera photograph of him was clearer. A prison guard recognised the ex-prisoner robber by the name of Jerry Clapper who was duly arrested and admitted having committed the bank robberies, including the two for which Deckinga had been convicted. Deckinga's conviction was quashed and he was released from prison.

is consistent with the empirical evidence showing little statistical relationship between such measures of verbal recall as accuracy, completeness, consistency and fluency and accuracy of witness recognition performance (Pigott and Brigham, 1985).[14]

A parade may occasionally involve a witness being asked to identify an object used in the commission of a crime such as vehicles, premises, firearms and other weapons, tools or instruments or clothing (*R v. Hickin and others* (1996) Crim.L.R. 584, CA) or other physical objects or even an animal. The same legal principles apply to both person and object identification parades (*R v. Turnbull* (1976) WLR 445). Interestingly, the experimental psychological literature on line-ups has been exclusively concerned with person identification. From the court's point of view, the line-up is used to make certain that the ability of the witness to recognise the suspect or an object has been fairly and adequately tested. In most countries such parades are normally conducted at police stations for a number of reasons but occasionally there is a need to do so elsewhere, including inside a prison. In addition to providing identification evidence for the courts, identification parades can also be used by police investigators to eliminate a suspect from an investigation early on or to put pressure on a suspect to confess. In view of the fact that photo-board identification may be prejudicial to the accused and its use prior to a line-up may result in unconscious transference, a line-up is, therefore, generally preferred to photo identification since a line-up also means the accused is present and in a position to comment on its fairness. A line-up rather than photo identification should be used at the evidence-gathering stage.

The existing empirical literature (see Penrod and Cutler, 1995a and b; Ross et al. 1994; Wells et al., 1998, 1999 for literature reviews) has identified a range of factors that contribute to biases in line-up procedures which result in apparently alarmingly high rates of false identifications. In common law countries alleged offenders are presumed innocent until proven guilty in a court of law or until they, of their own volition, decide to plead guilty. Consequently, biased line-ups are just not acceptable. As mentioned in chapter 7, the calling of an experimental psychologist to give expert evidence regarding the unreliability of identification evidence is not permitted in Australia (*R v. Smith* (1987) VR 907). Drawing on Freckelton and Selby's (2002) excellent work on the expert witness, expert evidence on eyewitness identification may not be given in the United States (*Dyas v. United States* 376 A 2d 827 (DC 1977); *Nelson v. State* 362 So 2d 10107 (Fla 1978); *United States v. Amaral* 488 F 2d 1148) and Canada (see *R v. Audy* (No.2) (1977) 34 CCC (2d) 231). But what is meant by 'fair' line-up? Wells et al. (1993) offer the following definition: 'A good line-up task is one that minimises the likelihood that an innocent suspect will be (falsely) identified and maximises the likelihood that a guilty suspect will be (accurately) identified' (p. 835). There is, however, disagreement as to whether the distractors/foils should resemble the suspect or match the eyewitness' description of the suspect (see below).

Before considering empirical evidence pertaining to sources of bias in identification performance, it is important to note that many of the studies concerned can be said to be low on external validity because they have used young students as subjects and, also, as Ainsworth (2000a) rightly argues, 'Although laboratory-based research studies examining identification procedures have been helpful in many areas, they are unable to replicate the tension which a real suspect [and witness] on a real identification parade might experience. For this reason, it is not easy to call upon reliable research evidence to establish the extent to which wrongly accused suspects can be picked out as guilty' (p. 173). The reader should note that many simulation studies of line-up identification accuracy have misused the term 'false identification'. This is partly because of a certain amount of conceptual confusion about the meaning of the terms 'culprit', 'suspect' and 'distractor/foil', which appears to have led so many identification evidence researchers to confuse all three or two of these three terms. By definition, a standard police line-up includes a suspect. The suspect who, of course, may be innocent, is suspected of being the culprit of the crime. Positive identification of the suspect has serious consequences. A distractor/foil is innocent and if the witness selects a distractor it has no consequences (Wells et al., 1994:227). In the same context, a distinction also needs to be made between 'false identification' and 'identification error' by a witness. Wells et al. (1994:228) 'reserve the term false identification for instances in which the eyewitness identifies an innocent suspect; if the eyewitness identifies a distractor we call this a foil identification or distractor identification', and, 'a false identification cannot occur when the actual culprit is a member of the line-up' (p. 228). Often researchers are actually reporting 'distractor identifications' that are of no real significance in real life other than a source of police frustration and disappointment. High rates of false identifications in the target-present condition have seldom been reported. In a real line-up, of course, a witness has no way of knowing for certain whether the one the police suspect of committing the crime is in fact the culprit. The distinctions made by Wells et al. (1994) have implications for how one decides the similarity between the suspect and the foils.

4.1 Sources of Bias

4.1.1 Police Practices, Knowledge, Attitudes and Intentions

It is standard police practice worldwide when a crime is being reported to them and/or when an eyewitness is available, to ask for a verbal description of the culprit/s. One of the techniques used by police in criminal investigations is to ask witnesses to assist them with constructing a composite face image of the suspect by verbally describing facial features or simply selecting them from a collection provided by the police. This task can be performed manually or with the aid of computers. In fact, such state-of-the-art software is fast making the police artist an endangered species. Some well-known examples of commercially available software of face composites are the American Identi-Kit III, the British Photo-Fit and E-Fit and the Australian FACE. They all involve a witness selecting individual level characteristics from data bases of facial (hair, eyebrows, nose, chin, eyes, etc.) and other features (for example, hats, glasses) which are put together to construct a composite face. Individual characteristics are then exchanged or edited using computer graphics in order to reduce discrepancies between the composite and the image of a face in the witness' memory. Sometimes, publicising a face-composite image of the suspect/s is the only avenue of inquiry available to detectives in their search for crime suspects.

The E-Fit is widely used in nineteen countries (Turner, 2000) and, therefore, some details concerning its use would appear justified. According to Bennet et al. (2000), before a facial composite is constructed the witness is interviewed by the system operator to ascertain how well they saw the perpetrator. Only if the witness had an adequate exposure to the perpetrator will the operator proceed. A second stage of selection takes place after the composite has been constructed. When the final composite has been produced, the witness is asked to give a 'rating' score of how good a likeness the composite is compared to their memory of the perpetrator. If the rating is below a certain amount, the composite is deemed 'negative' and is not used further in the police investigation of the case. Bennet et al. predicted that a composite is in many ways similar to a witness providing a confidence rating and would thus be expected to bear little relationship to how good a likeness the composite actually is. In a number of field studies in which trained E-Fit operators worked with participant-witnesses to a live, staged crime a very low correlation was found between the rating scores provided by witnesses and the accuracy of the composite. According to Turner (2000), there are two types of E-Fit construction types: 'piecemeal' and 'jigsaw'. In the piecemeal technique the witness selects each feature individually, while in the jigsaw technique a witness begins by selecting features individually but each feature is left on view while subsequent features are added. One factor which may affect the quality of E-Fit is a form of 'overshadowing', which can occur when seeing similar but incorrect feature exemplars during the composite construction process.[15]

Of course, as far as the outcome of criminal investigations is concerned, the use of a face composite is but one of many factors that can contribute to a crime being cleared up. Also, there is evidence that, when not instructed to do so, only 4 per cent of witnesses report focusing on facial cues (Tooley et al., 1984, cited in Deffenbacher, 1989:566). Finally, likely difficulties in communication between the witness and the operator of the computer-witness interaction system mean that the hard-copy generated is at best a poor likeness of the suspect (Davies, 1981, 1983, 1986b). Having witnesses directly produce the computer image would not be feasible because of the heterogeneity of crime victims, time considerations and implications for police resources. In addition, there is evidence that having a witness (children aged five and six years) make a drawing of the suspect as an intervening task between witnessing an event and line-up identification two weeks later is correlated with more false line-up identifications (Vilhelmy, 2000).

Evaluation data on the operational effectiveness of face composites is rather scarce. Despite what some police members may think, the available empirical evidence indicates that such face composites only contribute to the apprehension of offenders in a small minority of cases. An early survey by the British Home Office (Darnborough, 1977, cited by Clifford and Davies, 1989:54) reported that the Photo-Fit proved significantly useful in solving a crime in 22 per cent of applicable cases. In the absence of data regarding the types of crimes involved and the time interval between the offence and when composites were constructed, it is impossible to evaluate Darnborough's finding. Bennett (1986) sent questionnaires to 512 police officers in one Metropolitan Police area in London who had been supplied with a Photo-Fit image. With a response rate of 70 per cent, it was found that only 3.8 per cent indicated the Photo-Fit had led to an arrest. In fact, in four of the fourteen cases cleared up, the image was judged a poor likeness of the person arrested. The present author carried out a study (unpublished) on behalf of the Victoria Police, Australia, of 200 colour computer face composites (representing an 18 per cent response rate by detectives) using FACE (Facial Composition and Editing) provided to operational police in Melbourne by the force's specialist six-member Criminal Identification Squad during July 1995 to June 1996. The squad members had been trained in the cognitive interview technique six months prior to the commencement of the study.

It was found that the main crimes involved were theft (22 per cent), burglary (20 per cent), armed robbery (12 per cent) and assault (10 per cent); 54 per cent of the witnesses were female, 21 per cent were aged 11 to 20, 21 to 30 (44 per cent) and 35 per cent over thirty years. It was also found that utilising FACE, police were able to charge someone in 19 per cent of the cases while in 23 per cent the FACE assisted in confirming a suspect. Out of fifty-two cases where it was possible for police to rate the FACE composite on a 5-point scale in terms of its likeness to the offender, 46 per cent attracted a rating of 4 and 69 per cent a rating of 3 or greater. Finally, there were significant between-squad member differences regarding the proportion of their composite FACE images that contributed directly to an offender being arrested and charged – it ranged from 6.9 per cent to 33 per cent. The findings reported concerning the apparent usefulness of FACE composites should be treated with caution, however, due to the low response rate by detectives and the possibility that the memory of many of the witnesses was probably adversely affected by the fact that witnesses were interviewed for a FACE more than three days after the offence had been committed and had, by then, been interviewed by different police members, and the memory of 25 per cent had been further interfered with by being asked to look through photo albums of suspects at a police station before being interviewed for FACE composite. Nevertheless, the study does provide limited support for police use of computer FACE composites.

Newlands (2000) reported a study which investigated the efficacy of facial composites. Two days after seeing a mock perpetrator for the first time, witnesses were interviewed, gave descriptions of the suspect and helped to create computerised composites of his face using E-Fit. The witnesses rated the likeness of the composites to the perpetrator from their memories of him and the most highly rated composites were chosen for use in the study. A total of seventy people to whom the perpetrator was known were shown the composite. Half saw the composite only and half saw the composite and also heard a tape of the witness' description of the perpetrator, obtained using a cognitive interview. Identification accuracy in the composite and description condition was significantly higher than in the composite-only condition. Newlands' finding supports the use of other evidence in conjunction with that gained from composite systems. Finally, Vazel and Somat (2000) compared two face-composite software packages used by French police forces, namely the CD-fit and FACES, when combined with either a standard French police interview or a 'guided interview', which is adapted from the cognitive interview. They found a greater degree of composite accuracy for the CD-fit combined with the 'guided interview'. The need for more research in this area cannot be overemphasised, especially concerning the interactive nature of the composite face interviews and how to enhance the interviewer–witness communication.

When asking a witness for a verbal description of the suspect/s, police are in no position to know whether a line-up will later be required, and a good physical description of the culprit/s is needed to be communicated to patrol units, unmarked cars and even to a police helicopter if an operation is to be mounted to apprehend one or more serious offenders making their getaway from the scene of the crime. Schooler and Engstler-Schooler (1990) reported that the very act of asking eyewitnesses for a verbal description of the culprit can impair performance on a delayed line-up identification test. The researchers termed this phenomenon 'verbal overshadowing'. The identification impairment was not found, however, if the subjects did the line-up test soon after describing the culprit.

On the basis of Schooler and Engstler's verbal overshadowing hypothesis, we would expect this police practice to impact on an eyewitness' line-up identification performance. Indeed, Comish (1987) found that the identification performance of subjects who had earlier tried to construct an Identi-kit composite image of a suspect showed more false identifications than for control subjects if the foils in the line-up resembled the experimental subjects' errors when attempting the Identi-kit image. According to Lindsay, D.S. (1994:46), the effects reported by Schooler and Engstler-Schooler (1990) and Comish (1987) can be described in terms of source monitoring processes, that is, without being aware subjects draw on memories from different sources: at the encoding stage, when describing the face (the interpolated material) and when seeing it in a photo line-up, because of similarity in the information involved. Lindsay, D.S. suggests, therefore, that warning witnesses about these effects may well help to avoid them.

4.1.2 The Composition of the Line-up

A basic proposition by Wells et al. (1994:225) in the context of their numerous constructive recommendations on how to properly conduct line-up identifications, is that 'The purpose of a line-up is to uncover information in an eyewitness' recognition memory that was not available in recall. (Luus and Wells, 1991)'. Line-ups can differ in terms of their size (see below) as well as the extent of similarity between the suspect and the foils. In the typical line-up procedure used in Britain, Australia and New Zealand, for example, a suspect is included in a line together with seven foils (innocent 'distractors') side-by-side and the suspect can choose his or her position in the line. The witness gets to view the line-up simultaneously. As Thomson (1995a:143) points out, 'the standard method of identification parades is not unlike multiple-choice exam questions'. Such a procedure, of course, means that there is scope for each foil to somehow 'let the witness know' that they are not the suspect and, if for some reason, all or some of the foils know who the suspect is, the potential is there for them to communicate that knowledge to the witness in a subtle way, whether consciously or unconsciously (Thomson, 1995a).

A line-up may be 'unfair', 'biased', 'suggestive' when one person stands out from the rest in such a way that anyone equipped with the original verbal description given by the witness can pick him/her out irrespective of whether they were present at the scene of the crime (Clifford, 1981:25). A person could stand out in a line-up because of the colour of their hair, their ethnic background, their clothing (especially if one of the line-up members happens to be wearing clothes similar to those worn by the offender when seen by the witness) or because other line-up members are not standing close to a particular person or they keep looking at him (Lloyd-Bostock, 1988:14).

The inclusion of reasonably look-alike foils in a line-up is meant to ensure that a witness identifies a suspect on the basis of their memory of what the suspect looks like and not by deduction (that is, by knowing who the police suspect of having committed the offence in question and thus identifying that same person as the perpetrator, as might be happening with show-ups). In Britain and Australia, line-ups (until recently most of them live ones) are presented simultaneously. We saw in chapters 2 to 4 that police investigators should expect that eyewitnesses will often only be able to furnish them with incomplete and inaccurate descriptions of culprits. If the police use the witness' description to select the foils it will probably mean that in a number of cases they will not be very similar in appearance to the person the police suspect. In Britain, however, whatever the description given by a witness, Annex A of the revised edition (effective from 1 April, 1991) of Code of Practice D (*Police and Criminal Evidence Act* (1984)) specifically states that the members of a line-up selected by the police must, 'as far as possible resemble the suspect in age, height, general appearance and position in life' (cited by McKenzie, 1995). In the case of *Quinn* (*The Times*, 15 March 1994) Lord Taylor, CJ, stated that the idea is not to produce a line-up comprising seven clones of the suspect (cited in McKenzie, 1995:203).

Psychologists have examined the impact on identification performance of the degree of similarity between the target and foils in a line-up as well as whether the choice of foils should be on the basis of the description given by a witness (Luus and Wells, 1991; Wells et al., 1993) or on the basis of what rather than a ratio of suspects to total line-up members' (p. 229). In such a line-up, there is a 16.6 per cent probability of chance identification of an innocent suspect. The same authors argue that the fact that Nosworthy and Lindsay (1990) chose foils on the basis of foil-suspect similarity instead of matching them with witnesses' description of the suspect, 'might have implications for the shape of the function relating the number of good distractors to the risk of false identifications of the suspect' (p. 229).

As already mentioned above, line-up bias refers to how far the suspect stands out in the line-up. Line-up bias often overlaps with line-up size (Brigham and Pfeiffer, 1994:202). A psychologist could be used, as has been the case especially in the United States, to inform the court about the fairness of a line-up. Doing so would require working out the likelihood of any line-up member being picked out by a witness by chance alone. The formula for this is $1/N$ where N equals the size of the parade. This approach was in fact used by Buckhout (1976)[16] to inform the jury in *State of Florida v. Richard Campbell* that the line-up in which the defendant had been identified had been biased. Buckhout reported that college students, who had not seen the defendant before, selected him 52 per cent of the time when in a six-member line-up his chance level would be only 16.7 per cent.

Regarding measures of line-up size fairness, a number of them have been proposed, namely: the effective size (Malpass, 1981; Malpass and Devine, 1983); acceptable foils (Malpass and Devine, 1983); defendant bias (Malpass and Devine, 1983); proportions (Doob and Kirschenbaum, 1973) and, finally, the functional size technique (Wells et al., 1979). Brigham and Pfeiffer (1994) provide a good account of all these techniques but Navon (1990ab) and Wells and Luus (1990b) would be worth reading. Such techniques basically involve the use of mock witnesses who have not witnessed a crime and are asked to attempt to identify the suspect in a line-up. In a six-person line-up there is a 16.6 per cent probability that a mock-witness would pick the suspect by chance alone. The techniques below basically compare expected chance identifications we would anticipate with identifications by mock-witnesses. On the basis of their empirical assessment, Brigham et al. (1990) opt for the proportions technique as the most useful of the five line-up bias measures, both in terms of discriminability and sensitivity. This post-hoc measure of line-up fairness developed by psychologists is also known as the 'diagnosticity ratio'. This refers to the ratio of correct identifications in a target-present line-up to false identifications in a target-absent one.

The suggestion for a double line-up, only one of which contains the suspect (Wells, 1984), would also point to unreliable witnesses who select an innocent foil in the blank line-up because they are anxious to select anyone or because their memory of what the culprit looked like is poor. This procedure would also reduce the pressure on the witness to select the suspect from a line-up which the witness has been 'informed' contains the suspect. The witness would, of course, be told that only one of the line-ups contains the suspect. Research reported by Brigham and Pfeiffer (1994) found that three line-up fairness measures based on college student mock-witnesses were statistically

The 'Multiple-Choice-Sequential-Large' (MSL) is a promising approach in increasing line-up accuracy.

related to direct evaluations of line-up fairness by forty law officers and provide further support for the use of student subjects in developing such indices (pp. 216–17). Furthermore, such indices can form the basis of guidelines to the courts to decide the question of whether a particular line-up was fair or not (Wells et al., 1979).

A rather original argument has been put forward by Avraham Levi (2001) in favour of using what he calls 'Multiple-Choice-Sequential-Large' (MSL) line-up. The MSL: (a) consists of at least about forty members; (b) is sequential rather than simultaneous; and (c) allows the witness to choose more than one person in the line-up. For practical reasons, it is conducted either on video or with photos. On the basis of his experiments, Levi maintains that each of the three line-up modifications mentioned contributes to reducing single choices of a line-up member in perpetrator-absent line-ups. When combined with asking the witnesses to give their confidence with each choice, they make line-up identifications diagnostic of guilt. Drawing, also, on a meta-analysis of previous studies in which witnesses gave their confidence in each choice, Levi has come to the conclusion that, 'it is possible to clearly differentiate accurate from inaccurate "identifications" from multiple choices. The prosecution gets the evidence to convict all culprits, while the innocent are exonerated'. No doubt, Levi's work needs to be replicated before deciding whether or not to adopt the MSL line-up. While the question of feasibility would not be an issue since the MSL does not require a live line-up, implementing Levi's suggestion would require changes to existing legislation in most countries.

4.1.4 Biased Instructions

An identification police officer can also influence the witness' identification of the suspect by the instruction/s he/she gives the witness. This was also the view of the sixty-three eyewitness experts surveyed by Kassin et al. (1989). The same experts also believed the effect was reliable enough for them to so testify about it in court. Relative to twenty other factors listed, line-up instructions were perceived by the same experts to be the second-most reliable phenomena in eyewitness research. It has long been reported by a number of researchers that telling a witness the culprit is in the line-up produces high rates of mistaken identification (Cutler et al., 1987; Foster et al., 1994; Paley and Geiselman, 1989). Köhnken and Maass (1988, Experiment 1) challenged generalising research on biased instructions to actual line-ups on the basis that their own findings indicate that 'the instructional bias effect observed in previous experiments is limited to subjects who are fully aware that they are participating in an experiment' and the fact they failed to find a significant increase in false identifications as a function of biased instructions 'suggests that eyewitnesses are better than their reputation' (p. 369).

Cutler and Penrod's (1995a) discussion of the evidence, including Paley and Geiselman (1989), led them to the conclusion that 'biased instructions influence identification performance even when subjects are given the option of providing no response (that is, "don't know")' (p. 122). Biased instructions studies, however, have not, as a rule, taken into account the gender of the witness and whether the line-up is presented simultaneously or sequentially. It should also be remembered in this context that the biased instructions effect which inflates the false identification rate has been found in target-absent line-ups (Paley and Geiselman, 1989). Furthermore, Foster et al. (1994) found that male witnesses were more influenced by such instructions than female ones. On the basis of the existing empirical evidence, we can conclude that a biased instructions effect has indeed been demonstrated but the way it operates is not as simple as first thought. Of course, the scope for the police to give biased line-up instructions is limited when the law specifies how a witness is to be instructed and what to be told. In Britain, for example, Code of Practice D (Annexe A, para.14) (PACE, 1984) states that the identification officer shall tell the eyewitness that, 'the person he saw may or may not be in the parade and [that] if he cannot make a positive identification he should say so'. How far operational police comply with this requirement is not known. If they do not, it would be a ground for the defence counsel asking the court not to admit the identification evidence concerned and if the court of first instance nevertheless admits such identification evidence, it would be a ground for an appeal against the conviction.

4.1.5 How a Line-up is Presented

The police are also in a position to influence the bias and the outcome of a line-up identification by the very procedure they use, that is, whether they present a line-up simultaneously or sequentially. A line-up can be presented live, as has traditionally been the practice within British, American, Canadian and New Zealand police forces as well as those in other Commonwealth countries, or using a set of photographs or, finally, on video. Video identification has been introduced in Victoria, Australia, combined with the use of a one-way viewing, and is also provided for in England and Wales. A body of empirical studies have examined whether presenting a line-up simultaneously or sequentially influences identification accuracy[17] (see Cutler and Penrod, 1995a, and Ross et al., 1994, for literature reviews). Such studies have tended to use line-ups or photo-arrays usually consisting of a target and five to seven foils. It has been consistently found that identification performance is not influenced by the type of presentation in the target-present condition. By definition, of course, an identification parade/line-up contains a suspect. As mentioned above, however, there are jurisdictions where there are no guidelines regarding the composition, size and so forth of line-ups or how they are to be conducted. The empirical evidence shows that:

- Presentation style does not significantly affect identification accuracy in a target-present line-up or photo-array.
- It is only in target-absent line-ups that witnesses yield an alarmingly high rate of false identifications when a line-up or a photo-array is presented simultaneously.

- The high rate of false identifications in target-absent line-ups is significantly reduced in sequential presentations for both children and adult witnesses (Parker and Ryan, 1993; Cutler and Penrod, 1995a:135). Sequential presentations also reduce the impact of biased instructions and the beneficial effects of sequential presentation are reduced if subjects have the opportunity of a target-absent practice trial or get a second chance, especially with a simultaneous presentation, after they have been exposed to all the members of a line-up sequentially.

Thomson (1995a:142–3) lists four advantages of presenting line-ups sequentially: 'it reduces the witness's tendency to select the person in the line-up who best fits the witness's memory of the offender rather than selecting the person who is positively recognised ... the opportunity for the other participants in the parade to cue, consciously or unconsciously, the witness as to who is the suspect will be significantly reduced ... it is possible to preserve the suspect's right to select the order in which he or she appears and not convey to the other members of the parade that he is the suspect [and it] will more easily allow witnesses to observe members of the line-up re-enacting the activities that had previously taken place'.

Bearing in mind the need for standardisation of suspect identification police procedures, Thomson's suggestion to vary the size of line-ups so that the witness does not know how many individuals will be presented and, consequently, his/her temptation to select any member or foil is reduced would not be feasible because it would lead to inconsistent police procedures. In addition, even if police were to accept such a suggestion, defence attorneys would most likely attack identification evidence so obtained in cross-examination and would appeal against a conviction based on witness identification evidence obtained by police using rather inconsistent procedures. The rest of the advantages listed by Thomson (1995a) and the policy recommendations that follow from them should be taken very seriously by law reform commissions and police alike when revising witness identification law and procedure.

Finally, one factor that has been neglected by line-up accuracy researchers is the potential danger for identification accuracy of intervening line-ups. Hinz and Pedzek (2001) describe the following hypothetical situation: a crime takes place, the police arrest an innocent suspect who is subsequently put in a line-up and the witness rejects the line-up. The police later arrest a new suspect and the witness is asked for the second time to identify him/her in another line-up that includes the innocent suspect and the new suspect (the actual criminal) and four foils (in the United States). Hinz and Pedzek have found that the effect of the intervening line-up with an innocent suspect is that the witness is significantly more likely to identify him/her second time round than the true perpetrator. In England and Wales, the Code of Practice under the *Police and Criminal Evidence Act* (1984) provides that such a danger is non-existent because a new line-up would be completely new (see above), that is, the suspect that has not been identified by the witness is not brought back to participate in another line-up. As we shall see below, many of the recommendations by Wells et al. (1998) to improve the conducting of line-ups in the States and to protect the innocent have been in place in England since 1984.[18]

4.1.6 Identification Test Medium

Given that there are different ways of presenting a suspect to a witness for identification – show-ups, live line-ups, videotaped live line-ups, or photo-arrays, Cutler et al. (1994:164–6) mention a number of practical issues in choosing the identification test medium, namely availability of suitable foils, the time it takes to construct it and where it can take place. Photo-arrays, however, allow a greater pool of persons to select foils from, are transportable, they prevent line-up members influencing the witness in any way while he or she is viewing the line-up, and avoid the anxiety which most crime victims/ crime witnesses would naturally feel when confronting the perpetrator of a crime face-to-face. The videotape is an increasingly more popular alternative to both live line-ups and photo-arrays and, as Cutler et al. point out, it can provide a witness with the same information as a live line-up, it is less expensive and time-consuming to construct, requires less personnel and, finally, it prevents the witness being cued by foils as to who the suspect is. Another advantage of the videotape that can be added to the list is that it provides a record of the line-up for the purposes of the trial and thus avoids frequent legal arguments about alleged police improprieties in conducting the line-up that delay the processing of criminal cases through the courts. There can be no doubt that the videotape will eventually replace live line-ups, but do different identification test media produce different identification performance?

Turnbull and Thomson (1984)[19] compared the identification performance of subjects who witnessed an abrasive exchange between the lecturer and a stranger and whose memory of the perpetrator was tested in target-present and target-absent conditions using either a live line-up or a photo-display. They found that in the target-present condition, there were no significant differences in identification accuracy. Similar findings had earlier been reported by Hilgendorf and Irving (1978) and Shepherd et al. (1982). Turnbull and Thomson, however, also found that in the target-absent condition, false identifications were three times higher in the photo-display than in the live line-up condition. Cutler et al. (1994) carried out a meta-analysis of eight studies comparing identification test media and found that the type of medium (live line-ups, videotaped line-ups, photo-arrays, slides and line drawings, produced comparable identification performances (p. 179). Consequently, they concluded that 'identifications from photoarrays should therefore not be given less weight in investigations or in trials than identifications from live line-ups. Another conclusion is that, given the apparent comparability of live line-ups and photo-arrays, it is not worth the trouble and expense to use live line-ups' (p. 181). Cutler et al. do remind their readers, however, that in deciding which identification test medium to use, one should take into account relevant legal provisions requiring, for example, that the suspect's legal counsel be present at any of them (Wells and Cutler, 1990).[20] Cutler et al. do not, however, consider their meta-analytic findings the last word on the subject but urge future researchers to examine the effects of identification test media in field experiments that are forensically more relevant. Finally, on the basis that videotape technology allows faces to be blown up larger than life, persons to be shown in motion, and a line-up to be shown repeatedly, the same authors maintain that 'it is conceivable that videotaped line-ups might improve identification accuracy rates in comparison to live line-ups'.

4.1.6.1 Video Film Identification Code D:2(10–12) of PACE (1984) provides that, if a suspect refuses to participate in an identification parade or group identification and the identification officer is of the view that for this or other reasons it would be the most satisfactory course of action to take in the circumstances, he/she may show a witness a video-film of the subject in accordance with Annex B. The suspect's consent should be sought but the identification officer may proceed even if the suspect does not consent if it is practicable to do so. The procedure for video identification is almost identical to that for identification parades. *Inter alia*, Annex B provides that: the suspect and the other eight people shall as far as possible be filmed in the same positions or carrying the same activity and under identical conditions; reasonable time is to be given the suspect and his/her solicitor, friend, or other appropriate adult, to see the film before it is shown to the witness. Annex B also provides for the security of the tape and its destruction if the suspect is not prosecuted or, if prosecuted, is cleared of the charge/s against him/her (D.13–14).

4.1.6.2 Identification from Video Footage According to British researchers Pike, Brace and Kemp (2000), video footage, whether it is from closed-circuit television or police surveillance cameras, is increasingly being used to identify offenders. When this footage is of a high resolution and frames are in colour and show a clear, unobstructed close-up view of the person's face, it can be used as convincing evidence as to the identity of the perpetrator. However, often the footage is of low resolution, the face is but a small part of the image and is only in view for a few frames. Various facial comparison techniques have been developed to enable one to compare an image captured from video footage with the image of the suspect. The effectiveness of these techniques is being evaluated. Pike et al. reported a study of the effectiveness of facial comparison techniques (that is, the accuracy with which operators can determine facial orientation and the location of features in video images) in which they manipulated the ethnicity of the target face in images of varying resolution. They found that care needs to be taken using video footage to identify a perpetrator, particularly of a different race.

5 Voice Identification

People have stereotypes of what sort of individuals speak with what kind of voices, and this applies also to stereotypes of different kinds of criminals

5.3 Delay

How much time elapses between actual earwitnesses hearing a voice and when they are asked to identify it varies from case to case. There has been no consistency in the findings reported about the effect of retention interval on voice recognition accuracy. McGehee (1937) had subjects listen to a fifty-word passage read by an unseen speaker at different time intervals. Later subjects were asked to identify the speaker from among four others reading the same passage. It was found that identification accuracy was 83 per cent at two days, 68 per cent at two weeks, 35 per cent at three months, and 13 per cent at five months. Other researchers found no significant decrease in accuracy 24 hours later (Saslove and Yarmey, 1980) while others have reported a significant negative effect over 24 hours (Clifford et al., 1981; Hammersley and Read, 1985), one week (Thompson, 1985a) or two weeks (Goldstein and Chance, 1985). A week after subjects in the Thompson (1985a) study heard a reader's voice, they were asked to select the voice from an array of six voices. Some subjects' voice recognition accuracy was no better than chance. Van Wallendael et al. (1994) reported that retention interval (0 days, 7 days, and 14 days) had no detrimental effect on voice recognition accuracy in both target-present and target-absent conditions (pp. 666–7). Finally, Yarmey and Matthys (1992) found that while voice recognition accuracy did not differ significantly over a one-week period, the false alarm rate increased over the same delay. As Yarmey (1995) points out, 'forgetting over time depends upon the extent of original learning; some voices because of their distinctiveness may be more easily learned and less affected by delay in testing' (p. 267).

5.4 Listener Characteristics

As far as the age of the earwitness is concerned, it is known that infants under six months of age can differentiate their mother's voice from that of strangers (Friedlander, 1970). Conflicting findings have been reported about whether voice recognition accuracy in children increases with age. Peter's (1987) study of children aged 3 to 8 years found that identification performance was generally poor irrespective of the age of the children when their recognition was tested 24 and 48 hours following a visit to the dentist's and conversing with the target speaker for 5 minutes. An earlier study by Mann et al. (1979) reported that voice recognition accuracy increases from age 6 to 10 but declines during the ages 10 to 14. Differences have also been reported for different adult age-groups. Bull and Clifford (1984) reported that individuals under 21 years of age and those over 40 showed inferior voice recognition accuracy than those aged 21 to 40. Bull and Clifford (1999:199) point out, however, this finding may reflect age differences in attention deployment and perception of social situations. Regarding the question of whether adults' voice recognition accuracy is significantly better than children's, Mann et al. (1979) found that accuracy among children aged 10 approached that of adults. Available evidence shows that both children and adults are equally poor at voice-identification (Clifford, 1997; Clifford and Toplis, 1996). More research into age differences in voice recognition accuracy is needed before definitive conclusions can be drawn about the children vs. adults issue.

As far as gender differences are concerned, McGehee (1937) found male subjects better only at recognising female voices. Clifford et al. (1980) reported that in general female listeners were better than male listeners. Thompson (1985a) had subjects identify a reader's voice from an array of six voices. One week later, no gender differences were found. Finally, Yarmey and Matthys (1992:375) varied voice-sample duration (18 seconds, 36 seconds, 120 seconds, and 6 minutes) and, like Yarmey (1986), found no gender differences, with one exception – 'Females were reliably inferior to males in hit scores with the 6-minute voice sample'. Yarmey and Matthys offer no theoretical reason for the one specific gender difference they found. The available literature, therefore, does not point to gender differences in voice recognition (Yarmey, 1995:267; Bull and Clifford, 199:199).

Regarding the importance of the race of the speaker and the earwitness, Goldstein et al. (1981) could find no clear evidence of cross-racial difficulties in speaker identification. In their report to the British Home Office, Clifford et al. (1980:100) concluded that sighted listeners are not as accurate at recognising a voice as blind listeners. However, Winograd, Kerr and Spence (1984) did not find a difference between blind and sighted people.

Empirical studies of the nature of the relationship between earwitness confidence and accuracy have found some support for a positive relationship. More specifically, a positive correlation was reported by Clifford and Bull (1984), a small but significant correlation by Saslove and Yarmey (1980), a significant correlation in the target-absent condition (Yarmey, 1991) and, finally, a significant positive relationship with voice-sample duration of 2 or 6 minutes but not 18 or 36 seconds (Yarmey and Matthys, 1992). Yarmey et al. (1994), however, found no significant relationship between confidence and voice recognition accuracy in show-ups and six-voice line-ups in both target-present and target-absent conditions. Taking into account more recent research (Clifford and Bulloch, 1999),[30] the available evidence indicates that, as in the case of eyewitness testimony, earwitness' confidence is not a reliable criterion by which to judge the accuracy of earwitness' accuracy.

Commonsense would lead us to predict that highly skilled, experienced phoneticians would show significantly better voice recognition accuracy than non-voice experts. Ladefoged (1981, in Yarmey, 1995) appears to be the only study to have investigated this hypothesis and found that nine of the eleven phoneticians tested made correct identifications of all eleven familiar target speakers, but five of the 'experts' also falsely identified an unfamiliar speaker. Correct identification of unfamiliar voices poses difficulties even for phoneticians. The McGehee (1944) study reported some evidence that it might be possible to train people in voice recognition. Later research, however, has failed to find support for trainability (Clifford et al., 1980).

5.5 Post-event Interference

As in the case of eyewitness testimony, there is empirical support for post-event interference on subsequent voice recognition. Subjects in Thompson's (1985b) study listened to a tape-recorded message and 2 to 7 days later they listened to another voice that was either the same as the original voice or a lure and had to identify it. One month later their voice recognition accuracy was tested with a six-voice line-up that included both the original and the lure voice. Thompson found that subjects who had been exposed to the lure were significantly more likely to falsely identify it as the original voice than those who had not been exposed to the lure between hearing the original voice and the test. The adverse effect of an interpolated test that plants new information in earwitnesses' memory (that is, contaminates it) for voices could easily be produced by police investigators who sometimes test witnesses' memory of a suspect's voice on more than one occasion for operational reasons. Such a practice should definitely be avoided.

5.6 Identification Procedure Used

In view of the fact that voice line-ups are more time consuming to arrange than show-ups, police investigators might be interested in the finding that voice recognition accuracy has been found to be poor in both procedures by Yarmey et al. (1994). Clifford et al. (1980:100) reported that identification accuracy is decreased by the size of the voice parade.

5.7 Voice Identification Accuracy: Conclusions

On the basis of the available literature it can be concluded that while in many situations human listeners are capable of accurate voice identification, the reliability of earwitness testimony is affected by a number of factors, namely the duration of the verbal communication listened to and the number of voices listened to at the time a crime is being perpetrated. Additional factors are the pitch of the voice, delay in an earwitness being asked to identify the suspect's voice, whether the witness has been an unexpected earwitness and whether the earwitness has conversed with the speaker. Finally, the emotional state at the time of encoding as well as the age and the gender of the witness and whether the voice is disguised impact on voice recognition accuracy. It would appear that voice recognition is more difficult than visual identification (Legge et al., 1984; McAlister et al., 1993).

In view of the limitation of human voice identification accuracy, Clifford et al. (1980:101) concluded that, 'the complexities of criminal identification by voice are no greater than by visual means' and that 'While verbal identification like any evidence of identification will need to be treated with caution there is no evidence that it should be ignored'. Since then a great deal of research has been carried out. Hammersley and Read (1995) point out in their review of the literature that earwitness performance in experimental studies may have frequently been found to be poor because the researchers used recognition tasks that are intrinsically too difficult. They urge caution in interpreting earwitness accuracy findings from well-controlled laboratory studies. They also state that recognition of a familiar voice is a more feasible task but one that has attracted the attention of few researchers. They conclude that while 'Generally, voice identification or recognition does not guarantee the speaker's identity and one should be pessimistic about the likelihood of recognition' (p. 147), they concede that such identification can be possible and can be tested in a voice line-up on the condition that the voice line-up is valid and the results are not misinterpreted. They suggest future research looks at the questions of how voice and speech processing interact, whether listeners develop a holistic representation of someone's voice with enough exposure to them and, finally, how such exposure, its duration, how it is spaced out as well as its content, influence the accuracy of subsequent voice recognition (p. 147).

Bull and Clifford (1999) concluded their literature review stating that, 'For the criminal justice system, the current findings suggest that police and courts should treat voice identification made by auditory-visual witnesses with caution' (p. 169). Of course, this is not to deny that voice identification can indeed be very accurate. However, normally the circumstances under which a crime victim/witness listens to someone's voice are such that Yarmey (1995) recommends that, in most circumstances, a case should not proceed if it is based exclusively on voice identification; even then, however, voice identification should satisfy three criteria, namely: there was very good opportunity for the witness to listen; the witness was intentionally prepared to remember the perpetrator's voice; and, finally, the appropriate identification procedures have been followed (pp. 270–1).

6 Conclusions

The extent of similarity between visual and voice identification is exemplified by the finding that when listeners attending a voice parade were instructed that the target voice might be absent, they were still reluctant to indicate its absence, that is, earwitnesses, too, approach their task with a set to select someone (Clifford et al., 1980:101). As Wells et al. (1994:224) points out, no eyewitness author has as yet proposed a coherent theoretical framework to account for the social and cognitive processes involved in deciding whether or not to select a particular line-up member as the suspect. The same authors refer to such social and cognitive processes as 'the eyewitness identification process' (p. 224).

Without ignoring limitations of psychological studies of identification procedures, undesirable police practices are a major cause of eyewitness misidentification. While there is some limited empirical evidence that police computer face-composite images appear to be useful to police hard-pressed to apprehend offenders, the range of identification procedures considered in this chapter are fraught with risks for the innocent. As McKenzie (1995) puts it, have to confront the argument that, generally speaking, scores on such tests do not predict future performance. This, of course, does not mean that psychometric tests do not say something about individuals; rather, it points to the importance of such factors as faking by test-takers and the possibility that what a police psychologist might be trying to predict may well be influenced by stress, physical exhaustion, and other factors present in an operational context, that militate against the predictive value of psychological tests.

The police selection field is also plagued by the simple fact that there is no general agreement on what qualities a good recruit should possess and there is a lack of information concerning those who are not recruited. Ainsworth (1993)[5] reported a study in which a small sample of British police officers attending a course at Manchester University listed the following qualities in order of importance: a sense of humour, communication skills, adaptability, common sense, resilience, assertiveness, sensitivity, tolerance, integrity, literacy, honesty, and problem-solving ability. As Ainsworth (1995) points out, while some of these traits can be reliably measured, others cannot (p. 137). A key question in police psychology is whether some types of people (in terms of their values, attitudes or personality) are more likely to want to become police officers and it is this that explains characteristics of serving police personnel (the 'pre-dispositional' model) or whether such police characteristics reflect the impact of training and socialisation into the police role (the 'socialisation' model). This section draws partly on Burbeck and Furnham's (1985) review.

The selection process usually comprises medical and fitness tests, psychological testing and interview/s. On the basis of both US and British studies of police values, utilising, for example, the Rokeach Value Survey,[6] Burbeck and Furnham (1985) concluded that, 'police officers' values seem pretty representative of those of people from their own age and class, though these are not very close to the population at large. However, some of these values appear to change with the experience of being a police officer' (p. 60).

According to Worden (1993), the stereotypical police officer holds a jaundiced view of citizens, and the insularity and isolation of the job is thought to encourage an 'us against them' mentality (pp. 210–11). At the same time, because the perceived role of police emphasises fighting crime and especially their prosecutorial role (Stephenson, 1992:114), operational police appear to have a 'concern for the truth: in what actually happens, rather than what they might wish to happen' (Brown, 1988).[7]

It does appear that police are generally perceived, and especially by young people, as authoritarian and conservative. But are they? The answer to this question is important (Hollin, 1989) because, as Brown and Willis (1985) pointed out, authoritarianism is a recurring theme in police research and also because it relates to hostile police attitudes and behaviour which should not be tolerated and is also associated with unacceptable treatment of racial minorities (Scarman, 1981).

Research into police attitudes on both sides of the Atlantic[8] has been criticised for inadequate matching of controls and because results reported are difficult to interpret in view of the likely possibility that subjects fake their responses to impress (Burbeck and Furnham, 1985). Not surprisingly, such studies of police attitudes have reported conflicting findings. In an interesting study by Brown and Willis (1985) a revised version of the F (fascism) scale was administered to two groups of police recruits, one in the north (N = 54 Ms and 19 Fs) and one in the south of England (N = 30 Ms and 6 Fs). A third group of sixteen fire-service recruits were also administered the scale. Recruits completed the scale during the first week, twelve to thirteen weeks upon completion of training and after three months in the job. The researchers also interviewed twenty-five police inspectors and chief inspectors about their reactions to the preliminary findings. Brown and Willis found support for the socialisation model as recruits were low on authoritarianism during training but experience on the beat increased their authoritarianism. It was also found that the impact of operational policing experience was greater for those who worked in a high-crime area and in a police force that used a more traditional approach to policing. Brown and Willis' findings emphasise the importance of the well-established practice whereby more experienced police members pass on the police subculture (also termed 'locker room culture' by Holdaway, 1983, with its norms for malpractice and emphasis on excitement and taking risks) to the neophytes who are in no position to question 'advice' given them by the station sergeant, for example. The Brown and Willis (1985) study has a number of weaknesses. However, as they themselves admit, the version of the F scale used means their results are not comparable with those of other studies; furthermore, sixteen fire-service recruits cannot be said to be an adequate control group.

Partial support for the socialisation model has been reported by Australian researchers, Wortley and Homel (1995). They administered the Beswick and Hills' (1972) Australian Ethnocentricism (E) scale to measure prejudice, as well as Ray's (1972) Balanced F (BF) scale and a shortened version of the Marlowe-Crowne Social Desirability (SD) scale to help control motivational distortion, to 412 recruits at the New South Wales Police Academy at recruitment, after six months' full-time academy training and after twelve months' police experience. There was some evidence that respondents would not acknowledge their ethnocentricism in order to give a good impression. Wortley and Homel found that:

- Ethnic recruits and females were generally less ethnocentric than Anglo and male recruits. Also, female recruits were less authoritarian than males.
- Recruit training reduced authoritarianism.
- Recruits became more ethnocentric and authoritarian during the field experience. Ethnocentricism increased especially in those recruits sent to police districts with a large Aboriginal population.

Wortley and Homel concluded that police attributes develop as a function of particular policing experience and that training alone is unlikely to overcome the problem of police prejudice. It is unfortunate that Wortley and Homel did not have a control group to test the importation vs socialisation hypothesis. In considering authoritarianism among police officers one should control for age and education. A Canadian study by Perrot and Taylor (1995) compared 123 constables and 36 non-commissioned officers and found that: (a) the latter (who reported significantly greater job satisfaction) were more authoritarian than the former; and (b) education was a significant predictor of authoritarianism (p. 332). Perrot and Taylor's findings would seem to provide some support to the socialisation model.

Worden (1993) did not focus on either ethnocentricism or authoritarianism in her survey of gender differences among 740 police officers (10 per cent females) who had been in the job for no more than seven years in twenty-four police departments in three metropolitan areas in the United States. Worden reported that, taking relevant variables into account, the gender of a police officer was not related to his/her attitudes (pp. 228–9). The literature discussed provides support for both the importation and the socialisation model of police authoritarian attitudes, while a police officer's gender does not appear of itself to be a relevant variable in this context.

2 Predicting Success Within the Force

Burbeck and Furnham (1985) concluded that neither intelligence nor education guarantee success in the police; in fact, they allude to the possibility that, 'Higher levels of education may paradoxically give rise to more dissatisfaction and higher wastage' (p. 62), a hypothesis worth testing at a time when more university graduates are applying to join the police in western countries than a few years ago. To the disappointment, perhaps, of police psychologists, Burbeck and Furnham also concluded, like Lester (1983), that psychological testing does not predict a recruit's later performance and that part of the difficulty may lie in the fact that there is so much variation in what being a police officer entails that, 'it is not necessary to be expected that one common denominator will be found' (p. 64). In addition, there is no consensus on what is meant by 'success' and 'failure' in this context and 'what is needed is a multidimensional, reliable and robust set of criterion measures on which police officers could be judged by superiors, peers and junior officers. Discriminant analysis can then be used to determine what factors discriminate between successful and unsuccessful police officers' (p. 64). The same argument can be made regarding selection of detectives, utilising already available knowledge about the skills and abilities required to carry out the role of a police detective successfully (see McGurk et al., 1994). The need for the kind of research advocated by Burbeck and Furnham (1985) cannot be over-emphasised because psychological testing has also been shown not to be useful in predicting future performance of police officers even in cases where candidates are selected for entry into a police force against recommendations based on psychological testing (Lester et al., 1980). In other words, psychological testing at present is not particularly useful in either screening in or screening out police applicants. This conclusion is at variance with Hollin's

(1989) more optimistic conclusion on the basis of his review of the relevant literature, namely that psychometric and interview data can predict success at police work but 'the exact predictors of success await definition' (p. 139).

Assuming that one can reliably detect deception in law-enforcement applicants using, for example, such widely used tests as the Minnesota Multiphasic Personality Inventory (see Borum and Stock, 1993), paper-and-pencil psychological tests are easy to administer and score, do not cost much money and are usually supplemented with interviews. Since both of these selection methods are shown to have no significant predictive utility, there is a strong argument for making greater use of assessment centres (see Reinke, 1977; Wigfield, 1996). This method is more commonly used to select officers in the armed forces and senior civil service personnel. It usually involves applicants spending two or three days at a centre where they undergo a range of exercises, and tests, including job-simulation exercises to ascertain whether they possess qualities required for a particular position. More recent American research into the predictive utility of one such centre for police recruits (Pynes and Bernardin, 1992) found that whereas psychological testing predicted academy performance better than the centre, the latter was better at predicting on-the-job performance. Pynes and Bernardin used one-day assessment, three candidates at a time, a written examination on three role-play exercises and a multiple-choice test after viewing a crime-related video, and requiring applicants to speak to a home-owner who had reported vandalism. The assessment produced ratings on eight 'skill clusters': directing orders, interpersonal skills, perception, decision-making, decisiveness, adaptability, oral communication and written examination (p. 45). Assessment centres have a number of advantages over more subjective methods such as interview panels, primarily because 'they allow a standardised evaluation of a number of different aspects of behaviour, thereby allowing a better assessment to be made of each person's strengths and weaknesses' (Ainsworth, 2000b:53). One limitation of the assessment centre is that because of its nature and financial cost, this method can only be used when selecting a small number of candidates. Nevertheless, given the cost to train a police recruit and the financial and other loss when he/she resigns, or is advised to resign or is found to be corrupt and is prosecuted, more thought should be given by police executives to using assessment centres.

3 Encounters With the Public

The tradition of the police uniform is as old as the history of modern law enforcement. This section draws on a literature review by Johnson (2001). The familiar dark blue para-military uniform of the London 'Bobbies' dates back to 1829 (p. 27). On the basis of social psychological studies of the social significance of clothing in how we perceive someone (Connor et al., 1975), it comes as no surprise to learn that available empirical evidence (cited by Johnson, 2001) indicates the following positive and negative correlates of the police uniform:

- It is the most likely uniform to induce feelings of safety (Balkin and Houlden, 1983).
- In contrast to casual clothes, it conveys an image of a more competent, reliable, intelligent and helpful person (Singer and Singer, 1985).
- The mere presence of a person wearing it induces conformity to traffic regulations (Sigelman and Sigelman, 1976). According to Johnson (2001), however, studies of the influence of a uniform's colour indicate that, 'Because of citizens' negative psychological perception of dark colours, they may perceive a police officer in a negative manner partly because of the officer's uniform colour' (p. 31).
- A dirty and/or creased uniform or a badly worn duty belt sends the message to criminal suspects that a police officer is unprofessional and incompetent and, consequently, can invite violence (Pinizzotto and Davis, 1992).

We can see that while the police uniform conveys the power and authority of the person wearing it, it also has a subconscious psychological influence on people the nature of which depends on a person's preconceived feelings about police officers (Johnson, 2001:31). For this reason, police administrators should think seriously about their policies concerning the uniform.

Police–public relations are problematic in many countries but especially in such multiracial societies as the United States (Nietzel and Hartung, 1993), the UK (Ainsworth, 1995:130–4),[9] Australia[10] and New Zealand. In fact, 'Complaints arising from police-citizen contacts account for much of the attention police receive' (Goldstein, 1994:323). Some authors would argue that as psychologists come to play a bigger role in police training, such important skills as listening, counselling, stress awareness, communication, decision-making and conflict-resolution skills (Reiser and Klyver, 1987:453) on recruit, sub-officer and officer courses can be transferred to the workplace and improve police encounters with the public (Bull and Horncastle, 1986; Bull et al., 1987). Bull and his co-workers evaluated the 'human awareness training' (HAT) programme introduced into the Metropolitan Police's recruit training in June 1982 which was based on a skills-based model of police training. The focus of HAT has been threefold, namely to improve 'interpersonal skills (comprising conversational skills and purposive encounter skills); self-awareness (comprising self-knowledge through tests and participation in structured experience); and community relations – comprising race awareness and cultural awareness' (Bull, 1985:109).

The comprehensive five-year-long evaluation of the effectiveness of HAT by Bull and his co-workers (see Bull and Horncastle, 1994, for an overview) was carried out in three phases. Because this research is a very good example of how psychologists can contribute to improving police training by evaluating changes introduced, it will be described in some detail, drawing on Bull and Horncastle (1994).

In phase 1, three groups of about thirty officers each completed three questionnaires in week one of recruit training, and at the end of recruit training (week twenty), as well as at six months and at twelve months in their probationary period. The three questionnaires were: a social-evaluative anxiety questionnaire (measures social avoidance and distress); a self-esteem questionnaire (measures perceived interpersonal threat, self-esteem, faith in people, and sensitivity to criticism); and an interpersonal relations questionnaire (measures need to establish satisfactory relationships, need to control them and need for affection). In addition, a recruit training questionnaire (RTQ) was administered to two groups of officers (N = 30) on the four testing occasions. The RTQ assesses attitudes and behaviours which HAT intended the recruits to acquire.

In phase 2, the first three questionnaires as in phase 1 and a self-monitoring questionnaire (measures amount of self-observation and self-control) were administered to three cohorts of forty officers twenty, forty and sixty-six weeks after initial training during which time the new recruits were into their probationer training programme. In addition, a revised version of the RTQ, subsequently called district training questionnaire (DTQ), was administered to two groups of officers (totalling sixty-one) on the same testing occasions. By now HAT was retitled Policing Skills Training (PST). As part of phase 2, an observational study was carried out by one or two researchers of sixty-four police officers in eight police stations with 28 to 43 months' service while on patrol. Observers recorded data on 550 police–citizen encounters. On fifty occasions the observer/s also interviewed the constable concerned and the encountered member of the public separately at the end of the encounter.

Bull and his co-workers found that, generally, HAT trainees were more satisfied with training than were their predecessors and HAT-trained officers attracted fewer complaints during their first three years of service than a matched control group. Regarding the extent to which HAT-trained police officers use HAT skills in their work, Bull et al. (1987) reported a follow-up to forty-three months after completing recruit training that found some evidence for the transfer of HAT skills to the workplace resulting in improved police–public relations. Bull (1985) concluded that, 'of the three components of HAT, "interpersonal skills" is clearly the best; the component described as "self-awareness" is of a reasonable standard; and that described as 'community relations is, as yet, rather poor … HAT is a very substantial improvement over that which it preceded. HAT also compares very favourably indeed with training in other forces around the world' (p. 121).

Regarding the extent to which the effects of PST were manifested in police constables' behaviour, Bull and Horncastle (1994) reported phase 2 of their evaluation found 'little evidence to suggest that the concepts and skills which Policing Skills Training sought to impart to recruits were significantly undermined by those recruits' subsequent operational experience' (p. 149). Bull and Horncastle identified the following areas which needed to be addressed by the London Metropolitan Police command: (a) enhancement of the self-evaluation and self-awareness components of PST; (b) misunderstandings about the nature and objectives of PST within the force; and (c) enhance officers' understanding and sympathy towards victims.

It is encouraging to be told by Bull and Horncastle (1994) that, 'Since receiving our final report the London Metropolitan Police has acted on all its recommendations' (p. 149). It remains to be seen how many of the police forces in England and Wales have benefited from the experience of the London Metropolitan Police experience with PST.

The research thus far shows that, unless a systematic programme to minimise some negative influences exerted by more experienced colleagues on probationary police officers in the process of being inducted into the police subculture and occupational deviance accompany steps taken to improve recruit training, any improvements in police attitudes and behaviour are likely to be ephemeral.

North American and Australian tourists in the UK are often surprised to find that British police on the beat carry no firearms. While the explanation for this characteristic of the British 'bobby' is more historical, British police forces would be well-advised to resist the call to be armed when on duty in view of the rather low risk of serious physical injury or death to which they are exposed, unlike their patrol officer counterparts in some parts of the United States. Furthermore, there is empirical evidence that the presence of a sidearm has an adverse effect on public perceptions of the police. Boyanowsky and Griffiths (1982) carried out a field experiment to examine weapon presence and eye contact as instigators or inhibitors of aggressive arousal in police–public encounters during the normal course of performing traffic patrol duties. Four constables were recruited in Surrey, British Columbia, for the study. They stopped eighty-seven men and forty-six women and told them they were either going to give them a traffic ticket or that they were merely making enquiries and/or making a records check. The constable would be wearing or not wearing a gun and sunglasses. The researcher observed the encounter and straight after gave the motorist a questionnaire to complete. It was found that: (a) a constable wearing sunglasses was perceived more negatively; and (b) motorists who were told they were getting a ticket expressed the most anger on their faces and reported more aggression when the police wore a gun than when no weapon was visible.

Stephenson (1992:121) points out, that 'there are very few in-depth studies of the effects of police–citizen interaction on attitudes of citizens'. One such study by Cox and White (1988) surveyed 460 students who had received a traffic citation and compared their responses with those of 373 who had not. The former were found to have negative perceptions of the police as far as police demeanour (for example, brutality) but not as far as police competence is concerned. These findings point to the need to differentiate between specific and general public attitudes towards the police.

4 Stress

Police associations and police management worldwide are concerned about the long-term effects of stress on their members, which include medical problems, absenteeism, alcohol abuse, marital problems and staff turnover. The available evidence indicates that it is not uncommon for police who stay in the job for their working career to continue to experience professional exhaustion, otherwise known as 'burnout' (Oligny, 1994). Kroes' (1985) study of 2300 police officers from twenty-nine different stations or squads painted the following picture of stress indicators: marital problems (37 per cent), health problems (36 per cent), drinking problems (23 per cent), having children with emotional problems (20 per cent) and using tranquillisers (10 per cent). There is a large body of literature on the topic of police stress (Reiser and Klyver, 1987). What follows is an overview of what has been reported about the topic and draws partly on Hollin's (1989) review.[11]

Terry (1981) distinguished four categories of stress:[12]

1 *External* (for example, feeling under siege by an antagonistic public, seeing offenders convicted of serious offences receiving very lenient sentences).

2 *Internal* (for example, a feeling that nepotism underpins promotion decisions, feeling there is no hope of promotion, having to be content with obsolete technology). An interesting study of inter-personal trust among ninety-two officers by Skellington (2001) in Scotland obtained both questionnaire and seem-structured interview data and found that: (a) young officers scored higher on inter-personal trust; (b) lack of trust may be attributed to police experience; and (c) suspicion of the police by 'outsiders' combined with 24-hour police accountability hindered the development of between-police officer trust.

3 *Task-related* (for example, emotional burnout due to seeing the dark side of human nature too often).

4 *Serious concerns about one's own personal safety* (for example, knowing that there is a high risk of getting shot at in some areas one has to patrol and that there has been a significant number of both fatal and non-fatal shootings of colleagues already). It should be noted in this context that an assumption of dangerousness in police–citizen routine traffic stop encounters by the US Supreme Court has led it to allow police officers during traffic stops to order drivers (*Pennsylvania v. Mimms*, 434, US, 106, 1977) and passengers (*Maryland v. Wilson*, 117 US 882, 1997) from their car without suspicion to ensure the safety of police officers. However, Lichtenberg and Smith (2001) examined ten years of national US data on traffic stops, police homicide and assaults and has cast doubt on the Supreme Court's assumption.

Police officers would appear vulnerable to stress because of the very nature of some of their duties (Bull et al., 1983:112–37) but also because one feature of police 'canteen culture' is the macho style that discourages officers from talking about stressors, preferring instead to 'keep a stiff upper lip' – a mechanism which is 'over-used and inadequate' (Manolias, 1991; see, also, Pogrebin and Poole, 1991). Regarding the kind of officer most vulnerable to burnout, a Quebec study reported by Oligny (1994) identified the following characteristics: being a perfectionist and highly committed to one's duties, not confiding in others, having a very strong will and, finally, the type who blames others for his/her problems (p. 23).

A British study by Cooper et al. (1982) of 200 police officers ranging in rank from sergeant to superintendent found that the most significant stressors were: work overload, lack of personal recognition and unfulfilled work aspirations, perceived unnecessary obstacles that undermine the police function, and the consequences of autocratic management. Complaints about the police accounted for 2.6 per cent of the variance. Another study of perceptions of stress among random samples of 1125 chiefs and 302 sheriffs in the United States found that: (a) sheriffs reported higher levels of stress than did chiefs; (b) chiefs with greater autonomy and with a perception that they had control over the hiring process reported less stress; and, finally, (c) chiefs with lower levels of education (especially those with a high school diploma or less) were more likely to perceive stress (Crank et al., 1993). As stated in social psychology textbooks, role ambiguity is a major cause of conflict and stress. Tabol and Ainsworth (2000) administered a questionnaire to forty police officers from a force in northern England and found that role conflict was inversely related to job satisfaction, job satisfaction was inversely related to depression and, finally, that encountering individuals with conflicting expectations in the course of police work was predictive of a police officer's stress score. Utilising the Life Events Inventory and the Bodily Sensations Questionnaire, Gudjonsson (1983) investigated sources of stress experienced by 100 British police officers the previous year, comparing them with a sample of hospital administrators. The three most frequently reported stressors were promotion difficulties, difficulties with their own children, as well as with their spouses. It was also found, however, that the police officers were no different to the hospital administrators in what they had experienced as stressful and what bodily sensations they had as a result.

Intuitively, one might expect stress to be related to how long one has been a police member but it turns out that the picture is not so straightforward. Gudjonsson and Adlam (1982) reported that senior ranks were more likely to point to work overload and paperwork as their sources of stress while the lower ranks cited having to deal with violent confrontations and having to respond to nasty car accidents. These findings show that British police officers, like their American counterparts, experience different sources of stress depending on their rank which correlates with length of service and type of duties performed.

In an Australian study, Evans et al. (1992) administered the Jenkins Activity Survey (Jenkins et al., 1979) and the State-trait Anxiety Inventory – Form Y (Spielberger et al., 1983) to 120 Victoria Police and 151 Federal Police officers. They found that officers with more than twelve years of service had significantly lower trait anxiety scores even though they scored higher on the Hard-driving and Competitive dimension of the Jenkins Activity Survey. As Evans et al. point out, these behavioural differences over length of service may reflect changes in how officers perceive their jobs and themselves (see also Perrot and Taylor, 1995) or they may reflect the fact that those who are not happy as police officers, or think of themselves as unsuitable for the job, simply leave. Interestingly, there is some evidence to suggest that years of experience in the job tend to render police officers 'more accepting of legal restrictions, but also more narrowly focused on crime fighting, more resistant to rules, more inclined to favour selective enforcement, and more motivated by money' (Worden, 1993:221).

In what appears to be a unique study, Alexander and Wells (1991) followed up ninety-one Scottish police officers involved in body-handling duties following the Piper Alpha disaster in the North Sea in 1988 when 167 men were killed, and compared them with a control group matched for age, sex, marital status, and band scores on the Hospital Anxiety Depression (HAD) Scale (Zigmond and Smith, 1983), pre-disaster data (HAD and the Eysenck Personality Questionnaire Eysenck and Eysenck, 1975); and post-disaster data (Revised Impact of Event Scale – Horowitz et al., 1979; a body-handling questionnaire, and a coping strategy scale). Alexander and Wells reported that the police officers concerned 'emerged relatively unscathed, and some even seem to have gained from the experience' (p. 551). It was also reported that 'over half of the officers found the anticipation of what was facing them more stressful than the work itself' (p. 553) and that humour and talking to colleagues were the ways most officers found useful in coping with the experience (p. 550). In accepting Alexander and Wells' findings, however, a certain degree of caution is warranted because of the lack of normative data for Eysenck's lie scale. This means that the absence of significant evidence for stress as a result of the body-handling experience may be due to some police officers lying in accordance with the macho image but not being detected by the lie scale.

Regarding stress management, there is no shortage of advice on how to both recognise stress (Ainsworth and Pease, 1987) and how to cope with it (see Ainsworth and Pease, 1987; Stein, 1986)). Counselling is discussed by Bull et al. (1983) who also recommend relaxation, meditation, dietary control and exercise. They also argue that, 'organizationally much can be done to reduce the risk of stress and strain by obviating role conflict and role ambiguity, and by managing job content and work loads' (p. 134). Both junior and senior officers themselves made the following suggestions for police command on how to reduce stress (Gudjonsson and Adlam, 1982; Gudjonsson, 1983): (a) better training on how to cope with demanding situations; (b) greater support from senior colleagues; (c) better familiarity with police procedures; (d) improved police–community relations; and (e) fewer bureaucratic obstacles. For such suggestions to be implemented, changes at an organizational level are needed (Ainsworth and Pease, 1987).

5 Questioning Suspects

The police clear-up rate for major/indictable/index crime is generally low in western countries. This is especially the case with property offences. In those jurisdictions with an adversarial system, the major role for the police is to construct the case for the prosecution (Sanders, 1987).[13] While police officers generally spend a small proportion (13 per cent) of their time during a tour of duty on tasks related to crime enquiries/investigation, historically, being a detective confers status on a police member, especially if he/she happens to belong to an elite squad of detectives. A British study by McGurk et al. (1994) used both questionnaires and interviews to collect data from 334 detectives in four police forces (the Metropolitan, Greater Manchester, Hertfordshire and Cambria Constabulary), and found that in 98 per cent their work involved interviewing.

Not surprisingly, therefore, one of the core attributes expected of a good detective is detecting a lot of crime by being effective and efficient at questioning suspects. A significant number of criminal suspects confess, and obtaining a confession is strategically important because police are more likely to formally charge a suspect and to end up with a conviction. Therefore, it comes as a big surprise to be told that questioning suspects is not a skill which, despite its importance and the availability of textbooks on how to go about the task (see, for example, Inbau et al., 1986; Royal and Schutt, 1976; Yeschke, 1993) is apparently poorly taught even to detectives and that the whole process of suspect questioning is rather inadequately supervised (Irving and Hilgendorf, 1980; Stephenson, 1992). An interactive computer programme has been jointly created by interviewing and interrogating instructors from the FBI's Academy and members of the Johns Hopkins University's Applied Physics Laboratory which simulates an interrogation. Its purpose is to enhance basic and important skills (see Einspahr, 2000). Dubious practices of police investigators are reduced when they are legally obliged to have the questioning tape-recorded as is the case in England and in Australia (Heaton-Armstrong, 1995b; Shepherd, 1995). For a number of years now, the Homicide Squad of the Victoria Police in Australia routinely conducts its questioning of suspects on video and such evidence is admissible in court. If there is a reasonable basis for suspecting that someone has committed an offence, police are required by law to caution the suspect before questioning them. Such a legal requirement, of course, does not stop police questioning a suspect outside a police station (for example, in a police car), or in the cells, or before the tape-recorder or video camera is switched on (see Torpy, 1994). According to Moston (1996), this suspicion is reinforced by the finding that most admissions in the study by Moston et al. (1992) tended to be at the start of the interviews. Research by Irving and McKenzie, 1988, 1989) established that the use of some interviewing ploys declined following the introduction of PACE (1984) in England although the number of admissions of guilt by suspects did not decline (Moston and Stephenson, 1993). In the United States an undercover officer in the prison context is not required to caution another inmate when asking them questions (see chapter 9). Gudjonsson (1992) provides a good discussion of the literature on the broad topic of police questioning of suspects, as does Stephenson (1992). This section draws on both these reviews as well as on the work of other researchers.

Apparently, a high proportion (48 per cent) of suspects who are subsequently convicted and imprisoned initially deny their involvement in crime and a number (41 per cent) are unwilling to confess when first questioned (Gudjonsson and Bownes, 1992). However, a significant proportion of suspects questioned by police make full or partial admissions/confessions. Softley et al. (1980) reported that 47.6 per cent of the 218 suspects questioned at four police stations in England made full confessions while an additional 13.4 per cent made partial confessions. A number of factors appear to be important in whether suspects confess. Research with prisoners in England (Moston, 1996), in Iceland (Gudjonsson and Petursson, 1991) and in Northern Ireland (Gudjonsson and Bownes (1992) has identified three reasons why suspects confess: (a) proof (that is, the strength of the evidence against the suspect); (b) internal pressure (that is, a need to tell the investigator about the crime); and (c) external pressure (that is, police persuasion, fear of confinement).

A significantly higher admission/confession rate for suspects without a criminal record has been reported by Neubauer (1974) and Softley et al. (1980) but Baldwin and McConville's (1980b) study of confessions in London and Birmingham reported the opposite trend. The likelihood of a confession decreases significantly as a suspect's age increases.[14] Moston et al. (1992) found that when there is strong evidence against a suspect, juveniles are more likely to deny an allegation while older suspects are more likely neither to admit nor to deny (p. 36). Finally, with the notable exception of Baldwin and McConville (1980b), it has generally been found that property offenders are significantly more likely to make an admission/confession than those charged with crimes against the person (Mitchell, 1983; Neubauer, 1974). It is quite possible, of course, that the higher confession rate of property offenders (who are known to be highly prolific as far as their criminal activity is concerned) can be attributed to their following a practice whereby they agree to confess on the understanding that the police will take other offences into consideration.

In examining correlates of making a confession one needs to also take into account whether a suspect has had legal advice before being questioned by the police, a factor which has been found to significantly reduce the likelihood of a confession (Moston et al., 1992 and see below). Finally, in considering studies of false confessions it is important to take into account the types of criminal cases examined (that is, whether serious or minor) and, in the case of England and Wales, whether a study was carried out before the *Police and Criminal Evidence Act*, 1984 (s.60), which introduced the tape-recording of police interviews with suspects. Code E of PACE provides that: the code of practice itself shall be readily available for consultation by police officers, detained persons and members of the public at every police station to which an order under s.60 applies (E.1). Code E provides detailed guidance for:

- Recording and the sealing of master tapes.
- Interviews to be tape-recorded.

- The interview (commencement, special warnings to be given, interviews with the deaf, objections and complaints by the suspect, changing tapes, taking a break during the interview, failure of recording equipment and conclusion of the interview).
- After the interview. Tape security. On 26 May 1989, Lord Lane CJ, sitting in the Court of Appeal (Criminal Division), issued a practice direction concerning the preparation of evidence of tape-recorded interviews for court.[15]
- Code E (4C) provides that a suspect who is interviewed after arrest fails or refuses to answer certain questions, or to answer them satisfactorily, after due warning, a court or jury may draw a proper inference from this silence under sections 36 and 37 of the *Criminal Justice and Public Order Act 1994*. In that context, however, in the case of *Murray v. UK*, 22 EHRR 29 at 67, ECHR), the European Court of Human Rights held that delaying access to legal advice, whatever the justification, is incompatible with the right to a fair trial guaranteed by Article 6 of the *European Convention on Human Rights*.

Horgan (1979)[16] defines the goals of interrogation as including: (a) learning the truth of the crime and how it occurred; (b) securing an admission/a confession of guilt from the suspect; (c) obtaining all the facts in order to ascertain the *modus operandi* and the circumstances of the crime; (d) collecting information that will enable the investigators to draw logical conclusions; and (e) furnishing the prosecutor with the evidence required.

Available literature on police questioning techniques almost exclusively describes procedures used by law-enforcement in the United States 'where the legal restrictions on questioning show a marked difference to those set out in PACE' (Moston, 1996:93). Leo (1994) informs us that police use five psychological techniques of influence: persuasion, deception, neutralisation and normalisation. On the basis of his participant observation field study of more than five hours in three police departments, Leo (1996) concluded that contemporary US police interrogation 'can be best understood as a confidence game based on the manipulation and betrayal of trust' (p. 259). Moston (1996) lists the following 'feedback' persuasive techniques, psychological ploys, that are commonly used by British police interviewers when suspects who have made an initial denial, both in the absence of evidence and in the use of evidence:

- In the absence of incriminating evidence: simple repetition of the suspect's answers, commenting on the suspect's body language[17] and expressing sympathy for the victim.
- When incriminating evidence is available: emphasise victim/independent witness evidence, accomplice evidence.

Using eighteen cases in which the suspects had been interviewed by police in connection with serious criminal offences between April 1991 and July 1996, Pearse and Gudjonsson (1999) examined whether more powerful and hostile dynamics are utilised by police officers in England and Wales to overcome a suspect's resistance. They examined the importance of thirty-three variables and found that the police resorted to manipulative coercive tactics, namely: intimidation, robust challenge, manipulation, question style and soft challenge. They also found that the nature and frequency of the tactics used was related to the likelihood that the courts would rule the evidence inadmissible.

Con/scam/bunco artists/fraudsters pose a special challenge for police interviewers because they feel no remorse for obtaining money or some other financial advantage from people by deceiving them, are confident, intelligent, accomplished liars and it is difficult for the prosecution to prove *mens rea* (guilty intent) in deception offences (O'Neal, 2000:17). However, 'With the proper preparation and strategic approach on the part of investigators, evidence produced from subject interviews of con artists can become the key to successful prosecutions' (p. 17). The unusual fraudster in the case study that follows proved very difficult when questioned by Victoria Police Major Fraud Group detectives in the early 1990s in Melbourne, Australia, about her criminal activities (Krambia-Kapardis, 2001):

Case Study

An untypical fraudster who proved difficult to question

The A$1 250 000 fraud was committed by a 47-year-old grandmother accountant who had been dismissed by her previous employer for committing fraud. Acting out of greed she exploited weak internal accounting controls. A lack of segregation of duties allowed her to be both in charge of personnel records as well as responsible for paying salaries. She defrauded her employer of the stated amount by means of fraudulent transactions. Using a variety of methods to cover up her frauds, she misappropriated cheques issued by her employer who was a foreign government and had them paid into her own account. She did this by getting subordinates to sign 'pay cash' cheques or by forging cheques to alter the amount stated to a larger amount and had the difference paid into her account. She also misappropriated bills (meant to pay employees' salaries) upon their maturity by adding 'or pay cash'. She believed she had a very good chance of getting away with her frauds. With a salary of only A$27 000 and employment of about ten years the offender managed to own four houses in her name, buy another two for family members, pay school fees for grandchildren and to hold cash deposits of A$1 million. It is unknown why a number of her assistants or even upper management co-operated with her and banked the cheques or even authorised the alterations. No charges were laid against those people. She was found out by the bank when she tried to have a bill paid into her own account which had already been paid. When interviewed by the police, she first appeared naive and used the language barrier as an excuse not to communicate. Her command of English improved miraculously when she was confronted with numerous discrepancies between her account of how she came to so much wealth and the evidence in the hands of the police. She showed no remorse and remained confident she would get away with it through all the police interviews. Fortunately, the documentary evidence she had left behind was irrefutable and she went to prison.

O'Neal (2000) provides practical advice on how best to question a con artist, including: thorough preparation for the interview; having an inexhaustible supply of patience and listening very carefully to first extract the subject's own full story; confronting him/her with discrepancies between what the investigator knows to have happened and what is claimed has happened (starting with minor issues first); elicit more incriminating admissions; and, finally, elicit broad statements of confession. Basically, the investigator offers the con artist ample opportunity to talk freely, knowing that self-confidence will most likely compel him/her to continue the deception during the interview, thus furnishing the investigator with the opportunity 'to elicit significant proof of criminal intent in the form of false exculpatories and admissions' (p. 21).

In the light of criticisms levelled against British police interviewing skills over the years, an attempt has been made to identify skill gaps in specialist investigative interviewing (see Bull and Cherryman, 1995). It has been necessary first, however, to provide a generally agreed working definition of specialist investigative interviewing (SII). Bull and Cherryman analysed, both quantitatively and qualitatively, data from 194 police officers from thirteen forces in England and Wales and have reported the following definition of SII: 'The fair questioning or facilitative interviewing by a well-trained, experienced officer with "in-depth" knowledge of a specific area, of a suspect, witness or victim in offences of a special nature or in unusual circumstances' (p. ii).

In recent years in western countries there has been a shift away from physically coercive to psychologically manipulative tactics in police questioning of suspects. Interrogation is nowadays referred to as 'interviewing a suspect' to denote a shift which is part of a large change in policing whereby social control has become more subtle, more sophisticated, yet potentially more dominating than in the past. The shift has paralleled legislative changes and concomitant changes in police standing order/codes of practice.

There is no shortage of advice on how to interrogate criminal suspects (Inbau et al., 1986; McDonald, 1993).[18] According to Tousignant (1991), a prerequisite for a successful interrogation is for the interrogator to 'treat suspects in a civilised manner, no matter how vicious or serious the crime might have been' (p. 16). Another essential rule stated by the same author is that 'investigators should adopt a compassionate attitude and attempt to establish a rapport with suspects' (p. 16). Such treatment is said to encourage suspects to be 'open, forthright and honest'. Tousignant's (1991) basic premises are:

- Committing a crime gives rise to psychological and physiological pressures in people which they are motivated to alleviate by communicating and explaining the circumstances under which the crime was committed. In other words, 'most suspects feel a need to confess' (p. 17). Empirical evidence supporting this view has been provided by Gudjonsson and Bownes (1992) who found that 56 per cent of the prisoners they surveyed in Northern Ireland had confessed to the police because of an internal need to 'get it off their chest'.

- Suspects confess when their internal anxiety caused by their deception is greater than their perceptions of the consequences of the crime (p. 17).[19]
- A guilty individual who confesses is, from the start, looking for the 'proper opening during the investigation to communicate their guilt to the interrogators' (p. 17).[20] Fear of punishment combined with a loss of pride in confessing to a crime inhibit suspects from communicating their guilt (p. 17).
- To communicate about the circumstances of the crime, suspects must feel comfortable during the interrogation and have confidence in the investigator. Two basic qualities of a good interrogator is being a good listener and allowing suspects to describe in their own time and words the circumstances surrounding the crime.
- To overcome a suspect's inhibitions about communicating the circumstances of a crime questions should focus on what motivated the suspect to commit the crime and not on the crime itself. This encourages the suspect to begin to rationalise, to explain what made them do it.
- When suspects make an admission, however insignificant, it indicates a breakthrough in the interrogation because the suspect's 'defence mechanisms are diminished, and at this point, the investigators may push through to elicit the remaining elements of confession' (p. 17).

One basic assumption made by Tousignant (1991) is that, 'Both the hard core criminals and first time offenders suffer from the same pangs of conscience' (p. 17). The validity of this assumption, however, is questionable.

In the British study of SII by Bull and Cherryman (1995) a questionnaire was constructed on the basis of in-depth interviews with ninety-three police officers experienced in SII. The officers concerned were asked what skills they considered to be the most important in officers who conduct SII as well as in themselves. 'Listening' was found to be considered the most important in SII. Bull and Cherryman also found that the skills that were most often missing in police officers who conduct SII were said to be 'preparation', 'open-mindedness' and 'flexibility'.

Assuming we have a good interrogator (that is, one who possesses both good intelligence and understanding of human behaviour, is skilled at getting on with other people, is patient and persistent – Inbau et al., 1986, cited by Gudjonsson, 1992:29) and a suspect who is willing to communicate with the investigator, what approach should one follow to secure a confession? Inbau et al. (1986) recommend a total of nine steps:

1   'Direct positive confrontation'.
2   'Theme development' (for example, to reduce an emotional suspect's guilt or to assist a non-emotional suspect to see the futility of continuing to deny his/her part in the crime).
3   'Handling denials'.
4   'Overcoming objections'.
5   'Procurement and retention of a suspect's attention'.
6   'Handling the suspect's passive mood'.

7 Handling the suspect's 'resenting an alternative question'.
8 Having the suspect 'orally relate various details of the offence'.
9 'Converting an oral confession to a written confession'.

The last step would be unnecessary in jurisdictions which provide for the tape-recording of police interrogations, usually for the more serious crimes termed felonies/indictable offences. Of course, adequately documenting and reporting a confession with a signed statement is essential for securing a conviction (Burke, 2001). But what can psychologists tell police investigators about the process of questioning itself?

According to Stephenson (1992), interviewing is basically a question-and-answer information-gathering exercise and 'interviewing skill may be evaluated in terms of the interviewer's success in eliciting relevant and accurate information' (p. 125). It follows that the interviewer may be unsuccessful in obtaining relevant and accurate information and/or a confession if he/she conducts the interview on the basis of unfounded assumptions and/or does not allow the suspect enough opportunity to give a full account of their position vis-à-vis the crime. At the same time, a suspect who provides the interviewer with a plausible but untruthful account, or says very little or even says nothing, can undermine the success of the interview. To illustrate, Evans and Webb (1991), two serving British police officers, analysed a random sample of sixty tape-recorded interviews of male and female suspects aged 10 to 16 years by police on Merseyside in May 1990. It was found that interviews of children and young persons, in which a parent, guardian or other responsible adult would often be present, take a lot less time – an average of 7 minutes compared with 21 to 22 minutes for adults. As Evans and Webb point out, this finding may well be due to the presence of others during the interview and/ or the police having decided to caution the child or young person and, consequently, wanting to 'get it over and done with as quickly as possible'. The same researchers also found, however, that the police interviews in their sample exhibited 'a rather didactic, and dismissive, handling of the interviewees who spoke for about a third of the woefully short period of time' (p. 45).

A common concern of detectives is having to cope with a suspect who simply refuses to answer their questions, and especially one who does so while being tape-/video-recorded. What, then, can a detective do in response to the 'no comment' problem? How can he/she overcome the suspect's resistance? According to Shepherd (1991a), an investigator should remember that it is not only suspected offenders who resist questioning; the aetiology of resistance is much more complex. Shepherd argues that appropriate conversation and conversation management help an investigator to cope with resistance. This strategy entails: 'respect for the person, empathy, supportiveness, a non-judgemental attitude, straightforward talk and a conversational style signalling a commitment to talk across as equals, not up-down or as pseudo-equals' (pp. 6–7).

Shepherd maintains that the following are conducive for creating resistance in suspects: poor conversation management; inappropriate pacing (impatiently rushing in as soon as the suspect has answered a question); inappropriate forms of assertion and listening (that is, disruptive talk, overtalking, counterproductive questions, inappropriate listening (for example, assuming the answer before it is given)); inappropriate content of assertions which lead the suspect to the conclusion that the interviewer does not have sufficient knowledge about the crime, or what he/she knows about it is rather vague. Such practices by the interviewer, Shepherd argues, result in 'Alienation, antipathy, mistrust, loss of confidence in the interviewer and loss of interviewer credibility and loss of self-confidence' (p. 9). One major reason why police investigators find it difficult to cope with a suspect who does not answer their questions is the fact that 'the general pattern of investigative training – as exemplified by CID training – is not training to develop skills but crash courses in the law and procedures' (p. 11). As Moston et al. (1992:38) pointed out, most British police officers receive no interview training and, in fact, training courses are a relatively new development 'which is still under-researched and under-resourced' (p. 38).

5.1 How Police Officers Approach the Task

Stephenson and Moston (1991, 1994) and Moston et al. (1992) reported a large study of police questioning of suspects at ten Metropolitan Police stations in London. The researchers investigated a consecutive series of fifty or more interviews of suspects by detectives at each police station, giving a total of 1067 cases, ranging in seriousness from minor offences to rape and murder. Each detective was asked to complete two short questionnaires – one before and one after the interview. It was found that in the majority of cases the detectives' aim was to secure a confession as either main evidence or additional evidence (Stephenson and Moston, 1991:30). It was also found that most interviewing officers (73 per cent) were sure of the guilt of the suspect they were interviewing before the interview got under way, largely on the basis of their perception of the strength of the evidence against the suspect. Officers were particularly prejudiced against suspects with previous convictions (p. 32).

In their research for the British Home Office, Bull and Cherryman (1995) analysed sixty-nine videotaped recordings of interviews with suspects provided by a number of different police forces which fell into the category of SII. Four experienced analysts rated independently each interview for the overall skill with which the police officers concerned carried out the interview as well as whether the interview was or was not characterised by twenty-nine factors. Bull and Cherryman reported that, 'The weaknesses most commonly observed in the interviews were the failure to use pauses and silences, the lack of rapport, the lack of empathy/compassion, inflexibility, and the use of leading questions. Comparison between those interviewers rated as skilled with those not rated as skilled revealed several differences, with communication skills, flexibility and empathy/compassion showing the largest differences' (p. iii).

Regarding how effective British detectives are in getting suspects to confess, Stephenson and Moston (1991) reported that there was no statistical relationship between a detective's assumption of guilt and the outcome of the interrogation. Although London detectives would probably like us to think otherwise, 'few suspects were "persuaded" to confess' (p. 33). Furthermore, the decision to admit an allegation during the interrogation was in the main associated with three factors, namely strength of evidence, legal advice and the criminal history of the suspect (Moston et al., 1992). Full admissions were found to drop 20 per cent in cases where a suspect had made contact with a solicitor (Moston et al., 1992:36). Further support for the importance of the strength of evidence against a suspect in whether he/she confesses to a crime has been reported by Gudjonsson and Bownes (1992). They found that proof was the factor most commonly (60 per cent) given by the prisoners they surveyed for making a confession to the police which they did not subsequently retract.

Whether a suspect has a criminal record is another relevant factor in this context. Suspects in the Moston et al. study with a criminal record were 20 per cent less likely to make an admission even in the face of strong evidence against them – 59 per cent of them did compared with 78 per cent of the first offenders. There was also significant variation between different police stations in the percentage of suspects who admitted allegations put to them during questioning. This is an interesting finding that awaits an explanation. Virtually all of the suspects who confessed were charged but detectives favoured female suspects in that they were significantly less likely to be charged (53 per cent) compared with male suspects (66 per cent). Finally, the same study also found that the style of questioning differed depending on the strength of the evidence against a suspect. In cases where the evidence was strong, detectives used accusatorial questioning strategies; where the evidence was weak, information-gathering strategies (for example, asking open-ended questions) were more likely to be used (Moston et al., 1992:38).

The experience of criminal suspects of police questioning methods internationally provides myriads of examples of sheer police brutality, more so in some countries than in others. It is generally the case, that for most suspects the interrogation context is still rather coercive without the need for manacles, handcuffs and hoods (Gudjonsson, 1992; Stephenson, 1992:129). The suspects may be physically exhausted, embarrassed, harbouring a strong sense of guilt, very anxious and feeling at a disadvantage *vis-à-vis* the police investigators. Realistically speaking, the interrogator has control of the situation and can determine whether a suspect gets 'rewards' or is 'punished', he/she is in a position to manipulate the information available to the suspect about the evidence against them in order to increase the suspect's level of anxiety and lead to the conclusion that there is no sense in continuing to deny his/her involvement in the crime. From the present author's knowledge of many hardened, career criminals, and on the basis of discussions with detectives in different police forces, there is a minority of criminal suspects who have had extensive experience of being interrogated, have read books on the subject, do not mind lying (and some of them can do so very convincingly) but may prefer to say as little as possible and, finally, the worst punishment if they are charged – prison – does not worry them in the least. Most people, however, would find the experience of being questioned by police as a suspect for a crime a rather unpleasant one. Legislation in the UK (*Police and Criminal Evidence Act*, 1984, and relevant Practice Codes) with the requirement that interrogations be tape-recorded, has been shown to reduce police use of coercive tactics (Irving and McKenzie, 1988).[21] Interestingly, the same researchers reported that such reduction does not lead to a reduction in the proportion of suspects who confess. Similar legislation has existed in Australian jurisdictions since the late 1980s but their impact on police questioning practices remains to be ascertained.

Interrogative pressure, of course, is a double-edged sword in the hands of the interviewer since it has been shown to sometimes have a boomerang effect. Gudjonsson (1995) describes four cases (two incest, one murder and one conspiracy to commit sexual offences) which show that 'interrogative pressure can result in a marked shift in lowering subjects' suggestible behaviour' (p. 317). Utilising Ofshe and Christman's (1986) 'two-process theory', Gudjonsson states that his finding 'can be interpreted … as an effective discontinuation of reactive behaviour and activation of strategic coping' (p. 317).

6 False Confessions[22]

As mentioned in chapter 9, some police investigators feel confident they know how to 'spot a liar' on the basis of 'obvious' clues, coupled with an assumption that most suspects routinely lie. Interviewer bias against the suspect and the coerciveness of the whole questioning context and process has been shown to occasionally result in false confessions, especially by suggestible suspects (Torpy, 1994). Ainsworth (1995:41) describes the case of George Heron in North East England who in 1993 was cleared of the murder of a 7-year-old girl. He had confessed to the murder after four days' of intensive police questioning and after other members of his family had also been arrested by the police. He claimed he decided to make a confession to the police to put an end to what the police were doing to him and members of his family. While the idea of interrogative suggestibility goes back to Binet (1900), the results of empirical studies and a number of highly publicised miscarriages of justice, like the Birmingham Six and the Guildford Four, in which defendants were convicted and served terms of imprisonment largely on the basis of having confessed to crimes while undergoing interrogation by police, has focused attention on pressures on police investigators to be successful and some dubious practices by police as well as on the question of the voluntariness of confessions and some suspects' vulnerability to falsely confessing to a crime. There can be no doubt that a confession is one of the strongest forms of evidence that influences the outcome of a criminal trial. However, as McCann (1998:441) reminds us, tension is endemic within the criminal justice system because of the need, on the one hand, to protect individual rights and, on the other hand, the need to protect the public from violent criminal offenders. Not surprisingly, therefore, confessions during police interviews have become a source of controversy. The psychology of confessions by suspects has attracted a great deal of attention on both sides of the Atlantic since the early 1980s. Gudjonsson (1992a) provides a very comprehensive discussion of the topic of false confessions and this section partly draws on his work (see also Kassin, 1997).

As for how frequently false confessions occur, Richardson (1991)[23] reported that 23 per cent of sixty juveniles in a residential forensic unit, who apparently had no ulterior motive for such a claim, claimed to have made a false confession to the police, largely out of loyalty and in order to protect a peer or a friend (48 per cent). Gudjonsson and Sigurdsson (1994) approached all offenders admitted to prisons in Iceland (a country with an inquisitorial legal system) during the period August 1991 to July 1992 and 95 per cent of them (N = 229) agreed to be interviewed. It was found that 12 per cent of the inmates claimed to have made a false confession in the past during a police interview and the majority of them (78 per cent) were subsequently convicted of the offence in question; female inmates were approximate three times more likely more likely to have made such a claim; most (78 per cent) had not retracted their alleged false confession because they considered it futile to do so; 52 per cent said they had made a false confession to avoid police pressure or in order to get out of police custody while slightly less (48 per cent) of them did it to protect someone else. Gudjonsson and Sigurdsson concluded that their findings 'corroborate the results of Richardson (1991) among adolescent delinquents in England and suggest that false confessions do occur with greater frequency than is commonly believed' (p. 24). Gudjonsson and Sigurdsson do point out, however, that their findings tell us how frequently persons interviewed by the police in Iceland falsely confess in general, but also give an indication of the frequency of false confessions among prison inmates in Iceland. One crucial issue which Gudjonsson and Sigurdsson do not really address is the truthfulness of the claims made by the inmates.

In the course of an interrogation an investigator is usually in control of the situation and in a position to place psychological demands on a suspect, communicate excessive expectations and, also, manipulate the suspect's emotions, especially since 'Suspects are never quite sure of exactly what information investigators possess' (Tousignant, 1991:15). Experimental evidence shows that being told that one should remember certain non-existent facts in a memory task results in some subjects accepting more false clues relating to those facts than if no such expectation is communicated and the interview contains no such demands (Gudjonsson and Hilton, 1989). With a combination of the experimenter effect, the coercive circumstances of being questioned in a police station (Irving and Hilgendorf, 1980), a suggestible suspect (for example, one low on self-esteem and/or of low intelligence[24] and investigators who are bent on securing a confession, a false confession becomes a real possibility. Some authors have expressed strong concern about the reliability of confessions made by drug users while intoxicated or under the influence of drugs or suffering from withdrawal symptoms or drug-induced illnesses (Davison and Forshaw, 1993). The same concern has been voiced about the reliability of confessions made by individuals of low cognitive ability when questioned by the police (Torpy, 1994).

Following the quashing in March 1991 by the Court of Appeal in England of the conviction for murder of the Birmingham Six, the Royal Commission on Criminal Justice was established with a brief to scrutinise the operation of the criminal justice system, to examine how effective it was in securing the conviction of the guilty and the acquittal of the innocent against the backdrop of efficient use of resources. To assist the Commission in its task, the British Home Office funded twenty-two research reports.[25] One of the research projects was that by Gudjonsson et al. (1994) who investigated the psychological characteristics of adult subjects before being interviewed by the police in order to identify those vulnerable to interrogative suggestibility and thus at risk and candidates for safeguards provided in the *Police and Criminal Evidence Act* (PACE), (1984). They interviewed an unbiased sample of 156 suspects at two London police stations. About two-thirds of the suspects had previous convictions and more than one in three had already served a prison sentence. Seven per cent of the suspects were found to be suffering from mental illness, 3 per cent from mental handicap, 3 per cent were illiterate and 2 per cent had language problems; in other words, 15 per cent were vulnerable to suggestibility. The police, who were somewhat unlikely to identify those suspects suffering from clinical depression, only summoned an appropriate adult to be present during the questioning (as provided in PACE) in only 4 per cent of those cases. There was some evidence that Afro-Caribbean subjects were more suggestible than others. Gudjonsson et al.'s findings emphasise the need for operational police to be trained and to have clear criteria for identifying mental disorder and suggestibility.

Gudjonsson and McKeith (1988) distinguished three kinds of false confessions:

1   *A voluntary false confession:* in this case, one confesses falsely for one's own very good reason and without having been pressured to do so. Possible reasons in this context might be a wish by an individual to be in the limelight, or to be punished or to cover up the real culprit.

2   *A coerced-compliant false confession:* here someone agrees to make a confession which they know to be untrue in order, for example, to avoid further physical pain, or to be allowed to sleep, or to go home, or on a promise that the investigator/s will 'have a word with the magistrate/judge' about a lenient sentence.

3   *A coerced-internalised false confession:* in such cases suspects come to believe that they are guilty because they no longer trust their own memory of certain details (see Ofshe, 1989, for details of how this kind of confession can be constructed by an interrogator).[26] Later on, of course, such a person may come to realise that they falsely confessed but it may be rather late because a retracted confession has been show still to influence jurors.

Gudjonsson and Clark (1986) put forward a theory of suggestibility (see Gudjonsson, 1992a:116–30) which postulates that 'most people would be susceptible to suggestions if the necessary conditions of uncertainty, inter-personal trust and heightened expectations are present' (p. 121). Implicit in such a model is the assumption that interrogative suggestibility is a distinct type of suggestibility (Gudjonsson, 1992a:123). Gudjonsson also points out that, 'Suggestibility is, to a certain extent, influenced by situational factors and experience' (p. 163). Gudjonsson has constructed a suggestibility scale (Gudjonsson Suggestibility Scale (GSS) – now there is GSS1[27] and GSS2)[28] but, as he himself acknowledges, 'One of the most difficult questions with regard to suggestibility relates to the extent to which one can generalise from a GSS test score to a trait concept of interrogative suggestibility' (p. 164). The GSS, developed for both research and clinical purposes, consists of twenty statements which are answered either 'True' or 'False' and, finally, the items are loaded on two factors: (a) avoidance of conflict and confrontation; and (b) eagerness to please. Fifteen of the questions are leading and five are nor leading.

Gudjonsson (1984) tested his scale by comparing the GSS score of twelve alleged confessors and eight resisters. The former group made confessions during police interrogation which they subsequently retracted. The latter group were defendants who continued denying their crime involvement even though there was forensic evidence linking them with the crime. Gudjonsson found that resisters scored less on the GSS. Gudjonsson admits two limitations of that study: the small number of subjects in each group and that the differ-ences in IQ between the two groups could have influenced their suggestibility scores. Stephenson (1992:132) has pointed out two more limitations: (a) that 'the scores of the false confessors fell within the normal range of scores on this test'; and (b) 'What has to be explained is the remarkably low scores of the deniers (that is, people who deny having committed a crime), most of whom, it almost has to be said, were found guilty of the offence with which they were charged'. When examining whether the GSS discriminates reliably between those who are high and those who are low on interrogative suggestibility one needs to also take into account such relevant factors as whether suspects are first offenders or recidivists used to being questioned by the police, as well as whether suspects have received legal advice before being questioned. Moston et al. (1992) found that first offenders were twice as likely to be interviewed by police without having seen a solicitor (p. 33) and, furthermore, 50.4 per cent of those without legal advice made admissions to the police but only 29.4 per cent of those who had had legal advice did so (p. 35).

Gudjonsson and Lebegue (1989) reported evidence supporting the validity of the GSS in the form of a higher score by a man who had confessed to the murder of a close friend he was subsequently shown not to have committed. Gudjonsson (1991) reported further evidence that the GSS reliably differ-entiates between resisters (N = 20) and false confessors (N = 20). He measured their suggestibility and compliance and controlled for age, sex, intelligence and memory capacity and found significant differences between the two groups on both suggestibility and compliance – two constructs which are theoretically constructed as overlapping. Gudjonsson (1989) also found that suggestibility assessment discriminated between the two groups independent of their level of intelligence. He also compared resisters and false confessors as groups but there were individual differences within each group. Gudjonsson (1991) does admit, however, that 'it is almost certain that not all of the alleged false confessors in the present study are innocent of the crime with which they were charged' (p. 151). It will be interesting to know what became of the four false confessors whose cases were pending at the time. It does seem that convincing evidence for the validity of the GSS has yet to be provided. At the time of writing his paper five out of the twenty false confessors had in fact been convicted. Consequently, the question about the validity of the GSS remains unresolved. It needs to be remembered in this context that a suspect's suggestibility is not the only factor relevant to whether he/she successfully resists the interrogator's suggestions and pressures but it 'is undoubtedly due to the combination of situational and interrogational factors on the one hand, and the suspect's mental state, motivation, personality and coping ability, on the other' (Gudjonsson, 1992a:157).

As far as predicting the likelihood of a confession is concerned, Pearse et al. (1998) used the GSS and biographical data to assess 160 suspects for a number of factors (including psychological vulnerability) when they were detained at two London police stations but before they were interviewed by police. They found that:

- Vulnerable suspects were no more likely to confess than non-vulnerable suspects. As the researchers admit, their finding may be attributable to the fact that they were dealing with minor cases and little pressure was put on the suspects by the police to confess.
- Suspects were more likely to confess if they reported having taken an illegal drug in the previous 24 hours.
- Younger suspects were more likely to confess.
- Suspects interviewed in the presence of a lawyer or who had experience of prison or custodial remand were less likely to confess.

However, Pearse et al.'s failure to control for the strength of incriminating evidence against the suspect may well have confounded their results (Kebbell, 1999).

Gudjonsson et al. (2000) asked eighty-six consultant psychiatrists, twenty-six forensic medical examiners, eighty-seven lawyers and 121 police officers to complete a questionnaire concerning a suspect's fitness to be interviewed according to psychological vulnerabilities which had to do with his history of mental problems and current problems with communication (p. 78). The most commonly identified vulnerabilities were: confusion and disorientation, withdrawing from heroin, communication problems, a paranoid belief, and not appearing to understand simple questions. In contrast, the respondents did not think the following factors rendered the suspect unfit to be interviewed: claiming amnesia, depression and appearing suggestible and eager to please.

Sigurdsson and Gudjonsson (2001) reported a study of 509 prison inmates in Iceland which examined the extent to which psychological (N = 17), criminological and substance abuse variables (N = 16) differentiate between alleged false confessors (12 per cent of the sample) and other prisoners. Discriminant function analysis revealed that two factors (number of previous criminal convictions and the score on the Gough Socialization Scale of the California Psychological Inventory: Megargee, 1972) correctly classified 93 per cent of the non-false confessors and 32.3 per cent of the alleged false confessors. Sigurdsson and Gudjonsson concluded that their findings suggest that antisocial personality characteristics and the number of previous terms of imprisonment are the best predictors of Icelandic offenders claiming to have made a false confession to the police and, finally, that among Icelandic prisoners, making a false confession is a feature of their criminal lifestyle.

Evidence challenging the validity of the GSS1 has been reported by Bain and Baxter (2000). While a number of studies have concerned themselves with interviewees'/suspects' characteristics that would predispose them to make a false confession, there is limited literature on the role of interviewer behaviour. In an experimental study that used mainly psychology undergraduates as subjects Bain and Baxter (2000) tested the hypothesis that the greater the psychological distance created between the interviewer and the interviewee by a general demeanour adopted throughout the interview, the higher SSS1 scores will be. Ss were administered the GSS1 under a 'friendly' or an 'abrupt' interviewing condition. They found that two of the GSS1 measures appear to be biased significantly by interviewer style. Ss tested in the 'abrupt' condition gained higher scores for 'Shift' and 'Total Suggestibility' than those in the 'friendly' condition. If Bain and Baxter's findings are replicated Gudjonsson would need to seriously consider revising his suggestibility scale.

In view of the emphasis by law-enforcement personnel on obtaining a confession from criminal suspects, the empirical evidence for the use of coercion that results in coerced confessions and false confessions, the crucial significance of a confession as far as the outcome of trial is concerned and the evidence for interrogative suggestibility, some authors (for example, Wakefield and Underwager, 1998) maintain that expert testimony may be necessary to help jurors understand the circumstances that lead to non-voluntary confessions.

For his part, Shepherd (1991b) has argued that unethical police interviews of suspects are founded on valuing expediency (p. 48), has proposed a change of approach in how police interviews are conducted and has outlined the following six principles of ethical interviewing: the prior investigation, sincerity, disclosure, open-mindedness, tolerance and the integrity principle.

Such moral principles, if adhered to by criminal investigators, would go a long way in eliminating improper practices during police questioning of suspects. However, it is unlikely that they will be readily embraced by a large proportion of criminal investigators who would have serious difficulties, for example, telling a suspect where some of their knowledge about a crime has come from. In the world of real, serious, violent crime and offenders, including organised crime, to divulge such information to a suspect could well result in the murder of a police informer or the compromise of an undercover operative, or a long-term surveillance operation. Is Shepherd (1991b) suggesting that such police methods are unethical and should cease? Like changes in police procedures legislated in a number of countries in recent years, it remains to be seen whether the ethical style of interviewing proposed by Shepherd, appealing though it may be, has an effect on false confessions. Despite some pragmatic reservations about some of Shepherd's (1991b) moral principles, many would probably agree with him that, 'Doing the job in response to a call to cope with a rise in crime or to catch the perpetrator of an outrageous crime can never be taken to be a licence to act with expediency when dealing with information or with people' (p. 55).

7 Conclusions

Psychologists have a great deal to contribute in the area of law enforcement, as exemplified by the cognitive interview, for example, but they need to seriously address the limitations of tests used to select personnel. Incorporating findings from the psychological literature into police training can help improve police–citizen encounters, but only to a certain degree. The all-too-familiar dark blue police uniform appears to be a mixed blessing, as far as police–citizen encounters are concerned. Traditional, and apparently not very effective, methods of questioning suspects need to give way to interviewing methods that are informed by psychological knowledge and safeguard the rights of suspects without jeopardising the effectiveness of the work of investigators. Reflecting on the contributions to police work thus far and taking note of some of the limitations is necessary if psychology is to meaningfully contribute to move police work generally into the twenty-first century.

12 Conclusions

The contents of this book show that a great deal has been happening at the interface of psychology and law. Especially since the 1980s, major advances have been made in our knowledge on a broad range of issues and the influence of psychology and law has been a two-way process. The maturity of legal psychology as a discipline in its own right and its contributions to society, both diverse and significant, are of special interest in view of a number of impediments in the process of bridging the gap between psychology and law.

As legal psychology continues to evolve, the indications are that psycholegal researchers are more cognisant than they used to be of the need to use a range of research methods and to conduct research that is ecologically valid. Of course, however forensically relevant research might be, 'there is always some risk when generalising from scientific studies to real world analogs' (Bruck and Ceci, 1995:309).

The discussion of empirical studies in the preceding chapters also shows that legal psychology's advances are more evident in some areas than in others and some summits still wait to be conquered. As Kadane (1993) has noted, there is undoubtedly an imbalance in the amount of attention psychologists have paid to different areas within law and legal processes. This imbalance probably reflects the fact that: (a) some issues are more amenable to study by the experimental method (psychologists' preferred method); and (b) the contemporary sociolegal climate in a country is such as to make some research topics the focus of psycholegal researchers' attention. In the process, important topics such as legal advocacy in and out of court, or how real crime victim/witnesses fare in their interaction with lawyers in their chambers, in busy court corridors or in the courtroom and/or operational police on the street or in police stations, have been neglected by psychologists.

Despite limitations of some of the empirical literature discussed in the preceding chapters and the imbalance mentioned, euphoric about their successes, legal psychologists run the risk of overselling psychology to the lawyers and overlooking the few but major difficulties that remain in bridging what gap is left between the two disciplines. Such differences include their different models of anthropos and preferred methodology, difficulties within legal psychology and its relationship with both academic and practising lawyers and a tendency for many psycholegal researchers not to locate their work in a contemporary critical sociolegal context.

As legal psychology approaches its adulthood and soldiers on in the beginning of the twenty-first century, legal psychologists have a lot to be proud of. At the same time, there is reason to expect that the scope of psycholegal research will continue to be widened, psychologists' communication with academic and practising lawyers will become more frequent and more constructive, and the feeling of frustration that has characterised members of the legal and psychological professions will dissipate. Optimistic psychologists can, therefore, look forward to the day in the near future when, to borrow Carson and Bull's (1995a:3) words, 'the legitimacy of the offspring of the relationship between psychology and law' will cease to be an issue.

Discussion in the preceding chapters has identified a number of gaps in our knowledge about various psycholegal issues. They include the following, and tackling them poses a challenge for legal psychologists:

- Utilising a range of research methods (including follow-up studies of real crime victims/witnesses as they are processed through the criminal justice process system) to determine the interaction effects of key factors known to impact adversely on the accuracy of adult and child witnesses.
- To identify the merits and defects, as far as jury decision-making is concerned, of different alternatives in the jury reform debate such as laypersons vs professional judges alone or laypersons vs a combination of lay persons and professional judges.
- To identify good predictors of successful legal advocacy in a variety of contexts and how to teach the skills involved efficiently and effectively to law students and legal practitioners.
- To ascertain the comparative effectiveness of different methods of detecting deception and to provide a theory that accounts for success at both deceiving others and at detecting deception.
- To contribute more to law enforcement by improving the predictive utility of different methods of selecting police personnel, both generally as well as for specialist roles in operational policing.
- Finally, historical and sociological research into the development of legal psychology as a discipline and how and why some of its 'successes' and 'failures' have come about will be of great interest and practical use to all those legal psychologists who like to reflect on their discipline and to 'take stock'.

All those with an interest in legal psychology can look forward to the discipline's increasing growth in terms of both the quantity and quality of the research conducted and courses taught at tertiary and other institutions.

three and, finally, in 1989 the right was removed altogether (Lloyd-Bostock, 1996:353). The abolition of the peremptory challenge means that it is not possible to ensure a racially mixed jury. A defendant can still challenge jurors for cause but the scope is very limited because only a juror's name and address are known.

11 See Vidmar (2000a) for detailed accounts of the jury systems of twelve countries.

12 See S.42(1) *Criminal Justice and Public Order Act* (1994) for England and Wales.

13 Under the *Contempt of Court Act* (1981).

14 Darbyshire (1991:743) attributes her comments on these Latin terms to Cornish (1968:12).

15 However, see *Lewis v. United States*, 116, S.Ct 2163 (1996) for a Supreme Court ruling by a 5 to 4 majority that defendants who are prosecuted in a single case for more than one petty offence do not have the constitutional right to jury trial.

16 Cited by Cammack (1995:481).

17 Lloyd-Bostock (1995:350).

18 Darbyshire (1991:751).

19 The occasional vetting of jurors by the Director of Public Prosecutions in England and Wales in trials where strong political motives are involved, for example, adds further to the unrepresentativeness of the jury.

20 King (2000:117).

21 Brown and Neal (1988:127–8), Darbyshire (1991:741,746), Evans (1995). In the mid 1990s in England and Wales juries were used in approximately twelve to fourteen civil trials a year (Lloyd-Bostock, 1996); in other words, the civil jury 'to all practical purposes [has] been abolished' (Lloyd-Bostock, 1995:351).

22 Blom-Cooper (1974).

23 Blom-Cooper (1974).

24 Willis (1983).

25 Willis (1983).

26 Blom-Cooper (1974).

27 Bevan et al. (1958:447), Kerr (1987:63).

28 Queensland Criminal Justice Commission (1991).

29 Barber and Gordon (1976), Nathanson (1995), Pickel (1995).

30 Ogloff and Vidmar (1994), Sue et al. (1974).

31 Green (1990).

32 Kramer et al. (1990).

33 Bevan et al. (1958).

34 Darbyshire (1991:746), Dunstan et al. (1995:42).

35 See the case of *Kemp, The Times*, 25 April 1994.

36 Cadzow (1995:16), Margolic (1995), Slind-Flor (1992), Feldman and Bell (1991), Shuman et al. (1994).

37 Kerr (1987:63), Nathanson (1995), Severance et al. (1992), Williams (1963).

38 Kerr (1987:63).

39 Mark (1973) but see Zander (1974) for a rebuttal.

40 Stephenson (1992).

41 Baldwin and McConville (1979,1980a), Kalven and Zeisel (1966), McCabe and Purvis (1974), Stephenson (1992), Zander and Henderson (1994).

42 Darbyshire (1991:744), Dunstan (1995:33).

43 Darbyshire (1991:748).

44 Blom-Cooper (1974).

45 Darbyshire (1991:741).

46 Blom-Cooper (1974). An exception to this would be some jurisdictions in the United States where long terms of incarceration can be imposed on even minor repeat offenders to keep them out of circulation under the 'three-strikes-and-you-are-out' approach.

47 Blom-Cooper (1974).

48 Kerr (1987:63), Roskill Committee (1986).

49 Duff and Findlay (1988).

50 Heuer and Penrod (1995:527).

51 Heuer and Penrod (1995:527).

52 Brett (1962:74), Devlin (1974).

53 Diamond and Caspar (1992).

54 Nietzel et al. (1999:39).

55 McCabe (1975), Sealy (1975).

56 Zander and Henderson (1994).

57 Diamond and Casper (1992), Harding (1988), Thompson (1989).

58 Bornstein (1994), Hans and Lofquist (1992).

59 Galiber et al. (1993). See Clarke (2000) for an account of the origins and historical evolution of jury nullification (that is, the jury's power not to adhere to the law).

60 Heuer and Penrod (1995:527).

61 In the English study conducted by Baldwin and McConville (1979) the jury sometimes ignored the judge's direction to acquit the defendant, especially where the defendant was black. Such verdicts were deemed to be perverse acquittals.

62 Zander and Henderson (1994:47).

63 Zander and Henderson (1994:46).

64 Jackson (1996:331); Cutler and Hughes (2001); Boatright (2001).

65 See Lloyd-Bostock (1996:350) for an account of the growth of Magistrates' Courts at the expense of jury trials.

66 See Werner et al. (1985) for one of the reports from that project.

67 See also Hans and Vidmar (1991).

68 However, as far as it has been possible to ascertain, it would be illegal to tape jury deliberations in any western common law or civil law country.

69 Devine et al. (2001) give a compound figure of 7 per cent for both retrospective surveys and interviewing ex-jurors (p. 627).

70 Hastie, Penrod and Pennington (1983), King (1986), Lloyd-Bostock (1996), McEwan (2000).

71 See issues of *Indiana Law Review*, 1995, vol.70 (3,4).

72 Robert Maxwell was alleged to have 'plundered' his companies' pension fund.

73 Cited by Hoffmann (1995:1137).

74 See Bersoff and Ogden (1987), Hans and Vidmar (1986:233–4), Kassin and Wrightsman (1988:39).

75 See Anderson (1974).

76 It is likely, of course, that cases in which there is strong evidence against the defendant or plaintiff may well be settled out of court and never reach jury trial.

77 See, for example, the English *Criminal Evidence Act* (1898) upon which are based such provisions in each Australian jurisdiction (Waight and Williams, 1995).

78 As would have been expected, Nietzel et al. (1999) found that 'enhancing' judicial instructions by translating them into non-technical English makes them more comprehensible to the jurors and, thus, more effective.

79 See also Hans and Vidmar (1986), Kassin and Wrightsman (1988), Potas and Rickwood (1984).

80 Cited in Hollin (1989:168).

81 Cited by Levine (1992:152).

82 See also Izzett and Leginski (1974), Landy and Aronson (1969), Ostrom et al. (1978).

83 See Arce (1989, cited by Arce, 1995:566–7).

84 Kalven and Zeisel (1966), Zeisel (1971), Nemeth (1977), Saks (1977), Kerr and MacCoun (1985), Foss (1981).

85 See Hastie (1993b) for a discussion.

86 Both studies are cited by Antonio and Hans (2001:69).

Chapter 6 *Sentencing As A Human Process*

1 See Feeley and Rubin (1999) for an account of how the judiciary in the United States reformed the country's prisons.

2 See Tata and Hutton (1998b) regarding computer support systems for discretionary judicial decision-making in sentencing.

3 See Freiberg and Ross (1995) for a discussion of the experience in recent years in Victoria, Australia, with sentencing legislation in theory and practice.

4 See, for example, the [British] *Magistrates' Association's Sentencing Guidelines* (1997), von Hirsch (1988).

5 In the context of the European Union, according to Baker (1999), Community Law has a lot to say about the regulation and operation of the criminal justice system of the member states, including their sentencing laws.

6 See McConville and Mirsky (1995) for an interesting ethnographic study of how guilty pleas are socially constructed.

7 However, the committee that reviewed the Criminal Courts of England and Wales under the chairmanship of Lord Justice Auld (2001) has proposed a formalised system of plea-bargaining whereby the earlier the plea of guilty, the higher the sentence discount.

8 For a discussion of the various rationales for sentencing see Ashworth (1997: 1096–102) and Ashworth (2000:62–78), Braithwaite (1989) and Walker (1980). See also Wexler (2001) regarding therapeutic jurisprudence (in other words, the study of the role of law as a therapeutic tool).

9 See *Herald Sun*, 1995, for some interesting Australian cases that illustrate this difficulty.

10 See Kapardis (1985:23–4) for a discussion of the concept. See Wrightsman (1999) for a discussion of how US Supreme Court judges decide a case and the role of the Chief Justice.

11 See the English Court of Appeal decision in *Reid* (1982) 4 CrAppR (S) 280 and the Australian High Court's decision in *Ryan v The Queen* [2001] HCA 21. Also, Walker and Padfield (1996).

12 See Kannai (1999) regarding structuring of judicial discretion in Israel by the Goldberg Committee and van Zyl Smit (1999) for mandatory sentences in South Africa.

13 Freiberg (1999) explores the question of whether the sentencing policies of one country or jurisdiction can be said to be more or less severe than that of another and argues that one needs to distinguish sentence severity from the broader concept of 'penal severity'.

14 See Lovegrove (1999) for a discussion of theoretical and methodological issues in

the psychological study of judicial sentencing. See Kapardis (1985) for a detailed discussion of the different methods used to study variations in sentencing, and more, especially early, studies that have utilised each of the methods.

15 See also Everson (1919), Willett (1964).

16 See also Baab and Furgeson (1967), Hogarth (1971), Sutton (1978).

17 See also Carlen (1976), Darbyshire (1980), Konečni and Ebbesen (1979), Stewart (1980).

18 See Heidensohn (1997) for detailed discussion of this view.

19 For England and Wales, see *Sex Discrimination Act* (1991).

20 Atkinson and Newman (1970), Pope (1975), Wilbanks (1986).

21 Carter and Cleland (1979), Clarke and Koch (1980), Rapaport (1991).

22 Also, see Aboud and Levy (1999) for a detailed discussion of various measures to reduce racial prejudice and discrimination in society.

23 For early research findings that a physically attractive person will be perceived more positively on a broad range of personality attributes see Dion et al. (1972), Goldman and Lewis (1977) and Miller (1970).

24 See Bierhoff et al. (1989), Efran (1974), Landy and Aronson (1969), Sigall and Ostrove (1975).

25 See also Ho and Venus (1995), Rose (1965), Solimine and Wheatley (1995).

26 See Bowen (1965), Gibson (1978), Hogarth (1971).

27 See Schubert (1959), Walker (1972).

28 See Hogarth (1971), Kapardis (1984, 1985), Spreutels (1980).

29 See Lovegrove (1997) for an Australian simulation study and a model of sentencing which also considers judges' intuition in deciding on what sentence to impose.

30 See Segal and Spaeth's (1993) book *The Supreme Court and the Attitudinal Model*.

Chapter 7 The Psychologists as Expert Witnesses

1 See also Kargon (1986) regarding the historical development of the expert witness and the Special Issue of *Law and Human Behaviour* 16(3) on expert evidence.

2 For a detailed discussion of the roles of the forensic psychologist see the book by Gudjonsson and Haward (1998) and Blau's (1998) book (2nd edn) for a thorough text on the psychologist as expert witness in the United States.

3 Citing Hodgkinson (1990:52).

4 See chapters 3, 6, 4, 7 and 5 respectively in Freckelton and Selby (2002) for detailed discussion of the five rules.

5 See Carson (1992), Edmondson (1995), Freckelton (1990, 1993), Gudjonsson (1992b, 1995) and Nijboer (1995) for discussions of this and Loftus and Ketcham (1991) regarding the experience of appearing as an expert witness for the defence in American courts.

6 See Smith (1995) for some difficulties in the idea of a court expert.

7 See American Psychology Law Society (1991) and Committee on Ethical Guidelines for Forensic Psychologists (1991) for details.

8 The expert concerned was William Marston, a pioneer in the use of the polygraph to detect deception.

9 Quoted in Landsman (1995:155).

10 See Gatowski et al. (2001:434) for details of the authors concerned.

11 See Gutheil and Stein (2000) for a discussion of the challenges posed by *Daubert* and its progeny *Joiner* and *Kumho* for psychology and psychiatry.

12 Cited by Gutheil and Stein (2000:246).

13 Voice identification is recognised as an expert field in England (see *R v. Robb* (1991) 93 Cr. App.R. 161 at 165; EE, 1(1):20).

14 In *R v. McFlin* (1985) the New Zealand Court of Appeal also endorsed the safeguards concerning evidence under hypnosis in s.795 (a)(3)(D) of the Californian Evidence Code but allowed the judge discretion as to how far to comply with those safeguards (Freckelton and Selby, 2002:208).

15 See Freckelton (1990:56) who cites *R v. Holland* (1981) 6 WCB 177; *R v. Scoppelliti* (1981) 34 OR (2d) 524 at 531; *R v. Clark* (1983) 1 DLR (4d) 46.

16 See Freckelton (1993:111) for details.

17 See Freckelton and Selby (2002:706–14) for detailed advice to expert witnesses by two very experienced and highly respected barristers.

Chapter 8 Persuasion in the Courtroom

1 Examples of 'great advocates' mentioned by the same authors are: Lord Birkett (1962), Lord Macmillan (1952), Hastings (1923), Jackson (1959) and Parry (1923) (p. 190).

2 See Du Cann (1964), Evans (1995), Glissan (1991), Lubert (1993), Pannick (1992), Phillips (1985), Munkman (1951, 1986), Wells (1988), Selby (2000).

3 See, however, Tronk and Dearden's (1993) *Advocacy Basics for Solicitors*, for a long-awaited focus on the humble solicitor and advocacy in the lower courts.

4 According to Mauet and McCrimmon (1993), courtroom advocacy skills are called for after: completing interrogatories; pre-trial motions; negotiations with the other party to achieve settlement of the dispute in question have failed; a case file has been compiled that contains court documents, evidence and counsel notes; a notebook is by now also available in the name of effectiveness and efficiency; the lawyer has constructed a 'theory of the case' (that is, the chosen position and approach to all the evidence the lawyer anticipates will be presented at trial; witnesses have been prepared for trial and, finally, a decision has been made on which witnesses to call and in what order.

5 See Leippe (1994) for a model.

6 Cited in Du Cann (1964:47).

7 See the American Bar Association's *ABA Standards for Criminal Justice Prosecution Function and Defense Function*, pp. 123–11, regarding the responsibilities of 'effective' counsel.

8 See McEwan (1995b:495) for detailed discussion of adversarial and inquisitorial proceedings.

9 The one not included concerns counsel's position and delivery and has already been mentioned.

10 See Glissan (1991:39–44) for a detailed discussion of these issues and relevant Australian case law.

11 As Bartlett and Memon (1995) point out, 'probabilistic statements of guilt tend to be more persuasive in that they confirm the opinion of those who already agree and require less change in the opinion of those who initially disagreed' (p. 549).

Chapter 9 Detecting Deception

1 See also Block et al. (1992), Jacobs (1993a, 1993b), Pogrebin and Poole (1993) regarding the use of undercover agents by the police.
2 See Hyman (1989:140–3) for non-human deception.
3 See Vrij (2000) for a comprehensive review.
4 Citing Goldberg et al. (1991), Ones et al. (1993) and Sackett et al. (1989).
5 See, also Navarro and Schafer (2001) for similar but more comprehensive advice by two FBI special agents.
6 It was said by President Nixon during the Watergate affair (DePaulo, 1998, cited in the *Sunday Times*, 24 May 1998, p. 14).
7 Cited by Miller and Stiff (1993).
8 Personal communication, Sergeant Chris Ward, Nottingham, England.
9 See Raskin (1989b) and Iacono (1995) for details of the procedure used with this and the other techniques.
10 See Ames' KGB controller's interview in the *Sunday Times* (8 February 1998, p. 21), explaining how he helped him to pass polygraph tests.
11 See Gudjonsson (1988) for a good discussion of this topic.
12 The results were presented at the 2001 annual meeting of the Society for Neuroscience in San Diego, California (*The Times*, 12 November 2001, p. 11).
13 Patty Hearst came from a wealthy family and was imprisoned for a number of crimes (including armed robbery) which she committed while a member of the Symbionese Liberation Army. At her trial it was alleged she had been brainwashed into joining that terrorist organisation while she was its captive.
14 See Gudjonsson (1992a) for discussion of this technique.
15 The criteria are also listed in Marxsen et al. (1995:445).
16 CBCA criteria listed by Vrij (2000:117) are adapted from Steller and Kohnken (1989).
17 Citing Sapir (1991, 1993).

Chapter 10 Witness Recognition Procedures

1 (Cmnd 2315).
2 Brandon and Davies (1973) listed seventy cases in which an innocent person had been convicted, largely as a result of eyewitness identification.
3 See *R v. Burchielli* ((1981) VR 611) regarding similar guidelines for the judiciary in Victoria, Australia.
4 See Joyce (1993) for evidence that only a minority of the general public in England might be able to understand properly a lot of the information contained in the (1991) revised Codes of Practice, *Police and Criminal Evidence Act* (1984).
5 See Borchard (1932), Brandon and Davies (1973), Frank and Frank (1957), Rattner (1988).
6 Cited by Davies (1989).
7 See *Police and Criminal Evidence Act* (1984) Annex B, for details of the procedures to be followed where a video parade is to be arranged in England and Wales.
8 See *Police and Criminal Evidence Act* (1984), Annex D for procedures to be followed for a showing of photographs in England and Wales.
9 See *Downey* (1994) *The Times*, 5 April, and *Fremantle v. R* (1994) *The Times*, 7 July, for cases where the warning was not given but the appeal failed.

10 See Brown et al. (1977), Hilgendorf and Irving (1978), Loftus (1974, 1976).

11 See Brigham (1989), Malpass and Devine (1983), Wagenaar and Veefkind (1992).

12 See *R v. Cormack* ((1981) 5 CrLJ 163); *R v. Kehagias, Leone and Durkic* ((1985) V.R 107).

13 Examples of such advice are to be found, for example, in: Victoria Police, Detective Training School (1994). *Identification*. Police Headquarters, Melbourne, Australia; Victoria Police (1995). *Prosecutor's Manual* (chapter 43, 43.1–43.11). and, finally, in police standing orders worldwide.

14 Cited in Wells et al. (1994:225).

15 See Turner (2000) for an attempt to overcome 'overshadowing' by constructing the E-Fit within a 'minimal face' which provides a face context without the possibility of overshadowing.

16 Cited in Clifford (1981).

17 See Cutler and Penrod (1988), Lindsay and Wells (1985), Lindsay et al., (1991a and b), Parker and Ryan (1993) and Sporer (1993).

18 See Davies and Valentine's (1999) discussion of Wells et al.'s (1998) (panel of experts) recommendations in the United States.

19 Cited in Thomson (1995:142).

20 Cited by Cutler et al. (1994:181).

21 See Bull (1981), Bull and Clifford (1984), Clifford et al. (1980), Clifford and Davies (1989), Hammersley and Read (1995), Thomson (1995:133–5) and Yarmey (1994, 1995) for literature reviews.

22 Reported in *Expert Evidence*, 1994, 3(2):87.

23 *United States v. Hauptman* (1935) *Atlantic Report*, 180, 809–29, cited in Yarmey (1995:262).

24 See *R. v. Gilmore*, ((1977 2 NSWLR, 935); *R. v. McHaardie and Danilson* ((1983 2 NSWLR,763); *R. v. Robb*, (93 Cr.App.R. 161).

25 See Hammersley and Read (1995) for a review of the empirical literature on earwitness identification.

26 Goldstein and Chance (1985), Hammersley and Read (1985), Read and Craik (1995), Yarmey and Matthys (1992).

27 Cited in Yarmey (1995).

28 Cited in Yarmey (1995).

29 Clifford (1980), Clifford and Denot (1982), Orchard (1993), Reich and Duke (1979, cited in Yarmey, 1995), Saslove and Yarmey (1980).

30 Cited by Bull and Clifford (1999:2000).

Chapter 11 Psychology and the Police

1 See Blackburn (1993), Feldman (1993).

2 See Kapardis (1988, 1989, 1990a).

3 See Blumberg (1994), Fridell and Binder (1992), Kapardis (1990a), Vrij et al. (1995).

4 Mortimer (1991), Stalans and Finn (1995).

5 Cited in Ainsworth (1995:136–7).

6 See Bennett and Greenstein (1975) Griffeth and Cafferty (1977), Teahan (1975).

7 Cited by Stephenson (1992:115–16).

8 See Bayley and Mendelsohn (1969), Carlson et al. (1971), Colman and Gorman (1982).

9 See, also, Feldman (1993: 98), Policy Studies Institute (1983), Scarman (1981).

10 See Cunneen (1990), Hazlehurst (1988), Johnston (1991).

11 See Bull et al. (1983), Ainsworth (1995), Stein (1986).

12 The examples given to illustrate are the present author's.

13 Cited in Stephenson (1992:126).

14 See Baldwin and McConville (1980b), Leiken (1970), Softley et al. (1980).

15 Practice Direction (Crime: Tape Recording of Police Interviews: Preparation for Proceedings in the Crown Court), 89 Cr.App.R. 132.

16 This technique is ethically very questionable because of its likely impact on an innocent suspect, including the likelihood of eliciting a false confession (Moston, 1996:94).

17 Cited by Tousignant (1991).

18 See, for example, the 'Reid Technique of Interviewing and Interrogation' (also known as 'Behavioral Analysis Interview') which is taught widely in the United States (Reid and Arther, 1954)

19 Citing Reid & Associates (1986:44).

20 Citing Swanson et al. (1988:210).

21 Cited in Stephenson (1992).

22 See Archbold (2000:1464–96) regarding confessions and related matters under the *Police and Criminal Evidence Act* (1984).

23 Cited in Gudjonsson and Sigurdsson (1994).

24 See Richardson and Kelly (1995), Torpy (1994).

25 See Home Office Research and Statistics Department, Research Bulletin No. 35, (1994).

26 Cited in Ainsworth (1995).

27 See Gudjonsson (1984).

28 See Gudjonsson (1987).

References

Aboud, F.E. and Levy, S.R. (eds) (1999). Introduction: are we ready to translate research into programs? *Journal of Social Issues*, 55(4), 621–25.

Abwender, D.A. and Hough, K. (2001). Interactive effects of characteristics of defendant and mock juror on U.S. participants' judgement and sentencing recommendations. *Journal of Social Psychology*, 141(5), 603–15.

Aguirre, A. and Baker, D.V. (1990). Empirical research on racial discrimination in the imposition of the death penalty. *Criminal Justice Abstracts*, 135–51.

Ainsworth, P. (2000a). *Psychology and Crime: Myths and Reality*. London: Longman.

Ainsworth, P. (2000b). Psychology and police investigation. In J. McGuire et al. (eds), 39–63.

Ainsworth, P. (2001). Getting confusion: unconscious transference in media reporting. In R. Roesch, R. R. Corrado and R. Dempster (eds), pp. 241–51.

Ainsworth, P.B. (1981). Incident perception by British police officers. *Law and Human Behavior*, 5, 231–6.

Ainsworth, P.B. (1995). *Psychology and Policing in a Changing World*. Chichester: Wiley.

Ainsworth, P.B. and Pease, K. (1987). *Police Work*. London: The British Psychological Society and Methuen.

Akehurst, L., Bull, R. and Vrij, A. (2000). Training British police officers, social workers and students to detect deception in children using criteria-based content analysis. Manuscript submitted for publication. Cited by Vrij (p. 153).

Akehurst, L., Köhnken, G. and Hofer, E. (2001). Content credibility of accounts derived from live and video presentations. *Legal and Criminological Psychology*, 6, 65–83.

Akehurst, L., Köhnken, G., Vrij. A. and Bull, R. (1996). Lay persons' and police officers' beliefs regarding deceptive behavior. *Applied Cognitive Psychology*, 10, 461–71.

Alexander, D.A. and Wells, A. (1991). Reactions of police officers to body-handling after a major disaster: a before-and-after comparison. *British Journal of Psychiatry*, 159, 547–55.

Allen, H. (1987). The logic of gender in psychiatric reports to the courts. In D.C Pennington and S. Lloyd-Bostock (eds), 104–16.

Allen, J. J., Iacono, W. G. and Danielson, K. D. (1992). The identification of concealed memories using the event-related potential and implicit behavioral measures: a methodology of prediction in the face of individual differences. *Psychophysiology*, 29, 504–22.

Allen, R. J. and Miller, J.S. (1995). The expert as educator: enhancing the rationality of verdicts in child sex abuse prosecutions. *Psychology, Public Policy, and Law*, 1, 323–38.

Allport, G.W. and Postman, L. (1947). *The Psychology of Rumor*. New York: Henry Holt.

Alonso-Quecuty, M.L. (1992). Deception detection and reality monitoring: a new answer to an old question? In F. Lösel, D. Bender and T. Bliesener (eds), 328–32.

American Bar Association. (1993). *ABA Standards for Criminal Justice Prosecution Function and Defense Function* (third edition), 123–211.

American Professional Society on the Abuse of Children (1990). *Guidelines for psychological evaluation of suspected sexual abuse in young children*. Unpublished manuscript.

American Psychiatric Association (1993). *Statement on Memories of Sexual Abuse*. Adopted by the Board of Trustees of the APA, 12 December.

American Psychological Association (1990). *Craig v. Maryland: Brief of the American Psychological Association*. Washington, DC. (Reprinted as G.S. Goodman, M. Levine, G.B. Melton and D.W. Ogden (1990)). *Law and Human Behavior*, 15, 13–29.

American Psychological Association (1991). Minutes of the Council of Representatives. *American Psychologist*, 46, 722.

American Psychology Law Society (1991). Speciality guidelines for forensic psychologists. *American Psychology Law Society News*, 11, 8–11.

Anderson, K. (1987). Sentencing in Magistrates' Courts. In I. Potas (ed.), *Sentencing in Australia: Issues, Policy and Reform* (pp. 191–206). Canberra: Australian Institute of Criminology.

Anderson, N.H. (1974). Cognitive algebra. In. L. Berkowitz (comp.), *Advances in Experimental Social Psychology*. New York: Academic Press.

Antonio, M.E. and Hans, V.P. (2001). Race and the civil jury: how does a juror's race shape the jury experience? In R. Roesch et al. (eds), 69–81.

Applegate, B.K., Wright, J.P. and Dunaway, R.G et al. (1994). Victim–offender race and support for capital punishment: a factorial design approach. *American Journal of Criminal Justice*, 18, 95–115.

Arce, R. (1995). Evidence evaluation in jury decision making. In R. Bull and D. Carson (eds), 565–80. Chichester: Wiley.

Arce, R., Farina, F. and Real, S. (1996). Empirical assessment of the escabinato jury system. *Psychology, Crime and Law*, 2, 175–83.

Arce, R., Farina, F., Novo, M. and Seijo, D. (1999). In search of causes of hung juries. *Expert Evidence*, 6, 243–60.

Arce, R., Sobral, J., Farina, F. (1992). Verdicts of psychosocially biased juries. In F. Lösel, et al. (eds), 435–9.

Archbold. (2000). *Criminal Pleading, Evidence and Practice*. London: Sweet and Maxwell.

Arndt, B. (1995). Dark memories. In 'Focus', *The Weekend Australian*, July 1–2, 28.

Aronson, E. (1980). *The Social Animal* (third edition). San Francisco: Freeman.

Aronson, E., Wilson, T.D. and Akert, R.M. (2002). *Social Psychology* (fourth edition). New Jersey: Prentice Hall.

Aschermann, E., Dannenberg, U. and Scholz, A.P. (1998). Photographs as retrieval cues for children. *Applied Cognitive Psychology*, 12, 55–66.

Ashmore, R.D., Solomon, M.R. and Longo., L.C. (1966). Thinking about fashion models' looks: a multi-dimensional approach to the structure of perceived physical attractiveness. *Personality and Social Psychology Bulletin*, 22, 1083–104.

Ashworth, A. (1995). Reflections on the role of the sentencing scholar. In C. Clarkson and R. Morgan (eds), *The Politics of Sentencing Reform*, 251–66.

Ashworth, A. (1997). Sentencing. In M. Maguire, R. Morgan and R. Reiner (eds), *The Oxford Handbook of Criminology* (second edition), 1095–135. Oxford: Clarendon Press.

Ashworth, A. (2000). *Sentencing and Criminal Justice*. London: Butterworths.

Atkinson, J. and Walker, E. (1955). The affiliation motive and perceptual sensitivity to faces. *Journal of Abnormal Social Psychology*, 53, 38–41.

Atkinson, R.C. and Shiffrin, R.M. (1968). Human memory: a proposed system and its control processes. In K.W. Spence and J.T. Spence (eds), *The Psychology of Learning and Motivation: Advances in Research and Theory* (vol. 2). New York: Academic Press.

Auld, Lord Justice (2001). *Review of the Criminal Courts of England and Wales* [The Auld Report]. London: HMSO.

Australian Law Reform Commission and Human Rights and Equal Opportunity Commission (1997). *Seen and Heard: Priority for Children in the Legal Process*. Sydney: Australian Government Publishing Service.

Australian Psychological Society. (1995). *Guidelines Relating to Recovered Memories*. Melbourne.

Avery, G., Baker, E. and Kane, B. (1984). *Psychology at Work: Fundamental and Applications*. Sydney: Prentice-Hall.

Avio, K.L. (1988). Capital punishment in Canada: statistical evidence and constitutional issues. *Canadian Journal of Criminology*, 30, 331–45.

Baab, G.W. and Furgeson, W.R. (1967) Texas sentencing practices: a statistical study. *Texas Law Review*, 472–503.

Bagby, R.M., Parker, J.D., Rector, N.A. and Kalemba, V. (1994). Racial prejudice in the Canadian legal system: juror decisions in a simulated rape trial. *Law and Human Behavior*, 18, 339–50.

Bain, S.A. and Baxter, J.S. (2000). Interrogative suggestibility: the role of interviewer behaviour. *Legal and Criminological Psychology*, 5, 123–33.

Baker, E. (1999). The impact of EC law on sentencing. Paper presented at the Sentencing and Society Conference, University of Strathclyde, June 24–26, Glasgow, Scotland.

Baker, T. and Carter D.L. (eds) (1994). *Police Deviance* (third edition). Cincinatti, OH: Anderson Publishing.

Baker-Ward, L. and Ornstein, P.A. (2002). Cognitive underpinnings of children's testimony. In H.L. Westcott et al. (eds), 21–35.

Baldus, D.C., Pulaski, C. and Woodworth, G. (1983). Comparative review of death sentences: an empirical study of the Georgia experience. *Journal of Criminal Law and Criminology*, 74, 661–753.

Baldwin, J. (1994). The role of legal representatives at police stations. Royal Commission on Criminal Justice Study no. 3. *Research Bulletin*, no. 35, 11–12. London: Home Office Research and Statistics Department.

Baldwin, J. and McConville, M. (1979). *Jury Trials*. Oxford: Clarendon Press.

Baldwin, J. and McConville, M. (1980a). Juries, foremen and verdicts. *British Journal of Criminology*, 20, 35–44.

Baldwin, J. and McConville, M. (1980b). *Confessions in Crown Court Trials*. Royal Commission on Criminal Procedure, Research Study no. 5. London: HMSO.

Balkin, S. and Houlden, P. (1983). Reducing fear of crime through occupational presence. *Criminal Justice and Behavior*, 10, 13–33.

Ballard, P.B. (1913). Obliviscence and reminiscence. *British Journal of Psychology Monograph Supplements*, 1, 1–82.

Bandura, A. (1986). *Social Foundations of Thought and Action: A Social Cognitive Theory*. Englewood Cliffs, NJ: Prentice-Hall.

Barber, D. and Gordon, G. (eds) (1976). *Members of the Jury*. London: Wildwood House.

Barclay, C.D., Cutting, J.E. and Kozlowski, L.T. (1978). Temporal and spatial factors in gait perceptions that influence gait recognition. *Perception and Psychophysics*, 23, 145–52.

Barker, T. and Carter, D.L. (1994). Police lies and perjury: a motivation-based taxonomy. In T. Barker and D.L. Carter (eds), 139–52.

Barland, G.H. (1988). The polygraph test in the USA and elsewhere. In G. Gale (ed.), 73–95. London: Sage.

Barnes, J.A. (1994). *A Pack of Lies: Towards a Sociology of Lying*. Cambridge: Cambridge University Press.

Barnett, A. (1985). Some distribution patterns for the Georgia death sentence. *University of California, Davis Law Review*, 18, 1327–74.

Bartholomews, B. (1973). Voice identification by nursery school children. *Canadian Journal of Psychology*, 27, 464–72.

Bartlet, D. and Memon, A. (1995). Advocacy. In R. Bull and D. Carson (eds), 543–54.

Bartlett, F. (1932). *Remembering: A Study in Experimental and Social Psychology*. Cambridge: Cambridge University Press.

Bartlett, J.C. and Fulton, A. (1991). Familiarity and recognition of faces in old age. *Memory and Cognition*, 19, 229–38

Bartlett, J.C. and Leslie, J.E. (1986). Aging and memory for faces versus single views of faces. *Memory and Cognition*, 14, 371–81.

Bartol, C. (1996). Police psychology: then, now and beyond. *Criminal Justice and Behavior*, 23, 70–89.

Bartol, C.R. and Bartol, A.M. (1994). *Psychology and Law: Research and Application* (second edition). Pacific Grove: Brooks/Coole.

Bashore, T.R. and Rapp, P.E. (1993). Are there alternatives to traditional polygraph procedures? *Psychological Bulletin*, 113, 3–22.

Bass, E. and Davis, L. (1988). *The Courage to Heal: A Guide for Women Survivors of Childhood Sexual Abuse*. New York: Harper and Row.

Batterman-Faune, J.M. and Goodman, G.S. (1993). Effects of context on the accuracy and suggestibility of child witnesses. In G.S Goodman and B.L. Bottoms (eds), 301–30.

Bavelas, J.B., Black, A., Chovil, N. and Mullett, J. (1990). *Equivocal Communication*. Newbury Park, CA: Sage.

Bayley, D. and Mendelsohn, H. (1969). *Minorities and the Police: Confrontation in America*. New York: The Free Press.

Behrman, B.C. and Davey, S.L. (2001). Eyewitness identification in actual criminal cases: an archival analysis. *Law and Human Behavior*, 25(5), 475–91.

Bekerian, D.A. (1993). In search of the ideal eyewitness. *American Psychologist*, 48, 574–6.

Bell, B.E. and Loftus, E.F. (1988). Degree of detail of eyewitness testimony and mock juror judgement. *Journal of Applied Social Psychology*, 18, 1171–92.

Belli, R.F. (1989). Influences on misleading postevent information: misinformation interference and acceptance. *Journal of Experimental Psychology: General*, 118, 72–85.

Bennet, P., Pike, G., Brace, N. and Kemp, R. (2000). Accuracy and confidence in E-FIT construction. Paper presented at the 10th European Conference of Psychology and Law, Limassol, Cyprus, April 12–14.

Bennet, W.S. and Feldman, M.S. (1981). *Reconstructing Reality in the Courtroom*. New Brunswick: Rutgers University Press.

Bennett, P. (1986). Face recall: a police perspective. *Human Learning*, 5, 197–202.

Bennett, P. and Gibling, F. (1989). Can we trust our eyes? *Policing*, 5, 313–21.

Bennett, R.R. and Greenstein, T. (1975). The police personality: a test of the predispositional model. *Journal of Police Science and Administration*, 3, 439–45.

Bennett, T. and Lupton, R. (1992). A national activity survey of police work. *Howard Journal*, 31(3), 200–23.

Ben-Shakhar, G. (1989). Non-conventional methods in personnel selection. In P. Herriott (ed.), *Assessment and Selection in Organizations* (pp. 469–85). Chichester: Wiley.

Berliner, L. and Williams, L.M. (1994). Memories of child sexual abuse: a response to Lindsay and Read. *Applied Cognitive Psychology*, 8, 379–87.

Berman, G.L. and Cutler, B.L. (1996). Effects of inconsistencies in eyewitness testimony on mock-juror decision making. *Journal of Applied Psychology*, 81, 170–7.

Berman, G.L., Narby, D.J. and Cutler, B.L. (1995). Effects of inconsistent statements on mock jurors' evaluations of the eyewitness, perceptions of defendant culpability and verdicts. *Law and Human Behavior*, 19, 79–88.

Bernardin, H.J. and Cooke, D.K. (1993). Validity of an honesty test in predicting theft among convenience store employees. *Academy of Management Journal*, 36, 1097–108.

Berry, M.J., Robinson, C.A. and Bailey, J. (1999). The use of hypnosis to recover evidence from convicted offenders: issues and implications. Paper presented at the International Psychology and Law Conference, University College, Dublin, 6–9 July, 1999.

Bersoff, D.N. and Ogden, D.W. (1987). In the Supreme Court of the United States: Lockhart v. McCree. *American Psychologist*, 42, 59–68.

Beswick, D.G. and Hills, M.D. (1972). A survey of ethnocentrism in Australia. *Australian Journal of Psychology*, 24, 153–63.

Bevan, W., Albert, R., Loiseaux, P., Mayfield, P. and Wright, G. (1958). Jury behavior as a function of the prestige of the foreman and the nature of his leadership. *Journal of Public Law*, 7, 419–49.

Bierhoff, H.W., Buck, E. and Klein, R. (1989). Attractiveness and respectability of the offender as factors in the evaluation of criminal cases. In H. Wegener, F. Lösel and J. Haisch (eds), 192–207.

Billig, M. and Milner, D. (1976). A spade is a spade in the eyes of the law. *Psychology Today*, 21, 13–15; 62.

Binet, A. (1896). *Psychology of postigitation*. Annual Report of the Board of Regents of the Smithsonian Institution, 1894, 555–71. Washington, DC: GPO.

Binet, A. (1900). *La Suggestibilité*. Paris: Doin and Fils.

Binet, A. (1905). La science du témoigne. *Année Psychologique*, 1, 128: 38.

Birch, D. (2000). A better deal for vulnerable witnesses? *Criminal Law Review*, 223–49.

Birch, D.J. (1992). Children's evidence. *Criminal Law Review*, 262–76.

Birkett, Lord. (1962). *Six Great Advocates*. Harmondsworth: Penguin.

Blackburn, R. (1993). *The Psychology of Criminal Conduct: Theory, Research and Practice*. Chichester: Wiley.

Blackburn, R. (1996). What is forensic psychology? *Legal and Criminological Psychology*, 1, 3–16.

Blackburn, R. (2000). Risk assessment and prediction. In J. McGuire, T. Mason and A. O'Kane (eds), 177–204.

Blackstone, W. (1776). *Commentaries*, vol. IV.

Blaney, P.H. (1986). Affect and memory: a review. *Psychological Bulletin*, 99, 229–46.

Blau, T.H. (1998). *The Psychologist as Expert Witness* (second edition). New York: Wiley.

Block, A., Marx, G., Leo, R.A. et al. (1992). Issues and theories on covert policing. *Crime, Law and Social Change*, 18, 1–217.

Blom-Cooper, L. (1974). The jury on trial. *Guardian*, 10 June, 9.

Blumberg, M. (1994). Police use of deadly force: exploring some key issues. In T. Barker and D.L. Carter (eds), *Police Deviance*, 201–21.

Boat, B.W. and Everson, M.D. (1993). The use of anatomical dolls in sexual abuse evaluations: current research and practice. In G.S. Goodman and B.L. Bottoms (eds), 47–69.

Boatright, R.G. (2001). Generational and age-based differences in attitudes towards jury service. *Behavioral Science and the Law*, 19, 285–304.

Boaz, T.L., Perry, W.P., Raney, G., Fischler, J.R. and Shuman, D. (1991). Detection of guilty knowledge with event-related potentials. *Journal of Applied Psychology*, 76, 788–95.

Boccaccini, M.T. and Brodsky, S.L. (2001). Characteristics of the ideal criminal defense attorney from the client's perspective: empirical findings and implications for legal practice. *Law and Psychology Review*, 25, 81–117.

Bogoch, B. (1999). Judging in a 'different' voice: gender and the sentencing of violent offences in Israel. *Journal of the Sociology of Law*, 27, 51–78.

Bok, S. (1978). *Lying: Moral Choice in Public and Private*. New York: Pantheon Books.

Bond, R.A. and Lemon, N.E. (1979). Changes in magistrates' attitudes during the first year on the bench. In D.P. Farrington, K. Hawkins and S. Lloyd-Bostock (eds), 125–42.

Bonto, M.A. and Payne, D.G. (1991). Role of environmental context in eyewitness memory. *American Journal of Psychology*, 104, 117–34.

Boon, J. and Noon, E. (1994). Changing perspectives in cognitive interviewing. *Psychology, Crime and Law*, 1, 59–69.

Boon, J.C.W. and Davies, G.M. (1987). Rumors greatly exaggerated: Allport and Postman's experimental study. *Canadian Journal of Behavioral Science*, 19, 430–40.

Borchard, E. (1932). *Convicting the Innocent: Errors of Criminal Justice*. New Haven: Yale University Press.

Boring, E. (1963). *The Psychology of Controversy*. New York: Academic Press.

Bornstein, B.H. (1994). David, Goliath and Reverend Bayes: prior beliefs about defendants' status in personal injury cases. *Applied Cognitive Psychology*, 8, 233–58.

Bornstein, B.H. (1995). Memory processes in elderly eyewitnesses: what we know and what we don't know. *Behavioral Sciences and the Law*, 13, 337–48.

Bornstein, B.H. (1999). The ecological validity of jury simulations: is the jury still out? *Law and Human Behavior*, 23, 75–91.

Borum, R. and Stock, H.V. (1993). Detection of deception in law enforcement applicants. *Law and Human Behavior*, 17, 157–66.

Bothwell, R.K., Brigham, J.C. and Malpass, R.S. (1989). Cross-racial identification. *Personality and Social Psychology Bulletin*, 15, 19–25.

Bothwell, R.K., Brigham, J.C. and Pigot, M.A. (1987a). An exploratory study of personality differences in eyewitness memory. *Journal of Social Behaviour and Personality*, 2, 335–43.

Bothwell, R.K., Deffenbacher, K.A. and Brigham, J.C. (1987b). Correlations of eyewitness accuracy and confidence: optimality hypothesis revisited. *Journal of Applied Psychology*, 72, 691–5.

Bottoms, B.L. and Goodman, G.S. (1996). *International Perspectives on Child Abuse and Children's Testimony: Psychological Research and Law*. Thousand Oaks, CA: Sage Publications.

Botwinick, J. and Shock, N.W. (1972). Age differences in performance decrement with continuous work. *Journal of Gerontology*, 7, 41–6.

Bowen, R.A. (1965). The explanation of judicial voting behavior from sociological characteristics of judges. Unpublished doctoral dissertation, Yale University. Cited by J.B. Grossman, (1966) Social backgrounds and judicial decision-making. *Harvard Law Review*, 79, 1551–61, at 1561.

Bower, G. (1967). A multicomponent theory of memory trace. In K.W. Spence and J.T. Spence (eds), *The Psychology of Learning and Motivation*, vol. 1.

Bower, G.H. (1981). Mood and memory. *American Psychologist*, 36, 129–48.

Bower, G.H., Black, J.B. and Turner, T.J. (1979). Scripts in memory for text. *Cognitive Psychology*, 11, 177–220.

Bowers, W. (1995). The capital jury project: rationale, design, and preview of early findings. *Indiana Law Review*, 70, 1043–102.

Boyanowsky, E.O. and Griffiths, C.T. (1982). Weapon and eye contact as instigators or inhibitors of aggressive arousal in police citizen interaction. *Journal of Applied Social Psychology*, 12, 398–407.

Brabin, P.J. and Berah, E.F. (1995). *Psychiatry, Psychology and Law*, 2(2), 165–71.

Bradfield, A.L. and Wells, G.L. (2000). The perceived validity of eyewitness identification testimony: a test of the five *Biggers* criteria. *Law and Human Behavior*, 24(5), 581–94.

Bradley, B.P. and Baddley, A.D. (1990). Emotional factors in forgetting. *Psychological Medicine*, 20, 351–5.

Brahams, D. (2000). 'Repressed memories' and the law. *Medico-Legal Journal*, 68(3), 79–80.

Braithwaite, J. (1989). *Crime, Shame and Reintegration*. Cambridge: Cambridge University Press.

Brandon, I.S. (1999). Recovered memories: some aspects of the controversy. *Medico-Legal Journal*, 67, 25–34.

Brandon, R. and Davies, C. (1973). *Wrongful Imprisonment: Mistaken Convictions and their Consequences*. London: George Allen and Unwin.

Bray, R.M. and Kerr, N.L. (1982). Methodological considerations in the study of the psychology of the courtroom. In R.M. Bray and N.L. Kerr (eds), *The Psychology of the Courtroom* (pp. 287–323). New York: Academic Press.

Breci, M.G. (1997). What motivates officers to continue their college education? *Journal of Criminal Justice Education*, 8(1), 51–60.

Brekke, N.J. and Borgida, E. (1988). Expert psychological testimony in rape trials: a social cognitive analysis. *Journal of Personality and Social Psychology*, 55, 372–86.

Brennan, M. (1993). The battle for credibility. *New Law Journal*, 143, 623–6.

Brenner, M., Branscomb, H.H. and Schwartz, G.E. (1979). Psychological stress evaluator: two tests of vocal measure. *Psychophysiology*, 16, 351–7.

Brewer, S. and Wilson, C. (eds) (1995). *Psychology and Policing*. Hillsdale, NJ: Erlbaum.

Breyer, H. (1992). The battered woman syndrome and the admissibility of expert testimony. *Criminal Law Bulletin*, 28, 99–115.

Brickner, P. and Bruzansky, S. (1966). Effects of stimulus context and duration on talker identification. *Journal of Acoustical Society of America*, 40, 1441–9.

Brigham, J.C. (1983). Psychological factors in eyewitness identifications. *Journal of Criminal Justice*, 11, 47–56.

Brigham, J.C. (1986). The influence of race on face recognition. In H.D. Ellis, M.A. Jeeves, F. Newcombe and A. Young (eds), *Aspects of Face Processing* (pp. 170–7). Dordrecht, Netherlands: Martinus Nijhoff.

Brigham, J.C. (1989). Disputed eyewitness identifications: can experts help? *The Champion*, 8, 10–18.

Brigham, J.C. (1990). Target person distinctiveness and attractiveness as moderator variables in the confidence–accuracy relationship in eyewitness identifications. *Basic and Applied Social Psychology*, 11, 101–5.

Brigham, J.C. and Bothwell, R.K. (1983). The ability of prospective jurors to estimate the accuracy of eyewitness identifications. *Law and Human Behavior*, 7, 19–30.

Brigham, J.C. and Pfeiffer, J.E. (1994). Evaluating the fairness of lineups. In D.F. Ross, J.D. Read and M.P. Toglia (eds), 201–22.

Brigham, J.C. and Wolfskiel, M.P. (1983). Opinions of attorneys and law enforcement personnel on the accuracy of eyewitness identifications. *Law and Human Behavior*, 7, 337–49.

Brigham, J.C., Maass, A., Snyder, L.D. and Spaulding, K. (1982). The accuracy of eyewitness identifications in a field setting. *Journal of Personality and Social Psychology*, 42, 673–81.

Brigham, J.C., Ready, D.J. and Spier, S.A. (1990). Standards for evaluating the fairness of photograph lineups. *Basic and Applied Social Psychology*, 11, 149–63.

Brigham, J.C., Van Verst, M. and Bothwell, R.K. (1986). Accuracy of children's eyewitness identification in a field setting. *Basic and Applied Social Psychology*, 7, 295–306.

British Psychological Society Working Group on the Use of the Polygraph in Criminal Investigation and Personnel Screening (1986). *Bulletin of the British Psychological Society*, 39, 81–94.

Brooks, K. and Siegal, M. (1991). Children as eyewitnesses: memory, suggestibility, and credibility. *Australian Psychologist*, 26, 84–8.

Broughton, F. (1995). The memory debate in perspective: and some future directions. *Psychiatry, Psychology and Law*, 2(1), 91–6.

Brown, A. (1988). *Watching the Detectives*. London: Hodder and Stoughton.

Brown, D. and Neal, D. (1988). Show trials: the media and the gang of twelve. In M. Findlay and P. Duff (eds), *The Jury Under Attack* (pp. 126–39). Sydney: Butterworths.

Brown, E., Deffenbacher, K. and Sturgill, W. (1977). Memory for faces and the circumstances of the encounter. *Journal of Applied Psychology*, 62, 311–18.

Brown, I. and Hullin, R. (1992). A study of sentencing in the Leeds magistrates' courts: the treatment of ethnic minority and white offenders. *British Journal of Criminology*, 32, 41–53.

Brown, L. and Willis, A. (1985). Authoritarianism in British police recruits: importation, socialization or myth? *Journal of Occupational Psychology*, 58, 97–108.

Brown, M.R. (1926). *Legal Psychology: Psychology Applied to the Trial of Cases, to Crime and its Treatment, and to Mental States and Processes*. Indianapolis, IN: Bobbs-Merrill.

Brown, R. and Kulik, J. (1977). Flashbulb memories. *Cognition*, 5, 73–93.

Bruce, V. (1988). *Recognising Faces*. London: LEA.

Bruck, M. and Ceci, S.J. (1995). Amicus brief for the case of New Jersey v. Margaret Kelly Michaels presented by committee of concerned social scientists. *Psychology, Public Policy, and Law*, 1, 272–322.

Bryan, W.J. (1971). *The Chosen Ones*. New York: Vantage Press.

Buckhout, R. (1974). Eyewitness testimony. *Scientific American*, 231, 23–31.

Buckhout, R. (1976). Experimental testimony by psychologists. *Social Action and the Law*. Center for Responsive Psychology, 3, 41–53.

Budai, P. (1995). Rehabilitation of child sexual assault cases. *Current Issues in Criminal Justice*, 7, 223–30.

Bulkley, J.A. and Horowitz, M.J. (1994). Adults sexually abused as children: legal actions and issues. *Behavioral Sciences and the Law*, 12, 65–87.

Bull, R. (1974). The importance of being beautiful. *New Society*, 30, 412–14.

Bull, R. (1979). The influence of stereotypes on person perception. In Farrington et al. (eds), 184–193.

Bull, R. (1981). Voice identification by man and machine: a review of research. In S. Lloyd-Bostock (ed.), (1981a), 28–42.

Bull, R. (1985). Police awareness training. *Policing*, 1, 109–23.

Bull, R. (1992). Obtaining evidence expertly: the reliability of interviews with child witnesses. *Expert Evidence*, 1, 5–12.

Bull, R. (1995a). Interviewing children in legal contexts. In R. Bull and D. Carson (eds), 235–46.

Bull, R. (1995b). Interviewing children with learning disabilities. In R. Bull and D. Carson (eds), 247–60.

Bull, R. and Carson, D. (eds) (1995). *Handbook of Psychology in Legal Contexts*. Chichester: Wiley.

Bull, R. and Cherryman, J. (1995). *Helping to Identify Skills in Specialist Investigative Interviewing: Enhancement of Professional Skills*. London: Home Office, Police Department, Police Research Group.

Bull, R. and Clifford, B. (1999). Earwitness testimony. In A. Heaton-Armstrong, E. Shepherd and D. Wolhover (eds), *Analysing Witness Testimony: A Guide for Legal Practitioners and Other Professionals* (pp. 194–206). London: Blackstone Press.

Bull, R. and Clifford, B.R. (1984). Earwitness voice recognition accuracy. In G.L. Wells and E.F. Loftus (eds), 92–123.

Bull, R. and Davies. G. (in press). Child witness research in England. In B. Bottoms and G. Goodman (eds), *International Perspectives on Children's Testimony*. Newbury Park, CA: Sage.

Bull, R. and Green, J. (1980). The relationship between physical appearance and criminality. *Medicine, Science and the Law*, 20, 79–83.

Bull, R. and Horncastle, P. (1986). Metropolitan police recruit training: an independent evaluation. London: The Police Foundation.

Bull, R. and Horncastle, P. (1994). Evaluation of police recruit training involving psychology. *Psychology, Crime and Law*, 1, 143–9.

Bull, R. and Reid, R. (1975). Recall after briefing: television versus face-to-face presentation. *Journal of Occupational Psychology*, 48, 73–8.

Bull, R., Bustin, B., Evans, P. and Gahagan, D. (1983). *Psychology for Police Officers*. Chichester: Wiley.

Bull, R., Horncastle, P., Jones, C. and Mason, D. (1987). *Metropolitan Police Recruit Training in 'Policing Skills' (Phase 2): An Independent Evaluation. Executive Summary*. London: Police Foundation.

Burbeck, E. and Furnham, A. (1985). Police officer selection: a critical review of the literature. *Journal of Police Science and Administration*, 13, 58–69.

Burk, T.T. (2001). Documenting and reporting a confession with a signed statement: a guide for law enforcement. *FBI Law Enforcement Bulletin*, 17–22.

Burman, S. and Allen-Meaves, P. (1994). Neglected children of murder: children's witness to parental homicide. *Social Work*, 39, 28–34.

Burt, H.E. (1925). Measurement of confusion between similar trade names. *Illinois Law Review*, 19, 320–42.

Burt, H.E. (1931). *Legal Psychology*. New York: Prentice-Hall.

Bussey, K. (1995). Allegations of child sexual abuse: accurate and truthful disclosures, false allegations, and false denials. *Current Issues in Criminal Justice*, 7, 176–92.

Bussey, K., Lee, K. and Grimbeek, E.J. (1993). Lies and secrets: implications for children's reporting of sexual abuse. In G.S. Goodman and B.L. Bottoms (eds), 147–68.

Bussey, K., Ross, C. and Lee, K. (1991). The effect of the transgressor's presence on children's truthfulness. Manuscript in preparation.

Butler-Slos, J. (1992). *Inquiry into Child Abuse in Cleveland*. London: HMSO Comnd 412.

Buxton, R. (1990a). Challenging and discharging jurors – 1. *Criminal Law Review*, 225–35.

Buxton, R. (1990b). Challenging and discharging jurors – 2. *Criminal Law Review*, 284–91.

Byrne, K. (1988). Distinguishing genuine from fabricated child sexual abuse. In D. Greig and I. Freckelton (eds), *International Perspectives on Psychiatry, Psychology and Law* (pp. 186–91). Melbourne, Australia: Australian and New Zealand Association of Psychiatry, Psychology and Law.

Byrne, K. and Maloney, L. (1991). Brainwashing of children in family law cases: is there a cure? In I. Freckelton., D. Greig and M. MacMahon (eds), *Forensic Issues in Mental Health*. Proceedings of the Twelfth Annual Congress of the Australian and New Zealand Association of Psychiatry, Psychology and Law. Melbourne, Australia (pp. 307–14).

Byrne, P. (1988). Jury reform and the future. In M. Findlay and P. Duff (eds), 190–208.

Byrne, P. (1991). Children as witnesses – legal aspects. In J. Vernon (ed.), *Children as Witnesses* (pp. 3–18) Conference Proceedings no. 8, Canberra: Australian Institute of Criminology.

Cadzow, J. (1995). Witness to the prosecution. *Good Weekend (The Age* Magazine), 4 February, pp. 14–20.

Cairns, H. (1935). *Law and the Social Sciences*. London: Kegan Paul, Trench Trubner and Co.

Camara, W.J. and Schneider, D.L. (1994). Integrity tests: facts and unresolved issues. *American Psychologist*, 49, 112–19.

Cammack, M. (1995). In search of the post-positivist jury. *Indiana Law Journal*, 70(2), 405–89.

Candel, I., Merckelbach, H. and Muris, P. (2000). Measuring interrogative suggestibility in children: reliability and validity of the Bonn Test of Statement Suggestibility. *Psychology, Crime and Law*, 6, 61–70.

Canter, D. (1992). An evaluation of the 'cumsum' stylistic analysis of confessions. *Expert Evidence*, 1, 93–9.

Canter, D. (1995). Psychology of offender profiling. In R. Bull and D. Carson (eds), 345–456.

Cantor, C., Brodie, J. and McMillen, J. (1991). Firearms victims – who are they? *Medical Journal of Australia*, 155, 442–6.

Carey, S. (1981). The development of face perception. In G.M. Davies, H. Ellis and J. Shepherd (eds), *Perceiving and Remembering Faces* (pp. 9–38). London: Academic Press.

Carlson, H., Thayer, R.E. and Germann, A.C. (1971). Social attitudes and personality differences among members of two kinds of police departments (innovative vs traditional) and students. *Journal of Criminal Law, Criminology and Police Science*, 62, 564–7.

Carroll, J.S. and Payne, J.W. (1977). Judgements about crime and the criminal: a model and a method for investigating parole decisions. In B.D. Sales (ed.), *Perspectives in Law and Psychology. vol. 1: The Criminal Justice System* (pp. 191–239). New York: Plenum Press.

Carson, D. (1990). *Professionals and the Courts: A Handbook for Expert Witnesses.* Birmingham: Venture Press.

Carson, D. (1992). Beyond the ultimate issue. In Lösel et al. (eds), 447–64.

Carson, D. (1995a). Individualism: its importance in law and psychology. In R. Bull and D. Carson (eds), 43–53.

Carson, D. (1995b). Law's premises, methods and values. In R. Bull and D. Carson (eds), 29–40.

Carson, D. (1995c). Regulating the examination of children. *Expert Evidence*, 4, 2–9.

Carson, D. and Bull, R. (1995a). Psychology in legal contexts: idealism and realism. In R. Bull and D. Carson (eds), *Handbook of Psychology in Legal Contexts* (pp. 3–11). Chichester: Wiley.

Carson, D. and Bull, R. (1995b). Psychology and law: future directions. In R. Bull and D. Carson (eds), 645–50.

Carson, R.C., Butcher, J.N. and Mineka, S. (2000). *Abnormal Psychology and Modern Life.* Boston: Allyn and Bacon.

Casburn, M. (1979). *Girls will be Girls: Sexism and Juvenile Justice in a London Borough.* London: Women's Research and Resources Centre.

Cashmore, J. (1990). The use of video technology for child witnesses. *Monash Law Review*, 16, 228–50.

Cashmore, J. (1991). Problems and solutions in lawyer–child communication. *Criminal Law Journal*, 193–202.

Cashmore, J. (1992). The use of closed-circuit television for child witnesses in the ACT. Sydney: Australian Law Reform Commission.

Cashmore, J. (2002). Innovative procedures for child witnesses. In H.L. Westcott et al. (eds), 203–17.

Cashmore, J. (with Dhaas, N.). (1992). *The Use of Closed Circuit Television for Child Witnesses in the ACT.* Sydney: Australian Law Reform Commission.

Casper, J.D. and Benedict, K.M. (1993). The influence of outcome information and attitudes on juror decision making in search and seizure cases. In R. Hastie (1993a) (ed.), 65–83.

Casper, J.D., Benedict, K.M. and Perry, J.L. (1989). Juror decision making, attitudes and the hindsight bias. *Law and Human Behavior*, 13, 291–310.

Cassell, W.S. and Bjorklund, D.E. (1995). Developmental patterns of eyewitness memory and suggestibility: an ecologically-based short-term longitudinal study. *Law and Human Behavior*, 19, 507–32.

Cattell, J.M. (1895). Measurement of the accuracy of recollection. *Science*, 2, 761–6.

Cattermole, G.A. (1984). The psychologist as an expert witness. In M. Nixon (ed.), *Issues In Psychological Practice* (pp. 121–32). Melbourne: Longman Cheshire.

Cavoukian, A. and Heslegrave, R.J. (1979). The admissibility of polygraph evidence in court. Some empirical findings. *Law and Human Behavior*, 4, 117–31.

Ceci, S.J. and Leichtman, M. (1992). 'I know you know that I know that you broke the toy': a brief report of recursive awareness among 3-year-olds. In S. J. Ceci, M. Leichtman and M. Putnik (eds), *Cognitive and Social Factors in Early Deception*, 1–9. Hillsdale, NJ: Erlbaum.

Ceci, S.J. and Bruck, M. (1993). Suggestibility of the child witness: a historical review and a synthesis. *Psychological Bulletin*, 113, 403–39.

Ceci, S.J. and Bruck, M. (1995). *Jeopardy in the Courtroom: A Successful Analysis of Children's Testimony.* Washington, DC: American Psychological Association.

Ceci, S.J. and Leichtman, M. (1992, March). Group distortion effects in preschoolers' reports. In D. Peters (Chair) Issues related to the witness child. Symposium presented at the American Psychology and Law Biennial Meeting, San Diego, CA.

Ceci, S.J. and Loftus, E.F. (1994). 'Memory work': a royal road to false memories? *Applied Cognitive Psychology*, 8, 351–64.

Ceci, S.J., Bruck, M. and Rosenthal, R. (1995). Children's allegations of sexual abuse: forensic and scientific issues: a reply to commentators. *Psychology, Public Policy, and Law*, 1, 494–520.

Ceci, S.J., Huffman, M.L.C., Smith, E. and Loftus, E.F. (1996). Repeatedly thinking about a non-event: source misattributions in the creation of false beliefs among preschoolers. In K. Pedzek and W. Banks (eds), *The Recovered Memory/False Memory Debate* (pp. 225–44). San Diego, CA: Academic Press.

Ceci, S.J., Lind, E.A. and Bermant, G. (1987). *Jury Service in Lengthy Jury Trials*. Washington, DC: Federal Judicial Center.

Ceci, S.J., Loftus, E.F., Leichtman, M.D. and Bruck, M. (1994). The possible role of source misattributions in the creation of false beliefs among preschoolers. *International Journal of Clinical and Experimental Hypnosis*, 42, 304–20.

Ceci, S.J., Toglia, M.P. and Ross, D.F. (eds) (1997). *Children's Eyewitness Memory*. New York: Springer Verlag.

Chahal, K. and Cassidy, T. (1995). Deception and its detection in children: a study of adult accuracy. *Psychology, Crime and Law*, 1, 237–45.

Chaiken, S. (1979). Communicator physical attractiveness and persuasion. *Journal of Personality and Social Psychology*, 37, 1387–97.

Chaiken, S., Liberman, A. and Eagly, A.H. (1989). Heuristic and systematic processing within and beyond the persuasion context. In J.S. Uleman and J.A. Bargh (eds), *Unintended Thought* (pp. 212–52). New York: Guilford.

Chambliss, W.J. and Seidman, R.B. (1971). *Law, Order, and Power*. Reading, Mass: Addison-Wesley.

Champagne, A., Shuman, D. and Whitaker, E. (1991). An empirical examination of the use of expert witnesses in American courts. *Jurimetrics Journal*, 31, 375–92.

Chance, J., Goldstein, A. and McBride, L. (1975). Differential experience and recognition memory for faces. *Journal of Social Psychology*, 97, 243–53.

Chance, J., Turner. A.L. and Goldstein, A.G. (1982). Development of differential recognition of own- and other-race faces. *Journal of Psychology*, 112, 29–37.

Chappel, D., Grabosky, P., Wilson, P. and Mukherjee, S. (1988). Firearms and violence in Australia. Report no. 10, Trends and Issues in Justice and Criminal Justice series. Canberra: Australian Institute of Criminology.

Chen, Y.Y. and Geiselman, R.E. (1993). Effects of ethnic stereotyping and ethnically-related cognitive biases on eyewitness recollections of height. *American Journal of Forensic Psychology*, 11, 1–7.

Child Witness Project (1991). Reducing the system-induced trauma for child sexual abuse victims through court preparation, assessment and follow-up. London, Ontario: Family Court Clinic.

Chiricos, T.G. and Waldo, G.P. (1975). Socio-economic status and criminal sentencing: an empirical assessment of a conflict proposition. *American Sociological Review*, 40, 753–72.

Chisholm, R. and Nettheim, G. (1992). *Understanding Law: An Introduction to Australia's Legal System*. Sydney: Butterworths.

Christiansen, R.E., Sweeney, J.D. and Ochalek, K. (1983). Influencing eyewitness descriptions. *Law and Human Behavior*, 7, 59–65.

Christianson, S.A. (1984). The relationship between induced emotional arousal and amnesia. *Scandinavian Journal of Psychology*, 25, 147–60.

Christianson, S.A. (1989). Flashbulb memories: special, but not so special. *Memory and Cognition*, 17, 435–43.

Christianson, S.A. (1992). Emotional stress and eyewitness memory: a critical review. *Psychological Bulletin*, 112, 284–309.

Christianson, S.A. (ed.) (1992). *The Handbook of Emotion and Memory: Research and Theory*. Hillsdale, NJ: Erlbaum.

Christianson, S.A. and Hubinette, B. (1993). Hands up!: a study of witnesses' emotional reactions and memories associated with bank robberies. *Applied Cognitive Psychology*, 7, 365–79.

Christianson, S.A., Goodman, J. and Loftus, E.F. (1992). Eyewitness memory for stressful events: methodological quandaries and ethical dilemmas. In S.A. Christianson (ed.), 217–41.

Christianson, S.A., Karlsson, I. and Persson, L.G.W. (1998). Police personnel as eyewitnesses to a violent crime. *Legal and Criminological Psychology*, 3, 59–72.

Clark, N.K., Stephenson, G.M. and Rutter, D.R. (1986). Memory for a complex social discourse: the analysis and prediction of individual and group recall. *Journal of Memory and Language*, 25, 295–313.

Clark, S.E. and Tunnicliff, J.L. (2001). Selecting line-up foils in eyewitness identification experiments: experimental control and real-world simulation. *Law and Human Behavior*, 25(3), 199–216.

Clarke, J. (2000). The social psychology of jury nullification. *Law and Human Behavior*, 24: 39–57.

Clarke, S.H. and Koch, G.G. (1976). The influence of income and other factors on whether criminal defendants go to prison. *Law and Society Review*, 11, 57–92

Clarkson, C. and Morgan, R. (eds) (1995). *The Politics of Sentencing Reform*. Oxford: Clarendon Press.

Clifford, B.R. (1978). A critique of eyewitness research. In M.M. Gruneberg, P.E. Morris and R.W. Sykes (eds), *Practical Aspects of Memory*. New York: Academic Press.

Clifford, B.R. (1979). Eyewitness testimony: the bridging of a credibility gap. In D. Farrington et al. (eds), (1979a), 167–83.

Clifford, B.R. (1980). Voice identification by human listeners: on earwitness reliability. *Law and Human Behavior*, 4, 373–94.

Clifford, B.R. (1981). Towards a more realistic appraisal of the psychology of testimony. In S.M.A. Lloyd-Bostock (ed.), (1981a), 19–27.

Clifford, B.R. (1983). Memory for voices: the feasibility and quality of earwitness evidence. In S.M.A. Lloyd-Bostock and B.R. Clifford (eds), 189–218.

Clifford, B.R. (1993). Witnessing: a comparison of adults and children. *Issues in Criminological and Legal Psychology*, no. 20, 15–21.

Clifford, B.R. (1995). Psychology's premises, methods and values. In R. Bull and D. Carson (eds), 13–27.

Clifford, B.R. (1997). A comparison of adults' and children's face and voice identification. Paper presented at the Fifth European Congress of Psychology, 1–6 July 1997, Dublin, Ireland.

Clifford, B.R. (2002). Methodological issues in the study of children's testimony. In H.L. Westcott et al. (eds), *Children's Testimony* (pp. 331–44). Chichester: Wiley.

Clifford, B.R. and Bull, R. (1978). *The Psychology of Person Identification*. London: Routledge & Kegan Paul.

Clifford, B.R. and Bulloch, G. (1999). Face and voice identification by children under sequential and simultaneous lineups. Cited by Bull, R. and Clifford, B.R. (1999) as 'under review' at the time.

Clifford, B.R. and Davies, G.M. (1989). Procedures for obtaining identification evidence. In D.C. Raskin (ed.), 47–95.

Clifford, B.R. and Denot, H. (1982). Visual and verbal testimony and identification under conditions of stress. Unpublished manuscript, North East London Polytechnic, London, England.

Clifford, B.R. and George, R. (1995). A field evaluation of training in three methods of witness/victim investigative interviewing. *Psychology, Crime and Law*, 2, 1–18.

Clifford, B.R. and Gwyer, P. (1999). The effects of the cognitive interview and other methods of context reinstatement on identification. *Psychology, Crime and Law*, 5, 61–80.

Clifford, B.R. and Hollin, C.R. (1981). Effects of the type of incident and the number of perpetrators on eyewitness memory. *Journal of Applied Psychology*, 66, 364–70.

Clifford, B.R. and Richards, G. (1977). Comparison of recall by policemen and civilians under conditions of long and short durations of exposure. *Perceptual Motor Skills*, 45, 39–45.

Clifford, B.R. and Scott, J. (1978). Individual and situational factors in eyewitness memory. *Journal of Applied Psychology*, 63, 352–9.

Clifford, B.R. and Toplis, R. (1996). A comparison of adults' and children's witnessing abilities. In N. Clark and G. Stephenson (eds), *Investigative and Forensic Decision*

Making: Issues in Criminological and Legal Psychology. Leicester: British Psychological Society.

Clifford, B.R., Bull, R. and Rathborn, H. (1980). *Voice identification.* The final report to the Home Office. (Res.741/1/1). 207 pages, Department of Psychology, North-East London Polytechnic.

Clifford, B.R., Rathborn, H. and Bull, R. (1981). The effects of delay on voice recognition accuracy. *Law and Human Behavior*, 5, 201–8.

Clyde, The Lord. (1992). The Report of the Inquiry into the Removal of Children from Orkney in February 1991. Edinburgh: Her Majesty's Stationery Office.

Cockburn, J.S. and Green, T.A. (eds) (1988). *Twelve Good Men and True: The Criminal Trial Jury in England, 1220–1800.* NJ: Princeton University Press.

Cody, M.J., Marston, P.J. and Foster, M. (1984). Deception: paralinguistic and verbal leakage. In R.N. Bostrom (ed.), *Communication Yearbook* 8 (pp. 464–90). Beverly Hills, CA: Sage.

Coffin, F.M. (1994). *On Appeal: Courts, Lawyering, and Judging.* New York: W.W. Norton & Co.

Coghlan, A., Kiernan, V. and Mullins, J. (1995). Nowhere to hide. *Technospy (New Scientist Supplement)*, 4–7, 4 November.

Cohler, B.J. (1994). Memory recovery and the use of the past: a commentary on Lindsay and Read from psychoanalytic perspectives. *Applied Cognitive Psychology*, 8, 365–78.

Coleman, B.L. Stevens, M.J. and Reeder, G.D. (2001). What makes recovered-memory testimony compelling to jurors? *Law and Human Behavior*, 25(4), 317–38.

Colgrove, F.W. (1899). Individual memories. *American Journal of Psychology*, 10, 228–55.

Colman, A.M. and Gorman, L.P. (1982). Conservatism, dogmatism, and authoritarianism in British police officers. *Sociology*, 16, 1–11.

Colman, A.M. and Mackay, R.D. (1993). Legal issues surrounding the admissibility of expert psychological and psychiatric testimony. *Issues in Criminological and Legal Psychology*, 20, 46–50.

Colman, A.M. and Mackay, R.D. (1995). Psychological evidence in court: legal developments in England and the United States. *Psychology, Crime and Law*, 1, 261–8.

Comish, S.E. (1987). Recognition of facial stimuli following an intervening task involving the identi-kit. *Journal of Applied Psychology*, 72, 488–91.

Committee on Ethical Guidelines for Forensic Psychologists (1991). Specialty guidelines for forensic psychologists. *Law and Human Behavior*, 15, 655–65.

Connor, B., Peters, K. and Nagasawa, R. (1975). Person and costume: effects on the formation of first impressions. *Home Economics Research Journal*, 4, 32–41.

Connors, E., Lundregan, T., Miller, N. and McEwen, T. (1996). *Convicted by Juries, Exonerated by Science: Case Studies in the use of DNA Evidence to Establish Innocence After Trial.* NIH Research Report: US Department of Justice.

Cook, P.J. (1983). The influence of gun availability on violent crime patterns. In M. Tonry and N. Morris (eds), *Crime and Justice: An Annual Review of Research*, vol. 2, 211–68. Chicago: University of Chicago Press.

Cooke, Judge P.K. (1987). The practical problems of the sentencer. In D.C. Pennington and S. Lloyd-Bostock (eds), 57–60.

Cooney, M. (1994). Evidence as partisanship. *Law and Society Review*, 28, 833–57.

Cooper, C.L., Davidson, M.J. and Robinson, P. (1982). Stress in the police service. *Journal of Occupational Medicine*, 24, 30–6.

Cooper, J. and Hall, J. (2000). Reaction of mock jurors to testimony of a court appointed expert. *Behavioral Sciences and the Law*, 18, 719–29.

Cooper, J. and Neuhaus, I.M. (2000). The 'hired gun' effect: assessing the effect of pay, frequency of testifying, and credentials on the perception of expert testimony. *Law and Human Behavior*, 24, 149–71.

Coppersmith, S. and Gilberts, R. (1982). *Manual for the Behavioral Academic Self Esteem Scale.* Palo Alto, CA: Consulting Psychologists Press.

Corbett, C. (1987). Magistrates' and court clerks' sentencing behaviour: an experimental study. In D.C. Pennington and S. Lloyd-Bostock (eds), 204–16.

Cornish, W.R. (1968). *The Jury.* London: Penguin.

Corso, J.F. (1981). *Aging Sensory Systems and Perception.* New York: Praeger.

Costanzo, S. and Costanzo, M. (1994). Life or death decisions: an analysis of capital jury decision making under the special issues sentencing framework. *Law and Human Behavior*, 18, 151–70.

Cox, T.C. and White, M.F. (1988). Traffic citations and student attitudes toward the police: an examination of selected interaction dynamics. *Journal of Police Science and Administration*, 16, 105–21.

Coyle, M. (1995). Death juries get it wrong – study: survey reports they mishear judges. *National Law Journal*, 13 March, 17, A6.

Craik, F.I.M. (1977). Age differences in human memory. In J.E. Birren and K.W. Schaie (eds), *Handbook of the Psychology of Aging*. New York: Van Nostrand Reinhold.

Crank, J.P., Regoli, B., Hewitt, J.D. and Culbertson, R.G. (1993). An assessment of work stress among police executives. *Journal of Criminal Justice*, 21, 313–24.

Croft, S. (1995). Helping victims to remember. *Police*, November, 13–14.

Crombag, H.E.M., Wagenaar, W.A. and Van Koppen, P.J. (1996). Crashing memories and the problem of 'source monitoring'. *Applied Cognitive Psychology*, 10, 95–104.

Crombag, H.F. M. (1994). Law as a branch of applied psychology. *Psychology, Crime and Law*, 1, 1–9.

Cross, J., Cross, J. and Daly, J. (1971). Sex, race, age and beauty as factors in recognition of faces. *Perception and Psychophysics*, 10, 393–6.

Crow, I. and Cove, J. (1984). Ethnic minorities and the courts. *Criminal Law Review*, 413–17.

Crowley, A.E. and Hoyer, W.D. (1994). An integrative framework for understanding two-sided persuasion. *Journal of Consumer Research*, 20, 561–74.

Crowley, M.J., O'Callaghan, M.G. and Ball, P.J. (1994). The juridical impact of psychological expert testimony in a simulated child sexual abuse trial. *Law and Human Behavior*, 18, 89–105.

Cunneen, C. (1990). Aboriginal–police relations in Redfern: with special reference to the 'police raid' of 8 February 1990 (Report commissioned by the National Inquiry into Racist Violence).

Cunningham, J.L. and Bringmann, W.G. (1986). A re-examination of William Stern's classic eyewitness research. *Perceptual and Motor Skills*, 63, 565–6.

Curran, P. (1991). Discussions in the judge's private room. *Criminal Law Review*, 79–86.

Cutler, B.L. and Fisher, R.P. (1993). Identifying Ivan: some thoughts on the application of psychological research. *Expert Evidence*, 1, 119–26.

Cutler, B.L. and Hughes, D.M. (2001). Judging jury service: results of the North Carolina administrative office of the courts survey. *Behavioral Science and the Law*, 19, 305–20.

Cutler, B.L. and Penrod, S.D. (1988). Improving the reliability of eyewitness identification: lineup construction and presentation. *Journal of Applied Psychology*, 73, 281–90.

Cutler, B.L. and Penrod, S.D. (1995a). *Mistaken Identification: The Eyewitness, Psychology, and the Law*. Cambridge: Cambridge University Press.

Cutler, B.L. and Penrod, S.D. (1995b). Assessing the accuracy of eyewitness identifications. In R. Bull and D. Carson (eds), 193–213.

Cutler, B.L., Berman, G.L., Penrod, S. and Fisher, R.P. (1994). Conceptual, practical, and empirical issues associated with eyewitness identification test media. In Ross et al. (eds), 163–81.

Cutler, B.L., Penrod, S.D. and Dexter, H.R. (1989). The eyewitness, the expert psychologist, and the jury. *Law and Human Behavior*, 13, 311–32.

Cutler, B.L., Penrod, S.D. and Dexter, H.R. (1990). Juror sensitivity to eyewitness evidence. *Law and Human Behavior*, 14, 185–91.

Cutler, B.L., Penrod, S.D. and Martens, T.K. (1987). The reliability of eyewitness identification: the role of system and estimator variables. *Law and Human Behavior*, 11, 233–58.

Cutler, B.L., Penrod, S.D. and Stuve, T.E. (1988). Juror decision making in eyewitness identification cases. *Law and Human Behavior*, 12, 41–56.

Cutting, J.E. and Proffitt, D.R. (1981). Gait perception as an example of how we may perceive events. In R. Walk and H.I. Pick (eds) *Intersensory Perceptions and Sensory Integration*, 249–73. New York: Plenum Press.

Dahmen-Zimmer, K. and Kraus, M. (1992). Phenomenal Causality. In *Eyewitness Report*. In Lösel et al. (eds), 321–27.

Daly, K. (1987). Structure and practice of familial-based justice in a criminal court. *Law and Society Review*, 21, 267–90.

Darbyshire, P. (1991). The lamp that shows that freedom lives: is it worth the candle? *Criminal Law Review*, 740–52.

Darnborough, M. (1977). The use of facial reconstruction methods by the police. Paper presented at the Annual Conference of the British Psychological Society, Exeter, Devon, England.

Daudistel, H.C., Hosch, H.M., Holmes, M.D. and Graves, J.B. (1999). Effects of defendant ethnicity on juries' dispositions of felony cases. *Journal of Applied Social Psychology*, 29, 317–36.

Davenport, G.C. (1992). *Essential Psychology*. London: Collins Educational.

Davies, E. and Seymour, F.W. (1997). Child witnesses in the criminal courts: furthering New Zealand's commitment to the United Nations convention on the rights of the child. *Psychiatry, Psychology and Law*, 4(1), 13–24.

Davies, G. and Valentine, T. (1999). Codes of practice for identification. *Expert Evidence*, 7, 59–65.

Davies, G., Wilson, C., Mitchell, R. and Milsom, J. (1995). *Videotaping Children's Evidence: An Evaluation*. London: Home Office.

Davies, G.M. (1981). Face recall systems. In G.M. Davies, H.D. Ellis and J.W Shepherd (eds), *Perceiving and Remembering Faces* (pp. 227–50). London: Academic Press.

Davies, G.M. (1983). Forensic free recall: the role of visual and verbal information. In S.M.A. Lloyd-Bostock and B.R. Clifford (eds), 103–23.

Davies, G.M. (1986a). Context effects on episodic memory: a review. *Cahiers de Psychologie Cognitive*, 6, 157–74.

Davies, G.M. (1986b). The recall and reconstruction of faces: implications for theory and practice. In H.D. Ellis, M.A. Jeeves, F. Newcomb and A.W. Young (eds), *Aspects of Face Processing* (pp. 388–97). Dodrecht: Martinus Nijhoff.

Davies, G.M. (1989). The applicability of facial memory research. In A.W. Young and H.D. Ellis (eds), *Handbook of Research on Face Processing* (pp. 557–62). Elsevier Publishers.

Davies, G.M. (1991). Children on trial? Psychology, videotechnology and the law. *The Howard Journal*, 30, 177–91.

Davies, G.M. (1992). Influencing public policy on eyewitnessing: problems and possibilities. In F. Lösel, D. Bender and T. Bleisener (eds), *Psychology and Law: International Perspectives* (pp. 265–74). New York: Walter de Gruyter.

Davies, G.M. (1993a). Witnessing events. In G.M. Davies and R.H. Logie (eds), *Memory in Everyday Life* (pp. 367–401). Amsterdam: Elsevier Science Publishers.

Davies, G.M. (1993b). Children's identification evidence. In S.L. Sporer, R.S. Malpass and G. Köhnken (eds), *Psychological Issues in Eyewitness Identification* (pp. 223–58). NJ: Erlbaum.

Davies, G.M. (1994). Children's testimony: research findings and policy implications. *Psychology, Crime and Law*, 1, 175–80.

Davies, G.M. (1995). Evidence: psychological perspective. In R. Bull and D. Carson (eds), 179–91.

Davies, G.M. (1996). Mistaken identification: where law meets psychology head on. *The Howard Journal*, 35(4), 232–41.

Davies, G.M., Lloyd-Bostock, S., McMurran, M. and Wilson, C. (eds) (1996). *Psychology, Law and Criminal Justice: International Developments in Research and Practice*. New York: de Gruyter.

Davies, G.M. and Noon, E. (1991). An evaluation of the live link for child witnesses. London: Home Office.

Davies, G.M. and Noon, E. (1993). Video links: their impact on child witness trials. *Issues in Criminological and Legal Psychology*, no. 20, 22–6.

Davies, G.M., Stevenson-Robb, Y. and Flin, R. (1988). Tales out of school: children's memory for an unexpected event. In M. Gruneberg, P.E. Morris and R.N. Sykes (eds), *Practical Aspects of Memory: Current Research and Theory*. Chichester: Wiley.

Davies, M. (1994). *Asking the Law Question*. Sydney: Law Book Company.

Davis, J. (1989). Psychology and law: the last 15 years. *Journal of Applied Social Psychology*, 19, 199–230.

Davis, J.H., Stasson, M., Ono, K. and Zimmerman, S. (1988). Effects of straw polls on group decision making: sequential voting pattern, timing and local majorities. *Journal of Personality and Social Psychology*, 55, 918–26.

Davison, S.E. and Forshaw, D.M. (1993). Retracted confessions: through opiate withdrawal to a new conceptual framework. *Medicine, Science and the Law*, 33(4), 285–90.

De Luca, J.R. (ed.) (1981). Fourth Special Report to the US Congress on Alcohol and Health. Rockville, Maryland: National Institute of Alcohol and Alcoholism.

Deffenbacher, K.A. (1983). The influence of arousal on reliability of testimony. In S.M.A. Lloyd-Bostock and B.R. Clifford (eds), 235–51.

Deffenbacher, K.A. (1989). Forensic facial memory: Time is of the essence. In A.W. Young and H.D. Ellis (eds), 563–70.

Deffenbacher, K.A. and Loftus, E.F. (1982). Do jurors share a common understanding concerning eyewitness behavior? *Law and Human Behavior*, 6, 15–30.

DeLoache, J.S. (1995). The use of dolls in interviewing young children. In M.S. Zaragozza, J.R. Graham, G.C.N. Hall, R. Hirschman and Y.S. Ben-Porath (eds), *Memory and Testimony in the Child Witness* (pp. 160–78). Thousand Oaks, CA: Sage.

Dent, H. (1988). Children as witnesses. In H. Dent and R. Flin (eds), *Children as Witnesses* (pp. 1.1–1.17). Seminar papers, Leo Cussen Institute and Law Institute of Victoria, Melbourne, Australia.

Dent, H. and Flin, R. (eds) (1992). *Children as Witnesses*. Chichester: Wiley.

Dent, H.R. (1977). Stress as a factor influencing person recognition in identification parades. *Bulletin of the British Psychological Society*, 30, 339–40.

Deosoran, R. (1993). The social psychology of selecting jury forepersons. *British Journal of Psychology*, 33, 70–80.

Department of Defense, US (1984). *The Accuracy and Utility of Polygraph Testing*. Washington, DC.

DePaulo, B.M., Kashy, D.A., Kirkendol, S.E., Wyer, M.M. and Epstein, J.A. (1996). Lying in everyday life. *Journal of Personality and Social Psychology*, 70, 979–95.

DePaulo, B.M., Stone, J.I. and Lassiter, G.D. (1985). Deceiving and detecting deceit. In B.R. Schlenker (ed.), *The Self in Social Life* (pp. 323–70). New York: McGraw Hill.

DePaulo, B.M., Zuckerman, M. and Rosenthal, R. (1980). Humans as lie detectors. *Journal of Communication*, 30, 129–39.

DePaulo, P.J. and DePaulo, B.M. (1989). Can deception by salespersons and customers be detected through nonverbal behavior cues? *Journal of Applied Social Psychology*, 19, 1552–7.

Dessoir, M. (1893). The psychology of legerdemain. *The Open Court*, 7, 3599–602, 3608–11, 3616–19, 3633–4.

Devine, D.J., Clayton, L.D., Dunford, B.B., Seying, R.P. (2001). Jury decision making: 45 years on deliberating groups. *Psychology, Public Policy and Law*, 7(3), 622–727.

Devlin, K. (1971). Sentencing offenders in magistrates' courts: a study of legal factors affecting the sentencing process. Unpublished manuscript, School of Social Sciences, Brunel University, England.

Devlin, Lord P. (1976). Report to the Secretary of State for the Home Department of the Departmental Committee on Evidence on Identification in Criminal Cases. London: HMSO.

Devlin, P.A., Sir. (1956). *Trial by Jury*. Hamlyn Lecture Series. London: Stevens.

Devlin, P.A., Sir. (1974). Trial by jury. *The Guardian*, 10 June, 9.

Diamond, R. and Carey, S. (1977). Developmental changes in the representation of faces. *Journal of Experimental Child Psychology*, 23,1–22.

Diamond, S.J. and Casper, J.D. (1992). Blindfolding the jury to verdict consequences: damages, experts and the civil jury. *Law and Human Behavior*, 26, 515–63.

Diamond, S.S. (1992). Foreword. In D.K. Kagehiro and W.S. Laufer (eds), v–ix.

Dietze, P.M. and Thomson, D.M. (1993). Mental reinstatement of context: a technique for interviewing child witnesses. *Applied Cognitive Psychology*, 7, 97–108.

Diges, M., Rubio, M.E. and Rodriguez, M.C. (1992). Eyewitness memory and time of day. In Lösel et al. (eds), 317–20.

Dillehay, R.C. and Nietzel, M.T. (1985). Juror experience and jury verdicts. *Law and Human Behavior*, 9, 179–91.

Dion, K.E., Berscheld, E. and Walster, E. (1972). What is beautiful is good. *Journal of Personality and Social Psychology*, 24, 285–90.

Doob, A.N. (1977). Canadian jurors' view of the criminal jury trial. Law Reform Commission of Canada, *Studies on the Jury* 29, 60–4.

Doob, A.N. (1995). The United States Sentencing Commission Guidelines: if you don't know where you are going you might not get there. In C. Clarkson and R. Morgan (eds), 199–250.

Doob, A.N. and Kirschenbaum, H.M. (1973). Bias in police lineups: partial remembering. *Journal of Police Science and Administration*, 1, 287–93.

Doris, J. (ed.) (1991). *The Suggestibility of Children's Recollections*. Washington, DC: American Psychological Association.

Doris, J., Mazur, R. and Thomas, M. (1995). Training in child protective services: A commentary on the amicus brief of Bruck and Ceci (1993/1995). *Psychology, Public Policy and Law*, 1, 479–93.

Douglas, R. (1988). Tolerated contests: plea and sentence in the Victorian magistrates' courts. *Journal of Criminal Justice*, 16, 269–90.

Douglas, R. (1989). Does the magistrate matter? Sentencers and sentence in the Victorian magistrates' courts. *Australian and New Zealand Journal of Criminology*, 22, 40–59.

Douglas, R. (1992). A different kind of justice: trial and punishment in the rural Magistrates' Courts. *Law in Context*, 10, 63–90.

Douglas, R. (1994). Social class and court outcomes: making sense of the empirical literature. *Law in Context*, 12, 97–129.

Douglas, R., Weber, T. and Braybrook, E.K. (1980). *Guilty, Your Worship: A study of Victoria's Magistrates' Courts*. Occasional Monograph no. 1, Legal Studies Department, La Trobe University, Melbourne, Australia.

Doyle, J.M. (1989). Legal issues in eyewitness evidence. In D.C. Raskin (ed.), 125–47.

Driscoll, L.N. (1994). A validity assessment of written statements from suspects in criminal investigations using the scan technique. *Police Studies*, vol. XVII, 77–87.

Dristas, W.J. and Hamilton, V.L. (1977). Evidence about evidence: effect of presupposition, item salience, stress, and perceived set on accident recall. Unpublished manuscript, University of Michigan.

Du Cann, R. (1964). *The Art of the Advocate*. Harmondsworth, England: Penguin.

Duff, P. and Findley, M. (1988). The politics of jury reform. In M. Findlay and P. Duff (eds), 209–26.

Duncan, K.L. (1996). 'Lies, damned lies, and statistics'? Psychological syndrome evidence in the courtroom after *Daubert*. *Indiana Law Journal*, 7, 753–71.

Dunning, D. and Stern, L.B. (1992). Examining the generality of eyewitness hypermnesia: a close look at time delay and question type. *Applied Cognitive Psychology*, 6, 643–57.

Dunning, D. and Stern, L.B. (1994). Distinguishing accurate from inaccurate eyewitness identifications via inquiries about decision process. *Journal of Personality and Social Psychology*, 67, 818–35.

Dunning, D., Li, J. and Malpass, R. (March 1998). Basketball fandom and cross-race identification among European Americans: another look at the contact hypothesis. Paper presented at the American Psychology Law Society Biennial Conference, Relondo Beach, California. Cited by A. Memon and D. B. Wright (2000). Factors influencing witness evidence. In J. McGuire et al. (eds), 65–81.

Dunstan, S., Paulin, J. and Atkinson, K.A. (1995). *Trial by Peers? The Composition of New Zealand Juries*. Wellington, New Zealand: Department of Justice.

Durham A.M. III, (1989). Judgements of appropriate punishment: the effect of question type. *Journal of Criminal Justice*, 17, 75–85.

Durkin, K. and Jeffery, L. (2000). The salience of the uniform in young children's perception of police status. *Legal and Criminological Psychology*, 5, 47–55.

Durso, F.T., Reardon, R. and Jolly, E.J. (1985). Self-nonself segregation and reality monitoring. *Journal of Personality and Social Psychology*, 48, 447–55.

Dutton, D.G. (1986). The public and the police: training implications of the demand for a new model police officer. In J.C. Yuille (ed.), *Police Selection and Training: The Role of Psychology* (pp. 141–57). Dordrecht: Martinus Nijhoff.

Eagly, A.H., Ashmore, R.D., Makhijani, M.G. and Longo, L.C. (1991). What is beautiful is good, but … a meta-analytic review of research on the physical attractiveness stereotype. *Psychological Bulletin*, 110, 109–28.

Easterbrook, J.A. (1959). The effect of emotion on cue utilization and the organization of behavior. *Psychological Review*, 66, 183–201.

Ebbinghaus, H. (1885). *Uber das Gedachtnis*. Leipzig. Dunker. H. Ruyer and C.E. Bussenins (translation) *Memory*. Teachers College Press, New York, 1913.

Edelstein, R.S., Goodman, G.S., Ghetti, S., Weede Alexander, K., Quas, J.A., Redlich,A.D., Scaaf, J.M. and Cordon, I.M. (2002). Child witnesses' experiences post-court: effects of legal involvement. In Westcott et al. (eds), 261–77.

Edmondson, J. (1995). The psychologist as expert witness. *Forensic Update*, no. 42, 28–33.

Edwards, D. and Middleton, D. (1986). Joint remembering: constructing an account of shared experience through conversation discourse. *Discourse Processes*, 9, 42–59.

Efran, L. (1974). The effects of physical appearance on the judgement of guilt, interpersonal attraction and severity of recommended punishment in a simulated jury task. *Journal of Research in Personality*, 8, 44–54.

Egeth, H.E. (1993). What do we know about eyewitness identification? *American Psychologist*, 48, 577–80.

Eggleston, E. (1976). *Fear, Favour or Affection: Aborigines and the Criminal Law in Victoria, South Australia and Western Australia*. Canberra: Australian National University.

Eichelbaum, Sir Thomas. (2001). *The Peter Ellis Case: Report of the Ministerial Inquiry for the Honourable Phil Goff*. Auckland, New Zealand: Department of Justice.

Einspahr, O. (2000). The interview challenge. *FBI Law Enforcement Bulletin*, 16–20.

Ekman, P. (1985). *Telling Lies: Clues to Deceit in the Marketplace, Politics and Marriage*. New York: W.W. Norton & Co.

Ekman, P. and Friesen, W.V. (1972). Hand movements and deception. *Journal of Communication*, 22, 353–74.

Ekman, P. and O'Sullivan, M. (1989). Hazards in detecting deceit. In D.C. Raskin (ed.), 297–332.

Ekman, P. and O'Sullivan, M. (1991). Who can catch a liar? *American Psychologist*, 46, 913–20.

Ekman, P., Davidson, R.J. and Friesen, W.V. (1990). The Duchenne smile: emotional expression and brain physiology. *Journal of Personality and Social Psychology*, 58, 342–53.

Elaaad, E. and Ben-Shakkar, B. (1997). Effects of item repetition and variations on the efficiency of the guilty knowledge test. *Psychophysiology*, 34, 107–20.

Elaad, E. (1990). Detection of guilty knowledge in real-life criminal investigations. *Journal of Applied Psychology*, 75, 521–9.

Elaad, E. (1998). The challenge of the concealed knowledge test. *Expert Evidence*, 6, 161–87.

Elaad, E. and Kleiner, M. (1990). Effects of polygraph chart interpreter experience on psychophysiological detection of deception. *Journal of Police Science and Administration*, 17, 115–23.

Elaad, E., Ginton, A. and Jungman, N. (1992). Detection measures in real-life criminal guilty knowledge tests. *Journal of Applied Psychology*, 77, 587–96.

Elion, V.H. and Megargee, E.I. (1979). Racial identity, length of incarceration, and parole decision-making. *Journal of Research in Crime and Delinquency*, 16, 232–45.

Elliott, R. (1991). On the alleged prosecution-proneness of death qualified juries and jurors. In P.J Juedfeld and P.E. Terlock (eds), *Psychology and Social Policy* (pp. 255–65). New York: Hemisphere Publishing Corporation.

Elliott, R. (1993). Expert testimony about eyewitness identification: a critique. *Law and Human Behavior*, 17, 423–37.

Elliott, R., Farrington, B. and Mannheim, H. (1988). Eyewitness credible and discredible. *Journal of Applied Social Psychology*, 18, 1411–22.

Ellis, H.C. and Ashbrook, P.W. (1988). Resource allocation model of the effects of depressed mood states on memory. In K. Fielder and J. Forgas (eds), *Affect, Cognition and Social Behavior*. Toronto, Canada: Hogrefe.

Ellis, H.C. and Ashbrook, P.W. (1991). The 'state' of mood and memory research. In D. Kuiken (ed.), *Mood and Memory* (pp. 1–21). California: Sage Publications.

Ellis, H.D. (1975). Recognising faces. *British Journal of Psychology*, 66, 409–26.

Ellis, H.D. (1984). Practical aspects in face memory. In G.L. Wells and E.F. Loftus (eds), 2–37.

Ellis, H.D., Shepherd, J.W., Flin, R.H. and Davies, G.M. (1989). Identification from a computer-driven retrieval system compared with a traditional mug-shot album search. *Ergonomics*, 32, 167–77.

Ellsworth, P.C. (1993). Some steps between attitudes and verdicts. In R. Hastie (ed.), (1993a), 42–64.

Epstein, S. (1994). Integration of the cognitive and the psychodynamic unconscious. *American Psychologist*, 49, 709–24.

Ericson, R. and Baranek, P.M. (1982). *The Ordering of Justice: A Study of Accused Persons as Dependents in the Criminal Process*. Toronto: University of Toronto Press.

Esam, E. (2002). Young witnesses. In Westcott et al. (eds), *Children's Testimony* (pp. 309–23). Chichester: Wiley.

Esplin, P.W., Houed, T. and Raskin, D.C. (1988). Application of statement validity assessment. Paper presented at the meeting of the NATO Advanced Study Institute on Credibility Assessment, Maratea, Italy.

Estes, W.K. (1955). Statistical theory of spontaneous recovery and regression. *Psychological Review*, 62, 145–54.

Evans, B.J. (1994). Introduction. In B.J. Evans and R.O. Stanley (eds), 1–5.

Evans, B.J. and Stanley, R.O. (eds) (1994). *Hypnosis and the Law: Principles and Practice*. (Special Issue) *Australian Journal of Clinical and Experimental Hypnosis*. Melbourne.

Evans, B.J., Coman, G.J. and Stanley, R.O. (1992). The police personality: type A behavior and trait anxiety. *Journal of Criminal Justice*, 20, 429–41.

Evans, G. and Webb, M. (1991). High profile, but not that high profile: interviewing of young persons. *Issues in Criminological and Legal Psychology*, 18, 37–46.

Evans, K. (1995). *Advocacy in Court: A Beginner's Guide* (second edition). London: Blackstone Press.

Everson, G. (1919). The human element in justice. *Journal of Criminal Law and Criminology*, 10, 90–9.

Ewart, B. and Pennington, D.C. (1987). An attributional approach to explaining sentencing disparity. In D.C. Pennington and S. Lloyd-Bostock (eds), 181–92.

Exline, R.E., Thibault, J., Hickey, C.B. and Gumpert, P. (1970). Visual interaction in relation to Machiavellianism and an unethical act. In R. Christie and F.L. Geis (eds), *Studies in Machiavellianism* (pp. 53–75). New York: Academic Press.

Eysenck, H.J. (1977). *Crime and Personality* (3rd edition) London: Paladin.

Eysenck, H.J. and Eysenck, S.B. (1975). *Manual of the Eysenck Personality Questionnaire*. Sevenoaks, Kent: Hodder and Stoughton.

Eysenck, M. (1982). *Attention and Arousal. Cognition and Performance*. Berlin: Springer-Verlag.

Fanselow, M. (1975). How to bias an eyewitness. *Social Action and the Law*, 2, 3–4.

Farewell, L.A. and Donchin, E. (1991). The truth will out: interrogative polygraphy ('lie detection') with event-related potentials. *Psychophysiology*, 28, 531–47.

Farrington, D.P. (1978). The effectiveness of sentences. *Justice of the Peace*, 4 February, 68–71.

Farrington, D.P. and Lambert, S. (1993). Predicting violence and burglary offenders from victims, witness and offence data. Paper presented at the First NISCALE Workshop on Criminality and Law Enforcement, The Hague, Netherlands, October, 1993.

Farrington, D.P. and Morris, A. (1983). Sex, sentencing and reconviction. *British Journal of Criminology*, 23, 229–48.

Farrington, D.P. and Tarling, R. (eds) (1985). *Prediction in Criminology*. Albany: State University of New York Press.

Farrington, D.P., Hawkins, K. and Lloyd-Bostock, S.M. (1979a). *Psychology, Law and Legal Processes*. London: Macmillan.

Farrington, D.P., Hawkins, K. and Lloyd-Bostock, S.M. (1979b). Introduction: doing psycholegal research. In D.P. Farrington, K. Hawkins and S.M. Lloyd-Bostock (eds), *Psychology, Law and Legal Processes*, xiii–xvii.

Farrington, D.P., Hollin, C. and McMurran, M. (2001). *Sex and Violence: The Psychology of Crime and Risk Assessment*. London: Routledge.

Faust, D. and Ziskin, J. (1988). The expert witness in psychology and psychiatry. *Science*, 241, 31–5.

Feely, M.M. (1979). *The Process is the Punishment: Handling Cases in a Lower Criminal Court*. Russell Sage Foundation.

Feeley, M.M. and Rubin, E.L. (1999). *Judicial Policy Making and the Modern State*. Cambridge: Cambridge University Press.

Feingold, A. (1992). Good-looking people are not what we think. *Psychological Bulletin*, 111, 304–41.

Feinman, S. and Entwistle, D.R. (1976). Children's ability to recognize other children's faces. *Child Development*, 47, 506–10.

Feldman, P. (1993). *The Psychology of Crime*. Cambridge: Cambridge University Press.

Feldman, T. and Bell, R.A. (1991). Crisis debriefing of jury after a murder trial. *Hospital and Community Psychiatry*, 42, 79–81.

Felson, R.B. (1981). Physical attractiveness and perceptions of deviance. *Journal of Social Psychology*, 114, 85–9.

Findlay, M. and Duff, P. (eds) (1988). *The Jury Under Attack*. Sydney: Butterworths.

Finegan, J. (1978). The effects of non-legal factors on the severity of sentence in traffic court. Unpublished MA thesis, University of Toronto.

Fischer, K. and Bullock, D. (1984). Cognitive development in school-age children: conclusions and new directions. In W. Collins (ed.), *Development During Middle Childhood: The Years from Six to Twelve* (pp. 70–146). Washington, DC: National Academy Press.

Fisher, C.B. and Fyrberg, D. (1994). Participant partners: college students weigh the costs and benefits of deceptive research. *American Psychologist*, 49, 417–27.

Fisher, R., McCauley, M.R. and Geiselman, R.E. (1994). Improving eyewitness testimony with the cognitive interview. In Ross et al. (eds), 245–69.

Fisher, R.D., Mello, E.W. and McCauley, M.R (1999). Are jurors' perceptions of eyewitness credibility affected by the cognitive interview? *Psychology, Crime and Law*, 5, 167–76.

Fisher, R.P. (1995). Interviewing victims and witnesses of crime. *Psychology, Public Policy and Law*, 1, 732–64.

Fisher, R.P., Geiselman, R.E., Raymond, D.S., Jurkevitch, L.M. and Warhaftig, M.L. (1987). Enhancing enhanced eyewitness memory: refining the cognitive interview. *Journal of Police Science and Administration*, 15, 291–7.

Fisher, R.P. and Geiselman, R.E. (1992). *Memory Enhancing Techniques for Investigative Interviewing: The Cognitive Interview*. Springfield, IL: Charles Thomas.

Fitzgerald, M. (1994). Ethnic minorities and the criminal justice system. *Research Bulletin*, no. 35, 49–50.

Fitzgerald, R. and Ellsworth, P.C. (1984). Due process vs. crime control: death qualification and jury attitudes. *Law and Human Behavior*, 8, 31–51.

Fitzmaurice, C. and Pease, K. (1986). *The Psychology of Judicial Sentencing*. Manchester: Manchester University Press.

Fitzmaurice, C., Rogers, D. and Stanley, P. (1996). Predicting court sentences: a perilous exercise. In G. Davies et al. (eds), 305–13.

Fitzpatrick, K.M. and Boldizar, J.P. (1993). The prevalence and consequences of exposure to violence among African American Youth. *Journal of the American Academy of Child and Adolescent Psychiatry*, 32, 424–30.

Fivush, R. (1993). Developmental perspectives on autobiographical recall. In G.S. Goodman and B.L. Bottoms (eds), 1–24.

Fivush, R. (2002). The development of autobiographical memory. In H.L. Westcott et al. (eds), 55–68.

Fivush, R. and Hammond, N.R. (1990). Autobiographical memory across the preschool years: toward reconceptualizing childhood amnesia. In R. Fivush and J.A. Hudson (eds), 223–48.

Fivush, R. and Hudson, J.A. (eds) (1990). *Knowing and Remembering in Young Children*. Cambridge: Cambridge University Press.

Fivush, R. and Shukat, J.R. (1995). Content, consistency and coherence of early autobiographical recall. In Zaragozza et al. (eds), 5–23.

Fivush, R., Gray, J.T. and Fromhoff, F.A. (1987). Two year olds talk about the past. *Cognitive Development*, 2, 393–410.

Fivush, R., Hammond, N.R., Harsch, N., Singer, N. and Wolf, A. (1991). Content and consistency in early autobiographical recall. *Discourse Processes*, 14, 373–88.

Flemming, R.B. (1986). Client games: defense attorney perspectives on their relations with criminal clients. *American Bar Foundation Research Journal*, 2, 253–77.

Flin, R.H. (1992). Child witnesses in British courts. In Lösel et al. (eds), 365–73.

Flin, R.H. (1993). Hearing and testing children's evidence. In G.S Goodman and B.L. Bottoms (eds), 279–99.

Flin, R.H. (1995). Children's testimony: psychology on trial. In Zaragozza et al. (eds), 214–54.

Flin, R.H. and Shepherd, J.W. (1986). Tall stories: eyewitnesses' ability to estimate height and weight characteristics. *Human Learning*, 5, 29–38.

Flin, R., Boone, J. Knox, A. and Bull, R. (1992). The effect of a five-month delay on children's and adults' eyewitness memory. *British Journal of Psychology*, 83, 323–36.

Flin, R.H., Davies, G. and Tarrant, A. (1988). *The Child Witness. Report to the Scottish Home and Health Department*. Aberdeen: Robert Gordon Institute of Technology.

Flood, J. (1991). Doing business: the management of uncertainty in lawyers' work. *Law and Society Review*, 25, 41–71.

Foley, L.A. and Pigott, M.A. (1997). Race, age and jury decisions in a civil rape trial. *American Journal of Forensic Psychology*, 15, 37–55.

Fontaine, G. and Emily, C. (1978). Causal attribution and judicial discretion: a look at the verbal behavior of municipal court judges. *Law and Human Behavior*, 2, 323–37.

Forslund, M.A. (1970). A comparison of negro and white crime rates. *Journal of Criminal Law, Criminology and Police Science*, 61, 214–17.

ForsterLee, L., Horowitz, I.A., Athaide-Victor, E. and Brown, N. (2001). The bottom line: the effect of written expert witness statements on juror verdicts and information processing. *Law and Human Behavior*, 25(4), 299ff.

ForsterLee, L., Horowitz, I.A., ForsterLee, R., King, K. and Ronlund, L. (1999). Death penalty attitudes and juror decisions in Australia. *Australian Psychologist*, 43(1), 64–9.

ForsterLee, L., Horowitz, I.A. and Bourgeois, M. (1994). Effects of note taking on verdicts and evidence processing in a civil trial. *Law and Human Behavior*, 18, 567–8.

Forsyth, W.M.A. (1852). *History of Trial by Jury*.

Foss, R.D. (1981). Interactions between jurors as a function of majority vs. unanimity decision rules. *Journal of Applied Psychology*, 7, 38–56.

Foster, R.A., Libkuman, T.M., Schooler, J.W. and Loftus, E.F (1994). Consequentiality and eyewitness person identification. *Applied Cognitive Psychology*, 8, 107–21.

Fox, R.G. (1987). Controlling sentencers. *Australian and New Zealand Journal of Criminology*, 20, 218–46.

Fox, R.G. (1995). On punishing infringements. In A. Kapardis (ed.), *Sentencing. Law in Context* (Special Issue), 13, 7–38.

Fox, R.G. and Freiberg, A. (1990). Ranking offence seriousness in reviewing statutory maximum penalties. *Australian and New Zealand Journal of Criminology*, 23, 165–91.

Foxhall, K. (2000). Bridging law and psychology together. *Monitor on Psychology*, 31(1), 38.

Frank, J. and Frank, B. (1957). *Not Guilty*. London: Gollancz.

Frank, Judge J. (1949). *Law and the Modern Mind*. London: Stevens & Sons.

Frase, R.S. (1995). Sentencing guidelines in Minnesota and other American States: A Progress report. In C. Clarkson and R. Morgan (eds), 169–98.

Freckelton, I. (1987). *The Trial of the Expert*. Melbourne: Oxford University Press.

Freckelton, I. (1990). Psychiatry and psychology: mistrusted guests at the legal table: contemporary operation of the common knowledge rule. In D. Greig and I. Freckelton (eds), 49–68.

Freckelton, I. (1993). Science and the legal culture. *Expert Evidence*, 2, 107–14.

Freckelton, I. (1996). Repressed memory syndrome: counterintuitive or counterproductive? *Criminal Law Journal*, 20, 7–33.

Freckelton, I. (1997a). Admissibility of false memory evidence: R v Bartlett [1996] 2 VR 687 per P. Winneke, J.A. Charles and A.J.A. Southwell, *Psychology, Psychiatry and Law*, 4(2), 241–4.

Freckelton, I. (1997b). The diagnostic expertise of forensic psychologists: *Whitbread v The Queen* (1995) 78 A Crim R 452.

Freckelton, I. and Selby, H. (2002). *Expert Evidence: Law, Practice, Procedure and Advocacy*. Sydney: Lawbook Co.

Freckelton, I. and Selby, H. (eds) (1993–). *Expert Evidence*. Sydney: Law Book Co. (Looseleaf Service).

Freckelton, I., Greig, D. and McMahon, M. (eds) (1991). Forensic issues in mental health. Proceedings of the Twelfth Annual Congress of the Australian and New Zealand Association of Psychiatry, Psychology and Law. Melbourne.

Freckelton, I., Knowles, A. and Mulvany, J. (eds) (1992). *Current controversies in psychiatry, psychology and law*. Proceedings of the Thirteenth Annual Congress of the Australian and New Zealand Association of Psychiatry, Psychology and Law. Melbourne.

Freckelton, I., Reddy, P. and Selby, H. (1999). *Australian Judicial Perspectives on Expert Evidence: An Empirical Study*. Melbourne: Australian Institute of Judicial Administration.

Freckelton, I., Reddy, P. and Selby, H. (2001). *Australian Magistrates' Perspectives on Expert Evidence: A Comparative Study*. Melbourne: Australian Institute of Judicial Administration.

Freiberg, A. (1999). What's it worth? Across-jurisdictional comparison of sentence severity. Paper presented at the Sentencing and Society Conference, University of Strathclyde, Glasgow, Scotland, 24–26 June.

Freedman, J.L., Adam, E.K., Davey, S.A. and Koegl, C.J. (1996). The impact of a statement: more detail does not always help. *Legal and Criminological Psychology*, 1, 117–30.

Freeman, R.J. and Roesch, R. (1992). Psycholegal education: training for forum and function. In D.K. Kagehiro and W.S. Laufer (eds), 567–76.

Freud, S. (1906/1959). Psycho-analysis and the establishment of facts in legal proceedings. In J. Strachey (ed.), *Standard Edition of the Complete Works of Sigmund Freud*, vol. 9, 103–14. London: Hogarth.

Freud, S. (1940). An outline of psychoanalysis. In J. Strachey (ed.), *Standard Edition of the Complete Works of Sigmund Freud*, vol. 23. London: Hogarth.

Fridell, L.A. and Binder, A. (1992). Police officer decisionmaking in potentially violent confrontations. *Journal of Criminal Justice*, 20, 385–99.

Friedlander, B.Z. (1970). Receptive language development: issues and problems. *Merrill-Palmer Quarterly of Behavior and Development*, 16, 7–15.

Friedman, W.J. (1993). Memory for time of past events. *Psychological Bulletin*, 113, 44–66.

Fukurai, H., Butler, E. and Krooth, R. (1993). *Race and the Jury: Racial Disenfranchisement and the Search for Justice*. New York: Plenum Press.

Fukurai, H., Butler, E.W. and Krooth, R. (1991). Cross-sectional jury representation or systematic jury representation? Simple random and cluster sampling strategies in jury selection. *Journal of Criminal Justice*, 19, 31–48.

Furedy, J.J. (1996). Some elementary distinctions among, and comments concern-ing, the 'control' question 'test' (CQT) polygraphers' many problems: a reply to Honts, Kircher and Raskin. *International Journal of Psychophysiology*, 22, 53–9.

Fyfe, N.R. (2001). *Protecting Intimidated Witnesses*. London: Ashgate.

Gabora, N.J., Spanos, N.P. and Joab, A. (1993). The effect of complainant age and expert psychological testimony in a simulated child sexual abuse trial. *Law and Human Behavior*, 17, 103–19.

Gale, G.H. (ed.) (1988). *The Polygraph Test: Truth, Lies and Science*. London: Sage Publications/The British Psychological Society.

Galiber, J.L., Latzer, B. and Dwyer, M, et al. (1993). Law, justice, and jury nullification: a debate. *Criminal Law Bulletin*, 29, 40–69.

Galton, Sir. F. (1985). Terms of imprisonment. *Nature*, 20 June, 174–6.

Gardner, D. (1933). The perception and memory of witnesses. *Cornell Law Quarterly*, 18, 391–409.

Gardner, R.W., Holzman, P.S., Klein, G.S., Linton, H.B. and Spence, D.P. (1959). Cognitive control: a study of individual consistencies in cognitive behavior. *Psychological Issues* (Monograph 4).

Garkawe, S. (1994). The role of the victim during criminal court proceedings. *University of New South Wales Law Journal*, 17, 595–616.

Garrido, E. and Masip, J. (1999). How good are police officers at spotting lies? *Forensic Update*, 58, 14–21.

Garrido, E. and Masip, J. (2001). Experienced officers', police recruits', and non-officers' general beliefs and knowledge about deception and its detection. Paper presented at the Eleventh European Conference of Psychology and Law, 5–8 June 2001, Lisbon, Portugal.

Garrido, E., Masip, J., Herrero, C., Tabernero, C. and Vega, M.T. (1997). Policemen's ability to discern truth from deception of testimony. Unpublished manuscript. Cited by Garrido and Masip (1999: 16).

Garrido, V. and Redodo, S. (1992). Psychology and law in Spain. In F. Losel, D. Bender and T. Bliesener (eds), 526–34.

Garry, M., Manning, C.G., Loftus, E.F. and Sherman, S.J. (1996). Imagination inflation: imagining a childhood event inflates confidence that it occurred. *Psychonomic Bulletin and Review*, 3, 208–14.

Gatowski, S.I., Dobbin, S.A., Richardson, J.T., Ginsburg, G.P., Merlino, M.L. and Dahir, V. (2001). Asking the gatekeepers: a national survey of judges on judging expert evidence in a post-*Daubert* world. *Law and Human Behavior*, 25(5), 433–58.

Geis, G. (1991). Sanctioning the selfish: the operation of Portugal's new 'bad Samaritan' statute. *International Review of Victimology*, 1, 297–313.

Geiselman, R.E., Fisher, R.P., Firstenberg, I., Hutton, L.A., Sullivan, S., Artisan, I. and Prosket, A. (1984). Enhancement of eyewitness memory: an empirical evaluation of the cognitive interview. *Journal of Police Science and Administration*, 12, 74–80.

Geiselman, R.E. and Padilla, J. (1988). Interviewing children witnesses with the cognitive interview. *Journal of Police Science and Administration*, 16, 236–42.

Geiselman, R.E., Fisher, R.P., MacKinnon, D.P. and Holland, H.L. (1985). Eyewitness memory enhancement in the police interview: cognitive retrieval mnemonics versus hypnosis. *Journal of Applied Psychology*, 70, 401–12.

Geiselman, R.E., Fisher, R.P., MacKinnon, D.P. and Holland, H.L. (1986). Enhancement of eyewitness memory with the cognitive interview. *American Journal of Psychology*, 99, 385–401.

Geiselman, R.E., Haghighi, D. and Stown, R. (1996). Unconscious transference and characteristics of accurate and inaccurate eyewitnesses. *Psychology, Crime, and Law*, 2, 197–209.

Geiselman, R.E., Saywitz, K. and Bornstein, G.K. (1990). Cognitive questioning techniques for child victims and witnesses of crime (unpublished technical report, SJI-88-11J-D-016). State Justice Institute.

Geiselman, R.E., Saywitz, K.J. and Bornstein, G.K. (1993). Effects of cognitive questioning techniques on children's recall performance. In G.L. Goodman and B.L. Bottoms (eds), 71–93.

Gelsthorpe, L. and McWilliam, W. (eds) (1993). *Minority Ethnic Groups and the Criminal Justice System*. Cambridge: Institute of Criminology, University of Cambridge.

George, R. (1991). A field and experimental evaluation of three models of interviewing witnesses/victims of crime. Unpublished manuscript. North-East London Polytechnic.

Gibb, F. (2001). The Auld Report: judges may have their performance checked. *The Times*, 9 October 2001.

Gillies, P. (1987). *Law of Evidence in Australia*. (first edition) Sydney: Legal Books.

Gillies, P. (1993). *Criminal Law* (third edition). Sydney: Law Book Co.

Gisbert, A. (1990). *El futuro tribunal espanol*. Barcelona: PPU. Cited by Arce (1995).

Glaser, D. and Collins, C. (1989). The response of young, non-sexually abused children to anatomically correct dolls. *Journal of Child Psychology and Psychiatry*, 30, 547–60.

Glissan, J.L. (1991). *Cross-examination Practice and Procedure*. Sydney: Butterworths.

Goldberg, H. (1995). A random choice of jury? *The Times*, 13 June.

Goldberg, L.R., Grenier, J.R., Guion, R.M., Sechrest, L.B. and Wing, H. (1991). *Questionnaires used in the prediction of trustworthiness in pre-employment selection decisions: an APA Task Force Report*. Washington, DC: American Psychological Association.

Golding, J.M., Sego, S.A. and Poly Sanchez, R. (1999). The effect of multiple childhood sexual assaults on mock-jurors' perceptions of repressed memories. *Behavioral Sciences and the Law*, 17, 483–93.

Golding, S.L. (1992). Increasing the reliability, validity and relevance of psychological expert evidence: an introduction to the special issue on expert evidence. *Law and Human Behavior*, 16, 253–6.

Goldman, N. (1963). *The Differential Selection of Juvenile Offenders for Court Appearances*. U.S. National Council on Crime and Delinquency.

Goldman, W. and Lewis, P. (1977). Beautiful is good: evidence that the physically attractive are more socially skilful. *Journal of Experimental Social Psychology*, 13, 125–30.

Goldstein, A.G. and Chance, J.E. (1985). Voice recognition: the effects of faces, temporal distribution of 'practice', and social distance. Paper presented at the Midwestern Psychology Association meeting. Chicago, Illinois.

Goldstein, A.G., Knight, P., Bailis, K. and Conover, J. (1981). Recognition memory for accented and unaccented voices. *Bulletin of Psychonomic Society*, 17, 217–20.

Goldstein, H. (1994). Controlling and reviewing police-citizen contacts. In T. Barker and D.C. Carter (eds), 323–54.

Gonzalez, R., Ellsworth, P.C. and Pembroke, M. (1993). Response biases in lineups and showups. *Journal of Personality and Social Psychology*, 64, 525–37.

Goodman, G. S., Bottoms, B.L., Schwartz-Kenney, B. and Rudy, L. (1991). Children's testimony about a stressful event: improving children's reports. *Journal of Narrative and Life History*, 7, 69–99.

Goodman, G., Rudy, L., Bottoms, B. and Aman, C. (1990). Children's concerns and memory: ecological issues in the study of children's eyewitness testimony. In R. Fivush and J. Hudson (eds), 249–84.

Goodman, G.S., Taub, E., Jones, D.P.H., England, P., Port, L.K., Rudy, L. and Prado, L. (1992). Testifying in criminal court: emotional effects on child sexual assault victims. *Monographs of the Society for Research in Child Development*, 57 (5, serial no. 229).

Goodman, G.S. and Aman, C.J. (1990). Children's use of anatomically detailed dolls to recount an event. *Child Development*, 61, 1859–71.

Goodman, G.S. and Bottoms, B.L. (eds) (1993). *Child Victims, Child Witnesses: Understanding and Improving Testimony*. New York: The Guildford Press.

Goodman, G.S. and Hahn, A, (1987). Evaluating Eyewitness Testimony. In I. Weiner and A. Hess (eds), 258–92.

Goodman, G.S., Aman, C. and Hirschman, J. (1987). Child sexual and physical abuse: children's testimony. In S.J. Ceci, M.P. Toglia and D.F. Ross (eds), *Children's Eyewitness Memory* (pp. 1–23). New York: Springer-Verlag.

Goodman, G.S., Bottoms, B.L., Rudy, L., Davis, S.L. and Schwartz-Kenney, B.M. (2001). Effects of past abuse experiences on children's eyewitness memory. *Law and Human Behavior*, 25(3), 269–98.

Goodman, G.S., Hirschman, J.E., Hepps, D. and Rudy, L. (1991). Children's memory for stressful events. *Merrill-Palmer Quarterly*, 37, 109–57.

Goodman, G.S., Jones, D.P.H., Pyle, E.A., Prado-Estrada, L., Port, L.K., England, P., Mason, R. and Rudy, L. (1988). The emotional effects of criminal court testimony on child sexual assault victims: a preliminary report. In G. Davies and J. Drinkwater (eds), The child witness: do the courts abuse children? (*Issues in Criminological and Legal Psychology*, no. 13, pp. 46–54). Leicester: The British Psychological Society.

Goodman, G.S., Quas, J.A., Bulkley, J. and Shapiro, C. (1999). Innovations for child witnesses: a national survey. *Psychology, Public Policy and Law*, 5, 255–81

Goodman, G.S., Tobey, A.E., Batterman-Faunce, J.M., Thomas, S., Shapiro, C. and Sachsenmaier, T. (1998). Face-to-face confrontation: effects of closed-circuit technology on children's eyewitness testimony and jurors' decisions. *Law and Human Behavior*, 22, 165–203.

Goodman, J., Loftus, E.F. and Greene, E. (1991). Money, sex and death: gender bias in wrongful damage awards. *Law and Society Review*, 25, 263–85.

Goodman, K.C. and Gareis, K.C. (1993). The influence of status on decisions to help. *Journal of Social Psychology*, 133, 23–31.

Gorenstein, G. and Ellsworth, P. (1980). Effect of choosing an incorrect photograph on a later identification by an eyewitness. *Journal of Applied Psychology*, 5, 616–22.

Gowan, M.A. and Gatewood, R.D. (1995). Personnel selection. In N. Brewer and C. Wilson (eds), 205–28.

Grabosky, P. and Rizzo, C. (1983). Dispositional disparities in courts of summary jurisdiction: the conviction and sentencing of shoplifters in South Australia, 1980. *Australian and New Zealand Journal of Criminology*, 16, 146–62.

Granhag, P.A. and Spjut, E. (2001). Children's recall of the unfortunate fakir: a further test of the enhanced cognitive interview. In R. Roesch et al. (eds), 209–22.

Granhag, P.A. and Stromwall, L.A. (2000). Effects of preconceptions on deception detection and new answers to why lie-catchers often fail. *Psychology, Crime and Law*, 6, 197–218.

Granhag, P.A., Stromwall, L.A. and Olson, C. (2001). Fact or fiction? Adults' ability to assess children's veracity. Unpublished paper presented at the Eleventh European Conference of Psychology and Law, 5–8 June 2001, Lisbon, Portugal.

Grant, J.D., Grant, J. and Toch, H.G. (1982). Police–citizen conflict and decisions to arrest. In V. Konečni and E. Ebbesen (eds), (1982a), 133–58.

Gray, P. (1999). *Psychology*. New York: Worth Publishers.

Green, E. (1990). Media effects on jurors. *Law and Human Behavior*, 14, 439–50.

Green, E., Downey, C. and Goodman-Delahunty, J. (1999). Juror decisions about damages in employment discrimination cases. *Behavioral Sciences and the Law*, 17, 107–21.

Greene, E. and Dodge, M. (1995). The influence of prior record evidence on juror decision making. *Law and Human Behavior*, 19, 67–78.

Greer, D.S. (1971). Anything but the truth: the reliability of testimony in criminal trials. *British Journal of Criminology*, 11, 131–54.

Greig, D. and Freckelton, I. (eds) (1988). *International Perspectives on Psychiatry, Psychology and Law*. Proceedings of the Ninth Annual Congress of the Australian and New Zealand Association of Psychiatry, Psychology and Law. Melbourne, Australia.

Greig, D. and Freckelton, I. (eds) (1989). Emerging issues for the 1990s in psychiatry, psychology and law. Proceedings of the Tenth Annual Congress of the Australian and New Zealand Association of Psychiatry, Psychology and Law. Melbourne, Australia.

Greig, D. and Freckelton, I. (eds) (1990). The patient, the law and the professional. Proceedings of the Eleventh Annual Congress of the Australian and New Zealand Association of Psychiatry, Psychology and Law. Melbourne, Australia.

Greuel, L. (1992). Police officers' beliefs about cues associated with deception in rape cases. In F. Lösel, D. Bender and T. Bliesener (eds), 234–9.

Griffith, R.W. and Cafferty, T.P. (1977). Police and citizens value systems: some cross-sectional comparisons. *Journal of Applied Social Psychology*, 3, 191–204.

Gross, H. (1898). *Kriminalpsychologie*. Graz: Leuschner and Lubensky.

Gross, H. (1911). *Criminal Psychology* (fourth edition). (Kallen, M., translation). Mount Claire, NJ: Paterson Smith.

Groth, A.N. (1979). The older rape victim and her assailant. *Journal of Geriatric Psychiatry*, 11, 203–15.

Gruhl, J., Spohn, C. and Welch, S. (1981). Women as policy makers: the case of trial judges. *American Journal of Political Sciences*, 25, 308–22.

Grunhut, M. (1956). *Offenders Before the Courts*. Oxford: Oxford University Press.

Gudjonsson, G. (1993). *The Psychology of Interrogations, Confessions and Testimony*. Chichester Wiley.

Gudjonsson, G.H. (1983). Life events stressors and physical reactions in senior police officers. *Police Journal*, 56, 66–7.

Gudjonsson, G.H. (1984). A new scale of interrogative suggestibility. *Personality and Individual Differences*, 5, 303–14.

Gudjonsson, G.H. (1985). Psychological evidence in court: results from the BPS survey. *Bulletin of the British Psychological Society*, 38, 327–30.

Gudjonsson, G.H. (1987). A parallel form of the Gudjonsson Suggestibility Scale. *British Journal of Clinical Psychology*, 26, 215–21.

Gudjonsson, G.H. (1988). How to defeat the polygraph tests. In A. Gale (ed.), 126–36.

Gudjonsson, G.H. (1989). Compliance in an interrogation situation: a new scale. *Personality and Individual Differences*, 10, 535–40.

Gudjonsson, G.H. (1991). Suggestibility and compliance among alleged false confessors and resisters in criminal trials. *Medicine, Science and the Law*, 31, 147–51.

Gudjonsson, G.H. (1992a). *The Psychology of Interrogations, Confessions and Testimony*. Chichester: Wiley.

Gudjonsson, G.H. (1992b). The admissibility of expert psychological and psychiatric evidence in England and Wales. *Criminal Behaviour and Mental Health*, 2, 245–52.

Gudjonsson, G.H. (1993). The implications of poor psychological evidence in court. *Expert Evidence*, 2, 120–4.

Gudjonsson, G.H. (1995a). The vulnerability of mentally disordered witnesses. *Medicine, Science, and Law*, 35, 101–6.

Gudjonsson, G.H. (1995b). Psychology and assessment. In R. Bull and D. Carson, (eds), 55–66.

Gudjonsson, G.H. (1995c). The effects of interrogative pressure on strategic coping. *Psychology, Crime and Law*, 1, 309–8.

Gudjonsson, G.H. (1996). Forensic psychology in England: one practitioner's experience and viewpoint. *Legal and Criminological Psychology*, 1, 131–42.

Gudjonsson, G.H. and Adlam, K.R.C. (1982). Factors reducing occupational stress in police officers: senior officers' view. *Police Journal*, 55, 365–9.

Gudjonsson, G.H. and Bownes, I. (1992). The reasons why suspects confess during custodial interrogation: data for Northern Ireland. *Medicine, Science and the Law*, 32, 204–12.

Gudjonsson, G.H. and Clark, N.K. (1986). Suggestibility in police interrogation: a social psychological model. *Social Behavior*, 1, 83–104.

Gudjonsson, G.H. and Haward, L.R.C. (1998). *Forensic Psychology: A Guide to Practice*. Chichester: Wiley.

Gudjonsson, G.H. and Hilton, M. (1989). The effects of instructional manipulation on interrogative suggestibility, *Social Behavior*, 4, 189–93.

Gudjonsson, G.H. and Lebegue, B. (1989). Psychological and psychiatric aspects of a coerced-internalized false confession. *Journal of the Forensic Science Society*, 29, 261–9.

Gudjonsson, G.H. and McKeith, J.A.C. (1988). Retracted confessions: legal, psychological and psychiatric aspects. *Medical Science and Law*, 28, 187–94.

Gudjonsson, G.H. and Petursson, H. (1991). Custodial interrogation: why do suspects confess and how does it relate to their crime, attitude and personality? *Personality and Individual Differences*, 12, 295–306.

Gudjonsson, G.H. and Sartory, G. (1983). Blood-injury phobia: a 'reasonable excuse' for failing to give a specimen in case of suspected drunken driving. *Journal of Forensic Science Society*, 23, 197–201.

Gudjonsson, G.H. and Sigurdsson, J.F. (1994). How frequently do false confessions occur? an empirical study among prison inmates. *Psychology, Crime and Law*, 1, 21–6.

Gudjonsson, G.H., Clare, C., Rutter, S. and Pewarse, J. (1994). Persons at risk during interviews in police custody: the identification of vulnerabilities. Research Bulletin, no. 35, 31–2. London: Home Office Research and Planning Unit.

Gudjonsson, G.H., Hayes, G.D. and Rowlands, P. (2000). Fitness to be interviewed and psychological vulnerability: the views of doctors, lawyers and police officers. *Journal of Forensic Psychiatry*, 11(1), 75–92.

Gutheil, T.G. and Stein, M.D. (2000). Daubert-based gatekeeping and psychiatric/psychological testimony in court: review and proposal. *Journal of Psychiatry and Law*, 28, 235–51.

Haaga, D.A.F. (1989). Mood-state-dependent retention using identical or non-identical mood induction at learning and recall. *British Journal of Clinical Psychology*, 28, 75–83.

Hagan, J. (1975). Law, order and sentencing: a study of attitude in action. *Sociometry*, 38, 374–84.

Hagan, J. (1977). Finding discrimination: a question of meaning. *Ethnicity*, 4, 167–76.

Hagan, J. and Bernstein, L.N. (1979). Conflict in context: the sanctioning of draft resisters, 1963–76. *Social Problems*, 27, 109–22.

Hagen, A.M. (1991). Note: tolling the statute of limitations for adult survivors of childhood sexual abuse. *Iowa Law Review*, 76, 355.

Hain, P. (1976). *Mistaken Identity: The Wrong Face of the Law*. London: Quartet Books.

Halevy, T. (1995). Racial discrimination in sentencing? A study with dubious conclusions. *Criminal Law Review*, 267–71.

Ham, P. (1996). You must remember this … and this … and this. *The Australian Magazine*, 26–31.

Hamlyn-Harris, S. (1992). The limits of expert evidence. In Freckelton et al. (eds), 79–93.

Hammersley, R. and Read, J.D. (1985). The effect of participation in a conversation on recognition and identification of the speakers' voices. *Law and Human Behavior*, 9, 71–81.

Hammersley, R. and Read, J.D. (1995). Voice identification by humans and computers. In S.L. Sporer, R.C. Malpass and G. Köhnken (eds), *Suspect Identification: Psychological Knowledge, Problems and Perspective* (pp. 117–52). Hillside, NJ: Erlbaum.

Hammersley, R. and Read, J.D. (1996). Voice identification by humans and computers. In R. Malpass and G. Koehnken (eds), *Psychological Issues in Eyewitness Identification*. Manwah, NJ: Erlbaum.

Hammond, N.R. and Fivush, R. (1990). Memories of Mickey Mouse: young children recount their trip to Disneyworld. *Cognitive Development*, 6, 433–48.

Hampel, His Honour Justice G. (1993). Preface. In T.A Mauet and L.A. McCrinnon (1993).

Hampton, R.E. (1979). Sexual sentencing in children's court. *Australian and New Zealand Journal of Criminology*, 12, 24–32.

Hand, L. (1901). Historical and practical considerations regarding expert testimony. *Harvard Law Review*, 15, 40–58.

Haney, C. (1980). Psychology and legal change: on the limits of factual jurisprudence. *Law and Human Behavior*, 4, 147–99.

Haney, C. (1993). Psychology and legal change: the impact of a decade. *Law and Human Behavior*, 17, 371–98.

Haney, C., Sontag, S. and Costanzo, S. (1994). Deciding to take a life: capital juries, sentencing instructions, and the jurisprudence. *Journal of Social Issues*, 50, 149–76.

Hannaford, P.L., Hans, V.P. and Munsterman, G.T. (2000). Permitting jury discussions during trial: impact of the Arizona reform. *Law and Human Behavior*, 24(3), 359–82.

Hans, V.P. (1992). Jury decision making. In D.K. Kagehiro and W.S. Laufer (eds), 56–76.

Hans, V.P. (1995a). Jury decision making in complex trials. In R. Bull and D. Carson (eds), 527–41.

Hans, V.P. (1995b). How juries decide death: the contributions of the capital jury project. *Indiana Law Journal*, 70, 1233–40.

Hans, V.P. and Lofquist, W.S. (1992). Jurors' judgements of business liability in tort cases: implications for the litigation explosion. *Law and Society Review*, 26, 85–115.

Hans, V.P. and Vidmar, N. (1982). Jury selection. In N.L. Kerr and R.M. Bray (eds), 39–82.

Hans, V.P. and Vidmar, N. (1986). *Judging the Jury*. New York: Plenum.

Hans, V.P. and Vidmar, N. (1991). The American Jury at twenty-five years. *Law and Society Inquiry*, 16, 323–51.

Harding, R. (1988). Jury performance in complex cases. In M. Findlay and P. Duff (eds), 74–94.

Harding, S. and Phillips, D. (1986). *Contrasting Values in Western Europe: Unity, Diversity and Change* (Studies in the Contemporary Values of Modern Society). London: Macmillan.

Hare, R.D. (1970). *Psychopathy: Theory and Research*. New York: Wiley.

Hare, R.D. (1996). Psychopathy: a clinical construct whose time has come. *Criminal Justice and Behavior*, 23, 25–54.

Harlow, R.E., Darley, J.M. and Robinson, P.H. (1995). The scaling of intermediate penal sanctions: a psychophysical scaling approach for obtaining community perceptions. *Journal of Quantitative Criminology*, 11, 71–95.

Harman, H. and Griffith, J (1979). *Justice Deserted: The Subversion of the Jury*. London: National Council for Civil Liberties.

Harnon, E. (1982). Evidence obtained by polygraph: an Israeli perspective. *Criminal Law Review,* 340–8.

Harrison, A., Halem, M. and Raney, D.F. (1978). Cue to deception in an interview situation. *Social Psychology*, 4, 156–61.

Harry, B. (1986). A diagnostic study of the criminal alias. *Journal of Forensic Sciences*, 31, 1023–8.

Harsch, N. and Neisser, U. (1989). Substantial and irreversible errors in flashbulb memories of the Challenger explosion. Poster presented at the meeting of the Psychonomic Society, Atlanta, GA.

Hartshorne, H. and May, M.A. (1928). *Studies in Deceit*. New York: Macmillan.

Hasher, L. and Zacks, R. (1979). Automatic and effortful processes in memory. *Journal of Experimental Psychology*: General, 108, 356–88.

Hastie, R. (ed) (1993a). *Inside the Juror: The Psychology of Juror Decision Making*. Cambridge: Cambridge University Press.

Hastie, R. (1993b). Introduction. In R. Hastie (ed.), 3–41.

Hastie, R. (1993c). Algebraic models of juror decision making. In R. Hastie (ed.), 84–115.

Hastie, R., Penrod, S.D. and Pennington, N. (1983). *Inside the Jury*. Cambridge, MA: Harvard University Press.

Hastings, P. (1923). *Cases in Court*. London: Heinemann.

Hatcher, C., Mohandie, K., Turner, J. and Michael, G. (1998). The role of the psychologist on crisis/hostage negotiations. *Behavioral Sciences and the Law*, 16, 455–72.

Haugaard, J.J. and Crosby, C. (1989). Children's definitions of the truth and their competency as witnesses in legal proceedings. Paper presented at the Southeastern Psychological Association Conference, Washington, DC.

Havatny, N. and Strack, F. (1980). The impact of a discredited key witness. *Journal of Applied Social Psychology*, 10, 490–509.

Haward, L.R.C. (1979). The psychologist as expert witness. In Farrington et al. (eds) (1979a), 44–53.

Haward, L.R.C. (1981). *Forensic Psychology*. London: Batsford.

Haward, L.R.C. (1981a). Expert opinion based on evidence from forensic hypnosis and lie-detection. In S.M.A. Lloyd-Bostock (ed.), (1981a), 107–18.

Haward, L.R.C. (1981b). *Forensic Psychology*. London: Batsford.

Hazlehurst, K.M. (1988). Racial tension, policing, and public order: Australia in the eighties. In I. Freckelton and H. Selby (eds), *Police in Our Society* (pp. 8–25). Sydney: Butterworths.

Heaton-Armstrong, A. (1995a). Editorial: eyewitness testimony and judicial studies. *Medicine, Science, and Law*, 35, 93–4.

Heaton-Armstrong, A. (1995b). Recording and disclosing statements by witnesses: law and practice. *Medicine, Science and the Law*, 35, 136–43.

Hecker, M.H., Stevens, K.N., von Bismarck, G. and Williams, C.E. (1968). Manifestations of task-induced stress in the acoustic speech signal. *Journal of the Acoustical Society of America*, 44, 993–1001.

Hedderman, C. (1987). *Children's Evidence: The Need for Corroboration*. Home Office Research and Planning Unit, Paper no. 41. London: Home Office.

Hedderman, C. (1994). Decision-making in court: observing the sentencing of men and women. *Psychology, Crime and Law*, 1, 165–73.

Heidensohn, F.M. (1992). *Women in Control? The Role of Women in Law Enforcement*. Oxford: Oxford University Press.

Heider, F. (1958). *The Psychology of Interpersonal Relations*. New York: Wiley.

Heilbrun, K. (1992). The role of psychological testing in forensic assessment. *Law and Human Behavior*, 16, 257–72.

Henning, T. (1995). Psychological explanations in sentencing women in Tasmania. *Australian and New Zealand Journal of Criminology*, 28, 298–322.

Herkov, M.J., Myers, W.C. and Burket, R.C. (1994). Children's reactions to serial murder. *Behavioral Sciences and the Law*, 12, 251–9.

Hermann, D. and Gruneberg, M. (1993). The need to expand the horizons of the practical aspects of memory movement. *Applied Cognitive Psychology*, 7, 553–65.

Hernandez-Fernaud, E. and Alonso-Quecuty, M. (1995). The cognitive interview and lie detection: a new magnifying glass for Sherlock Holmes? Paper presented at European Psychology and Law Conference, Budapest, Hungary.

Hershkowitz, I. (2001). Children's responses to open-ended utterances in investigative interviews. *Legal and Criminological Psychology*, 6, 49–63.

Hessing, D.J., Elffers, H. and Wigel, R.H. (1988). Exploring the limits of self-reports and reasoned action: an investigation of tax evasion behavior. *Journal of Personality and Social Psychology*, 54, 405–13.

Heuer, F. and Reisberg, D. (1990). Vivid memories of emotional events: the accuracy of remembered minutiae. *Memory and Cognition*, 18, 496–506.

Heuer, L. and Penrod, S. (1988). Increasing jurors' participation in trials: a field experiment with jury note taking and question asking. *Law and Human Behavior*, 12, 231–61.

Heuer, L. and Penrod, S.D. (1989). Instructing jurors: a field experiment with written and preliminary instructions. *Law and Human Behavior*, 13, 409–30.

Heuer, L. and Penrod, S. (1994a). Juror note taking and question asking during trials: a national field experiment. *Law and Human Behavior*, 18, 121–50.

Heuer, L. and Penrod, S. (1994b). Trial complexity: its meaning and effects. *Law and Human Behavior*, 18, 29–51.

Heuer, L. and Penrod, S. (1995). Jury decision-making in complex trials. In R. Bull and D. Carson (eds), 527–41.

Hilgendorf and Irving, (1978). False positive identification. *Medicine, Science and the Law*, 18, 255–62.

Hill, P. and Hill, S. (1987). Videotaping children's testimony: an empirical view. *Michigan Law Review*, 85, 809–33.

Himelein, M., Nietzel, M.T. and Dillehay, R.C. (1991). Effects of prior juror experience on jury sentence. *Behavioral Sciences and the Law*, 9, 97–106

Hindley, G. (1990). *The Book of Magna Carta*. London: Constable & Co.

Hinsz, V.B. (1990). Cognitive and consensus processes in group recognition memory performance. *Journal of Personality and Social Psychology*, 59, 715–18.

Hinz, T. and Pezdek, K. (2001). The effect of exposure to multiple line-ups on face identification accuracy. *Law and Human Behavior*, 25 (2), 185–98.

Ho, R. and Venus, M. (1995). Reactions to a battered woman who kills her abusive spouse: an attributional analysis. *Australian Journal of Psychology*, 47, 153–9.

Hodgkinson, T. (1990). *Expert Evidence: Law and Practice*. London: Sweet and Maxwell.

Hofer, E., Akehurst, L. and Metzger, G. (1996). Reality monitoring: a chance for further development of CBCA? Paper presented at the Annual Meeting of the European Association of Psychology and Law in Siena, Italy, August 1996.

Hoffman, H.G., Loftus, E.F., Greenmun, C.N. and Dashiell, R.L. (1992). The generation of misinformation. In Lösel et al. (eds), 292–301.

Hoffmann, J.L. (1995). Where's the buck?: juror misperception of sentencing responsibility in death penalty cases. *Indiana Law Journal,* 70, 1137–60.

Hogarth, J. (1971). *Sentencing as a Human Process*. Toronto: University of Toronto Press.

Holdaway, S. (1983). *Inside the British Police*. Oxford: Blackwell.

Holdsworth, Sir. W.A. (1903). *A History of English Law*, vol. 1, 7th edition.

Hollien, H., Bennett, G. and Gelfer, M.P. (1983). Criminal identification comparison: aural versus visual identifications resulting from a simulated crime. *Journal of Forensic Sciences*, 28, 208–21.

Hollin, C. (1980). An investigation of certain social, situational and individual factors in eyewitness memory. Unpublished doctoral dissertation, North-East London Polytechnic.

Hollin, C.R. (1989). *Psychology and Crime: An Introduction to Criminological Psychology*. London: Routledge.

Hollin, C.R. (1995). *Clinical Approaches to Working With Young Offenders*. Chichester: Wiley.

Hollin, C.R. (ed.) (1996). *Working With Offenders: Psychological Practice in Offender Rehabilitation*. Chichester: Wiley.

Hollinger, R.C. and Clark, J.P. (1983). *Theft by Employees*. Lexington, MA: Lexington Books.

Holmes, O.W. (1897). The path of the law. *Harvard Law Review*, 10, 457–78.

Holst, V.F. and Pezdek, K. (1992). Scripts for typical crimes and their effects on memory for eyewitness testimony. *Applied Cognitive Psychology*, 6, 573–87.

Home Office (1998). *Speaking up for Justice: Report of the Interdepartmental Working Group on the Treatment of Vulnerable or Intimidated Witnesses in the Criminal Justice System*. London: Home Office.

Home Office Research and Statistics Department (1994). Research undertaken for the Royal Commission of Criminal Justice. *Research Bulletin*, vol. 35, special edition. London.

Honts, C.R. and Perry, M.V. (1992). Polygraph admissibility: changes and challenges. *Law and Human Behavior*, 16, 357–78.

Honts, C.R. and Raskin, D.C. (1988). A field study of the validity of the directed lie control question. *Journal of Police Science and Administration*, 16, 373–85.

Honts, C.R., Raskin, D.C. and Kircher, J.C. (1994). Mental and physical countermeasures reduce the accuracy of polygraph tests. *Journal of Applied Psychology,* 79, 252–9.

Hood, R. (1962). *Sentencing in Magistrates' Court*. London: Stevens.

Hood, R. (1972). *Sentencing the Motoring Offender: A Study of Magistrates' Views and Practices*. London: Heinemann.

Hood, R. (1992). *Race and Sentencing: A Study in the Crown Court. A Report for the Commission for Racial Equality*. Oxford: Oxford University Press.

Hood, R. (1995). Race and sentencing: a reply. *Criminal Law Review*, 272–9.

Hood, R. and Sparks, R. (1970). *Key Issues in Criminology*. World University Library.

Horgan, J.J. (197). *Criminal Investigation* (second edition). New York: McGraw Hill Book Co.

Horne, J.A. (1992). Stay awake, stay alive. *New Scientist*, 4, 20–4.

Horne, J.A. and Ostberg, O. (1976). A self-assessment questionnaire to determine morningness-eveningness in human circadian rhythms. *International Journal of Sociology*, 4, 97–110.

Horowitz, I.A. and ForsterLee, L. (2001). The effects of note-taking and trial transcript access on mock jury decisions in a complex civil trial. *Law and Human Behavior*, 25(4).

Horowitz, M., Wilner, M. and Alvarez, W. (1979). Impact of event scale: a measure of subjective stress. *Psychosomatic Medicine*, 41, 209–18.

Horowitz, S.W., Lamb, M.E., Esplin, P.W., Boychak, T.D., Krispin, O. and Reiter-Lavery, L. (1997). Reliability of criteria-based content analysis of child witnesses. *Legal and Criminological Psychology*, 2, 11–21.

Horvath, F. (1979). Effect of different motivational instructions on detection of deception with the psychological stress evaluator and the galvanic skin response. *Journal of Applied Psychology*, 64, 323–30.

Hosch, H. (1994). Individual differences in personality and eyewitness identification. In Ross et al. (eds), 328–47.

Hosch, H.M. and Cooper, S.D. (1982). Victimization as a determinant of eyewitness accuracy. *Journal of Applied Psychology*, 67, 649–52.

Hosch, H.M. and Platz, S.J. (1984). Self-monitoring and eyewitness accuracy. *Personality and Social Psychology Bulletin*, 10, 289–92.

Hosch, H.M., Bothwell, R.K., Sporer, S.L. and Saucedo, C. (1990). The accuracy of witness choice: facial recognition ability, reaction time and confidence. Southwestern Psychological Association, Houston, TX.

Hosch, H.M., Bothwell, R.K., Sporer, S.L. and Saucedo, C. (1991). Assessing eyewitness identification accuracy: an individual differences approach. New Orleans, LA: Southeastern Psychological Association.

Hosch, H.M., Leippe, M.R., Marchione, P.M. and Cooper, D.S. (1984). Victimization, self-monitoring, and eyewitness identification. *Journal of Applied Psychology*, 69, 280–8.

House of Commons Employment Committee (1985). Third Report from the Employment Committee Session 1984–1985. The implications for industrial relations and employment of the introduction of the polygraph. Together with the Proceedings of the Committee. London: HMSO.

Houston, T.C. (1980). Reporting and nonreporting of observed crimes: moral judgement of the act and actor. *Journal of Applied Social Psychology*, 10, 56–70.

Houts, M. (1963). *From Evidence to Guilt*. Springfield IL: Charles C. Thomas.

Howells, K. (1994). Child sexual abuse: Finkelhor's precondition model revisited. *Psychology, Crime and Law*, 1, 201–14.

Howells, K. and Blackburn, R. (1995). Clinical psychology and offenders: Part I an introduction. *Psychology, Crime and Law*, 2, 1–4.

Howells, L.A.L., Furnell, J.R.G., Puckering, C. and Harris, J. (1996). Children's experiences of the Children's Hearing System: a preliminary study of anxiety. *Legal and Criminological Psychology*, 1, 233–50.

Howels, T.H. (1983). A study of ability to recognize faces. *Journal of Abnormal and Social Psychology*, 123, 173–4.

Howie, P.M. and Dowd, H.J. (1996). Self-esteem and the perceived obligation to respond: effects on children's testimony. *Legal and Criminological Psychology*, 1, 197–209.

Hudson, B. (1989). Discrimination and disparity: the influence of race on sentencing. *New Community*, 16, 23–34.

Hudson, J.A. (1986). Memories are made of this: general event knowledge and the development of autobiographic memory. In K. Nelson (ed.), 97–118.

Hudson, J.A. (1990). The emergence of autobiographic memory in mother–child conversations. In R. Fivush and J.A. Hudson (eds), 166–96.

Hudson, J.A. and Fivush, R. (1987). As time goes by: sixth graders remember a kindergarten experience. *Emory Cognition Project Report* no. 13, Emory University, Atlanta.

Hudson, J.A. and Fivush, R. (1991). As time goes by: sixth grade children remember a kindergarten experience. *Applied Cognitive Psychology*, 5, 347–60.

Huff, C.R., Rattner, A. and Sagarin, E. (1986). Guilty until proven innocent: wrongful conviction and public policy. *Crime and Delinquency*, 32, 518–44.

Huffman, M.L. (1995). Can CBCA discriminate between accurate and false reports of preschoolers? A validation attempt. Manuscript submitted for publication.

Huffman, M.L., Crossman, A.M. and Ceci, S.J. (1997). Are false memories permanent? An investigation of the long-term effects of source misattribution. *Consciousness and Cognition*, 6, 48–90.

Humphrey, G.F. (1992). Scientific fraud: the McBride case. *Medicine, Science and Law*, 32, 199–203.

Hunt, R.R. and Einstein, G.O. (1981). Relational and item-specific information in memory. *Journal of Verbal Learning and Verbal Behavior*, 20, 497–514.

Hunter, I.M.L. (1957). *Memory: Facts and Fallacies*. Harmondsworth: Penguin.

Hunter, I.M.L. (1968). *Memory*. Harmondsworth: Penguin.

Hurvich, L.M. (1981). *Color Vision*. Sunderland: MA: Sinauer Associates.

Hurwitz, D., Wiggins, N. and Jones, L. (1975). Semantic differential for facial attributions: the face differential. *Bulletin Psychonomic Science*, 6, 370–2.

Hurwitz, S.D., Miron, M.S. and Johnson, B.T. (1992). Source credibility and the language of expert testimony. *Journal of Applied Social Psychology*, 22, 1909–39.

Hutchins, R. and Slesinger, D. (1928). Some observations on the law of evidence: spontaneous exclamations. *Columbia Law Review*, 28, at 432.

Hutchins, R.M. and Slesinger, D. (1929a). Legal psychology. *Psychological Review*, 36, 13–26.

Hutchins, R.M. and Slesinger, D. (1929b). Some observations on the law of evidence-consciousness of guilt. *University of Pennsylvania Law Review*, 77, 725–48.

Hyman, I.E., Husband, T.H. and Billings, F.J. (1995). False memories of childhood experiences. *Applied Cognitive Psychology*, 9, 181–97.

Hyman, R. (1989). The psychology of deception. *Annual Review of Psychology*, 40, 133–54.

Iacono, W.G. (1995). Offender testimony: detection of deception and guilty knowledge. In N. Brewer and C. Wilson (eds), 155–71.

Iacono, W.G. and Lykken, D.T. (1997). The validity of the lie detector: two surveys of scientific opinion. *Journal of Applied Psychology*, 82, 426–33.

Iacono, W.G., Cerri, A.M., Patrick, C.J. and Fleming, J.A.E. (1987). The effect of antianxiety drugs on the detection of deception. *Psychophysiology*, 24, 594.

Iacono, W.G., Cerri, A.M., Patrick, C.J. and Fleming, J.A.E. (1992). Use of antianxiety drugs as countermeasures in the detection of guilty knowledge. *Journal of Applied Psychology*, 77, 60–4.

Inbau, F.E., Reid, J.E. and Buckley, J.P. (1986). *Criminal Interrogation and Confessions* (third edition). Baltimore: Williams and Wilkins.

Ingram, R.E. and Reed, M. (1986). Information encoding and retrieval processes in depression: findings, issues and future directions. In R.E. Ingram (ed.), *Information Processing Approaches to Clinical Psychology* (pp. 131–50). Orlando, FL: Academic Press.

Irving, B. and McKenzie, B. (1989). *Regulating Custodial Interviews: The Effects of the Police and Criminal Evidence Act 1984: vol. II*. London: Police Foundation.

Irving, B. and Hilgendorf, L. (1980). Police interrogation: the psychological approach. Royal Commission on Criminal Procedure (Research Study no. 1). London: HMSO.

Irving, B. and McKenzie, B. (1988). *Regulating Custodial Interviews*. London: Police Foundation.

Isenberg, D.J. (1986). Group polarisation: a critical review and meta-analysis. *Personality and Social Psychology*, 50, 1141–51.

Israel, M. (1998). Ethnic bias in jury selection in Australia and New Zealand. *International Journal of the Sociology of Law*, 26, 35–54.

Izzett, R. and Leginski, W. (1974). Group discussion and the influence of defendant characteristics in a simulated jury setting. *Journal of Social Psychology*, 93, 271–9.

Jack, M. and Yeo, T. (1992). Foreword. *Memorandum of Good Practice On Video Recorded Interviews With Child Witnesses for Criminal Proceedings*. Home Office in conjunction with department of Health. London: HMSO.

Jackson, J. (1994). Trial by jury and alternative modes of trial. In J. McConville and L. Bridges (eds), *Criminal Justice in Crisis* (pp. 255–63). London: Edward Elgar.

Jackson, J. (1995). Evidence: legal perspective. In R. Bull and D. Carson (eds), 163–77.

Jackson, J. (1996). Juror decision-making in the trial process. In G. Davis, S. Lloyd-Bostock, M. McMurran and C. Wilson (eds), *Psychology, Law and Criminal Justice* (pp. 327–36). Berlin: de Gruyter.

Jackson, L.A. and Ervin, K.S. (1992). Height stereotypes of women and men: the liability of shortness for both sexes. *Journal of Social Psychology*, 132, 433–45.

Jackson, R. (1959). *The Chief: A Biography of Lord Hewitt, Lord Chief Justice, 1922–40*.

Jacobs, B.A. (1993a). Getting narced: neutralization of undercover identity discreditation. *Deviant Behavior: An Interdisciplinary Journal*, 14, 187–208.

Jacobs, B.A. (1993b). Undercover detection clues: a case of restrictive deterrence. *Criminology*, 31, 281–99.

Jalbert, N.L. and Getting, J. (1992). Racial and gender issues in facial recognition. In F. Lösel et al. (eds), 309–16.

James, W. (1890). *The Principles of Psychology*, vol. 2. New York: Holt.

Jastrow, J. (1900). *Fact and Fable in Psychology*. Cambridge, MA: Riverside Press.

Jefferson, T. and Walker, M.A. (1992). Ethnic minorities in the criminal justice system. *Criminal Law Review*, 83–95.

Jenkins, C.D., Zyzanski, S.J. and Rosenman, M.D. (1979). *Jenkins Activity Survey Manual* (Form C). New York: The Psychological Corporation.

Jobe, J.B., Tourangeau, R. and Smith, A.F. (1993). Contributions of survey research to the understanding of memory. *Applied Cognitive Psychology*, 7, 567–84.

Joffe, R. (1992). Criteria-based content analysis: an experimental investigation with children. Unpublished doctoral dissertation, University of British Columbia, Vancouver.

Johnson, M.K. (1983). A multiple-entry modular memory system. In G.H. Bower (ed.), *The Psychology of Learning and Motivation*, vol. 17, 81–123. New York: Academic Press.

Johnson, M.K. and Raye, C.L. (1981). Reality monitoring. *Psychological Rreview*, 88, 67–85.

Johnson, M.K. and Raye, C.L. (1998). False memories and confabulation. *Trends in Cognitive Sciences*, 2, 137–45.

Johnson, M.K., Foley, M.A., Suengas, A.G. and Raye, C.L. (1988). Phenomenal characteristics of memories for perceived and imagined autobiographical events. *Journal of Experimental Psychology: General*, 117, 107–10.

Johnson, M.K., Hashtroudi, S. and Lindsay, D.S. (1993). Source monitoring. *Psychological Bulletin*, 114, 3–28.

Johnson, R. (2001). The psychological influence of the police uniform. *FBI Law Enforcement Bulletin*, 27–32.

Johnston, E. (1991). *National Report of the Royal Commission into Aboriginal Deaths in Custody* (vol. 2). Canberra: Australian Government Publishing Service.

Jonas, K., Eagly, A.H. and Stroebe, W. (1995). Attitudes and persuasion. In M. Argyle and A.M. Colman (eds), *Social Psychology* (pp. 1–19). London: Longman.

Joyce, D. (1993). How comprehensible are PACE Codes of Practice to the majority of persons who might wish to read them? *Issues in Criminological and Legal Psychology*, no. 20, 70–4.

Judd, J.J., Judd, F.K. and Burrows, G.D. (1994). Hypnosis and the Australian legal process. In B.J. Evans and R.O. Stanley (eds), 71–9.

Jung, C.G. (1905). Die psychologische diagnoses des Tatbestands Schweizerische *Zeitschrift für Strafrecht*, 18, 368–408.

Juthjak Ivkovich, S. (1999). *Lay Participation in Criminal Trials: The Case of Croatia*. San Francisco: Austin & Winfield.

Kadane, J.B. (1993). Sausages and the law. In R. Hastie (ed.), 229–34.

Kagan, J., Rosman, B.L., Day, D., Albert, J. and Phillips, W. (1964). Information processing in the child: significance of analytic and reflective attitudes. *Psychological Monographs*, 78 (Whole no. 578).

Kagehiro, D.K. and Laufer, W.S. (eds) (1992). *Handbook of Psychology and Law*. New York: Springer.

Kalbfleisch, P.J. (1985). Accuracy in deception detection: a quantitative review. Unpublished doctoral dissertation, Michigan State University, East Lansing. Cited by Miller, G.R. and Stiff, J.B. *Deceptive Communication*. New York: Sage.

Kalven, H. and Zeisel, H. (1966). *The American Jury*. Chicago: University of Chicago Press.

Kannai, R. (1999). Structuring sentencing in Israel: the proposal of the Goldberg Committee. Paper presented at Sentencing and Society Conference, University of Strathclyde, Glasgow, Scotland, 24–26 June.

Kanovitz, J. (1992). Hypnotic memories and civil sexual abuse trials. *Vanderbilt Law Review*, 45, 1185.

Kapardis, A. (1984). *A Psychological Study of Magistrates' Decision Making*. Doctoral dissertation, Institute of Criminology, Cambridge University.

Kapardis, A. (1985). *Sentencing by English Magistrates as a Human Process*. Nicosia, Cyprus: Asselia Press.

Kapardis, A. (1988). *They Wrought Mayhem: An Insight into Mass Murder*. Melbourne: River Seine Press.

Kapardis, A. (1989). One hundred armed robbers in Melbourne: myths and reality. In D. Challinger (ed.), *Armed Robbery* (pp. 37–47). Canberra: Australian Institute of Criminology.

Kapardis, A. (1990a). Stranger homicides in Victoria, January 1984 – December 1989. *Australia and New Zealand Journal of Criminology*, 23, 241–58.

Kapardis, A. (1990b). *Firearms Training in the Victoria Police Force: A Consultancy Report*. Melbourne: Police Headquarters.

Kapardis, A. (1993). Killed by a stranger in Victoria, Jan. 1990 – April 1992. In H. Strang (ed.), *Homicide: Patterns, Prevention and Control* (pp. 121–32). Canberra: Australian Institute of Criminology.

Kapardis, A. (1994) Police and computer composite images of real criminals' faces: a survey of 1636 crime victim/witnesses and a follow-up of 200 composites. Unpublished consultancy report to the Victoria Police Identification Squad.

Kapardis, A. and Cole, B. (1988). Characteristics of homicide in Victoria. *Australia Police Journal*, 42, 130–2.

Kapardis, A. and Farrington, D.P. (1981). An experimental study of sentencing by magistrates. *Law and Human Behavior*, 5, 107–21.

Kargon, R. (1986). Expert testimony in historical perspective. *Law and Human Behavior*, 10, 15–27.

Kassin, S.M. (1985). Eyewitness identification: retrospective self-awareness and the accuracy–confidence correlation. *Journal of Personality and Social Psychology*, 49, 88–93.

Kassin, S.M. (1997). The psychology of confession evidence. *American Psychologist*, 52, 221–33.

Kassin, S.M. and Wrightsman, L.S. (1983). The construction and validation of juror bias scale. *Journal of Research in Personality*, 17, 423–42.

Kassin, S.M. and Wrightsman, L.S. (1988). *The American Jury on Trial*. New York: Hemisphere.

Kassin, S.M., Ellsworth, P.C. and Smith, V.L. (1989). The 'general acceptance' of psychological research on eyewitness testimony: a survey of experts. *American Psychologist*, 44, 1089–98.

Kassin, S.M., Ellsworth, P.C. and Smith, V.L. (1994). Déjà vu all over again: Elliott's critique of eyewitness experts. *Law and Human Behavior*, 18, 203–10.

Kebbell, M. (1999). Predicting the likelihood of a confession. Brief report and discussion of Pearse et al. (1998). *Expert Evidence*, 6, 293–4.

Kebbell, M.R. and Johnson, S.D. (2000). Lawyers' questioning: the effect of confusing questions on witness confidence and accuracy. *Law and Human Behavior*, 24(6), 629–41.

Kebbell, M.R. and Wagstaff, G.F. (1998). Hypnotic interviewing: the best way to interview eyewitnesses? *Behavioral Sciences and the Law*, 16, 115–29.

Kebbell, M.R., Milne, R. and Wagstaff, G.F. (1999). The cognitive interview: a survey of its forensic effectiveness. *Psychology, Crime and Law*, 5, 101–15.

Keil, T.J. and Vito, G.F. (1990). Race and the death penalty in Kentucky murder trials: an analysis of post-Gree outcomes. *Justice Quarterly*, 7, 189–207.

Kelley, H.H. (1967). Attribution theory in social psychology. In *Nebraska Symposium on Motivation* (pp. 192–238). Lincoln: University of Nebraska Press.

Kelly, L. (2002). Remembering the point: a feminist perspective on children's evidence. In H.L. Westcott et al. (eds), 361–76.

Kennedy, L.W. and Silverman, R.A. (1990). The elderly victim of homicide: an application of the routine activities approach. *Sociological Quarterly*, 31, 307–19.

Kerkoff, G. (1985). Interindividual differences in the human circadian system: a review. *Biological Psychology*, 20, 83–112.

Kerr, J.F. (1987). *A Presumption of Wisdom: An Expose of the Jury System of Injustice*. Sydney: Angus & Robertson.

Kerr, N.L. (1993). Stochastic models of juror decision making. In R. Hastie (ed.), 116–35.

Kerr, N.L. and Bray, R.M. (eds) (1982). *The Psychology of the Courtroom*. New York: Academic Press.

Kerr, N.L. and MacCoun, R. (1985). The effects of jury size and polling method on the process and product of jury deliberation. *Journal of Personality and Social Psychology*, 48, 349–63.

Kerr, N.L. and MacCoun, R.J. (1985). The effects of jury size and polling method on the process and product of jury deliberation. *Journal of Personality and Social Psychology*, 48, 349–63.

Kidd, R.F. (1985). Impulsive bystanders: why do they intervene? In D.P. Farrington and J. Gunn (eds) *Reactions to Crime: The Public, the Police, Courts and Prisons* (pp. 21–39). Chichester: Wiley.

King, M. (1986). *Psychology in and Out of Court: A Critical Examination of Legal Psychology*. Oxford: Pergamon.

King, N.J. (2000). The American Criminal Jury. In N. Vidmar (ed.) (2000a), *World Jury Systems* (pp. 93–124). Oxford: Oxford University Press.

Kirby, Justice M.D. (1981). Psychology and evidence law reform. Paper presented at the Second Australian Congress on Psychiatry, Psychology and Law, Melbourne, 6 November 1981.

Kircher, J.C and Raskin, D.C. (1988). Human versus computerized evaluations of polygraph data in a laboratory setting. *Journal of Applied Psychology*, 73, 291–302.

Kleck, G. (1985). Life support for ailing hypotheses, modes for summarizing the evidence for racial discrimination in sentencing. *Law and Human Behavior*, 9, 271–84.

Kleck, R. and Rubenstein, C. (1975). Physical attractiveness, perceived attitude similarity and interpersonal attraction in an opposite-sex encounter. *Journal of Personality and Social Psychology*, 31, 107–14.

Kneller, W. and Stevenage, S. (2000). The effects of line-up presentation mode, construction method and target presence on eyewitness identification accuracy and decision making strategies. Paper presented at the Tenth European Conference on Psychology and Law, Limassol, Cyprus, 12–14 April.

Knittel, E. and Seiler, D. (1972). The merits of trial by jury. *Cambridge Law Journal*, 56, 223–8.

Kogan, N. (1971). Educational implications of cognitive styles. In G.S. Lesser (ed.), *Psychology and Educational Practice* (pp. 242–92) Glenview, IL: Scott, Foresman.

Kogan, N. and Wallach, M.A. (1967). Risk taking as a function of the situation, the person, and the group. In G. Mandler, P. Mussen, N. Kogan and M.A. Wallach (eds), *New Directions in Psychology III* (pp. 111–278) New York: Holt, Rinehart and Winston.

Köhnken, G. (1992). The cognitive interview: a meta-analysis. Paper presented at the Third European Conference on Psychology and Law, Oxford.

Köhnken, G. (2002). A German perspective on children's testimony. In H.L. Westcott et al. (eds), 233–44.

Köhnken, G. and Brockman, C. (1987). Unspecific postevent information, attribution of responsibility and eyewitness performance. *Applied Cognitive Psychology*, 1, 197–207.

Köhnken, G. and Maass, A. (1988). Eyewitness testimony: false alarms on biased instructions? *Journal of Applied Psychology*, 73, 363–70.

Köhnken, G., Finger, M. and Nitschke, N. (1991). Statement validity analysis and the cognitive interview with child witnesses. Unpublished manuscript, Germany: University of Kiel.

Köhnken, G., Milne, R., Memon, A. and Bull, R. (1999). The cognitive interview: a meta-analysis. *Psychology, Crime and Law*, 5, 3–27.

Konečni, V.J. and Ebbesen, E.B. (1979). External validity of research in legal psychology. *Law and Human Behavior*, 3, 39–70.

Konečni, V.J. and Ebbesen, E.B. (1982a). *The Criminal Justice System: A Social Psychological Analysis*. San Francisco: W.H. Freeman and Co.

Konečni, V.J. and Ebbesen, E.B. (1982b). An analysis of the sentencing system. In V.J. Konečni and B. Ebbesen (eds) (1982a).

Konečni, V.J. and Ebbesen, E.B. (1992). Methodological issues in research on legal decision making, with special reference to experimental simulation. In Lösel et al. (eds) (1982), 413–23.

Koocher, G.P., Goodman, G.S., White, C.S., Sivan, A.B. and Reynolds, C.R. (1995). Psychological science and the use of anatomically detailed dolls in child sexual-abuse assessment. *Psychological Bulletin*, 118, 199–222.

Kopelman, M.D. (1987). Amnesia: organic and psychogenic. *British Journal of Psychiatry*, 150, 428–42.

Krambia-Kapardis, M. (2001). *Enhancing the Auditor's Fraud Detection Ability: An Interdisciplinary Approach*. Frankfurt am Main, Germany: Peterlang.

Kramer, G.P., Kerr, N.L. and Carroll, J.S. (1990). Pretrial publicity, judicial remedies and jury bias. *Law and Human Behavior*, 14, 409–38.

Kramer, H.T., Buckhout, R. and Eugenio, P. (1990). Weapon focus, arousal and eyewitness memory. *Law and Human Behavior*, 14, 167–84.

Krauss, D.A. and Sales, B.D. (2001). The effects of clinical and scientific expert testimony on juror decision making in capital sentencing. *Psychology, Public Policy and Law*, 7, 267–310.

Krauss, Stanton, D. (1995). Thinking clearly about guilt, juries and jeopardy. *Indiana Law Journal*, 70, 921–7.

Krauss, Stephen, J. (1995). Attitudes and the prediction of behavior: a meta-analysis of the empirical literature. *Personality and Social Psychology Bulletin*, 21, 58–75.

Kraut, R.E. and Poe, D. (1980). Behavioral roots of person perception: the deception judgements of custom inspectors and laymen. *Journal of Personality and Social Psychology*, 39, 784–98.

Kritzer, H.M. and Uhlmann, T.M. (1977). Sisterhood in the courtroom: sex of judge and defendant in criminal case disposition. *Social Science Journal*, 14, 366–79.

Kroes, W.H. (1985). *Society's victim – The Policeman: An Analysis of Job Stress in Policing*. New York: Charles C. Thomas.

Kuehn, L.L. (1974). Looking down a gun barrel: person perception and violent crime. *Perception and Motor Skills*, 39, 1159–64.

Kutnjak Ivkovich, S. (1999). *Lay Participation in Criminal Trials: The case of Croatia*. San Francisco: Austin and Winfield.

Ladefoged, P. (1981, April). Expectation affects identification by listening. Paper presented at the 94th meeting of the Acoustical Society of America. New York.

Lamb, M.E. (1994). The investigation of child sexual abuse: an interdisciplinary consensus statement. *Expert Evidence*, 2, 151–6.

Lamb, M.E., Strenberg, K. and Esplin, P. (1995). Making children into competent witnesses: reactions to the amicus brief in *re Mihaels*. *Psychology, Public Policy and Law*, 1, 438–49.

Landry, K. and Brigham, J. (1992). The effects of training in Criteria-Based Content Analysis on the ability to detect deception in adults. *Law and Human Behavior*, 16, 663–76.

Landsman, S. (1995). Of witches, madmen, and products liability: an historical survey of the use of expert testimony. *Behavioral Sciences and the Law*, 13, 131–57.

Landy, D. and Aronson, E. (1969). The influence of the character of the criminal and his victim on decisions of simulated jurors. *Journal of Experimental Social Psychology*, 5, 141–52.

Landy, F.J. (1992). Hugo Münsterberg: victim or visionary? *Journal of Applied Psychology*, 77, 6, 787–802.

Larson, J.A. (1932). *Lying and its Detection: A Study of Deception and Deception Tests*. Chicago: Chicago University Press.

Lass, N.J., Hughes, K.R. and Bowyer, M.D. (1976.) Speaker sex identification from voiced, whispered and filtered isolated vowels. *Journal of the Acoustical Society of America*, 59, 675–8.

Lasswell, H.D. (1948). The structure and function of communication in society. In L. Bryson (ed.), *The Communication of Ideas: Religion and Civilization Series* (pp. 37–51). New York: Harper & Row.

Laster, K. (1989). Infanticide: a litmus test for feminist criminological theory. *Australian and New Zealand Journal of Criminology*, 22, 151–66.

Latane, B. and Darley, J.M. (1970). *The Unresponsive Bystander: Why Doesn't He Help?* New York: Appleton-Century-Crofts.

Latane, B. and Naida, S. (1981). Ten types of research on group size and helping. *Psychological Bulletin*, 89, 308–24.

Laughery, K.R. and Wogalter, M.S. (1989). Forensic applications of facial memory research. In A.W. Young and H.D. Ellis (eds), 519–55.

Laughery, K.R., Alexander, T. and Lane, A. (1971). Recognition of human faces: effects of target exposure time, target position, and type of photograph. *Journal of Applied Psychology*, 55, 477–83.

Law Reform Commission of New South Wales (1985). *The Jury in a Criminal Trial*. Sydney, Australia.

Law Reform Commission of Victoria (1985). *The Jury in a Criminal Trial*. Melbourne, Australia.

Law Reform Commission of Western Australia (1991). Report on Evidence of Children and Other Vulnerable Witnesses. Project no. 87. Perth, Western Australia.

Law Reform Committee (1995). Jury Service in Victoria. Issue Paper no. 2. Melbourne: Parliament of Victoria, Australia.

Law Society (1994). *Police Station Skills for Legal Advisers*. London: The Law Society.

Lawrence, J. and Homel, R. (1987). Sentencing in magistrates' courts: the magi-strate as professional decision maker. In I. Potas (ed.), *Sentencing in Australia: Issues, Policy and Reform* (pp. 151–90). Canberra: Australian Institute of Criminology.

Lawrence, T. Judge. (1993). Judicial appointments: a system fit for change? *Medicine, Science and the Law*, 33, 279–84.

Lecont, P. (1988). Les rhythmicités de l'efficience cognitive. *L'Anné'e Psychologique*, 88, 215–36.

Lee, K. and Bussey, K. (1999). The effects of misleading and inconsistent post event information on children's recollections of criterion-learned information. *Journal of Experimental Child Psychology*, 73, 161–82.

Lee, T. and Geiselman, R.E. (1994). Recall of perpetrator height as a function of eyewitness and perpetrator ethnicity. *Psychology, Crime and Law*, 1, 11–19.

Leeman-Conley, M. and Crabtree, J. (1989). Providing assistance to victims of bank hold-ups. In D. Challinger (ed.), *Armed Robbery* (pp. 101–9). Canberra: Australian Institute of Criminology.

Legge, D. (1975). *An Introduction to Psychological Science*. London: Methuen.

Legge, G.E., Grossman, C. and Pieper, C.M. (1984). Learning unfamiliar voices. *Journal of Experimental Child Psychology*, 10, 298–303.

Leichtman, M.D. and Ceci, S.J. (1995). The effects of stereotypes and suggestions on pre-schoolers' reports. *Developmental Psychology*, 31, 568–78.

Leiken, L.S. (1970). Police interrogation in Colorado: the implementation of *Miranda*. *Denver Law Review*, 47, 1–53.

Leippe, M.R. (1980). Effects of integrative and memorial cognitive processes on the correspondence of eyewitness accuracy and confidence. *Law and Human Behavior*, 4, 261–74.

Leippe, M.R. (1985). The influence of eyewitness non-identifications on mock-jurors' judgements of a court case. *Journal of Applied Social Psychology*, 15, 656–72.

Leippe, M.R. (1994). The appraisal of eyewitness testimony. In Ross et al. (eds), 385–418.

Leippe, M.R., Manion, A.P. and Romanczyk, A. (1993). Discernibility or discrimination? Understanding jurors' reactions to accurate and inaccurate child and adult witnesses. In G.S. Goodman and B. Bottoms (eds), 169–202.

Leippe, M.R., Romanczyk, A. and Manion, A.P. (1991). Eyewitness memory for a touching experience: accuracy differences between child and adult witnesses. *Journal of Applied Psychology*, 76, 267–379.

Lempert, R.O. (1975). Uncovering 'non-discernible' differences: empirical research and the jury-size cases. *Michigan Law Review*, 73, 643–708. Cited by Arce (1995).

Leo, R.A. (1994). Police interrogation and social control. *Social and Legal Studies*, 3, 93–120.

Lerner, R.M. and Korn, S.J. (1972). The development of body-build stereotypes in males. *Child Development*, 43(3), 908–20.

Lester, D. (1980). The personalities of English and American Police. *Journal of Social Psychology*, 111, 153–4.

Lester, D. (1983). The selection of police officers: an argument for simplicity. *Police Journal*, 56, 53–55.

Lester, D., Babcock, S.D., Cassisi, J.P. and Brunetta, M. (1980). Hiring despite the psychologist's objections. *Criminal Justice and Behavior*, 7, 41–9.

Levi, A.M. (2000). Multiple choices in the MSL line-up: some are highly predictive of guilt. Paper presented at the Tenth European Conference on Psychology and Law, Limassol, Cyprus, 12–14 April.

Levine, F. and Tapp, J. (1971). The psychology of criminal identification: the gap from Wade to Kirby. *University of Pennsylvania Law Review*, 121, 1079–132.

Levine, J.P. (1992). *Juries and Politics*. Pacific Grove, CA: Brooks/Cole Publishing Co.

Levine, M.L. (ed.) (1995). *Law and Psychology*. Aldershot: Dartmouth.

Lewis, M., Sreanger, C. and Sullivan, M.W. (1989). Deception in 3-year-olds. *Developmental Psychology*, 25, 439–43.

Lichtenberg, I.D. and Smith, A. (2001). How dangerous are routine police-citizen traffic stops? A research note. *Journal of Criminal Justice*, 29, 419–28.

Liggett, J. (1974). *The Human Face*. London: Constable.

Light, L.H. (1991). Memory and aging: four hypotheses in search of data. *Annual Review of Psychology*, 42, 333–76.

Lilli, W. (1989) The perception of social events and behavior consequences. In Wegener et al. (eds), 216-27.

Lind, E.A. and Ke, G.Y. (1985). Opening and Closing Statements. In S.M. Kassin and L.S. Wrightsman (eds), *The Psychology of Evidence and Trial Procedure* (pp. 229–52). Beverly Hills, CA: Sage.

Lindsay, D.S. (1994). Memory source monitoring and eyewitness testimony. In Ross et al. (eds), 27–55.

Lindsay, D.S. and Read, J.D. (1994). Psychotherapy and memories of childhood sexual abuse: a cognitive perspective. *Applied Cognitive Psychology*, 8, 281–338.

Lindsay, R.C.L. (1986). Confidence and accuracy of eyewitness identification from lineups. *Law and Human Behavior*, 10, 229–39.

Lindsay, R.C.L. (1994a). Expectations of eyewitness performance: jurors' verdicts do not follow their beliefs. In Ross et al. (eds), 362–83.

Lindsay, R.C.L. (1994b). Biased lineups: where do they come from? In Ross et al. (eds), 182–200.

Lindsay, R.C.L. and Harvie, V.L. (1988). Hits, false alarms, correct and mistaken identification: the effects of method of data collection on facial memory. In M. Gruneberg et al. (eds), *Practical Aspects of Memory: Current Research and Issues* (pp. 47–52). Chichester: Wiley.

Lindsay, R.C.L. and Johnson, M.K. (1987). Reality monitoring and suggestibility: children's ability to discriminate among memories from different sources. In S.J. Ceci, M.P. Toglia and D.F. Ross (eds), *Children's Eyewitness Memory* (pp. 92–121). New York: Springer-Verlag.

Lindsay, R.C.L. and Wells, G.L. (1980). What price justice? Exploring the relationship of lineup fairness to identification accuracy. *Law and Human Behavior*, 4, 303–14.

Lindsay, R.C.L. and Wells, G.L. (1983). What do we really know about cross-race eyewitness identification? In S.M.A. Lloyd-Bostock and B.R. Clifford (eds), 219–33.

Lindsay, R.C.L. and Wells, G. L. (1985). Improving eyewitness identifications from lineups: simultaneous versus sequential lineup presentation. *Journal of Applied Psychology*, 70, 556–64.

Lindsay, R.C.L., Lea, J.A. and Fulford, J.A. (1991a). Sequential lineup presentation: technique matters. *Journal of Applied Psychology*, 76, 741–5.

Lindsay, R.C.L., Lea, J.A., Nosworthy, G.J., Fulford, J.A. et al. (1991b). Biased lineups: sequential presentation reduces the problem. *Journal of Applied Psychology*, 76, 796–802.

Lindsay, R.C.L., Martin, R. and Webber, L. (1994a). Default values in eyewitness descriptions: a problem for the match-to-description lineup foil selection strategy. *Law and Human Behavior*, 18, 527–41.

Lindsay, R.C.L., Nosworthy, G.J., Martin, R. and Martynuck, C. (1994b). Using mugshots to find suspects. *Journal of Applied Psychology*, 79, 121–30.

Lindsay, R.C.L., Pozzulo, J.D., Craig, W., Lee, K. and Corber, S. (1997). Simultaneous line-ups, sequential line-ups and show-ups: eyewitness identification decisions of adults and childern. *Law and Human Behavior*, 21, 391–404.

Lindsay, R.C.L., Wallbridge, H. and Drennan, D. (1987). Do the clothes make the man? An exploration of the effect of lineup attire on eye-witness identification accuracy. *Canadian Journal of Behavioural Science*, 19, 463–78.

Lindsay, R.C.L., Wells, G.L. and Rumpel, C. (1981). Can people detect eyewitness identification accuracy within and across situations? *Journal of Applied Psychology*, 66, 79–89.

Ling, J. and Blades, M. (1995). Children's memory for colour. *Forensic Update*, Issue 41, April, 23–9.

Lipovsky, J.A., Tidwell, R., Crisp, J., Kilpatric, D.G., Saunders, B.E. and Dawson, V.L. (1992). Child witnesses in criminal courts: descriptive information from three southern states. *Law and Human Behavior*, 16, 635–50.

Lipton, J.P. (1977). On the psychology of eyewitness testimony. *Journal of Applied Psychology*, 66, 79–89.

Lisman, S.A. (1974). Alcoholic 'blackouts': state-dependent learning. *Archives of General Psychiatry*, 30, 46–53.

List, J. (1986). Age and schematic differences in the reliability of eyewitness testimony. *Developmental Psychology*, 22, 50–7.

Lloyd-Bostock, S. (1996). Juries and jury research in context. In G. Davies, S. Lloyd-Bostock, M. McMurran and C. Wilson (eds), 349–59.

Lloyd-Bostock, S.M.A. (1988). *Law in Practice: Applications of Psychology to Legal Decisionmaking and Legal Skills*. London: Routledge/British Psychological Society.

Lloyd-Bostock, S.M.A. (1994). Research and teaching in legal psychology: an outline of British developments. *Psychology, Crime and Law*, 1, 159–64.

Lloyd-Bostock, S.M.A. (ed.) (1981a). *Psychology In Legal Contexts: Applications and Limitations*. London: Macmillan.

Lloyd-Bostock, S.M.A. (ed.) (1981b). Psychology and law: a critical review of research and practice. *British Journal of Law and Society*, 8, 1–28.

Lloyd-Bostock, S.M.A. (ed.) (1984). *Children and the Law*. Oxford: Centre for Socio-Legal Studies.

Lloyd-Bostock, S.M.A. and Clifford, B.R. (eds) (1983). *Evaluating Witness Evidence: Recent Psychological Research and New Perspectives*. Chichester: Wiley.

Loftus, E.F. (1981). Eyewitness testimony: psychological research and legal thought. In M. Tonry and N. Morris (eds), *Crime and Justice: An Annual Review of Research*, vol. 3 (pp. 105–51). Chicago: University of Chicago Press.

Loftus, E.F., Greene, E.L. and Doyle, J.M. (1989). The psychology of eyewitness testimony. In D. C. Raskin (ed.), (1989a), 3–45.

Loftus, E.F. (1974). Reconstructing memory: the incredible witness. *Psychology Today*, 8, 116–19.

Loftus, E.F. (1976). Unconscious transference in eyewitness identification. *Law and Psychology Review*, 2, 93–8.

Loftus, E.F. (1979). *Eyewitness Testimony*. Cambridge, MA: Harvard University Press.

Loftus, E.F. (1980). Impact of expert psychological testimony on the unreliability of eyewitness identification. *Journal of Applied Psychology*, 65, 9–15.

Loftus, E.F. (1993). The reality of repressed memories. *American Psychologist*, 48, 518–37.

Loftus, E.F. and Burns, T.E. (1982). Mental shock can produce retrograde amnesia. *Memory and Cognition*, 10, 318–23.

Loftus, E.F. and Doyle, J.M. (1987). *Eyewitness Testimony: Civil and Criminal*. New York: Kluwer Law Book Publishers.

Loftus, E.F. and Ketcham, K.E. (1983). The malleability of eyewitness accounts. In S.M.A. Lloyd-Bostock and B.R. Clifford (eds), 159–71.

Loftus, E.F. and Ketcham, K.E. (1991). *Witness for the Defense*. New York: St Martin's Press.

Loftus, E.F. and Palmer, J.C. (1974). Reconstruction of automobile destruction: an example of the interaction between language and memory. *Journal of Verbal Learning and Verbal Behavior*, 13, 585–9.

Loftus, E.F. and Pickrel, J.E. (1995). The formation of false memories. *Psychiatric Annals*, 25, 720–5.

Loftus, E.F. and Zanni, G. (1975). Eyewitness testimony: the influence of the wording of a question. *Bulletin of the Psychonomic Science*, 5, 86–8.

Loftus, E.F., Banaji, M.R., Schooler, J.W. and Foster, R.A. (1987c). Who remembers what? Gender differences in memory. *Michigan Quarterly Review*, xxvi, 64–85.

Loftus, E.F., Loftus, G.R. and Messo, J. (1987a). Some facts about 'weapon focus'. *Law and Human Behavior*, 11, 55–62.

Loftus, E.F., Miller, D.G. and Burns, H.J. (1978). Semantic integration of verbal information into a visual memory. *Journal of Experimental Psychology: Human Learning and Memory*, 4, 19–31.

Loftus, E.F., Schooler, J.W., Booye, S.M. and Kline, D. (1987b). Time went by so slowly: overestimation of event duration by males and females. *Applied Cognitive Psychology*, 1, 3–13.

Logie, R., Wright, R. and Decker, S. (1992). Recognition memory performance and residential burglary. *Applied Cognitive Psychology*, 6, 109–23.

Lord, C.G., Ross, L. and Lepper, M.R. (1979). Biased assimilation and attitude polarization: the effects of prior theories on subsequently considered evidence. *Journal of Personality and Social Psychology*, 37, 2098–109.

Lösel, F. (1992). Psychology and law: overtures crescendos and reprises. In F. Lösel, D. Bender and T. Bliesener (eds) (1992a), 3–21.

Lösel, F., Bender, D. and Bliesener, T. (eds) (1992a). *Psychology and Law: International Perspectives*. New York: Walter de Gruyter.

Lösel, F., Bender, D. and Bliesener, T. (1992b). International perspectives on psychology and law: an introduction. In F. Lösel, D. Bender and T. Bliesener (eds), (1992a), vii–xvii).

Lovegrove, A. (1984). An empirical study of sentencing disparity among judges in an Australian criminal court. *International Review of Applied Psychology*, 33, 161–76.

Lovegrove, A. (1997). *The Framework of Judicial Sentencing*. Cambridge: Cambridge University Press.

Lubert, S. (1993). *Modern Trial Advocacy: Analysis and Practice*. Notre Dame, Indiana: National Institute of Trial Advocacy.

Luginbuhl, J. and Howe, J. (1995). Discretion in capital sentencing: guided or misguided? *Indiana Law Journal*, 70, 1161–85.

Luntz, H. and Hambly, A.D. (1992). *Torts: Cases and Commentary* (third edition). Sydney, Australia: Butterworths.

Luria, A.R. (1932). *The Nature of Human Conflicts*. W. Wortley Grantt (trans.).

Luus, C.A. and Wells, G.L. (1994a). Eyewitness identification confidence. In Ross et al. (eds), 348–61.

Luus, C.A.E. and Wells, G.L. (1991). Eyewitness identification and then selection of distractors for lineups. *Law and Human Behavior*, 15, 43–57.

Luus, C.A.E. and Wells, G.L. (1994b). The malleability of eyewitness confidence: co-witness and perseverance effects. *Journal of Applied Psychology*, 79, 714–23.

Lykken, D.T. (1959). The GSR in the detection of guilt. *Journal of Applied Psychology*, 43, 385–8.

Lykken, D.T. (1988). The case against polygraph testing. In A. Gale (ed.), 111–25.

Lyon, T.D. (1995). False allegations and false denials in child sexual abuse. *Psychology, Public Policy, and Law*, 1, 429–37.

Maass, A. and Köhnken, G. (1989). Eyewitness identification: simulating the 'weapon effect'. *Law and Human Behavior*, 13, 397–408.

MacCoun, R. (1990). The emergence of extralegal bias during jury deliberation. *Criminal Justice and Behavior*, 17, 303–14.

MacDowell, D.M. (1978). *The Law in Classical Athens*. London: Thames & Hudson.

Machura, S. (1999). Interaction between lay assessors and professional judges in German mixed courts. Paper presented at the conference, Lay participation in the criminal trial in the 21st century, at the International Institute for Higher Studies in the Criminal sciences, Siracusa, Italy. Cited by Antonio and Hans (2001).

Mackay, R.D. (1993). The consequences of killing very young children. *Criminal Law Review*, 21–30.

MacLeod, M.D. (1987). Psychological dynamics of the police interview. Unpublished doctoral dissertation, University of Aberdeen.

MacLeod, M.D. and Shepherd, J.W. (1986). Sex differences in eyewitness reports of criminal assaults. *Medicine, Science and the Law*, 26, 311–18.

MacLeod, M.D., Frowley, J.N. and Shepherd, J.W. (1994). Whole body information: its relevance to eyewitnesses. In Ross et al. (eds), 125–43.

Macmillan, Lord. (1952). *Law and Other Things*. London: Macmillan.

Magistrates' Association (1993). *Sentencing Guidelines*. London.

Magner, E. (1991). Wigmore confronts Münsterberg: present relevance of a classic debate. *Sydney Law Review*, 13(2), 121–37.

Magner, E. (1995). Recovered memories: the Australian position. *Expert Evidence*, 3(4), 157.

Magner, E.S. (1995). Improving witness memory: an interdisciplinary reseaech agenda. *Current Issues in Criminal Justice*, 7, 25–35.

Maguire, J., Mason, T. and O'Kane, A. (2000). *Behaviour, Crime and Legal Processes: A Guide for Forensic Practitioners*. Chichester: Wiley.

Mair, G. (1986). Ethnic minorities, probation and the courts. *British Journal of Criminology*, 26, 147–55.

Malleson, K. (1999). *The New Judiciary: The Effects of Expansion and Activism*. Aldershot: Ashgate.

Malpass, R.S. (1981). Effective size and defendant bias in eyewitness identification. *Law and Human Behavior*, 5, 299–309.

Malpass, R.S. and Devine, P.G. (1981). Realism and eyewitness identification research. *Law and Human Behavior*, 4, 347–58.

Malpass, R.S. and Devine, P.G. (1983). Measuring the fairness of eyewitness identification lineups. In S.M.A. Lloyd-Bostock and B.R. Clifford (eds), 81–102.

Mandler, G. (1975). *Mind and Emotion*. New York: Wiley.

Mann, V., Diamond, R. and Carey, S. (1979). Development of voice recognition: parallels with face recognition. *Journal of Experimental Child Psychology*, 27, 153–65.

Mannheim, H. et al. (1957). Magisterial policy in the London courts. *British Journal of Delinquency*, 8, 13–33, 119–39.

Manolias, M. (1986). The psychologist as an agent for change. In J.C. Yuille (ed.), 347–51.

Manolias, M. (1991). Police stress. *International Criminal Police Review*, 13–17.

Manstead, A.S.R. and Lee, J.S. (1979). The effectiveness of two types of witness appeal signs. *Ergonomics*, 22, 1125–40.

Margolick, D. (1995). Strain of Simpson trial takes toll on one juror: asks judge to be removed from the case. *New York Times*, April 21, 144, A8, A14.

Mark, Sir R. (1973). Minority verdict. Dimbleby Lecture, British Broadcasting Corporation, 8–14.

Marshall, G. (1975). The judgement of one's peers: some aims and ideals of jury trial. In N.D. Walker and A. Pearson (eds), *The British Jury System: Papers Presented at the Cropwood Round-Table Conference*, December 1974. Cambridge: Institute of Criminology.

Marshall, J. (1969). *Law and Psychology in Conflict*. New York: Doubleday-Anchor. (Original work published in 1966).

Marx, G.T. (1988). *Undercover: Police Surveillance in America*. Berkeley, CA: University of California Press.

Marxsen, D., Yuille, J.C. and Nisbett, M. (1995). The complexities of eliciting and assessing children's statements. *Psychology, Public Policy and Law*, 1, 450–60.

Mason, M.A. (1991). A judicial dilemma: expert witness testimony in child sexual abuse cases. *Journal of Psychiatry and Law*, 19(3–4), 185–219.

Mather, L.M. (1979). *Plea Bargaining on Trial*. Lexington, MA: Lexington Books.

Mauet, T.A. and McCrimmon, L.A. (1993). *Fundamentals of Trial Techniques*. Australian Edition. Melbourne: Longman.

Mauro, R. (1991). Tipping the scales toward death: the biasing effects of death qualification. In P. Suedfeld and P.E. Tetlock (eds), *Psychology and Social Policy* (pp. 243–54). New York: Publishing Corporation.

Mawby, R.I. (1977). Sexual discrimination and the law. *Probation Journal*, 24, 38–43.

May, R. (1998). Jury selection in the United States: are there lessons to be learned? *Criminal Law Review*, 270–3.

Mayer, J.D. and Bower, G.H. (1986). Detecting mood-dependent retrieval. In P.H. Blainey (Chair) *Mood and Memory: Current Research Issues*. Symposium conducted at the meeting of the American Psychological Association, Washington, DC.

Mazzella, R. and Feingold, A. (1994). The effects of physical attractiveness, race, socioeconomic status, and gender of defendants and victims on judgements of mock jurors: A meta-analysis. *Applied Social Psychology*, 24, 1315–44.

Mazzoni, G.A.L., Loftus, E.F., Seitz, A. and Lynn, S.J. (1999). Changing beliefs and memories through dream interpretation. *Applied Cognitive Psychology*, 13, 125–44.

McAlister, H., Dale, R. and Keay, C. (1993). Effects of line-up modality on witness credibility. *Journal of Social Psychology*, 133, 365–6.

McCabe, S. (1975). Discussions in the jury room: are they like this? In N.D. Walker (ed.), *The British Jury System* (pp. 22–8). Cambridge: Institute of Criminology.

McCabe, S. and Purves, R. (1972a). By-passing the jury: a study of changes of plea and directed acquittals in higher courts. Oxford University Penal Research Unit, Occasional Paper 3.

McCabe, S. and Purves, R. (1972b). The jury at work: a study of jury trials in which the defendant was acquitted. Oxford University Penal Research Unit, Occasional Paper 4.

McCabe, S. and Purves, R. (1974). *The Jury at Work*. Oxford: Blackwell.

McCann, J.T. (1992). Criminal personality profiling in the investigation of violent crime: recent advances and future directions. *Behavioral Sciences and the Law*, 10, 475–81.

McCann, J.T. (1998). A conceptual framework for identifying types of confessions. *Behavioral Sciences and the Law*, 16, 441–53.

McCarthy, B.R. and Smith, B.L. (1986). The conceptualization of discrimination in the juvenile justice process: the impact of administrative factors and screening decisions on juvenile court dispositions. *Criminology*, 24, 42–64.

McCarty, D.G. (1929). *Psychology for the Lawyer*. New York: Prentice-Hall.

McCloskey, M. and Egeth, H. (1983). Eyewitness identification: what can a psychologist tell the jury? *American Psychologist*, 38, 573–5.

McCloskey, M. and Zaragoza, M. (1985). Misleading postevent information and memory for events: arguments and evidence against memory impairment hypothesis. *Journal of Experimental Psychology*, 114, 1–16.

McCloskey, M., Egeth, H. and McKenna, J. (1986). The experimental psychologist in court: the ethics of expert testimony. *Law and Human Behavior*, 10, 1–13.

McCloskey, M., Wible, C.G. and Cohen, N.J. (1988). Is there a special flashback memory mechanism? *Journal of Experimental Psychology*, 117, 171–81.

McConkey, K. (1995). Hypnosis, memory and the ethics of uncertainty. *Australian Psychologist*, 30, 1–10.

McConkey, K.M. (1992). The social sciences, the humanities and science and technology in economic development: the place of psychology. *Bulletin of the Australian Psychological Society*, 14(6), 3–6.

McConkey, K.M. and Roche, M. (1989). Knowledge of eye-witness memory. *Australian Psychologist*, 24(3), 377–84.

McConkey, K.M. and Sheehan, P.W. (1988). Forensic hypnosis: current legislation and its relevance to practice. *Australian Psychologist*, 23(3), 323–34.

McConville, M. and Mirsky, C. (1995). Guilty plea courts: a social disciplinary model of criminal justice. *Social Problems*, 42, 216–34.

McDonald. P. (1993). *Make 'Em Talk!: Principles of Military Interrogation*. Boulder, CO: Paladin Press.

McDowell, D.M. (1978). *The Law in Classical Athens*. London: Thames and Hudson.

McEwan, J. (1988). Child evidence: more proposals for reform. *Criminal Law Review*, 813–22.

McEwan, J. (1990). In the box or on the box? The Pigot report and child witness. *Criminal Law Review*, 363–70.

McEwan, J. (1995). Adversarial and Inquisitorial proceedings. In R. Bull and D. Carson (eds), 495–608.

McEwan, J. (2000). Decision making in legal settings. In Maguire et al. (eds), *Behaviour, Crime and Legal Processes,*111–31. Chichester: Wiley.

McGehee, F. (1937). The reliability of the identification of the human voice. *Journal of General Psychology*, 17, 249–71.

McGehee, F. (1944). An experimental study of voice recognition. *Journal of General Psychology*, 31, 53–65.

McGeoch, J.A. (1932). Forgetting and the law of disuse. *Psychological Review*, 39, 352–70.

McGinley, G. and Waye, V. (1994). *Evidence Handbook*. Sydney: Law Book Company.

McGough, L.S. (1995). For the record: videotaping investigative interviews. *Psychology, Public Policy and Law*, 1, 370–86.

McGuire, J., Mason, T. and O'Kane, A. (eds) (2000). *Behaviour, Crime and Legal Processes: A Guide for Forensic Practitioners*. Chichester: Wiley.

McGuire, W.J. (1972). Attitude change: the information processing paradigm. In C.G. McClintock (ed.), *Experimental Social Psychology* (pp. 108–41). New York: Holt, Rinehart & Winston.

McGuire, W.J. (1985). Attitudes and attitude change. In G. Lindzey and E. Aronson (eds), *The Handbook of Social Psychology* (vol. 2, pp. 233–346). New York: Random House.

McGurk, T., Platton, T. and Gibson, R.L. (1994). Detectives: a job and training needs analysis. *Issues in Criminological and Legal Psychology*, 21, 24–31.

McIntosh, J.A. and Prinz, R.J. (1993). The incidence of alleged sexual abuse in 603 family court cases. *Law and Human Behavior*, 17, 95–101.

McKenzie, I. (1995). Psychology and legal practice: fairness and accuracy in identification parades. *Criminal Law Review*, 200–8.

McLean, M. (1995). Quality investigation? Police interviewing of witnesses. *Medicine, Science and Law*, 35, 116–22.

McMahon, M. and Knowles, A. (1995). Confidentiality in psychological practice: a decrepit concept? *Australian Psychologist*, 30, 164–8.

McNair, D.M., Lorr, M. and Drappelman, M. (1971). *Manual for the Profile of Mood States (POMS)*. San Diego: Educational and Industrial Testing Service.

Medical Research Council Applied Psychology Unit (1986). *Fraud Trials Committee: Improving the Presentation of Information to Juries in Fraud Trials*. London: HMSO.

Megargee, E.I. (1972). *The California Personality Inventory Handbook*. London: Jossey-Bass Inc.

Mehrabian, A. and Williams, M. (1969). Nonverbal concomitants of perceived and intended persuasiveness. *Journal of Personality and Social Psychology*, 13, 37–58.

Mellers, B.A. and Baron, J. (eds) (1993). *Psychological Perspectives on Justice: Theory and Applications*. Cambridge: Cambridge University Press.

Melton, G.B., Monahan, J. and Saks, M.J. (1987). Psychologists as law professors. *American Psychologist*, 42, 502–9.

Memon, A. and Bull, R. (1991). The Cognitive Interview: its origins, empirical support and practical implications. *Journal of Community and Applied Psychology*, 1, 291–307.

Memon, A. and Bull, R. (1999). *Handbook of Investigative Interviewing*. Chichester: Wiley.

Memon, A. and Higham, P. (1999). A review of the cognitive interview. *Psychology, Crime and Law*, 5, 177–96.

Memon, A. and Shuman, D. (1998). Juror perception of experts in civil disputes: the role of race and gender. *Law and Psychology Review*, 22, 179–97.

Memon, A. and Wright, D.B. (2000). Factors influencing witness evidence. In J. McGuire et al. (eds), 65–81.

Memon, A., Bull, R. and Smith, M. (1995). Improving the quality of the police interview: can training in the use of cognitive techniques help? *Policing and Society*, 5, 53–68.

Memon, A., Cronin, O., Eaves, R. and Bull, R. (1993). The cognitive interview and child witnesses. *Issues in Criminological and Legal Psychology*, no. 20, 3–9.

Memon, A., Wark, L., Bull, R. and Köhnken, G. (1997). Isolating the effects of the cognitive interview techniques. *British Journal of Psychology*, 88, 179–97.

Memon, A., Wark, L., Holley, A., Bull, R. and Köhnken, G. (1997). Eyewitness performance in cognitive and structured interviews. *Memory*, 5, 639–55.

Memorandum of Good Practice on Video Recorded Interviews with Child Witnesses for Criminal Proceedings. Home Office in conjunction with Department of Health, 1992. London: HMSO.

Messick, S. and Damarin, F. (1964). Cognitive styles and memory for faces. *Journal of Abnormal and Social Psychology*, 69, 313–18.

Metcalfe, J. (1990). Composite holographic associative recall model (CHARM) and blended memories in eyewitness testimony. *Journal of Experimental Psychology: General*, 119, 145–60.

Meudell, P.R., Hitch, G.J. and Kirby, P. (1992). Are two heads better than one? Experimental investigations of the social facilitation of memory. *Applied Cognitive Psychology*, 6, 525–43.

Michon, J.A. and Pakes, F.J. (1995). Judicial decision making: a theoretical perspective. In R. Bull and D. Carson (eds), 509–25.

Milgram, S. (1974). *Obedience to Authority: An Experimental View*. New York: Harper & Row.

Miller, A.G. (1970). Role of physical attractiveness in impression formation. *Psychonomic Science*, 19, 241–3.

Miller, A.G., Ashston, W. and Mishal, M. (1990). Beliefs concerning features of constrained behaviour: a basis for the fundamental attribution error. *Journal of Personality and Social Psychology*, 59, 635–50.

Miller, G.R. and Stiff, J.B. (1993). *Deceptive Communication*. Newbury Park CA: Sage Publications.

Miller, N., Maruyama, G., Beaber, R. and Valone, K. (1976). Speed of speech and persuasion. *Journal of Personality and Social Psychology*, 34, 615–24.

Milne, R. and Bull, R. (1995). Children with mild learning disability: the cognitive interview and suggestibility. Paper presented at the Fifth European Psychology and Law Conference, Budapest, Hungary, September, 1995.

Milne, R. and Bull, R. (1999). *Investigative Interviewing: Psychology and Practice*. Chichester: Wiley.

Milne, R. and Shaw, G. (1999).Obtaining witness statements: the psychology, best practice and proposals for innovation. *Medicine, Science and the Law*, 39(2), 127–38.

Milne, R., Bull, R., Köhnken, G. and Memon, A. (1994). The cognitive interview and suggestibility. Paper presented at the Fourth European Conference of Law and Psychology. Barcelona.

Milne, R., Bull, R., Köhnken, G. and Memon, A. (1995). The cognitive interview and suggestibility. *Issues in Criminological and Legal Psychology*, 22, 21–7.

Milne, R., Clare, I.C. and Bull, R. (1999). Using the cognitive interview with adults with mild learning disabilities. *Psychology, Crime and Law*, 5, 81–99.

Mirrles-Black, C. (1992). Using psychometric personality tests in the selection of firearms officers. London: Home Office Research and Planning Unit, Paper 68.

Mitchell, B. (1983). Confessions and police interrogations of suspects. *Criminal Law Review*, 596–604.

Mitchell, K., Livorsky, M. and Mather, M. (1998). The weapon focus effect revisited: the role of novelty. *Legal and Criminological Psychology*, 3, 287–303.

Moloney, L. (1986). Cross-examination of social workers and psychologists in the Family Court. *Australian Psychologist*, 21(3), 377–87.

Monahan, J. and Loftus, E.F. (1982). The psychology of law. *Annual Review of Psychology*, 33, 441–75.

Monahan, J. and Walker, L. (1985). *Social Science in Law: Cases and Materials*. Mineola, New York: The Foundation Press.

Montaya, J. (1995). Lessons from *Akiki* and *Michaels* on shielding child witnesses. *Psychology, Public Policy and Law*, 1, 340–69.

Moore, L.E. (1973). *Tool of Kings, Palladium of Liberty*. Cincinatti OH: W.H. Anderson.

Morgan, J. and Zedner, L. (1992a). The victim's charter: a new deal for child victims? *The Howard Journal*, 31, 294–307.

Morgan, J. and Zedner, L. (1992b). *Child Victims: Crime, Impact and Criminal Justice*. Oxford: Clarendon Press.

Morgan, M. (1995). *How to Interview Sexual Abuse Victims, Including the Use of Anatomical Dolls*. Thousand Oaks, CA: Sage.

Morgan, P., Moxon, D. and Tarling, R. (1987). The implications of sentencing for the criminal justice system. In D.C. Pennington and S. Lloyd-Bostock (eds), 159–70.

Morgan, R. and Clarkson, C. (1995). The politics of sentencing reform. In C. Clarkson and R. Morgan (eds), 1–16.

Morris Committee (1965). Jury Service. London: HMSO: Cmnd. 2627.

Morse, C.K., Woodward, E.M. and Zweigenhaft, R.L. (1993). Gender differences in flashbulb memories elicited by the Clarence Thomas hearings. *Journal of Social Psychology*, 133, 453–8.

Morse, W. and Beattie, R.H. (1932). A study of the variances in sentences imposed by circuit judges. In J.R. Klonoski and R.I. Mendelsohn (eds), *The Politics of Local Justice* (pp. 175–86). London: Little Brown.

Mortimer, A. (1991). 'A case of': patterns in police officers' perceptions of offences. *Issues in Criminological and Legal Psychology*, 18, 13–29.

Morton, A. (1978). *Literary Detection: How to Prove Authorship in Literature and Documents*. London: Bowker.

Morton, A. and Michaelson, S. (1990). *The Q sum Plot*. Department of Computer Science, University of Edinburgh.

Morton, J., Hammersley, R.H. and Bekerian, D. (1985). Headed records: a model for memory and its failures. *Cognition*, 20, 1–23.

Moston, S. (1990). How children interpret and respond to questions: situation sources of suggestibility in eyewitness interviews. *Social Behavior*, 5, 155–67

Moston, S. (1996). From denial to admission in police questioning of suspects. In G. Davies et al. (eds), 91–9.

Moston, S. and Engelberg, T. (1992). The effect of social support on children's testimony. *Applied Cognitive Psychology*, 6, 61–75.

Moston, S. and Stephenson, G.M. (1993). The changing face of police interrogation. *Community and Applied Social Psychology*, 3, 101–15.

Moston, S., Stephenson, G. and Williamson, T.M. (1992). The effects of case characteristics on suspect behaviour during police questioning. *British Journal of Psychology*, 32, 23–40.

Mugford, S. and Gronfors, M. (1978). Racial and class factors in the sentences of first offenders. *Australian and New Zealand Journal of Sociology*, 14, 58–61.

Müller, D.E., Blackman, D.E. and Chapman, A.J. (eds) (1984). *Psychology and Law*. Chichester: Wiley.

Mulroy, T.M. (1993). How to examine a psychologist in a custody case. *American Journal of Family Law*, 7, 65–72.

Mungham, G. and Bankowski, Z. (1976). The jury in the legal system. In P. Carlen (ed.), *The Sociology of Law* (pp. 202–25). Sociological Review Monograph 23, University of Keele, UK.

Mungham, G. and Thomas, P.A. (1979). Advocacy and the solicitor-advocate in magistrates' courts in England and Wales. *International Journal of the Sociology of Law*, 7, 169–95.

Munkman, J.H. (1951). *The Technique of Advocacy*. London: Stevens & Sons.

Munkman, J.H. (1986). *The Technique of Advocacy*. London: Sweet Maxwell.

Münsterberg, H. (1908). *On the Witness Stand: Essays on Psychological Crime*. New York: Clark Boardman.

Murphy, K.R. (1995). Integrity testing. In N. Brewer and C. Wilson (eds), 205–28.

Murray, K. (1995). *Live Television Link: An Evaluation of of its use by the Child Witnesses in Scottish Criminal Trials*. Edinburgh: The Scottish Office, HMSO.

Myers, B. and Arbuthnot, J. (1997). Polygraph testimony and juror judgements: a comparison of the guilty knowledge test. *Journal of Applied Social Psychology*, 27, 1421–37.

Myers, J.E.B. (1993). The competence of young children to testify in legal proceedings. *Behavioral Sciences and the Law*, 11, 121–33.

Myers, M.A. and Talarico, S.M. (1987). *The Social Context of Criminal Sentencing*. New York: Springer.

Myklebust, T. and Alison, L. (2000). The current state of police interviews with children in Norway: how discrepant are they from models based on current issues in memory and cognition? *Psychology, Crime and Law*, 6, 331–51.

Nagel, S.S. (1961). Political party affiliation and judges' decisions. *American Political Science Review*, 55, 844–50.

Narby, D.J. and Cutler, B.L. (1994). Effectiveness of voir dire as a safeguard in eyewitness cases. *Journal of Applied Psychology*, 79, 274–9.

Nathanson, H.S. (1995). Strengthening the criminal jury: long overdue. *Criminal Law Quarterly*, 38, 217–48.

National Committee on Violence (1990). *Violence: Directions for Australia*. Canberra: Australian Institute of Criminology.

Navarro, J. and Schafer, J.R. (2001). Detecting deception. *FBI Law Enforcement Bulletin*, July, 9–13.

Navon, D. (1990a). How critical is the accuracy of an eyewitness's memory? Another look at the issue of lineup diagnosticity. *Journal of Applied Psychology*, 75, 506–10.

Navon, D. (1990b). Ecological parameters and non-lineup evidence: a reply to Wells and Luus. *Journal of Applied Psychology*, 75, 517–20.

Naylor, B. (1989). The child in the witness box. *Australian and New Zealand Journal of Criminology*, 22(2), 82–94.

Neisser, U. (1967). *Cognitive Psychology*. New York: Appleton-Century-Crofts.

Neisser, U. (1982). Snapshots or Benchmarks? In U. Neisser (ed.), 43–8.

Neisser, U. (ed.), (1982). *Memory Observed*. San Francisco: W.H. Freeman.

Neisser, U. (1986). Nested structure of autobiographical memory. In D.C. Rubin (ed.), *Autobiographical Memory* (pp. 71–81). Cambridge: Cambridge University Press.

Neisser, U. and Harsch, N. (1992). Phantom flashbulbs: false recollections of hearing the news about Challenger. In E. Winograd and U. Neisser (eds).

Nelson, J.F. (1992). Hidden disparities in case processing: New York State, 1986–1986. *Journal of Criminal Justice*, 20, 181–200.

Nelson, K. (1986). *Event Knowledge: Structure and Function in Development*. Hillsdale, N.J: Erlbaum.

Nelson, K., Fivush, R., Hudson, J. and Lucariello, J. (1983). Scripts and the development of memory. In M. Chi (ed.), *Current Trends in Memory Research* (pp. 52–69). New York: Springer-Verlag.

Neubauer, D.W. (1974). Confessions in prairie city: some causes and effects. *Journal of Criminal Law and Criminology*, 65, 103–12.

New South Wales Children's Evidence Taskforce. (1997). Audio and videotaping of children's out-of-court Statements. Sydney: NSW Attorney General's Department.

New South Wales Law Reform Commission (1985). The jury in a criminal trial. Discussion paper no. 12. Sydney, Australia.

New South Wales Law Reform Commission. (1996). Sentencing. Discussion paper no. 33. Sydney, Australia.

Newlands, P. (2000). Investigating suspect identification: do you recognise this man? Paper presented at the Tenth European Conference of Psychology and Law, Limassol, Cyprus, 12–14 April.

Newman, S.A. (1994). Assessing the quality of expert testimony in cases involving children. *Journal of Psychiatry and Law*, 22, 181–234.

Newton, P., Reddy, V. and Bull, R. (2000). Children's everyday deception and performance on false-belief tasks. *British Journal of Developmental Psychology*, 18, 297–317.

Nicholson, R.A. and Norwood, S. (2000). The quality of forensic psychological assessments, reports and testimony: acknowledging the gap between promise and practice. *Law and Human Behavior*, 24(1), 9–44.

Nietzel, M.T. and Hartung, C.M. (1993). Psychological research on police: an introduction to a special section on the psychology of law enforcement. *Law and Human Behavior*, 17, 151–5.

Nietzel, M.T., McCarthy, D.M. and Kery, M. (1999). Juries: the current state of the empirical literature. In R. Roesch, S.D. Hart and J.R. Ogloff (eds), 23–52.

Nightingale, N.N. (1993). Juror reaction to child victim witnesses: factors affecting trial outcome. *Law and Human Behavior*, 17, 679–700.

Nijboer, H. (1995). Expert evidence. In R. Bull and D. Carson (eds), 555–64.

Nisbett, R.E. and Wilson, T.D. (1977). Telling more than we can know: verbal reports of mental processes. *Psychological Review*, 84, 231–59.

Noon, E. and Hollin, C.R. (1987). Lay knowledge of eyewitness behaviour: a British survey. *Applied Cognitive Psychology*, 1, 143–53.

North, C.S. et al. (1989). Short-term psychopathology in eyewitnesses to mass murder. *Hospital and Community Psychology*, 40, 1293–95.

Nosworthy, G.J. and Lindsay, R.C.L. (1990). Does nominal lineup size matter? *Journal of Applied Psychology*, 75, 358–361.

O'Connor, J. and Seymour, J. (1990). *Introducing Neuro-Linguistic Programming*. London: Harper Collins.

O'Grady, C. (1996). *Child Witnesses and Jury Trials*. Perth: Western Australia Ministry of Justice.

O'Neal, S. (2000). Interviewing self-confident con artists. *FBI Law Enforcement Bulletin*, 16–21.

O'Barr, W.M. (1982). *Linguistic Evidence: Language, Power and Strategy in the Courtroom*. New York: Academic Press.

Odubekum, L. (1992). A structural approach to differential gender sentencing. *Criminal Justice Abstracts*, 24, 343–60.

Office of Technology Assessment, US Congress (1983). *Scientific Study of Polygraph Testing: A Research Review and Evaluation*. Washington, DC: US Government Printing Office.

Office of Technology Assessment, US Congress. (1990). *The Use of Integrity Tests for Pre-Employment Screening* (OTA-SET-442). Washington, DC: US Government Printing Office.

Ofshe, R. (1989). Coerced confessions: the logic of seemingly irrational action. *Cultic Studies Journal*, 6, 1–15.

Ofshe, R. and Christman, K. (1986). A two-process theory of social behavior. In A.R. Harris (ed.), *Rationality and Collective Belief*. NJ: Ablex Publishing Corporation.

Ogloff, J.R.P. (1992). *Law and Psychology: The Broadening of the Discipline*. Durham, NC: Academic Press.

Ogloff, J.R.P. (2000). Two steps forward and one step backward: the law and psychology movement(s) in the 20th century. *Law and Human Behavior*, 24(4), 457–83.

Ogloff, J.R.P. (2001). Jingoism, Dogmatism and other evils in legal psychology: lessons learned in the 20th century. In R. Roesch et al. (eds), 1–17.

Ogloff, J.R.P. and Finkelman, D. (1999). In R. Roesch et al. (eds), 1–20.

Ogloff, J.R.P. and Vidmar, N. (1994). The impact of pretrial publicity on jurors: a study to compare the relative effects of television and print media in a child sex abuse case. *Law and Human Behavior*, 18, 507–25.

Oligny, M. (1994). Burnout in the police environment. *International Criminal Law Review*, 22–5.

O'Neil, M.J. (1992). Juridical situation of child witnesses in Canada. In Lösel et al. (eds), 399–410.

Ones, D.S., Viswesvaran, C. and Schmidt, F.L. (1993). Meta-analysis of integrity testing. Findings and implications for personnel selection and theories of job performance. [Monograph]. *Journal of Applied Psychology*, 78, 679–703.

Orchard, T. and Yarmey, A.D. (1995). The effects of whispers, voice-sample duration, and voice distinctiveness on criminal speaker identification. *Applied Cognitive Psychology*, 9, 249–60.

Orchard, T.L. (1993). Factors affecting voice identification accuracy. Unpublished master's thesis, University of Guelph, Ontario, Canada.

Orne, M.T. (1979). The use and misuse of hypnosis in court. *International Journal of Clinical and Experimental Hypnosis*, 27, 311–41.

Orne, M.T., Soskis, D.A., Dinges, D.F. and Orne, E.C. (1984). Hypnotically induced testimony. In G.L. Wells and E.F. Loftus (eds), 171–213.

Ornstein, P.A., Shapiro, L.R., Clubb, P.A., Follmer, A. and Baker-Ward, L. (1997). The influence of prior knowledge on children's memory for salient medical experiences. In N. Stein, P.A. Ornstein, C.J. Brainerd and B. Tversky (eds), *Memory for Everyday and Emotional Events* (pp. 83–111). Hillsdale: Erlbaum.

Osborne, Y.H., Rappaport, N.B. and Meyer, R.G. (1986). An investigation of persuasion and sentencing severity with mock juries. *Behavioral Sciences and the Law*, 4, 339–49.

Osner, N., Quinn, A. and Crown, G. (eds) (1993). The Royal Commission on Criminal Justice. *Criminal Justice Systems in Other Jurisdictions*. London: HMSO.

Ostrom, T.M., Werner, C. and Saks, M. (1978). An integration theory analysis of jurors' presumption of guilt or innocence. *Journal of Personality and Social Psychology*, 36, 436–50.

Oswald, M.E. (1992). Justification and goals of punishment and the attribution of responsibility in judges. In Lösel et al. (eds), 424–34.

Oswald, M.E. and Drewniak, R. (1996). Attitude and behaviour of male and female judges concerning the punishment of offenders. In G. Davies et al. (eds), 297–304.

Otani, H. and Hodge, M.H. (1991). Does hypermnesia occur in recognition and cued recall? *American Journal of Psychology*, 104, 101–16.

O'Toole, D.M. (1988). Crime under the influence: the effects of alcohol intoxication during a crime on subsequent physiological detection of deception. Unpublished doctoral dissertation, University of British Columbia, Vancouver. Cited by Raskin (1989b).

Ouston, J. (1984). Delinquency, family background and educational attainment. *British Journal of Criminology*, 24, 2–26.

Overton, D.A. (1964). State-dependent or dissociated learning procedure with pentobarbital. *Journal of Comparative Physiological Psychology*, 57, 3–12.

Oxford, T. (1991). Spotting a liar. *Police Review*, 15 February, 328–9.

Ozcan, Y.Z. and Caglar, A. (1994). Who are the future police elites? Socio-economic background of the students at the police academy in Turkey. *Policing and Society*, 3, 287–301.

Paley, B. and Geiselman, R.E. (1989). The effects of alternative photospread instructions on suspect identification performance. *American Journal of Forensic Psychology*, 7, 3–13.

Palmiotto, M.J. (1983). An historical review of lie-detection methods used in detecting criminal acts. *Canadian Police College Journal*, 7(3), 206–16.

Palys, T.S. and Divorski, S. (1986). Explaining sentencing disparity. *Canadian Journal of Criminology*, 28, 347–62.

Pannell, W.K., Hosch, H.M. and Sands, S. (1992). Self-monitoring and event related potentials as predictors of facial recognition. Manuscript submitted for publication.

Pannick, D. (1992). *Advocates*. New York: Oxford University Press.

Parker, A.D. and Brown, J. (2000). Detection of deception: Statement Validity Analysis as a means of determining truthfulness or falsity of rape allegations. *Legal and Criminological Psychology*, 5, 237–59.

Parker, E.S.P., Birnbaum, I.M., Weingartner, H., Hartley, J.T., Stillman, R.C. and Wyatt, R.J. (1980). Retrograde enhancement of human memory with alcohol. *Psychopharmacology*, 69, 219–22.

Parker, J.F. and Carranza, L.E. (1989). Eyewitness testimony of children in target-present and target-absent lineups. *Law and Human Behavior*, 13, 133–49.

Parker, J.F. and Ryan, V. (1993). An attempt to reduce guessing behavior in children's and adults' eyewitness identifications. *Law and Human Behavior*, 17, 11–26.

Parker, K.D. and Ray, M.C. (1990). Fear of crime: an asssessment of related factors. *Sociological Spectrum*, 10, 29–40.

Parkinson, P. (1991). The future of competency testing for child witnesses. *Criminal Law Journal*, 15, 186–92.

Parrick, C.J. and Iacono, W.G. (1989). Psychopathy, threat, and polygraph test accuracy. *Journal of Applied Psychology*, 74, 347–55.

Parrick, C.J. and Iacono, W.G. (1991). Validity of the control question polygraph test: the problem of sampling bias. *Journal of Applied Psychology*, 76, 229–38.

Parry, E.A. (1923). *The Seven Lamps of Advocacy*. London: Unwin.

Paterson, B. and Bull, R. (1999). Young children's recall after long delays. Paper presented at the Annual Conference of the European Psychology and Law Association, Dublin.

Payne, D.G. (1987). Hypermnesia and reminiscence in recall: a historical and empirical review. *Psychological Bulletin*, 101, 5–27.

Pearse, J. and Gudjonsson, G.H. (1999). Measuring influential police interviewing tactics: a factor analytic approach. *Legal and Criminological Psychology*, 4, 221–38.

Pearse, J., Gudjonsson, G.H., Clare, I.C.H. and Rutter, S. (1998). Police interviewing and psychological vulnerabilities: predicting the likelihood of a confession. *Journal of Community and Applied Psychology*, 8, 1–21.

Pedzek, K. and Hinz, T. (2002). The construction of false events in meory. In H.L. Westcott et al. (eds), *Children's Testimony* (pp. 99–116). Chichester: Wiley.

Pedzek, K. and Hodge, D. (1999). Planting false childhood memories in children: the role of event plausibility. *Child Development*, 70, 887–95.

Pennington, D.C. and Lloyd-Bostock S.M.A. (eds) (1987). *The Psychology of Sentencing: Approaches to Consistency*. Oxford: Centre for Socio-Legal Studies.

Pennington, N. and Hastie, R. (1986). Evidence evaluation in complex decision making. *Journal of Personality and Social Psychology*, 51, 242–58.

Pennington, N. and Hastie, R. (1990). Practical implications of psychological research on juror and jury decision making. *Personality and Social Psychology Bulletin*, 16(1), 90–105.

Pennington, N. and Hastie, R. (1993). The story model for juror decision making. In R. Hastie (ed.), 192–221.

Penrod, S., Loftus, E.F. and Winkler, J.D. (1982). The reliability of eyewitness testimony: a psychological perspective. In N.L. Kerr and R.M. Bray (eds), 119–68.

Penrod, S.D., Solomon, M., Fulero, J.D. and Cutler, B.L. (1995). Expert psychological testimony on eyewitness reliability before and after *Daubert*: the state of the law and science. *Behavioral Sciences and the Law*, 13, 229–59.

Perlman, N.B., Erickson, K.I., Esses, V.M. and Isaacs, B. (1994). The developmentally handicapped witness: competency as a function of question format. *Law and Human Behavior*, 18, 171–87.

Perrot, S.B. and Taylor, D.M. (1995). Attitudinal differences between police constables and their supervisors: potential influences of personality, work environment, and occupational role. *Criminal Justice and Behavior*, 22(3), 326–39.

Perry, C. and Gold, A.D. (1995). Hypnosis and the elicitation of true and false memories of childhood sexual abuse. *Psychiatry, Psychology and Law*, 2(2), 127–38.

Perry, N.W. and Wrightsman, L. (1991). *The Child Witness: Legal Issues and Dilemmas.* Newbury Park, CA: Sage.

Peters, D.P. (1985). A naturalistic study of earwitness evidence: does the addition of a voice to a lineup influence accuracy and/or confidence? Paper presented at the annual meeting of the Eastern Psychological Association.

Peters, D.P. (1987). The impact of naturally occurring stress on children's memory. In Ceci et al. (eds), 122–41.

Peters, D.P. (1991). Confrontational stress and children's testimony: some experimental findings. In J. L. Doris (ed.), 60–76.

Peterson, C. (1999). Children's memory for medical emergencies: 2 years later. *Developmental Psychology*, 35, 1493–506.

Peterson, C.C., Peterson, J.L. and Seeto, D. (1983). Developmental changes in ideas about lying. *Child Development*, 54, 1529–35.

Petty, R.E. and Cacioppo, J.T. (1984). The effects of issue involvement on responses to argument quantity and quality: central and peripheral routes of persuasion. *Journal of Personality and Social Psychology*, 46, 69–81.

Petty, R.E., Cacioppo, J.T. and Goldman, R. (1981). Personal involvement as a determinant of argument based persuasion. *Journal of Personality and Social Psychology*, 41, 847–55.

Petty, R.E., Wegener, D.T. and Fabrigar, L.R. (1997). Attitudes and attitude change. *Annual Review of Psychology*, 48, 609–47.

Pezdek, K. (1994). The illusion of illusory memory. *Applied Cognitive Psychology*, 8, 339–50.

Phillips, J. (1985). *Advocacy With Honour*. Sydney: The Law Book Co.

Phillpots, G.J. and Lancucki, L.B. (1979). *Previous Convictions, Sentence and Reconviction: A Statistical Study of a Sample of 5000 Offenders Convicted in January 1971*. London: Home Office, Research Study no. 53.

Piaget, J. (1972). *Judgement and Reasoning in the Child.* (M. Warden, trans.) Littlefield, Adams: Totawa, NJ (originally published in 1924).

Pickel, K.L. (1995). Inducing jurors to disregard inadmissible evidence: a legal explanation does not help. *Law and Human Behavior*, 19, 407–24.

Pickel, K.L. (1998). Usualness and threat as possible sources of 'weapon focus'. *Memory*, 6(3), 277–95.

Pickholz, G. and Pickholz, J. (2001). Manipulation. *Journal of Financial Crime*, 9(2), 117–33.

Pigot, His Honour Judge. (1989, December). Report of the National Advisory Group on Video Evidence. London: Home Office.

Pigott, M.A. and Brigham, J.C. (1985). Relationship between accuracy of prior description and facial recognition. *Journal of Applied Psychology*, 70, 547–55.

Pike, G. and Kemp, R. (1995). Turning heads. *Forensic Update*, Issue 40, 23–7.

Pike, G., Brace, N. and Kemp, R. (2000). Facial mapping of low resolution CCTV images. Paper presented at the Tenth European Conference of Psychology and Law, Limassol, Cyprus, 12–14 April.

Piliavin, I. and Briar, S. (1964). Police encounters with juveniles. *American Journal of Sociology*, 70, 206–14.

Piliavin, J.A., Dovidio, J.F., Gaertner, S.L. and Clark, R.D. (1981). *Emergency Intervention*. New York: Academic Press.

Pillemer, D. and White, S.H. (1989). Childhood events recalled by children and adults. In H.W. Reese (ed.), *Advances in Child Development and Behavior* (vol. 22, pp. 297–346). New York: Academic.

Pinizzotto, A. and Davis, E. (1992). Cop killers and their victims. *FBI Law Enforcement Bulletin*, 9–11.

Pipe, M.E. and Goodman, G.S. (1991). Elements of secrecy; implications for children's testimony. *Behavioral Science and the Law*, 9, 33–41.

Pipe, M.E., Salmon, K. and Priestley, G.K. (2002). Enhancing children's accounts: how useful are non-verbal techniques? In H.L. Westcott et al. (eds), 161–74.

Pitchert, J.W. and Anderson, R.C. (1977). Taking perspectives on a story. *Journal of Educational Psychology*, 69, 309–15.

Ploscowe, M. (1951). The court and the correctional system. In P. Tappan (ed.), *Contemporary Correction*. New York: McGraw-Hill. Cited by Green, E. (1961). *Judicial Attitudes: A Study of the Factors Underlying the Sentencing Practice of the Criminal Court of Philadelphia*. London: Macmillan.

Plotnikoff, J. and Woolfson, R. (2002). What do judges know about young witnesses? In H.L. Westcott et al. (eds), 295–307.

Podlesny, J.A. and Raskin, D.C. (1977). Physiological measures and the detection of deception. *Psychological Bulletin*, 84, 782–99.

Podlesny, J.A. and Raskin, D.C. (1978). Effectiveness of techniques and physiological measures in the detection of deception. *Psychophysiology*, 15, 344–58.

Pogrebin, M.R. and Poole, E.D. (1991). Police and tragic events: the management of emotions. *Journal of Criminal Justice*, 19, 395–403.

Pogrebin, M.R. and Poole, E.D. (1993). Vice isn't nice: a look at the effects of working undercover. *Journal of Criminal Justice*, 21, 383–94.

Police and Criminal Evidence Act (1984). Codes of Practice, Revised edition-effective 1 April, 1991. London: HMSO, 1992.

Policy Studies Institute (1983). *Police and People in London*. London: Policy Studies Institute.

Polk, K. and Tait, D. (1988). The use of imprisonment by the magistrates' courts. *Australian and New Zealand Journal of Criminology*, 21, 31–44.

Pollack, I., Pickett, J. and Sumby, W. (1954). On the identification of speakers by voice. *Journal of the Acoustical Society of America*, 26, 403–6.

Pope, H.G., Oliva, P.S. and Hudson, J.L. (1999). The scientific status of research on repressed memories. In D.L. Faigman, D.H. Kaye, M.J. Saks and J. Sanders (eds), *Modern Scientific Evidence: The Law and Science of Expert Testimony*, vol. 1 (pp. 112–55). St Paul, MN: West Group.

Popper, K.R. (1939). *The Logic of Scientific Discovery*. London: Hutchinson.

Porter, S. and Yuille, J.C. (1995). Credibility assessment of criminal suspects through statement analysis. *Psychology, Crime and Law*, 1, 319–31.

Porter, S., Woodworth, M. and Birt, A.R. (2000). Truth, lies and videotapes: an investigation of the ability of federal parole officers to detect deception. *Law and Human Behavior*, 24(6), 643–58.

Potas, I. and Rickwood, D. (1984). *Do Juries Understand*? Canberra: Australian Institute of Criminology.

Powel, M.B. and Thomson, D.M. (1994, March). A study of children's memory about a specific episode of a recurring event. Paper presented by the first author at the First National Conference on Child Sexual Abuse, Radisson Hotel, Melbourne.

Power, D.J. (1977). Memory, identifications and crime. *Medicine, Science and Law*, 17, 132–9.

Powers, P.A., Andriks, J.L. and Loftus, E.F. (1979). Eyewitness account of females and males. *Journal of Applied Psychology*, 64, 339–47.

Pozzulo, J.D. and Lindsay, R.C.L. (1998). Identification accuracy of children versus adults: a meta-analysis. *Law and Human Behavior*, 22, 549–70.

Pozzulo, J.D. and Lindsay, R.C.L. (1999). Elimination line-ups: an improved identification procedure for child witnesses, *Journal of Applied Psychology*, 84(2), 167–76.

Pynes, J. and Bernardin, H.J. (1992). Entry-level police selection: the assessment center is an alternative. *Journal of Criminal Justice*, 20, 41–52.

Pynoos, R. and Eth, S. (1984). The child as witness to homicide. *Journal of Social Issues*, 40, 87–108.

Quattrone, G.A. and Jones, E.E. (1980). The perception of variability with in-groups and out-groups: implications for the law of small numbers. *Journal of Personality and Social Psychology*, 38, 141–52.

Queensland Criminal Justice Commission (1991). Report of an investigative hearing into alleged jury interference. Brisbane, Australia.

Quinn, K. (1999). Lay Participation in the criminal trial in the 21st century: country study: republic of Ireland. Paper presented at the conference 'Lay participation in the criminal trial in the 21st century', International Institute for Higher Studies in the Criminal Sciences, Siracusa, Italy, May 1999.

Rabbitt, P.M.A. (1981). Applying human experimental psychology to legal questions about evidence. In S.M.A. Lloyd-Bostock (ed.) (1981a), 3–18.

Ragg, M. (1995). Proof positive or negative? *The Bulletin*, 13 June, 14–17. Canberra, Australia.

Raskin, D.C. (ed.) (1989a). *Psychological Methods in Criminal Investigation and Evidence*. New York: Springer.

Raskin, D.C. (1989b). Polygraph techniques for the detection of deception. In D.C. Raskin (1989a) (ed.), 247–95.

Raskin, D.C. and Esplin, P.W. (1991) Statement validity assessment: interview procedures and content analysis of children's statements of sexual abuse. *Behavior Assessment*, 13, 265–91.

Raskin, D.C. and Esplin, P.W. (1991). Assessment of children's statements of sexual abuse. In J. Doris (ed.), 153–64.

Raskin, D.C. and Yuille, J.C. (1989). Problems in evaluating interviews of children of sexual abuse. In S. Ceci, D. Ross and M. Toglia (eds), *Perspectives on Children's Testimony* (pp. 184–207). New York: Springer-Verlag.

Rattner, A. (1988). Convicted but innocent: wrongful conviction and the criminal justice system. *Law and Human Behavior*, 12, 283–94.

Ray, J.J. (1972). A new balance F scale and its relation to social class. *Australian Psychologist*, 7, 155–66.

Read, D. and Craik, F. (1995). Earwitness identification: some influences on voice recognition. *Journal of Experimental Psychology: Applied*, 1, 6–18.

Read, J.D. and Lindsay, D.S. (1994). Moving toward a middle ground on the 'false memory debate': reply to commentaries on Lindsay and Read. *Applied Cognitive Psychology*, 8, 407–35.

Read, J.D., Tollestrup, P., Hammersley, R., McFazden, E. and Christensen, A. (1990). The unconscious transference effect: are innocent bystanders ever misidentified? *Applied Cognitive Psychology*, 4, 3–31.

Read, J.D., Yuille, J.C. and Tollestrup, P. (1992). Recollections of a robbery: effects of arousal and alcohol upon recall and person identification. *Law and Human Behavior*, 16, 425–46.

Rector, N.A. and Bagby, R.M. (1995). Criminal sentence recommendations in a simulated rape trial: examining juror prejudice in Canada. *Behavioural Sciences and the Law*, 13, 113–21.

Redmayne, M. (1994). The royal commission's proposals on expert evidence. *Expert Evidence*, 2, 157–63.

Regan, P.C. and Berscheid, E. (1995). Gender differences in beliefs about the causes of male and female sexual desire. *Personal Relationships*, 2, 345–58.

Reich, A. and Duke, J. (1979). Effects of selected vocal disguises upon speaker identification by listening. *Journal of the Acoustical Society of America*, 66, 1023–8.

Reid, J. and Associates (1986). *The Reid Technique of Interviewing and Interrogation*. Chicago, IL: Reid & Associates.

Reid, J.E. and Arther, R.O. (1954). Behavior symptoms of lie-detector subjects. *Journal of Criminal Law, Criminology, and Police Science*, 44, 104–8.

Reifman, A., Gusick, S.M. and Ellsworth, P.C. (1992). Real jurors' understanding of the law in real cases. *Law and Human Behavior*, 16, 539–54.

Reinke, R. (1977). *Selection Through Assessment Centers*. Washington, DC: Police Foundation Publication.

Reisberg, D., Heuer, F., Maclean, J., and O'Shaughnessy, M. (1988). The quantity, not the quality of affect predicts memory vividness. *Bulletin of the Psychonomic Society*, 26, 100–3.

Reiser, M. (1989). Investigative hypnosis. In D.C. Raskin (ed.), 151–90.

Reiser, M. and Klyver, N. (1987). Consulting with the police. In I.B. Weiner and H.K. Hess (eds), 437–59.

Report of the Inquiry into Child Abuse in Cleveland (1987). London: HMSO.

Report of the Royal Commission on Criminal Procedure (1981). London: HMSO.

Reskin, B.F. and Visher, C.A. (1986). The impacts of evidence and extralegal factors in jurors' decisions. *Law and Society Review*, 20, 423–38.

Rhodes, W.M. (1977). A study of sentencing in the Hennepin County and Ramsay County District Courts. *Journal of Legal Studies*, 6, 333–53.

Richardson, G. (1991). A study of interrogative suggestibility in an adolescent forensic population. MSc dissertation, University of Newcastle-upon-Tyne.

Richardson, G. and Kelly, T.P. (1995). The relationship between intelligence, memory and interrogative suggestibility in young offenders. *Psychology, Crime and Law*, 1(4), 283–90.

Roberts, H. and Glasgow, D. (1993). *Issues in Criminological and Legal Psychology*, 20, 10–14.

Robertson, B., Vignaux, G.A. and Egerton, I. (1994). Stylometric evidence. *Criminal Law Review*, 645–9.

Rock, P. (1991). Witness and space in a Crown Court. *British Journal of Criminology*, 31, 266–79.

Roesch, R., Corrado, R.R., and Dempster, R. (eds) (2001). *Psychology in the Courts: International Advances in Knowledge*. London and New York: Routledge.

Roesch, R., Hart, S.D. and Ogloff, J.R.P. (eds) (1999). *Psychology and Law: The State of the Discipline*. New York: Kluwer Academic/Plenum Publishers.

Rose, G. (1965). An experimental study of sentencing. *British Journal of Criminology*, 5, 314–19.

Rosefeld, J.P., Angell, A., Johnson, M. and Qian, J. (1991). An ERP-based, control-question lie detector analog: algorithms for discriminating within individuals' average waveforms. *Psychophysiology*, 28, 319–55.

Rosen, J. (1992). Jury mandering: a case against peremptory challenges. *New Republic*, 30 November, 15–16.

Rosenbaum, D. (1989). Prayer was a turning point, a juror says. *New York Times*, 5 May, p. A.19.

Rosenthal, R. (1995). *State New Jersey v. Margaret Kelly Michaels*: an overview. *Psychology, Public Policy and Law*, 1, 246–71.

Roskill, Lord P.C. (1986). *Fraud Trials Committee Report*. London: HMSO.

Ross, D.F., Ceci, S.J., Dunning, D. and Toglia, M.P. (1994b). Unconscious transference and lineup identification: toward a memory blending approach. In Ross et al. (1994a) (eds), 80–100.

Ross, D.F., Ceci, S.J., Dunning, D. and Toglia, M.P. (1994c). Unconscious transference: when a witness misidentifies a familiar but innocent person. *Journal of Applied Psychology*, 79, 918–30.

Ross, D.F., Dunning, D., Toglia, M.P. and Ceci, S. (1990). The child in the eyes of the jury: assessing mock jurors' perceptions of the child witness. *Law and Human Behavior*, 14, 5–23.

Ross, D.F., Hopkins, S., Hanson, E., Lindsay, R.C.L., Hazen, K. and Eslinger, T. (1994d). The impact of protective shields and videotape testimony on conviction rates in a simulated trial of child sexual abuse. *Law and Human Behavior*, 18, 553–66.

Ross, D.F., Read, J.D. and Toglia, M.P. (eds) (1994a). *Adult Eyewitness Testimony: Current Trends and Developments*. Cambridge: Cambridge University Press.

Rowland, C.K. and Carp, R.A. (1996). *Politics and Judgement in Federal District Courts*. Lawrence KS: University Press of Kansas.

Royal Commission on Civil Liability and Compensation for Personal Injury (The Pearson Commission, Chairman, Lord Pearson). Cmnd. 7054–1 London: HMSO, 1978.

Royal Commission on Criminal Justice (1993). (Cmnd. 2262). London: HMSO.

Royal Commission on Criminal Justice (1993). Report. Cmnd. 2263. London: HMSO.

Royal Commission on Criminal Procedure (1984). London: HMSO.

Royal Commission on Gambling (1978). Final Report (The Rothschild Report). London, HMSO; Cmnd. 7200, 1978.

Royal, R.F. and Schutt, S.R. (1976). *The Gentle Art of Interviewing and Interrogation*. New Jersey: Prentice-Hall.

Ruck, M.D. (1996). Why children think they should tell the truth in court: developmental considerations for the assessment of competency. *Legal and Criminological Psychology*, 1, 103–16.

Rudy, L. and Goodman, G.S. (1991). Effects of participation on children's reports: implications for children's testimony. *Developmental Psychology*, 27, 527–38.

Rue, L. (1994). *By the Grace of Guile: The Role of Deception in Natural History and Human Affairs*. New York: Oxford University Press.

Runciman, Lord. (1993). *Report of the Royal Commission on Criminal Justice*. Cmnd. 2263. London: HMSO.

Russell, J.A. (1995). Facial expression of emotion: what lies beyond minimal universality? *Psychological Bulletin*, 118, 379–91.

Russell, K. (1986). Polygraph use in the United Kingdom. *Yearbook of Law Computers and Technology*, 126–9.

Sackett, P.R. (1985). Honesty research and the person-situation debate. In W. Terris (ed.) *Employee Theft*. Chicago, IL: London House Press.

Sackett, P.R., Burris, L.R. and Callahan, C. (1989). Integrity testing for personnel selection: an update. *Personnel Psychology*, 42, 491–529.

Saks, M. (1977). *Jury Verdicts: The Role of Group Size and Social Decision Rule*. Mass., Heath: Lexington.

Saks, M. and Hastie, R. (1978). *Social Psychology in Court*. London: van Nostrand.

Saks, M.J. (1986). The law does not live by eyewitness-testimony alone. *Law and Human Behavior*, 10, 279–80.

Saks, M.J. (1992). Normative and empirical issues about the role of expert witnesses. In D.K. Kagehiro and W.S. Laufer (eds), 185–203.

Sales, B.D. (ed.) (1977). *Perspectives in Law and Psychology* vol 1: The Criminal Justice System. New York: Plenum.

Sales, B.D., Shuman, D.W. and O'Connor, M. (1994). In a dim light: admissibility of child sexual abuse memories. *Applied Cognitive Psychology*, 8, 399–406.

Sallmann, P. and Willis, J. (1984). *Criminal Justice in Australia*. Melbourne: Oxford University Press.

Sanborn, J.B. (1993). The right to a public jury trial: a need for today's juvenile court. *Judicature*, 76, 230–8.

Sanders, A. (1987). Constructing the case for the prosecution. *Journal of Law and Society*, 14, 229–53

Sanders, A. (1997). From suspect to trial. In M. Maguire, R. Morgan and R. Reiner (eds), *The Oxford Handbook of Criminology* (pp. 1051–93). Oxford: Clarendon Press.

Sanders, G.S. (1986). On increasing the usefulness of eyewitness research. *Law and Human Behavior*, 10, 333–5.

Sanders, G.S. and Warnick, D.H. (1981). Truth and consequences: the effects of responsibility on eyewitness behavior. *Basic and Applied Social Psychology*, 12, 67–79.

Sandoval, V.A. and Adams, S.H. (2001). Subtle skills for building rapport using neurolinguistic programming in the interview room. *FBI Law Enforcement Bulletin*, 1–5.

Sandys, M. (1995). Cross overs: capital jurors who change their minds about the punishment: a litmus test for sentencing guidelines. *Indiana Law Journal*, 70, 1183–221.

Sandys, M. and Dillehay, R.C. (1995). First-ballot votes, predeliberation dispositions, and final verdicts in jury trials. *Law and Human Behavior*, 19, 175–95.

Santila, P., Roppola, H., Runnti, M. and Niemi, P. (2000). Assessments of child witness statements using Criteria-based Content Analysis (CBCA): the effects of age, verbal ability, and interviewer's emotional style. *Psychology, Crime and Law*, 6, 159–79.

Sapir, A. (1991). Scientific Content Analysis course presentation. March 1992. Detroit, Michigan.

Sapir, A. (1993). SCAN advanced workshop. 1–3 June, Washington, DC.

Sarason, I. and Stroops, R. (1978). Test anxiety and the passage of time. *Journal of Consulting and Clinical Psychology*, 46, 189–97.

Sarat, A. (1995). Violence, representation and responsibility in capital trials: the view from the jury. *Indiana Law Journal*, 70, 1103–39.

Saslove, H. and Yarmey, A.D. (1980). Long-term auditory memory: speaker identification. *Journal of Applied Psychology*, 65, 111–16.

Sattar, G. and Bull, R. (1994). Preparing the child witness. *Policing*, 11(3), 155–70.

Sattar, G. and Bull, R. (1999). Ethnicity: an ignored issue in child witness research. Paper presented at the Psychology and Law International Conference, University College Dublin, 6–9 July 1999.

Saunders, W. (1984). *Alcohol Use in Britain: How Much is Too Much*? Edinburgh.

Saywitz, K.J. (1987). Children's testimony: age-related patterns of memory errors. In S.J. Ceci, M.P. Toglia and D.F. Ross (eds), 36–52.

Saywitz, K.J. (2002). Developmental underpinnings of children's testimony. In H.L. Westcott et al. (eds), 3–19.

Saywitz, K.J. and Snyder, L. (1991, April). Preparing child witnesses: the efficacy of comprehension monitoring training. Paper presented at the biennial convention of the Society for Research on Child Development, Seattle, WA. Cited by Saywitz and Snyder (1993).

Saywitz, K.J. and Snyder, L. (1993). Improving children's testimony with preparation. In G.S. Goodman and B.L. Bottoms (eds), 117–46.

Saywitz, K.J., Geiselman, R.E. and Bornstein, G.K. (1993). Effects of cognitive interviewing and practice on children's recall performance. *Applied Psychology*, 77, 744–56.

Saywitz, K.J., Goodman, G.S., Nicholas, E. and Moan, S. (1991a). Children's memories of physical examinations involving genital touch: implications for reports of child sexual abuse. *Journal of Consulting and Clinical Psychology*, 59, 682–91.

Saywitz, K.J., Moan, S. and Lamphear, V. (1991b, August). The effect of preparation on children's resistance to misleading questions. Paper presented at the annual meeting of American Psychological Association, San Francisco, CA.

Saywitz, K.J., Snyder, L. and Lamphear, V. (1990, August). Preparing child witnesses: their efficacy of memory strategy training. Paper presented at the annual convention of the American Psychological Association, Boston, MA.

Scarman, Rt Hon., Lord. (1981). The Brixton Disorders 1–12 April 1981: Report of an Enquiry by Rt Hon. Lord Scarman. Cmnd. 8427. London: HMSO.

Schacter, L., Kagan, J. and Leichtman, M.D. (1995). True and false memories in children and adults: a cognitive neuroscience perspective. *Psychology, Public Policy and Law*, 1, 411–28.

Schare, M.L., Lisman, S.A. and Spear, N.E. (1984). The effects of mood variation on state-dependent retentions. *Cognitive Therapy Research*, 8, 387–408.

Scheflin, A.W. (1994). Forensic hypnosis and the law: the current situation in the United States. In B.J. Evans and R.O. Stanley (eds), 25–48.

Schiff, W., Banka, L. and Bordes Galdi, G. (1986). Recognising people seen in events via dynamic 'mugshots'. *American Journal of Psychology*, 99, 219–31.

Schiffman, H.R. and Bobko, D. J. (1974). Effects of stimulus complexity of the perception of short temporal durations. *Journal of Experimental Psychology*, 103, 156–9.

Schill, T. (1966). Effects of approval motivation and varying conditions of verbal reinforcement on incidental memory for faces. *Psychological Reports*, 19, 55–60.

Schneider, D.J. (1995). Attribution of social cognition. In M. Argyle and A. M. Colman (eds), *Social Psychology* (pp. 38–56). London: Longman.

Schooler, J.W. and Engstler-Schooler, T.Y. (1990). Verbal overshadowing of visual memories: some things are better left unsaid. *Cognitive Psychology*, 22, 36–71.

Schor, D.P. and Sivan, A.B. (1989). Interpreting children's labels for sex-related body parts of anatomically explicit dolls. *Child Abuse and Neglect*, 13, 523–31.

Schubert, G. (1959). *Quantitative Analysis of Judicial Behavior*. Glencoe, IL: The Free Press.

Schubert, G. (1965). *The Judicial Mind: Attitudes and Ideologies of Supreme Court Justices, 1946–1963*. Evanston, IL: Northwestern University Press.

Schubert, G. (1974). *The Judicial Mind Revisited: Psychometric Analysis of Supreme Court Ideology*. New York: Oxford University Press.

Schuller, R.A., Terry, D. and McKimme, B. (2001). The impact of an expert's gender on jurors' decisions. *Law and Psychology Review*, 25, 59–79.

Schum, D.A. (1993). Argument structuring and evidence evaluation. In R. Hastie (ed.), 175–91.

Schwalb, B.L. (1991). Child abuse trials and the confrontation of traumatized witnesses: defining 'confrontation' to protect both children and defendants. *Harvard Civil Rights-Civil Liberties Law Review*, 26, 185–217.

Scrivner, E. and Safer, M.A. (1988). Eyewitnesses show hypermnesia for details about a violent event. *Journal of Applied Psychology*, 73, 371–7.

Scrivner, E.M. (1986). Assessment strategy for special unit assignments: an alternative to psychological tests. In J.C. Yuille (ed.), 251–5.

Sealy, A.P. (1975). What can be learned from the analysis of simulated juries? In N.D. Nalker (ed.), 12–21.

Sealy, A.P. (1989). Decision processes in the jury room. In Wegener et al. (eds), 163–80.

Sealy, A.P. and Cornish, W.R. (1973). Juries and the rules of evidence. *Modern Law Review*, 208–23.

Sedlak, A.J. and Broadhurst, D.D. (1996). *Third National Incidence Study of Child Abuse and Neglect: Final Report*. Washington, DC: US Department of Health and Human Resources, Administration for Children and Families.

Segal, J.A. and Spaeth, H.J. (1993). *The Supreme Court and the Attitudinal Model*. Cambridge: Cambridge University Press.

Selby, H. (2000). *Winning in Court: An Introduction to Advocacy*. Melbourne: Oxford University Press.

Seltzer, R., Venuti, M.A. and Lopes, G.M. (1991). Juror honesty during voir dire. *Journal of Criminal Justice*, 19(5), 451–62.

Sentencing Committee [Victoria]. (1988). *Report of the Victorian Sentencing Committee*, vol. 1. Melbourne: Attorney-General's Department.

Severance, L.J., Goodman, J. and Loftus, E.F. (1992). Inferring the criminal mind: toward a bridge between legal doctrine and psychological understanding. *Journal of Criminal Justice*, 20, 107–20.

Shakoor, B.H. and Chalmers, D. (1991). Co-victimization of African-American children who witness violence: effects on cognitive, emotional, and behavioral development. *Journal of the National Medical Association*, 83, 233–8.

Shapiro, P.N. and Penrod, S. (1986). Meta-analysis of facial identification studies. *Psychological Bulletin*, 100, 139–56.

Shapland, J. (1987). Who controls sentencing? Influences on the sentencer. In D.C. Pennington and S. Lloyd-Bostock (eds), 77–87.

Shaw, J.S., Garven, S. and Wood, J.M. (1997). Co-witness information can have immediate effects on eyewitness memory reports. *Law and Human Behavior*, 21, 503–23.

Shaw, J.S., Zerr, T.K. and Woythaler, K.A. (2001). Public eyewitness confidence ratings can differ from those held privately. *Law and Human Behavior*, 25(2), 141–54.

Shea, P. (1996). *Psychiatry in Court* (second edition). Sydney: Hawkins Press.

Sheehan, P.W. (1989). Response to suggestions of memory distortions in hypnosis: sampling cognitive and social factors. In V.A. Gheorgiu et al. (eds), *Suggestion and Suggestibility: Theory and Research* (pp. 295–303). Berlin: Springer.

Sheehan, P.W. (1994). Issues in forensic hypnosis. In B.J. Evans and R.O. Stanley (eds), 61–79.

Sheehan, P.W. and McConkey, K. (1994). Lying in hypnosis: a conceptual analysis of the possibilities. In B.J. Evans and R.O. Stanley (eds), 125–33.

Sheingold, K. and Tenney, Y.J. (1982). Memory for a salient childhood event. In U. Neisser (ed.), 201–2.

Sheldon, D.H. and McCleod, M.D. (1991). From normative to positive data: expert psychological evidence re-examined. *Criminal Law Review*, 811–20.

Sheldon, W.H. (1942). *The Varieties of Temperament: A Psychology of Constitutional Differences*. New York: Harper.

Shepherd, E. (1991a). Resistance in interviews: the contribution of police perceptions and behaviour. *Issues in Criminological and Legal Psychology*, 18, 5–11.

Shepherd, E. (1991b). Ethical interviewing. *Issues in Criminological and Legal Psychology*, 18, 46–55.

Shepherd, E. (1995). Representing and analysing the interviewee's account. *Medicine, Science and the Law*, 35, 122–35.

Shepherd, E., Mortimer, A., Turner, V. and Watson, J. (1999). Spaced cognitive interviewing: facilitating therapeutic and forensic narration of traumatic memories. *Psychology, Crime and Law*, 5, 117–43.

Shepherd, J.W., Ellis, H.D. and Davies, G.M. (1982). *Identification Evidence: A Psychological Evaluation*. Aberdeen: The University Press.

Sherman, S.J. (1995). The capital jury project: the role of responsibility and how psychology can inform the law. *Indiana Law Journal*, 70, 1241–8.

Shoemaker, D., South, D. and Lowe, J. (1973). Facial stereotypes of deviants and judgements of guilt or innocence. *Social Forces*, 51, 427–33.

Shuman, D.W., Hamilton, J.A. and Daley, C.E. (1994). The health effects of jury service. *Law and Psychology Review*, 18, 267–307.

Siegal, M. and Peterson, C.C. (1995). Memory and suggestibility in conversations with children. *Australian Journal of Psychology*, 47, 38–41.

Sigall, H. and Ostrove, N. (1975). Beautiful but dangerous: effects of offender attractiveness and nature of the crime on juridic judgements. *Journal of Personality and Social Psychology*, 31, 410–14.

Sigelman, C. and Sigelman, L. (1976). Authority and conformity: violation of a traffic regulation. *Journal of Social Psychology*, 100, 35–43.

Sigurdsson, J.F. and Gudjonsson, G.H. (2001). False confessions: the relative importance of psychological and substantive abuse variables. *Psychology, Crime and Law*, 7, 275–89.

Silets, H.L. and Overbey, D.L. (2000). Where does advocacy end and obstruction begin? *Journal of Financial Crime*, 8(1), 68–82.

Simon, R.J. (1967). *The Jury and the Defence of Insanity*. Boston: Little Brown & Co.

Singer, M. and Singer, A. (1985). The effect of police uniforms on interpersonal perceptions. *Journal of Psychology*, 119, 157–61.

Skellington, K. (2000). Interpersonal trust in the police. Paper presented at the Eleventh European Psychology and Law Conference, Lisbon, Portugal, 5–8 June, 2001.

Skinner, J. and Berry, K. (1993). Anatomically detailed dolls and the evaluation of child sexual abuse. *Law and Human Behavior*, 18, 399–421.

Skyrme, T. Sir. (1979). *The Changing Image of the Magistracy*. London: Macmillan.

Slind-Flor, V. (1992). Counties begin to help jurors cope afterward. *National Law Journal*, January 20(14), 3.

Slora, K.B. (1989). An empirical approach to determining employee deviance base rates. Paper presented at the 97th Annual Convention of the American Psychological Association, New Orleans, LA.

Slovenko, R. (1993). The 'revival of memory' of childhood sexual abuse: is the tolling of the statute of limitations justified? *Journal of Psychiatry and Law*, 21, 7–34.

Small, M.A. (1993). Advancing psychological jurisprudence. *Behavioral Sciences and the Law*, 11, 3–16.

Small, M.A. and Melton, G.B. (1994). Evaluation of child witnesses for confrontation with criminal defendants. *Professional Psychology: Research and Practice*, 25, 228–33.

Smith, A.D. and Winogard, E. (1978). Adult age differences in remembering faces. *Developmental Psychology*, 14, 443–4.

Smith, D. (1997). Race, crime and criminal justice. In M. Maguire, R. Morgan and R. Reiner (eds), *The Oxford Handbook of Criminology*. Oxford: Clarendon Press.

Smith, J.C. (1995). *Criminal Evidence*. London: Sweet and Maxwell.

Smith, V.L. and Ellsworth, P.C. (1987). The social psychology of eyewitness accuracy: misleading questions and communicator expertise. *Journal of Applied Psychology*, 72, 294–300.

Smith, V.L., Kassin, S.M. and Ellsworth, P.C. (1989). Eyewitness accuracy and confidence: within- versus between-subjects correlation. *Journal of Applied Psychology*, 74, 356–9.

Snel, B. (1978). Observation in the courtroom. *Netherlands Journal of Applied Psychology*, 74, 294–300

Snyder, M. (1979). Self-monitoring processes. In L. Berkowitz (ed.), *Advances in Experimental Social Psychology* (vol. 12, pp. 85–128). New York: Academic Press.

Snyder, M. (1987). *Public Appearance/Private Realities*. New York: W.H. Freeman.

Softley, P., Brown, D., Forde, B., Mair, G. and Moxon, D. (1980). *Police Interrogation: An Observational Study in Four Police Stations*. London: HMSO.

Solimine, M.E. and Wheatley, S.E. (1995). Rethinking feminist judging. *Indiana Law Journal*, 70, 891–920.

Spencer, J. and Flin, R. (1990). *The Evidence of Children: The Law and the Psychology*. London: Blackstone.

Spencer, J. and Flin, R. (1993). *The Evidence of Children: The Law and the Psychology* (second edition). London: Blackstone.

Spiegel, R. (1989). *Psychopharmacology: An Introduction*. Chichester: Wiley.

Spielberger, C.D., Gorsuch, R.L., Lushene, R.E., Vagg, P.R. and Jacobs, G.A. (1983). *State-Trait Anxiety Inventory Manual*. Palo Alto, CA: Consulting Psychologists Press.

Spohn, C. (1992). An analysis of the 'jury trial penalty' and its effect on black and white offenders. *Justice Professional*, 7, 93–112.

Spohn, C. and Cederblom, J. (1991). Race and disparities in sentencing: a test of the liberation hypothesis. *Justice Quarterly*, 8, 305–27.

Spohn, C., Gruhl, J. and Welch, S. (1981–2). The effect of race on sentencing: a re-examination of an unsettled question. *Law and Society Review*, 16, 72–88.

Sporer, S.L. Penrod, S., Read, D. and Cutler, B. (1995). Choosing, confidence, and accuracy: a meta-analysis of the confidence-accuracy relation in eyewitness identification studies. *Psychological Bulletin*, 118, 315–27.

Sporer, S.L. (1989). Verbal and visual process in person identification. In Wegener et al. (eds), 303–24.

Sporer, S.L. (1993). Eyewitness identification accuracy, confidence and decision times in simultaneous and sequential lineups. *Journal of Applied Psychology*, 78, 22–33.

Sporer, S.L. (1997). The less travelled road to truth: verbal cues in deception detection in accounts of of fabricated and self-experienced events. *Applied Cognitive Psychology*, 11, 373–97.

Spreutels, J.P. (1980). Giving reasons for sentence at the Crown Court. *Criminal Law Review*, 486–95.

Stalans, L.J. and Finn, M.A. (1995). How novice and experienced officers interpret wife assaults: normative and efficiency frames. *Law and Society Review*, 29, 287–321.

Steblay, N.M. (1992). A meta-analytic review of the weapon focus effect. *Law and Human Behavior*, 16, 413–24.

Steele, C.M. and Josephs, R.A. (1990). Alcohol myopia: its prized and dangerous effects. *American Psychologist*, 45, 921–33.

Steffensmeier, D.J., Kramer, J. and Streifel, C. (1993). Gender and imprisonment decisions. *Criminology*, 31, 411–46.

Steffensmeier, D.J. and Terry, R.M. (1973). Deviance and respectability: an observational study of reactions to shoplifting. *Social Forces*, 51, 417–26.

Stein, F.M. (1986). Helping young policemen cope with stress and manage conflict situations. In J.C. Yuille (ed.), 301–5.

Steller, M. and Boychuk, T. (1992). Children as witnesses in sexual abuse cases: investigative interview and assessment techniques. In H. Dent and R. Flin (eds), 47–71.

Steller, M. and Köhnken, G. (1989). Criteria-based content analysis. In D.C. Raskin (ed.), 217–45.

Steller, M. (1989). Recent developments in statement analysis. In J.C. Yuille (ed.).

Stephenson, G. and Moston, S.J. (1991). Attitudes and assumptions of police officers when questioning criminal suspects. *Issues in Criminological and Legal Psychology*, 18, 30–6.

Stephenson, G.M. (1992). *The Psychology of Criminal Justice*. Oxford: Blackwell.

Stephenson, G.M. (1995). Looking to the future: a psychologist's comments on Richard Abel's *Contested Communities*. *Journal of Law and Society*, 22, 133–9.

Stephenson, G.M. and Moston, S.J. (1994). Police interrogation. *Psychology, Crime and Law*, 1, 151–7.

Stephenson, G.M., Abrams, D., Wagner, W. and Wade, G. (1986a). Partners in recall: collaborative order in the recall of police interrogation. *British Journal of Social Psychology*, 25, 341–3.

Stephenson, G.M., Brandstatter, H. and Wagner, W. (1982). An experimental study of social performance and delay on the testimonial validity of story telling. *European Journal of Social Psychology*, 13, 175–91.

Stephenson, G.M., Clark, N.K. and Kniveton, B.H. (1989). Collaborative testimony by police officers: a psycho-legal issue. In Wegener et al. (eds), 254–70.

Stephenson, G.M., Clark, N.K. and Wade, G.S. (1986b). Meetings make evidence? An experimental study of collaborative and individual recall of a simulated police interrogation. *Journal of Personality and Social Psychology*, 50, 1113–22.

Stephenson, G.M., Kniveton, B.H. and Wagner, W. (1991). Social influences on remembering: intellectual, interpersonal and intergroup components. *European Journal of Social Psychology*, 21, 463–75.

Stern, L.B. and Dunning, D. (1994). Distinguishing accurate from inaccurate eyewitness identifications: a reality monitoring approach. In Ross et al. (eds), 273–99.

Stern, L.W. (1910). Abstracts of lectures on the psychology of testimony and on the study of individuality. *American Journal of Psychology*, 21, 270–82.

Stern, L.W. (1939). The psychology of testimony. *Journal of Abnormal and Social Psychology*, 34, 3–20.

Stevens, P. and Willis, C.F. (1979). *Race, Crime and Arrests*. London: Home Office, Study no. 58.

Steward, M. (1992). Preliminary findings from the University of California-Davis, child memory study. *The Advisor*, 5, 11–13.

Stewart, J.E. (1980). Defendant's attractiveness as a factor in the outcome of criminal trials: an observational study. *Journal of Applied Social Psychology*, 10, 348–61.

Stiff, J.B. and Miller, G.R. (1986). 'Come to think of it': interrogative probes, deceptive communication, and deception detection. *Human Communication Research*, 12, 339–57.

Stone, E.F. and Stone, D.L. (1990). Privacy in organizations: theoretical issues, research findings, and protection mechanisms. In G. Ferris and K. Rowland (eds), *Research in Personnel and Human Resources Management* (vol. 8, pp. 349–411). Greenwich, CT: JAI Press.

Stone, M. (1991). Instant lie detection? Demeanour and credibility in criminal trials. *Criminal Law Review*, 821–30.

Stone, R.W. (1990). Commentary: twelve good men (or women) and true. *Police Journal*, 63, 283–5.

Strodtbeck, F.L., James, J. and Hawkins, C. (1957). Social status in jury deliberations. *American Sociological Review*, 22, 713–19.

Stuesser, L. (1992). Admitting prior inconsistent statements for their truth. *Canadian Bar Review*, 71, 48–76.

Sue, S., Smith, R.E. and Gilbert, R. (1974). Biasing effects of pretrial publicity on judicial decisions. *Journal of Criminal Justice*, 2, 163–71.

Swanson, C.R., Chamelin, N. and Territo, L. (1988). *Criminal Investigation* (fourth edition). New York: Random House.

Sweeney, L.T. and Haney, C. (1992). The influence of race on sentencing: a meta-analytic review of experimental studies. *Behavioral Sciences and the Law*, 10, 179–95.

Szasz, J.S. (1957). Psychiatric expert testimony: its court meaning and social function. *Psychiatry*, 20, 313–16.

Tabol, C.E. and Ainsworth, P.B. (2000). Police conflict and role ambiguity amongst a sample of British police officers: implications for psychological well being. Paper presented at the Tenth European Psychology and Law Conference, Limassol, Cyprus, 12–14 April 2000.

Tanford, S. and Penrod, S. (1986). Jury deliberations: discussion, content and influence processes in jury decision making. *Journal of Applied Social Psychology*, 16, 322–47.

Tanford, S., Penrod, S. and Collins, R. (1985). Decision making in joined criminal trials: the influence of charge similarity, evidence similarity and limiting instructions. *Law and Human Behavior*, 9, 319–37.

Tapp, J.L. (1976). Psychology and the Law: An Overture. In M.L. Rosenzweig and L.W. Porter (eds), *Annual Review of Psychology*, vol. 27. Palo Alto, CA: Annual Reviews.

Tapp, J.L. and Levine, F.J. (eds) (1977). *Law, Justice and the Individual in Society*. New York: Holt, Rinehart and Winston.

Tata, C. and Hutton, N. (1998a). What 'rules' in sentencing? Consistency and disparity in the absence of 'rules'. *International Journal of the Sociology of Law*, 26, 339–64.

Tata, C. and Hutton, N. (1998b). The application of judicial intelligence and 'rules' to systems supporting discretionary judicial decision-making. *Artificial Intelligence and Law*, 6, 203–30.

Taylor, P.J. and Kopelman, M.D. (1984). Amnesia for criminal offences. *Psychological Medicine*, 14, 581–8.

Taylor, S.E. and Crocker, J. (1980). Schematic basis of social information processing. In E.T. Higgins et al. *Social Cognition, The Ontario Symposium*, vol. 1. Hillsdale, NJ: Erlbaum.

Teahan, J.E. (1975). A longitudinal study of attitude shifts among black and white police officers. *Journal of Social Issues*, 31, 47–56.

Terr, L. (1991). *Too Scared to Cry*. New York: Harper & Row.

Terry, W.C. (1981). Police stress: the empirical evidence. *Journal of Police Science and Administration*, 9, 61–75.

The Times (2001). Britain's one-card trick yields superior lie test. 12 November, 11.

Thomas, D. (1979). *Principles of Sentencing* (second edition). London: Heinemann.

Thomas, D. (1987). Sentencing: some current questions. In D.C. Pennington and S. Lloyd-Bostock (eds), 13–23.

Thomas, G.C. and Pollack, B.S. (1992). Rethinking guilt, juries and jeopardy. *Michigan Law Review*, 91, 1–33.

Thomas-Peter, B.A. and Warren, S. (1998). Legal responsibilities of forensic psychologists. *Expert Evidence*, 6, 79–106.

Thomassin, L. and Michael, A. (1990). Performance of eyewitnesses when giving evidence and making eyewitness identification. *Canadian Police College Journal*, 14, 233–46.

Thompson, C.P. (1985a). Voice identification: speaker identification and a correction of the record regarding sex effects. *Human Learning. Journal of Practical Research and Applications*, 4, 19–28.

Thompson, C.P. (1985b). Voice identification: attempted recovery from a biased procedure. Human Learning. *Journal of Practical Research and Applications*, 4, 213–24.

Thompson, C.P. (1987). A language effect in voice identification. *Applied Cognitive Psychology*, 1, 121–31.

Thompson, W.C. (1989). Are juries competent to evaluate statistical evidence? *Law and Contemporary Problems*, 52, 9–41.

Thomson, D.M. (1981). Person identification influencing the outcome. *Australian and New Zealand Journal of Criminology*, 14, 49–54.

Thomson, D.M. (1984). Towards a more efficient judicial system: observations of an experimental psychologist. In M. Nixon (ed.), *Issues in Psychological Practice* (pp. 107–32). Melbourne: Longman Cheshire.

Thomson, D.M. (1988). A matter of justice: protecting the rights of the victim and the accused in child sexual abuse cases. In *Children as Witnesses* (pp. 2.1–2.18). Melbourne: Leo Cussen Institute of Victoria.

Thomson, D.M. (1991). Reliability and credibility of children as witnesses. In J. Vernon (ed.), 43–52.

Thomson, D.M. (1995a). Eyewitness testimony and identification tests. In N. Brewer and C. Wilson (eds), 121–153.

Thomson, D.M. (1995b). Allegations of childhood sexual abuse: repressed memories or false memories? *Psychiatry, Psychology and Law*, 2, 97–106.

Thomson, E. (1997). Discrimination and the death penalty in Arizona. *Criminal Justice Review*, 22(1), 65–76.

Thornton, P. (1995). The admissibility of expert psychiatric and psychological evidence: judicial training. *Medicine, Science and the Law*, 35, 143–9.

Tickner, A. and Poulton, E. (1975). Watching for people and actions. *Ergonomics*, 18, 35–51.

Toch, H. (1961). *Legal and Criminal Psychology*. New York: Holt, Rinehart and Winston.

Todd, C. and Perlmutter, M. (1980). Reality recalled by preschool children. In M. Perlmutter (ed.), *New Directions for Child Development, no. 10: Children's Memory* (pp. 69-86). San Francisco: Jossey-Bass.

Tollestrup, P.A., Turtle, J.W. and Yuille, J.C. (1994). Actual victims and witnesses to robbery and fraud: an archival analysis. In Ross et al. (eds), 144–60.

Tooley, V., Brigham, J., Maass, A. and Bothwell, R.K. (1987). Facial recognition: weapon effect and attentional focus. *Journal of Applied Social Psychology*, 17, 845–9.

Tooley, V., Brigham, J.C., Maass, A. and Bothwell, R.K. (1984). Facial recognition: weapon effect and attentional focus. Unpublished manuscript, Florida State University, Tallahassee.

Torpy, D. (1994). You must confess. *Issues in Criminological and Legal Psychology*, 21, 21–3.

Toussignant, D.D. (1991). Why suspects confess. *FBI Law Enforcement Bulletin*, 60(3), 14–18.

Trankell, A. (1972). *The Reliability of Evidence: Methods of Analysing and Assessing Witness Statements*. Stockholm: Beckmans.

Traverso, G. and Bagnoli, L. (eds) (2001), *Psychology and Law in a Changing World: New Trends in Theory, Practice and Research*. London: Routledge.

Traverso, G. and Manna, O. (1992). Law and psychology in Italy. In F. Lösel, D. Bender and T. Bliesener (eds), 535–45.

Traverso, G.B. and Verde, A. (2001). Psychology and law at the end of the century. In R. Traverso and L. Bagnoli (eds), 1–15.

Treadway, M. and McCloskey, M. (1987). Cite unseen: distortions of the Allport and Postman study in the eyewitness testimony literature. *Law and Human Behavior*, 11, 19–25.

Treadway, M. and McCloskey, M. (1989). Effects of racial stereotypes on eyewitness performance: implications of the real and rumored Allport and Postman studies. *Applied Cognitive Psychology*, 3, 53–64.

Tremper, C.R. (1987). Organized psychology's efforts to influence judicial policy-making. *American Psychologist*, 42, 496–501.

Tremper, C.R. (1987). Sanguinity and disillusionment where law meets social science. *Law and Human Behavior*, 11, 267–76.

Triplett, N. (1900). The psychology of conjuring deceptions. *American Journal of Psychology,* 11, 439–510.

Tronk, K. and Dearden, I. (1993). *Advocacy Basics for Solicitors.* Sydney: The Law Book Co.

Tucker, A., Mertin, P. and Luszcz, M. (1990). The effect of a repeated interview on young children's eyewitness memory. *Australian and New Zealand Journal of Criminology*, 23, 117–24.

Tulving, E. (1974). Cue-dependent forgetting. *American Scientist*, 62, 74–82.

Tulving, E. (1983). *Elements of Episodic Memory*. Oxford: Oxford University Press.

Tuohy, A.P., Wrennall, M.J., McQueen, R.A. and Stradling, S.G. (1993). Effect of socialization factors on decisions to prosecute. *Law and Human Behavior*, 17, 167–81.

Turnbull, D.G. and Thomson, D.M. (1984, May). Eyewitness testimony: photographic versus live line-ups. Paper presented at the Experimental Psychology Conference, Deakin University, Geelong, Australia.

Turner, J. (2000). Applying perceptual research to E-FIT construction: a minimal face experiment. Paper presented at the Tenth European Conference of Psychology and Law, Limassol, Cyprus, 12–14 April.

Turnstall, O., Gudjonsson, G., Eysenck, H. and Howard, L. (1982). Professional issues arising from psychological evidence presented in court. *Bulletin of the British Psychological Society*, 35, 329–31.

Turtle, J.W. and Yuille, J.C. (1994). Lost but not forgotten: repeated eyewitness recall leads to reminiscence but not hypermnesia. *Journal of Applied Psychology*, 79, 260–71.

Twining, W. (1983). Identification and misidentification in legal processes: redefining the problem. In S.M.A. Lloyd-Bostock and B.R. Clifford (eds), 255–84.

Tzeng, O.J.L. and Cotton, B. (1980). A study-phase retrieval model of temporal coding. *Journal of Experimental Psychology*, 6, 705–16.

Underwood, G. and Milton, H. (1993). Collusion after a collision: witnesses' reports of a road accident with and without discussion. *Applied Cognitive Psychology*, 7, 11–22.

Undeutsch, U. (1982). Statement reality analysis. In A. Trankell (ed.), *Reconstructing the Past: The Role of Psychologists in Criminal Trials* (pp. 27–56). Stockholm: P.A. Norsted and Sons.

US Bureau of the Census. (1994). US Department of Commerce, Statistical Tracts of the United States: 213 (114th edition).

Van Koppen, P.J. and Lochun, S.K. (1997). Portaying perpetrators: the validity of offender descriptions by witnesses. *Law and Human Behavior*, 21, 661–85.

Van Koppen, P.J., Boelhouwer, A.J.W., Merekelbach, H.L.G.J. and Verbaten, M.N. (1996). *Leugendetectie in actie: Het gebruik van polygraaf in de praktijk.* Leiden: Netherlands Studiecentrum Criminaliteit en Rechtshandhaving. Cited in Vrij (2000:245).

Van Wallandael, L.R., Surace, A., Parsons, D.B. and Brown, M. (1994). Earwitness' voice recognition: factors affecting accuracy and impact on jurors. *Applied Cognitive Psychology*, 8, 661–77.

Vandermaas, M.O., Hess, T.M. and Baker-Ward, L. (1993). Does anxiety affect children's reports of memory for a stressful event? *Applied Cognitive Psychology*, 7, 109–27.

Van Zyl Smit, D. (1999). Mandatory sentences: a conundrum for the new South Africa? Paper presented at the Sentencing and Society Conference, University of Strathclyde, Glasgow, Scotland, 24–26 June.

Vazel, M.A. and Somat, R. (2000). Memory for faces and photofits: to a new method of cognitive interview adapted to photofits. Paper presented at the Tenth European Conference of Psychology and Law, Limassol, Cyprus, 12–14 April.

Verinis, J.S. and Walker, V. (1970). Policemen and the recall of criminal details. *Journal of Social Psychology*, 81, 217–21.

Vernon, J. (ed.) (1991). *Children as Witnesses*. Canberra: Australian Institute of Criminology.

Winograd, E. and Soloway, R.M. (1985). Reminding as a basis for temporal judgements. *Journal of Experimental Psychology: Learning, Memory and Cognition*, 11, 262–71.

Winograd, E., Kerr, N. and Spence, M. (1984). Voice recognition: effect of orienting task, and a test of blind versus sighted listeners. *American Journal of Psychology*, 97, 57–70.

Wippich, W. (1989). Remembering social events and activities. In Wegener et al. (eds), 228–41.

Witkin, H.A., Dyke, R.B., Faterson, H.F., Goodenough, D.R. and Karp, S.A. (1962). *Psychological Differentiation*. New York: Wiley.

Wojcikiewicz, J. (2001). Polygraphy in Poland. In G.B. Traverso and L. Bagnoli (eds), 263–9.

Wolfgang, M.E. and Reidel, M. (1975). Rape, race and the death penalty in Georgia. *American Journal of Orthopsychiatry*, 45, 658–68.

Wood, W. (1982). Retrieval of attitude relevant information from memory: effects on susceptibility to persuasion and on intrinsic motivation. *Journal of Personality and Social Psychology*, 42, 798–810.

Wooley, R.M. and Hakstian, A.R. (1992). An examination of the construct validity of personality-based and overt measures of integrity. *Educational Psychological Measurement*, 52, 475–89.

Wooton, B. (1959). *Social Science and Social Pathology*. London: Allen and Unwin.

Worden, A.P. (1993). The attitudes of men and women in policing: testing conventional and contemporary wisdom. *Criminology*, 31, 203–41.

Wortley, K.R. and Homel, R.J. (1995). Police prejudice as a function of training and outgroup contact: a longitudinal investigation. *Law and Human Behavior*, 19, 305–31.

Wright, D.B. (1993). Recall of the Hillsborough disaster over time: Systematic biases of 'flashbulb' memories. *Applied Cognitive Psychology*, 7, 129–38.

Wright, D.B. and McDaid, A.T. (1996). Comparing system and estimator variables using data from real line-ups. *Applied Cognitive Psychology*, 10, 75–84.

Wright, P. (1991). *The Spycatcher's Encyclopedia of Espionage*. Melbourne, Australia: Heinemann.

Wrightsman, L.S. (1999). *Judicial Decision Making: Is Psychology Relevant?* New York: Kluwer Academic/Plenum Publishers.

Wrightsman, S.L. (1987). *Psychology and the Legal System*. Pacific Grove, CA: Brooks Cove Publishing.

Yanagihara, T. and Petersen, R.C. (eds) (1991). *Memory Disorders: Research and Clinical Practice*. New York: Dekker.

Yarmey, A.D. (1979). *The Psychology of Eyewitness Testimony*. New York: Free Press.

Yarmey, A.D. (1986a). Perceived expertness and credibility of police officers as eyewitnesses. *Canadian Police College Journal*, 10, 31–52.

Yarmey, A.D. (1986b). Verbal, visual, and voice identification of a rape suspect under different conditions of illumination. *Journal of Applied Psychology*, 71, 363–70.

Yarmey, A.D. (1990). *Understanding Police and Police Work*. New York: New York University Press.

Yarmey, A.D. (1991). Voice identification over the telephone. *Journal of Applied Social Psychology*, 21, 1868–76.

Yarmey, A.D. (1994). Earwitness evidence: memory for a perpetrator's voice. In Ross et al. (eds), 101–24.

Yarmey, A.D. (1995). Earwitness and evidence obtained by other senses. In R. Bull and D. Carson (eds), 261–73.

Yarmey, A.D. and Jones, H.P.T. (1983). Accuracy of memory of male and female eyewitnesses to a criminal assault and rape. *Bulletin of the Psychonomic Society*, 21, 89–92.

Yarmey, A.D. and Kent, J. (1980). Eyewitness identification by elderly and young adults. *Law and Human Behavior*, 4, 359–71.

Yarmey, A.D. and Matthys, E. (1992). Voice identification of an abductor. *Applied Cognitive Psychology*, 6, 367–77.

Yarmey, A.D. and Pauley, T. (1993). The effects of weapon focus and perceived violence on voice identification. Unpublished manuscript, University of Guelph, Ontario, Canada.

Yarmey, A.D. and Tressillian Jones, H.P. (1982). Police awareness of the fallibility of eyewitness identification. *Canadian Police College Journal*, 6, 113–24.

Yarmey, A.D., Yarmey, A.L. and Yarmey, M.J. (1994). Face and voice identifications in showups and lineups. *Applied Cognitive Psychology*, 8, 453–64.

Yerkes, P.M. and Berry, C.S. (1909). The association reaction time method of mental diagnosis. *American Journal of Psychology*, 20, 22–37.

Yerkes, R.M. and Dodson, J.D. (1908). The relation of strength of stimulus to rapidity of habit-information. *Journal of Comparative Neurology of Psychology*, 18, 459–82.

Yeschke, C.L. (1993). *Interviewing: A Forensic Guide to Interrogation* (second edition). Springfield, IL: Charles C. Thomas.

Young, A.W. and Ellis, H.D. (eds) (1989). *Handbook of Research on Face Recognition.* Amsterdam: North Holland.

Yuille, J.C. (1986). Meaningful research in the police context. In J.C. Yuille (ed.), 225–43.

Yuille, J.C. (1989). *Credibility Assessment.* Netherlands: Kluwer Academic Publisher.

Yuille, J.C. (1992). Psychologists and the police. In Lösel et al. (eds), 205–11.

Yuille, J.C. (ed.) (1986). *Police Selection and Training: The Role of Psychology.* Dordrecht: Martinus Nijhoff.

Yuille, J.C. and Cutshall, J.L. (1989). Analysis of the statements of victims, witnesses and suspects. In J.C. Yuille (ed.).

Yuille, J.C. and Kim, C.K. (1987). A field study of the forensic use of hypnosis. *Canadian Journal of Behavioral Science*, 193, 418–35.

Yuille, J.C. and McEwan, N.H. (1985). Use of hypnosis as an aid to eyewitness testimony. *Journal of Applied Psychology*, 70, 389–400.

Yuille, J.C. and Tollestrup, P.A. (1990). Some effects of alcohol on eyewitness memory. *Journal of Applied Psychology*, 75, 268–73.

Yuille, J.C. and Tollestrup, P.A. (1992). A model of the direct effects of emotion on eyewitness memory. In S.A. Christianson (ed.), 201–15.

Yuille, J.C. and Wells, G.L. (1991). Concerns about the application of research findings: the issue of ecological validity. In J. Doris (ed.), 118–28.

Yuille, J.C. and Cutshall, J.L. (1986). A case study of eyewitness memory for a crime. *Journal of Applied Psychology*, 71, 291–301.

Yuille, J.C., Davies, G.M., Gibling, F., Marxsen, D. and Porter, S. (1994). Eyewitness memory of police trainees for realistic role plays. *Journal of Applied Psychology*, 79, 931–6.

Yuille, J.C., Hunter, R., Joffe, R. and Zaparniuk, J. (1993). Interviewing children in sexual abuse cases. In G.S. Goodman and B.L. Bottoms (eds), 95–115.

Yuille, J.C., Marxsen, D. and Menard, K. (1993). Report to the Ministry of Social Services of British Columbia on the Systematic Interviewing Project. Vancouver, BC. Authors.

Zander, M. (1974). Why I disagree with Sir Robert Mark. *Police*, April, 16.

Zander, M. and Henderson, P. (1994). The Crown Court study. Royal Commission on Criminal Justice Study no. 19. *Research Bulletin*, no. 35, 46–8. London: Home Office Research and Statistics Department.

Zaparniuk, J., Yuille, J.C. and Taylor, S. (1995). Assessing the credibility of true and false statements. *International Journal of Law and Psychiatry* (in press).

Zaragoza, M.S. and Koshmider, J.W. III. (1989). Misled subjects may know more than their performance implies. *Journal of Experimental Psychology: Learning, Memory and Cognition*, 15, 246–55.

Zaragoza, M.S., Jamis, M. and McCloskey, M. (1987). Misleading postevent information and recall of the original event: further evidence against the memory impairment hypothesis. *Journal of Experimental Psychology: Learning, Memory, and Cognition*, 13, 36–44.

Zaragoza, M.S., Graham, J.R., Hall, G.C.N., Hirschman, R. and Ben-Porath, Y.S. (eds) (1995). *Memory and Testimony in the Child Witness.* Thousand Oaks, CA: Sage.

Zeisel, H. (1971). ' … And then there were none': the diminution of federal jury. *University of Chicago Law Review*, 35, 35–54.

Zeisel, H. and Diamond, S.S. (1987). Convincing empirical evidence on the six-member jury. In L.S. Wrightsman, S.M. Kassin and C.E. Willis (eds), *In the Jury Box: Controversies in the Courtroom* (pp. 193–208). Newbury Park, CA: Sage.

Zerman, M. (1977). *Call the Final Witness: the People vs. Mather as Seen by the 11th Juror.* New York: Harper & Row.

Zigmond, A.S. and Smith, R.P. (1983). The hospital anxiety and depression scale. *Acta Psychiatrica Scandinavica*, 67, 361–70.

Zimbardo, P.G. and Leippe, M.R. (1991). *The Psychology of Attitude and Social Influence*. New York: McGraw-Hill.

Zuckerman, M. and Driver, R. (1985). Telling lies: verbal and non-verbal correlates of deception. In A. W. Siegman and S. Feldstein (eds), *Nonverbal Communication: An Integrated Perspective* (pp. 129–47). Hillsdale, NJ: Lawrence Erlbaum.

Author index

Subject index